MILE MARKERS

40 INTIMATE JOURNEYS

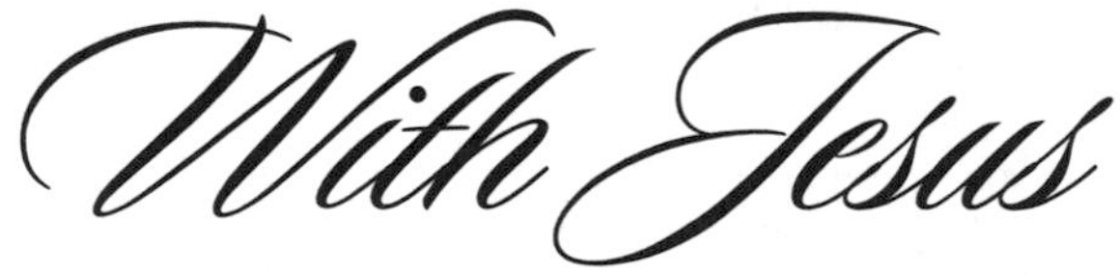

DONALD E. DEMARAY

Mile Markers: 40 Intimate Journeys with Jesus

Requests for information should be addressed to:
Evangel Publishing House
2000 Evangel Way
P.O. Box 189
Nappanee, Indiana 46550
Phone: (800) 253-9315
Email: info@evangelpublishing.com
Website: www.evangelpublishing.com

Unless otherwise indicated, biblical quotations are the author's own translation.

Cover design by Larry Stuart
Edited by Mark Garratt

ISBN-13: 978-1-928915-96-6
Library of Congress Control Number: 2007931566

Printed in the United States of America

5 6 7 8 9 EP 8 7 6 5 4 3 2 1

For

Jack and Jeanne

"Read this book if you hunger for a more intimate relationship with Jesus, and if you want to know how to 'do life' in His company. Don's writing is crisp and fresh. Each selection is a letter of spiritual counsel to actual people, but before you know it, he is writing just to you. I love the way he tells Gospel stories, relates life experiences, and weaves insights from great Christian classics. Follow his embedded reading suggestions and this little book quickly turns into a short course on the Christian life."

C. Reginald Johnson,
Professor of Spiritual Formation
Asbury Theological Seminary

"...The book is carefully organized, the spiritual direction given is bite-sized.... Best of all it is designed to lead the new believer from the threshold of faith into a relationship with Jesus Christ that is both spiritually vital and knowledgeable. Any new Christian, young or old, can profit from following the Mile Markers that Demaray clearly sets out. And for the well-motivated there are extra resources aplenty to enrich a new faith."

Donald N. Bastian, Bishop Emeritus
The Free Methodist Church

Table of Contents

Foreword

When the Green Bay Packers lost a football game, Coach Vince Lombardi would get the team back on the winning track by having them reconnect with the basics: blocking, tackling, running, passing and the like. The wise coach knew that games are won or lost in relation to the basics. He was aware that even seasoned veterans need to revisit the fundamentals from time to time.

Dr. Don Demaray has provided us with an excellent overview of the basics of spiritual formation, and he has done so through a contemporary use of the ancient practice of spiritual direction through letter writing. Functioning as a wise spiritual director, he motivates us with brief guidance, first to ponder, then enact. Post-modern seekers will find an invitation to travel with Jesus in this book, but so will older folks who've been around for a while!

By centering in the "I am" sayings of Jesus, we are also rooted in Scripture and a sound Christocentric spirituality—two emphases often missing in a more generic approach. The result is a 40-day journey that leaves plenty of room for personal exploration, while simultaneously establishing a good foundation for growing in grace. And in the process of doing this, we also sense the heartbeat of the author himself—which itself is a delight.

Dr. Steve Harper
Asbury Theological Seminary
Orlando, Florida

2

Beginnings

A freshly brewed pot of afternoon tea stood on the tray with scones, butter, and jam. But before my wife Kathleen and I could take our first sip, the door bell rang.

On our doorstep stood the Hamiltons, a couple we had recently befriended. "Adam and Megan!" I exclaimed. "Come right in. Kathleen and I have tea made and would love to have you join us."

The four of us sat in my study making small talk, but after a while Megan turned the conversation toward the reason they came to visit. "Adam and I want to grow as Christians." We talked at some length about this, until Megan finally ventured, "Would you consider mentoring us?"

"You want spiritual direction, then?" I asked.

"What's that?" Megan inquired. The question surprised me because she had enrolled in seminary where we do a lot of talking about spiritual direction. But realizing she had only started theological studies, I explained, "Spiritual direction actually relates to something even more important—spiritual formation. God desires His people to become more and more like Jesus Christ, to be *formed* in His image. The spiritual director simply assists in this journey; he helps earnest seekers grow into mature disciples."

As our conversation flowered, I sensed this young couple's eagerness and I got excited about helping them. This is what I live for—to see people get serious about Jesus!

Before going any further, I invited Megan and Adam to join my Christian Devotional Classics course at the seminary. There they would study great Christian writers like Brother Lawrence, Thomas à Kempis and St. Francis of Assisi; also authors from our own time like Richard Foster and Dallas Willard. The idea sounded good to them.

Then we got down to specifics about the three of us meeting. "Could you give just the two of us an hour once in a while?" they asked.

"Well, of course," I answered without hesitation. Adam and Megan reminded me of a single sentence by E. Stanley Jones, longtime missionary to India and evangelist to the world: "My spiritual maturity will depend not on my years but on my yearnings." My friends clearly yearned for closeness to God, and I was not about to let them down!

Over the next three years we met time and again, always with profit. God, His Word and His Son, Jesus Christ, came naturally into our discussions. We aimed at clear Bible teaching on many topics. Often we focused on how to practice the Christian gospel, praying for the grace to put feet to what we learned. Knowledge alone will not make disciples, we agreed. So we discussed the spiritual disciplines—Bible reading, prayer, service, meditation, study, fasting and all the rest. We did not cover every subject during their time in our seminary community, but we always found our conversations rich and growth-producing.

Recently they wrote to me and I've decided to answer them in a series of letters that will take them on a 40-day adventure into the heart of Jesus. It is the same adventure to which I am now inviting you! Before we set out, however, you will want to see the letter Adam and Megan wrote, along with my reply in which I offer a roadmap for the journey before us.

March 3

Dear Dr. Don:

We want to thank you for your time with us over the past few months. We have always come away from our sessions with new information and fresh inspiration.

But we have a problem. We took very few notes. When absorbed in conversation, who wants to do a lot of writing? So could you put some of what we talked about into writing?

You would know immediately why we want the spiritual formation principles recorded. We need hard copy reminders of the truths we have talked about. Please help us if you can.

Sincerely,

Adam and Megan Hamilton

March 12

Dear Adam and Megan:

I cannot tell you how your letter excites me! Of course I accept the invitation! In the days since I received your request, I have carefully considered how I want to write about the spiritual formation principles we discussed. Please allow me to share my fourfold approach to the writing I intend to do for you.

First, since Jesus is our model, I purpose to make Him central in every aspect of our study and reflection. Second, because His Word is our source of information, it will be the authority that grounds our understanding. Third, the classic Christian devotional writers—Thomas à Kempis, Brother Lawrence, St. Francis, and many others—reveal to us what happens when we get intimate with God. I will refer to them often. And fourth, personal experiences and observations about life also factor into our perception of God and His will. So I will share freely from my own journey with God as well.

The pattern of my writing will look something like this:

The great I AM declarations of Jesus will serve as the basis of the letters.

The seven I AMs will make up the seven legs of the 40-day pilgrimage. These are the Mile Markers, the larger themes that inform each day's journey.

I will put the seven I AMs, in their full context from John's Gospel, into paraphrases, using language understandable to our times. In other words, I will translate these rich passages of Scripture into everyday English.

Under each paraphrased Scripture portion I will write you a full-length letter of devotional commentary, from time to time using the Christian classics, along with stories from our
common human experience, to assist in the interpretation. In this way we will review some basic truths about spiritual formation, using Scripture as our foundational guide.

Because many others also want what you request, I intend to publish my material in book form. Once in print, you may want to use the book to teach a class in your home or church. The 40 days of Lent might prove to be a good time frame for such a course, meeting once a week at agreed times.

Sincerely yours,

Donald E. Demaray

PS: When the published book finally appears, you will want to read the Introduction carefully. In it I detail a good way to process spiritual formation material.

PPS: Letters lend themselves particularly well to the spiritual intimacy we're after. I must write to you from my soul, and I trust you will read my "little epistles" with your souls. So soul speaks to soul.

Acknowledgments

The conversation took on the warm and animated spirit that comes with a cup of tea. My literature loving daughter, Elyse, and I talked about metaphors. An editor from a publishing house had suggested I write a book on Biblical figures of speech. Of the hundreds of Scriptural figures, I pondered which I should choose. Conversation turned to a classic set of metaphors, the Great I AMs of the Gospel of John. "Why not decide on those?" Elyse suggested.

Reading, pondering and making notes, the I AMs took hold of my imagination. Before long the design of the book was underway. Thank you, Elyse, for the comment that issued in an exciting project.

Better than three years later, the manuscript in hand, friend Harold Burgess engaged me in conversation. Dr. Burgess read the print-out, liked the creativity and substance of it, and suggested Evangel Publishing House publish it. Roger L. Williams, executive director at Evangel, took the idea to his editorial Board. That began a stimulating dialog resulting in Mark Garratt taking on the editorial task. A knowledgeable, efficient and gracious penman, Mark and I spent happy hours revising and honing the text. I stand in debt to my editor, Mark Garratt.

Before Mr. Garratt saw the material, Kathleen, my wife and in-house editor, examined the manuscript with the enthusiasm and objectivity characteristic of everything she does. Kathleen critiques, to my great benefit, all I write.

At Evangel Publishing House office, Marlene Slabaugh has patiently fielded questions and, even over e-mail, exudes a warm and affirming spirit.

Encouragers along the way, in addition to those mentioned above, include (oh dear, I'm sure to leave someone out) Jodi Hopkins, Steve and Jeannie Harper, Donald Bastian, Howard Snyder, James Demaray

and his son Christopher, Cherith Davenport, David McKenna, and many more. Every writer knows the motivation that comes with an affirming word.

Soli Deo Gloria,

Donald E. Demaray

The Road Ahead

Doug, a seminary student of mine, wanted desperately to know Jesus in depth. An engineer by profession, he lived in an upscale house with his beautiful family, had money to buy the latest computer and software, but gave up his affluent job and lifestyle to go into Christian ministry.

Strangely, that major step did not satisfy his urgent need to know Jesus intimately. Not even seminary filled that craving.

Then one day the door opened to discovery: *Jesus* must come first; not software, not even seminary grades, only Jesus.

With that awakening about the way to meet his hunger, he surrendered his entire being to the Savior. Now he found the Scriptures, prayer, and meditation taking on a whole new meaning. The smile on his face, the delight in his life and walk with Jesus—even his body language—all demonstrated the validity of his new discovery.

The British evangelicals call this getting "thick" with Christ. American evangelicals term this getting "close" to Him. Some talk about "falling in love" with Christ. The classic devotional writers refer to "intimacy" with Him.

But how do you and I get to this place of intimacy with Jesus and walk closely with Him? Madame Guyon (1648-1717), a French devotional writer (she influenced people like John Wesley and Hudson Taylor), offers two simple steps: "praying the Scripture" and "beholding the Lord" (or "waiting in His presence").

Madame Guyon's *Experiencing the Depths of Jesus Christ* spells out how to pray the Scriptures and how to come into the Lord's presence. Read each verse carefully, quietly, slowly. Never hurry, she adds. Read only a small passage at a time. Let the message filter right down into the center of your mind and into the recesses of your heart.

You will notice that in the book you now hold, my paraphrases of Scripture come in small portions. I have put the passages from the Gospel of John into contemporary English so the intended meaning has a chance to seep into your soul. This seeping into the soul makes it possible to *sense deeply* the "very heart of what you have read," says Madame Guyon. She goes on to suggest turning the Scripture that has moved you into prayer.

When you move on to the meditations that follow each Scripture paraphrase, read in the same way, unhurried, pausing when a line or phrase strikes you as important. Allow God to speak and always be ready to dialog with Him.

I say "dialog with Him" because you will come to "beholding the Lord" or "waiting on the Lord." In other words, relating intimately with Jesus Christ Himself! Whatever unveils Jesus in your reading and contemplations brings you into fresh contact with Him.

At this point in your quiet time, however, you will likely come up against a big challenge. And we must face this now, before our adventure begins.

The challenge? Mind-wandering. One ancient devotional writer talks about opening the door of the heart to God, but because of the terrible busyness of our lives, lions and tigers come rushing in to chase away God's presence. How true! So we must work patiently at eliminating the lions and tigers and acclimating ourselves to the vision of Christ. That may take time. The 40-day period offered in this guide will suit you well in learning to see and hear Jesus only.

W. E. Sangster, the English preacher of the mid-twentieth century, gave wise instruction about handling the lions and tigers. Sometimes they are legitimate prayer concerns; in that case, says Dr. Sangster, pray about those needs, then return to the focus at hand. For us in meditation, that focus is the presence of Jesus.

The issue here is how easily we can let the wandering thoughts go on (not all of them are legitimate prayer concerns!), falling into a trap that keeps us from returning to The Presence. To make sure you come

back to Him, you may need to look again at some part of the daily Scripture passage and meditation. Quietly, surely, gently, yet with a firm hold on your focus, let The Presence invade your very being. The key word for what eventually comes is *experience—experience of the living Christ.* You will find that He refreshes your soul and brings a whole new spiritual awareness to your total being. When the Lord invades your spirit, entering into the deepest recesses of your person, you will discover yourself in the Holy of Holies. Oh, what a place! There you will find grace to meet all your needs, the greatest of which is simply to be in His presence.

You can read and meditate in this way because you have only two or three pages before you for each day's journey. Rushing in order to "do my devotional duty" will only block the voice of heaven and the presence of Jesus. Reading thoughtfully will open your heart's door to the intimacy eager Christians crave.

My friends, we crave this intimacy with Him because our hearts know the great rewards: peace, joy, love, trust, hope. No wonder these rewards become themes in the readings that follow.

Donald E. Demaray
Wilmore, Kentucky

12

MILE ONE

Days 1-6

"I am the bread of life"

14

Bread for the journey

In John 6:1-14 the Apostle John tells us this astonishing story:

Jesus crossed the Sea called Galilee, sometimes known as the Sea of Tiberias. A very large crowd walked around the lake to where Jesus and the disciples had tied up their boat. They followed Him because they had seen Him heal many people who suffered from all kinds of illnesses.

Jesus, needing to rest, went to the hills with His disciples and sat down. He looked at all the people coming toward him, and then said to Philip, "How can we get bread to feed all these people?" He asked this question to test Philip, because He already knew how to handle the challenge.

Philip's reply revealed the puzzle in his mind: "Eight months' wages earned by a worker would not buy all these people even a little bit of bread."

Then Andrew, Simon Peter's brother, said a young fellow in the crowd had brought his lunch: two loaves of bread made out of barley, and two fish. "But," exclaimed Andrew, "what good would such a small lunch do in this situation?"

The disciples looked at Jesus in wonder when He told them to invite everyone to sit down on the lush green grass. Counting the men only, there were about 5,000 people there!

Now Jesus picked up the loaves, gave thanks to His Father for them, and then had the disciples pass the pieces of the barley bread to the people. He did the same thing with the portions of fish.

Would you believe everyone ate as much as they wanted! In fact, after all had eaten and were satisfied, Jesus asked the disciples to collect the food left over. "We do not want to waste food," He said.

The disciples followed Jesus' instructions, and filled twelve baskets.

When the people saw what Jesus had done, they exclaimed, "A prophet has come to our world!"

Dear Adam and Megan:

I grew up during America's Great Depression. At that time, my dad was teaching at a Christian college. I recall that one year his contract called for a salary of $500.00, but the college could not even pay that over the twelve months. My father preached on weekends to supplement his income for a growing family, and did a lot of his own carpentry and repair work in our house. Sometimes we had only nickels, dimes and quarters, but we never went without a meal.

More than once, our compassionate neighbors, the Johnstons, left a sack of food on our doorstep. They had served as missionaries in Africa, but evidently inherited some money. They never grew tired of sharing. The Johnstons even gave us their used car when they got a new one.

Our neighbors' bold generosity demonstrates what is truly remarkable about the feeding of the 5,000—Jesus' *initiative* in providing the food. That's the story of God's non-stop love for His children, made so clear over and over again in the Bible.

God's people found food along the roads (Psalm 49:9); they did not hunger or thirst (49:10). The first verse of Isaiah 55 vibrates with the cry of the hungering heart: "…every one who thirsts, come to the waters; and he who has no money, come, buy and eat! Come, buy wine and milk without money and without price" (RSV).

Psalm 111:5 assures us that God will provide food for those who fear Him, while in 37:25 an old man recalls that, during the course of his long life, he never once saw God's people begging for bread. All through the Bible God promises His children adequate food, from the first chapter of Genesis (v. 30), through the manna in the wilderness story (Exodus 16), into the Gospels (e.g., Luke 6:21) and beyond.

We all know the story of manna in the desert. How would the children of Israel get food in such a desolate place? The people, just days out of Egypt, were complaining: "We could have had all the food we wanted back in Egypt," they grumbled. The Lord promised Moses He would drop bread from heaven; that it would, in fact, "rain" down. Each day the people would gather the heavenly bread, the gift of God. They could not store the bread, however; they must get it fresh daily.

Friends, I have noticed, and you have, too, that God provides bread for our souls, as well as our bodies; that it comes in adequate supply, and that He provides fresh bread daily. That bread sustains and invigorates us, inspires and motivates us to do God's assignments. But unlike the manna, the barley loaves, and fish that lasted only for a time, we have Jesus' promise that if we feast on Him, the bread of life, we will be satisfied *forever!*

Sincerely and with deep appreciation for God's provision,

Don

PS: For further nourishment, read Henry Nouwen's *Bread for the Journey: A Daybook of Wisdom and Faith* (Harper, 1997).

18

Day 2

The bread that lasts

In John 6:26-34, crowds continue to follow Jesus, and we hear the following dialog:

"You did not want to find Me because you saw God in the multiplication of the loaves. You wanted to find Me because you filled your stomachs with the food I provided. But do not think primarily about satisfying your physical needs; go for the food that does not spoil—for the eternal bread which I will give you.

"The Holy Spirit puts His seal on My promise to you."

They replied, "How can we take advantage of this offer?"

Jesus said, "Believe in the One God has sent to you."

They pressed Him further: "Can't you show us a sign, something we can see to demonstrate proof and make us believe? Moses gave our people bread in the desert."

Jesus told them they missed His point: "The Moses story is not so much about manna filling stomachs as it is God giving life with a capital L, Life for this life and the next. No mere human being like Moses can give you this kind of bread; only God Himself can do that."

They appeared to respond with eagerness: "Then by all means give us this bread; we want it now and every day!"

Dear Megan and Adam:

Fast food creates obesity. Even kids suffer from excess weight today. The other night on the news, I saw a young

man, grossly overweight, who is attempting to sue McDonald's for feeding him hamburgers and fries during his growing-up years. He claims the unhealthy food damaged his body and threatens his future. Today, spiritual fast food options tug and pull at us. Eastern religions, cults, New Age teachings—any of the substitutes—can deceive us. Our world, filled with all sorts of enticing edibles, easily and subtly leads us away from God. But these meals satisfy only for a time.

During my years as a college teacher, one of our students succumbed to a cult. The leader of the religious group, wearing a beard like an Eastern guru, claimed to do miracles (he boasted of feeding 5000 as well!), and told his followers what to eat as well as what to believe. He even got our student to accept a pseudo-religious experience, of which he then spoke publicly. His manner came across as terribly deceptive, using some of the same spiritual language Christians do.

My heart went out to that young man. He gorged himself on the fast food of deception, and paid a great price. I am also concerned about the fast food that has found its way into our evangelical churches, and pray we will refuse outside influences that steer us away from Jesus. It is not that we overtly teach and preach cultic beliefs, but that our sometimes frothy, feel-good religion lacks Biblical nutrients.

Eat the bread of life, and you will avoid fast food religion.

Adam and Megan, have you examined the quality of your devotional diet? Have you given attention to the classics? Thomas à Kempis, Brother Lawrence, and St. Francis of Assisi stand out as examples, as do more recent writers like Richard Foster, A. W. Tozer, and Dallas Willard. You will want to process these writers slowly, taking small bites.

Good! That only helps digestion and, best of all, builds strong spiritual bodies. No flab there!

Sincerely,

Don

PS: Since New Age thinking threatens many people today—even some in the church—try Bob Larson's book, *Straight Answers on the New Age* (Nashville: Thomas Nelson, 1989).

22

"I am the life-giving bread"

Jesus makes a remarkable claim in John 6:35-40:

"I am the life-giving bread; all who identify with Me will never go hungry again, nor will they get thirsty.

"But what puzzles Me is this: You have seen Me in action, yet you still do not believe in Me. Listen! Everyone the Father gives Me will surely come to Me, and I will never abandon those who come. This explains why I came from heaven—to do the Father's will, not My own.

"And the Father's will? That what He gave Me—absolutely everything—will come to its intended fulfillment. This goes for every person who is given to Me, so that when God winds up history, all My people will actually be whole. This defines God's will: Each person who says "Yes!" to the Son and His actions identifies with Him, and will have never-ending life. I Myself will see to it that every believer comes to fulfilled life."

Dear Adam and Megan:

God's will and its fulfillment—that gets at the heart of this passage.

The great spiritual writers all talk about God's will. Thomas R. Kelly, the Quaker writer, says, "Utter dedication of will to God is open to all.... Where the will to will God's will is present, there is a child of God."

You may recognize Soren Kierkegaard's famous sentence: "Purity of heart is to will one thing." He also talks about

bringing the will into conformity with God's unchangeable will.

In line with Kierkegaard, François Fénelon, the seventeenth and eighteenth century French author, calls for an undivided will. He exhorts us not to divide our will between God and something else. God wants to make us pliable in His hand so that we will desire only what He wants. In this state of mind, Fénelon observes, life goes right, and even idle moments of relaxation turn to good.

To get serious with God, we must live like Jesus, totally submitted to God's plan. God sent Jesus to save the lost and to keep the saved in His grip. God saved us to stay in His grip. And in His hand, we live intimately with Him.

We all struggle with how to live in submission to God's will. Few Christians argue against submission, though recently I read of a theologian who believed this was demeaning to human beings. Incredible! "Make me a captive Lord, and then I shall be free," cried George Matheson in his great hymn. Yes, the road to joy and freedom lies here: centering down into God's will. It is just what the Scottish pastor Matheson did...even though he was blind!

But how do we really surrender? I do not believe we can, at least not in the energy of the flesh. This takes an act of God. Our task, the lesser one, is simply to say "Yes"—with no subtle game playing—and God will grace us with His will. Some struggle with that. In fact, some wrestle a long time, much like Jacob and the angel. Augustine struggled, but finally surrendered and no longer found his will "split into different wills." It was then that he entered a rich, productive life for God, and became one of the leading lights in all of Christian history.

St. Paul declared that he died every day. The Acts of the Apostles saw people filled with the Spirit over and over again. And it was for them as it is for us: the door to the Spirit is surrender.

Sincerely for daily and intimate identification with God and His will,

Don

PS: You can trace the will-of-God motif in an anthology like the one by Richard Foster and James Smith, *Devotional Classics* (Harper, 1993). And, for your own library, you will need Leslie D. Weatherhead's little classic, *The Will of God* (Abingdon).

26

"I am the life-giving bread" (part two)

John 6:41-51 reveals that, despite opposition, Jesus continues to insist that all who follow Him on the journey will be set free to live fully, both in this world and in the world to come:

The Jews complained because Jesus claimed to be the bread of life from heaven. They argued like this: "Surely he is an ordinary member of our own community, the son of Joseph—we know this family and they're just like us. How can a commoner like Jesus say he came down from heaven?"

Jesus told them to stop arguing. "No one can come to Me unless the Father, who sent Me, draws them to Himself. Those who are drawn to Me I will bring to life at the resurrection, at the end of time.

"The Prophets wrote that God will teach His own, and everyone who has heard and learned from the Father will come to Me. Do not misread this: no one has seen the Father except the One He sent—only He has seen the Father.

"I tell you without the slightest doubt that anyone who believes has eternal life. I am the life-giving bread. Your ancestors ate manna in the wilderness; they died. The bread I give you comes right out of heaven; eat heaven-sent bread and you will not die!

"I am the living bread, the bread that came down from heaven. Anyone who eats this bread will live forever. The bread I will give—give for the life of all in the world—that bread is my flesh."

Dear Megan and Adam:

Jesus comes across with self-giving generosity in this passage. He dialogs patiently with those who oppose Him.

Moreover, the giving of Himself even in death is subtly, yet clearly evident in His comments about offering His life for the world.

Jesus models self-giving generosity for us. One of the hallmarks of people who live close to God is bighearted, ungrudging liberality. St. Paul rightly declares that "God loves a cheerful giver" (II Corinthians 9:7), and Jesus told us it's "more blessed to give than to receive" (Acts 20:35). The author of Proverbs 22:9 observes that, "Those who are generous are blessed…." In fact, the Bible says a great deal about the rewards given to generous hearts, especially free and open contact with God.

Conversely, greed closes the lines of communication with God. That's why St. Bernard of Clairvaux cried, "It is folly and extreme madness always to be longing for things that cannot only never satisfy but cannot even blunt the appetite." Such grasping persons, Bernard declared, live in "restless sighing after what is missing." Things and experiences take the place of the Creator, says Paul in Romans 1. Of course, it is God that the human heart wants, and indeed craves. So we read St. Augustine's famous statement about our hearts being restless until they find their rest in God; also Pascal's equally well known comment that a God-shaped vacuum exists in every human being.

The other night in my Devotional Classics class, I showed the Zeffirelli film, "Brother Sun, Sister Moon," on the life of St. Francis. You have probably seen that movie and will recall how Francis gave up his father's offer of business and wealth; he even removed his clothes, which his father had given him, as a symbol of his total independence. Francis, now freed from the burden of money, could give himself away. And that he did! He gave his energy to rebuild a

church, his organizational gifts to start the Franciscans, his love to feed the hungry—he gave all he had to glorify God.

Some have said that Francis lived more like Christ than anyone since Jesus. One of my students got so excited that he purchased "Brother Sun, Sister Moon," and spent an hour talking to his wife about St. Francis' *Little Flowers*!

Sincerely for a warm and generous heart,

Don

PS: You can get into the heart of St. Francis by reading his *Little Flowers*, which I have put into everyday English (Staten Island: Alba Press, 1992).

30

"My words are spirit and life"

In John 6:53-56, 60-65, Jesus speaks about Himself with authority and purpose:

Jesus, responding to the question of how anyone could eat His flesh, declared openly that unless one eats the flesh of the Son of Man and drinks His blood, he cannot have life. But those who eat His flesh and drink His blood—they have life!

Hearing this, many of His followers puzzled over such a statement. "Who on earth could believe that?" they asked.

Jesus, fully aware of His adherents' reaction, said to them, "Why do My words offend you? How would you react if you saw Me ascending to where I came from? Know this: the Spirit gives life; the flesh doesn't give life; My words are Spirit and life. But some of you will not believe."

Jesus said this because He knew in advance who would not believe and also who would betray Him. "This," said Jesus, "explains My comment that no one comes to Me unless the Father draws him."

Dear Adam and Megan:

Let me encourage you to think deeply about the meaning of the Lord's Supper. Did you notice, in the story of Jesus feeding the 5,000, that after He broke the bread He gave *thanks*? Interestingly, the word for *thanks* in the Greek text relates to one of our terms for Holy Communion, *Eucharist*. In fact, *Eucharist* means *thanks*.

The Eucharist signifies many things for which to give thanks. These include the atonement (Jesus died for me!), life and nourishment from the bread and wine, the communion of believers, and the Lord's return (I Corinthians 11:26). But especially we must express thanks for His presence in the Supper.

It is here, my friends, you will find an open door to intimacy with Christ—as you understand the Presence in the Eucharist. This explains in part why Henri Nouwen, wherever he went, developed what he called a "Eucharistic community," a little band of people who would celebrate the presence of Christ in His Supper each morning. Recently, I have followed Nouwen's pattern in some of my classes, telling the students that God wants us to live and study and work in the presence of Christ who creates a bonded community. So we celebrate the Lord's Supper at the beginning of each class session. You cannot believe how that binds us together and alerts us to the presence of the Lord Jesus in our study times!

So think with me about His presence. Ask yourself what you believe about His presence in the Eucharist. To help you ponder how Christians have perceived the Presence, think through the various theories. For example, John Calvin found the *mystical* Presence of Christ in the Supper. He believed in Jesus' spiritual presence, in some unexplainable or mystical, yet real way. He saw the Supper as a pledge to believers that God had done a work for them, and that the values of the cross apply to the believing heart.

Zwingli, a Swiss reformer like Calvin (they both lived in the 16th century), did not put the emphasis on the real Presence but on the *memory* of Christ's death and sufferings. Zwingli did not say much about what the sacrament itself

does for the believer but thought of it as a kind of memorial of the death of our Lord.

The Roman Catholics believe in *transubstantiation*; i.e., that when the priest consecrates the bread and wine they become the *actual* body and blood of our Lord. In this way Catholics literally eat the body and blood of Jesus, taking at face value His words in John 6, telling us to eat "My body."

Martin Luther believed in what he called *consubstantiation*. He said Jesus' Presence is *in, with, under, and around* the bread and wine. While he believed that our Lord's presence is there locally, Luther could not accept transubstantiation.

I personally do not think Zwingli went far enough. Yes, when we take the broken bread and the sip of wine or grape juice, we remember Jesus' death for us. We must! But if I understand the New Testament passages on the Lord's Supper, Jesus is, in some real way, *in* the bread and wine. That's why I can never take the Eucharist casually. In some mysterious way, Jesus is there!

You must come to your own conclusions about the Lord's Supper, but let us agree on this much: to take the Supper seriously, openly, receptively, welcoming Jesus into our hearts freshly. After all, what is more intimate than taking in His presence?

Sincerely for a more serious look at the Holy Eucharist,

Don

PS: My little book, *Basic Beliefs* (Indianapolis: Light and Life, revised, 1996) contains a chapter on Holy Communion. You may find this helpful.

34

Day 6

Hang in there!

John 6:66-71 tells the sad story of some who dropped out on their journey with Jesus:

After all this squabbling and debate about Jesus being the bread of life, many of His followers opted out, refusing to go with Him any longer.

So Jesus asked the twelve closest to Him, "Are you going to give up, too?"

Peter responded: "Who else would we follow, Lord? You guide us with heaven's language, the language that takes us to eternal life. We believe You, and because we have followed You all this way, we have come to know You as the Holy One God has sent."

Jesus answered, speaking to all twelve: "Yes, I chose each of you, but unfortunately one of you is a devil!" Jesus was referring to Judas, son of Simon Iscariot, because he, though one of the twelve, would betray Him.

Dear Megan and Adam:

One of the greatest clues to hanging in there on the journey relates to the food that energizes us.

Jesus Himself is our food. That helps explain John 6. In fact, the whole story of Jesus—even His birth—tells us He is our source of nourishment. For after His birth in the stable, Mary put Him in a manger. And a manger, as you know, is a feed box.

You will also remember that Jesus was born in the town called Bethlehem. The word *Bethlehem* literally means *house of bread*.

Today, over the site where tradition says Jesus began His earthly life, stands the Church of the Nativity, built during Constantine's reign in the fourth century. Here we can learn a great deal about our need, and yes, our reluctance to be fed.

Inside this majestic structure, we meet with two powerful images: an altar, and, just beyond it, the cave where the holy birth took place. The altar and the cave become metaphors of something very relevant to our nourishment in worship. Altars call us to kneel with humble hearts, to pray, to ask, to receive Him. Yet, while people eat and drink at the Lord's Table, not everyone wants to kneel. Ruskin, the famous nineteenth century art critic, loved the cathedral—the nave, the grand Gothic arches, the stained glass windows—but one part he did not like: the altar. Many people simply do not want to humble themselves to partake of Jesus as Lord of their lives. But where else can one get food?

The cave also speaks of humility. Jesus never asks us to take on a posture He Himself did not assume. And Joseph must have suffered humiliation as well when he could not take Mary to a suitable place to give birth. No innkeeper had a room. They ended up in a stable in a cave, says tradition. Imagine it! Smelly, cold, anything but nice—the birthplace of a king!

Humbly kneeling at the altar, bowing in worship in the starkness of the cave—this is the place of the Lord's Supper, and here we are fed.

Believe me, to feed often will keep us steadily on the journey. No wonder the early Christians celebrated the Lord's Supper frequently. John Wesley took it several times a week. For Amy Carmichael, that remarkable missionary in India, it was a daily practice. Some need to do this, but when we come eagerly and sincerely to daily prayer and devotion—whatever form that takes—we have found the secret!

Yours for daily, adequate feeding,

Don

38

MILE TWO

Days 7-12

"I am the light of the world"

40

Light for the road

In John 8:12-20, Jesus establishes Himself as the light for the journey:

Jesus declared, "I am the light of the world; therefore, the ones following Me cannot walk in the dark. Instead, they all enjoy the light that translates life into Life."

The Pharisees had a hard time with His statement. They asked, "What makes you think you can talk about yourself like that? You're just plain wrong."

Jesus had an answer for their accusation: "Yes, I say I am the light of the world because I know where I come from, and I know where I'm headed. You judge by mere human experience; I don't judge like you do. I have heaven's help in My judgments. Even in your own law, it takes two to prove a point; well, I have My Father's confirmation when I say I am the light and the life."

The Pharisees snapped back with a sneer: "Where is this 'Father' of yours?"

Jesus answered, "It's clear that you do not know My Father; nor do you know Me. If you did identify Me for who I am, you would know My Father too."

Jesus taught like this in the treasury part of the temple, but no one arrested Him because the years of His teaching had not come full circle.

Dear Adam and Megan:

William Barclay, the well-known Scottish preacher and commentator, penned a book called *The Promise of the Spirit*, and in the chapter on "The Holy Spirit and the Church Today," he quotes from A. S. M. Hutchison's novel, *If Winter Comes* (1921). Mark, one of the novel's central figures,

wants light. He talks to his friend, Hapgood: "…I tell you, Hapgood, that…down in the crypt and abyss of every man's soul is a hunger, a craving for other food than this earthly stuff. And the churches know it…." But instead of giving him what he actually wants—"light, light—…they invite him to dancing and picture-shows, and you're a jolly good fellow, and religion's a jolly fine thing and no spoil-sport…." But one can get all these things outside the church, so he cries out again, "Light, light! He wants light, Hapgood." Mark goes on: the pastors drink beer with the church members, watch boxing, and dance with them. The preachers say they want to show that religion is alive and fun. "Lift the hearts of the people to God, they say, by showing them that religion is not incompatible with having a jolly fine time. *And there's no God there that a man can understand for him to be lifted to.*" Then he makes the telling observation that no one could care less about giving up something if they could only be sure of "*light*" (Barclay, p. 107).

The walk to Emmaus, recorded in the last chapter of Luke's Gospel, speaks eloquently of the human need for light. Two of Jesus' followers, walking toward Emmaus, discussed the cross and the dark things that had happened in the last few days. Then Jesus Himself came near to walk and talk with them. They were so discouraged that they could not recognize Him. The Greek language describes their dark and blind posture in the clearest of terms: "…their eyes were kept from recognizing Him" (Luke 24:16). Jesus asked them about their discussion, but "They stood still looking sad" (v. 17). Jesus and His friends proceeded to talk at length, their disappointment reaching its fullest expression when they declared, "But we had hoped that He was the One to redeem Israel" (v. 21). Their words revealed that the angel's message about the empty tomb hadn't gotten through to them.

Notice what Jesus says now: "Oh, how foolish you are, and how slow of heart to believe all that the prophets have declared!" (v. 25). Then Jesus proceeded to interpret the Bible prophecies. A little while later, while eating together, "…their eyes were opened, and they recognized Him…" (v. 31; quotations from the NRSV).

When Jesus comes close, the dawn breaks through.

Substitutes for Jesus will not bring light. No, dancing and movies, even with those in the church, and simply talking about the problems of the world—these do not illuminate our spirits. Jesus does!

This reality explains the "magnificent obsession" the saints and mystics had and still have with our Lord.

Passionate about the light of the world, I am your fellow traveler,

Don

PS: In my copy of the *Classics Devotional Bible* (Zondervan, 1996, p. 1229), I found a beautiful prayer about light from the pen of Jacob Boehme (1575-1624) that you will love reading:

"O God, the source of eternal light, You provide temporal light for the earth, ruling over the sun and the moon that all creatures may live and thrive…the gentle beams of the moon and stars remind us that Your Word is alive and active even when we can see only dimly. Guide me to find my rightful place in Your creation, that in some small way I may add to the beauty of Your handiwork. And may Your eternal light shine in the darkest corners of my soul, that all shadow of sin may be expelled." Amen.

Day 8

Walking in light and freedom

In John 8:31-38, Jesus reveals the power of truth to give us freedom on our journey through life:

"If you hang in there with Me and what I say, you will in fact be My disciples; you will actually know the truth, and that truth will make you free persons."

This statement took them by surprise, so they said, "Abraham is our original father; none of us has suffered under slavery, so how can you say the truth will free us?"

Seeing they had missed the point, He talked about sin: "Every person who sins ends up a slave to sin. A slave cannot really feel at home in his own house, but the son feels perfectly at home—he's free to go in and out as he chooses. So if the Son gives you freedom, enjoy it! You're really free!

"Yes, I know you're Abraham's children, but I also know you want to destroy Me because you do not want to hear what I have to say. You are making a serious mistake here; I have learned the truth from My Father, while you go on living by what you think your father Abraham said."

Dear Megan and Adam:

In the freedom Jesus talked about to the Pharisees, He tried to persuade them that light (truth) stands strong, and darkness (prison) crouches ready to pounce out of the shadows of uncertainty and failure.

Phillips Brooks, that remarkable New England preacher and bishop, loved to write poetry. On one occasion he penned these lines:

Tomb, thou shalt not hold Him longer,
    Death is strong, but life is stronger;
Stronger than the dark, the light;
    Stronger than the wrong, the right;
Faith and hope triumphant say
    Christ will rise on Easter day.

Well, of course He *did* rise. And what a metaphor of truth and freedom!

The first century *Epistle of Barnabas* spells out the way of truth and freedom by a straightforward itemizing of what that means:

*Love the God who created you.

*Glorify God who redeemed you from death.

*Be simple in heart.

*Be rich in spirit.

*Hate doing what displeases God.

*Do not exalt yourself, but take on a lowly manner.

*Love your neighbor more than yourself.

*Do not murder a child by abortion or destroy it after birth.

*See trials as good things.

*Give without complaining.

*Confess your sins.

"This," says the writer of the *Epistle of Barnabas,* "is the way of light."

Then the writer goes on to itemize the way of dark and imprisoned living:

*Idolatry.

*Overconfidence.

*Arrogance in power.

*Hypocrisy.

*Double-mindedness.

*Adultery and rape.

*A haughty spirit.

*Deceit.

*Malice.

*Avarice.

*The absence of any respect for God.

*Persecuting good.

*Hating truth.

*Refusing to take care of widows and orphans and other needy ones.

*Killing children.

*Unkindness to suffering people.

(See *The Apostolic Fathers*, with an English translation by Kirsopp Lake, Vol. 1, pp. 401ff.)

This simple listing of good and bad (light and dark) lifestyles refreshes me, Adam and Megan. The reminder confirms and affirms the light which is Christ Jesus. It also makes me ask if I, a human being, can truly live in the light.

Thomas Merton wrote a wonderful little book called *Life and Holiness.* In it he asks if we believe we can put into practice the life of Christ, the light. Merton says many lay persons, even many religious (monks, nuns), don't believe human beings have that ability. Then he comes up with a comforting and strengthening sentence: "If we are called by God to holiness of life, and if holiness is beyond our natural power to achieve (which it certainly is) then it follows that God Himself must give us the light, the strength, and the courage to fulfill the task He requires of us." Then he offers this quick sentence, wonderfully assuring: "He [God] will certainly give us the grace we need" (New York: Herder and Herder, 1963, pp. 10-11).

This divine promise lies behind St. Paul's admonition in Romans 13 to avoid the works of darkness and put on the armor of light. In Ephesians 5, Paul reminds us to live as children of light.

By God's grace I want to do that. I have lived long enough and read enough to know that joyous freedom comes with walking in the light!

By grace alone,

Don

You can be sure of the truth

Unbelieving Jews attacked Jesus, declaring He did not really have the truth. In the argument that completes John 8, Jesus wins. He wins for those who believe; unbelief never hears with understanding.

John 8:39-59 reveals the conflict:

The questioning Jews tackled Jesus by talking about their ancestor, Abraham. "He is our father," they declared.

Jesus responded like this: "If you really followed Abraham, you would act like him. But you want to kill Me, a man who reveals the truth I heard from God Himself."

The unbelievers continued to argue: "We're not illegitimate children; we claim God as our Father!"

Jesus came right back at them: "If you really lived like God your Father, you would love Me. After all, I came from God, so how can you plug your ears to what I say?

"I'll tell you why: you cannot tolerate the truth about yourselves. You really act like the devil's your father. The devil, a murderer from the beginning, refuses to identify with truth because he's totally foreign to it. Of course he lies! What do you expect? That's his nature; he promotes lies.

"In contrast, I tell you truth; that's what troubles you."

Well, after that, these unbelievers accused Jesus of having a demon. Jesus tried to settle that argument, and went on to say that to believe in Him, the truth, means eternal life, not death. They would not listen to that either and said such nonsense only proved He had a demon. After all, Jesus, not even fifty years old, could hardly have seen Abraham or the prophets.

Then He declared that He was alive before Abraham, and that made the unbelievers so angry they picked up stones to kill him. Jesus escaped.

Dear Adam and Megan:

Norman Grubb, author of the famous missionary biography, *C. T. Studd: Cricketer and Pioneer* (London: Lutterworth, 1933), came to the college where I taught in my early years as a professor. He spoke during the chapel service; afterwards, I was so intrigued with this follower of Jesus that I met with him personally. Somehow we hit it off and I found myself going to lunch with a saint, this man who lived intimately with God.

He had startled me in chapel by saying that "Jesus lives literally in the life of the Christian." As a child I sang, "Into my heart, Lord Jesus; come into my heart…." But I had never thought Jesus actually lived in my heart. When I experienced conversion at age nine, I knew He stood *with* me in a special way, but that He lived *in* me—that, listening to Norman Grubb, now struck me as very new.

Mr. Grubb explained that the Spirit of Jesus, who is very real, does in fact live *in* His children. Literally. Reflecting on the teaching of the New Testament, I realized immediately that His Spirit *does* reside in us. And that explains, too, the great significance of the word *intimacy* for the Christian.

The Presence in our lives is in fact the light Jesus talked about. Yes, it makes some people angry, because, as Jesus said, they do not want to hear the truth. That explains why some people do not go to church—they fear learning something about themselves they do not want to know. Actually, we all live with a measure of that fear, especially when we are young. But, as we grow, we learn that contact

with God is the remedy. The closer we get to God, the more fear is swallowed up by the increase of trust and love.

With Christ *in* us, the light shines, alerting those around us to the truth that sets us free from fear, and roots and grounds us in genuine security.

Sincerely for growing in the light and an unshakable truth,

Don

52

Day 10

Light and deliverance

John 9:1-7 tells the story of a man born blind and how Jesus gave him sight so he could see light for the first time:

While on a walk, Jesus saw a man blind from birth. The disciples asked Jesus a question, the kind of question lots of people ask: "Teacher, did this man cause his blindness or did his parents' sin bring it about?"

Jesus spoke straightforwardly to His disciples: "Why do you ask a wrong question like that? Clearly this man did not cause his own blindness; equally clear, his parents did not make him blind.

"The real question? How will God reveal Himself in this man?

"Listen! It is day, but the dark of night will come when the light will go away; then, no one can see to work. While I'm in the world, I am the light."

Now wanting to bring home His point so everyone watching and listening could see Himself as the light, He spit, made mud, then put it on the blind man's eyes. Then He said, "Go wash off the mud in the pool of Siloam" (which means Sent*).*

The man did just that and came back seeing!

Dear Megan and Adam:

Blindness, an analogy for groping in the dark, calls for deliverance. But when deliverance (light) doesn't come, what then?

This poor man, blind from birth, probably never expected to see. Caught in a bad marriage, some couples never hope to enjoy a loving, joy-filled home life. Suffering from chronic illness, many cannot even dream of healing. Deep in debt, a business person may see only bankruptcy ahead.

Can God really bring light? I often quote Jesus' comforting words, "Come to Me, all you that are weary and are carrying heavy burdens, and I will give you rest. Take My yoke upon you, and learn from Me; for I am gentle and humble in heart, and you will find rest for your souls. For My yoke is easy, and My burden is light" (Matthew 11:28-29 NRSV). I find great comfort in these verses, and I love what St. Augustine said: "I have read in Plato and Cicero sayings that are very wise and very beautiful, but I never read in either of them: 'Come unto Me all ye that labor and are heavy laden.'"

Does God send light and, along with it, deliverance? He does. But you must know, my friends, that He always responds to the cries of our hearts with surprise answers. God's middle name is Surprise!

Reading Robert Schuller's autobiography, I note that he experienced one crisis after another: money problems, family accidents, enemies, impossible real estate dilemmas, and…well, you name it, he faced it. But with each daunting challenge—sometimes so daunting he thought he would either resign from ministry or collapse in it—God came to the rescue. Like the time he had to meet a deadline in buying property but needed $10,000. A couple completely unknown to him appeared in his office and provided the money required to purchase ten acres of land for his ministry!

Have you looked at the deliverance passages in the Old Testament recently? Look, for example, at Deuteronomy 7:17-19 and see how God delivered Israel: "If you say to yourself, 'These nations are more numerous than I; how can I dispossess them?' do not be afraid of them. Just remember what the Lord your God did to Pharaoh and to all Egypt, the great trials that your eyes saw, the signs and wonders, the mighty hand and the outstretched arm by which the Lord your God brought you out. The Lord your God will do the same to all the peoples of whom you are afraid."

Look, too, at Psalm 46 and note God's promise of rescue. The Psalm begins with the famous words, "God is our refuge and strength, a very present help in trouble." Then the psalmist rehearses his fears and imagines awful things happening, but concludes with the comforting, strengthening words, "The Lord of hosts is with us; the God of Jacob is our refuge."

Read Isaiah 43:2 and see how God will take you safely through fierce trials: "When you pass through the waters, I will be with you; and through the rivers, they shall not overwhelm you; when you walk through fire you shall not be burned, and the flame shall not consume you."

In the New Testament, read again that last verse of the Book of Matthew and refresh your souls in the comforting words of Jesus, "I am with you always…." (Scripture quotations NRSV)

The saints knew full well that getting intimate with God is not child's play; it's a matter of developing spiritual muscle through testing. No wonder these people have been called the "athletes of the Spirit!"

The passages above tell you how to grapple with the "impossibilities" of life, whether outward or inward, only to say that God never turns a deaf ear to you, that He loves you passionately and has chosen you as His friends, and will deliver you in His time.

With a prayer for your patience in the dark times,

Don

PS: For a straightforward discussion of the "muscular" challenges of life in the Spirit, see Dallas Willard, *The Spirit of the Disciplines* (Harper, 1988).

Walking with patience

The account of the blind man's healing continues in John 9:8-25. It would come across as downright funny if the story did not have all the earmarks of the tragedy of darkened minds:

Some neighbors asked if the cured man was in fact the blind beggar. Some said "Yes." Others said "No, he just looks like him."

But the beggar himself cleared up the argument: "I am the man."

Once everybody had heard this declaration, the neighbors buzzed with questions like, "So how did you get your sight?"

He also answered that question directly: "The one called Jesus healed me. He made clay, pasted it over my eyes, then told me to go to the pool called Siloam (which means Sent*) and wash off the clay. I did what He said and have been able to see ever since."*

The neighbors wanted to know where Jesus went, but the healed beggar did not know.

These same neighbors brought the beggar to the Pharisees. And the first thing they noticed? Jesus had broken the Sabbath! That infuriated them. The Pharisees quizzed him about how he had received his sight.

The poor man had to repeat the story about the clay and washing in the pool all over again!

The Pharisees, terribly irritated, now argued that Jesus could not have come from God because He broke the Sabbath. But some of those listening wondered aloud how a sinner could do such a healing miracle.

With that, the group divided. A few went on to quiz the beggar further: "Since you're the one who got healed, what do you have to say about this man?"

He answered in his now characteristic way: "Why! He is a prophet."

Would you believe, the stubborn, uncomprehending Jews still had a problem with this! In fact, they refused to acknowledge that the man had even suffered blindness! They got disturbed all the more when they talked to his parents: "Was your son actually born without the use of his eyes?"

They said, "Yes."

The Pharisees then asked, with a lot of acid in their tone, "How, then, did he get his sight?"

His parents, frightened the Pharisees would exclude them from worshipping in the synagogue if they said Jesus was the Christ, dodged the question by saying, "Ask our son yourself; he's an adult. We do not know who opened his eyes, nor do we know how he got healed."

The Pharisees, unwilling to leave the question, demanded the beggar give God praise by denying that Jesus—this sinner!—healed him.

The healed man's customary straightforwardness did not fail him: "A sinner or not, He did in fact open my eyes. I can't possibly doubt this because once I couldn't see, but now I can!"

Dear Adam and Megan:

The undercurrent of this vigorous dialog with unbelievers is the unspoken *patience* of God. God's purposes for the blind beggar's life surfaced only after decades of suffering!

I'm reminded of St. Augustine's story. He tells it in his autobiography called the *Confessions.* (You may wish to get your own copy of this spiritual autobiography.

E. M. Blaiklock translated the edition in my library. It was published by Thomas Nelson of Nashville in 1983.) In it Augustine recounts the years he spent running from God and engaging in serious sin. Monica, his devout mother, had raised him as a Christian, but evidently his father's rejection of the Gospel influenced Augustine toward a sinful lifestyle.

Later, he took up rhetoric in Milan and there came under the influence of Ambrose, a great Christian preacher. His life began to turn around. But Augustine could not extricate himself from sexual addiction. He asked God to cure him "but not yet." His habit was that strong!

That "not yet" tells us a great deal about this chapter in Augustine's life. His mother prayed earnestly for him over a long period of time. Once she threw herself at the feet of her bishop, pleading with him to pray for her son. Her bishop did a beautiful thing: he picked her up and assured her that God could not say "No" to her tears.

You may have read the famous account of Augustine's conversion. He heard a child's voice from a neighboring house say, "Pick it up and read it, pick it up and read it." He picked up a copy of the Epistles and turned to Romans 13:13-14 where he read, "…not in orgies and drunkenness, not in promiscuity and licentiousness, not in rivalry and jealousy. But put on the Lord Jesus Christ, and make no provision for the desires of the flesh." Augustine said he did not need to read more. "Instantly at the end of this sentence, as if a light of confidence had been poured into my heart, all the darkness of my doubt fled away" (Blaiklock, p. 204).

The saving light had finally come! God had heard Monica's fervent prayers.

I have learned, as perhaps you have, that *patience* plays a very important role in our spiritual formation. Augustine converted late. Some, on the other hand, believe early in life. As for me, I had turned nine years of age. The truth is, all of us experience the initial rebirth, and other steps in faith development, at our own rate. Often that seems terribly slow.

Here we have a fundamental principle: *light will come, but at its own rate and in its own time.* God holds time in His hand. And God wastes nothing. Augustine not only behaved sinfully, he also engaged in a heresy called Manichaeism (a fusion of Persian, Christian and Buddhist elements) and taught it for nearly a decade. And yet God brought great good out of all this, showing him how to distinguish the light (truth) from the dark (error), honing Augustine's mind and conditioning him to see life in perspective. The result we all know: he became one of the defining theologians of all time. He also built philosophical foundations for the Christian faith. Additionally, his insight into human behavior causes some authorities to call him the first psychologist.

The clear message? Hang in there! Whether you're praying for the salvation of your children, or wrestling with your own spiritual growth, or trying to help a slow learner, in God's own *kairos*, light will come.

Perhaps you know that Greek term, *kairos*. Just in case you have not come across this word, you will want to know that it refers to a special kind of time—God's time. The Greek language calls human or earthly time *chronos.* We get our word *chronology* from that term. A watch, a calendar, the seasons function with chronological time. But heaven counts time in terms of what the New Testament calls *kairos*—i.e., when readiness comes full circle. Only God can

determine that. In His time He saves us. I find that profoundly comforting, for He knows best when to free us, when to deliver us from the darkness of despair to the light of hope and peace. He also knows when repentance and conversion—all the steps of a developing faith in Christ—will have their divinely-intended influence.

Praying for the grace of waiting,

Don

62

The simplicity of light and truth

John 9:26-41 concludes the "I am the light of the world" portion of John's Gospel, which comprises all of chapters 8 and 9. In the final section, Jesus defines Himself clearly, showing the difference between embracing and refusing Him as the truth:

The man born blind, now seeing and knowing the truth, continued to irritate the Pharisees.

"What did this man [Jesus] *do to you?" they asked. "Tell us how he opened your eyes!"*

The beggar showed astonishment at this question: "Look! I already told you the facts, but you refused to open your ears. Do I need to rehearse the story again? Or maybe you're ready to follow Him as His disciples!"

Now they got really angry: "Clearly you're one of his disciples, but we wouldn't think of being disciples of anyone except Moses. We know God spoke through Moses, but this *man? Where does he come from?"*

The man now answered like this: "Well now! What a marvel! You do not know where He comes from, yet He opened my eyes. We know very well God does not listen to sinners, but He does listen to people who honor God and do His will. Not since the beginning of time has anyone heard of a man healed of blindness."

Even more angry at this, they replied, "You're scum, born in sin, so how can you teach us?"

With that, they threw him out, totally rejecting him.

Jesus heard about this and went to look for the man. Having found him, Jesus asked, "Do you believe in the Son of man from your heart?"

He answered Jesus, "Sir, please let me know: who is He so I can believe in Him?" Then Jesus said, "You're looking at Him. I'm the One, the One talking to you."

With that the man replied, "I believe." And he worshiped Him.

Jesus continued in this telling way: "Let Me share with you why I came into the world: I came to define truth, and to take the blindfold off pretenders; in other words, to expose fakes."

Some of the Pharisees standing nearby heard this. "So are you trying to tell us we're fakes? That we're really blind but won't admit it?"

Jesus said to them: "If you do not know you are walking in the dark, how can God judge you? But because you pretend to see truth, when actually you're quite blind, God judges you and holds you accountable for your pretense."

Dear Megan and Adam:

Pretense. That word strikes me as a perfect description of the Pharisees' attitude in this story. They engaged insincerely in dialog with Jesus and the blind man. Have you noticed that people who pretend are complicated? To be a fake requires a lot of work, fabricating awkward questions, weaving complex arguments.

Simplicity marks the honest person. I wonder if you have seen Richard Foster's fine book, *Freedom of Simplicity*. Simplicity takes many forms. It is not only freedom from unnecessary and convoluted thinking, but liberation from material things and "keeping up with the Joneses."

The great devotional writers lead me to believe that to get intimate with God, we must "uncomplicate" our lives. Elaborately woven arguments as well as materialism get in the way of intimacy. God relates to unvarnished honesty.

St. John of the Cross urges us not to desire more but less.

Thomas Kelly, the deeply spiritual Quaker, tells us that God never leads us into "an intolerable scramble of panting feverishness." Simplicity leads us, he says, into "the deep silences of the heart for which we were created."

François Fénelon, the French mystic, talks about purity of heart which robs us of the trouble of wondering what others think of us. He cries out against false modesty, and urges us to that "interior simplicity" which makes us frank and natural, open and gentle, innocent, joyful and serene. This simplicity he calls "the pearl of the gospel."

The Pharisees needed openness of mind, but facing the truth threatened them. What they did not see was that saying a simple "Yes" to truth would give them joy and freedom. Sincere belief would prove far less threatening than artificiality, if they only knew it!

Thomas Kelly believes that holy obedience and simplicity go together, that simplicity is in fact the fruit of obedience. With this comes humility, a humility that rests on what Kelly calls "holy blindness, like the blindness of him who looks steadily into the sun. For whenever he turns his eyes on earth, there he sees the sun. The God-blinded soul sees naught of self, naught of personal degradation or of personal eminence, but only the Holy Will…" (*A Testament of Devotion,* pp. 62-63).

Sincerely for coming to God just as we are,

Don

PS: I highly recommend Richard Foster's *Celebration of Discipline* (San Francisco: Harper, revised edition, 1988) as well as his *Freedom of Simplicity* (San Francisco: Harper, 1981). Along with those books, Thomas Kelly's *A Testament of Devotion* (New York: Harper, 1941) will uncover the subtle intricacies that rob us of life close to God.

MILE THREE

Days 13-17

"I am the good shepherd"

Day 13

Shepherding the sheep

John 10:1-5 introduces the good shepherd narrative (which extends through v. 21). Here we see Jesus' tender heart contrasted with that of a stranger:

"Please understand," says Jesus speaking from His heart, "that anyone who tries to climb into the sheep pen instead of entering through the door—well, that one is a thief and a robber.

"On the other hand, the one entering the sheep pen by the door is a true shepherd of the sheep. The doorkeeper welcomes the true shepherd, and the sheep recognize his voice as soon as he calls to them; when it's time to go out to pasture, they follow him. He even knows the sheep by name; this explains why he can lead them.

"When he has all the sheep outside the sheep pen, he leads the way in front of them and the sheep follow easily because they recognize the sound of his voice.

"And as for a stranger? They will never follow him because they do not recognize the sound of a different voice. In fact, they run away from a shepherd they do not know."

Dear Adam and Megan:

Your strong desire to get intimate with God leads me to believe you will eventually become shepherds, lay or ordained. People with your spiritual passion inevitably become contagious, even eager to care for God's flock.

St. Augustine enlightens us about shepherding in his *Homilies on Ministry*. As I write to you, I'm using the edition entitled *"We Are Your Servants"* edited by John E. Rotelle (Augustinian Press, 1986). Augustine refers to Timothy's

good record as a servant, and contrasts him with those who seek "their own interests, not those of Jesus Christ" (see Philippians 2:19-21). Augustine says these bad shepherds work toward their own ends, do not really love Christ, pursue worldly rewards, and long for honor. Quoting Matthew 6:5b—"Truly I tell you, they have received their reward"—Augustine drives his point home. "You will know them by their fruits" (Matthew 7:16) becomes St. Augustine's litmus test of good shepherding.

Zeal, or eager willingness, says Augustine, marks the true shepherd. Both of you, Adam and Megan, demonstrate a motivation marked by zeal, and I celebrate that!

Handel picked up Isaiah 40:11 to use in his famous oratorio, "The Messiah." A modern translation of that verse comes across so clearly, I want to share it with you: "He will feed his flock like a shepherd; he will gather the lambs in his arms, and carry them in his bosom, and gently lead the mother sheep" (NRSV).

This reminds me of the ancient story in which a flock of sheep came to a ravine so threatening they refused to cross. The shepherd took a lamb in his arms, crossed the gully, and when the mother sheep saw her lamb on the other side, she followed. Naturally the other sheep followed too. (See William Barclay's *The Daily Study Bible* on John 10.)

The truly good shepherd is a caring leader.

Are you familiar with the Moses legend? Moses, feeding his father-in-law's sheep in the wilderness, discovered a lamb had run off from the flock. Moses followed it to a drinking place, where he spoke to the little one: "I did not know that you ran away because you were thirsty. Now you must be weary." Then he put the lamb on his shoulders

and carried it back to the flock. God now spoke to Moses: "Because you have shown pity in leading back one of a flock belonging to a man, you shall lead my flock Israel" (Ibid).

From time to time we must retrieve one of our sheep, often a young disciple. And this kind of leadership means further opportunities for ministry in spiritual direction.

Nothing, Megan and Adam, offers so great a reward as introducing people to Jesus, the good shepherd who guides hungry lambs to the feeding station. I celebrate your infectious enthusiasm for giving away what you yourselves have received!

Yours very truly,

Don

72

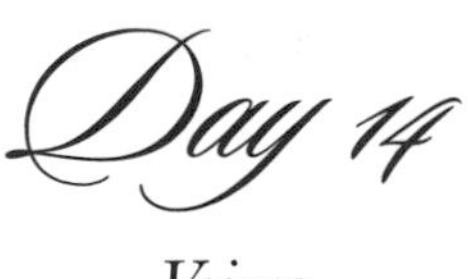

Voices

Jesus repeats the imagery of the shepherd, the door and the sheep in a slightly different way in John 10:6-10:

The people listening to Jesus could not grasp the scene He was painting, so He tried again.

"Please listen carefully," He began. "I Myself am the door at the entrance of the sheep pen. The thieves and robbers who try to take My place do not get a response from the sheep. They cannot hear the voices of these pretenders.

"I am the door and no one else. When the sheep come through Me into the sheep pen, they save themselves from the bad shepherds who kill and destroy the sheep. They go in and out of the sheep pen easily, grazing here and there, enjoying life to the full."

Dear Megan and Adam:

William Barclay, quoting H. V. Morton who wrote so much about Jesus and the Holy Land, says much about the shepherd's voice. Morton tells of two flocks sheltered together in a cave for the night. In the morning each flock returned to their own shepherd because they knew the sound of his voice calling to them.

On a visit to the Middle East, Morton himself listened to shepherds calling their animals. In the hills behind Jericho he witnessed weird, singsong vocal sounds, the likes of which he had never heard before. In his writing, Morton describes a shepherd of a herd of goats descending into a valley, then climbing the slope of an opposite hill.

Crying out, the shepherd talked to the goats in "a language that Pan must have spoken on the mountains of Greece. It was uncanny because there was nothing human about it. The words were animal sounds arranged in a kind of order." As soon as he spoke the animals answered with a bleat that "shivered over the herd...." One or two goats turned their heads in their shepherd's direction. "From the distance came the strange laughing call of the shepherd, and at the sound of it the entire herd stampeded into the hollow and leapt up the hill after him" (*The Daily Study Bible* on John chapter 10).

What a story! My friends, I want to recognize my Shepherd's voice, not the intruder's sounds. One of my mentors, E. Stanley Jones, taught me something about how to distinguish the Spirit's voice from the foreign voices. Brother Stanley, as we called him, *listened.* He spent quiet time in the morning and in the evening praying and listening. I cannot read Dr. Jones' books without sensing that he knew the Inner Voice.

The Inner Voice always speaks with the Bible. Anything contrary to the revealed Word cannot be God's voice.

The Inner Voice also harmonizes with the hymns of the Church. I read the hymns of John and Charles Wesley, John Newton and William Cowper, Isaac Watts and Augustus Toplady, and some of the more recent hymn writers, too, like Andrae Crouch and Richard Blanchard. They sing their way into my soul, inspire me, and give me direction.

When I hear true preaching, I sense God's voice. My former pastor, Dean Cook, soaks in the Scriptures, listens to the Spirit, exercises the skills he learned in seminary,

relates to his people—no wonder the congregation hears God speak!

You will know other ways in which God talks, for in every move of His hand, God makes Himself known.

Eager to recognize His voice, I am your fellow traveler,

Don

The good shepherd

John 10:11-15 paints a most beautiful picture of Jesus looking after His sheep, even if wild animals threaten His life:

"I am the good shepherd," declares Jesus. "A good shepherd will even die for his sheep. Not so with a bad shepherd—he runs away when he sees a wolf coming. After all, these sheep are not really his, so he leaves them to fend for themselves. The wolf kills some of the sheep and the rest scatter over the pasture land, filled with fear.

"The sheep don't matter to the false shepherd. But they do to Me! I am the good shepherd; I know My own sheep; and they know Me just as My Father knows Me.

"Yes, I will lay down My life for My sheep—that's how much I care!"

Dear Adam and Megan:

Sheep come into the Biblical picture so often, one cannot doubt that the metaphor of the good shepherd resonated with ancient Hebrews and early Christians. You will recall that Abraham, Moses and David all served as shepherds. Ezekiel 34:11-16 reveals God Himself as a shepherd. Jesus thought of His vocational goal as shepherding His sheep, as clearly stated in John chapter 10. I Peter 5:2 shows that tending God's flock describes the pastoral leadership role in the early Church: "Shepherd the flock of God that is among you, exercising oversight…" (ESV).

I can hardly believe what I recently saw pictured in the *Bible Review* magazine: a piece of sculpture dated 1600 A.D., from Goa, India. The ladder-style work at first looks

Hindu in origin, but upon further examination reveals itself as a clearly Christian artifact. Here we have Jesus holding a lamb, while under His feet stand Mary, His mother, and St. John, and between them a spout of water representing baptism. At the bottom of the creation appears Mary Magdalene absorbed in reading Scripture.

The art object depicts Jesus standing at the top, while other figures and symbols appear in descending order. Here we see the true pattern of intimacy with our Shepherd: Jesus comes first, sources of inspiration and grace follow. (Information from *Bible Review*, Vol. XVII, No. 3, June 2001, p. 56.)

My primary source of peace comes from Jesus Himself. Philip Keller's famous book, *A Shepherd Looks at Psalm 23* (Zondervan, 1970), makes it clear that when we go through tough times, our Protector watches over us. More, He makes the difficult paths a way to deeper intimacy with God.

Note, for example, what Keller says on p. 85: "Again and again I remind myself, 'O God, this seems terribly tough, but I know for a fact that in the end it will prove to be the easiest and gentlest way to get me onto higher ground.'" He continues: "Then when I thank Him for the difficult things, the dark days, I discover that He is there with me in my distress." This, he says, paves the way to calm instead of panic—i.e., "quiet confidence in His care." Well, yes! After all, God stands in control of our lives.

Here lies an enormous reward of intimacy with God. People who do not walk closely with Him often panic. Alarm laced with fright leads to the worsening of a bad situation. The trusting heart always receives grace not only to go through the dark times but to use them for an even better solution than one could have possibly imagined.

This morning, Adam and Megan, I finished reading Robert Schuller's autobiography, *My Journey* (Harper Collins, 2001). The ups and downs of his life come seemingly non-stop. No sooner does he get one problem solved (usually an overwhelming crisis like a million dollars to meet a deadline, or the amputation of his daughter's leg after a motorcycle accident), when another provocation rears its head. The mountaintops provide great inspiration, but the downers take Schuller's breath away. He stabilizes himself with the certain knowledge that the Shepherd will rescue him. And He always does.

Evidently human beings must have crises in order to relish the delicious experience called fulfillment. When landscapers make a golf course, the challenging physical contours (hills, valleys, ponds, etc.) must often be created if they do not occur naturally. God made us to rise to the challenges, but only with the strong support and grace of the Shepherd. Don't blame God for devising the hard times—wolves attack sheep! Do credit Him with rescuing us and treating our wounds, then fashioning something beautiful out of these ordeals.

Did you know that the Chinese character for *crisis* means *opportunity?*

Lovingly,

Don

PS: Let me share Martin Luther's secret of victory over the dark places. Perhaps you know Luther fought depression. When attacked, he repeated two Latin words over and over—*Baptizatus sum,* which means *I have been baptized.* James Stewart, the great Scottish preacher, comments that Luther meant God claimed him for His own and had

begun and would continue His work in him (James S. Stewart, *Walking with God,* Edinburgh: Saint Andrew Press, 1996, p. 61).

Day 16

Sacrifice

John 10:16-18 portrays Jesus' willingness to die for all those who call Him their shepherd:

"I have other sheep not in this sheep pen," Jesus said. "I must lead them as well, and they will recognize My voice.

"In this way, the sheep in this sheep pen and My sheep from other pens will all come together because I am the shepherd of them all.

"My Father loves me because I'm willing to give My life for all My sheep, and the Father gives Me freedom to know when I need to sacrifice Myself."

Dear Megan and Adam:

Today, sheep farmers shear their animals with power tools; in ancient times they used primitive instruments. Whether now or then, sheep often suffer bruises, even bleeding, when the shearer cuts away the wool. Yet, despite the rough treatment, sheep tend not to rebel against their shepherds. On a gut level, they seem to understand their need to be cared for and protected.

Evidence of this comes from Australia, which has more sheep than people. There, eagles represent the greatest threat to the flock. The huge birds swoop down with great power and snatch lambs, carrying them away in mid-air, landing, then devouring the helpless creatures. On one occasion a herder noticed a sheep lying motionless in the distance. Curious, he drove across the acreage to the site.

Sure enough, no movement. He noticed the eyes of the sheep were missing—pecked out by the eagles—and bits and pieces of the sheep's body removed—an ear, swatches of flesh. The shepherd gently reached out to the animal, hoping it was still alive, only to watch it topple. Amazingly, however, the farmer found a lamb under the mothering sheep, fully protected, and very much alive!

Sheep know how to care for their young just as a shepherd knows how to protect each animal.

William Barclay, through his *Daily Study Bible*, has helped me better understand the shepherd's sacrificial duty. He observes that Old Testament law required a shepherd who lost a sheep to prove that he could not possibly have saved the animal's life. Amos 3:12 refers to a shepherd rescuing just two legs and a piece of an ear from the mouth of a lion. Exodus 22:13 tells us that if beasts attacked a sheep, the herdsman must bring the mangled remains as evidence.

Barclay also talks about the difference between good and bad shepherds. One is only a hired hand who works for money but does not really care about his sheep. In contrast, good shepherds make sheep their world. They love their animals and often take care of a flock for years. David, a shepherd from his youth, while he did not lose his life, killed a bear and a lion to save his sheep. Sadly, some shepherds actually do pay the ultimate price.

Friends, when I think of Jesus, my shepherd, going to the cross to make salvation possible, I feel profoundly grateful. This spiritual reality puts me in intimate contact with Him.

Sincerely for deeper appreciation of my Shepherd's sacrifice,

Don

Day 17

For or against?

John 10:19-21 reveals the continuing division among the people:

Again the listeners disagreed among themselves because of Jesus' difficult-to-understand words. Some said He had a demon and raved on and on, so why listen to Him?

Others said a demon-possessed person could not possibly open the eyes of a blind man.

Dear Adam and Megan:

Sometimes I wonder if people who oppose Jesus, the good shepherd, really understand their need for His guidance!

Time and again the Scriptures employ the figure of shepherds and sheep to illustrate how God relates to His people. So central is this imagery to the story of the Bible that it would be difficult not to conclude that human beings are designed to be guided and nurtured by their Creator.

David often writes of his boyhood vocation. In fact, the book of Psalms abounds with these images. Psalm 23, which we call the shepherd's Psalm, begins, "The Lord is my shepherd." Psalm 77:20 contains this beautiful line: "You led your people like a flock by the hand of Moses and Aaron." Psalm 95:7 paints the essential relationship: "For He is our God, and we are the people of His pasture, and the sheep of His hand."

The same gentle care of sheep shines through in the New Testament. Luke 15:4 asks, "Which one of you, having a

hundred sheep and losing one of them, does not leave the ninety-nine in the wilderness and go after the one that is lost until he finds it?" (NRSV).

My friends, when I think of how Jesus, the good shepherd, has followed and cared for me over the years, I find myself in a place of genuine thankfulness!

Doesn't all of this remind you of I Peter 2:25? "For you were going astray like sheep, but now you have returned to the shepherd and guardian of your souls." Put that famous verse with the great benediction of Hebrews 13:20, "Now may the God of peace, who brought back from the dead our Lord Jesus, the great shepherd of the sheep, by the blood of the eternal covenant, make you complete in everything good so that you may do His will, working among us that which is pleasing in His sight, through Jesus Christ, to whom be the glory forever and ever. Amen" (NRSV).

How can one possibly oppose this loving leadership? Unlike the people in Jesus' day, we can never afford to second-guess the character or motives of One so committed to our wholeness!

With affection for Jesus, my Shepherd, I am as always your friend,

Don

MILE FOUR

Days 18–23

"I am the resurrection and the life"

86

A crisis along the way

After the announcement of Lazarus' illness at the beginning of John chapter 11, for a couple of days Jesus refused to go to Bethany where Mary, Martha, and Lazarus lived. We pick up the story there, in verses 11-15:

"Our friend, Lazarus, has gone to sleep," Jesus said to His disciples, "but I plan to awaken him."

The disciples replied, "Well, if he's gone to sleep because he is sick, he will wake up and feel better."

But Jesus had used sleep as a metaphor for death, so now He spoke to them directly: "Lazarus is dead." Then He added, "Actually, I'm glad I wasn't there because, in order to deepen your faith, I'm going to give you new evidence about who I am."

With that, He said they should go directly to Lazarus.

Dear Megan and Adam:

Sometimes when God seems absent He is really present. For years I have wanted to write a book on the *ministry of presence and absence.* The two go together.

Some time ago, I went to see a man dying of cancer. "Last night," the man in the bed began, "I couldn't find Him," his voice breaking as he spoke. However, as we talked, I could sense the man was becoming aware of Christ's Spirit once again. Oh, yes! He *will* come after His absences, and even the absences have their purpose! I had no doubt that

the man's faith took a leap forward because he sensed the Presence again.

Sometimes He comes to us through a person. My pastor dad, along with Kathleen and me, went on vacation in England. We stopped to see an authentic Elizabethan village. The three of us looked in wonder and awe at a very charming thatched roof cottage. As we sat in our rental car admiring the place, the owner emerged. Graciously, she invited us in to see her house. We had to bend low to get through the doorways—most people in Queen Elizabeth's day did not grow very tall. What a delight it was to tour this alluring sixteenth century home!

As we exited, Dad engaged the homeowner in conversation. She had lost her husband less than a year before. I could overhear her as she said, "God seems so far away."

Then came Dad's loving reply: "In sorrow, God always seems far away." His gentle tone let that dear woman know God had not gone far; in fact, He was right there in the conversation.

Tears come to my eyes as I recall that powerful moment, for inevitably God makes Himself known again and He always comes freshly alive in us. That English woman's faith, like that of the man with cancer, could only grow.

Lovingly,

Don

Day 19

Balancing Mary and Martha

In John 11:17-27, Jesus arrives in Bethany, the home of His friends, Mary and Martha. On a road just outside the city, He speaks with Martha about life and the life to come:

So Jesus came to Bethany and found Lazarus dead just as He had said. In fact, he had already lain in the tomb four days.

Bethany, only about two miles from Jerusalem, had drawn many of Mary and Martha's friends who had come to grieve with them for their brother. And when Martha heard Jesus was coming, she went out to meet Him on the road to Bethany, while Mary waited in the house. Martha said, "Lord, if you had only come earlier, my brother would not have died. But even now I know that whatever you ask God for He will give you."

Jesus responded like this: "Your brother will live again."

Martha replied immediately, "Yes, of course. I know he will rise again in the resurrection at the end of time."

But Jesus said, "I am life right now, *and anyone—and I do mean anyone—who believes in Me will live even if he dies. In fact, he will live forever!"*

With that, He asked Martha, "Do you believe this?"

She replied, "Yes, my Lord, I believe you are God's Son, the One God sent into our world."

Dear Adam and Megan:

Have you noticed how Mary and Martha always stand in such contrast with one another? Mary waits; Martha

works. Mary listens; Martha speaks. Mary sits at home; Martha runs out to meet Jesus. In today's world we are tempted, as Martha, to give Mary the failing grade. After all, the go-getters win, right?

Evelyn Underhill, the British mystic, flies a caution flag here. We get so tied up in busyness that we *lose* life. Martha, always *doing* things—even very good things—runs the risk of losing contact with the Source of Life. Underhill uses strong language: we *maim* ourselves by overdoing. With exhaustion comes "loss of depth and of vision." This results in the "vagueness and ineffectuality of a great deal of the work that is done for God." She goes on to say that total surrender to the "click-click" of life and its demands results in spiritual deadness.

Underhill insists that we must engage in "quiet contact" with the world of the supernatural. But, she observes, we use our lives conjugating three verbs: to Want, to Have, and to Do. "Craving, clutching, and fussing, on the material, political, social, emotional, intellectual—even on the religious—plane, we are kept in perpetual unrest: forgetting that none of these verbs has ultimate significance, except so far as they are transcended by and included in, the fundamental verb, to Be: and that Being, not wanting, having, and doing, is the essence of a spiritual life" (*Classics Devotional Bible*, p. 1250).

How then do we combine Mary and Martha? Martha, bless her, served (John 11:2, Luke 10:40), but she fussed about it: "Lord, do You not care that my sister has left me to serve alone?" (Luke 10:40). Jesus replied, "Martha, Martha, you are anxious and troubled about many things; one thing is needful. Mary has chosen the good portion, which shall not be taken away from her" (Luke 10:41 RSV).

We need Marthas—the world could not function without them. We also need Marys—the world could not survive without the quiet listeners.

But just maybe between Luke 10 and John 11 Martha made some progress. Notice in John's Gospel her avid attention to Jesus' words. Observe her affirmation of the Resurrection. Consider her further affirmation of Jesus as the Messiah. Clearly she is drawing closer to Jesus; she's making progress!

This, then, becomes the gut level question for you and me, Adam and Megan: Are *we* maturing by living in the balance of being and doing?

Yours for the balance,

Don

92

Facing the reality of death—and life!

The story of Jesus, Mary, and Martha continues to engage us in John 11:28-37:

After her conversation with Jesus, Martha went to Mary and told her that their Teacher had arrived and wanted to see her too. So Mary got up quickly and came to Him out on the road where Martha and Jesus had talked together.

Some of their Jewish friends followed her; they thought she would go to the tomb to morn. But Mary went to Jesus. She fell at His feet and cried, "Lord, if you had only been here! Lazarus would not have died."

When Jesus saw Mary weeping, and noticed her Jewish friends crying as well, He also felt troubled in His spirit and asked, "Where have you put Lazarus?"

"Come and see," everyone replied.

Now Jesus cried too, and the Jews said, "See how much He loved Lazarus!"

But some of them had to say, "Well, why didn't He stop Lazarus from dying? After all, anyone who can open a blind man's eyes can surely heal a man with a terminal disease."

Dear Megan and Adam:

Note that Jesus did not deny death. Cults may say death does not exist (Christian Science, e.g.), but the Christian faith, taking the clue from Jesus, never denies death.

Denial, one of the common stages of grief, seems to rob us of facing a loved one's death. We just can't believe that person has gone, never to return.

A friend shared with me that after his wife's passing, he had a moment, after a few days of mourning, when he fully realized, "Mildred has died. She will not come back." Emotionally, he said, he came to freedom and release. This is one reason we have open-casket viewings. The human psyche tends to hide from the threat of trauma, from bad news.

My wife's mother, joyful that she went to her husband Grover's viewing, said, "I'm so glad I went. Some people told me not to go to the funeral home to see Dad in the casket, but I did the right thing." Interestingly, she said that with a tone and expression of release.

Jesus did not deny death. But He did alert us to life. He wanted us to know the fact of resurrection both in the next life and in this one, too.

Rob sat in my seminary classes. Little did I know he had served time in prison. One day he told me. He never shared what put him behind bars, but his radiant faith demon-strated a personal resurrection from what must have struck authorities as a fairly serious crime. Rob, now a seminary graduate, serves in Gospel ministry.

Resurrection in this life, yes! And also in the next.

Perhaps you heard the National Public Radio interview with Robert Shaw, that remarkable musician/conductor who elevated the Atlanta Symphony and Chorus to international renown. Shaw and the interviewer discussed Bach's deeply spiritual "B Minor Mass." In the PBS

interview, the reporter asked, "Do you really believe what Bach is saying in the Mass?" Shaw's forthright answer brought a delighted laugh to my lips. Said Shaw, "After you've listened to the opening chorus of the "B Minor," you'd be a fool not to believe in the possibility of heaven!" Amen!

Jesus declared Himself the resurrection and the life, and that those who believe in Him never die. People who do not live close to Christ tend to doubt both resurrection and eternal life. We, however, echo the faith of Martin Luther, who declared that when we pray without ceasing we lose the fear of death.

Your fellow believer in resurrection and life,

Don

Day 21

"Let him go!"

One of the most remarkable events recorded in all of literature appears in John 11:38-44. And it's a true story!

Jesus, deeply mourning within Himself, came to Lazarus' tomb, a cave with a stone rolled in front of it. He asked some people standing by to lift the stone away.

Lazarus' sister, Martha, objected at first, remarking that the body would smell after four days in the grave.

Not bothered in the least by this, Jesus said, "Didn't I tell you that if you believe you would see God at work in a most glorious way?"

With that, they removed the stone and Jesus lifted His face to heaven: "Father, thank You for hearing Me. You always listen to Me, but all these people standing here need to know that You hear Me so they can believe You sent Me."

Having said these words, He cried out in a very loud voice, "Lazarus, come out!"

He came out, his hands and feet tied up with the grave clothes and his face wrapped around with a napkin.

Jesus said to the mourners standing by, "Cut away the grave clothes and let him go."

Dear Adam and Megan:

J. C. Eversole recently celebrated his 100th birthday. Three hundred fifty friends and relatives showed up for the party. All congratulated the founder and CEO of First Federal Savings and Loan Bank in Hazard, Kentucky.

Molly Toler, his granddaughter, declared, "He looked a lot younger than some of the other people at the celebration. He was as happy as he could be."

Eversole started First Federal in 1960 at retirement age. From that time until he broke his hip just a few weeks before his birthday, Joe reported to the bank virtually every day. Actually, he resigned as CEO five years before his centennial, but continues as an active director of the bank! On the Friday after the party, he said he would take a couple days off, "but I'll be back in the bank on Monday."

I love to think of the people who, though advanced in years, made significant contributions to the world. Grandma Moses, Franz Josef Haydn, Col. Sanders—the list goes on and on. I recall a pastor who came out of retirement to serve as president of a seminary. And remember Art Linkletter? Now past 90, he annually addresses numerous gatherings, mostly universities and churches. His humor and inspiring words bring hope and helpful information to thousands.

Living the life of creative possibilities, whatever one's age, has a way of announcing itself with the unexpected. Do you know the story of the railroad stationmaster who received a box of watches through the railway mail system? He tried to deliver them to the jeweler to whom the box was addressed. The jeweler refused them. The stationmaster could not return the box. He tried to give the box away; he couldn't find a soul to accept it. Then he got an idea. He drew pictures of the watches with prices indicated, and produced duplicated sales sheets. Wouldn't you know it, the watches sold. And with that one small success, the Sears catalog was launched!

I have discovered that when we live close to God, He stimulates our creativity. . .no matter what our age. *Life* in the Gospel of John has a larger meaning than heaven.

Let me remind you that the Greek word for *life* in John is *zoe*, or *abundant life*. That's the kind of life that makes you eager to get up in the morning! Today, Lord, cut off our grave clothes and let us go!

Eagerly yours,

Don

100

Day 22

The way of the Cross

Jesus' miracles always caused an uproar, especially in the hearts and minds of the Pharisees. John 11:45-53 tells us about the dialog that went on after Lazarus was raised:

Many of the Jews who had come with Mary, and who saw what Jesus did, now believed in Him. Many others did not. They went to the Pharisees and told them what had happened.

With that the chief priests called a meeting of the Council to ask what they should do in the light of Jesus' miracles. "If we let Him go on doing these remarkable things, won't everyone believe in Him?" they asked. "And if they do, the Romans will take away our positions of authority and even our nation!"

However, Caiaphas, the chief priest for that particular year, said, "You don't really understand what's going on here. Let Jesus alone; He will eventually put Himself in a corner and be killed. In that way He will die for us all, as it were. Then we will not have to fear the Romans."

Little did Caiaphas know what he predicted! He spoke as a prophet without knowing it and without realizing the implications of what he said. Actually Jesus' death would bring together all *God's children, even those scattered in many places.*

With the comment by Caiaphas, the Jewish authorities worked at finding a way to eliminate Jesus.

Dear Megan and Adam:

Gregory of Nyssa, a fourth century bishop and wonderful spiritual writer, tells us that if the "chambers of the soul" open wide, God Himself will come to live in us. On the

contrary, says Gregory, if we keep the "inner man" occupied with ungodly thoughts—even if we could go to Golgotha, or the Mt. of Olives, or to the place of the resurrection—we will "be as far away from receiving Christ. . .as one who has not even begun to confess him" (*Classics Devotional Bible*, p. 1268).

The Bible comes through loud and clear on this central truth: those who really want God have Him; those who oppose Him cannot have Him. The Pharisees did not want to believe in Jesus, so they forfeited the joy, freedom, peace and love He provides.

Do you read the celebrated and very old *Book of Common Prayer*? That Anglican worship book, which John Wesley considered the best of all worship guides, got into my heart many years ago. Despite the outdated language, I hope you will use it once in a while. These lines on the death and resurrection of our Lord summarize the Christian faith in all its power and victory: "But chiefly are we bound to praise Thee for the glorious resurrection of Thy Son Jesus Christ our Lord, for He is the very paschal lamb, who was sacrificed for us, and hath taken away the sin of the world; who by His death hath destroyed death, and by His rising to life again hath won for us everlasting life."

Please carefully consider that profoundly true and liberating prayer. I tell my ministerial students that if they believe in the Cross and empty tomb, they can communicate the Gospel. A clergy friend of mine went to the hospital to call on a church member. There he found a colleague, head buried in his hands, sitting near the room of one of his own parishioners. "Ben, what's the matter?" His distraught friend replied, "I can't visit my church member in there. . .I don't believe Jesus' cross saves us and I do not believe He rose from the dead. I have no real message for that dying woman."

My friends, I must agree with C. S. Lewis in his statement so well known you must have heard it more than once: "Christianity, if false, is of no importance, and, if true, of infinite importance. The one thing it cannot be is moderately important."

Yes! Either the Gospel story of the Cross and Resurrection stand absolutely true or the crucifixion becomes nothing more than a piece of theater and the empty tomb a myth to bring the play to a nice conclusion.

I rehearse the awesome truth of the Cross and Resurrection often, because I simply can't get over the fact that Jesus died for me, yes *me*, and that His resurrection guarantees my own eternal life. Really believing this bonds me to Jesus all the more.

In deep gratitude for the amazing Gospel of Jesus Christ,

Don

PS: Evelyn Underhill said this about Jesus' resurrection: "The primary declaration of Christianity is not 'This do!' but 'This happened!'"

104

Angry people

Jesus had a way of slipping through the fingers of the Pharisees and the Jewish authorities who did not like Him. In verse 54 to the end of John chapter 11, we see hints of His enemies' schemes:

No wonder Jesus avoided walking around where everyone could see Him. He hid Himself in the country near the desert city called Ephraim; there He spent time with His disciples.

The Passover Feast was about to take place in Jerusalem. Jesus became the hot topic of conversation. People walked toward Jerusalem and made themselves ready for the festival. While they walked they talked: "Do you suppose Jesus will come to the festival? Not likely!" After all, the chief priests and the Pharisees had commanded that anyone who saw Him must let them know. They were planning to arrest Him.

Dear Adam and Megan:

The chief priests and Pharisees did not grasp the fact that anger kills. Anger eats away at people, consuming the soul and, eventually, the body as well. So, in trying to kill Jesus they really took steps toward killing themselves.

I wonder if you have come across the writings of Redford and Virginia Williams of Duke University. The husband and wife team did a break-through book called *Anger Kills* (Random House, 1993). Their hostility questionnaire makes it possible to assess one's own anger levels.

Experience as a pastoral counselor tells me most people do not look at themselves realistically. They pretend they have no anger. Wow! I'm sure the Pharisees in today's Scripture

passage would balk at taking the Williams' hostility questionnaire!

I'm reminded of a marvelous little passage from Soren Kierkegaard. He helps his readers look honestly at James 1:22-25, those verses on looking in the mirror. People who will not look at themselves realistically gaze into the mirror but go away forgetting what they're like. The great Danish theologian gives his people three ways to get real:

(1) Don't look at the mirror "in order to inspect it"…look at yourself. When reading Scripture, refuse to get caught up in the interpretation of it; rather, read it for what it actually says and profit from it.

(2) When reading the Bible, remind yourself to say that it's speaking to *me*; "I am the one it is talking about." He goes on to say that if you see God's Word as only doctrine—a belief that is out there somewhere—you will not make it your own. A doctrine could be about as helpful as a wall!

(3) Finally, Kierkegaard asks us to remember what we really look like in the mirror. This means I must determine to remember how I appear, robbing myself of the ability to forget. (See John Baillie, *A Diary of Readings*, Day 312.)

Jesus had a way, by His personal presence and His poignant words, of penetrating the human heart. Pharisee-type people do not like this. They want to examine the mirror, focusing on mere doctrine, and so forget who they really are.

When I read Scripture, or listen to the Holy Spirit, or sing a hymn, or reflect on a sermon, I want the Spirit to speak to me. I must prepare myself to say "Yes" to His voice, but I know that only He can make me look at Jesus and myself

realistically. By God's grace I will accept Jesus simply for who He is, because when I do, joy and freedom, peace and love will flood my soul!

Do you ever puzzle over why people say "No" to Jesus, or even get angry at Him? Especially when He is their only source—their only hope—of happiness?

Lovingly and, by God's grace, wanting to be honestly His and yours,

Don

PS: Thomas à Kempis observed that when we get angry, wisdom vanishes.

108

MILE FIVE

Days 24-28

"I am the way, the truth and the life"

The greatest blessing

One of the most comforting verses in all Scripture occurs in John 14:1:

Jesus told His disciples not to allow trouble to enter their hearts. "Believe in God," He declared with a great sense of authority; "and believe in Me too."

Dear Megan and Adam:

Playing with etymology makes for some exciting discoveries! "The Word of the Day" comes from my seminary library onto my computer screen; this service traces word histories. *Benison* appeared on the screen this morning. It means *blessing* or *benediction*. Here's the example sentence: "The travelers stopped at the tiny country church and sought the *benison* of the priest before continuing their arduous journey."

Benison and *benediction* mean the same thing. They come from the Latin root, *benedicere*, meaning *to speak well of* or *to bless*.

Benison, I learned, has a longer history in the English language than *benediction.* Actually, *benison* had its beginning in the fourteenth century, while *benediction* first appeared a century later.

Jesus' words, "Let not your hearts be troubled" are a benison. It takes its place among the ancient benedictions as one of the greatest of all blessings. Jesus' clear intention? To comfort His disciples. Jesus would soon leave them. Jesus' benison is grief-processing in advance of the cross.

Belief in Me, Jesus says, will give you the security you need when I leave. I will never forget family prayers the morning I left for New York and my first year of seminary. Dad read an appropriate passage of Scripture, Mother prayed, I prayed, then my father prayed. Seldom have I seen my father cry; I did that morning. I knew he loved me and gave me his best blessing.

Then we got in Dad's Chevy and went to the Los Angeles train station. During that first year of graduate studies I never once doubted the intimate bond between my father and myself. The letters, the money he sent, his unfailing belief in me—all let me know without a shadow of a doubt that his benison had clothed me like a well-tailored suit.

Jesus bonds with us, knows our struggles, and invites us to speak very personally with Him. This explains the intimate language often seen in the great hymns.

Johann Franck (1618-1677) begins a hymn with this couplet:

> Jesus, priceless treasure,
> Source of purest pleasure

and ends it with this triplet:

> Yes, whate'er we here must bear,
> Still in Thee lies purest pleasure,
> Jesus, priceless treasure!

Or take these words from Bernard of Clairvaux (1091-1153):

> Jesus, the very thought of Thee
> With sweetness fills my breast;

But sweeter far Thy face to see,
And in Thy presence rest.

St. Bernard's fourth stanza reads like this:

But what to those who find? Ah, this
Not tongue nor pen can show:
The love of Jesus, what it is
None but His loved ones know.

The final verse lets us know He does not break His bond with us either in this life or the next:

Jesus, our only joy be Thou,
As Thou our prize wilt be:
Jesus, be Thou our glory now,
And through eternity.

Jesus Himself is the ultimate *benison.*

Sincerely with gratitude for the grace of His closeness,

Don

Day 25

On the way home

Jesus lets His disciples in on a glorious promise, wonderfully personal and reassuring. You will find it in John 14:2-3:

"In My Father's heavenly Kingdom there are many spacious houses. Yes, it's true—I would have let you know if I was only kidding! What is more, I am going there to prepare homes for you in God's Kingdom. Once I have made your accommodations ready, I will come to get you, and I will take you back to heaven with Me."

Dear Adam and Megan:

Do you love the old cathedrals? I do. Once inside, I marvel at the carved pulpit, the Gothic columns, the chancel, and the stained glass windows. Often the windows are most striking because of their exquisite beauty.

If you happen to visit a cathedral at noon, you may have the added pleasure of an organ concert. The powerful music fills the nave, echoing off the pillars and walls, and engages the soul in the richest of harmonies.

Do you know why the medieval Church erected cathedrals? To give us a glimpse of heaven. Just as the Eastern Orthodox think of icons as windows into eternity, so western European Christians conceive of these massive buildings, with richly colored glass, statuary, frescoes, carvings and music, as introducing us to heaven with all its grandeur.

What an exciting glimpse of all that awaits us! Jesus has gone on ahead to prepare for us what the King James

Version called "mansions." And to guarantee that we will actually get there, He promises to show us the way. In fact, He *is* the way. Yes, to follow Him assures our safe arrival.

When I meditate on heaven, I feel close to Jesus. It explains why I love to linger in the great cathedrals. And it reminds me of my kinship with the devout Christians through the ages who also thought a lot about eternal life. After all, we will *all* see Jesus face to face!

Grateful that we know the way to heaven,

Sincerely,

Don

PS: Just for fun, get a blank sheet of paper and draw or paint a scene representing what heaven means to you. Or, start a scrapbook collection of images that reflect heaven's beauty and majesty. Use your creation during quiet times as a tangible reminder of God's presence and His promise of eternal life!

The way, the truth and the life

In John 14:4-7, Jesus dialogs with Thomas about an issue of infinite importance:

"You know the way I'm going," Jesus announced.

Thomas addressed the Lord: "We don't know where You will go, so how can we feel secure about You returning and taking us back?"

Jesus answered like this: "I Myself am the way, also the truth; even more, I am the life. This explains why My Father guarantees your safe passage through Me. If you had really understood Me, you would know My Father speaks the truth about who I am. But now that I've told you this, you do know Him and can feel totally secure in what He says."

Dear Megan and Adam:

Jesus addresses life with a capital L. I want you to see what the German theologian, Dietrich Bonhoeffer said about life. His famous theme of "costly grace" comes into the quotation, as you can see here: "Costly grace is the treasure hidden in the field, for the sake of it a man will gladly go and sell all that he has. It is costly because it costs a man his life, and it is grace because it gives a man the only true life" (*The Cost of Discipleship*, London: SCM Press Ltd., 1959, pp. 36-37).

Yes! "He who loses his life shall find it," said Jesus with the kind of authority that makes us know that here we have a truly freeing principle of fulfilled living. *Zoe*, the word translated *life* in John's Gospel, means *abundant life*.

Zoe relates to the *joie de vive*—the joy of life. That kind of existence, says Jesus, comes from God Himself who created us. When we live life like that we identify with Him. That's intimacy with the Divine!

I wonder if you have seen the A. B. Simpson poem on experiencing God which shows the contrast between half trust and full faith. I want to share it with you because it makes crystal clear the difference between "almost" surrender and "total" self-giving, the key to life with a capital L:

Once it was the blessing, now it is the Lord;
Once it was the feeling, now it is His Word;
Once His gift I wanted, now, the Giver own;
Once I sought for healing, now Himself alone.

Once 'twas painful trying, now 'tis perfect trust;
Once a half salvation, now the uttermost;
Once 'twas ceaseless holding, now He holds me fast;
Once 'twas constant asking, now my anchor's cast.

Once 'twas busy planning, now 'tis trustful prayer;
Once 'twas anxious caring, now He has the care;
Once 'twas what I wanted, now what Jesus says;
Once 'twas constant asking, now 'tis ceaseless praise.

Once I hoped in Jesus, now I know He's mine;
Once my lamps were dying, now they brightly shine;
Once for death I waited, now His coming hail;
And my hopes are anchored safe within the veil.

All in all forever,
Only Christ I'll sing;
Ev'rything is in Christ,
And Christ is ev'rything.

Again, yes! This poem describes the quality of life—intimate, abundant, freeing, joyous, fulfilled—that God craves for us.

I'm on board for that!

As always your fellow traveler,

Don

120

Philip and Jesus

John 14:8-11 lets us see and hear Philip's struggle, which mirrors our own inner wrestling:

Philip now addressed Jesus: "If you show us Your Father, we will feel a lot better."

Jesus answered like this: "I've spent a long time with you, yet do you really know who I am, Philip?

"Let Me explain again: You have seen Me, so you have seen My Father also. How, then, can you ask to see the Father? Do you believe I'm alive in the Father and the Father's alive in Me? Here's an example: My words are really My Father's words; I speak with His authority. Yet the Father who lives in Me does His works through Me. So believe Me, Philip—believe that I live in the Father. And if that's hard for you to understand, at the very least believe the miraculous works that I do."

Dear Adam and Megan:

Poetry sometimes speaks deeply to my heart. You too? Thomas Aquinas, that unusual 13th century Italian theologian, would help Philip (and us) understand Jesus in "Godhead Here in Hiding:"

Godhead here in hiding, whom I do adore
Masked by these bare shadows, shape and nothing more,
See, Lord, at Thy service low lies here a heart
Lost, all lost in wonder at the God Thou art.

Seeing, touching, tasting are in Thee deceived;
How says trusty hearing? that shall be believed;

What God's Son has told me, take for true I do;
Truth himself speaks truly or there's nothing true.
On the cross Thy godhead made no sign to me;
Here Thy very manhood steals from human ken:
Both are my confession, both are my belief,
And I pray the prayer of the dying thief.

I am not like Thomas, wounds I cannot see,
But can plainly call Thee God and Lord as he;
This faith each day deeper be my holding of,
Daily make me harder hope and dearer love.

O thou our reminder of Christ crucified,
Living Bread the life of us for whom He died,
Lend this life to me then: feed and feast my mind,
There be Thou the sweetness man was meant to find....

Jesu, whom I look at shrouded here below,
I beseech Thee send me what I thirst for so,
Some day to gaze on Thee face to face in light,
And be blest for ever with Thy glory's light.

"Send me what I thirst for so...." What a phrase! Underneath the struggle over Jesus' identity, Philip actually wanted to drink at the spring of living water. The inner conflict between belief and wanting desperately to satisfy our deepest craving—we are all engaged in this wrestling match.

When belief comes at last, then settles in and finds nurture, the life John talks about in his Gospel becomes wonderfully real. But the learning curve takes its own time. We cannot rush it. We dare not throw in the towel when doubts threaten. We just hang in there, and little by little we mature in Christ, "the way, the truth and the life."

And there's more good news! As Aquinas says at the end of his remarkable poem, we will see Him face to face in heaven!

Growing in love for Jesus, the Christ,

Don

124

Day 28

"Even greater works!"

In John 14:12-14 Jesus makes a huge promise:

"I really want you to hear and believe in Me, because if you do, you will do the same works I do. . .no, even greater works! This will happen when I go to the Father.

"So, whatever you ask in My name, that I will do, so that the Father will get the credit through the Son. Listen! Whatever you ask in My name, I will do it."

Dear Megan and Adam:

This passage has always excited me! As a child I heard an adult say in Sunday School that Jesus' promise of "greater works" referred to modern science. I believe this, at least to a point, because medical research continues to make some incredible breakthroughs.

But I wonder if Jesus also meant other things. For example, have you noticed that the ministry of healing has returned to the Church? The openness of God's people to healing services, and the amazing number of healings, reminds me of the New Testament miracles.

Also, the Gospel has now reached more than two-thirds of the world. Those who study missionary work today chart the progress of world evangelization. From tiny Palestine (Jesus never preached outside that little strip of land), on to Asia Minor with St. Paul, then to Europe, later to Africa, Asia and beyond—breathtaking! More, the current growth rate of Christianity, with thousands of new believers being

added every day, makes us stand in awe of the mighty works of God. . .and He invites us to participate in that growth!

I feel compelled to say another word about the progress of the Gospel. Today, musicians, actors and writers in Hollywood, engineers, teachers, plumbers, and house builders—all witness for Christ in their places of work and in their communities. We don't hear a lot about this, but they practice life in Christ in a quiet but influential way.

Have you noticed that the people who are most energized and successful in the work of the Gospel live close to God? These people also do "the greater works." I celebrate them and God's power expressed in their lives!

Eager to participate in still more "greater works,"

Don

PS: Jesus often reminded His followers that with God, "all things are possible." Sometimes we fail to see the "greater works" because we cannot accept the reality of this promise. As a daily exercise, examine your thinking, identifying those attitudes which sell God short. Ask the Holy Spirit to replace your doubt with faith, and watch the possibilities grow!

MILE SIX

Days 29–34

"I am the true vine"

128

Day 29

Life in the vineyard

The first three verses of John 15 provide a picture of Jesus as the vine, His children the branches, and His Father the farmer who keeps the grapevines cleared of dead and useless growth:

Jesus, painting this new picture, declares, "I am the true, the real vine; My Father is the keeper of the vineyard. Every branch that does not bear fruit, the Father prunes away so that the grapes will come in big, rich clusters. Actually, My words to you have already pruned you clean of dead growth."

Dear Adam and Megan:

Jesus said, "I am the vine." He added, ever so graciously, "and you are the branches." And yet, by calling us branches, was Jesus really all that gracious? Branches must undergo pruning, which involves radical cutting. Vineyardists know that vines produce both good and bad wood. The Hebrews would not even use the discarded wood for altar fires on which they offered sacrifices. Bad wood must go!

That goes for bad grapes, as well. In Isaiah 5 we read a parable: A lavish vineyard is prepared and planted, but there are no edible grapes found on the vines! The bad fruit tastes sour, so Isaiah says the entire vineyard must be destroyed!

The sweet fruit—the quality fruit—of the Spirit, my friends, only comes from intimate contact with God and seasoning in the Spirit. Yes, He prunes us, and sometimes

that hurts. He also cultivates us, and that brings satisfying rewards.

A young lady came into my office complaining. Believe me, I like the kind of complaining I heard! She said, "I don't see the fruit of the Spirit in my life." I asked, "What's your devotional life like?" Her reply struck me as honest and unvarnished: "Hit and miss." Then I asked, "Do you eat your meals like that?" Then came something I did not expect: "I used to eat hit and miss. I nearly lost my health."

So, I need to remind myself, as well as you two, to read rich intimacy literature like John Wesley's *Christian Perfection*, Thomas Kelly's *A Testament of Devotion*, Oswald Chambers' *My Utmost for His Highest* and other classic works like you will find in the bibliography at the close of this book.

Da Vinci's *Last Supper*, painted on the wall of a monastery in Milan, Italy, gives us a beautiful picture of the intimacy we're after. Da Vinci placed the figures facing the dining room of the monastery. When the monks ate they dined across from Jesus and the Apostles. To sit at the feet of the masters of devotional writing is to sit facing Jesus and His special followers!

I want to eat and drink with Jesus and His close friends.

Your friend at the feast,

Don

Stay attached to the vine

Verses 4 and 5 of John 15 tell us how to stay secure and productive in Jesus:

"A branch cannot produce grapes by itself; it must stay attached to the vine. In the same way, you cannot bear fruit unless you live in Me.

"Let Me underscore what I just said: I Myself am the vine, and you are the branches. So the ones who stay attached to Me will recognize My attachment to them. These are the ones who will produce grapes.

"Why? Because living apart from Me means you can produce nothing at all."

Dear Megan and Adam:

My friend Steve Harper asks how clergy can thrive over the long haul. He answers that question in such a significant way, I want to share it with you because lay people must also grow and carry on productively despite demanding workloads.

Steve offers these seven imperatives for lifelong ministry:

*Offer yourself up.

*Pray yourself full.

*Study yourself sharp.

*Devote yourself completely.

*Relate yourself transparently.

*Keep yourself healthy.

*Guard yourself constantly.

Dr. Harper concludes his mini-essay with a quotation from Oswald Chambers: "We must work out what God has worked in." Steve's commentary on that statement comes in a single sentence: "This is not 'self-help'—it is response to grace" (from "Companion-Ships" for November 4, 2002, published at Asbury Theological Seminary, Orlando).

I want to share with you the story of my friend Harlow Snyder. He was a busy executive for a medical supply company, but never allowed his time with God to take a back seat. He showed me his little study room in the basement of his Boulder, Colorado, home. I saw on his bookshelves above the desk, the works of C. S. Lewis and other Christian writers. He confided that he got up at five each morning and spent a couple hours in reading and meditation. You can know I felt deeply moved. Harlow means business with God. He wants more than anything to get intimate with Jesus.

Harlow Snyder, my friend for over half a century, exhibits the Spirit of Jesus. His kind and considerate manner, his active work in the local church, his relationship with his family—all spell out closeness to Jesus Christ.

Friends, perhaps God has already revealed the quiet time He wants you to have daily. I learned many years ago that God tailor-makes a program for each one who earnestly desires Him. Harlow is an early bird, so he enjoys the early morning, as I do. Hopefully one of you is an early riser and the other a later riser, so that your meditation periods do not collide. Of course, you can each have your own space

at home if you both get up early or if the two of you retire late in the evening. I once knew a man who took his coffee breaks to meditate on Scripture. Some like to find a suitable place to eat a sack lunch and study God's Word at noon.

Enough said for this letter. I found writing you today refreshing because it reminded me of the great value of quiet in the presence of God.

As always your fellow disciple,

Don

PS: Take some time to reflect on each of Steve Harper's seven imperatives and how they relate to your own life of worship and service to God. Invite the Holy Spirit to reveal areas of weakness or weariness. Your quiet times spent listening, praying, and learning from God's Word will build, the spiritual "muscle" needed for staying attached to Jesus, the vine.

134

The pruning process

John 15:6-8 tells us what God does with dead wood:

"If you do not stay attached to Me, you will dry up and die. And the keeper of the vineyard, having pruned you away along with the other useless branches, must put you on the refuse pile and burn all that dead wood.

"On the other hand, if you stay attached to Me and My words, you can ask anything at all, and, if it's according to My will, you get it. You see, My Father's desire is for you to produce big, rich clusters of grapes; this shows you are really My disciples."

Dear Adam and Megan:

When the Master Gardener cuts away the non-productive branches, how do we handle the suffering that inevitably comes?

Before I answer that question—and mind you, I have only suggestions, no final answer!—we need to face some very real pitfalls of pruning. For one, I could become cynical and question, even ridicule, the work of the Gardener. Or I could lapse into pessimism, seeing my life and everyone around me in dark hues. I dare not embrace those two options.

What I *do* need to embrace—and now come my suggested answers—is the suffering I'm going through. To pretend it's not there only generates inner festering and therefore worsens the agony. But to face squarely what's happening

liberates me to rise to the challenge and handle it with sincere thankfulness.

This leads into the substance of what I want to say about the pruning and burning every devoted Christian experiences. Though gratitude is often difficult, we always move the healing and learning process forward by authentic thanksgiving.

Let me make a few suggestions about how to express thanks:

(1) Get a good, solid understanding of the word *gratitude.* It comes from the Latin *gratus*, meaning *pleasing*, or *thankful.* From that Latin root we get words like *grateful* and *gratitude*, which suggest an *appreciation for benefits received*. Appreciation comes as a natural response to a heart filled with gratitude. The term *grace* also relates to *gratus.* Signifying *beauty* or *favor*, it describes the kindness of God which fertilizes our own gratefulness. *Gratus* also finds its way into a positive term like *congratulate* and into negative terms like *ingrate* or *ingratitude*. An ingrate is inevitably a sour person, and ingratitude produces the bitter fruit of greed, which is anything but grace.

(2) Decide to be thankful. Gratitude opens the door wide to intimacy with God. Ingratitude closes the door. Pure, simple thankfulness does wonders for contact with our Father. As soon as you adopt that posture, you can *feel* His Presence. But to say, "Thank you," only to add, "If only," or, "Why me?" or, "But I'm so unworthy"—those negative qualifiers only throw us back into a dark, depressive mode which slams the door on God in a big hurry. So when the temptations come, make a firm decision to *be grateful.* I like what the Swiss theologian Karl Barth said about gratitude: It's like a suit of clothes, he commented; a suit of clothes to put on.

(3) Anticipate the benefits of thankfulness. We can never predict what wonders will emerge from a thankful spirit. Sometimes, for example, healing comes. Do you remember the story of Catherine Marshall's battle with tuberculosis? She wrestled and struggled, prayed and prayed some more; then one day, it struck her that she must thank God. Yes, thank Him for her illness! So she did. And God healed her! You can read about it in her book, *A Man Called Peter.* She lived many years after she wrote and published that biography of her husband.

Depend on this: a spirit of gratitude yields rich rewards. Healing is one; joy is another; liberation still another. And the best prize of all? Intimacy with the sovereign God!

Lovingly and with a prayer for the grace of gratitude,

Don

PS: One more thing. The causes of suffering lie couched in mystery; we don't know all the dynamics. What we do know is that God uses our hurts to mold us into people who are more like Jesus. Gratitude gives God permission to use our pain as a pruning, refining instrument, and that puts us into ever closer communion with Him.

Day 32

Love, the original blessing

John 15:9-10 gives us the key to living consistently in the security of Jesus' love:

"I love you the same way the Father loves Me—so now remain in My love.

"If you obey My rules you remain in My love. I keep My Father's rules, which proves I remain in His love."

Dear Megan and Adam:

The problem, of course, is that we do *not* always keep His rules. We don't because of original sin. Disobedience bars us from that intimacy for which our hearts long so deeply. So what's the answer to this puzzling enigma?

Henri Nouwen talks about our woundedness due to original sin, but also about "the original blessing." He defines the original blessing as God's unconditional love, present in God long before our conception. "It touches you from before your beginning until after your death. It embraces you forever." Nouwen even goes so far as to announce, and announce boldly, that, "You are the blessed one. That is your identity."

I love what Henri Nouwen says next about broken bread. To take the bread, to bless it, to break it, and to give it summarizes "the whole movement of God's love." In the same way, Jesus takes us, blesses us, breaks us, and gives us Himself so we can give ourselves to others. To know that

He blesses us before He breaks us opens wide the door of intimacy with God. Jesus breaks us, Nouwen believes, not because of our faults but because "we are blessed sons and daughters, like Jesus."

Of course we must give our love away—that's the nature of love. So Nouwen summarizes his message on the original blessing in this way: Our brokenness makes possible giving ourselves to the world as bread for the hungry. We see Jesus doing this over and again: He takes, blesses, breaks and gives Himself. That pattern characterizes His ministry. Nouwen does not want us to forget that. Like Jesus, God takes, blesses, breaks and gives us. Why? Because He loves His sons and daughters and has from our very beginning.

That original blessing—love, unconditional and revealed to us through both God's written and living Word—creates the richest of opportunities to get intimate with God. Here lies the heart of our desire to love and obey Him!

Yours in the unconditional love of Jesus,

Don

PS: You can read more of Nouwen's thoughts in *From Fear to Love: Lenten Reflections on the Parable of the Prodigal Son* by Henri J. M. Nouwen and edited by Mark Neilsen for *Creative Communications for the Parish,* 1564 Fencorp Drive, Fenton, MO 63026.

Day 33

Joy!

Verse 11, one of the most important single verses in John's Gospel, reveals Jesus' deep desire for His children and assures us of His great gift:

"Why have I told you all these things? I think you know the answer: the all-embracing joy that characterizes Me will come to fulfillment in you."

Dear Adam and Megan:

I love what Bernard of Clairvaux said: "Jesus is honey in the mouth, music in the ear and a shout of joy in the heart." Yes, Bernard!

Hear the shouts of joy from other great spiritual writers, because they give us an injection of inspiration, which in turn renews us in intimacy with God. Oswald Chambers asks where saints get their joy. Their joy is so great, he says, that one would think they have no burdens. "But we must take the veil from our eyes," he insists. "The fact that the peace, light, and joy of God is in them is proof that a burden is there as well." He explains: Burdens squeeze the grapes and produce sweet wine, but we tend to see only the wine and not the burden. Then comes the great truth: "No power on earth or in hell can conquer the Spirit of God living within the human spirit; it creates an inner invincibility."

C. S. Lewis was "surprised by joy;" John Wesley experienced heaven's joy at Aldersgate on May 24, 1738; Fyodor Dostoevsky, knowing that his life would soon end, declared, ". . .every day that is left me I feel how my earthly

life is in touch with a new, infinite, unknown, but approaching life, the nearness of which sets my soul quivering with rapture, my mind glowing and my heart weeping with joy." Fénelon sensed enormous joy when he received a fresh discovery of the faith, "like a miser who has found a treasure."

Come to think of it, my friends, tracing joy in the writings of the spiritual giants—that would make an exciting devotional experience, building our faith and putting us in fresh touch with God! If you find yourselves motivated to do such a study, you might begin in the *Classics Devotional Bible* (Zondervan, 1996), then move on to Foster and Smith's *Devotional Classics* (Harper, 1993) and another anthology Richard Foster worked on, *Spiritual Classics* (Harper, 2000).

John Wesley declared that, "Sour godliness is the devil's religion." Of course! Authentic relationship with God cannot help but bring joy. It is the natural, inevitable produce of our awareness that God loves us.

Yours for an increasing joy in Christ,

Don

PS: I wonder if you have come across Henri Nouwen's *Lifesigns*, in which he says a great deal about joy. In fact, he calls joy "ecstasy," a fitting description of the free and happy heart of the Spirit-filled Christian. Nouwen has a passage so delightful and authentic, I must share part of it with you: "The joy that Jesus offers His disciples is His own joy, which flows from His intimate communion with the One who sent Him. It is a joy that does not separate happy days from sad days, successful moments from moments of failure, experiences of honor from experiences of dishonor,

passion from resurrection." Now listen to this: "This joy is a divine gift that does not leave us during times of illness, poverty, oppression, or persecution." More, it keeps us away from fear and secures us in love (*Lifesigns: Intimacy, Fecundity, and Ecstasy in Christian Perspective,* pp. 98-99).

Love and friendship

John 15:12-17 assures us of Jesus' love—love that opens the way to friendship with God and other people:

"The foundational rule—my ultimate commandment—is simply this: love everybody as I love you.

"Now let me talk about ultimate love and friendship. No one can prove friendship more than to die for a friend. I want you to know that you are My friends if you follow this self-sacrificing rule of love.

"I also want you to know that I no longer call you servants. Servants never know what the master is doing, but I call you My friends, and the proof is that I have told you everything. That is to say, everything the Father has shared with Me I have passed on to you.

"You did not take the initiative in this friendship; I did. What is more, I have chosen you to be productive, to yield big, rich clusters of grapes, grapes that don't rot but serve their intended purpose. For this reason, ask anything you want from the Father—ask for it in My name—and He will give it to you.

"And remember the key to this high level of productivity: love one another!"

Dear Megan and Adam:

Sometimes a rather obscure writer catches my attention. I came across St. Aelred of Rievaulx (1110-1167), who lived in Northern England. A gentle soul, he understands the love principle Jesus addresses in John 15:12-17, and expresses himself in beautiful, intimate terms. He wrote

extensively on love and friendship, and what I want to quote here leads us straight to our closest Friend, Jesus Christ: "It is no small consolation in this life to have someone who can unite with you in an intimate affection and the embrace of a holy love." He explains that we need friends with whom our spirits can rest, with whom we can pour out our hearts. In addition, true friends will listen when we talk about the many troubles of our world. Together, we can shed tears about our worries, be happy when things go well, and search for answers to problems. All this means ties of love that go to the depths of your heart. This is heart speaking to heart, soul mingling with soul, and the two of you becoming one.

We relate in the same way to Christ, our Friend. St. Aelred writes, "And suddenly and insensibly, as though touched by the gentleness of Christ close at hand, you begin to taste how sweet He is and to feel how lovely He is. Thus from that holy love with which you embrace your friend, you rise to that love by which you embrace Christ" (quoted in Bert Ghezzi, *Voices of the Saints*, NY: Image Books/Doubleday, 2000, pp. 2-3).

I sometimes ask my students, especially struggling ones, if they know that God loves them. If they really do not know, we work together to make that discovery. And when the awareness of God's love comes—wow! A genuine "Aha!" moment.

Actually, we all need fresh assurance of His love, and sometimes that results in new "Aha!" moments. In any event, our sense of His deep and continual affection for us inevitably renews intimacy.

In the awareness of God's love,

Don

MILE FIVE

Days 35–40

"I am the Son of God"

Jesus at the Feast of Lights

In John 10:22-42, the Jewish Feast of Dedication, or Feast of Lights, becomes the backdrop for Jesus' revelation of Himself as God's Son. In the first paragraph of this section, verses 22-30, John uses the sheep and shepherd theme as his vehicle for communicating Jesus' heavenly relationship:

The Feast of Dedication (or Feast of Lights) was the center of Jerusalem's focus. Winter had come and Jesus walked along the Porch of Solomon in the Temple area. There some Jews gathered around Him and they asked a question: "How long will you keep us in suspense? Are you the Messiah? If so, tell us plainly."

Jesus answered, "I already told you but you would not believe Me. Haven't you seen the works I do in My Father's name? These tell you who I am.

"However, you do not believe, and I can tell you why. You are not My sheep. My sheep recognize My voice; I know them—that's why they follow Me.

"These sheep of Mine will enjoy eternal life. They will never die, and no one will snatch them out of My hand. My Father gave these sheep to Me, and He is greater than anything you can think of. So no one can snatch them out of my Father's hand either.

"I speak with authority because I and the Father are one."

Dear Adam and Megan:

The Feast of Dedication, sometimes called the Feast of Lights, came in the Jewish month of Chislew, our month of December. In every devout Jewish home, the lights of Hanukkah, another name for the festival, burn at this season of the year.

The origin of the Hanukkah lights goes back to Antiochus Epiphanes, a Syrian king, who tried to force Greek religion on the Jewish people. He polluted the Temple, and turned the altar, where the priests made burnt offerings, into a pagan altar. The pagan king also removed the sacred lights of the Temple.

Many Jews lost their lives in their rebellion against Antiochus, but a man called Judas Maccabaeus rescued the Temple and God's people, and he made possible the rededication of the Temple and the restoration of the lights.

The legend about the restoration of the lights goes like this: With the rededication of the Temple came the relighting of the great seven-branched candlestick. But authorities could find only one container of unpolluted oil, enough to burn candles for just one day. But God did a miracle—the oil lasted eight days. So for eight days the candles burned in the Temple. To this day Jewish homes light eight candles at Hanukkah.

And it was on this occasion, the Feast of Lights, that Jesus chose to illuminate His true identity. The light that shone on Bethlehem's stable now blazed in Jerusalem's Temple, as Jesus declared His oneness with the Father. The light of the world had come with the ability and desire to burn in the hearts of men and women everywhere, bringing them into living contact with God.

Friends, I find that light flooding my soul with Himself, His truth and His daily revelations.

In praise of His all-encompassing brightness,

Don

A careful look at Jesus

Jesus had enemies. Unbelievers accused Him of blasphemy because He declared that He was the Son of God. John 10:31-33 introduces the conflict between Jesus and these unbelieving Jews:

Angered, the Jews picked up stones, ready to kill Jesus. But Jesus had an answer for their hatred: "Look! I have done many good works, works that really help people. I have done them through My Father's power. Which of these good works makes you want to stone Me?"

They answered Him like this: "We have no intention of stoning you for your good works, but for blasphemy. You, only a man, claim to be God."

Dear Megan and Adam:

Blasphemy is defined as assigning the works of God to human beings. In other words, putting people in the place of God. The Jews had strict laws against blasphemy; in fact, anyone guilty of it must die by stoning (Leviticus 24:16).

Jesus answers the arguments of the unbelievers in terms of His works. Time and again in John's Gospel He tells them to look at what He does—He meets the real needs of real people by healing the sick, restoring sight to the blind, feeding the hungry.

Oh, that these objectors would have fully examined the life of our Lord: His righteous life, His pure motivations, His

identity with God the Father, and the evidence of His divinity in the miracles!

To keep your eyes on Jesus, and the holiness of His being and doing—there lies the key to embracing truth. People intimate with Jesus understand that; skeptics don't.

While a student in seminary, I heard that a well-known church leader had behaved inappropriately. My dad drove several hundred miles to visit me just to say one thing—words so important I cannot forget them after half a century: "Don," he began, "never focus on human beings; they will let you down. Keep your eyes on Jesus; He can never let you down."

The scribes and Pharisees, blinded by their legalism, did not really look at Jesus. Frequently, my friends, I must examine my own focus. I notice that if my eyes veer from the Lord, my perspective becomes increasingly chaotic and fragmented. When I see Him, the pieces of life's puzzle come together to make a workable and beautiful picture.

When Jesus is God for us, life works.

Sincerely in Him,

Don

Day 37

"I am the Son of God"

John 10:34-36 reveals Jesus as the unique Son of God. The story unfolds in a most interesting way:

Again Jesus answered the accusing unbelievers, this time quoting the Scriptures: "Doesn't the inspired Word tell us that God said, 'You are gods' [Psalm 82:6]*? The Word does not lie. Why, then, does it seem strange to you when I, the unique One, call Myself God? The Father sent Me, fully prepared, into the world. Why would you want to accuse Me of blasphemy?*

"The fact is I am *the Son of God."*

Dear Adam and Megan:

Dr. Fred Craddock, the much loved teacher of preaching, tells an amazing story. He met a stranger at a restaurant somewhere in the South. The man opened up to Dr. Craddock, sharing about his unhappy childhood. An illegitimate child, he felt excluded by his classmates. Rejected and lonely, he sensed no real bond with anyone.

One Sunday he went to hear a new pastor in his small town. The preacher captured his attention and when the minister concluded, the boy just sat in the pew, lost in thought, even after the closing prayer of the service.

Finally the boy got up to leave, but his shy spirit kept him from shaking hands with the minister. The pastor, however, took the initiative, placed a firm hand on the young man's

shoulder, and in a spirit of joy asked the boy his name. "Whose son are you?" the pastor wanted to know.

The young fellow couldn't say a word before the pastor announced, "I know who you are. I know who your family is. There is a distinct family resemblance. Why, you're the son of God."

The pastor also added: "Now, go claim your inheritance!"

When the man in the restaurant brought his story to a close, he looked into Craddock's face and said, "You know, those words changed my life." With that he walked out the door. Still gripped by the story, Fred asked the waitress to identify the man if she could.

To his astonishment she replied, "Why, that was Ben Hooper, two-term governor of Tennessee!"

Friends, just as Jesus says in today's Scripture reading, we are sons of God. No, not *the* Son of God—that is Jesus Himself. But God made us in His image, and when we claim that inheritance—wow! Who knows what will happen? And who knows what will happen to the people we treat as God's unique creation?

With a fresh desire to relate to people as sons and daughters of the Almighty,

Don

God with and within us!

In John 10:37-39, Jesus argues with the greatest clarity:

"If I do not do the good works of My Father, then don't believe me. Suppose you ignore for a moment what I have said about My own identity. Just focus on the works. If you turn your attention to what I do you will see that I work in the Father's energy. Then you cannot miss Our common goals and Our oneness.

"Now can you see that the Father lives in Me and I live in the Father?"

Dear Megan and Adam:

Jesus models for us the indwelling God. St. Augustine taught that He can live in us: "Jesus departed from our sight that He might return to our heart. He departed, and behold, He is here." Martin Luther put this truth in poetic language:

"Ah! dearest Jesus, holy child,
  Make Thee a bed, soft, undefiled,
Within my heart, that it may be
  A quiet chamber kept for Thee."

The Incarnation and the indwelling Christ are intimately related. E. Stanley Jones' famous picture story illustrates that. I do not remember where I first read Brother Stanley's story, but it spoke clearly to my heart:

A small boy, looking at a picture of his absent father, turned to his mother and said longingly, "I wish my father would step out of the picture."

"This little boy," Jones comments, "expressed the deepest yearning of the human heart." We see God in nature and know about Him in Scripture, but we want most of all to have God Himself. Oh, that He would step out of the indirect and impersonal and come to us in person!

Brother Stanley asks why the mere idea of God won't work for us. Why must we have a personal God? He answers with a poignant illustration. Suppose a child is crying for her mother, but instead someone talks to the little one about the idea of motherhood. The child would pay no attention and only go on crying. She doesn't want the idea of motherhood—she wants her mother!

But God *has* stepped out of the two-dimensional picture and given Himself in the form of a living person, Jesus Christ. "And the Word became flesh and lived among us, and we have seen His glory, the glory as of a father's only son, full of grace and truth" (John 1:14 NRSV). He is the fulfillment of the long-awaited *Immanuel,* or *God with us.*

E. Stanley Jones' story reminds me of what a little boy said: "Jesus is the best picture God ever took of Himself." We know God's character by looking at Jesus. And He makes us want to live like Him.

The only way we can live like Jesus is for His Spirit to live in us.

Yours in celebration of the desiring heart,

Don

PS: Brother Lawrence experienced the living Presence so strongly "that the time of business does not with me differ from the time of prayer, and in the noise and clatter of my kitchen. . .I possess God in as great tranquility as if I were upon my knees at the blessed sacrament."

Day 39

Back to where it all began

In John 10:39-40 we see how Jesus dealt with increasing opposition:

Those who hated Jesus now tried again to arrest Him, but He escaped. He crossed the Jordan and came to the place where John first baptized people, and He stayed there awhile.

Dear Adam and Megan:

I want you to notice Jesus' behavior in this brief passage. He knew His time had not yet come, so He escaped from his accusers. Wise! But observe *where* He went: to the place of His baptism, where His ministry began. John's baptism of Jesus proved a defining moment in His life.

Ask yourselves: Where did I begin? Where did God speak, launching me onto my spiritual journey and into His service?

I have a friend, a bishop in the Episcopal Church, who returns every year to his boyhood camp meeting. He knows that he must maintain contact with his roots. That camp and those people shaped his boyhood. They conditioned him to Christ and His Church. They "made" him.

When asked to preach an anniversary sermon at my home church, I responded with instant excitement! I would see my childhood friends, some of them very old now at this 85th year of the church; I would preach in the sanctuary where I had worshiped as a boy; I would see the Sunday

School, listen to the organ, hear the singing of my people. Believe me, I loved the experience!

God seems unusually close in our special places. Jesus returned to the scene of His baptism to hear the voice of God. The Voice becomes very important when in crisis or at some turning point in our lives.

Often we cannot return to that special, defining-moment location; we must go to a substitute site, a place where we can kneel in silence, uninterrupted, to hear the Voice.

A friend of mine did that on his 60th birthday. He went to a monastery, the Abbey of Gethsemane in Kentucky, where he could meditate, evaluate his life, and hear God's assignments. He needed to get away from the routine of daily tasks to focus on God. He returned to his work with fresh perspective.

Do you two get away sometimes, each by yourself? Do you give yourself the opportunity to recapture God's assignments? Do you allow Him the opportunity to give fresh definition to your lives?

Wanting most of all to hear His voice,

Don

Day 40

The attractive life

The story ends well. Despite His enemies, Jesus inspired many to follow Him. John 10:41-42 brings the passage to a close:

While on the other side of the Jordan, many people came to Him and they made an interesting observation: "John did no miracles, but everything he said about Jesus has come true."

No wonder many believed in Jesus right there along the Jordan River.

Dear Megan and Adam:

Yes, people do come to Jesus because of His works, and the greatest of all His works is the Cross and Resurrection. I found the following story in *The Interpreter,* a publication of St. Mark's United Methodist Church, Ocala, Florida. I love it because of its evangelistic power:

A Christian taking a photography class while at college got acquainted with a fellow student named Charles Murray. Charles, training for the summer Olympics, was a high diver.

Charles listened well as his new friend witnessed about Jesus and personal salvation. Murray, who had not grown up in a churchgoing home, listened with fascination. He even asked questions about forgiveness.

After listening to his student friend's testimony, the question came to Charles, "Do you sense your need of a Savior? Will you now believe in Him to save you?"

Charles felt guilty but could not respond in the affirmative. Yet for a number of days, Charles Murray thought deeply, then finally called his friend. He wanted to identify New Testament passages about salvation. He seemed troubled as he talked on the phone.

As an Olympic hopeful, Charles had special privileges at the university pool. Around 10 or 11 one evening, he decided to swim, to rehearse his dives. A huge and very bright moon shone in through the glass ceiling on that clear October night.

Charles walked up the ladder to the highest platform, ready to take his first dive. Just then God's Spirit moved him; he felt deep conviction, remembered the hours listening to his friend's testimony about Christ the Savior, and the Scriptures he had read—all flooded his mind.

Standing on the platform backwards, arms spread, he looked up at the wall and what greeted him came as a welcome and touching surprise. His own shadow made by the light of the moon became a cross. At that point he could no longer tolerate the weight of his sin. His broken heart caused him to sit down on the platform where he asked God to forgive him and come into his heart. There, over twenty feet above the pool deck, he trusted God to save him.

Just then the lights came on; the attendant had come to check on the pool. Would you believe the maintenance people had drained the pool for repairs? Charles had nearly gone to his death, but the cross of the Son of God had saved him.

What a powerful story! I must add this, then, to our 40-day journey: intimacy with God has its very personal

rewards, and to *share* what we have learned, as God leads us, not only keeps the learnings from drying up, it also spreads the Kingdom.

George Sweeting, once President of Moody Bible Institute, tells the story about Woodrow Wilson going to a barber shop. Mr. Moody also came to get a haircut that day:

Wilson, sitting in a barber's chair, became aware that a special person had entered the room. He had come in quietly, then sat in the chair next to Mr. Wilson. Every word the man uttered, though "not in the least didactic, showed a personal and vital interest in the man who was serving him…." Before Woodrow Wilson got through with his haircut he became "aware that I had attended an evangelistic service, because Mr. Moody was in the next chair." Wilson intentionally stayed in the room after Mr. Moody left and "noted the singular effect his visit had upon the barbers in that shop. They talked in undertones. They did not know his name, but they knew that something had elevated their thought. And I felt that I left that place as I should have left a place of worship" (*Great Quotes and Illustrations,* Word Books, 1985, p. 262).

Moody, who walked so closely with Christ, could not help but witness. Actually, our *lives* do the witnessing. People sense the Presence. This demonstrates spiritual formation in its truest form—our intimacy with God infecting all of life until it is reborn in the life of another!

Grateful for our journey together,

Don

The Continuing Journey

Resources for Spiritual Formation

Dear Adam and Megan:

As our 40 days traveling together draw to a close, a new adventure begins! After all, we're on a *lifetime* journey. To embrace the challenge of lifelong intimacy with God is an exciting business!

As a boy, I loved adventure tales, stories with plenty of action and danger. My favorite may surprise you—John Bunyan's *The Pilgrim's Progress*!

The Pilgrim's Progress reflects Bunyan's own difficult and adventurous journey. In fact, he wrote part of the book while in prison. The English government jailed him because he refused to obey the law requiring worship in the state-sanctioned Anglican Church. He preferred an Independent congregation.

Bunyan cleverly calls the book's characters Christian, Evangelist, Obstinate, Great Grace, Pliable, Faithful, Worldly Wiseman to name only a few. The story takes Christian from his conversion on earth to his permanent home in heaven. On the journey he comes to Doubting Castle, Celestial Country, the Delectable Mountains, the Slough of Despond and many other interesting, often dangerous, places.

Each striking metaphor makes the reader say, "I see *myself* on that *same* journey!" Haven't we all met Obstinate and Worldly Wiseman? Doesn't each of us, sooner or later, find

ourselves wandering in Doubting Castle and tempted to throw in the towel at the Slough of Despond? Fortunately, as Christ's followers, we also meet people like Great Grace and Faithful, encouragers who motivate us to persist to the finish line. This explains well my motivation for taking you two on your own pilgrims' journey—to resource your passion for God by encouraging you to run and finish well.

Spiritual formation does not happen automatically. The life you experienced during these weeks of study and reflection can quickly dry up if you settle back into old routines. For this reason, I suggest the following resources—my own "Top Ten" list, if you like!—which, when used as part of your daily devotions, allow for continued, rich, productive growth in your journey with Jesus:

(1) The Bible. This is no mere suggestion—it's a *must*! Wherever our life with God leads, the Scriptures ground us in truth with a capital T. But although God's Word never changes, its many translations and paraphrases do reflect the diversity of those who read and study it. So get the version that suits you. We all come to the Bible with our own personality, learning style and upbringing. This means we don't all understand in the same way—and understanding is what we're after! My wife Kathleen and I use the *New Living Translation* at breakfast. We find it easy to read; it makes some things clear we never quite understood before. You may want to try Eugene Peterson's *The Message.* The everyday language makes the stories come alive!

Look until you find a Bible that offers hardy multi-grain bread for the journey. You might want one of the spiritual formation editions; for example, *The Renovaré Spiritual Formation Bible* in the New Revised Standard Version and published by Harper San Francisco, 2005—a Bible rich in notes to help you mature in Christ.

(2) John Bunyan's *The Pilgrim's Progress.* This timeless work (which I described earlier) you can read over and over again, always with deeper insight into the journey of faith. One older friend of mine has read it at least 50 times!

A number of modern English versions are available if you find the language of the original hard to understand. Try *The Pilgrim's Progress in Modern English,* revised and updated, edited by L. Edward Hazelbaker, published by Bridge-Logos of Gainesville, FL, 1998.

(3) A hymnal, or worship song book. Poetry and music often accomplish what words alone cannot. The songs of the Church combine Scripture, history, and human emotion in one—a powerful unity of truth and shared experience! Keep your favorite songs accessible to your heart. Sing them out when you can. Meditate on their words. There you will find a vast spiritual reservoir and solid support in times of crisis, not to mention a valuable resource for learning Christian theology!

(4) Anything by Richard Foster! Foster, one of today's best-known spiritual formation writers, will help you forward. Look first at his *Celebration of Discipline*, revised edition, published by Harper and Row, 1988. His discussion of 13 disciplines can only stimulate your spiritual development in a Christ-ward direction.

(5) Richard Foster and James Bryan Smith's *Devotional Classics* (Harper San Francisco, revised edition, 2005), along with Richard Foster and Emilie Griffin's *Spiritual Classics* (Harper Collins, 2000), offer selections from the great spiritual writers that are sure to nourish your eager souls!

(6) Thomas à Kempis' *Imitation of Christ*, translated by Joseph N. Tylenda (Random House, revised edition, 1998).

You may also want to see my modern paraphrase of this work, published by Alba House in 1997.

(7) *Practice of the Presence of God* by Brother Lawrence (Whitaker House, 1982). I have produced a modern English version of this classic work as well (Alba House, 1997).

(8) The Internet. The swirl of online information holds a treasure trove of devotional and spiritual formation material. To avoid being overwhelmed by the sheer volume of information, limit your search to one topic or writer of interest at a time. Be creative! Ministries like Crosswalk.com, The Harvesters (www.harvestersonline.com), The Upper Room (www.upperroom.org) and Radio Bible Class (www.rbc.org) have daily devotionals you can read online, or even receive as daily emails. Find classic Christian art on the Web and use it as wallpaper for your desktop. Converse with fellow travelers through a spiritual formation message board or chat room.

Remember that wherever information abounds, so does *mis*information. Not everything that calls itself "spiritual" aligns with God's Holy Spirit. When in doubt, always refer to Resource Number One!

(9) In addition to this rich diet of reading and meditation, meet with a small group of like-minded people, one whose desire is to advance in Christ-likeness. If you can't find one, then form one! Regularly attending a local church, too, fosters spiritual growth, particularly when its leaders prioritize intimacy with God in their preaching and worship leading.

(10) Keep a journal. Make it a daily, or at the very least, a weekly practice to write down what you learn from your

times with God. Your own experiences and learnings represent an invaluable personal resource which no other writer can duplicate. It serves both as a growth chart for your own journey, and a valuable source of encouragement for those who follow.

Have you noticed that in offering you these resources, I have not prescribed a specific pattern for practicing the devotional life or any of the spiritual disciplines? The fact remains, no one can force you into a particular mold. Listen carefully. The Inner Voice of the Spirit will instruct you about the pattern (some older writers call it a "rule") to use, and God will design a daily program that fits your personality.

My friends, God's faithfulness to lead now requires your commitment to follow—to stay on the journey until He calls you home. *Eternal* intimacy with our heavenly Father is the ultimate goal, and keeping our lives on course opens a clear view to the finish line!

On the way, by God's grace,

Don

on Knowing

on Knowing

essays for the left hand

Expanded Edition

JEROME S. BRUNER

the Belknap Press of
Harvard University Press
Cambridge, Massachusetts
London, England
1979

The two lines from William Butler Yeats's "Among School Children" and the stanza from his "A Prayer for Old Age" are quoted by permission of The Macmillan Company, New York (*The Collected Poems of W. B. Yeats,* 1955). The lines from Louis MacNeice's "Postscript to Iceland for W. H. Auden" are quoted by permission of Faber & Faber, London (*Collected Poems, 1925–1948,* 1949). The last chapter, "Psychology and the Image of Man," is reprinted by permission of Oxford University Press, from H. Harris, ed., *Scientific Models and Man: The Herbert Spencer Lectures 1976,* © Oxford University Press 1979.

Library of Congress Catalog Card Number: 78-66286
ISBN 0-674-63475-6 (cloth)
ISBN 0-674-63525-6 (paper)

Printed in the United States of America

for Blanche

Preface to the Expanded Edition

There is something unique about the essay form. An essay posits for itself a topic and a set of constraints that limit the forms of comment one can make upon it. If the constraints are violated, the effect is to make the essay somehow slack, unserious, undisciplined. The essay is the literary counterpart of the "possible world" of the logician or like the "thought experiment" of the scientist. As with each of these, it begins with a set of connected familiars and seeks by rearranging them to leap to the higher ground of novelty, a novelty rooted in what was previously familiar.

On Knowing was originally written in the form of separate essays, each of them organized around some familiar matter—the impact of Freud on common sense, the concept of fate, the nature of the modern novel, the role of surprise in thinking, and so on. They were all matters that were "interesting" to me. It is not what made them interesting to *me* that now concerns me, but rather what might make them interesting to somebody else—and my focus is on the nature of intellectual interest rather than, say, upon why these particular matters should have occupied a university intellectual in the late 1950s and early 1960s. For I am fascinated with what it is that makes people try to think through certain issues, whether in an essay, a logically connected possible world, or in a scientific experiment.

As a start, let me propose that interior intellectual work is almost always a continuation of a dialogue. This is not a new point. Its most famous exponent is the Russian psycholinguist Vygotsky, who argues that the development of thought in the child is dependent upon his entering a dialogue and that, in

time and with practice, the dialogue becomes internalized. Not that thought consists solely of internal speech—there is ample evidence to warn us off that view. Indeed, even external dialogue is built upon shared, nonlinguistic presuppositions about the world, and these, in turn, are shaped by structures of mind that predispose us to experience "reality" in one way instead of others. Rather, it is the dialectical, almost dramaturgic quality of dialogue that provides a model for pursuing our own thoughts in the privacy of our own consciousness.

Each of the essays in this volume started in conversation. The Freud essay, for example, grew out of conversations with Grete Bibring, Robert Oppenheimer, and Elting Morison. Its preoccupation was with the manner in which a system of thought—however verified it might or might not be by the usual methods of putting a theory to test—could change or, better, crystallize a generation's mode of thought. My partners in dialogue were a psychoanalyst, a physicist (whose sympathies were very much with Freud although they were buffered in doubt), and a historian whose lifelong concern has been the relationship of power and ideas within a society. Each was a strong-willed protagonist. And in each conversation, the inevitable happened. By the very dynamics of dialogue you are constrained in two ways: first, you come to take the positions of the other rather for granted, and after a while it becomes an unfriendly act to challenge the other's presuppositions. It is like the life-term prisoners in the sick story who are so familiar with each other's jokes that it suffices to recount them by announcing their number. You begin to feel corseted in responding to *their* arguments or in noting settled agreements. The topic becomes interpersonally boring and, by unspoken mutual consent, it is either dropped or simply indicated by something like the life-termer's number.

Boredom is a powerful phenomenon—a poison to the intellectual in large doses. And like many poisons, it is a rather benign stimulant in small doses. I think it always infuses in-

tellectual work in some deep way. For all of the sciences and most of the humane disciplines of learning proceed by working with the familiar and attempting to rearrange it in certain ways so as to make the familiar generate something novel. It is inevitable that, from time to time, we get trapped in the familiar and suffer its boredom. Dialogue with others provides some escape from the procrustean familiarity of our "subject." But, alas, dialogue eventually goes the route of the life-termer's story.

But just here the essay as a form comes into its own. It is an invitation to ignore the constraints of the other that you encounter in dialogue, to consider and to unpack any presupposition without giving umbrage and to do it in a manner that permits a use of metaphor forbidden to the logician or scientist. Yet the essay form is tightly wrought enough to keep one's nose not so much to the grindstone as to the touchstone. Indeed, David Olson insists (and I think with good reason) that it is characteristic of the essay form, and may even be its historical origin, to try to transcend the constraints of dialogue and its context-bound definitions of truth—"the meaning is in the text," as Luther urged.

I remarked that each of the essays in the volume grew out of an encounter with certain matters that had interested me. Obviously, they come out of a common source, and friends have said to me that it is a very personal book. That may well be because the topics were ones I could not cope with by the universalized methods of experiment or logical analysis alone. Hence the subtitle: "Essays for the Left Hand." The left hand, *my* left hand, has known hard times since these essays were published. Or perhaps it would be better to say, left hands in the sixties and seventies were otherwise occupied, and principally with the politics of the revolution through which we have been living.

There has been Vietnam, the student uprising, the emergence of a Third World, and the battle against racial and

ethnic discrimination. It was impossible not to be involved. The clumsy cruelties of the student protests and the infamous "police bust" at Harvard in response drove me more deeply into an active role in the day-to-day life of the University. I became involved in school reform, in Africa, in Head Start. Were the times better suited for action than for reflection?

I recall sitting as chairman of the committee appointed by the president of Harvard to liquidate the Reserve Officers Training Corps at the university. Across the table were the representatives of the Navy and Army, serving officers with whom I disagreed but whom I greatly respected. I recall too, at the same time, the students and tutors in my Harvard house. I also admired their nerve and conviction in "trying on" new ideas and life styles. Though I didn't agree with them either, my respect for their integrity was complete. Perhaps I am the typical conflict-laden liberal, torn by an appreciation of contrary excellencies.

That period was a time for tracts rather than essays, particularly essays for the left hand. The essay form did not return my way for a decade, and then it emerged as the Herbert Spencer Lecture delivered at Oxford in 1976. It is the only new essay in this volume, and I am particularly pleased to have it included. It restored my faith in the importance of the essay as an intellectual experience.

In the seventeen years since the first publication of *On Knowing* there has been a steady polarization within psychology between the "hardnosed," psychonomic study of psychology and the more "humanistic," methodologically unconstrained approach. Those at the far reach of each movement have had a tendency to heap scorn on the other. Within the American Psychological Society, there are separate divisions where each lives, and the hardnosed genus of psychologist has set up a separate society—the Psychonomic Society. I see in both extremes a manifestation of anti-intellectualism: the one denigrating the processes that give rise to hypotheses, the other

damning the techniques designed for their testing. I find myself uneasy with both extremes. My idea has always been that the antic activities of the left hand offer gifts to the right for closer scrutiny and hardnosed testing.

In Great Britain, psychology is not much liked. It is seen as an upstart discipline and one without either a settled body of theory or a method of work and, supreme sin, cut off from the more humane and literary approaches to the study of man. It has been the reaction of some British psychologists to become even more implacably positivistic in their approach and to cultivate a connection with either biology or the computational sciences. The tempering effect of the psychology of language that has done so much to keep American psychology from dividing totally into separate fields is not nearly so evident in Britain. "Psychology and the Image of Man" was my effort to bring the two views of psychology back into single focus. It did not convince many of my Oxford friends who were initially of a contrary view, but unpopular views may at least seem to raise consciousness about alternatives. In any case, it created a good row—and that is always welcome on the British intellectual scene!

I don't think that psychology should enter the age-old battle to understand the nature of man with one hand tied behind its back—left *or* right. I can put it best in terms of a lament of a former postdoctoral fellow in my laboratory at Oxford—Michael Scaife who had just taken his degree in bird behavior and had been awarded a fellowship to be "retreaded" as a human psychologist. He said that when he worked on animal behavior he felt constantly deprived by the species difference between him and his subjects. He had always wanted to "get into their minds." Now that he was working on human beings he kept encountering critics who urged him to ignore the fact that he was the same species as his subjects. He had chosen to study how infants learned to share a common attentional focus with their mothers. How *could* he overlook what he already

knew as a human being about shared attention! It is surely foolish to pretend that it makes no difference that we are human beings when we begin to study human beings. It is enormously useful to have, in their full subjectivity, works such as A. R. Luria's accounts of the mind of a mnemonist and of the shattered world of one of his brain-injured patients. They are rich in evocation, a seedbed of hypotheses. And they are, each in its way, bits of literary art.

I hope we can encourage our students to use their own knowledge of the human condition, of themselves or their language or their families to derive, if not a hypothesis, at least a hunch that will start them on their way toward one. It would be a pity if we psychologists were to be condemned to a one-handed existence. It is a curious though not really an immodest thing to say, but I found that the rereading of these essays—my *own* essays—lured me back into a reconsideration of the unfinished business that had started them into existence in the first place. Perhaps, with some unpredictable luck, they may lead others back to some unfinished business of their own.

J. S. B.

Wolfson College
Oxford
January 1979

Preface

There are many debts to acknowledge and credits to be given—to the friends with whom one dines, to the colleagues with whom one works, to the students whose impatience helps keep a sense of doubt well nourished, to those administering spirits who keep chaos from descending, to foundations that have made some free time possible. The existence of a great university also makes a deep difference. Josiah Royce, commenting on the Harvard community, once remarked that for it talking was the most natural form of breathing.

Several close friends have been particularly generous in advice and encouragement. George Miller, Albert Guerard, and Elting Morison have been sources of instruction and models of patience. Elizabeth Weems Solomon could be counted on for arresting advice. Mark Saxton has labored with me long and generously in the process of making a continuity of the ideas expressed in these essays. Ruth and Richard Tolman, whose loss many of us still feel, encouraged me long ago in the pursuits reported here. My wife, Blanche Marshall Bruner, has been a constant and illuminating companion in the making of the book.

Museums and photographers are credited in the text. The following publishers and periodicals have given generous permission to reproduce material: Faber & Faber, Ltd., George Braziller, Inc., *Harvard Educational Review, International Journal of Psychology,* The Macmillan Company, *The Mathematics Teacher, Partisan Review, Psychological Review, The Reporter,* Rupert Hart-Davis, Ltd., and *Saturday Review Education Supplement.*

Cambridge, Massachusetts J. S. B.
January 1962

Contents

on

Knowing

Introduction

You are concerned, let us say, with the nature of myth and wherein it plays a role in man's thinking. An occasion arises—perhaps an invitation to speak or to contribute an article to a magazine—and you commit your thoughts to paper. Some years later there is another occasion: this time the topic, presumably a different one, may be freedom and the control of behavior. Only later, only in retrospect, does a continuity emerge. In any man's intellectual life there are only a few topics, only a limited set of persistent queries and themes.

This book took its origin in a collection of occasion pieces, essays written for the left hand, as I shall explain in a moment. The intent was to bring them out one day much as they had originally been written. But as I worked over them, they changed and merged and were no longer so occasional. The period of five years over which they had been written melted and the underlying themes emerged in their own right.

The themes are few enough in number. The first part of the book concerns itself with how we construct reality by the process of knowing: it deals with the act of knowing in itself and how it is shaped and in turn gives form to language, science, literature, and art. In effect, we shall be dealing with the issue of how we know and how knowledge reflects the structuring power of the human intellect.

But one's conception of knowing and of the nature of what

is known perforce lead one to a concern with how we impart knowledge, how we teach, how we lead the learner to construct a reality on his own terms. The second part of the book entertains conjectures on the nature of teaching and learning, conjectures that grew, in spirit if not in original sequence, from issues raised earlier. But sequence is a fiction, and in a human life what follows may have produced what went before.

Finally, the last part of the book examines how one's conception of reality, affected as it is by the uncertainties of seeking to know, influences action and commitment.

Since childhood, I have been enchanted by the fact and the symbolism of the right hand and the left—the one the doer, the other the dreamer. The right is order and lawfulness, *le droit*. Its beauties are those of geometry and taut implication. Reaching for knowledge with the right hand is science. Yet to say only that much of science is to overlook one of its excitements, for the great hypotheses of science are gifts carried in the left hand.

Of the left hand we say that it is awkward and, while it has been proposed that art students can seduce their proper hand to more expressiveness by drawing first with the left, we nonetheless suspect this function. The French speak of the illegimate descendant as being *à main gauche,* and, though the heart is virtually at the center of the thoracic cavity, we listen for it on the left. Sentiment, intuition, bastardy. And should we say that reaching for knowledge with the left hand is art? Again it is not enough, for as surely as the recital of a daydream differs from the well-wrought tale, there is a barrier between undisciplined fantasy and art. To climb the barrier requires a right hand adept at technique and artifice.

And so I have argued in one of the essays in this volume that the scientist and the poet do not live at antipodes, and I urge in another that the artificial separation of the two modes of knowing cripples the contemporary intellectual as an effec-

tive mythmaker for his times. But it is not principally in the role of a would-be mediator between the humanist and the scientist that I have written and then rewritten the essays that comprise this book. My objective, rather, is somewhat different, perhaps more personal.

It is to explore the range of the left hand in dealing with the nature of knowing. As a right-handed psychologist, I have been diligent for fifteen years in the study of the cognitive processes: how we acquire, retain, and transform knowledge of the world in which each of us lives—a world in part "outside" us, in part "inside." The tools I have used have been those of the scientific psychologist studying perception, memory, learning, thinking, and (like a child of my times) I have addressed my inquiries to the laboratory rat as well as to human beings. At times, indeed, I have adopted the role of the clinician and carried out therapy with children whose principal symptom presented at the clinic was a "learning block," an inability to acquire knowledge in a formal school setting, though their intelligence seemed normal or even superior. More recently, I have turned my attention to the nature of the teaching process in an effort to formulate the outlines of a "theory of instruction" and so better to understand what we seek to do when we guide another's learning either by a lecture or by that formidable thing known as a curriculum. Seeking the most beautifully simple case, I chose to study the learning and teaching of mathematics. But it was soon clear that the heart of mathematical learning was tipped well to the left. There have been times when, somewhat discouraged by the complexities of the psychology of knowing, I have sought to escape through neurophysiology, to discover that the neurophysiologist can help only in the degree to which we can ask intelligent psychological questions of him.

One thing has become increasingly clear in pursuing the nature of knowing. It is that the conventional apparatus of the psychologist—both his instruments of investigation and the

conceptual tools he uses in the interpretation of his data—leaves one approach unexplored. It is an approach whose medium of exchange seems to be the metaphor paid out by the left hand. It is a way that grows happy hunches and "lucky" guesses, that is stirred into connective activity by the poet and the necromancer looking sidewise rather than directly. Their hunches and intuitions generate a grammar of their own—searching out connections, suggesting similarities, weaving ideas loosely in a trial web. Once, having come in late to dine at King's College, Cambridge, with my friend Oliver Zangwill, I found myself seated next to a delightful older man whose name I had not caught in the hurried and mumbled introductions. We agreed that the climate of debate at Cambridge might be vastly improved if some far-sighted philanthropist would establish a chair of The Black Arts and Thaumaturgy, that the effort to know had become too aseptic and constrained. My neighbor at table turned out to be E. M. Forster.

The psychologist, for all his apartness, is governed by the same constraints that shape the behavior of those whom he studies. He too searches widely and metaphorically for his hunches. He reads novels, looks at and even paints pictures, is struck by the power of myth, observes his fellow men intuitively and with wonder. In doing so, he acts only part-time like a proper psychologist, racking up cases against the criteria derived from an hypothesis. Like his fellows, he observes the human scene with such sensibility as he can muster in the hope that his insight will be deepened. If he is lucky or if he has subtle psychological intuition, he will from time to time come up with hunches, combinatorial products of his metaphoric activity. If he is not fearful of these products of his own subjectivity, he will go so far as to tame the metaphors that have produced the hunches, tame them in the sense of shifting them from the left hand to the right hand by rendering them into notions that can be tested. It is my impression from ob-

serving myself and my colleagues that the forging of metaphoric hunch into testable hypothesis goes on all the time. And I am inclined to think that this process is the more evident in psychology where the theoretical apparatus is not so well developed that it lends itself readily to generating interesting hypotheses.

Yet because our profession is young and because we feel insecure, we do not like to admit our humanity. We quite properly seek a distinctiveness that sets us apart from all those others who ponder about man and the human condition—all of which is worthy, for thereby we forge an intellectual discipline. But we are not satisfied to forge distinctive methods of our own. We must reject whoever has been successful in the task of understanding man—if he is not one of us. We place a restrictive covenant on our domain. Our articles, submitted properly to the appropriate psychological journal, have about them an aseptic quality designed to proclaim the intellectual purity of our psychological enterprise. Perhaps this is well, though it is not enough.

It is well, perhaps, because it is economical to report the products of research and not the endless process that constitutes the research itself. But it is not enough in the deeper sense that we may be concealing some of the most fruitful sources of our ideas from one another. I have felt that the self-imposed fetish of objectivity has kept us from developing a needed genre of psychological writing—call it protopsychological writing if you will—the preparatory intellectual and emotional labors on which our later, more formalized, efforts are based. The genre in its very nature is literary and metaphoric, yet it is something more than this. It inhabits a realm midway between the humanities and the sciences. It is the left hand trying to transmit to the right.

I find myself a little out of patience with the alleged split between "the two cultures," for the two are not simply external ways of life, one pursued by humanists, the other by scientists.

They are ways of living with one's own experience. I recall a painfully withdrawn young physicist at the Institute for Advanced Study when I was a visiting member of that remarkable institution. His accomplishments as a flutist were magical; he could talk and live either music or physics. For all the rightness of his life, it was nonetheless a segmented one. What was lacking was not an institutionalized cultural bridge outside, but an internal transfer from the left to the right—and perhaps there was one, though my colleague could not admit it. It is a little like the amusing dialogue Louis MacNeice reports between himself and W. H. Auden on their trip to Iceland:

> And the don in me set forth
> How the landscape of the north
> Had educed the saga style
> Plodding forward mile by mile.
> And the don in you replied
> That the North begins inside,
> Our ascetic guts require
> Breathers from the Latin fire.

But the left hand is not all. For there is also in these pages much about the profound revolution that has been taking place in the sciences of man during the past decade and of the new dilemmas that have replaced the old ones. We know now, for example, that the nervous system is not the one-way street we thought it was—carrying messages from the environment to the brain, there to be organized into representations of the world. Rather, the brain has a program that is its own, and monitoring orders are sent out from the brain to the sense organs and relay stations specifying priorities for different kinds of environmental messages. Selectivity is the rule and a nervous system, in Lord Adrian's phrase, is as much an editorial hierarchy as it is a system for carrying signals.

We have learned too that the "arts" of sensing and knowing consist in honoring our highly limited capacity for taking in and processing information. We honor that capacity by learning the methods of compacting vast ranges of experience in

economical symbols—concepts, language, metaphor, myth, formulae. The price of failing at this art is either to be trapped in a confined world of experience or to be the victim of an overload of information. What a society does for its members, what they could surely not achieve on their own in a lifetime, is to equip them with ready means for entering a world of enormous potential complexity. It does all this by providing the means of simplification—most notably, a language and an ordering point of view to go with the language.

This has also been the decade in which the role of activity and environmental complexity has become clear to us—both in the maintenance of normal human functioning and in the development of human capacities. The isolation experiments have made it clear that an immobilized human being in a sensorially impoverished environment soon loses control of his mental functions. The daring and brilliant experiments inspired by Donald Hebb at McGill have shown the degree to which alertness depends on a constant regimen of dealing with environmental diversity. And as if this were not enough, we also know now that the early challenges of problems to be mastered, of stresses to be overcome, are the preconditions of attaining some measure of our full potentiality as human beings. The child is father to the man in a manner that may be irreversibly one-directional, for to make up for a bland impoverishment of experience early in life may be too great an obstacle for most organisms. Indeed, recent work indicates that for at least one species, the utilitarian rat, too much gray homogeneity in infancy may produce chemical changes in the brain that seem to be associated with dullness. One wonders, then, about the issue of the appropriate exercise of mind early in life as a condition for fullness later.[1]

Perhaps too, and for the first time, we have come to a sense

[1] For more details of this phase of work in psychology over the past decade, see Philip Solomon and others, eds., *Sensory Deprivation* (Cambridge: Harvard University Press, 1961).

of the nature of early mental life, indeed early intellectual life. My generation of psychologists has been fortunate in its exploration of early intellectual development—massively so in the flow of work that has come from Piaget at Geneva, and especially so in the quantitatively meager but brilliant work of the too-early dead Vygotsky at Moscow. Piaget has given us a respectful sense of the manner in which an intrinsic and self-contained logic characterizes mental operations at any stage of development, however primitive it may be. Vygotsky has given us a vision of the role of internalized dialogue as the basis of thought, a guarantor of social patterning in that most lonely sphere, the exercise of mind.

The decade in psychology and its allied fields has been energizing: the lock step of "learning theory" in this country has been broken, though it is still the standard village dance. It is apparent to many of us that the so-called associative connecting of physical stimuli and muscular responses cannot provide the major part of the explanation for how men learn to generate sentences never before spoken, or how they learn to obey the laws of the sonnet while producing lines never before imagined. Indeed, all behavior has its grammatical consistency; all of it has its consistency of style.

Perhaps the moment is uniquely propitious for the left hand, for a left hand that might tempt the right to draw freshly again, as in art school when the task is to find a means of imparting new life to a hand that has become too stiff with technique, too far from the scanning eye. In any case, the chapters that follow, mostly concerned with knowing and its significance, are written in that spirit.

PART I ◂

the Shape of Experience

I had been asked to study a highly productive invention group, attached to an industrial consulting firm of world-wide reputation. It was a curious group: though they worked on problems that might properly be called "engineering," the group contained no engineers. For a year, I sat in as a working member of this group, helping to design protective clothing for missile-loading teams that had to handle highly corrosive propellants. It was an illuminating experience in the sense that I discovered that I, with neither interest in nor knowledge of protective clothing or missiles or corrosives, could get deeply involved and, indeed, come up with some rather respectable ideas about how to get people into and out of protective suits. I even invented a technique for keeping the draft out of sleeping bags, a byproduct that properly ranks as beating swords into plowshares.

The effectiveness of the group members consisted in their sense of freedom to explore possibilities, in their devotion to elegant solutions, and in the interplay among them that, in effect, made each man stronger in the group than individually. During the year, I also had the benefit and pleasure of long discussion with two Cambridge friends, William J. J. Gordon and Jean MacKenzie Pool. The essay here, "The Conditions of Creativity," came out of my effort to bring together what I had observed and what I had seen and read before of creativity. There has been much work done in the field since 1959, when the piece was first written. Indeed, the work on the invention group has been admirably converted—through the analysis of tape recordings and statistical techniques—into a doctoral dis-

sertation at Radcliffe College, written by Dr. Betty Hosmer Mawardi, now on the staff of Western Reserve University.

"The Conditions of Creativity," then, is a first attempt, a preface to a more systematic analysis of creative invention. In greatly modified form, it first saw the light of day at a symposium on creative thinking held at the University of Colorado in the spring of 1959.

The next three essays in Part One were written in their first form during 1959 and 1960. The circumstances that led me to write them are all seemingly different. "Myth and Identity" was prepared for a symposium held by the American Academy of Arts and Sciences, a symposium since published in the pages of *Daedalus* and then in *Myth and Mythmaking* (New York: Braziller, 1960). "Identity and the Modern Novel" was given as a guest lecture in Albert Guerard's Harvard course on the modern novel. Guerard and I had talked for years about giving a joint course on the psychology of literature. We had spent many evenings together discussing Gide, Conrad, Hardy, and many younger novelists whose work he had led me to. An exchange of guest lectures was as close as we came to realizing our plan before he departed to take the chair in comparative literature created in honor of his father at Stanford University. The concluding section of the essay is based on a talk originally prepared for the celebration of Radcliffe College's seventy-fifth birthday. "Art as a Mode of Knowing" was written originally as a long letter to a painter friend, Mrs. Izler Solomon, who had been struggling bravely to teach me to paint and to look more wisely at pictures. The letter was eventually converted into a lecture for a course I was giving and finally into its present form.

There is a circumstance that relates the three pieces to each other. I was then studying learning blocks, the conditions that prevent children from learning, from exercising their normal curiosity. I had come upon the phenomenon of the "pre-

emptive metaphor" in that work: the technique by which many seemingly unrelated things are tied together by a common fear and a common avoidance. The joining of such disparate collections of fears seemed to be metaphoric. I was struck by the fact that metaphor, so often the vehicle for mythic leaping, could also be a device for a kind of cancerous illness. The cancerous quality was in the manner of the spread of a fear—akin to what in medicine is called metastasis, what in literary analysis is referred to as synecdoche. Let me illustrate from one of the cases then in treatment—a boy with a fatiguing load of pent-up hostility with the impossible, family-supported ideal of not expressing any of it. School learning had become extremely difficult for this fourteen-year-old; in his mind it had become associated with aggressive competition and rebellion within the confines of his family, literally a battle against a family image that cast boys and men in the role of intellectual ne'er-do-wells. The boy's father had accepted the role; indeed, it had been well established early when his then high-school sweetheart, his present wife, had helped him squeak through graduation. After that, the father had settled into a semiskilled job, perhaps somewhat uneasily, and the mother had taken on the mantle of family intellectual and doer of good works. An older sister had just finished high school with a strong record and was on her way through nurse's training.

The unconscious preoccupation of this boy was aggression and, when the preoccupation was aroused, he would freeze and, in his words, "turn stupid." Once rapport had been achieved between the boy and his therapist, it became clear how widely the fear had spread, what a range it had come to cover. In arithmetic, for example, he saw fractions as "cut-up numbers," and the operation of algebraic cancellation was "killing off numbers and letters on both sides of the equal sign." Graphing a simple arithmetic progression at one tutorial session, he was asked to guess where the line would go next, given several points already plotted. He said that when it got high

enough up on the graph it would explode and come back down. Once he commented to his tutor that pencils were dangerous because of their sharp points which were like knives, and then went on to muse that any piece of wood could also be dangerous because you could sharpen it, and it was plain that he could have carried this pre-emptive metaphor further if he had not been interrupted by the demands of the tutorial.

I had read a piece by Mark Schorer on metaphor ("Fiction and the 'Matrix of Analogy,'" *Kenyon Review,* XI, 1949) and the fine book by Calvin Hall dealing with the metaphoric devices found in dreams (*The Meaning of Dreams,* New York: Harper, 1953). It struck me that the metaphoric device of the dream and the metaphoric device of the poet are the same but for one thing—that ineffable thing, the work of the artist. Yet it was also clear to me that some dreams are rich and beautiful, others impoverished and crude, that dream work and the work of art might also share a certain discipline. What is characteristic of the great work of art is that its metaphoric artifice, its juxtapositions, have not only surprise value but also illuminating honesty. The two combine to create what we shall later refer to as "effective surprise." The work of art also has a cognitive economy in its metaphoric transformations, which make it possible for a seemingly limited symbol to spread its power over a range of experience. Neurotic symbolism and the metaphors of dreaming are somehow cloudy or even opaque.

Perhaps the surprise of the metaphoric juxtaposition where illness intervenes is too honest for the patient to face, given his responses. The result is defense and denial, an avoidance of the disturbing honesty at all costs. There is "overanticipating" of what is likely to be internally dangerous; too many things are put on the danger list. In consequence, the neurotic steers clear of what he anticipates as dangerous and is unable to learn whether he can cope with them. The economy of the mechanism is that the defensiveness is too efficient. Like Henry James's protagonist in "The Beast in the Jungle," the neurotic

avoids everything that *might* be dangerous and in the end is immobilized. It is this overefficient pre-emptiveness that makes such metaphoric activity sick, in contrast to the illuminating quality of great myth and great poetry.

All of these considerations led me to a concern with the positive side of metaphoric and literary thinking. What is the artifice that creates illumination rather than illness? The first essay explores myth itself and the manner in which life creates myth and then imitates it. The second essay treats some representative modern novels with a view to examining wherein the modern novel and the classic myth differ in their approach to metaphoric transformations of life. The last essay in the group concentrates on the devices of the painter and, when it is rewritten in some other guise some later day, it will show an even stronger stamp of the thinking of my friend Ernst Gombrich whose *Art and Illusion* is such a monumental achievement.

Our insights into mental functioning are too often fashioned from observations of the sick and the handicapped. It is difficult to catch and record, no less to understand, the swift flight of man's mind operating at its best.

The Conditions of Creativity

There is something antic about creating, although the enterprise be serious. And there is a matching antic spirit that goes with writing about it, for if ever there were a silent process it is the creative one. Antic and serious and silent. Yet there is good reason to inquire about creativity, a reason beyond practicality, for practicality is not a reason but a justification after the fact. The reason is the ancient search of the humanist for the excellence of man: the next creative act may bring man to a new dignity.

There is, alas, a shrillness to our contemporary concern with creativity. Man's search for the sources of dignity changes with the pattern of his times. In periods during which man saw himself in the image of God, the creation of works *ad majorem gloriam dei* could provide a sufficient rationale for the dignity of the artist, the artisan, the creative man. But in an age whose dominant value is a pragmatic one and whose massive achievement is an intricate technological order, it is not sufficient to be merely useful. For the servant can pattern himself on the master—and so he did when God was master and Man His servant creating works in His glory—but the machine is the servant of man, and to pattern one's function on the machine provides no measure for dignity. The machine is useful, the system in terms of which the machines gain their use is efficient, but what is man?

The artist, the writer, and to a new degree the scientist seek

an answer in the nature of their acts. They create or they seek to create, and this in itself endows the process with dignity. There is "creative" writing and "pure" science, each justifying the work of its producer in its own right. It is implied, I think, that the act of a man creating is the act of a whole man, that it is this rather than the product that makes it good and worthy. So whoever seeks to proclaim his wholeness turns to the new slogan. There is creative advertising, creative engineering, creative problem solving—all lively entries in the struggle for dignity in our time. We, as psychologists, are asked to explicate the process, to lay bare the essence of the creative. Make no mistake about it: it is not simply as technicians that we are being called, but as adjutants to the moralist. My antic sense rises in self-defense. My advice, in the midst of the seriousness, is to keep an eye out for the tinker shuffle, the flying of kites, and kindred sources of surprised amusement.

We had best begin with some minimum working definition that will permit us at least to look at the same set of things. An act that produces *effective surprise*—this I shall take as the hallmark of a creative enterprise. The content of the surprise can be as various as the enterprises in which men are engaged. It may express itself in one's dealing with children, in making love, in carrying on a business, in formulating physical theory, in painting a picture. I could not care less about the person's intention, whether or not he intended to create. The road to banality is paved with creative intentions. Surprise is not easily defined. It is the unexpected that strikes one with wonder or astonishment. What is curious about effective surprise is that it need not be rare or infrequent or bizarre and is often none of these things. Effective surprises, and we shall spell the matter out in a moment, seem rather to have the quality of obviousness about them when they occur, producing a shock of recognition following which there is no longer astonishment. It is like this with great formulae, as in that for the conserva-

tion of energy or for the brilliant insight that makes chemistry possible, the conservation of mass. Weber's stunning insight into the nature of a just noticeable sensory difference is of this order, that before a difference will be noticed it must be a constant fraction of the sensory intensity presently being experienced: $\Delta I/I = K$.

I think it is possible to specify three kinds of effectiveness, three forms of self-evidence implicit in surprise of the kind we have been considering. The first is predictive effectiveness. It is the kind of surprise that yields high predictive value in its wake—as in the instance of the formula for falling bodies or in any good theoretical reformulation in science. You may well argue that predictive effectiveness does not always come through surprise, but through the slow accretion of knowledge and urge—like Newton with his *hypothesis non fingo.* I will reply by agreeing with you and specifying simply that whether it is the result of intuitive insight or of slow accretion, I will accept it within my definition. The surprise may only come when we look back and see whence we have come.

A second form of effectiveness is best called formal, and its most usual place is in mathematics and logic—possibly in music. One of the most beautiful descriptions of the phenomenon is to be found in G. H. Hardy's engaging A *Mathematician's Apology.* It consists of an ordering of elements in such a way that one sees relationships that were not evident before, groupings that were before not present, ways of putting things together not before within reach. Consistency or harmony or depth of relationship is the result. One of the most penetrating essays that has ever been written on the subject is, of course, Henri Poincaré's in his *Science and Method.* He speaks of making combinations that "reveal to us unsuspected kinship between . . . facts, long known, but wrongly believed to be strangers to one another."

Of the final form of effectiveness in surprise it is more difficult to write. I shall call it metaphoric effectiveness. It, too, is effective by connecting domains of experience that were

before apart, but with the form of connectedness that has the discipline of art.

It is effective surprise that produces what Melville celebrated as the shock of recognition. Jung speaks of art that can produce such metaphoric connectedness as "visionary" in contrast to the merely psychological. It is, for example, Thomas Mann's achievement in bringing into a single compass the experiences of sickness and beauty, sexuality and restraint in his *Death in Venice*. Or it is the achievement of the French playwright Jean Anouilh who in *Antigone* makes Creon not only a tyrant but a reasonable man. What we are observing is the connecting of diverse experiences by the mediation of symbol and metaphor and image. Experience in literal terms is a categorizing, a placing in a syntax of concepts. Metaphoric combination leaps beyond systematic placement, explores connections that before were unsuspected.

I would propose that all of the forms of effective surprise grow out of combinatorial activity—a placing of things in new perspectives. But it is somehow not simply a taking of known elements and running them together by algorithm into a welter of permutations. One could design a computer to do that, but it would be with some embarrassment, for this is stupid even for a computer, and an ingenious computer programmer can show us much more interesting computer models than that. "To create consists precisely in not making useless combinations and in making those which are useful and which are only a small minority. Invention is discernment, choice." If not a brute algorithm, then it must be a heuristic that guides one to fruitful combinations. What is the heuristic? Poincaré goes on to urge that it is an emotional sensibility: "the feeling of mathematical beauty, of the harmony of numbers and forms, of geometric elegance." It is this that guides one in making combinations in mathematics. But it is surely not enough. One hears physicists speak of "physical intuition" as distinguishing

the good theorist from the mere formalist, the mathematician. I suspect that in each empirical field there is developed in the creating scientist a kind of "intuitive familiarity," to use a term that L. J. Henderson was fond of, that gives him a sense of what combinations are likely to have predictive effectiveness and which are absurd. What precisely this kind of heuristic consists of is probably difficult to specify without reference to the nature of the field in question, which is not to say that the working models are utterly different in different areas of empirical endeavor, for there is obviously some generality, too.

It seems unlikely that the heuristic either of formal beauty or of intuitive familiarity could serve for the artist, the poet, and the playwright. What genius leads Faulkner to create and combine a Temple Drake and a Popeye in *Sanctuary*? How does Dostoevsky hit upon the particular combination of the Grand Inquisitor and the Christ figure in *The Brothers Karamazov*? What leads Picasso to include particular objects in a painting? Picasso says to Christian Zervos: "What a sad thing for a painter who loves blondes but denies himself the pleasure of putting them in his picture because they don't go well with the basket of fruit! What misery for a painter who detests apples to have to use them all the time because they harmonize with the tablecloth! I put in my pictures everything I like. So much the worse for the things—they have to get along with one another." [1] However maddening such a remark may be coming from a painter, it does point up the essentially emotive nature of the painter's work and his criteria for judging the fitness of combination. So Yeats may write:

> God guard me from those thoughts men think
> In the mind alone;
> He that sings a lasting song
> Thinks in a marrow-bone.

[1] "Conversation with Picasso," *Cahiers d'Art* (Paris), 1935. Translated by Brewster Ghiselin in *The Creative Process* (New York: Mentor Books, 1952), p. 56.

But marrow-bones are not really enough for lasting songs. For if it is true, as Picasso and many before have said, that "a picture lives only through him who looks at it," then the artist must speak to the human condition of the beholder if there is to be effective surprise. I, for one, find myself compelled to believe that there are certain deep sharings of plight among human beings that make possible the communication of the artist to the beholder, and, while I object to the paraphernalia that Jung proposes when he speaks of the collective unconscious, I understand why he feels impelled to proffer the idea. The artist—whatever his medium—must be close enough to these conditions in himself so that they may guide his choice among combinations, provide him with the genuine and protect him from the paste.

The triumph of effective surprise is that it takes one beyond common ways of experiencing the world. Or perhaps this is simply a restatement of what we have been meaning by effective surprise. If it is merely that, let me add only that it is in this sense that life most deeply imitates art or that nature imitates science. Creative products have this power of reordering experience and thought in their image. In science, the reordering is much the same from one beholder of a formula to another. In art, the imitation is in part self-imitation. It is the case too that the effective surprise of the creative man provides a new instrument for manipulating the world—physically as with the creation of the wheel or symbolically as with the creation of $e = mc^2$.

One final point about the combinatorial acts that produce effective surprise: they almost always succeed through the exercise of technique. Henry Moore, who is unusually articulate both as craftsman and artist, tells us that he was driven to the use of holes in his sculpture by the technical problem of giving a sense of three-dimensionality to solid forms—"the hole connects one side to the other, making it immediately more three-dimensional," a discovery made while fretting over the puzzle

of how to avoid relief carving on brittle material like stone. Joseph Conrad and Ford Madox Ford sat before a scene trying to describe it to each other in the most economical terms possible. Katherine Anne Porter sat on a camp stool before a landscape trying to jot down everything before her—and finally decided that she could not train her memory that way. Technique, then, and how shall we combine it eventually with the doctrine of inspiration?

As soon as one turns to a consideration of the conditions of creativity, one is immediately met by paradox and antinomy. A "determinant" suggests itself, and in the next pulse its opposite is suggested. I shall honor these antinomies and what I have to say will, as a result, seem at times paradoxical.

Detachment and commitment. A willingness to divorce oneself from the obvious is surely a prerequisite for the fresh combinatorial act that produces effective surprise. There must be as a necessary, if not a sufficient, condition a detachment from the forms as they exist. There are so many ways in which this expresses itself in creative activity that one can scarcely enumerate them. Wallace Stevens, among many, has written of the alienation of the poet from society and reality, and the spirit of this alienation is caught in his searching poem, "Notes Towards a Supreme Fiction." It is in part a condition for exploring one's own individuality, in part a means of examining the possibilities of human connection. The University as an institution, protected within its walls, should and sometimes does provide a basis for detachment insofar as it recognizes the inviolate privacy of those who inhabit it. The preoccupation of the scholar, gating out all but what seems relevant to his theme—this too is a vehicle of detachment. The creative writer who takes his journey without maps or his voyage into the interior, whether in the subjective Africas of Graham Greene or Joseph Conrad or in the interior jungles of Henry James or Marcel Proust—again it is detachment.

But it is a detachment of commitment. For there is about it a caring, a deep need to understand something, to master a technique, to rerender a meaning. So while the poet, the mathematician, the scientist must each achieve detachment, they do it in the interest of commitment. And at one stroke they, the creative ones, are disengaged from that which exists conventionally and are engaged deeply in what they construct to replace it.

Passion and decorum. By *passion* I understand a willingness and ability to let one's impulses express themselves in one's life through one's work. I use it in the sense, "he has a passion for painting," or, "she has a passion for cooking." I do not wish to raise or explore the Bohemian dilemma—whether the condition for passion in work is its expression in other forms of life. I happen to believe that Freud's fixed quantity of libido (express it here and it must be withdrawn from there) is a kind of first-order nonsense. Passion, like discriminating taste, grows on its use. You more likely act yourself into feeling than feel yourself into action. In any case, it is true of the creative man that he is not indifferent to what he does, that he is moved to it. For the artist, if not for the scientist, there is a tapping of sources of imagery and symbolism that would otherwise not be available—as expressed in the beautiful refrain line of Rimbaud's *Les Illuminations:* "J'ai seul la clef de cette parade sauvage." As for the scientist and the scholar, it is perhaps the eighteenth-century French philosopher, Helvetius, who, in his *Treatise on Man,* has put it best: "A man without *passions* is incapable of that degree of attention to which a superior judgment is annexed: a superiority that is perhaps less the effect of an extraordinary effort than an habitual attention."

But again a paradox: it is not all urgent vitality. There is a decorum in creative activity: a love of form, an etiquette toward the object of our efforts, a respect for materials. Rimbaud's wild beasts in the end are caged. For all that *Lord Jim* is a turbulent book, with the full range of human impulse,

its raw power is contained by the decorum of the dispassionate gentlemanly narrator, Marlow. Herakles of the myth was not a hairy ape expressing his mastery indiscriminately: his shrewd trickery is the decorum. The wild flood of ideas that mathematicians like Hardy have described: eventually they are expressed in the courtesy of equations.

So both are necessary and there must surely be a subtle matter of timing involved—when the impulse, when the taming.

Freedom to be dominated by the object. You begin to write a poem. Before long it, the poem, begins to develop metrical, stanzaic, symbolical requirements. You, as the writer of the poem, are serving it—it seems. Or you may be pursuing the task of building a formal model to represent the known properties of single nerve fibers and their synapses: soon the model takes over. Or we say of an experiment in midstream that *it* needs another control group really to clinch the effect. It is at this point that we get our creative second wind, at the point when the object takes over. I have asked about a dozen of my most creative and productive friends whether they knew what I meant as far as their own work was concerned. All of them replied with one or another form of sheepishness, most of them commenting that one usually did not talk about this kind of personal thing. "This is when you know you're in and—good or bad—the thing will compel you to finish it. In a long piece of work it can come and go several times." The one psychologist among my informants was reminded of the so-called Zeigarnik completion tendency, suggesting that when the watershed was reached the task then had a structure that began to require completeness.

There is something odd about the phenomenon. We externalize an object, a product of our thoughts, treat it as "out there." Freud remarked, commenting on projection, that human beings seem better able to deal with stimuli from the outside than from within. So it is with the externalizing of a creative work, permitting it to develop its own being, its own

autonomy coming to serve *it*. It is as if *it* were easier to cope with there, as if this arrangement permitted the emergence of more unconscious impulse, more material not readily accessible.

There is still another possibility. Observing children in the process of learning mathematics, I have been struck repeatedly by the economical significance of a good mode of representing things to oneself. In group theory, for example, it is extraordinarily difficult to determine whether a set of transformations constitutes a closed group so that any combination of them can be expressed by a single one. The crutch provided by a matrix that gets all the combinations out of the head on to paper or the blackboard makes it possible to look at the group structure as a whole, to go beyond it to the task of seeing whether it has interesting properties and familiar isomorphs. Good representation, then, is a release from intellectual bondage.

I have used the expression "freedom to be dominated" by the object being created. It is a strange choice of words, and I should like to explain it. To be dominated by an object of one's own creation—perhaps its extreme is Pygmalion dominated by Galatea—is to be free of the defenses that keep us hidden from ourselves.

As the object takes over and demands to be completed "in its own terms," there is a new opportunity to express a style and an individuality. Likely as not, it is so partly because we are rid of the internal juggling of possibilities, because we have represented them "out there" where we can look at them, consider them. As one friend, a novelist and critic, put it, "If it doesn't take over and you are foolish enough to go on, what you end up with is contrived and alien."

Deferral and immediacy. There is an immediacy to creating anything, a sense of direction, an objective, a general idea, a feeling. Yet the immediacy is anything but a quick orgasm of completion. Completion is deferred. Let me quote at some

length from the conversation of Christian Zervos with Picasso:

With me a picture is a sum of destructions. I make a picture, and proceed to destroy it. But in the end nothing is lost; the red I have removed from one part shows up in another.

It would be very interesting to record photographically, not the stages of a painting, but its metamorphoses.[2] One would see perhaps by what course a mind finds its way towards the crystallization of its dream. But what is really very curious is to see that the picture does not change basically, that the initial vision remains almost intact in spite of appearance. I see often a light and a dark, when I have put them in my picture, I do everything I can to "break them up," in adding a color that creates a counter effect. I perceive, when this work is photographed, that what I have introduced to correct my first vision has disappeared, and that after all the photographic image corresponds to my first vision, before the occurrence of the transformations brought about by my will.[3]

This is not to say that there is not the occasional good luck, the piece that comes off lickety-split and finished, the theory hit upon at first fire. If ever Georges Simenon is acclaimed a great writer—and that he is more than simply competent is plain—then we will say he brings it off in a gush, in a quantum of pure energy and with such intensity, Carvel Collins tells us, that he has developed the custom of getting clearance from his doctor before he flings himself into a new novel.

Having read a good many journals and diaries by writers, I have come to the tentative conclusion that the principal guard against precocious completion, in writing at least, is boredom. I have little doubt that the same protection avails the scientist. It is the boredom of conflict, knowing deep down what one wishes to say and knowing that one has not said it. One acts on the impulse to exploit an idea, to begin. One also acts on the impulse of boredom, to defer. Thus Virginia Woolf, trying to finish *Orlando* in February 1928: "Always, always, the last chapter slips out of my hands. One gets bored. One whips oneself up. I still hope for a fresh wind and don't very

[2] My colleague Professor George Miller is now engaged in doing just this.—J. S. B.

[3] *The Creative Process,* pp. 56–57.

much bother, except that I miss the fun that was so tremendously lively all October, November, and December." [4]

The internal drama. There is within each person his own cast of characters—an ascetic, and perhaps a glutton, a prig, a frightened child, a little man, even an onlooker, sometimes a Renaissance man. The great works of the theater are decompositions of such a cast, the rendering into external drama of the internal one, the conversion of the internal cast into dramatis personae. Freud, in his searching essay on "The Poet and the Daydream," is most discerning about this device of the playwright.[5] There have been times when writers have come too close to their own personal cast in constructing a play, and even so able a craftsman of the theater as Goethe stumbled in his *Torquato Tasso,* an embarrassingly transparent autobiographical piece about the conflict between Tasso the poet and Antonio the politician. It is, perhaps, Pirandello among modern playwrights who has most convincingly mastered the technique, although a younger Italian dramatist, Ugo Betti, showed promise of carrying it further before his premature death a few years ago. In his brilliant *The Queen and the Rebels,* Betti includes an unforgettable scene at the political frontier of a mythical fascist state, the frontier guards searching a bus party for the fleeing queen. As the scene progresses, it becomes patent that the queen is a spineless nonentity; it is the prostitute in the party who emerges as the queen.

As in the drama, so too a life can be described as a script, constantly rewritten, guiding the unfolding internal drama. It surely does not do to limit the drama to the stiff characters of the Freudian morality play—the undaunted ego, the brutish id, the censorious and punitive superego. Is the internal cast a reflection of the identifications to which we have been com-

[4] *A Writer's Diary* (New York: Harcourt, Brace, 1953), p. 121.

[5] For a discussion of Freud's use of the same device in the development of psychoanalysis, see the chapter on "Freud and the Image of Man."

mitted? I do not think it is as simple as that. It is a way of grouping our internal demands and there are idealized models over and beyond those with whom we have special identification—figures in myth, in life, in the comics, in history, creations of fantasy.

There are some scripts that are more interesting than others. In some, there is a pre-empting protagonist in the center of the stage, constantly proclaiming, save for those moments when there are screamed intrusions from offstage, at which point the declaimer apologizes by pointing out that the voices are not really in the play. In others there is a richness, an inevitability of relationship, a gripping and constant exchange —or perhaps one should call it "inchange." These are dramatic personalities, producers of surprise.

I would like to suggest that it is in the working out of conflict and coalition within the set of identities that compose the person that one finds the source of many of the richest and most surprising combinations. It is not merely the artist and the writer, but the inventor too who is the beneficiary.

The dilemma of abilities. We have now looked at some of the paradoxical conditions that one might assume would affect the production of effective surprises—creativity. Nothing has been said about ability, or abilities. What shall we say of energy, of combinatorial zest, of intelligence, of alertness, of perseverance? I shall say nothing about them. They are obviously important but, from a deeper point of view, they are also trivial. For at any level of energy or intelligence there can be more or less of creating in our sense. Stupid people create for each other as well as benefiting from what comes from afar. So too do slothful and torpid people. I have been speaking of creativity, not of genius.

The chapter in Henry Adams' *Education*, "The Dynamo and the Virgin," is urbane, but beneath the urbanity there is a deep perplexity about what moves men, what moves history, what

makes art. Adams spent the summer and fall of 1900 haunting the Great Exposition in Paris, particularly the hall of dynamos, until the dynamos "became a symbol of infinity . . . a moral force, much as the early Christians felt the Cross." During the same summer he made excursions to Notre Dame of Amiens and to Chartres, and it was then that he came to realize that the Virgin as symbol was also a source of energy: "All the steam in the world could not, like the Virgin, build Chartres." I end with the same perplexity in attempting to find some way of thinking reasonably about the creative process. At the outset I proposed that we define the creative act as effective surprise—the production of novelty. It is reasonable to suppose that we will someday devise a proper scientific theory capable of understanding and predicting such acts. Perhaps we will understand the energies that produce the creative act much as we have come to understand how the dynamo produces its energy. It may be, however, that there is another mode of approach to knowing how the process generates itself, and this will be the way in which we understand how symbols and ideas like the Virgin capture men's thoughts. Often it is the poet who grasps these matters most firmly and communicates them most concisely. Perhaps it is our conceit that there is only one way of understanding a phenomenon. I have argued that just as there is predictive effectiveness, so is there metaphoric effectiveness. For the while, at least, we can do worse than to live with a metaphoric understanding of creativity.

Myth and Identity

We know now a new origin of the faint hissing of the sea in the conch shell held to the ear. It is in part the tremor and throb of the hand, resonating in the shell's chambers. Yet, inescapably, it is the distant sea. For Yeats, it would have been a reaffirmation of his proper query:

> O body swayed to music, O brightening glance,
> How can we know the dancer from the dance?

And so with myth. It is at once an external reality and the resonance of the internal vicissitudes of man. Richard Chase's somewhat cumbersome definition will at least get us on our way: "Myth is an esthetic device for bringing the imaginary but powerful world of preternatural forces into a manageable collaboration with the objective (i.e., experienced) facts of life in such a way as to excite a sense of reality amenable to both the unconscious passions and the conscious mind." [1]

That myth has such a function—to effect some manner of harmony between the literalities of experience and the night impulses of life—few would deny. Yet I would urge that we not be too easily tempted into thinking that there is an oppositional contrast between *logos* and *mythos,* the grammar of experience and the grammar of myth. For each complements the other, and it is in the light of this complementarity that I wish to examine the relation of myth and personality.

[1] *Quest for Myth* (Baton Rouge: Louisiana State University Press, 1949).

Consider the myth first as projection, to use the conventional psychoanalytic term. I would prefer the term "externalization" better to make clear that we are dealing here with the process mentioned earlier in connection with works of art, scientific theories, inventions in general—the human preference to cope with events that are outside rather than inside. Myth, insofar as it is fitting, provides a ready-made means of externalizing human plight by embodying and representing them in storied plot and characters.

What is the significance of this externalizing tendency in myth? It is threefold, I would say. It provides, in the first instance, a basis for communion among men. What is "out there" can be named and shared in a manner beyond the sharing of subjectivity. By the subjectifying of our worlds through externalization, we are able, paradoxically enough, to share communally in the nature of internal experience. By externalizing cause and effect, for example, we may construct a common matrix of determinism. Fate, the full of the moon, the aether—these and not our unique fears are what join us in common reaction. Perhaps more important still, externalization makes possible the containment of terror and impulse by the decorum of art and symbolism. Given man's search for art forms, it must surely be no accident that there is no art of internal feeling or impulse. We seem unable to impose what Freud once called the artifice of formal beauty upon our internal sensations or even upon our stream of seemingly uncontrolled fantasy. It is in the fact of fashioning an external product out of our internal impulses that the work of art begins. There is no art of kinesthesis, and, mindful of Aldous Huxley's fantasies, it is doubtful whether the titillation of the "feelies" could ever become an art form. Sharing, then, and the containment of impulse in beauty—these are the possibilities offered by externalization.

Of the economy provided by the externalized myth, little

need be said. Dollard and Miller, looking at the psychotherapeutic process, have commented upon the importance of sorting and "labeling" for the patient.[2] That is to say, if one is to contain the panicking spread of anxiety, one must be able to identify and put a comprehensible label upon one's feelings better to treat them again, better to learn from experience. Free-floating anxiety, as Freud's translators have vividly called the internal terror that seem causeless to the sufferer, cries for anchoring. Therapy, with its drawn-out "working through," provides an occasion for fashioning an anchor of one's own. So too with hope and aspiring. In boundless form, they are prologues to disenchantment. In time and as one comes to benefit from experience, one learns that things will turn out neither as well as one hoped nor as badly as one feared. Limits are set. Myth, perhaps, serves in place of or as a filter for experience. In the first of the world wars, the myth of the fearless soldier forced a repression of the fear one felt in battle. The result, often enough, was the dissociation and fugue of shell-shock. A quarter century later, a second world war, governed by a different concept of mythic human drama, had provided a means of containment through the admission of human fear. The case books of the two wars are as different as the myths that men use to contain their fears and fatigue. The economical function of myth is to represent in livable form the structure of the complexities through which we must find our way. But such representation, if it is to be effective, must honor the canons of economy that make art.

Let me illustrate my point by reference to Homer, particularly to the madness of Ajax in the *Iliad*. Recall the occasion of the death of Achilles and the determination of Thetis that the bravest man before Ilium shall have her slain son's arms. Agamemnon must make the fateful decision, and it is

[2] J. Dollard and N. E. Miller, *Personality and Psychotherapy* (New York: McGraw-Hill, 1950).

Odysseus and not Ajax who receives the gift of Hephaestus-forged armor. Ajax is lashed by human anger and a craving for vengeance in a proportion to match his heroic capacities. But before these impulses can be expressed, there is an intervention by Athene: Ajax is struck mad and slaughters the captive Trojan livestock, cursing Agamemnon, Odysseus, and Menelaus the while, in a manner that would be described today as a massive displacement of aggression. It is Athene, then, who saves Ajax from a more direct expression of his fury and saves the Greeks from a slaughter of their leaders. Again we have the ingenious and rational intervention of the gods, a formal working out of internal plight in a tightly woven and dramatic plot. It is much as E. R. Dodds has suggested in examining the containment of irrationality in Greek myth. The clouding and bewildering of judgment that is *ate*, or the seemingly unnatural access of courage that is *menos*—both of these sources of potential disruption of natural order are attributed to an external agency, to a supernatural intervention, whether of the gods or of the Erinys.

> I suggest that in general the inward monition, or the sudden unaccountable feeling of power, or the sudden unaccountable loss of judgment, is the germ out of which the divine machinery developed. One result of transposing the event from the interior to the external world is that the vagueness is eliminated: the indeterminate daemon has to be made concrete as some particular personal god.[3]

These were the gods that the Greeks shared, by virtue of whom a sense of causation became communal, through the nurturing of whom an art form emerged. The alternative, as Philip Rahv comments in discussing the governess in "The Turn of the Screw" and the chief protagonist in "The Beast in the Jungle," [4] is to give up one's allotment of experience. If one cannot externalize the demon where it can be enmeshed in the

[3] *The Greeks and the Irrational* (Boston: Beacon Press, 1957), pp. 14–15.

[4] *The Great Short Novels of Henry James* (New York: Dial Press, 1944), introduction.

texture of aesthetic experience, then the last resort is to freeze and block: the overrepression and denial treated so perceptively by Freud in *The Problem of Anxiety.*

What is the art form of the myth? Principally it is drama; yet for all its concern with preternatural forces and characters, it is realistic drama that, in the phrase of Wellek and Warren, tells of "origins and destinies." As they put it, it comprises "the explanations a society offers its young of why the world is and why we do as we do, its pedagogic images of the nature and destiny of man." [5] Ernst Cassirer senses a proper antinomy when he notes that the myth somehow emphasizes the facelike character of experience while at the same time it has the property of compelling belief. Its power is that it lives on the feather line between fantasy and reality. It must be neither too good nor too bad to be true, nor may it be too true. And if it is the case that knowing through art has the function of connecting through metaphor what before had no apparent kinship, then in the present case the art form of the myth connects the daemonic world of impulse with the world of reason by a verisimilitude that conforms to each.

But there is a paradox. On the one side we speak of myth as an externalization; on the other we speak of it as a pedagogic image. This is surely a strange source of instruction! But it is precisely here that the dramatic form of myth becomes significant, precisely here where Gilbert Murray perceived the genius of Homer and the Greeks: "This power of entering vividly into the feelings of both parties in a conflict is . . . the characteristic gift." [6]

I revert for a moment to a consideration of the human personality, to the nature of the vicissitudes that are externalized in myth. It is far from clear why our discordant impulses are bound and ordered in a set of identities—why one pattern

[5] René Wellek and Austin Warren, *Theory of Literature* (New York: Harcourt, Brace, 1942), p. 180.

[6] *The Literature of Ancient Greece* (Chicago: University of Chicago Press, 1957), p. 43.

of impulse is the self-pitying little man in us, another the nurturing protector, another the voice of moral indignation. Surely it is something more than the sum of identifications we have undertaken in the course of achieving balances between love and independence, coming to terms with those who have touched our lives. It is here that myth becomes the tutor, the shaper of identities; it is here that personality imitates myth in as deep a sense as myth is an externalization of the vicissitudes of personality.

Joseph Campbell writes:

> In his life-form the individual is necessarily only a fraction and distortion of the total image of man. He is limited either as male or as female; at any given period of his life he is again limited as child, youth, mature adult, or ancient; furthermore, in his life-role he is necessarily specialized as craftsman, tradesman, servant, or thief, priest, leader, wife, nun, or harlot; he cannot be all. Hence the totality—the fullness of man—is not in the separate member, but in the body of the society as a whole; the individual can be only an organ.[7]

But if no man is all, there is at least in what Campbell calls the "mythologically instructed community" a corpus of images and identities and models that provides the pattern to which growth may aspire—a range of metaphoric identities. We are accustomed to speaking of myth in this programmatic sense in reference to history, as when Sorel invokes the general strike of all workers as a dynamic image, or when Christians speak of the Second Coming for which men must prepare themselves. In the same sense, one may speak of the corpus of myth as providing a set of possible identities for the individual personality. It would perhaps be more appropriate to say that the mythologically instructed community provides its members with a library of scripts upon which the individual may judge the play of his multiple identities. For myth, as I shall now try to illustrate, serves not only as a pattern to which one aspires but also as a criterion for the self-critic.

[7] *The Hero with a Thousand Faces* (New York: Meridian Books, 1956), pp. 382–383.

Take as an example the myths that embody and personify man's capacity for happiness. They are not infinite in variety, but varied enough. An early version is the Greek conception of the Five Ages of Man, the first of which is the happy Age of Gold. As Robert Graves tells it: "These men were the so-called golden race, subjects of Cronus, who lived without cares or labor, eating only acorns, wild fruit, and honey that dripped from the trees . . . never growing old, dancing, and laughing much; death to them was no more terrible than sleep. They are all gone now, but their spirits survive as happy genii." [8] This is the myth of happiness as innocence, and in the Christian tradition we know it as Man before the Fall. Innocence ends either by a successful attempt to steal the knowledge of God or by aspiring to the cognitive power of the gods, *hubris*. And with the end of innocence, there is an end to happiness; knowledge is equated with temptation to evil. The issue appears to revolve around the acquisition and uses of knowledge.

I will oversimplify in the interest of brevity and say that from these early myths there emerge two types of mythic plot: the plot of innocence and the plot of cleverness—the former being a kind of Arcadian ideal, requiring the eschewal of complexity and awareness, the latter requiring the cultivation of competence almost to the point of guile. The happy childhood, the good man as the child of God, the simple plowman, the Rousseauian ideal of natural nobility—these are the creatures of the plot of innocence. At the other extreme there are Penelope, the suitors, and Odysseus. In Murray's words:

> Penelope—she has just learned on good evidence that Odysseus is alive and will return immediately—suddenly determines that she cannot put off the suitors any longer, but brings down her husband's bow, and says she will forthwith marry the man who can shoot through twelve axeheads with it! Odysseus hears her and is pleased! May it not be that in the original story there was a reason for Penelope to bring the bow, and for Odysseus to be pleased? It was a plot. He [Odysseus] meant Eurycleia [the old maidservant] to

[8] *The Greek Myths* (Baltimore: Penguin Books, 1955), p. 36.

recognize him [by his scar], to send the maids away, and break the news to Penelope. Then husband and wife together arranged the trial of the bow.[9]

Again and again in the Greek myths there are cleverness, competence, and artifice—Herakles, Achilles, Odysseus, Perseus—wherever you look. It is the happy triumph of clever competence with a supernatural assist. And yet there is also the ideal of the Age of Innocence. So too in the later Christian tradition and in our own times. The manner in which superior knowledge shows itself changes: the ideal of the crafty warrior, the wise man, the interpreter of the word of God, the Renaissance omnicompetent, the wily merchant, the financial wizard, the political genius. If it is true that in some way each is suspect, it is also true that each is idealized in his own way. Each is presented as satisfied. New versions arise to reflect the ritual and practice of each era—the modifications of the happiness of innocence and the satisfaction of competence.

The manner in which man has striven for competence and longed for innocence has reflected the controlling myths of the community. The medieval scholar, the Florentine prince, the guild craftsman, as well as the withdrawn monastic of Thomas à Kempis and the mendicant of St. Francis—all of these are deeply involved with the myths of innocence and competence and are formed by them. Indeed, the uncertainty in resolving the dichotomy of reason and revelation as ways to know God reflects the duality of the myth of happiness and salvation. It is not simply society that patterns itself on the idealizing myths, but unconsciously it is the individual man as well who is able to bring order to his internal clamor of identities in terms of prevailing myth. Life, then, produces myth and finally imitates it.

In our own time, in the American culture, there is a deep problem generated by the confusion that has befallen the myth of the happy man. It reflects itself in the American

[9] *The Literature of Ancient Greece,* pp. 39–40.

personality. There still lingers the innocent Christian conception that happiness is the natural state of man—or at least of the child and of man as innocent—and that it is something that we have done or failed to do as individuals that creates a rather Protestantized and private unhappiness. The impact of Freud has begun to destroy this myth, to replace it. Our popular films may now, with artistry, depict the child as murderer. A generation of playwrights has destroyed the remnants of Horatio Alger, replacing it with the image of Arthur Miller's salesman dying by entropy, an object of compassion. We are no longer a "mythologically instructed community." And so one finds a new generation struggling to find or to create a satisfactory and challenging mythic image.

Two such images seem to be emerging in the new generation. One is that of the hipsters and the squares; the other is the idealization of creative wholeness. The first is the myth of the uncommitted wandering hero, capable of the hour's subjectivity—its "kicks"—participating in a new inwardness. It is the theme of reduction to the essentially personal, the hero able to filter out the clamors of an outside world, an almost masturbatory ideal. Eugene Burdick in *The Reporter* gives the following account of a conversation in a San Francisco café between two members of the Beat Generation:

"Man, I remember something when I was little, a boy," somebody named Lee says. He is hunched forward, his elbows on the table, a tumbler of wine between his hands. "About a dog. Little miserable dog of mine."

"Yeah, man, go on," Mike says, his eyes lighting up.

"I get up real early to do my paper route. Los Angeles *Examiner*," Lee says. "Streets always empty, just a few milk trucks and bakery trucks and other kids like me. My dog goes along, see? Every day he trots along with me. Little mongrel dog."

"Yeah, yeah, go on, man," Mike says, impatient for the story, sure that it has meaning.

"There we are in all those big empty streets. Just me and the dog. Sun coming up, papers falling on the porches, me dreaming and walking and the dog trotting," Lee says. "Then far away, about as big as a black mosquito, I see this hopped-up Model A. Wonderful

pipes on it, blatting so sweet I could hear them for six blocks. I stand there on the curb, listening to that sweet sound and watching that car come weaving down that empty street. And the dog stands in the gutter, watching too. That Model A gets bigger and I can see the chrome pipes on the side, the twin Strombergs sucking air, just eating up the asphalt."

He pauses and Mike leans forward and says urgently, "Now man, come on, go. I wanna hear this."

"This Model A is a roadster and there is a Mexican driving and his girl with him," Lee says slowly, stalking the climax. "It weaves across the street, and me and the dog stare at it. And it comes for us in a big slow curve and hit that dog. His back broke in mid-air and he was dead when he hit the street again. Like a big man cracking a seed in his teeth . . . same sound, I mean. And the girl stare back at me and laughs. And I laugh. You see why, man?"

The two of them sit quietly, looking down at the wine and listening to the jazz. Mike glances once at Lee and then back at his glass. He has learned something secret and private about Lee, and that is good enough. After a while they sit back, smiling, and listen to the jazz.[10]

It is not easy to create a myth and to emulate it at the same time. James Dean and Jack Kerouac, Kingsley Amis and John Osborne, the Teddy Boys and the hipsters: they do not make a mythological community. They represent mythmaking in process as surely as Hemingway's characters or Scott Fitzgerald's. What is ultimately clear is that even the attempted myth must be a model for imitating, a drama to be tried on for fit. One sees the identities of a group of young men being "packaged" in terms of the unbaked myth. It is a mold, a prescription of characters, a plot. Whether the myth will be viable, whether it will fit the internal plight, we do not know. There are temporary myths, too. There was a myth of the supernatural birth of a dead woman's son, a myth Boas found in 1888 and again in 1900. By 1931 there was no trace of it.

What of the renewal of the myth of the full creative man? It is even more inchoate than the first, yet perhaps more

[10] "The Innocent Nihilists Adrift in Squaresville," *The Reporter,* 3 April 1958, p. 33.

important. It is, as we have seen in another context, the middle-aged executive sent back to the university by the company for a year, wanting humanities and not sales engineering; it is this man telling you that he would rather take life classes Saturday morning at the museum school than be president of the company; it is the adjectival extravaganza of the word "creative," as in "creative advertising." It is as if, given the demise of the myths of creation and their replacement by a scientific cosmogony that for all its formal beauty lacks metaphoric force, the theme of creating becomes internalized, creating anguish rather than, as in the externalized myths, providing a basis for psychic relief and sharing. Yet this self-contained image of creativity becomes, I think, the basis for a myth of happiness. But perhaps between the death of one myth and the birth of its replacement there must be a reinternalization, even to the point of a *culte de moi*. That we cannot yet know. All that is certain is that we live in a period of mythic confusion that may provide the occasion for a new growth of myth, myth more suitable for our times.

Indeed, one may ask whether the rise of the novel as an art form, and particularly the subjectification of the novel since the middle of the nineteenth century, whether these do not symbolize the voyage into the interior that comes with the failure of prevailing myths to provide external models toward which one may aspire. For when the prevailing myths fail to fit the varieties of man's plight, frustration expresses itself first in mythoclasm and then in the lonely search for internal identity. The novels of Conrad, of Hardy, of Gide, of Camus—paradoxically enough—provide man with guides for the internal search. One of Graham Greene's most tormented books, an autobiographical fragment on an African voyage, is entitled *Journey Without Maps*. Perhaps the modern novel, in contrast to the myth, is the response to the internal anguish that can find no external constraint in myth, a form of internal map.

But this is a matter requiring a closer scrutiny than we can give it here. Suffice it to say that the alternative to externalization in myth appears to be the internalization of the personal novel, the first a communal effort, the second the lone search for identity.

Identity and the Modern Novel

History has been described, probably too simply, as man's effort to make a home for himself in the world. It might better be described as an extension of those urges that impel man to find antecedents for his acts and his dilemmas, to find a prologue for his posture toward the future. The writing of history and the quest for identity share a paradox. A society's grasp of its history and a man's sense of his identity, when fully achieved, are final acts. But a community washed by the currents of growth does not easily come to a sharing of its conception of origins or the meaning of events. And no man answers easily the questions: "Who am I, where do I belong, and of what am I capable?"

Why are such issues so elusive? Perhaps it is as a brilliantly intuitive woman once put it in trying to understand the James-Lange theory of emotion: "Yes, yes, what William James must have begun with is, 'How do I know what I am until I feel what I do?'" Marlow voyages up the Congo toward Kurtz in "Heart of Darkness" and is in a constant anguish of action. Conrad's "The Secret Sharer" is no conversation piece between the young captain and his double, Leggatt. At the climax, the captain takes his ship—"on my conscience it had to be thus close"—to a point where "the black mass of Koh-ring, like the gate of the everlasting night, towered over the taffrail." The alienated narrator in Camus' *The Stranger* achieves a sense of his identity only by living out the consequences of a senseless

murder. It is not by accident that highly subjective novels are often mistaken for tales of adventure.

But surely the puzzle is deeper than the idea that identity inheres in action and that it is only through retrospection upon action that we find it. Whose action? Here, I think, lies the deeper puzzle to which the novelist addresses himself: the puzzle of retroflective knowledge about self and identity, the epistemologically impossible question, "who am I?" to which the philosopher Morris Cohen once replied, "and who is asking the question?" For there are many selves in a character, and their relation to each other is the matter that is often most obscure.

What complicates the search, then, is not the simple fact that identity inheres in action and must be sought there, but rather that the action is not single in its purpose. Once again we are looking for a cast, for a script, and for an *explication du texte*. This is why action is required, both in the novel and in life itself, why it is so difficult to know who you are until you feel what you do, what each "you" does. And that is not all—we must complicate the matter one degree further. It is Jung who has most strongly urged the complementary principle of human character: a function that is exercised has the effect of strengthening an opposite function. After a while the introvert develops strong extraversive needs; the man whose life has been governed exclusively by thinking craves in time the guide of feeling; the literal man searches eventually for ways of intuiting. So with the principal actors within the human character. Their rebellious understudies, if I may so designate them, are often of opposite persuasion, Jung's *Gegentypus*. Here is the origin of the "secret sharer" and "the double," here the core of what is so movingly funny about Walter Mitty.

The more intensely a life is lived, the more complete its singleness of purpose, the more compelling is the secret sharer. The more externally successful a life is, the more difficult it

usually becomes to admit the contrary double into the play that governs the life.

Character and the company of identities that constitute it seem to emerge at times of crisis in the life of man. Crises have a certain chronology and, while they differ in depth and content in each life, there are certain constants. I should like to consider four works of fiction—Camus' *The Stranger,* Fitzgerald's *The Great Gatsby,* Conrad's "The Secret Sharer," and a little-known novel of Jules Romain called *The Death of a Nobody.* But I cannot do so before sketching some of the more universal forms crisis takes when it creates characters. I am grateful to Erik Erikson for his searching examination of these matters, and I shall lean heavily upon his conception of identity crises in what follows.[1]

The first of the crises, first in the sense that it is likely to be the one that occurs earliest in the life of man, surrounds the issue of trust and mistrust in the meaningfulness of life and of one's own actions. Its pattern lies in the intensive relation between mother and infant when consistency of love and support is demonstrated by the mother's ability and willingness to give succor and warmth and rightness to the infant's life, to respond to the child's actions in a manner that lends meaning and predictability to them. In Camus' *The Stranger,* failure to achieve such a sense of meaning results in Meursault's sense of absurdity, his lack of caring whether he marries Marie or whether his firm sends him to Paris—nothing much matters. He is in the grownup world of the man who has come to expect nothing but capriciousness and meaninglessness—first from his mother, then from life itself. It is a stroke of art on Camus' part that the novel should begin with the death of such a mother, and that the issue of guilt in Meursault's trial

[1] Erik H. Erikson, *Childhood and Society* (New York: W. W. Norton, 1950).

should rest so heavily on his failure to cry at her funeral, his smoking at the death vigil, his acceptance of *café au lait* from the warder. For him, no action is appropriate, none inappropriate: neither going to a Fernandel film, sleeping with Marie the day after the funeral, nor the pointless shooting of the Arab. It is in a paroxysm of rage against the priest's insistence on meaningfulness in life and death that he finally achieves the primitive identity that comes from wanting to live: "It was as if that great rush of anger had washed me clean, had emptied me of hope, and gazing up at the dark sky spangled with its signs and stars, for the first time, the first, I laid my heart open to the benign indifference of the universe." At last a defense against meaninglessness, the strongest defense: none at all. At last identity in an absurd world.

The second crisis occurs in its earliest form when personal autonomy becomes the issue, and it involves the problem of creating a line of demarcation between oneself and the pressures and influences of the outside world. This is the stage of life in which the child exerts his negativism in the interest of his positive identity—to be free, if only by negation. It is at this moment in growth that the personal pronoun becomes a repetitive feature of the child's vocabulary, as if "I" and "me" were verbal probes for exploring the outer bounds of his living space. Like the crisis of trust, this one also is never finished; it recurs in later versions in richer contexts. Where failure to resolve the crisis of trust leads to doomed struggles with the sense of absurdity, failure here introduces the theme of "touch-me-not": one holds back, or strikes out compulsively, or is shamed by the power others have over one.

At this point, the range of crises begins to extend beyond the nucleus of family. The first one of this order involves initiative, the power to explore, to feel one's way, to take the initiative in action. Failure this time leads to a gnawing sense of guilt, of doubt in action. As school becomes increasingly important, there is the struggle to avoid a sense of inferiority and

mediocrity, to be able to exercise one's industry and competence, to make the initiative come to something that fits into a broader society. And on the heels of this another crisis is soon generated: concentration or diffuseness, the adolescent's struggle, continued in altered form through life, between a sense of one's own identity and the wish to be engaged, to belong, and to play many roles. This crisis bedevils the American, particularly the successful American—specters like Sinclair Lewis' Arrowsmith or Arthur Miller's Salesman. It is one of Gatsby's deep confusions, deeper perhaps than the dream of perpetual youth symbolized by Daisy.

With the end of adolescence there is the first crisis of adult love: intimacy or isolation. The popularity and flirtatiousness of the girl must be replaced by the fidelity and intimate sympathy of the woman; the exploitative, sentimental date mongering of the teen-age boy must change into the protective giving and receiving of love by the man. The countless false roads to intimacy and mutual sexuality between man and woman provide a never-ending source of themes. Promiscuity, violence, and the sinuous maneuvers whereby men attempt to turn their women into mothers to recapture an earlier and safer version of intimacy are among the means by which man isolates himself from intimacy.

Finally, there are the two typical crises of the middle years. In one man faces the possibility that he will either create or stagnate. In the other he sums up the personal balance, looking for integrity and fearing to find despair.

The crisis of creating comes at the moment when a man looks beyond his own life to a next generation—through his children, through his works. There is the emergence of a new responsibility. If the awareness of this new responsibility does not emerge, a man is beset by a sense of sterility. This essentially is the theme of Lorca's *Yerma*, an embittering crisis of childlessness.

The Spanish writer Calderón has put the meaning of in-

tegrity best. He calls it the conviction of the moral paternity of one's own soul. With this relationship accepted, one can understand how to follow and to lead, how to aid and be aided. But now when the search fails, there is despair and time seems too short to explore other roads. It is cruel to die and cruel to live. I suspect this is the crisis that impels the novelists whose works we shall examine now.

Of Conrad's "The Secret Sharer" much has already been written about its bearing on the sense of self. The young captain on his first command is standing the anchor watch. In the dark water there appears a swimmer, Leggatt. He is the fleeing mate of a vessel anchored in the same roadstead a few miles off. The mate comes aboard on the Jacob's ladder that has been inadvertently left over the side. He has escaped from irons on his own ship, the *Sephora,* where sometime earlier he had strangled a crew member; part of a heroic episode in which Leggatt had set a foresail that saved the ship from foundering in a wild sea. The captain hears out Leggatt's story, the tale of a competent but impulsive man. He hides him carefully in his own cabin, tortured by guilt and misgiving with the deceits that are required. Finally, the captain brings his ship perilously close to the shore to let Leggatt escape, having given him a hat and some coins. The puzzle is why he did hide Leggatt, an outlaw, and, having hid him, why he brought his own ship so dangerously close in on shore when Leggatt had obviously been able to swim a few miles to get from the *Sephora* to the foot of the captain's ladder. One need not repeat at length what all of us already know about the story: that the captain's identification with Leggatt is based on a recognition of likeness—there is a lawless and impulsive Leggatt in the captain as in all law-abiding men, symbolized by the headless appearance of the swimming figure that emerges from the phosphorescent water at the foot of the rope ladder. I should like, rather, to explore two puzzling

features of the story that are of especial interest. Why, indeed, does the captain have to take his ship so close to shore before coming about in order to let Leggatt slip over the side? The captain most surely knows that Leggatt must be a prodigious swimmer. And, then, what is the meaning of the final line, "my second self had lowered himself into the water to take his punishment; a free man, a proud swimmer striking out for a new destiny"?

The madly skillful maneuver of bringing the ship that close to Koh-ring has nothing to do with paying a debt to the captain's second self, but it is rather a symbolization of the crisis of competence, the third of the crises mentioned earlier. It is the captain testing his own limits, a full testing. Leggatt had already warned him of the folly of the maneuver, impulsive Leggatt: "'Be careful,' he murmured warningly, and I realized that all my future, the only future for which I was fit, would perhaps go irretrievably to pieces in any mishap to my first command." Yet take her in he must. There is an element of Russian roulette in the scene; the same rule prevails—that to gain identity, one must risk losing it altogether. It is the rule of coping with crisis. Leggatt had set the foresail, had risked his life. He had risked his impulse of anger too, had strangled the mutinous crew member. He had lost. By putting in that close to shore the captain was in his turn playing win all or lose all. In this deepest respect they were allies. It is not surprising, then, that it is the hat, the symbol of the head and of integrity, the hat thrown to Leggatt in the water, that provides a marker by which the captain is able to judge his steerageway when he has come hard alee. The prize, when he has won, is that he is now the sole master of the ship and in a sense is rid of Leggatt, but in a very special sense.

To the captain, the departing Leggatt is a free man and a proud swimmer seeking a new destiny. It would seem that the captain had freed not only himself but the stranger as well. What has happened is that a victory of discrimination has been

won. It is not that the secret sharer has been eliminated but that he has been recognized. The captain is no longer to be confused by his conflicting identities. Having risked the ordeal, he is now able to distinguish that part of himself which is the master of the ship, that part which is the double. Discriminated, the two of them are now at peace: "And I watched the hat, the expression of my sudden pity for his mere flesh. It had been meant to save his homeless head from the dangers of the sun. And now–behold–it was saving the ship. . . ." Not only is Leggatt free and proud; so too is the captain. The cast has been found, the text explicated. No despair here.

We have already commented upon the plight of Meursault, the narrator in *The Stranger*. His tragic situation, and it must be called that, is that his vision or myth of his own life–a life perceived by him as a set of self-sufficient existential moments, each providing its own meaning–does not mesh with the expectations that society lives by. The point is not that his understanding is better, or that the conventional morality and the conventional conception of cause and effect are more adequate; it is that there is no contact. And so at the critical moment of the trial, he says: "Just then I noticed that almost all the people in the courtroom were greeting each other, exchanging remarks and forming groups–behaving in fact as in a club where the company of others of one's own tastes and standing makes one feel at ease. That, no doubt, explained the odd impression I had of being *de trop* here, of being a gate crasher." And when the testimony unrolls, it seems to Meursault not to be about his life, his motives, his way of knowing the world at all. He is the stranger. And, indeed, each man is the stranger. I do not mean to be excessively clinical about the unfortunate Meursault, for it is obvious that Camus intended him as a symbol and not as a case study. Yet it is appropriate to note that there is something psychologically very special about him. Having failed to resolve what earlier we spoke of as the crisis of trust, having failed to find some meaningfulness,

it is impossible for him to be concerned with any of the other crises. Initiative, competence, intimacy—all are meaningless. But in the end, like the captain, he finds his integrity in *recognizing* the indifference of the universe, washed clean of rage.

Oddly enough, I think Jules Romain's short novel, *The Death of a Nobody,* gives a clue to the special psychological quality of Camus' narrator. The novel is an extended account of what Eliot put in a metaphoric image: we die not with a bang but a whimper. A retired railroad functionary comes to a somewhat shabby section of Paris to live, contracts an illness after an expedition to the Pantheon, dies quietly in his room. The concierge and the stock characters of the neighborhood are a bit shocked, but there are few ripples. A life comes anonymously to an end. That is all that happens. I am not doing full justice to the structure of the novel, but you will recognize that it is not a very good novel, though it is a brave attempt to capture urban anonymity and man's small place in the world. Romain's hero has never committed the murder precipitating the action that permits Meursault to capture his own autonomy. He only catches cold. The main event in his life is his death: and it is absurd. Like Camus, Romain is very French. For both of them, identity includes a conception of one's place in a greater scheme, a matching of personal meaning with some external meaning. Superficially, each writer concludes that there is none, yet more deeply each asserts that whatever there is suffices. One is freer by virtue of knowing the manner in which he is a victim. Both novelists are dealing with the crisis of autonomy: one successfully, the other not, but that makes no difference here. What makes the difference is knowledge of one's predicament.

The theme repeats itself in *The Great Gatsby,* but in a different setting and with a different resolution. Gatsby seeks to be his own creator—no roots, no background, infinite facade. His parties overflow, but in the end his funeral is unattended.

And for all that, what is the true despair is that the world to which he aspires, the world he seeks to create in which to live out his dream, is not only not worth creating but that Gatsby never recognizes this: "The truth is that Jay Gatsby of West Egg, Long Island, sprang from his Platonic conception of himself. He was a son of God—a phrase which if it means anything means just that—and he must be about his Father's business, the service of a vast, vulgar, and meretricious Beauty. So he invented just the sort of Jay Gatsby that a seventeen year old boy would be likely to invent, and to this conception he was faithful to the end." And to the end he could not face or master the crises that could give him an identity beyond the Platonic facade. Daisy herself destroys the dream of Daisy. In the end, with no awareness, the web of dreams that Gatsby had tried to build into a life dissolves.

Why does the novel replace the great unifying myths? The emergence of the novel as a "character art" very likely reflects the increase in self-consciousness that has been part of the development of our civilization, as various critics have suggested. The mythic form, serving as protoscience, protoreligion, and protoliterature, depended for its full effectiveness, as we have noted, upon a sharing of beliefs about origins—supernatural origins under the control of a personalized, deified destiny such as the Greek pantheon. Drama, thaumaturgy, and science, when such a culture prevails, are not so far removed each from the other, for the form of "scientific" explanation is more often than not a dramatic or magical one.

A corollary of this proposition is that the psychological novel, in contrast to the myth, exists as a recognition of the distinction between subjective and objective. Compare the relation between Leggatt and the captain, on the one hand, and that between Agamemnon and Ajax, on the other—or contrast Meursault in *The Stranger* and Sisyphus of the myth, each coping with ultimate absurdity. The contemporary novel is subjective, immanent, living in time, animated by human

impulses that lead to human actions. The myth is objective, transcendental, timeless, moved by impulses beyond man to meet inhuman demands. In the objective verisimilitude of myth lies the triumph of its externalization of man's inner experience. With the novel and its interior monologues, the effort is to save the subjectivity, to use it as cause. Meursault's sense of meaningless is not a divine condemnation: it is of his own flesh. He is not condemned, as Sisyphus was, to push the rock endlessly up a slope.

To consider the element of time in myth and the novel is revealing. Leon Edel in his *The Psychological Novel* makes much of the subjective conception of time in contemporary writing:

> We know that Proust studied briefly under Bergson and that he read his works. He mentions him only once, in *Cities of the Plain,* in connection with the effects of soporific drugs on memory. Memory, however, is at the heart of Bergson's explorations, as it is of Proust's. Bergson's concept of time—*la durée*—is the measure of existence. "The invisible progress of the past, that gnaws into the future," his thesis of the use of the past in the evolution of the creative act, his discussion of intuition and reality, his belief in the flux of experience—all these ideas are taken up and studied with extraordinary refinement by Proust. Like William James, Bergson taught that we are remoulded constantly by experience; that consciousness is a process of endless accretion, so long as mind and senses are functioning; that it is "the continuation of an indefinite past in a living present." And out of this comes also the preoccupation with time which is central to the psychological novel. The watch measures off the hours with continuing regularity, but consciousness sometimes makes an hour seem like a day, or a day like an hour. In the mind past and present merge: we suddenly call up a memory of childhood that is chronologically of the distant past; but in it, memory becomes instantly vivid and is relived for the moment that it is recalled. So, in setting down in the novel the thoughts as they are passing through the mind of the character, the novelist is catching and recording the present moment—and no other. It was no accident that Joyce sought to record a single day in *Ulysses* and that throughout Virginia Woolf there is a preoccupation with "the moment." [2]

[2] *The Psychological Novel* (London: Rupert Hart-Davis, 1955), pp. 28–29.

Myth, the realm of eternal representation, on the contrary, is replete with reference to eternities. Sisyphus is eternally with his rock; Prometheus is not involved in an episode. Indeed, the decline of the Golden Age in Greek myth is in the thousands of years. Time and space are impersonal, desubjectified, as they are in the science of the nineteenth century. Science having captured time, what is left as personal is *la durée*, the length and breadth of existence as experienced.

The crises of growth with which we started, Erikson's list of human vicissitudes, are all personal, all subjective, all elementary forms of a struggle for awareness. It is the struggle for awareness that is so poignantly summarized today in our preoccupation with the "quest for identity." It is not, in turning to literature, that we seek mythic models for action. Rather, the search is for models or images or paradigms of awareness and its paradoxes: it is not objective reality and what to do when up against it, but subjective reality and how to discern it. One cannot help but compare the autobiographical fragment left by Ghiberti, discussing the long period during which he worked on the famous doors of the Baptistery at Florence, with the personal writing, say, of a modern sculptor like Henry Moore. Ghiberti talks of the material that was "needed" to do the designs that were "required." It is as if it were all "out there." Moore is concerned with the creating of illusions and symbols, and self-awareness for him is as important as a stone chisel.

The modern novel in many ways is a reflection of the separation of ways of knowing into the literary, the scientific, and the religious. While they were of a piece, the myth was an appropriate vehicle for the clarifying externalization. Today, in our age of separatism, the novel seeks an art form suitable to the changing, increasingly subjective mind of modern man.

I think the transition from myth to novel can be well illustrated by a crisis in development that comes after all of Erik-

son's have gone by. It is the crisis involved in facing death, in dying. There has been an attenuation of the sense and significance of death. The instructing myth has eroded. Death now is the machine stopping. Once the shades were able to pay the boatman Charon for their passage across the Styx with a coin placed under the tongue of those who had died by those who had been left behind. Today death has become somehow impersonal and unnecessary, perhaps like a fatal vitamin deficiency that might have been prevented or at least delayed. Death in the abstract has been couched in such large numbers —one hundred thousand at Hiroshima, four million Jews exterminated, the holocaust properties of the new thermonuclear weapons—that we have at times lost sight of what individual dying means. The wonder drugs have shed still another abstract light on dying, and one reads drug advertising with the sense that death must be an error on the part of the consumer. John Sloan Dickey, writing of the contemporary American undergraduate, remarks that, because of the scattering of the extended family of great-aunts and grandparents, few have seen death close by. One dies nowadays in hospitals, hidden from view, victims of medical failure.

What has this to do with awareness of identity, with myth and novel? I would suggest in the spirit of an hypothesis that a concept of death and its dignity are always inherent in a culture that imparts a sense of meaning to life. If a life has a structure and a meaning, there must be times for dying that are more appropriate than others, ways of dying that are better than others. We must come to terms with death, and the image of the used-up machine provides no terms at all. It may well be that a sense of irreplaceability, connoting a felt uniqueness, is the hallmark of one who dies well and in continuity with life. Perhaps it is the anonymity of modern technological life that makes it so difficult, then, to have a "death of one's own." It is not as in Rilke's *Malte Laurits Brigge*, with the grandfather, Chamberlain Christoph Detlev,

roaring from room to room in the house over which he presided, dying with a desperate blend of protest and pride, yet knowing that the coin for Charon would be under his tongue: "It was the . . . death which the Chamberlain had carried within time and nourished in himself his whole life long. All excess of pride, will and lordly vigor that he himself had not been able to consume in his quiet days had passed into his death. . . . And when I think of the others I have seen or about whom I have heard: it is always the same. They all have had a death of their own."

Where technique grows without supporting compassion, as so often happens in a transitional phase of growth in our society, we lose sight of the cruelty of prolonging life, prolonging it because it is possible to do so and because we have been hard put to define when, if you will, a life has been spent. Should a man go on living though he has become a vegetable or only a mindless vehicle of pain? "Dying should be while there is still some taste in life to have made it worth living. It should be while a man is still loved and before he has become a hated burden or a fool." A friend put it that way, trying to fathom what might be meant by a "right death."

The myth of a hereafter is premised on a conception of a persistent fate, persistent no mater how fickle its execution. It requires a sense of the inexplicable magic of death, whether the brooding magic or even the faery touch of E. M. Forster's *Celestial Omnibus*. Technical intervention with death, however beneficent or violent, whether positively through medical practice or negatively through man-made slaughter reckoned in exponents, hastens the secularization of heaven into a cipher, leaving death with the sole meaning of no-life.

There have been many learned and wise words written about the decline in the power of the afterlife as a mythic symbol and a guiding religious idea. To trace the history of the decline is a monumental labor and need not concern us here. The enlightenment and skepticism of science, the divorce of

the concept of truth from the uses of poetry and metaphor and its canonical connection with objective proof, the encroachment of a feeling of human potency on what was formerly thought of as fate—all of these have made life more valued and death more neuter. The result is an increased demand for significance in life, for a sense of identity, for meaning in experience; and with it goes a loss of tolerance for absurdity or, better, a greater readiness to recognize absurdity as an immanent property of life.

While heaven prevailed, its externalizing myth could point outward beyond experience. With its erosion, a new literary symbolism became necessary. The inventions of a Poe or a Melville, Captain Ahab with his coffin prepared, the deep undertones of death in Camus' *The Plague,* Hesse's *Death and the Lover,* Freud's death instinct, Hemingway's preoccupation with dying well—all have replaced the heavenly treatment of death and after. All have been concerned not as in classic myth with what comes after death, but with what comes before it, with the style of awareness that gives death meaning in terms of life.

Though I have illustrated my point by choosing death as an example, I might as readily have taken love or competence or guilt. In each, subjectification and the demise of fate has been the historical rule. Compare the distant screen figure of Beatrice in Dante's *Vita Nuova* with Anna Karenina, or Kafka's figures with those of the Greek myths.

The novel has turned the uses of metaphor to an exploration of the ways and models of awareness. The change is as enormous, surely, as the difference between the concept of demonic possession and the concept of neurosis—the one emphasizing an outside origin, the other emphasizing origin from within.

Art as a Mode of Knowing

For all one's conviction that the world should be open to knowing, there are certain forms of knowledge that one fears. So it is with the subject of art and man's relationship to art as creator or beholder. It is not that one actually hopes the riddle of man will withstand the inquiry of the psychologist, nor is it the fear that knowledge will make man vulnerable to manipulation, for knowledge surely makes man proof against manipulation, too. It is neither of these things. It is more likely the fear that knowledge will negate the pleasures of innocence. This is not altogether a foolish or a sentimental attitude. For there is a deep question whether the possible meanings that emerge from an effort to explain the experience of art may not mask the real meanings of a work of art.

But risky as it is, I should like to consider four aspects of the experience of art—the connecting of experience that is the reward for grasping a work of art, the manner in which achieving understanding of a poem or picture requires an expression of human effort, what it is that is "moving" about experiencing an object of beauty, and wherein lies the generality of that which we find beautiful.

It is only fair to warn at the outset that psychology as an experimental and empirical enterprise has little to say about these matters and that Whitehead may not have been altogether wrong, though he was obscure, in suggesting that, both for the exploration of the metaphysical and the poetic, the

language of the poet may be the only appropriate medium.

Connectedness. Whoever reflects recognizes that there are empty and lonely spaces between one's experiences. Perhaps these gaps are the products of reflection or at least its fruits. Indeed, the conditional tense in grammar conserves a special mode for expressing our sense of these unfilled possibilities for experience. "What would it be like if . . .?" Science, by reducing the need for empiricism with its statement of general laws, fills these gaps only partly. Given $s = gt^2/2$, we may easily know the distance traversed by any falling object in the earth's gravitational field for any length of time, however limited our direct observation of specific objects falling. What is more striking still is that the equation specifies such distance for the ideal frictionless fall, a state of nature we can never directly observe. Friction may be added to the picture in the interest of "realism," but the law of falling bodies goes beyond realism. But this is somehow not enough, and we argue with Goethe's romantic view: "Gray is all theory; green grows the golden tree of life." The general scientific law, for all its beauty, leaves the interstices as yearningly empty as before.

If you travel from Florence, where you may see in the works of Cimabue at the Uffizi the peak of the thirteenth century in Italian painting, to Padua to look at the passionate, rude forms of Giotto in the Arena Chapel, you perceive a new image and something akin to a new unity in experience. Something happens between the end of the thirteenth and the beginning of the fourteenth century, for Giotto is the new century even if he lived in the old, and that something is a gain in unity. To go from the stylized, almost iconic representations of Cimabue (Figure 1) to the powerful combination of form and impulse in Giotto (Figure 2) is to break free from well-established representation to a new, more comprehensive unity. Of course, it is in poetry that one most vividly uses the new, even bizarre juxtapositions that provide the refreshing and instructive surprises of art. If form and the expression of impulse or

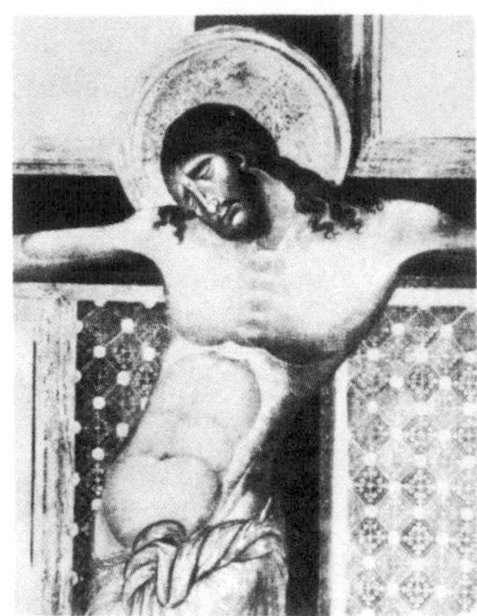

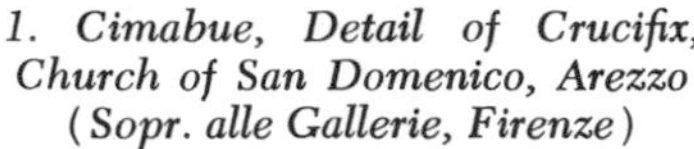

1. Cimabue, Detail of Crucifix, Church of San Domenico, Arezzo (Sopr. alle Gallerie, Firenze)

2. Giotto, Detail of Crucifixion, Arena Chapel, Padua (Alinari)

feeling are suddenly fused when painting departs from its iconized conventions, it is much the same order of recombining that we know in poetry. We find in Eliot's "Prufrock," for example, not solely the vein of contempt but also a basis for compassion—for the young reader, particularly, a new unity in experience. What is this experience of unity? First one has scorn for the figure who does not dare to eat a peach, who fears the mermaids will not sing to him; and then suddenly there is also compassion for this man who fears that he has measured out his life with coffee spoons, that he should have been a pair of ragged claws.

There are perhaps two processes that yield a clue about how art achieves this connecting, this comprehensiveness. One is the construction of the tautly economical symbol, a matter to which we shall turn presently. The other is the construction and exploitation of the category of possibility, the formulated but empty category through which we search out new experience. This is a method used by both art and science. The

nuclear physicist creates such empty categories out of the requirements of a theory of the nature of matter: for the nucleus of an atom to behave as it is supposed to behave, there *must* be a small particle with neither positive nor negative charge, a neutrino. The neutrino is created as a fruitful fiction. And in time a neutrino is found. But a comparable creation in art does not follow the necessities of strict logical implication. Contrast the created mythic category of centaurs, torso of man and powerful lower body of horse, with the equally untenanted class, "female presidents of the United States, past, present, and future." One is a symbolic achievement, the other a device for ticking off moderately interesting eventualities. To combine man with horse is to connect the image of man's rational gift with a renewed image of virility: sexuality and strength, the fleetness and mobility of Hermes, instinctual dignity. An image is created connecting things that were previously separate in experience, an image that bridges rationality and impulse. A centaur is not a device for exploring what it would be like if men and horses were combined in varying degree. In this respect it transcends the category of "female presidents" which is such a device and only that. The centaur is, rather, a metaphoric fusing of two spheres of experience. It is this fusing that makes Prufrock, too, a metaphoric achievement: the contemptible is also an object of compassion; two islands of experience have beneath them a single continent.

Return for a moment to the painting of Giotto. In the Christ figures of the twelfth century one sees a gradual humanizing process. The crucifixion figures at the beginning of the century are without pain, weightlessly suspended from their nails, calm-faced. Gradually, and subject to edict, Deity is permitted to suffer, stylistically, at least. But in Giotto, a new conception emerges. Here is the Christ, at the limit of endurance, coarse-haired, human, formed in suffering quite unstylized. The conception of God and of the human condition are fused. This is

the Son of God, a man, not an icon. One looks at this figure: it is Man, Christ, it could be a peasant in pain. It is a set of perspectives, joined in a single class, represented. We say of this truly awesome Christ that it is a painting of great unity. But just as properly we may say that it is an experience of great unity.

Metaphor joins dissimilar experiences by finding the image or the symbol that unites them at some deeper emotional level of meaning. Its effect depends upon its capacity for getting past the literal mode of connecting, and the unsuccessful metaphor is one that either fails in finding the image or gets caught in the meshes of literalness. We may say of a woman that "she is a peach"—peach by now connoting little more than "very nice"—and the effect is prosaic. But say now of a woman that "she is a garden" and the metaphoric process is renewed, with a skein of unpredictable though not altogether pleasing affective connections.

For, indeed, there is more to the metaphor of art than mere emotional connectedness. There is also the canon of economy that must operate, a canon that distinguishes the artfully metaphoric from that which is only floridly arty or simply "offbeat." It is the difference between the chaste interior of the Salzburg Dreifalltigskeitkirche of the young Fischer von Erlach, with the graceful oval of its cupola surmounted by a dove, and the heavily florid profusion of marbles of his later Karlskirche in Vienna. The first speaks quietly through its sparsely decorated geometry of man's celebration of a sophisticated Deity; the other merely boasts in opulence. Or it is the difference between an elaborate ceremonial canvas depicting the blend of power and piety of the sixteenth-century church and a painting by El Greco of one of its cruel and pious cardinals (Figure 3).

Though the idea of economy in metaphor is by no means novel, it is worth special mention in a discussion of art as knowing, for it is precisely in its economy that art shares a

3. *El Greco, Portrait of Cardinal Guevara, Metropolitan Museum, New York. Bequest of Mrs. H. O. Havemeyer, 1929. The H. O. Havemeyer Collection.*

fundamental principle with other forms of knowing. There is, perhaps, one universal truth about all forms of human cognition: the ability to deal with knowledge is hugely exceeded by the potential knowledge contained in man's environment. To cope with this diversity, man's perception, his memory, and his thought processes early become governed by strategies for protecting his limited capacities from the confusion of overloading. We tend to perceive things schematically, for example, rather than in detail, or we represent a class of diverse things by some sort of averaged "typical instance." The corresponding principle of economy in art produces the compact image or symbol that, by its genius, travels great distances to connect ostensible disparities.

Lest it seem that the modes of connecting in art and science are separated by an unbridgeable gap, that in all ways they are different modes of knowing, one primitive similarity should be mentioned—one that partakes of the nature of metaphor. It is the manner in which the scientist gets his hypothesis. Philosophers of science, who, characteristically, do not practice science but only reflect upon its more public forms of discipline, rarely touch on this theme. For these worthy men the labors of the scientist often begin with an hypothesis to be verified, or at least with rules of induction for discriminating nature's signal from her noise. Or, at even a further remove, they are concerned with the subtle and beautiful process of formalizing knowledge into the special symbolic language of mathematics. Yet the prescientific effort to construct a fruitful hypothesis may indeed be the place where the art of science, like all other art forms, operates by the law of economical metaphor. May it not be that without the myth of Sisyphus, forever pushing his rock up the hill, the concept of the asymptote in mathematics would be less readily grasped? What is Heraclitus' account but a giant metaphor on instability? He gropes for a picture of the universe. And so it is at the beginnings of insight. In a later chapter, we shall consider Freud

and the dramatic metaphor that made his first steps possible. So too in the other newer sciences that are in search of guiding "pictures." Surely the "mental evolution" conceived by the early anthropologists could only be taken in a metaphoric sense, for there is patently no correspondence between evolutionary genetics and the manner in which so biologically stable a race as man should emerge culturally from the savage state to the writing of philosophy. As Bertrand Russell comments, "Physics is mathematical not because we know so much about the physical world, but because we know so little: it is only its mathematical properties that we can discover." And until they are "discovered" in this more rigorous sense, one proceeds by intuition and metaphor, hoping to be led beyond to a new rigor. Until then, the economical combinings of the scientist and the artist share far more than we are often prepared to admit.

Effort. The art historian Ernst Gombrich, lecturing before an august group of British psychoanalysts, used an interesting illustration to underscore the role of work in aesthetic pleasure. He presented a very ordinary academic painting by Bonnencontre, typical of French academic technique of the final quarter of the last century (Figure 4). It is not a very pleasing piece of work and certainly not a moving one. Gom-

4. Bonnencontre, The Three Graces, Soho Gallery, London. The two reproductions on the right are seen as through rolled glass. "Psychoanalysis and the History of Art," Int. J. Psych., *1954. (Braun et Cie)*

brich then presented the picture covered with unevenly rolled, transparent glass, which had the effect of breaking up the idealized forms and the planes of the surface in much the same way as John Marin learned to do in his water colors. The effect was most striking. The picture was now interesting, and with an effort something could be made of it.

What is this effort? Perhaps it consists in departing from the habitual and literal ways of looking, hearing, and understanding in order to resolve the ambiguity that is a feature of works of art. But in a deeper sense, it is the effort to make a new connection between different perspectives. The trick used by Gombrich prevents an easy and literal perception of Bonnencontre's figures and forces the metaphoric mode on the beholder. This happens also when one encounters both piety and cruelty in an El Greco cardinal. What one feels is the effort to connect. It is not only for the creation of a work of art that one should use the expression *unitas multiplex,* but for the experience of knowing it as well.

But why is one willing to undertake the effort? Perhaps the effort of beholding art is its own reward, or the reward is the achievement of unity of experience, which is to say that it develops on itself. Taste begets better taste. Listen to enough Dvorak and a taste for Beethoven or Wagner will develop. If ever there were a pure instance of what Karl Bühler long ago called *Funktionslust,* pleasure in the exercise of a function, the realm of art is its home.

Somehow the image of the beholder of a painting as one who works, however much he enjoys his work and is rewarded by the enrichment it affords, is too Puritan an image. There is much in art that is undemandingly decorative. Does this differ from the kind of art we have been considering? Shall we honor the distinction Graham Greene makes between his "novels" and his "entertainments"? I think so. And I believe that the distinction is precisely in terms of the amount and the nature of the work demanded.

I happen to have a favorite period of decorative painting, that of the great Sienese school, and my particular favorite is Sassetta. Perhaps I shall sound insufficiently appreciative of such painting, but I am not. It has an elegant restfulness. Faith, Hope, and Charity ascending into the heavens in defiance of the laws of gravity are incomparably and uncomplicatedly feminine (Figure 5), and one loves this painting of St. Francis taking his vows to Poverty in the way that one loves to go back to innocent ways of hearing the fairy stories of childhood. For Sassetta's canvas to create the disturbance of art, to go from being decorative to being powerfully beautiful, there must be an infusion of productive paradox. For it is this that triggers the work of connecting. This is not to say that the work is enough. It must surely result, if successful, in the self-rewarding experience of connection.

But creating new unities is not all the work. There is also control and conversion of the impulses that are aroused in the experience of art, the exercise of restraint that permits the reader to maintain a distance from the hero of a novel and the playgoer to remain on his side of the proscenium arch. Here again the distinction between the decorative and beautiful is useful. For the decorative achieves its restfulness by permitting us to remain uninvolved, untempted. Indeed, an essay remains to be written on the defense against beauty, about those who, in the face of the awesomeness of a Gothic cathedral, can remain unshaken and find what they behold merely pleasing. But these are matters better treated more systematically, and to this we turn now.

Conversion of impulse. Any impulse, we have argued, can be turned to art: the urge to kill becomes the art of rudeness; curiosity produces the art of conversation; sexuality matures into the art of making love. It is a necessary but not a sufficient condition in each case that the impulse be held in check and converted from its original form. It is equally true that the successful *beholding* of a work of art involves a comparable

5. *Sassetta, Marriage of St. Francis and Poverty, Musée Conde, Chantilly (Bulloz)*

act of containing impulses that have been aroused. It is not necessary that there be a concordance in the impulse of the creator and the beholder, and, for our purposes, the matter of communicating an impulse from creator to receiver is not at issue.

Consider the beautiful piece of Renaissance statuary in the Toledo Cathedral known as the Santa Maria Blanca, a graceful half-smiling Virgin holding the Christ Child, who reaches up as if to chuck her under the chin (Figure 6). This White Virgin is all the faces of woman, mother, wife, flirt, daughter, sister, mistress, saint, and harlot. As one looks at it, there are impulses-in-restraint to father her, be mothered by her, make love to her, gossip with her, and just to watch how the face will change when the Child finally pokes her under the chin. It provides a fine example, for probably the conversion of impulse into a sense of beauty requires the arousing of several impulses at once. And here, if anywhere, one may speak of the experience of art as a mode of knowing. For when one looks at the White Virgin, the energy of all one's discordant impulses creates a single image connecting the varieties of experience in her extraordinary face.

Let us be more specific about how impulses are converted into the experience of art. Two types of cognitive activity are set in train when a need is aroused. One is at the center of awareness as desire: it is directed toward achieving an end and is specialized to the task of finding means. The other is at the fringes of awareness, a flow of rich and surprising fantasy, a tangled reticle of associations that gives fleeting glimpses of past occasions, of disappointments and triumphs, of pleasure and unpleasures. It is the stuff of which James's stream of consciousness was made, and we honor such a writer as Joyce for his insight into the technical problem of communicating this scarcely expressible fringe. To the degree that the direct expression of impulse can be kept in abeyance, to that degree it is possible for the fringes of association to elaborate themselves. And to this degree too there can be a merging of the

6. Santa Maria Blanca, The Cathedral, Toledo. Three views.

streams fed by different impulses, a joining of the scraps and images. For at this level, thinking is more symphonic than logical, one theme suggesting the next by a rule of letting parts stand for wholes. Where art achieves its genius is in providing an image or a symbol whereby the fusion can be comprehended and bound.

In short, the conversion of impulse into the experience of art comes from the creation of a stream of metaphoric activity and the restraining of any direct striving for ends. In essence, the connecting of experience is given its first impetus by the simultaneous presence of several such streams of fringe association. It is the formal artifice of the work of art itself, the genius of its economical imagery, that makes possible the final fusing of these inner experiences. The process we have described requires work from the beholder. Beholding an art object in a manner that may be called knowing is not a passive act. But when the beholder stops beholding, when there is too much involvement with the figures in a canvas, there is an end to the conversion of impulse, distance is lost, and in place of the experience of art there is either a daydream or merely action.

Generality. Any idea, any construct or metaphor, has its range of convenience or its "fit" to experience, and this is one feature that art and science as modes of knowing share deeply. A concept like "parthenogenesis," for example, fits certain reproductive phenomena in biology, but fails to fit or predict others. Our techniques for finding out about the range of convenience of ideas in science are rather straightforward, though it requires much ingenuity at times to devise operational techniques for verification. There is no direct analogue of verification in the experience of art. In its place, there is a "shock of recognition," a recognition of the fittingness of an object or a poem to fill the gaps in our own experience. In this sense, and it is a limited sense, we may say that art is not a universal mode of communication, for each man who beholds a picture or reads a poem will bring to the experience a matrix of life

that is uniquely his own. Though this is certainly the case, and though it is true that one's vision of the Santa Maria Blanca may not be the same as that of the sexton who lights the evening candles in the Toledo Cathedral, it is equally true to say that there are constant features of the human situation and that for all men there is the problem of reconciling the different faces of woman: harlot with wife, flirt with mother, and the rest. For one beholder this exquisite piece of Renaissance statuary may engage with this need for reconciliation, for another not. The predicament is differently shaped for each: for the intransigently religious man the Virgin and Child may pre-empt the entire experience.

This is scarcely to say that the communicability of a work of art is a function entirely of time, place, and condition. For if it were, one would not find such a shock of refreshment in the cave paintings of Altamira and Lascaux or in the artifacts of the second Pueblo period. One need not invoke a racial unconscious or archetypal images to account for this communicability across cultures and times: there are features of the human condition that change only within narrow limits whether one be a cave dweller, a don in medieval Oxford, or a Left Bank expatriate of the 1920s: love, birth, hate, death, passion, and decorum persist as problems without unique solution.

Can it ever be said, then, that life imitates art? If so, then art is the furthest reach of communication. There are perhaps two ways that are somewhat more than trivial. One is the effect of art in freeing us from the forms of instrumental knowing that comprise the center of our awareness; from the tendency to say that this figure here represents Christ, that over there is an apple; apples are good for eating, Christ for worshiping or admiring. When we see the possibility of connection in internal experience, we strive to recreate it and to live it.

The second sense in which life imitates art is in the manner in which the experience of art nourishes itself, so that having sensed connectedness one is impelled to seek more of it.

James Bryant Conant, presiding some years ago over a meeting of the Harvard faculty which was debating the relationship between engineering sciences and applied physics, remarked that the object of a science is to reduce empiricism. The intent of the scientist is to create rational structures and general laws that, in the mathematical sense, predict the observations one would be forced to make if one were without the general laws. To the degree that the rational structures of science are governed by principles of strict logical implication, to that degree prediction becomes more and more complete, leading eventually to the derivation of possible observations that one might not have made but for the existence of the general theory. Surely, then, science increases the unity of our experience of nature. This is the hallmark of the way of knowing called science.

Art as a form of knowing does not and cannot strive for such a form of unification. In its most refined form, the myth of Sisyphus is not the concept of the mathematical asymptote. The elegant rationality of science and the metaphoric nonrationality of art operate with deeply different grammars; perhaps they even represent a profound complementarity. For in the experience of art, we connect by a grammar of metaphor, one that defies the rational methods of the linguist and the psychologist. There has been progress in interpreting the metaphoric transformation of dreams, rendering the latent meaning from the manifest content, progress to which Freud contributed so greatly. Yet to interpret a dream as "a wish to be loved by one's rejecting mother" or to interpret Marlow's pursuit of Kurtz at the end of Conrad's "Heart of Darkness" as a man pursuing a bride, neither of these exercises, however revealing, catches fully the nature of metaphor. What is lost in such translations is the very fullness of the connection produced by the experience of art itself.

PART II ◂

the Quest for Clarity

The essays that follow—"The Act of Discovery," "On Learning Mathematics," and "After John Dewey, What?"—are all ostensibly concerned with the process of education. But education is a process that cannot, I think, be separated from what it is that one seeks to teach. It is much as in the study of the nature of knowing: one cannot pursue the investigation of how one comes to know without full heed of what it is that is known. It has always been disturbing to me that some psychologists have operated on the assumption that knowing anything is the same as knowing anything else—a pigeon pecking buttons discriminatively or a rat finding his way through a maze or an undergraduate withdrawing his finger from a switch when a light appeared represent the componentry out of which any higher order of knowledge is constructed. Perhaps I can sum up my dissent by the overly simple dictum that the whole is less than the sum of the parts. A house is not a matter of knowing about a collection of nails, shingles, wallboards, and windows. Nor can it be said that it is *more* than these things, for to say this is to make it seem that the organization of elements produces something more complex than the sum of these elements. Instead, higher-order mental organization, or cognitive structure as it is sometimes called, has the effect of supplanting the niggling complexities and Irish pennants of the less good orders that precede the imposition of more encompassing orders on experience.

If, then, the structure of knowledge has its own laws, makes its own contribution to the economical use of mind, one must necessarily look to such a structure for hints about the nature

and uses of mind. If it is the case that the power and significance of poetry resides in its capacity to condense and symbolize experience in a well-wrought metaphoric web, then it follows that the teaching of poetry must honor the nature of poetry by providing the learner an opportunity to discover and use its special powers. And so too with mathematics or any "subject" one chooses to understand or to teach.

So, though the essays that follow are ostensibly about teaching and learning, they are also about the nature of knowing and about the nature of things to be known. They are perhaps more "right-handed" than the essays that precede them, largely because they are more closely related to some of my most horny-handed experimental studies of perception, memory, and thinking—notably the work reported in *A Study of Thinking* (New York: John Wiley, 1956) and in *Contemporary Approaches to Cognition* (Cambridge: Harvard University Press, 1957).

"The Act of Discovery" first took form after my having seen two inspired teachers of mathematics at work at the University School of the University of Illinois—David Page and Max Beberman. Both of them practiced the canny art of intellectual temptation, and in a few hours I saw quite ordinary students in their classes discovering quite unself-consciously all manner of interesting mathematical relations. There is an informal seminar at Illinois made up of educators, psychologists, mathematicians, chemists, physicists, and others who care actively about how one teaches anything. My friend Lee Cronbach asked me if I would talk with the group about what had struck me in my visit. The seminar went on for many hours, and the basis of the essay published here is the set of notes I took then. It was later presented in a somewhat different form in an address to the Society for the Philosophy of Education and published in yet a different form in the *Harvard Educational Review* (Winter 1961).

"On Learning Mathematics" is, among other things, a summer conversation with my step-daughter Lyn who, during its

preparation, was getting ready to go off to Uganda to teach mathematics at the Demonstration School in Kampala. It was a summer in which there was much talk at home about how one gets children to think mathematically. I had been invited to talk before the National Council of Teachers of Mathematics; the conversations at home, correspondence with David Page, and the invitation all conspired to get me much involved in thinking about the tactics and strategy of mathematics teaching as a special and interesting case of teaching and learning. The following year I was also committed to a joint research project with the English mathematician, Z. P. Dienes, designed to investigate the nature of conceptual learning in mathematics. "On Learning Mathematics" served to clear my mind on some of the issues we were to face. Today I could not write the essay in its present form. "Mathematics learning" is now a right-handed subject for me, but the essay included here was a left-handed propaedeutic to what followed. The essay, in slightly altered form, first appeared in *The Mathematics Teacher* (December 1960).

The John Dewey piece appeared first in the *Saturday Review* (Suppl., June 17, 1961), and its origin is amusing. My wife and I had gone to Toronto in mid-winter to take part in a conference on revising the curriculum of the city schools. It was a joint enterprise of the university there and the board of education, and I had been asked to come because the Toronto project had been influenced by the work of the Woods Hole Conference reported in my *The Process of Education.* It took us three days of waiting in airports and circling helplessly in weather-bound airplanes to get back to Cambridge. Through good fortune, I happened to have with me John Dewey's *My Pedagogic Creed.* I read it aloud to my wife, with comments of course. I think she must have had a certain amount of difficulty figuring out which were my comments and which was text, for in the end she suggested that I write out my thoughts on the subject as an exercise in finding out what my own credo was. I did. She was quite right.

The Act of Discovery

Maimonides, in his *Guide for the Perplexed,* speaks of four forms of perfection that men might seek.[1] The first and lowest form is perfection in the acquisition of worldly goods. The great philosopher dismisses this on the ground that the possessions one acquires bear no meaningful relation to the possessor: "A great king may one morning find that there is no difference between him and the lowest person." A second perfection is of the body, its conformation and skills. Its failing is that it does not reflect on what is uniquely human about man: "he could (in any case) not be as strong as a mule." Moral perfection is the third, "the highest degree of excellency in man's character." Of this perfection Maimonides says: "Imagine a person being alone, and having no connection whatever with any other person; all his good moral principles are at rest, they are not required and give man no perfection whatever. These principles are only necessary and useful when man comes in contact with others." The fourth kind of perfection is "the true perfection of man; the possession of the highest intellectual faculties. . . ." In justification of his assertion, this extraordinary Spanish-Judaic philosopher urges: "Examine the first three kinds of perfection; you will find that if you possess them, they are not your property, but the property of others. . . . But the last kind of perfection is exclusively yours; no one else owns any part of it."

[1] Maimonides, *Guide for the Perplexed* (New York: Dover Publications, 1956).

Without raising the question of whether moral qualities exist without reference to others, it is a conjecture much like the last of Maimonides' that leads me to examine the act of discovery in man's intellectual life. For if man's intellectual excellence is the most his own among his perfections, it is also the case that the most personal of all that he knows is that which he has discovered for himself. How important is it, then, for us to encourage the young to learn by discovery? Does it, as Maimonides would say, create a unique relation between knowledge and its possessor? And what may such a relation do for a man—or, for our purposes, a child?

The immediate occasion for my concern with discovery is the work of the various new curriculum projects that have grown up in America during the last few years. Whether one speaks to mathematicians or physicists or historians, one encounters repeatedly an expression of faith in the powerful effects that come from permitting the student to put things together for himself, to be his own discoverer.

First, I should be clear about what the act of discovery entails. It is rarely, on the frontier of knowledge or elsewhere, that new facts are "discovered" in the sense of being encountered, as Newton suggested, in the form of islands of truth in an uncharted sea of ignorance. Or if they appear to be discovered in this way, it is almost always thanks to some happy hypothesis about where to navigate. Discovery, like surprise, favors the well-prepared mind. In playing bridge, one is surprised by a hand with no honors in it and also by one that is all in one suit. Yet all particular hands in bridge are equiprobable: to be surprised one must know something about the laws of probability. So too in discovery. The history of science is studded with examples of men "finding out" something and not knowing it. I shall operate on the assumption that discovery, whether by a schoolboy going it on his own or by a scientist cultivating the growing edge of his field, is in its essence a matter of rearranging or transforming evidence in such a way that one is enabled to go beyond the evidence so reassembled

to new insights. It may well be that an additional fact or shred of evidence makes this larger transformation possible. But it is often not even dependent on new information.

Very generally, and at the risk of oversimplification, it is useful to distinguish two kinds of teaching: that which takes place in the *expository mode* and that in the *hypothetical mode*. In the former, the decisions concerning the mode and pace and style of exposition are principally determined by the teacher as expositor; the student is the listener. The speaker has a quite different set of decisions to make: he has a wide choice of alternatives; he is anticipating paragraph content while the listener is still intent on the words; he is manipulating the content of the material by various transformations while the listener is quite unaware of these internal options. But in the hypothetical mode the teacher and the student are in a more cooperative position with respect to what in linguistics would be called "speaker's decisions." The student is not a bench-bound listener, but is taking a part in the formulation and at times may play the principal role in it. He will be aware of alternatives and may even have an "as if" attitude toward these, and he may evaluate information as it comes. One cannot describe the process in either mode with great precision of detail, but I think it is largely the hypothetical mode which characterizes the teaching that encourages discovery.

Consider now what benefits might be derived from the experience of learning through discoveries that one makes oneself. I shall discuss these under four headings: (1) the increase in intellectual potency, (2) the shift from extrinsic to intrinsic rewards, (3) the learning of the heuristics of discovering, and (4) the aid to conserving memory.

Intellectual potency. I should like to consider the differences among students in a highly constrained psychological experiment involving a two-choice machine.[2] In order to win chips, they must depress a key either on the right or the left

[2] J. S. Bruner, J. J. Goodnow, and G. A. Austin, *A Study of Thinking* (New York: John Wiley, 1956).

side of the apparatus. A pattern of payoff is designed so that, say, they will be paid off on the right side 70 percent of the time, on the left 30 percent, but this detail is not important. What is important is that the payoff sequence is arranged at random, that there is no pattern. There is a marked contrast in the behavior of subjects who think that there is some pattern to be found in the sequence—who think that regularities are discoverable—and the performance of subjects who think that things are happening quite by chance. The first group adopts what is called an "event-matching" strategy in which the number of responses given to each side is roughly commensurate to the proportion of times that it pays off: in the present case, 70 on the right to 30 on the left. The group that believes there is no pattern very soon settles for a much more primitive strategy allocating *all* responses to the side that has the greater payoff. A little arithmetic will show that the lazy all-and-none strategy pays off more if the environment is truly random: they win 70 percent of the time. The event-matching subjects win about 70 percent on the 70-percent payoff side (or 49 percent of the time there) and 30 percent of the time on the side that pays off 30 percent of the time (another 9 percent for a total take-home wage of 58 percent in return for their labors of decision).

But the world is not always or not even frequently random, and if one analyzes carefully what the event matchers are doing, one sees that they are trying out hypotheses one after the other, all of them containing a term that leads to a distribution of bets on the two sides with a frequency to match the actual occurrence of events. If it should turn out that there is a pattern to be discovered, their payoff could become 100 percent. The other group would go on at the middling rate of 70 percent.

What has this to do with the subject at hand? For the person to search out and find regularities and relationships in his environment, he must either come armed with an expectancy

that there will be something to find or be aroused to such an expectancy so that he may devise ways of searching and finding. One of the chief enemies of search is the assumption that there is nothing one can find in the environment by way of regularity or relationship. In the experiment just cited, subjects often fall into one of two habitual attitudes: either that there is nothing to be found or that a pattern can be discovered by looking. There is an important sequel in behavior to the two attitudes.

We have conducted a series of experimental studies on a group of some seventy schoolchildren over a four-year period.[3] The studies have led us to distinguish an interesting dimension of cognitive activity that can be described as ranging from *episodic empiricism* at one end to *cumulative constructionism* at the other. The two attitudes in the above experiments on choice illustrate the extremes of the dimension. One of the experiments employs the game of Twenty Questions. A child—in this case he is between ten and twelve—is told that a car has gone off the road and hit a tree. He is to ask questions that can be answered by "yes" or "no" to discover the cause of the accident. After completing the problem, the same task is given him, though this time he is told that the accident has a different cause. In all, the procedure is repeated four times. Children enjoy playing the game. They also differ quite markedly in the approach or strategy they bring to the task. In the first place, we can distinguish clearly between two types of questions asked: one is intended to locate constraints in the problem, constraints that will eventually give shape to an hypothesis; the other is the hypothesis as question. It is the difference between, "Was there anything wrong with the driver?" and "Was the driver rushing to the doctor's office for an appointment and the car got out of control?" There are children who precede hypotheses with efforts to locate constraint and there

[3] J. S. Bruner and others, *The Processes of Cognitive Development*, in preparation.

are those who are "potshotters," who string out hypotheses noncumulatively one after the other. A second element of strategy lies in the connectivity of information gathering: the extent to which questions asked utilize or ignore or violate information previously obtained. The questions asked by children tend to be organized in cycles, each cycle usually given over to the pursuit of some particular notion. Both within cycles and between cycles one can discern marked differences in the connectivity of the children's performances. Needless to say, children who employ constraint location as a technique preliminary to the formulation of hypotheses tend to be far more organized in their harvesting of information. Persistence is another feature of strategy, a characteristic compounded of what appear to be two factors: sheer doggedness and a persistence that stems from the sequential organization that a child brings to the task. Doggedness is probably just animal spirits or the need to achieve. Organized persistence is a maneuver for protecting the fragile cognitive apparatus from overload. The child who has flooded himself with disorganized information from unconnected hypotheses will become discouraged and confused sooner than the child who has shown a certain cunning in his strategy of getting information—a child who senses that the value of information is not simply in getting it but in being able to carry it. The persistence of the organized child stems from his knowledge of how to organize questions in cycles and how to summarize things to himself.

Episodic empiricism is illustrated by information gathering that is unbound by prior constraints, that is deficient in organizational persistence. The opposite extreme, what we have called cumulative constructionism, is characterized by sensitivity to constraint, by connective maneuvers, and by organized persistence. Brute persistence seems to be one of those gifts from the gods that make people more exaggeratedly what they are.

Before returning to the issue of discovery and its role in the

development of thinking, there is a word more to say about the ways in which the problem solver may transform information he has dealt with actively. The point arises from the pragmatic question: what does it take to get information processed into a form best designed to fit some future use? An experiment by R. B. Zajonc in 1957 suggests an answer.[4] He gave groups of students information of a controlled kind, some groups being told that they were to transmit the information later on, others that they were merely to keep it in mind. In general, he found more differentiation of the information intended for transmittal than of information received passively. An active attitude leads to a transformation related to a task to be performed. There is a risk, to be sure, in the possible overspecialization of information processing. It can lead to such a high degree of specific organization that information is lost for general use, although this can be guarded against.

Let me convert the foregoing into an hypothesis. Emphasis on discovery in learning has precisely the effect on the learner of leading him to be a constructionist, to organize what he is encountering in a manner not only designed to discover regularity and relatedness, but also to avoid the kind of information drift that fails to keep account of the uses to which information might have to be put. Emphasis on discovery, indeed, helps the child to learn the varieties of problem solving, of transforming information for better use, helps him to learn how to go about the very task of learning. So goes the hypothesis; it is still in need of testing. But it is an hypothesis of such important human implications that we cannot afford not to test it—and the testing will have to be in the schools.

Intrinsic and extrinsic motives. Much of the problem in leading a child to effective cognitive activity is to free him from the immediate control of environmental rewards and punishments. Learning that starts in response to the rewards of parental or teacher approval or to the avoidance of failure can

[4] R. B. Zajonc, personal communication (1957).

too readily develop a pattern in which the child is seeking cues as to how to conform to what is expected of him. We know from studies of children who tend to be early overachievers in school that they are likely to be seekers after the "right way to do it" and that their capacity for transforming learning into viable thought structures tends to be lower than that of children achieving at levels predicted by intelligence tests.[5] Our tests on such children show them to be lower in analytic ability than those who are not conspicuous in overachievement. As we shall see later, they develop rote abilities and depend on being able to "give back" what is expected rather than to make it into something that relates to the rest of their cognitive life. As Maimonides would say, their learning is not their own.

The hypothesis I would propose here is that to the degree that one is able to approach learning as a task of discovering something rather than "learning about" it, to that degree there will be a tendency for the child to work with the autonomy of self-reward or, more properly, be rewarded by discovery itself.

To readers familiar with the battles of the last half-century in the field of motivation, this hypothesis will be recognized as controversial. For the traditional view of motivation in learning has been, until very recently, couched in terms of a theory of drives and reinforcements: learning occurs because a response produced by a stimulus is followed by the reduction in a primary drive. The doctrine is greatly but thinly extended by the idea of secondary reinforcement: anything that has been "associated" with such a reduction in drive or need can also serve to reinforce the connection between a stimulus and the response that it evokes. Finding a steak will do for getting a food-search act connected with a certain stimulus, but so will the sight of a nice restaurant.

In 1959 there appeared a most searching and important criticism of this ancient hedonistic position, written by Robert White, reviewing the evidence of recently published animal studies, of work in the field of psychoanalysis, and of research

[5] See Note 3 above.

on the development of cognitive processes in children. Professor White comes to the conclusion, quite rightly I think, that the drive-reduction model of learning runs counter to too many important phenomena of learning and development to be either regarded as general in its applicability or even correct in its general approach. Let me quote some of his principal conclusions and explore their applicability to the hypothesis stated above.

I now propose that we gather the various kinds of behavior just mentioned, all of which have to do with effective interaction with the environment, under the general heading of competence. According to Webster, competence means fitness of ability, and the suggested synonyms include capability, capacity, efficiency, proficiency, and skill. It is therefore a suitable word to describe such things as grasping and exploring, crawling and walking, attention and perception, language and thinking, manipulating and changing the surroundings, all of which promote an effective—a competent—interaction with the environment. It is true, of course, that maturation plays a part in all these developments, but this part is heavily overshadowed by learning in all the more complex accomplishments like speech or skilled manipulation. I shall argue that it is necessary to make competence a motivational concept; there is *competence motivation* as well as competence in its more familiar sense of achieved capacity. The behavior that leads to the building up of effective grasping, handling, and letting go of objects, to take one example, is not random behavior that is produced by an overflow of energy. It is directed, selective, and persistent, and it continues not because it serves primary drives, which indeed it cannot serve until it is almost perfected, but because it satisfies an intrinsic need to deal with the environment.[6]

I am suggesting that there are forms of activity that serve to enlist and develop the competence motive, that serve to make it the driving force behind behavior. I should like to add to White's general premise that the *exercise* of competence motives has the effect of strengthening the degree to which they gain control over behavior and thereby reduce the effects of extrinsic rewards or drive gratification.

In 1934 the brilliant Russian psychologist Vygotsky charac-

[6] R. W. White, "Motivation Reconsidered: The Concept of Competence," *Psychological Review*, no. 66 (1959), pp. 317–318.

terized the growth of thought processes as starting with a dialogue of speech and gesture between child and parent.[7] Autonomous thinking, he said, begins at the stage when the child is first able to internalize these conversations and "run them off" himself. This is a typical sequence in the development of competence. So too in instruction. The narrative of teaching is of the order of Vygotsky's conversation. The next move in the development of competence is the internalization of the narrative and its "rules of generation" so that the child is now capable of running off the narrative on his own. The hypothetical mode in teaching, by encouraging the child to participate in "speaker's decisions," speeds this process along. Once internalization has occurred, the child is in a vastly improved position from several obvious points of view—notably that he is able to go beyond the information he has been given to generate additional ideas that either can be checked immediately from experience or can, at least, be used as a basis for formulating reasonable hypotheses. But over and beyond that, the child is now in a position to experience success and failure not as reward and punishment but as information. For when the task is his own rather than a prescribed matching of environmental demands, he becomes his own paymaster in a certain measure. Seeking to gain control over his environment, he can now treat success as indicating that he is on the right track, failure as indicating that he is on the wrong one.

In the end, this development has the effect of freeing learning from immediate stimulus control. When learning leads only to pellets of this or that in the short run rather than to mastery in the long run, then behavior can be readily "shaped" by extrinsic rewards. But when behavior becomes more extended and competence-oriented, it comes under the control of more complex cognitive structures and operates more from the inside out.

The position of Pavlov is interesting. His early account of

[7] L. S. Vygotsky, *Thinking and Speech* (Moscow, 1934).

the learning process was based entirely on a notion of stimulus control of behavior through the conditioning mechanism in which, through contiguity, a new conditioned stimulus was substituted for an old unconditioned stimulus. But even he recognized that his account was insufficient to deal with higher forms of learning. To supplement it, he introduced the idea of the "second signalling system," with central importance placed on symbolic systems, such as language, in mediating and giving shape to mental life. Or as Luria put it in 1959, the first signal system is "concerned with directly perceived stimuli, the second with systems of verbal elaboration." Luria, commenting on the importance of the transition from first to second signal system, says:

> It would be mistaken to suppose that verbal intercourse with adults merely changes the contents of the child's conscious activity without changing its form. . . . The word has a basic function not only because it indicates a corresponding object in the external world, but also because it abstracts, isolates the necessary signal, generalizes perceived signals and relates them to certain categories; it is this systematization of direct experience that makes the role of the word in the formation of mental processes so exceptionally important.[8]

It is interesting too that the final rejection of the universality of the doctrine of reinforcement in direct conditioning came from some of Pavlov's own students. Ivanov-Smolensky and Krasnogorsky published papers showing the manner in which symbolized linguistic messages could take over the place of the unconditioned stimulus and of the unconditioned response (gratification of hunger) in children.[9] In all instances, they

[8] A. L. Luria, "The Directive Function of Speech in Development and Dissolution," *Word*, no. 15 (1959), p. 12.

[9] A. G. Ivanov-Smolensky, "The Interaction of the First and Second Signal Systems in Certain Normal and Pathological Conditions," *Physiological Journal of the USSR*, XXXV, no. 5 (1949); Ivanov-Smolensky, "Concerning the Study of the Joint Activity of the First and Second Signal Systems," *Journal of Higher Nervous Activity*, I, no. 1 (1951); N. I. Krasnogorsky, *Studies of Higher Nervous Activity in Animals and in Man*, I (Moscow, 1954).

speak of these as *replacements* of lower first-system mental or neural processes by higher second-system controls. A strange irony, then, that Russian psychology, which gave us the notion of the conditioned response and the assumption that higher-order activities are built up out of colligations of such primitive units, has rejected this notion while much of the American psychology of learning until quite recently has stayed within the early Pavlovian fold—as, for example, a 1959 article by Spence in the *Harvard Educational Review,* reiterating the primacy of conditioning and the derivative nature of complex learning.[10] It is even more noteworthy that Russian pedagogic theory has become deeply influenced by this new trend and is now placing much stress upon the importance of building up a more active symbolical approach to problem solving among children.

In this matter of the control of learning, then, my conclusion is that the degree to which the desire for competence comes to control behavior, to that degree the role of reinforcement or "outside rewards" wanes in shaping behavior. The child comes to manipulate his environment more actively and achieves his gratification from coping with problems. As he finds symbolic modes of representing and transforming the environment, there is an accompanying decline in the importance of stimulus-response-reward sequences. To use the metaphor that David Riesman developed in a quite different context, mental life moves from a state of outer-directedness, in which the fortuity of stimuli and reinforcement are crucial, to a state of inner-directedness in which the growth and maintenance of mastery become central and dominant.

The heuristics of discovery. Lincoln Steffens, reflecting in his *Autobiography* on his undergraduate education at Berkeley, comments that his schooling paid too much attention to learning what was known and too little to finding out about what

[10] K. W. Spence, "The Relation of Learning Theory to the Technique of Education," *Harvard Educational Review,* no. 29 (1959), pp. 84–95.

was not known.[11] But how does one train a student in the techniques of discovery? Again there are some hypotheses to offer. There are many ways of coming to the arts of inquiry. One of them is by careful study of its formalization in logic, statistics, mathematics, and the like. If one is going to pursue inquiry as a way of life, particularly in the sciences, certainly such study is essential. Yet whoever has taught kindergarten and the early primary grades or has had graduate students working with him on their theses—I choose the two extremes for they are both periods of intense inquiry—knows that an understanding of the formal aspect of inquiry is not sufficient. Rather, several activities and attitudes, some directly related to a particular subject and some fairly generalized, appear to go with inquiry and research. These have to do with the *process* of trying to find out something and, though their presence is no guarantee that the *product* will be a great discovery, their absence is likely to lead to awkwardness or aridity or confusion. How difficult it is to describe these matters—the heuristics of inquiry. There is one set of attitudes or methods that has to do with sensing the relevance of variables—avoiding immersion in edge effects and getting instead to the big sources of variance. This gift partly comes from intuitive familiarity with a range of phenomena, sheer "knowing the stuff." But it also comes out of a sense of what things among many "smell right," what things are of the right order of magnitude or scope or severity.

Weldon, the English philosopher, describes problem solving in an interesting and picturesque way. He distinguishes among difficulties, puzzles, and problems. We solve a problem or make a discovery when we impose a puzzle form on a difficulty to convert it into a problem that can be solved in such a way that it gets us where we want to be. That is to say, we recast the difficulty into a form that we know how to work with—then we work it. Much of what we speak of as discovery consists of

[11] *Autobiography of Lincoln Steffens* (New York: Harcourt, Brace, 1931).

knowing how to impose a workable kind of form on various kinds of difficulties. A small but crucial part of discovery of the highest order is to invent and develop effective models or "puzzle forms." It is in this area that the truly powerful mind shines. But it is surprising to what degree perfectly ordinary people can, given the benefit of instruction, construct quite interesting and what, a century ago, would have been considered greatly original models.

Now to the hypothesis. It is my hunch that it is only through the exercise of problem solving and the effort of discovery that one learns the working heuristics of discovery; the more one has practice, the more likely one is to generalize what one has learned into a style of problem solving or inquiry that serves for any kind of task encountered—or almost any kind of task. I think the matter is self-evident, but what is unclear is the kinds of training and teaching that produce the best effects. How, for instance, do we teach a child to cut his losses but at the same time be persistent in trying out an idea; to risk forming an early hunch without at the same time formulating one so early and with so little evidence that he is stuck with it while he waits for appropriate evidence to materialize; to pose good testable guesses that are neither too brittle nor too sinuously incorrigible? And so on and on. Practice in inquiry, in trying to figure out things for oneself is indeed what is needed —but in what form? Of only one thing am I convinced: I have never seen anybody improve in the art and technique of inquiry by any means other than engaging in inquiry.

Conservation of memory. I have come to take what some psychologists might consider a rather drastic view of the memory process. It is a view that in large measure derives from the work of my colleague, George Miller.[12] Its first premise is that the principal problem of human memory is not storage but retrieval. In spite of the biological unlikeliness

[12] G. A. Miller, "The Magical Number Seven, Plus or Minus Two," *Psychological Review*, no. 63 (1956), pp. 81–97.

of it, we seem to be able to store a huge quantity of information—perhaps not a full tape recording, though at times it seems we even do that, but a great sufficiency of impressions. We may infer this from the fact that recognition, the ability to recall with maximum promptings, is so extraordinarily good in human beings and that spontaneous recall, with no promptings, is so extraordinarily bad. The key to retrieval is organization or, in even simpler terms, knowing where to find information that has been put into memory.

Let me illustrate with a simple experiment. We present pairs of words to twelve-year-olds. The children of one group are told only to remember the pairs and that they will be asked to repeat them later. Others are told to remember the pairs by producing a word or idea that will tie them together in a way that will make sense. The word pairs include such juxtapositions as "chair-forest," "sidewalk-square," and the like. One can distinguish three styles of mediators, and children can be scaled in terms of their relative preference for each: generic mediation, in which a pair is tied together by a superordinate idea: "chair and forest are both made of wood"; thematic mediation, in which the two terms are imbedded in a theme or a little story: "the lost child sat on a chair in the middle of the forest"; and part-whole mediation, in which "chairs are made from trees in the forest" is typical. Now the chief result, as you would predict, is that children who provide their own mediators do best—indeed, one time through a set of thirty pairs, they recover up to 95 percent of the second words when presented with the first ones of the pairs, whereas the uninstructed children reach a maximum of less than 50 percent recovered. Also, children do best in recovering materials tied together by the form of mediator they most often use.

One can cite a myriad of findings to indicate that any organization of information that reduces the aggregate complexity of material by imbedding it into a cognitive process a person has constructed for himself will make that material

more accessible for retrieval. We may say that the process of memory, looked at from the retrieval side, is also a process of problem solving: how can material be "placed" in memory so that it can be obtained on demand?

We can take as a point of departure the example of the children who developed their own technique for relating each word pair. The children with the self-made mediators did better than the children who were given ready-made ones. Another group of children were given the mediators developed by this group to aid them in memorizing—a set of "ready-made" memory aids. In general, material that is organized in terms of a person's own interests and cognitive structures is material that has the best chance of being accessible in memory. It is more likely to be placed along routes that are connected to one's own ways of intellectual travel. Thus, the very attitudes and activities that characterize figuring out or discovering things for oneself also seem to have the effect of conserving memory.

On Learning Mathematics

I take as my starting point a notion of the philosopher Weldon, one I have mentioned before. He said that one can discriminate among difficulties, puzzles, and problems. A difficulty is a trouble with minimum definition. It is a state in which we know that we want to get from here to there, both points defined rather rawly and without much of an idea of how to bridge the gap. A puzzle, on the other hand, is a game in which there is a set of givens and a set of procedural constraints, all precisely stated. A puzzle also requires that we get from here to there, and there is at least one admissible route by which we can do so, but the choice of route is governed by definite rules that must not be violated. A typical puzzle is that of the Three Cannibals and Three Missionaries, in which you must get three missionaries and three cannibals across a river in a boat that carries no more than two passengers. You can never have more cannibals than missionaries on one side at a time. Only one cannibal can row; all three missionaries can. Now Weldon proposes, you recall, that a problem is a difficulty upon which we attempt to impose a puzzle form. A young man, trying to win the favor of a young lady—a difficulty—decides to try out successively, with benefit of correction by experience, a strategy of flattery—an iterative procedure and a classic puzzle—and thus converts his difficulty into a problem. I rather expect that most young men do all this deciding at the unconscious level. The point of mentioning it is to emphasize that the con-

version of difficulties into problems by the imposition of puzzle forms is often not always done with cool awareness, and that part of the task of the mathematician is to work toward an increase in such awareness.

The pure mathematician is above all a close student of puzzle forms—puzzles involving the ordering of sets of elements in a manner to fulfill specifications. The puzzles, once grasped, are obvious, so obvious that it is astounding that anybody has difficulty with mathematics at all, as Bertrand Russell once said in exasperation. The answer to our puzzle is simple. The rowing cannibal takes over another cannibal and returns. Then he takes over the other cannibal and returns. Then two missionaries go over, and one of them brings back a nonrowing cannibal. Then a missionary takes the rowing cannibal over and brings back a nonrowing cannibal. Then two missionaries go over and stay, while the rowing cannibal travels back and forth, bringing the remaining cannibals over one at a time. And there are never more cannibals than missionaries on either side of the river. If you say that my statement of the solution is clumsy and lacking in generality, even though it is correct, you are quite right. But now we are talking mathematics.

For the mathematician's job is not pure puzzle mongering. It is to find the deepest properties of puzzles so that he may recognize that a particular puzzle is an examplar—trivial, degenerate, or important, as the case may be—of a family of puzzles. He is also a student of the kinship that exists among families of puzzles. So, for example, he sets forth such structural ideas as the commutative, associative, and distributive laws to show the manner in which a whole set of seemingly diverse problems have a common puzzle form imposed on them.

There probably are two ways in which one goes about both learning mathematics and teaching it. One of them is through a technique that I like to call unmasking, although it is some-

times called empirical generalization. Roughly, it consists in discovering or unmasking certain abstract properties that characterize solutions of more or less practical problems. Thus, the solving of surveying and triangulation problems in the ancient Nile valley, undertaken to reconstruct land boundaries after flooding, provided an empirical starting point for the development of abstract geometry and trigonometry. And so, too, in teaching we use "practical problems" or "concrete embodiments" to equip the learner with the experiences upon which later abstractions can be based. Such devices as the Cuisenaire rods, various of the block sets now on the market, and the "mathematical laboratory" are aids in this approach.

A second approach to mathematics teaching, which by no means excludes the first, is to work directly on the nature of puzzles themselves—on mathematics per se. If the first approach is somewhat semantic, going from things to the symbols used for characterizing them, then the second is principally syntactic in emphasis. For it is concerned not with what mathematical ideas and relations "stand for" or are "derived from" but rather with the grammar of mathematics as such. Empirical reference is put in a secondary position and, if one were to think of an example in teaching, the use of numbers to different bases than the base 10 is a nice one.

Obviously, both the working research mathematician and the person learning mathematics for the first time use both approaches in some optimum sequence.

In what follows, we shall be concerned with four aspects of the teaching or learning of mathematics. The first has to do with the role of *discovery* and if it is important or not that the learner discover things for himself. The second aspect is *intuition,* the class of nonrigorous ways by which mathematicians speed toward solutions or cul-de-sacs. The third is mathematics as an analytic language, and I shall concentrate on the problem of the *translation* of intuitive ideas into mathematics. This assumes that anything that can be said in mathematical

form can also be said in ordinary language, though it may take a tediously long time to say it and there will always be the danger of imprecision of expression. The fourth and final problem is the matter of *readiness:* when is a child "ready" for geometry or topology or a discussion of truth tables?

Discovery. Much has already been said in the preceding essay about the act of discovery. The learning of mathematics provides a test case for some of the notions considered there. Take first the distinction between an active, manipulative approach to learning and the passive approach—the first likened to a speaker's decisions in using language and the second to a listener's. We do a disservice to our subject by calling the stimulation of active thinking, "the method of discovery." For there is certainly more than one method and each teacher has his own tricks for stimulating the quest in his pupils. Indeed, I am impressed by the fact that almost anything that gets away from the usual approach to natural numbers and their mechanical manipulation has the effect of freshening the student's taste for discovering things for himself. It would be better to consider how discovery usually proceeds when it does occur.

My own observation is that discovery in mathematics is a byproduct of making things simpler. Perhaps this is true of growth in pursuing other intellectual disciplines as well, but that is an issue that should not divert us, though a good case can be made for it, I think.[1] In any case, where mathematics is concerned, the issue hinges on *how* simplification occurs. It results most often from a succession of constructing representations of things. We do something that is manipulative at the outset—literally, provide a definition of something in terms of action. A hole is to dig, a yard is to pace off or apply a ruler to, subtraction is to take away. That is the start. But it is a start that provides the material for a second step. For having

[1] See J. S. Bruner and R. R. Olver, "The Growth of Equivalence Transformations in Children," *Child Development Monographs,* in press.

acted—paced off, taken away, turned upside down, or whatnot—we are then able to turn around on our own actions and represent them. Having considered the ways of "saying-doing" how big or long things are by pacing, putting fingers next to each other, or using a ruler, we may simplify by characterizing all these activities as measuring. In the effort to relate these measuring actions one to the other, it is a very distracted child who will not rediscover the importance of the unit of measure as a means of getting all this welter of activity into a single, simpler framework. Then and only then can there be fruitful discussion of how we construct a unit of measure.

Learning to simplify is to climb on your own shoulders to be able to look down at what you have just done—and then to represent it to yourself. The constructing or doing that precedes the new representation can be well or poorly designed. The good teacher is one who can construct exercises (or, better, provide experiences) that cry for representation in the manner that the one shoe dropped on the floor above cries to have the second one drop. The poor teacher permits so much irrelevant action to occur in such self-obscuring sequences that only a genius could give a coherent account of what he had been up to. Indeed, we can revise a refrain of an earlier chapter to read, "How can I know what I think until I represent what I do?"

Manipulation and representation, then, in continuing cycles are necessary conditions for discovery. They are the antitheses of passive, listenerlike learning. Yet representation is not frenzied activity. Though active, it is still ratiocination, a going back over experience, a listening to oneself. Nor should we think that a teacher cannot play a role. Perhaps, in discussing the functions of teaching, we should make a special place for the art of teaching people to listen to what they have been doing so that their actions can be converted into representations of what they have done and what has resulted. If Percy Bridgman's argument in his long effort to persuade scientists

to define their concepts in terms of the operations employed in arriving at them could be turned around to read backward, it would fit our case well. Our task as teachers is to lead students to develop concepts in order to make sense of the operations they have performed. Bridgman's dictum should, I think, be converted into a two-way street.

Intuition. It is particularly when I see a child going through the mechanical process of manipulating numbers without any intuitive sense of what it is all about that I recall the lines of Lewis Carroll: "Reeling and Writhing, of course, to begin with . . . and then the different branches of Arithmetic—Ambition, Distraction, Uglification, and Derision." Or as Max Beberman has put it, much more gently, "Somewhat related to the notion of discovery in teaching is our insistence that the student become aware of a concept before a name has been assigned to the concept." I am quite aware that the issue of intuitive understanding is a very live one among teachers of mathematics, and even a casual reading of the twenty-fourth *Yearbook* of the National Council of Teachers of Mathematics makes it clear that they are also very mindful of the gap that exists between proclaiming the importance of such understanding and actually producing it in the classroom.

Intuition implies the act of grasping the meaning or significance or structure of a problem without explicit reliance on the analytic apparatus of one's craft. It is the intuitive mode that yields hypotheses quickly, that produces interesting combinations of ideas before their worth is known. It precedes proof; indeed, it is what the techniques of analysis and proof are designed to test and check. It is founded on a kind of combinatorial playfulness that is only possible when the consequences of error are not overpowering or sinful. Above all, it is a form of activity that depends upon confidence in the worthwhileness of the process of mathematical activity rather than upon the importance of right answers at all times.

I shall examine briefly what intuition might be from a psy-

chological point of view and consider what we can do about stimulating it among our students. Perhaps the first thing that can be said about intuition when applied to mathematics is that it involves the embodiment or concretization of an idea, not yet stated, in the form of some sort of operation or example. I watched a ten-year-old playing with snail shells he had gathered, putting them into rectangular arrays. He discovered that there were certain quantities that could not be put into such a rectangular compass, that however arranged there was always one left out. This of course intrigued him. He also found that two such odd-man-out arrays put together produced an array that was rectangular, that "the left-out ones could make a new corner." I am not sure it is fair to say that this child was learning much about prime numbers. But he most certainly was gaining the intuitive sense that would make it possible for him later to grasp what a prime number is and, indeed, what the structure of a multiplication table is.

I am inclined to think of mental development as involving the construction of a model of the world in the child's head, an internalized set of structures for representing the world around him. These structures are organized in terms of perfectly definite grammars or rules of their own, and in the course of development the structures change and the grammar that governs them also changes in certain systematic ways. The way in which we gain lead time for anticipating what will happen next and what to do about it is to spin our internal models just a bit faster than the world goes.

Now the child whose behavior I was just describing had a model of quantities and order that was implicitly governed by all sorts of seemingly subtle mathematical principles, many of them newly acquired and some of them rather strikingly original. He may not have been able to talk about them, but he was able to do all sorts of things on the basis of them. For example, he had "mastered" the very interesting idea of conservation of quantity across transformations in arrangement or,

as you would say, the associative law. Thus, the quantity 6 can be stated as $2 + 2 + 2$, $3 + 3$, and by such "irregular" arrangements as $2 + 4$, $4 + 2$, $2 + (3 + 1)$, $(2 + 3) + 1$, and so on. Inherent in what he was doing was the concept of reversibility, as Piaget calls it, the idea of an operation and its inverse. The child was able to put two sets together and to take them apart; by putting together two prime-number arrays, he discovers that they are no longer prime (using our terms now) but can be made so again by separation. He was also capable of mapping one set uniquely on another, as in the construction of two identical sets. This is a formidable amount of highbrow mathematics.

Now what do we do with this rather bright child when he gets to school? In our own way we communicate to him that mathematics is a logical discipline and that it has certain rules, and we often proceed to teach him algorisms that make it seem that what he is doing in arithmetic has no bearing on the way in which he would proceed by nonrigorous means. I am not, mind you, objecting to "social arithmetic" with its interest rates and baseball averages. I am objecting to something far worse, the premature use of the language of mathematics, its end-product formalism, which makes it seem that mathematics is something new rather than something the child already knows. It is forcing the child into the inverse plight of the character in *Le Bourgeois Gentilhomme* who comes to the blazing insight that he has been speaking prose all his life. By interposing formalism, we prevent the child from realizing that he has been thinking mathematics all along. What we do, in essence, is to remove his confidence in his ability to perform the processes of mathematics. At our worst, we offer formal proof (which is necessary for checking) in place of direct intuition. It is good that a student knows how to check the conjecture that $8x$ is equivalent to the expression $3x + 5x$ by such a rigorous statement as the following: "By the commutative principle for multiplication, for every x, $3x + 5x = x3 + x5$.

By the distributive principle, for every x, $x3 + x5 = x\ (3 + 5)$. Again by the commutative principle, for every x, $x\ (3 + 5) = (3 + 5)\ x$ or $8x$. So, for every x, $3x + 5x = 8x$." But it is hopeless if the student gets the idea that this and this only is *really* arithmetic or algebra or "math" and that other ways of proceeding are really for nonmathematical dolts. Therefore, "mathematics is not for me."

It is important to allow the child to use his natural and intuitive ways of thinking, indeed to encourage him to do so, and to honor him when he does well. I cannot believe that he has to be taught this. Instead, we should first end our habit of inhibiting intuitive thinking and then find ways of helping the child improve at it.

Translation. The mathematician David Page wrote to me last year: "When I tell mathematicians that fourth-grade students can go a long way into 'set theory,' a few of them reply, 'Of course.' Most of them are startled. The latter are completely wrong in assuming that the set theory is intrinsically difficult. Of course, it may be that nothing is intrinsically difficult—we just have to wait the centuries until the proper point of view and corresponding language is revealed!" How can we state things in such a way that ideas can be understood and converted into mathematical expression?

It seems to me there are three problems here. Let me label them the problem of structure, the problem of sequence, and the problem of embodiment. When we try to get a child to understand a concept, leaving aside now the question of whether he can "say" it, the first and most important condition, obviously, is that the expositors themselves understand it. I make no apology for this necessary point. Its implications are not well understood. To understand something well is to sense wherein it is simple, wherein it is an instance of a simpler general case. I know that there are instances in the historical development of knowledge in which this may not be true, as in physics before Mendeleev's table or in contemporary physics where

particle theory is for the moment seemingly moving toward divergence, rather than convergence, of principles. In the main, however, to understand something is to sense the simpler structure that underlies a range of instances, and this is notably true in mathematics.

In seeking to transmit our understanding of structure to another person, there is the problem of finding the language and ideas he would use if he were attempting to explain the same thing. If we are lucky, it may turn out that the language we would use would be within the grasp of the person we are teaching. When we are less fortunate, we are faced with the problem of finding a homologue that will contain our own idea moderately well and get it across without too much loss of precision—at least in a form that will permit us to communicate further at a later time.

For instance, we wish to tell the first-grade student that much of what we speak of as knowledge in science is indirect, that we talk about such things as pressure or chemical bonds or neural inhibition although we never encounter them directly. They are inferences we draw from certain regularities in our observations. This is all very familiar to us. It is an idea with a simple structure but with complicated implications. It is difficult to tell the truth to a young student, used to thinking of things as either existing or not existing, who asks whether pressure "really" exists. We wish to transmit the idea that there are certain observations we make or operations we perform that turn out to be quite regular and predictable. We weigh things or study the manner in which our instruments move under set conditions. "Pressure" is the construct we invent to represent the operations we perform and the regularities in experience that occur when we perform them. Does pressure exist? Well, yes, provided you have invented it!

Now there is a sequence. How do we get the child to progress from his present two-value logic of things that exist

and things that do not exist to a more subtle grasp of the matter? Take an example from the work of Inhelder and Piaget. They find that there are necessary sequences or steps in the mastery of a concept. In order for a child to understand the idea of serial ordering, he must first have a firm grasp of the idea of comparison—that one thing includes another or is larger than another. Or, in order for a child to grasp the idea that the angle of incidence is equal to the angle of reflection, he must first grasp the idea that for any angle at which a ball approaches a wall there is a corresponding unique angle by which it departs. Until he grasps this idea, there is no point in talking about the two angles being equal or bearing any particular relationship to each other, just as it is a waste to try to explain transitivity to a child who does not yet have a firm grasp on serial ordering.

The problem of embodiment then arises: how to embody illustratively the middle possibility of something that does not quite exist as a clear and observable datum? One group of chemists working on a new curriculum proposed as a transitional step in the sequence that the child be given a taped box containing an unidentified object. He may do anything he likes to the box: shake it, run wires through it, boil it, anything but open it. What does he make of it? I have no idea whether this gadget will get the child to the point where he can then more easily make the distinction between constructs and data. But the attempt is illustrative and interesting. It is a nice instance of how one seeks to translate a concept into a simpler form: that an object that cannot be seen can still be described—even if only indirectly. The object in this case "stands for" an invisible concept, albeit rather poorly, but it is a step in the right direction.

Surely all this argues for something akin to a spiral curriculum in which ideas are first presented in a form and language, honest though imprecise, which can be grasped by the

child, ideas that can be revisited later with greater precision and power until, finally, the student has achieved the reward of mastery.[2]

Readiness. One of the conclusions of the 1959 Woods Hole Conference of the National Academy of Sciences on curriculum in science was that any subject can be taught to anybody at any age in some form that is honest. It is a brave assertion, and the evidence on the whole is all on its side. At least there is no evidence to contradict it.

Readiness, that is, is a function not so much of maturation as it is of our intentions and our skill at translating ideas into the language and concepts of the age level we are teaching. But our intentions must be plain before we can start deciding what can be taught to children of what age, for life is short and art is long and there is much art yet to be created in the transmission of knowledge. So a word about our intentions as educators.

When one sits down to the task of trying to write a textbook or to prepare a lesson plan, it soon becomes apparent that there is an antinomy between two ideals: coverage and depth. Perhaps this is less of a problem in mathematics than in the field of history or literature, but it is not by any means negligible. In content, positive knowledge is increasing at a rate that is alarming when considered in terms of what one man can know in a lifetime. But fortunately, as the bulk of knowledge increases, the organizing structures that support it also grow. So that if there is ever more knowledge, it may indeed be the case that it is ever more related: the only possible way in which individual knowledge can keep proportional pace with the surge of available knowledge is through a grasp of the relatedness of knowledge. We may well ask of any item of information that is taught or that we lead a child to discover for himself whether it is worth knowing. I can think of

[2] See J. S. Bruner, *The Process of Education* (Cambridge: Harvard University Press, 1960).

only two good criteria and one middling one for deciding such an issue: whether the knowledge gives a sense of delight and whether it bestows the gift of intellectual travel beyond the information given, in the sense of containing within it the basis of generalization. The middling criterion is whether the knowledge is useful. It turns out, on the whole, as Charles Sanders Peirce commented, that useful knowledge looks after itself. So I would urge that we as schoolmen let it do so and concentrate on the first two criteria. Delight and travel, then.

It seems to me that the implications of this conclusion are that we opt for depth and continuity in our teaching, rather than coverage, and that we re-examine afresh what it is that gives a sense of intellectual delight to a person who is learning. To do the first of these, we must ask what it is that we wish the man of our times to know, what sort of minimum. What do we mean by an educated man? I think that, at the very least, an educated man should have a sense of what knowledge is like in some field of inquiry, to know it in its connectedness and with a feeling for how the knowledge is gained. An educated man must not be dazzled by the myth that advanced knowledge is the result of wizardry. The way to battle this myth is in the direct experience of the learner—to give him the experience of going from a primitive and weak grasp of some subject to a stage in which he has a more refined and powerful grasp of it. I do not mean that each man should be carried to the frontiers of knowledge, but I do mean that it is possible to take him far enough so that he himself can see how far he has come and by what means.

The principles of conservation in physics, which are useful elsewhere in this book, are vividly illustrative here. I mean the conservation of energy, mass, and momentum; and I would include the idea of invariance across transformation in order to include mathematics more directly. The child is told, by virtue of living in our particular society and speaking our particular language, that he must not waste his energy, fritter

it away. In common experience, things disappear, get lost. Bodies "lose" their heat; objects set in motion do not appear to stay in motion as in the pure case of Newton's law. Yet the most powerful laws of physics and chemistry are based on the conception of conservation. Only the meanest of purists would argue against the effort to teach the conservation principles to a first-grade student on the grounds that it would be "distorted" in the transmission. We know from the work of Piaget and others that, indeed, the child does not easily agree with notions based on conservation. A six-year-old child will often doubt that there is the same amount of fluid in a tall, thin glass jar as there was in a flat, wide one, even though he has seen the fluid poured from the latter into the former. Yet with time and with the proper embodiment of the idea—as in the film of the Physical Science Study Committee where a power plant is used as an example—it can be presented in its simplest and weakest form. The idea should be revisited constantly. It is central to the structure of the sciences of nature. In good time, many things can be derived from it that yield tremendous predictive power. Coverage in this sense, then, showing the range of things that can be related to this particular and powerful something, serves the ends of depth.

But what of delight? If you should ask me as a student of thought processes what produces the most fundamental form of pleasure in man's intellectual life, I think I would reply that it is the reduction of surprise and complexity to predictability and simplicity. But immediately there is a paradox. For it is the *act* of reducing surprise and complexity that gives pleasure. The road is better than the inn, for there is not all that much delight in simple unsurprisingness, and the cry "Not that *again!*" is surely a cry of dismay. It is precisely this readiness for new acts of simplification and surprise reduction that provides the thread of delight in what we have called a spiral curriculum. The great structural themes in learning lend themselves to just such an approach, to constant revisits yielding

new discovery, new surprise and its reduction, new and deeper simplification.

My choice of the conservation theorems in physics as an illustration to be repeated has not been adventitious. It is as basic and ramifying in one's growing understanding of nature as any theme could be. There are similar themes in other fields: the idea of biological continuity in nature that begins, perhaps, with the observation that giraffes have giraffe babies and not little elephants and progresses eventually to the "memory" of the large helical molecules of DNA that bring the feat off; the associative, distributive, and commutative laws in mathematics; the elaboration of the concept of tragedy in literature.

When we are clear about what we want to do in this kind of teaching, I feel reasonably sure that we shall be able to deal with the pseudoproblem of readiness. We shall have to use the unfolding of readiness to our advantage: to give the child a sense of his own growth and his own capacity to leap ahead. The evidence shows that the problem of translating concepts to this or that age level can be solved once we decide what it is we want to translate.

After John Dewey, What?

In 1897, at the age of thirty-eight, John Dewey published a stirring and prophetic work entitled *My Pedagogic Creed.* Much of his later writing on education is foreshadowed in this brief document. Five articles of faith are set forth. The first defines the educational process: "All education proceeds by the participation of the individual in the social consciousness of the race. This process begins unconsciously almost at birth, and is continually shaping the individual's powers, saturating his consciousness, forming his habits, training his ideas, and arousing his feelings and emotions."

The second article of faith embodies Dewey's concept of the school: "Education being a social process, the school is simply that form of community life in which all those agencies are concentrated that will be most effective in bringing the child to share in the inherited resources of the race, and to use his own powers for social ends. Education, therefore, is a process of living and not a preparation for future living." In the third thesis Dewey speaks to the subject matter of education: "The social life of the child is the basis of concentration or correlation in all his training or growth. The social life gives the unconscious unity and the background of all his efforts and all his attainments. . . . The true center . . . is not science, nor literature, nor history, nor geography, but the child's own social activities." A view of educational method gives form to Dewey's fourth article: "The law for presenting and treating material

is the law implicit in the child's own nature." For Dewey, the law was that of action: "the active side precedes the passive in the development of the child-nature. I believe that consciousness is essentially motor or impulsive; that conscious states tend to project themselves in action." And, finally, Dewey's fifth thesis: "Education is the fundamental method of social progress and reform."

One reads the document today with mixed feelings. Its optimism is classically American in its rejection of the tragic view of life. It defines truth in the pragmatic spirit: truth is the fruit of inquiry into the consequences of action. It expresses a firm faith not only in the individual's capacity to grow but in society's capacity to shape man in its own best image. The final lines of the creed are these: "Every teacher should realize the dignity of his calling; that he is a social servant set apart for the maintenance of proper social order and the securing of the right social growth. In this way the teacher always is the prophet of the true God and the usherer in of the true kingdom of heaven."

Yet the very wholesomeness—the optimism, the pragmatism, the acceptance of man's harmonious continuity with society—leaves one uneasy. For in the two thirds of a century between 1897 and today, there has been a profound change not only in our conception of nature but also of society and the world of social institutions. Perhaps more important, we have lived through a revolution in our understanding of the nature of man, his intelligence, his capabilities, his passions, and the forms of his growth.

Dewey's thinking reflected the changes, though he was limited by the premises of his philosophical position. But between Dewey's first premises and our day, there bristles a series of revolutionary doctrines and cataclysmic events that change the very character of the inquiry. Two world wars, the dark episode of Hitler and genocide, the Russian revolution, the relativistic revolution in physics and psychology, the Age

of Energy with its new technology, the sardonic reign of skeptical philosophy—all of these have forced a reappraisal of the underlying terms by which we construct a philosophy of education.

Let us then re-examine the terms, guided by what we know today of the world and of human nature. There is matter here, however, that is liable to some misinterpretation and we do well to clear it up at the outset. One writes against the background of one's day. Dewey was writing with an eye to the sterility and rigidity of school instruction in the 1890s—particularly its failure to appreciate the nature of the child. His emphasis upon the importance of direct experience and social action was an implied critique of the empty formalism that did little to relate learning to the child's world of experience. Dewey did mighty service in inspiring a correction. But an excess of virtue is vice. We, in our day, are reconsidering education against the background of such an excess.

Then, too, misunderstanding often converted Dewey's ideas into the sentimental practices he so deplored: "Next to deadness and dullness, formalism and routine," he wrote in his creed, "our education is threatened by no greater evil than sentimentalism." The sentimental cult of "the class project," of "life adjustment" courses, the reluctance to expose the child to the startling sweep of man and nature for fear it might violate the comfortable domain of his direct experience, the cloying concept of "readiness"—these are conceptions about children, often with no experimental support, that are justified in the name of Dewey. His was a noble yet tender view in his time. But what of our times? In what form shall we speak our beliefs?

What education is. Education seeks to develop the power and sensibility of mind. On the one hand, the educational process transmits to the individual some part of the accumulation of knowledge, style, and values that constitutes the culture of a people. In doing so, it shapes the impulses, the conscious-

ness, and the way of life of the individual. But education must also seek to develop the processes of intelligence so that the individual is capable of going beyond the cultural ways of his social world, able to innovate in however modest a way so that he can create an interior culture of his own. For whatever the art, the science, the literature, the history, and the geography of a culture, each man must be his own artist, his own scientist, his own historian, his own navigator. No person is master of the whole culture; indeed, this is almost a defining characteristic of that form of social memory that we speak of as culture. Each man lives a fragment of it. To be whole, he must create his own version of the world, using that part of his cultural heritage he has made his own through education.

In our time, the requirements of technology constrain the freedom of the individual to create images of the world that are satisfying in the deepest sense. Our era has also witnessed the rise of ideologies that subordinate the individual to the defined aims of a society, a form of subordination that is without compassion for idiosyncracy and respects only the instrumental contribution of a man to the progress of the society. At the same time, and in spite of ideologies, man's understanding of himself and of his world—both the natural and social world—has deepened to a degree that warrants calling our age an intellectually golden one. The need is now to employ our deeper understanding not only for the enrichment of society but also for the enrichment of the individual.

It is true, as Dewey said, that all education proceeds by the participation of the individual in the social consciousness of the race, but it is a truth with a double edge. For all education, good and bad alike, is of this order. We know now to what degree this is so. To take but one example, the very language one speaks conditions the style and structure of thought and experience. Indeed, as we have seen, there is reason to believe that thought processes themselves are internalizations of

social intercourse, an inner colloquy patterned by early external dialogues. It is this that makes education possible. But education, by giving shape and expression to our experience, can also be the principal instrument for setting limits on the enterprise of mind. The guarantee against limits is the sense of alternatives. Education must, then, be not only a process that transmits culture but also one that provides alternative views of the world and strengthens the will to explore them.

After a half century of startling progress in the psychological sciences, we know that mental health is only a minimum condition for the growth of mind. The tragedy of mental illness is that it so preoccupies the person with the need to fend off realities with which he cannot cope that it leaves him without either the nerve or the zest to learn. But mental health is only a state from which to start: the powers of mind grow with their exercise. Adjustment is too modest an ideal, if it is an ideal at all. Competence in the use of one's powers for the development of individually defined and socially relevant excellence is much more to the point. After a half century of Freud, we know that the freeing of instinct and inclination is not an end in itself but a way station along the road to competence. What is most prophetic for us about Freud in this second half of the century is not his battle against the fetters of rigid moralism, but his formula: "Where there was id, let there be ego."

Education must begin, as Dewey concluded his first article of belief, "with a psychological insight into the child's capacities, interests, habits," but a point of departure is not an itinerary. It is just as mistaken to sacrifice the adult to the child as to sacrifice the child to the adult. It is sentimentalism to assume that the teaching of life can be fitted always to the child's interests just as it is empty formalism to force the child to parrot the formulas of adult society. Interests can be created and stimulated. In this sphere it is not far from the truth to say that supply creates demand, that the provocation of what is

available creates response. One seeks to equip the child with deeper, more gripping, and subtler ways of knowing the world and himself.

What the school is. The school is an entry into the life of the mind. It is, to be sure, life itself and not merely a preparation for living. But it is a special form of living, one carefully devised for making the most of those plastic years that characterize the development of *homo sapiens* and distinguish our species from all others. School should provide more than a continuity with the broader community or with everyday experience. It is primarily the special community where one experiences discovery by the use of intelligence, where one leaps into new and unimagined realms of experience, experience that is discontinuous with what went before. A child recognizes this when he first understands what a poem is, or what beauty and simplicity inhere in the idea of the conservation theorems, or that measure is universally applicable. If there is one continuity to be singled out, it is the slow converting of the child's artistic sense of the omnipotence of thought into the realistic confidence in the use of thought that characterizes the effective man.

In insisting upon the continuity of the school with the community on the one side and the family on the other, John Dewey overlooked the special function of education as an opener of new perspectives. If the school were merely a transition zone from the intimacy of the family to the life of the community, it would be a way of life easily enough arranged. In the educational systems of primitive societies, there almost always comes a point, usually at puberty, where there is a sharp change in the life of the boy, marked by a *rite de passage* that establishes a boundary between childhood ways and the ways of the adolescent.

It would be romantic nonsense to pattern our practices upon those found in preliterate societies. I would only ask that we attend to one parallel: education must not confuse the child

with the adult and must recognize that the transition to adulthood involves an introduction to new realms of experience, the discovery and exploration of new mysteries, the gaining of new powers.

In the *shtetl* of Eastern Europe, the traditional Jewish ghetto, the scholar was a particularly important figure—the *talmid khokhem.* In his mien, his mode of conversation so rich in allusion, his form of poise, the wise man was the image not of a competent but, rather, of a beautiful person. Traditional Chinese society also had its image of the beautiful person, one who blended knowledge and sentiment and action in a beautiful way of life. The ideal of the gentleman served much the same function in the Europe of the seventeenth and eighteenth centuries. It is perhaps in this spirit that Alfred North Whitehead declared that education must involve an exposure to greatness if it is to leave its mark. For me the yeast of education is the idea of excellence, and that comprises as many forms as there are individuals to develop a personal image of excellence. The school must have as one of its principal functions the nurturing of images of excellence.

A detached conception of idealized excellence is not enough. A doctrine of excellence, to be effective, must be translatable into the individual lives of those who come in contact with it. What is compelling about the *talmid khokhem,* the Chinese scholar-administrator, and the eighteenth-century gentleman is that they embody ways of life to which any man can aspire in his own way and from which he can draw in his own style. I believe, then, that the school must also contain men and women who, in their own way, seek and embody excellence. This does not mean that we shall have to staff our schools with men and women of great genius but that the teacher must embody in his own approach to learning a pursuit of excellence. And, indeed, with the technical resources opened by television and its adjuncts, one can present the student and also his teacher with the working version of excellence in its

highest sense. In the years ahead, we shall find that the great scholar, scientist, or artist can speak as easily and honestly to the beginner as to the graduate student.

The subject matter of education. The issue of subject matter in education can be resolved only by reference to one's view of the nature of knowledge. Knowledge is a model we construct to give meaning and structure to regularities in experience. The organizing ideas of any body of knowledge are inventions for rendering experience economical and connected. We invent concepts such as force in physics, the bond in chemistry, motives in psychology, style in literature as means to the end of comprehension.

The history of culture is the history of the development of great organizing ideas, ideas that inevitably stem from deeper values and points of view about man and nature. The power of great organizing concepts is in large part that they permit us to understand and sometimes to predict or change the world in which we live. But their power lies also in the fact that ideas provide instruments for experience. Having grown up in a culture dominated by the ideas of Newton, and so with a conception of time flowing equably, we experience time moving inexorably and steadily, marked by a one-way arrow. Indeed, we know now, after a quarter of a century of research on perception, that experience is not to be had directly and neatly, but filtered through the programmed readiness of our senses. The program is constructed with our expectations and these are derived from our models or ideas about what exists and what follows what.

From this, two convictions follow. The first is that the structure of knowledge—its connectedness and the derivations that make one idea follow from another—is the proper emphasis in education. For it is structure, the great conceptual inventions that bring order to the congeries of disconnected observations, that gives meaning to what we may learn and makes possible the opening up of new realms of experience. The second con-

viction is that the unity of knowledge is to be found within knowledge itself, if the knowledge is worth mastering.

To attempt a justification of subject matter, as Dewey did, in terms of its relation to the child's social activities is to misunderstand what knowledge is and how it may be mastered. The significance of the concept of commutativity in mathematics does not derive from the social insight that two houses with fourteen people in each is not the same as fourteen houses with two people in each. Rather, it inheres in the power of the idea to create a way of thinking about number that is lithe and beautiful and immensely generative—an idea at least as powerful as, say, the future conditional tense in formal grammar. Without the idea of commutativity, algebra would be impossible. If set theory—now often the introductory section in newer curriculums in mathematics—had to be justified in terms of its relation to immediate experience and social life, it would not be worth teaching. Yet set theory lays a foundation for the understanding of order and number that could never be achieved with the social arithmetic of interest rates and bales of hay at so much per bale. Mathematics, like any other subject, must begin with experience, but progress toward abstraction and understanding requires precisely that there be a weaning away from the obviousness of superficial experience.

There is one consideration of cognitive economy, discussed in an earlier chapter, that is paramount. One cannot "cover" any subject in full, not even in a lifetime, if coverage means visiting all the facts and events and morsels. Subject matter presented so as to emphasize its structure will perforce be of that generative kind that permits reconstruction of the details or, at very least, prepares a place into which the details, when encountered, can be put.

What then of subject matter in the conventional sense? The answer to the question, "What shall be taught?" turns out to be the answer to the question, "What is nontrivial?" If one can first answer the question, "What is worth knowing about?"

then it is not difficult to distinguish between the aspects of it that are worth teaching and learning and those that are not. Surely, knowledge of the natural world, knowledge of the human condition, knowledge of the nature and dynamics of society, knowledge of the past so that it may be used in experiencing the present and aspiring to the future—all of these, it would seem reasonable to suppose, are essential to an educated man. To these must be added another: knowledge of the products of our artistic heritage that mark the history of our aesthetic wonder and delight.

A problem immediately arises concerning the symbolism in terms of which knowledge is understood and talked about. There is language in its natural sense and language in its mathematical sense. I cannot imagine an educated man a century from now who will not be largely bilingual in this special sense—concise and adept in both a natural language and mathematics. For these two are the tools essential to the unlocking of new experience and the gaining of new powers. As such, they must have a central place in any curriculum.

Finally, it is as true today as it was when Dewey wrote that one cannot foresee the world in which the child we educate will live. Informed powers of mind and a sense of potency in action are the only instruments we can give the child that will be invariable across the transformations of time and circumstance. The succession of studies that we give the child in the ideal school need be fixed in only one way: whatever is introduced, let it be pursued continuously enough to give the student a sense of the power of mind that comes from a deepening of understanding. It is this, rather than any form of extensive coverage, that matters most.

The nature of method. The process and the goal of education are one and the same thing. The goal of education is disciplined understanding; that is the process as well.

Let us recognize that the opposite of understanding is not ignorance or simply "not knowing." To understand something

is, first, to give up some other way of conceiving of it. Confusion all too often lies between one way of conceiving and another, better way. It is one of our biological inheritances that confusion produces emergency anxiety, and with anxiety there come the defensive measures—flight, fright, or freezing—that are antithetical to the free and zestful use of mind. The binding fact of mental life in child and adult alike is that there is a limited capacity for processing information—our span, as it is called, can comprise six or seven unrelated items simultaneously. Go beyond that and there is overload, confusion, forgetting. As George Miller has put it, the principle of economy is to fill our seven mental-input slots with gold rather than dross. The degree to which material to be learned is put into structures by the learner will determine whether he is working with gold or dross.

For this reason, as well as for reasons already stated, it is essential that, before being exposed to a wide range of material on a topic, the child first have a general idea of how and where things fit. It is often the case that the development of the general idea comes from a first round of experience with concrete embodiments of ideas that are close to a child's life. The cycle of learning begins, then, with particulars and immediately moves toward abstraction. It comes to a temporary goal when the abstraction can then be used in grasping new particulars in the deeper way that abstraction permits.

Insofar as possible, a method of instruction should have the objective of leading the child to discover for himself. Telling children and then testing them on what they have been told inevitably has the effect of producing bench-bound learners whose motivation for learning is likely to be extrinsic to the task—pleasing the teacher, getting into college, artificially maintaining self-esteem. The virtues of encouraging discovery are of two kinds. In the first place, the child will make what he learns his own, will fit his discovery into the interior world of culture that he creates for himself. Equally important, dis-

covery and the sense of confidence it provides is the proper reward for learning. It is a reward that, moreover, strengthens the very process that is at the heart of education—disciplined inquiry.

The child must be encouraged to get the full benefit from what he learns. This is not to say that he should be required to put it to immediate use in his daily life, though so much the better if he has the happy opportunity to do so. Rather, it is a way of honoring the connectedness of knowledge. Two facts and a relation joining them is and should be an invitation to generalize, to extrapolate, to make a tentative intuitive leap, even to build a tentative theory. The leap from mere learning to using what one has learned in thinking is an essential step in the use of the mind. Indeed, plausible guessing, the use of the heuristic hunch, the best employment of necessarily insufficient evidence—these are activities in which the child needs practice and guidance. They are among the great antidotes to passivity.

Most important of all, the educational process must be free of intellectual dishonesty and those forms of cheating that explain without providing understanding. I have expressed the conviction elsewhere that any subject can be taught to anybody at any age in some form that is honest. It is not honest to present a fifth-grade social-studies class with an image of town government as if it were a den of cub scouts presided over by a parent figure interpreting the charter—even if the image set forth does happen to mesh with the child's immediate social experience. A lie is still a lie—even if it sounds like familiar truth. Nor is it honest to present a sixth-grade science class with a garbled but concrete picture of the atom that is, in its way, as sweeteningly false as the suburban image of town government given them the year before. A dishonest image can only discourage the self-generating intellectual inquiry out of which real understanding grows.

The school and social progress. I believe that education is

the fundamental method of social change. Revolutions themselves are no better and are often less good than the ideas they embody and the means invented for their application. Change is swifter in our times than ever before in human history and news of it is almost instantaneous. If we are to be serious in the belief that school must be life itself and not merely preparation for life, then school must reflect the changes through which we are living.

The first implication of this belief is that means must be found to feed back into our schools the ever deepening insights that are developed on the frontiers of knowledge. This is an obvious point in science and mathematics, and continuing efforts are now being instituted to assure that new, more powerful, and often simpler ways of understanding find their way back into the classrooms of our primary and secondary schools. But it is equally important to have this constant refreshment from fields other than the sciences—where the frontiers of knowledge are not always the universities and research laboratories but political and social life, the arts, literary endeavor, and the rapidly changing business and industrial community. Everywhere there is change, and with change we are learning.

I see the need for a new type of institution, a new conception in curriculum. What we have not had and what we are beginning to recognize as needed is something that is perhaps best called an "institute for curriculum studies"—not one of them, but many. Let it be the place where scholars, scientists, men of affairs, and artists come together with talented teachers continually to revise and refresh our curriculums. It is an activity that transcends the limits of any of our particular university faculties—be they faculties of education, arts and science, medicine, or engineering. We have been negligent in coming to a sense of the quickening change of life in our time and its implications for the educational process. We have not shared with our teachers the benefits of new discovery,

new insight, new artistic triumph. Not only have we operated with the notion of the self-contained classroom but also with the idea of the self-contained school—and even the self-contained educational system.

The Nobel poet or the ambassador to the United Nations, the brilliant cellist or the perceptive playwright, the historian making use of the past or the sociologist seeking a pattern in the present—these men, like the student, are seeking understanding and mastery over new problems. They represent excellence at the frontiers of endeavor. If a sense of progress and change toward greater excellence is to illuminate our schools, there must be a constant return of their wisdom and effort to enliven and inform teacher and student alike. There is no difference in kind between the man at the frontier and the young student at his own frontier, each attempting to understand. Let the educational process be life itself as fully as we can make it.

PART III

the Idea of Action

The last three essays are concerned with the relation of thought and action: the first with the control of human behavior in a democratic society, the second with the impact of Freud on man's image of himself and his capacities, and the third with human effectiveness and its relation to the conception of fate in an age of science.

Action can be said to be determined by what a man knows, although I do not mean this in the rationalist's sense of calculus based on close reckoning of all alternatives. Rather, knowing has many faces and it is a linguistic pity that the word is a singular gerund. For we know in the light of many states, and it is man's fate that knowing in one light often precludes knowing in another at the same time—as in Niels Bohr's now-famous dictum that you cannot know somebody at the same time in the light of love and the light of justice. So we can say that, though action follows from what one knows, it is also the case that it never follows from *all* that one knows. Perhaps it is just as well, or else we should be in a persistent tetanus of indecision.

In any case, it would seem to me to follow from this principle that action can be understood in terms of the selective principle by which we use the knowledge available to us. It is for this reason that I have addressed the three remaining essays to the nature of the conceptions that underlie action in the modern world. Man does not respond to a world that exists for direct touching. Nor is he locked in a prison of his own subjectivity. Rather, he represents the world to himself and acts in behalf of or in reaction to his representations. The

representations are products of his own spirit as it has been formed by living in a society with a language, myths, a history, and ways of doing things. It is with these difficult issues that the final essays are concerned.

All three were prepared in their first versions for special celebrations. "The Control of Human Behavior" was presented in New York at the twenty-fifth anniversary of the Graduate Faculty of the New School for Social Research—the famous "University in Exile." The Freud essay was given at a special convocation of the American Academy of Arts and Sciences to honor the retirements of Percy Bridgman and Phillip Frank. It was later printed in the *Partisan Review* (Summer 1956) and *American Psychologist* (September 1956). A version of this also appeared in *Daedalus* (Winter 1958). "Fate and the Possible" was given at the Centenary of Massachusetts Institute of Technology as part of a panel discussion called "How Has Science in the Last Century Changed Man's View of Himself?" Since the tone and content of this essay was naturally and in some measure determined by the other panelists, I should record that they were the physicist Robert Oppenheimer, the novelist Aldous Huxley, and the theologian Paul Tillich.

The Control of Human Behavior

The most characteristic and indeed the defining thing about human behavior, or any behavior, is that it is virtually never random, that it is under the control of systematic processes impinging from outside or initiated from inside the organism. In the deepest sense, then, human behavior is always controlled. Many of the sources of control over behavior are, of course, other human beings and the societies they construct. And frequently societies and groups of human beings seek to gain control over aspects of human behavior that were formerly under the power of non-social forces, or of social forces that are considered wrong or unhealthy or illegal. I shall refer to controls of this order as deliberate controls, and they are well illustrated by laws, regulations, and certain kinds of formal education. But there are also forms of social control necessary for the operation of a society that are *not* deliberate; indeed, many of these may not even be recognized as existing—such inconspicuous influences as guiding myths and values and the various forms of child-rearing. This aspect of control is often referred to by anthropologists as "covert culture." I prefer the expression "latent culture" to avoid the pejorative meaning of the word covert.

Given the nature of societies, it is frequently the case that deliberate forms of control bear a seemingly capricious relation to the latent ones. As Clyde Kluckhohn has suggested, deliber-

ate controls may express the official aspirations of a culture, latent ones its practice. And one may also find instances in which the manifest effort at control is a guilt reaction against the informal or latent techniques of control—as in punitive legislation directed against illegitimate children. Finally, there are instances in which manifest and latent controls operate with admirable congruence, as in the accord between regulations and beliefs about compulsory education in the United States. To understand the control of human behavior, one must attend both to the manifest and the latent and to the manner of their interaction.

There are two approaches to the problem of control. One of them, the one that is least often a target for moral indignation, consists in seeking to control men by shaping their conception of the world in which they live. Once we have determined how men shall perceive and structure the world with which they have commerce, we can then safely leave their actions to them—in the sense that, if they believe themselves to be standing before a precipice, they will not step over it unless they intend suicide. This is cognitive control, controlling men's minds, to use that pompous phrase. Achieving such control is exceedingly difficult—or, rather, usurping it is difficult, for the control now rests in the culture and its ways of introducing members into its web of reality.

The second approach is more direct in the sense that it does not seek directly to alter the experience of the person, but only his acts. It utilizes punishments and rewards: when the former are the chief instruments it is called coercion; with the latter it is seduction. There is a great deal that is moot on the subject of what combination of coercion and seduction is most effective in controlling behavior and whether, once having controlled overt acts, one thereby changes the person's view of what the reality was to which he had reacted. A growing body of data points to the conclusion that people act themselves into a way of believing as readily as they believe themselves into a way

of acting. More simply, there is a strong human tendency toward construing one's acts as following from the reality of one's experience. Whether for reasons of cognitive economy or for the protection of self-esteem, people wish to see their acts as derived from, or congruent with, experience. The liking for absurdity is an acquired taste, and not widely distributed.

The distinction between cognitive control and control by coercion and seduction is a deep one. The one operates by intrinsic "self-administered" rewards and punishments; the other is regulated by gains and losses that are extrinsically administered. The distinction is familiar from its use in our earlier discussion of the act of discovery and in considering how one might fashion an ideal educational sequence. It is no exaggeration to say that the role given to each of these forms of control is a hallmark of any political theory of the state, and, by the same token, it is the single most telling feature of any psychological theory about the nature of man—whether one envisions man as ultimately captive of the shaping forces of his environment or as competent to shape a world of his own. It is an absorbing fact that psychological theory both in America and in the Soviet Union is sharply divided on this issue.[1]

There are certain generalizations one can make about the degree to which controls of all kinds can be made effective. Most of them are rather cheerful from the point of view of a pluralistic conception of democracy; none of them is particularly happy from the point of view of improving the conduct of man to make him a better citizen of a democracy. Two of these generalizations, the concept of monopolistic pre-emption and the concept of primacy, are closely related and worth considering here.

The concept of monopolistic pre-emption can be stated as follows. To the degree that one has monopolistic control of the

[1] See Raymond A. Bauer, *The New Man in Soviet Psychology* (Cambridge: Harvard University Press, 1952), and also my preface to L. Vygotsky's classic, *Thought and Language* (New York: John Wiley-Technology Press, 1962).

sources of information to which an individual is exposed and control over the order in which he encounters information, to that degree does one's opportunity for cognitive control increase. Similarly, in the realm of action, it follows that a monopoly over the means of coercion and seduction increases the potentiality for controlling human behavior. But just as the nature and order of information encountered must be manipulable to achieve cognitive control, so with coercion and seduction one must be able to reward or punish very quickly. If we know anything from the studies of the reinforcement of behavior in animals, it is that reward and punishment (but particularly the former) lose their power at a very sharp rate the further they are separated in time from the acts that they are supposed to be controlling. But we lose sight of the utopian conditions for all this—that *if* we had such monopolistic control, then we would be in good position to *attempt* to exercise control. It is not surprising that writers who are fond of fantasies about social control, like my colleague B. F. Skinner in his novel *Walden Two*, encourage themselves with tales set in a neatly arranged, benign, but nonetheless utterly monopolistic utopia.

A word now about primacy. Within interesting limits of error, it can be said that conceptions of reality early established tend to become the first editions of reality upon which later editions are fashioned. Though the later editions may change, they have a continuity or oppositional congruence with the earlier ones. In another place, I have written about the distinction between "line" and "filler" sources that people use in gaining information in an effort to maintain or modify their attitudes and values.[2] The filler sources may be found anywhere; line sources provide direct support to the more deeply selective principle in the person's approach to social reality. It is more often than not the case that the early versions of social

[2] See M. B. Smith, J. S. Bruner, and R. W. White, *Opinions and Personality* (New York: John Wiley, 1956).

reality have a pre-emptive power that makes them like line sources. I am not suggesting that people do not change their opinions and perspective on reality, but only that change always requires a reference point and that even violent change bears the mark of what was before. The passion of the ex-Communist become anti-Communist is all too familiar. Early emotionally organized beliefs and guides to action often may be stubbornly incorrigible, partly because they are isolated from the language-bound literal structure of reality that develops later. Such beliefs are hard to reach by the discourse of ordinary reason. It is thanks to one of Freud's great insights that psychoanalytic procedure can now bring some of them back into awareness where they can be linked to the day life of the ego. But psychoanalysis is for the few, and the ugly boast of Hitler, that if he could have the first dozen years of a child's life it mattered little who had the next twenty, still has nightmare quality.

One can go on almost endlessly speaking of the psychology of control without much reference to its implementation in society—talking as if the application of monopoly and primacy were simply matters of detail to be worked out later. Such a path deserves to be labeled *psychologist's fallacy*. It is the kind of misconception that leads some psychiatrists to argue that, if the hostility level of the man in the street could be lowered or diverted into other channels, there would be no war. It fails utterly to take into account the reality and complexity of social organization. It refuses to envisage the kind of social organization that would permit the impositions of those manifest and latent controls we know to be necessary if behavior is to be regulated. The fact of the matter is that only the most highly organized and ruthless totalitarian states ever consider the possibility of tackling the task. And they do so because they have a morality of government consonant with the administrative arrangements required. We do not. Although it is psychologically simpler and more spectacular to talk about such

totalitarian forms of control as brainwashing and the measured use of terror, it is more useful to consider the matter of behaviorial control as it actually exists in limited form in democratic societies.

The first thing that can be said about the ethics and the techniques of control in a democracy is that both of them rest heavily upon certain cultural values concerning the nature of the private sphere: there are sharp differences between the theory of control as exercised over the public sphere of life and the private. The public sphere is governed by codes of law and regulatory legislation, backed by police power and the force of public opinion, and adjudicated either by courts of law or regulatory commissions. It is quite plain that practices in the public sphere depend upon and change with the corpus of beliefs and opinions that develop as expressions of private morality. And where there is a conflict between the two domains, public and private, it is an occasion for crisis within a society. Two such crises beset us today, both matters of sharp concern in the United States and Great Britain where each is approached quite differently. One has to do with capital punishment and its justification either as a legitimate expression of moral indignation or as a presumably rational concern for deterring crimes of violence. Both justifications collide with a Christianized private ideal of compassion and rehabilitation. The other crisis is the view of homosexuality as crime, an issue recently given an airing by the Royal Commission under Lord Wolfenden. In both cases it can be shown that the body of laws and their spirit as interpreted by the courts have influenced private morality. But whereas control is exercised in the public realm by instruments of government, the case is usually quite different in matters of private belief and action. Here one may speak of the instruments of a culture as decisive. What are these instruments?

A short list would include: language and myth, affiliative pressure, anticipation of rejection and isolation, limitation of

opportunity, and variable compensation. Consider each of these in turn, and consider how each relates to monopoly and primacy.

Language and myth. It is perhaps Ernst Cassirer and Benjamin Lee Whorf who have made us most aware in recent times of the importance of myth and language in the shaping of man's conception of reality and of their consequent importance in the control of human behavior. Language and myth exercise this power by virtue of two circumstances—the first is the need to maintain communication because of the fractional competence of each individual in a society; the second is the requirement of conserving one's limited cognitive capacity. Myth and language each operate to accomplish both of these, and they maintain their controlling power because of their success. We have already considered the role of myth and language in shaping reality, but here a few words are needed to consider them as instruments of control.

Language is the human gift that is the chief guarantor of joint action, and it comes into its first use at a time when joint action is the only means whereby the young human organism can survive. Consequently, early language is essentially demand language, a two-way demand language. But language learning is also concept learning, and the price one pays for the gift of language is that one also learns to operate in terms of the concepts that are codified in a language—all the concepts of relationship, of modification, of cause and effect. I am not supporting the so-called strong form of Whorf's hypothesis—that language ineluctably molds the shape of thought—but rather the weaker form which holds that language predisposes a mind to certain modes of thought and certain ways of arranging the shared subjective reality of a linguistic community.

It is probably true that, given sufficient freedom of periphrasis, one can express any idea in any language, but the fact of the matter is that one usually does not. It is this cognitively predisposing property of a language that has been called its

Weltanschauung. Also, languages differ in their capacity to absorb and facilitate the use of new ideas that are not built-in features of a particular language. For example, Western languages may eventually absorb the idea of aspiration in a new structure of future tenses, adding to the future tense and the future conditional new forms that express the desired future state and the undesired one: on balance it will rain tomorrow, it could rain tomorrow, it should rain tomorrow, hopefully it will rain tomorrow, alas it will rain tomorrow. Our language absorbs such distinction easily. If Florence Kluckhohn is right in her claim that we are increasingly a "becoming" culture rather than a "being" one, then we are likely to develop such rules either formally or informally as a means of alerting the sensitivities of those who live in our culture. Perhaps we have already. The result in increased awareness represents a powerful form of control over reality.

Obviously, language and myth also play an enormous part, as we have already seen, in the conservation of cognitive capacity. What better way of coding and recoding experience than to catch its complexities in the constraining structure of words? As the social environment becomes increasingly complex, it becomes all the more important to have the words and concepts that can encompass the events and controls that we bring into being. We learn to segment the flow of events into "campaigns" or "crises" or "historical trends." Of course, a single participant in a linguistic community uses all the forms of regrouping experience that the culture provides. But there exists a linguistic and conceptual consensus that makes swift and widespread communication possible—and it is this consensus that provides yet another basis for the control of behavior, control in the sense that the result is a reduction in the variability of behavior.

And, to be sure, it is not only language and its concepts that operate in this fashion, but the myths and models provided by the society as well. A friend, a distinguished aeronautical

engineer, recently told me of his visit to the Soviet Union during which a gifted Russian colleague pressed him for details of his personal finances as a professor in a great American university. My friend, after carefully telling about his salary and his consulting fees, then went on to talk about his taxes each year. The Russian, a highly intelligent man, immediately seized upon this detail and exclaimed, "But under socialism, we have no taxes." "Come now," said my friend, "how do you pay for your space program, your armed forces, your beautiful subways?" The Russian, a thoughtful man, was visibly disturbed by the question. It had penetrated.

The question of mythmaking as a technique of control can be more sharply put. I have argued earlier that in our time the intellectual can reclaim his powerful position as mythmaker; that the scientist and humanist between them can offer new images of man's place in the universe we are coming to know. Friendly critics of widely different training have complained that I have failed to see the organic, unconscious nature of the growth of myth to which, so goes the claim, the intellectual only gives words and a voice. I think the point is a moot one. Indeed, there is evidence that even enduring folk art is almost always of minority origin, that it was first created by one man for a small audience. The impact of the intellectual and the technician on the magical conception of juju in West Africa is more than just amusing. A Nigerian educator told me of one change in his native village over the past fifteen or twenty years. Then, the children would take to the bush when the "injection man" appeared with small-pox vaccines. Today, the villagers line up for inoculations performed by uneducated Africans who inject distilled water, sold for a guinea a shot, as "white man's juju."

Nobody would doubt that the intellectual, by virtue of his sensitivity to the inappropriateness of existing myths, has played a great role as myth slayer. Perhaps his role in the years ahead will be considerably more positive.

Affiliation and rejection. Margaret Mead some years ago drew a distinction among forms of public opinion. Some are controlled ritualistically, as in Balinese society where issues are said to be settled by deriving a solution from a ritualized code. Others are managed affiliatively, where the decision depends upon the group membership and relationship of the contending parties, as among the Iatmul. And there might be still others, where resolution depends on individual values, in which opinion crystallizes spontaneously. It is not easy to pick a society where this occurs, though we like to think of our own in these terms. In any case, we have seen how language and myth operate as powerful ritualistic controls even if they are not readily manageable. A brief look at affiliation and the fear of losing it will, I believe, disclose a powerful controlling force and one much more easily manipulated.

A useful point of departure is the interesting literature now available on separation trauma in children. From the work of John Bowlby and others, it appears that quite early in life there is an important period in which the child develops a strong love-dependency relationship with a parental figure who looks after the child and supplies care and continuity—and the two together are critical. Brief separation from the parent figure produces a marked upset; somewhat longer separation leads to what appears to be a denial reaction in which the parent is not recognized after return from, say, the hospital. Continued separation with inadequate subsitution of another parent figure leads to certain irreversible changes that, in adulthood and adolescence, become what is best summarized as psychopathy. It consists of an inability to form identifications with people, to commit oneself for long periods to a line of work or an enterprise. People who have been subjected to such treatment (as in the aseptic nurseries for orphans in the twenties that operated on the misguided belief that too much love is not good for children and that they should not be comforted when they cry or allowed to become attached to one

nurse) characteristically slide into a "spiv" pattern, into petty thievery or casual prostitution, and they show various other forms of psychopathic drift through the demilegal borderlands of society. In short, they are hard to control by means other than confinement and coercion.

For the great majority who succeed in establishing affiliative identification with family, village, and society at large, there is a built-in vulnerability to control: the fear of ostracism. So far as I know, there is no society in which such isolation is not a source of dread. Perhaps, indeed, it is as widespread as the incest taboo.

Control of identification and manipulation of the threat of ostracism are the two great instruments by which human behavior is controlled by those who exert power—first in the family and later in the larger groups into which the person moves. It is central not only in the control of a democratic society but also in the totalitarian state. The renunciation of parental identification that is so much a part of the intense political schooling of China is not designed to destroy the capacity for identification but to transfer it to other symbols.

I have sometimes thought that we may have exaggerated the effects of childrearing practices on the adult personality as a general matter, but it has never crossed my mind that we have exaggerated the importance of identification in the childrearing process. Between the childrearing practices of one culture and another there is much in common that is dictated by the very nature of the task, whether in Detroit, in Peiping, or in Bali, and we have at times overlooked these communalities. But certainly it is clear that the capacity for identification, its quality, the transferability of identification, and the vividness and nature of the dread of isolation—all of these can be varied in striking ways by the handling of early dependency relationships.

What I should like to propose at this point is not that we seek to manipulate patterns of child training for achieving

official forms of control over man's behavior. Rather, it is here that I would look for defense against controls of a kind that are likely to be dangerous to the future of a democratic society. Whoever is sick with the fear of rejection, whoever has formed too strong and transferable an identification—he is the potential victim of forms of control that make men unfree. If public-health measures are understood in their most profound sense as expressions of a society's values, then surely here is a prime area for taking measures to ensure the survival of democracy.

Limitation of opportunity. Again it is some recent work on early deprivation that gives a new meaning to the limitation of opportunity as a technique for controlling human behavior.[3] Specifically, the work concerns sensory deprivation, and the subjects were animals, mostly dogs. (It is not possible to do the equivalent experiments on human beings.) Raising a dog in a highly impoverished environment, where there is little variety and no challenge to problem solving, produces a seemingly irreversible stupidity in the adult animal. The puppy who has been isolated needs many trials before he learns not to sniff the candle flame that burns his nose as a price for his curiosity. He is very deficient in learning how to go around a barrier to get food on the other side, and in general his behavior is lacking in variety and flexibility.

Relatively little is known as yet about the rehabilitation of such animals, save that it is a very slow process. Again, there seems to be a critical period during which isolation from the world of rich stimulation has its maximum deleterious effect—during the first year principally. But there is evidence that there are effects, more or less irreversible, that are produced by prolonged exposure to dulled and homogenized environments during the formative years of any mammal. My children have raised rats from the Wistar Institute in the usual chaos of a human habitat and these rats were considerably more

[3] See Philip Solomon and others, eds., *Sensory Deprivation* (Cambridge: Harvard University Press, 1961).

exploratory, venturesome, and intelligent personalities than the rats who lived in the gray atmosphere of the laboratory. Reviewing the literature in early sensory deprivation, I have come to the conclusion that one of the chief effects of such restriction is that, to put it metaphorically, the animals are prevented from developing adequate models of the environment in which they will eventually have to live—or, technically stated, there is interference with the formation of what Hebb has called cell assemblies and phase sequences, the hypothetical neural structures that are constructed in our brains to represent and abstract the texture of the environment.

The reader may properly wonder at this point whether I am proposing that such forms of deprivation be used for controlling behavior in the spirit, say, that Huxley's planners in *Brave New World* produced "gammas." On the contrary, I am suggesting that we are already inadvertently controlling behavior by imposing irreversible limits upon it with many of our practices in education, considering education now in the broad sense. We should be asking whether there are critical periods for the introduction of training in mathematics and language and guiding myths. There probably are. Are we mindful of what it takes by way of intensive exposure to certain forms of experience to unlock human capacities of certain kinds, whether for looking at art or for manipulating abstract symbols? I rather think we are not.

A final psychological point about limitation of exposure. Many students of human development have noted that there is a phenomenon by which supply creates demand. Gordon Allport has written of the functional autonomy of motives, the sequence whereby a habitual activity seems to acquire a motive of its own for its continuation. Karl Bühler, commenting on the development of language in children, has, you will recall, proposed the concept of *Funktionslust*—pleasure derived from the exercise of a newly developed function or skill. Donald Hebb and Robert White (whose views we visited in an earlier

essay) more recently have suggested that there seems to be an intrinsic pleasure or self-reward in gaining competence that feeds upon itself in the sense that the development of taste leads to increasing development of taste. How important this is in cultivating a taste for discovering we have already seen. It may well be that early sensory and intellectual deprivation prevents the kind of intellectual and emotional unfolding that nourishes early learning and makes later learning possible.

Compensation schedules. Finally, there is the thorny question of whether pay and its withholding is much of an instrument for the control of human behavior. For a psychologist this is unfamilar ground except insofar as rewards and punishments meted out in the training of laboratory animals and laboratory humans (by which I mean human beings made to respond in situations designed for animal response) are analogous to monetary or other forms of compensation and discipline. It is certainly plain that people can be paid for doing things, threatened with punishment if they do not do them, bribed, lured, or seduced by material rewards. Pay people adequately and reduce the noxious features of their work situation to a certain minimum and, in the main, they will do the job you hire them to do. A huge amount of the world's behavior is undoubtedly controlled in this way, notably in Western society. It constitutes a contractual arrangement where, in exchange for money or goods or prestige, an individual will sell to you the right to control his behavior within certain limits and for certain hours during a day. On the whole the system appears to work adequately.

This is all very well and may be just what it seems, but the startling thing to a psychologist is that the universal efficacy of the system is accepted so largely as a matter of faith. Not long ago I talked with the executive who designed and administers the compensation plan for an American corporation that hires about a third of a million employees. The company in question is enlightened, pays well, and gives large incen-

tives to its workers and managers to shoot high. But the conversation was oddly disillusioning. What struck me and what the executive openly confessed worry over was the lack of any systematic work on the extent to which money and other kinds of pay form a satisfying compensation for individual workers—what economists speak of as the utility function for the forms of pay. This particular company operates on the principle that for all supervisory personnel within any given level there should be a wide range in salary, an "incentive" range of at least 35 percent above the base rate. I asked the theory behind it and, while I was given an interesting rule-of-thumb answer, it was not one based on a study of what increases in compensation do for productivity or human satisfaction. I have mentioned compensation rates as a problem here largely because such a universal form of controlling behavior should be better understood from the psychological point of view. Economics, like any other field in the social sciences, is too important to leave entirely to its own practitioners.

All of which is not to say that compensation is not one of the great controlling factors in modern life. Rather, what strikes me is that once one is above some sort of minimum subsistence level—as all affluent societies are—the meaning of compensation ceases to have an "economic" significance in a narrow sense and takes on a symbolic significance in the broadest and haziest sense. In America, if one should ask a cross-section of workers whether they are earning enough money, most of them would look at the interrogator incredulously. Of course not. Yet we do not understand what the threshold of satisfaction in pay is, expressed in monetary terms.

Let me suggest, partly in a playful spirit, that we would do well to add a theorem to our list of theorems having to do with the economics of compensation. It is derived from a point made earlier, that supply creates demand. It might go something like this: above the subsistence level, you do not need any-

thing until you have it. That is to say, the anticipated value of money is not symmetrical with the value attached to the same amount of money once possessed and then lost. If one can say this for money, it can be said equally well for commodities or activities.

The theorem is based on the observation that to be deprived of an activity or of a habitual item of consumption is more disruptive of behavior than merely to want an activity or a thing that one has not had. We want any number of things and adjust with humor to our wants. But remove or diminish something around which we have organized a pattern of life, and a massive defense reaction is put into being.

Why should this be so psychologically? I think we have come upon part of the answer in what has already been discussed. Loss or reduction of compensation symbolizes withdrawal of support, a form of ostracism. So too with the symbolism of not being rewarded by raises at the same rate as those who appear to be doing the same work as you do. The traditional bitterness of the passed-over captain in our Navy is no exception. But beyond the symbolic spread of loss and reduction in compensation, there is one other powerful factor that operates. It is the stabilizing and simplifying role of expectation and habit in our daily lives—a subject about which William James wrote so brilliantly in his famous chapter on "Habit." Allport's doctrine of the functional autonomy of motives points in the same direction.

The implications of our hypothesis, and it should of course be treated as a very tentative one, is that economic affluence creates the condition for the use of compensation as a technique of blackmail—a most abhorrent conclusion. If indeed it is the case that the power of a system of compensation is the withdrawal of support from those who have become used to support, then the instrument of compensation (or, better, decompensation) is a powerful weapon for exacting compliance.

The great corporation of which we spoke, with its system of maintaining high variability from a base rate in paying its executives, is famous for the tensions and ulcers among them—and also for their efficiency. The techniques for beneficent blackmail, defined in terms of company objectives, are well built in. Money rewards (taken in the broadest sense) do not very likely operate as a simple utility function with effort or efficiency increasing as a function of increments in pay. A great deal of human behavior is indeed controlled by the contractual arrangement of wages, with services performed for money. But, in fact, the money or goods involved do not in themselves seem to do much by way of controlling the behavior. Rather, the nature of the job itself appears to provide the pattern of control. One gets a job as a mailman and one "behaves mailman," or if one is hired as a professor, one behaves that way. In time one develops what the French have long called *une déformation professionnelle,* a set of habits and outlooks to match the requirements of the job. One also develops an expectancy of support. To assure that the behaving is "professor" or "mailman" we use the coercive technique of withdrawal or reduction in support.

I would end with a conjecture about the control of human behavior. A colleague and friend has for some years been studying the social psychology of flattery. He distinguishes between normative and exploitative flattery—the former being the usual good manners involved in praising worthy efforts, the latter being perhaps too familiar to need much definition. He remarks that one of the costs of seeking to control others by flattery is that you forfeit an enormous amount of freedom in your own activity—who is controlled more by the flattery cycle, the flatterer or the flattered? So it is with control generally. The garrison state, the totalitarian state, the coercive institution all have it in common that they forfeit enormous resources to the maintenance of control. We have been con-

cerned with control in a democratic society. The guiding rule in such societies cannot be how to obtain maximum or even optimum control of human behavior, including now the most heinous forms of behavior. Rather, the question is how one obtains the necessary control while preserving the necessary variability that permits change, innovation, zest, and a lively sense that the invention of new alternatives is more important than the suppression of ones that may prove ugly.

Freud and the Image of Man

By the dawn of the sixth century before Christ, the Greek physicist-philosophers had formulated a bold conception of the physical world as a unitary material phenomenon. The Ionics had set forth a conception of matter as fundamental substance, transformation of which accounted for the myriad forms and substances of the physical world. Anaximander was subtle enough to recognize that matter must be viewed as a generalized substance, free of any particular sensuous properties. Air, iron, water, or bone were only elaborated forms, derived from a more general stuff. Since that time, the phenomena of the physical world have been conceived as continuous and monistic, as governed by the common laws of matter. The view was a bold one, bold in that it ran counter to the immediate testimony of the senses. It has served as an axiomatic basis of physics for more than two millennia. The bold view eventually became the obvious view, and it gave shape to our common understanding of the physical world. Even the alchemists rested their case upon this doctrine of material continuity and, indeed, they might even have hit upon the proper philosopher's stone.

The good fortune of the physicist—and these matters are always relative, for the material monism of physics may have impeded nineteenth-century thinking and delayed insights into the nature of complementarity in modern physical theory—this early good fortune or happy insight has no counterpart in the

sciences of man. Lawful continuity between man and the animal kingdom, between dreams and unreason on one side and waking rationality on the other, between madness and sanity, between consciousness and unconsciousness, between primitive and civilized man—each of these has been a cherished discontinuity preserved in doctrinal canons. There were voices in each generation, to be sure, urging the exploration of continuities. Anaximander had a passing good approximation to a theory of evolution based on natural selection; Cornelius Agrippa offered a plausible theory of the continuity of mental health and disease in terms of bottled-up sexuality. But Anaximander did not prevail against Greek conceptions of man's creation nor did Cornelius Agrippa against the demonopathy of the *Malleus Maleficarum*. Neither in establishing the continuity between the varied states of man nor in pursuing the continuity between man and animal was there conspicuous success until the nineteenth century.

I need not insist upon the social, ethical, and political significance of this image, for it is patent that the view one takes of man affects profoundly one's standard of what is humanly possible. And it is by the measure of such a standard that we establish our laws, set our aspirations for learning, and judge the fitness of men's acts. It is no surprise, then, that those who govern must perforce be jealous guardians of man's ideas about man, for the structure of government rests upon an uneasy consensus about human nature and human wants. The idea of man is of the order of *res publica*, and, by virtue of its public status, it is an idea that is not subject to change without public debate. The behavioral scientist, as some insist on calling him, may propose, but it is the society at large that disposes. Nor is it simply a matter of public concern. For man as individual has a deep and emotional investment in his image of himself. If we have learned anything in the last half century of psychology, it is that man has powerful and exquisite

capacities for defending himself against violations of his cherished self-image. This is not to say that Western man has not persistently asked: "What is man that thou art mindful of him?" It is only that the question, when pressed, brings us to the edge of anxiety where inquiry is no longer free.

Two figures stand out massively as the architects of our present-day conception of man: Darwin and Freud. Freud's was the more daring, the more revolutionary, and, in a deep sense, the more poetic insight. But Freud is inconceivable without Darwin.

Rear-guard fundamentalism did not require a Darwin to slay it in an age of technology. He helped, but this contribution was trivial in comparison with another. What Darwin did was to propose a set of principles unified around the conception that all organic species had their origins and took their form from a common set of circumstances—the requirements of biological survival. All living creatures were on a common footing. When the post-Darwin era of exaggeration had passed and religious literalism had abated into a new nominalism, what remained was a broad, orderly, and unitary conception of organic nature, a vast continuity from the monocellular protozoans to man. Biology had at last found its unifying principle in the doctrine of evolution. Man was not unique but the inheritor of an organic legacy.

As the summit of an evolutionary process, man could still view himself with smug satisfaction, indeed proclaim that God or Nature had shown a persistent wisdom in its effort to produce a final, perfect product. It remained for Freud to present the image of man as the unfinished product of nature: struggling against unreason, impelled by driving inner vicissitudes and urges that had to be contained if man were to live in society, host alike to seeds of madness and majesty, never fully free from an infancy that was anything but innocent.

What Freud was proposing was that man at best and at worst is subject to a common set of explanations: good and evil grow from a common process.

Freud was strangely yet appropriately fitted for his role as architect of a new conception of man. His qualifications are worth examining, for the image of man that he created was in no small measure founded on his painfully achieved image of himself and of his times. We are concerned not so much with his psychodynamics as with the intellectual traditions he embodies. A child of his century's materialism, he was wedded to the determinism and the classical physicalism of nineteenth-century physiology so boldly represented by Helmholtz. Indeed, the young Freud's devotion to the exploration of anatomical structures was a measure of the strength of this inheritance. But at the same time, as both Lionel Trilling and W. H. Auden have recognized with such sensitivity, there was a deep current of romanticism in Freud—a sense of the role of impulse, of the drama of life, of the power of symbolism, of ways of knowing that were more poetic than rational in spirit, of the poet's cultural alienation. It was perhaps this romantic sense of drama that led to his gullibility about parental seduction alleged by his first female patients and to his generous susceptibility to the fallacy of the dramatic instance.

Freud also embodies two traditions almost as antithetical as romanticism and nineteenth-century scientism. He was profoundly a Jew, not in a doctrinal sense but in his conception of morality, in his love of the skeptical play of reason, in his distrust of illusion, in the form of his prophetic talent, even in his conception of mature eroticism. His prophetic talent was antithetical to a utopianism either of innocence or of social control. Nor did it lead to a counsel of renunciation. Free oneself of illusion, of neurotic infantilism, and "the soft voice of intellect" would prevail. Wisdom for Freud was neither doctrine nor formula but the achievement of maturity. The patient who is cured is the one who is free enough of neurosis to

decide intelligently about his own destiny. As for his conception of mature love, it has always seemed to me that its blend of tenderness and sensuality combined the uxorious imagery of the Hasidic tradition and the sensual quality of the Song of Songs. And might it not have been Freud rather than a commentator of the Haftorahs who said, "In children, it was taught, God gives humanity a chance to make good its mistakes"? The modern trend of permissiveness toward children is surely a feature of the Freudian legacy.

But for all his Hebraic quality, Freud is also in the classical tradition—combining the Stoics and the great Greek dramatists. For Freud as for the Stoics, there is no possibility of man's disobeying the laws of nature. And yet for him it is in this lawfulness that the human drama inheres. His love for Greek drama and his use of it in his formulations are patent. The sense of the human tragedy, the inevitable working out of the human plight—these are the hallmarks of Freud's case histories. When Freud, the tragic dramatist, becomes a therapist, it is not to intervene as a directive authority. The therapist enters the drama of the patient's life, makes possible a play within a play, the transference, and when the patient has "worked through" and understood the drama, he has achieved the wisdom necessary for freedom. Again, like the Stoics, it is in the recognition of one's own nature and in the acceptance of the laws that govern it that the good life is to be found.

Freud's contribution lies in the continuities of which he made us aware. The first of these is the continuity of organic lawfulness. Accident in human affairs was no more to be brooked as "explanation" than was accident in nature. The basis for accepting such an obvious proposition had, of course, been well prepared by a burgeoning nineteenth-century scientific naturalism. It remained for Freud to extend naturalistic explanation to the heart of human affairs. The *Psychopathology of Everyday Life* is not one of Freud's deeper works, but "the

Freudian slip" has contributed more to the common acceptance of lawfulness in human behavior than perhaps any of the more rigorous and academic formulations from Wundt to the present. The forgotten lunch engagement, the slip of the tongue, the barked shin could no longer be dismissed as accident. Why Freud should have succeeded where novelists, philosophers, and academic psychologists had failed we shall consider in a moment.

Freud's extension of Darwinian doctrine beyond Haeckel's theorem that ontogeny recapitulates phylogeny is another contribution to continuity. It is the conception that, in the human mind, the primitive, the infantile, and the archaic exist side by side with the civilized and the evolved:

> Where animals are concerned we hold the view that the most highly developed have arisen from the lowest. . . . In the realm of mind, on the other hand, the primitive type is so commonly preserved alongside the transformations which have developed out of it that it is superfluous to give instances in proof of it. When this happens, it is usually the result of a bifurcation in development. One quantitative part of an attitude or an impulse has survived unchanged while another has undergone further development. This brings us very close to the more general problem of conservation in the mind. . . . Since the time when we recognized the error of supposing that ordinary forgetting signified destruction or annihilation of the memory-trace, we have been inclined to the opposite view that nothing once formed in the mind could ever perish, that everything survives in some way or other, and is capable under certain conditions of being brought to light again.[1]

What has now come to be common sense is that there is the potentiality for criminality in every man, and that these are neither accidents nor visitations of degeneracy, but products of a delicate balance of forces that under different circumstances might have produced normality or even saintliness. Good and evil, in short, grow from a common root.

Freud's genius was in his resolution of polarities. The distinction of child and adult was one. It did not suffice to

[1] *Civilization and Its Discontents* (London: Hogarth Press, 1930), pp. 14–15.

reiterate that the child was father to the man. The theories of infantile sexuality and the stages of psychosexual development were an effort to fill the gap, the latter clumsy, the former elegant. Though the alleged progression of sexual expression from oral, to anal, to phallic, to genital has not found a secure place either in common sense or in general psychology, the developmental continuity of sexuality has been recognized by both. Common sense honors the continuity in the baby-books and in the permissiveness with which young parents of today resolve their doubts. And the research of Beach and others has shown the profound effects of infantile experience on adult sexual behavior—even in lower organisms.

If today people are reluctant to report their dreams with the innocence once attached to such recitals, it is again because Freud brought into common question the discontinuity between the rational purposefulness of waking life and the seemingly irrational purposelessness of fantasy and dream. While the crude symbolism of Freud's early efforts at dream interpretation has come increasingly to be abandoned, the conception of the dream as representing disguised wishes and fears has become common coin. And Freud's recognition of deep unconscious processes in the creative act has gone far toward enriching our understanding of the kinship between the artist, the humanist, and the man of science.

It is our heritage from Freud that the all-or-none distinction between mental illness and mental health has been replaced by a more humane conception of the continuity of these states. The view that neurosis is a severe reaction to human trouble is as revolutionary in its implications for social practice as it is daring in formulation. The "bad seed" theories, the nosologies of the nineteenth century, the demonologies and doctrines of divine punishment—none of these provided a basis for compassion toward human suffering like that of our time.

One may argue, finally, that Freud's sense of the continuity of human conditions, of the universality of the human pre-

dicament, has made possible a deeper sense of the brotherhood of man. It has in any case tempered the spirit of punitiveness toward what once we took as evil and what we now see as sick. We have not yet resolved the dilemma posed by these two ways of viewing: its resolution is one of the great moral challenges of our age.

Why, after such initial resistance, were Freud's views so phenomenally successful in transforming common conceptions of man?

One reason we have already considered: the readiness of the Western world to accept a naturalistic explanation of organic phenomena and, concurrently, to be more prepared for such an explanation in the mental sphere. There had been at least four centuries of uninterrupted scientific progress, finally capped by a theory of evolution that brought man into continuity with the rest of the animal kingdom. The rise of naturalism was a way of understanding nature, and man saw a corresponding decline in the explanatory aspirations of religion. By the close of the nineteenth century, religion, to quote Morton White, "too often agreed to accept the role of a non-scientific spiritual grab-bag, or an ideological know-nothing." Elucidation of the human condition had been abandoned by religion and not yet adopted by science.

It was the inspired imagery, the prototheory of Freud, that was to fill the gap. Success in transforming the common conception of man did not come simply from adopting the cause-and-effect discourse of science. Rather it is Freud's imagery, I think, that provides the clue to his ideological power. It is an imagery of necessity, an imagery that combines the dramatic, the tragic, and the scientific views of necessity. It is here that Freud's is a theory or a prototheory peopled with actors. The characters are from life: the blind, energetic, pleasure-seeking id; the priggish and punitive superego; the ego, battling for its being by diverting the energy of the others to

its own use. The drama has economy and terseness. The ego develops canny mechanisms for dealing with the threat of id impulses: denial, projection, and the rest. Balances are struck among the actors, and in this balance are character and neurosis. Freud was using the dramatic technique of decomposition, where the actors are parts of a single life—a technique that he himself had recognized in fantasies and dreams, one which is honored in his essay, "The Poet and the Daydream," and which we have had occasion to discuss earlier.

The imagery of the theory, moreover, has an immediate resonance with the dialectic of experience. True, it is not the stuff of superficial conscious experience. But it fits the human dilemma, its conflict, its private torment, its impulsiveness, its secret and frightening urges, its tragic quality.

In its scientific imagery, the theory is marked by the necessity of the classical mechanics. At times the imagery is hydraulic: suppress one stream of impulses and it breaks out in a displacement elsewhere. The system is closed and mechanical, at times electrical, as when cathexes are formed and withdrawn like electrical charges. Such a way of thought accorded well with the common-sense physics of its age.

Finally, the image of man presented was thoroughly secular; its ideal type was the mature man free of infantile neuroticism, capable of finding his own way. This freedom from both utopianism and asceticism has earned Freud the contempt of ideological totalitarians of the right and the left. But the image has found a ready home in the rising liberal intellectual middle class. For them, the Freudian ideal type has become a rallying point in the struggle against spiritual regimentation.

I have said almost nothing about Freud's equation of sexuality and impulse. That equation surely was and still is a stimulus to resistance. But to say that Freud's success lay in forcing a reluctant Victorian world to accept the importance of sexuality is as empty as it is to hail Darwin for his victory over fundamentalism. Each had a far more profound effect.

Can Freud's contribution to the common understanding of man in the twentieth century be likened to the impact of such great physical and biological theories as Newtonian physics and Darwinian evolution? The question is an empty one. Freud's mode of thought is not a theory in the conventional sense; it is a metaphor, an analogy, a way of conceiving man, a drama. I would propose that Anaximander is the proper parallel: his view of the connectedness of physical nature was also an analogy, and a powerful one. Freud's work is the ground from which theory will grow, and he has prepared the twentieth century to nurture the growth. But, far more important, he has provided an image of man that has made him comprehensible without at the same time making him contemptible.

Fate and the Possible

Through history, man's notions about fate have corresponded to his changing ideas about himself. By setting forth some propositions about man's present conception of himself and his world and examining them closely, we may perhaps be able to draw some conclusions about the role of fate in an age of science.

1. A first proposition might be put this way. Man does not deal directly with nature; nature is a symbolic construct, a creature of man's powers to represent experience through powerful abstractions. As Ernst Cassirer might put it, man lives in a symbolic world of his own collective creation, a symbolic world that has as one of its principal functions the ordering and explication of experience. A change in one's conception of the world involves not simply a change in what one encounters but also in how one translates it.

2. Man's image of himself, perforce, is not independent of his image of the world. *Weltanschauung* places limits on and gives shape to *Selbstanschauung*. For it is characteristic of man not only that he creates a symbolic world but also that he then becomes its servant by conceiving of his own powers as limited by the powers he sees outside himself.

3. Perhaps the chief vehicle in the relation between man's subjective sense of himself and his sense of the world of nature is the idea of fate. Fate is that which is beyond one's control; it is an outer limit.

4. The inverse of fate is the sense of potency—what we

think is possible for us. That is to say, our view of fate shapes our sense of potency, and vice versa. Fate is the residuum that is left after one has run through the census of what is humanly possible. Each discovery of a way of proceeding, of a way of discovering, forestalling, or effecting, is, then, an incursion into fate that in effect rolls back what we take fate to be. There may one day be a beautiful formula that goes something like this: $e = p/f$, where e is the sense of human effectiveness, p the value of all outcomes thought to be determined by human effort, and f the value of all outcomes thought to be determined by fate.

5. The degree to which a society elaborates a technology determines the amount of division of labor in the society. The rationale of a technology is that its tools are not such that each individual can be equipped with a full set of them. With technological advance more things are possible, but social and technical organization is increasingly necessary to bring them off. In effect, then, the sense of potency—the idea of the possible—increases in scope, but the artificer of the possible is now society rather than the individual.

6. And one final proposition. Man's working image of himself is anchored in his sense of intimacy—in the events and relations that are the fabric of his immediate experience and make up his way of life. Change in the individual is a function of how much and in what manner an intimate way of life is altered.

Before exploring the consequences of these premises, there should be a word about the psychological structure of fate. At one extreme we may speak of a peopled fate, a realm over which one has no control, where purposeful and personalized forces operate. Dodds has given us a searching examination of the peopled fate of the classic Greeks in his *The Greeks and the Irrational.* At the other extreme is the view of fate as embodied in mathematical statistics and statistical mechanics. Fate is here equated with a conception of residual variance—the set of all remaining causes that cannot be accounted for

because of ignorance or, if all were known, pure unknowable randomness. The secular view of fate pits man as a systematic and controlling intelligence against ignorance and chaos. The religious view of fate pits man against a pantheon of controlling spirits.

In tracing the impact of science on man's image of himself, we might remind ourselves of the series of psychological upsets that served, presumably, to diminish that image. The fall of the heliocentric universe pushed man from the center of things, relegating him to a position on one of the satellites orbiting around a not very major star. The emergence of understanding about electricity and magnetism made it clear that one could no longer conceive of energy solely in the analogy of the human arm. The doctrine of evolution is said to have robbed man of his image of himself as unique. And within our own generation, Freud's insights have questioned man's rationalistic vanity in a degree comparable to the onslaught that nuclear fission and fusion have made on man's remaining sense of safety against annihilation by forces that are uncontrollable once freed.

Yet, if we look at the last century and man's changing image of himself, obviously we do not find man cringing before a swollen, chaotic fate. The style of the West, the style of the newly emerging states—with Nigeria's scheduling of the opening of five schools a month over a ten-year period—and even the style of the two most powerful Communist states are premised upon widely expanded conceptions of the possible: the technologically possible and the humanly possible. When one looks more deeply, there are new strains, to be sure, new forms of helplessness, new ways of defining incapacity. A modern Job might come to terms with the death of a child as science's failure to prevent this particular disease or death. But new also is the form of grief that leads one to give to a research institution so that others may be saved from dying senselessly.

There appear to be three loci of change that should be considered in discussing our propositions. The first is in the transition that occurs as man alters his image of fate and preempts the powers that were before seen as fateful. A second lies in the process of depersonalizing fate. Finally, there is change in the recognition that a scientific technology involves increasing dependence upon specialism within the society.

Perhaps the deepest but quietest change over the last century has been in man's view of himself as an intelligence. To put it more accurately, the change is less in his view of himself than in his conception of men as knowers, of their collective product, science. The idea of discovery as a result of engineered tinkering has given way to the concept of science as an enterprise of thinking—imperfectly understood, to be sure, but intuitively appreciated. The archetype of Edison as ingenious inventor has been replaced by one of Einstein as powerful thinker. The philosophical crises of our university seminars—Gödel's theorem of the inevitable paradox that is generated by any self-contained system of propositions, the principle of complementarity wherein certain forms of knowledge canonically exclude others, and the logico-linguistic relativities of Wittgenstein's "word games"—are finding their way into common sense and understanding as surely as did Newton's conceptions.

What has emerged as a result of this ferment is a reflective concern with the nature of knowledge and with the forms of intelligence that make knowledge possible. Indeed, out of our philosophical and scientific understanding of the informational processes we have created a new technology for the use of artificial intelligence as executed by computer programs. Not only have we reduced random fatefulness in industrial technology; we have delegated the policing of it to machine processes conceived of not as an extension of our arm but as an extension of our intelligence.

The depersonalization of fate is so deeply part of the history of the Western trend toward secularism that it cannot be treated apart from it. It is in the collapse of transcendental doctrines that we see the effects most clearly. In the first instance, there was the discomfort and disruption that came with the passing of religious absolutes, with the weakening of canons of absolute truth and goodness. Since then, it is interesting that we have either sought new guidance in the form of ersatz secular absolutes or have moved toward an intrinsic definition of the good and the beautiful from "inside out." There has been the secular absolutism of the right, with its deification of the state and racial destiny and with its genocide. On the equally absolute left, there has been the sanctification of a Marxist-Hegelian doctrine of historical inevitability, an inevitability that needed the support of police methods. Both solutions have been violently anti-intellectual, opposed to the definition of ideals in terms of individual reason and individual compassion. In the center, the effort has been to find a conception of rightness in an examination of the nature of man, to seek a humane ethic based not on an economic or political or religious view of man but on a psychological one.

There is perhaps no more meaningful index of this change than the manner in which we view children and their education. In one century we have moved from the moralism of McGuffey and his *Readers* to, and perhaps beyond, the child-centered and sometimes mawkish compassion of Dewey. It is Freud who gives the text: effectiveness is not a product of utopia but rests upon insight into the human condition. Indeed, the reform movement we see in American education today, the cultivation of individual excellence as an ideal, again moves from the inside out. It is an attempt to roll back fate through the increase of intellectual potency.

Finally, there is the revolution in society and economy that sprang from a century of technological and scientific innovation. The century has seethed with innovations in imagery,

efforts to find a new balance between a conception of society and a conception of man. We have witnessed new patterns of socialist organization and ideology in which social welfare has been converted from a political slogan into a difficult and not altogether consistent principle of administrative planning. Capitalism has altered its stance from the romanticism of perfect economic competition to a doctrine of public-service oligopoly. It would be difficult to infer from the British White Paper of 1925 on colonial education what in fact happened after the Second World War in Britain's wisely subtle liquidation of her overseas empire.

We are groping toward an arrangement of our industrial society, and the advent of automation makes the outcome unclear. The steady American trend over the past half century has been toward a universal middle class, with increasingly equal access to consumer goods made possible by steadily rising incomes falling within an ever narrower range. The prevailing ideal in this middle-class enterprise is "good management," a modestly activist image based again on confidence in the application of trained intelligence. We are as much shocked at Belgium's poor management of the transition in the Congo as we are by her earlier attitude of exploitation. It is perhaps most characteristic of our national enterprise that the concept of management rather than a doctrine of "planning" has become central. Management is planning that is subject to moment-by-moment revision by human intelligence. While it, like most emerging conceptions, is vaguely defined, its core is the exercise of decision based on human appraisal. That theories of decision making abound today is no historical accident.

Finally, what is the impact of all we have considered on the intimacy of life? Our ways have been changed not only by technology but by the new images of living that technology has made possible. Yet our taming of fate and our skills in the

management of enterprises has created malaise. We hear much of the search for identity. There has developed a wide disparity between our sense of what is possible and the private ways in which we live our immediate lives. The impact of the century has been powerfully and irreversibly energizing—but the sense of effectiveness, that resultant term in my mock formula for the relation of potency and fate, has not been given its full chance for expression. What we have now is a new frontier, a frontier for the full use of human beings. Perhaps I reveal my biases as a psychologist when I say that the cultivation of this frontier excites me far more than the prospects of exploring empty space.

Speaking at Massachusetts Institute of Technology in 1960, Edwin Land remarked that we had been puny in our conception of the new professions that are possible for men. Given, for example, the vast underdeveloped areas of the world, how do we arrange the use of our own human resources to bring these areas into the modern age speedily and without untoward suffering? Or, given the vast increase in knowledge in all fields of learning, how do we equip our men and women to impart that knowledge to new generations? I am not speaking of moral equivalents of war in James's sense: that is much too modest a conception. Rather, it is in developing the arts of peace that we shall find an expression for the new images that the century has produced. Until then, we shall not become the full beneficiaries of the change that science has wrought. A people who feel that they are living at the full limit of what is possible will have no crises of identity. Our challenge now is to use those portions of fate that we have taken over.

Psychology and the Image of Man

One sometimes agrees to deliver a lecture on a set theme, only to discover that the theme is not quite what one had expected. Having agreed to deliver a Herbert Spencer Lecture in Oxford on how psychology had affected common sense about man or had itself been affected by that common sense—thinking then that it would make an amusing summer interlude of historical writing—I soon discovered it would not go so easily. For once I had started on the inevitable first notes, it was plain to me that I was not embarked at all on a summer of intellectual history but on a much thornier enterprise, partly philosophical, partly psychological, and only trivially historical—trivial in the sense that it was no surprise that, in the later nineteenth century, psychology had modelled itself on those successful natural science neighbors in whose district it had decided to build its mansion, and had suffered the consequences thereafter.

I can recall my early dark thoughts. Little question, to begin with, that the most powerful impact on common sense had come from Freud. Yet Freud was, and is, peripheral to and grossly atypical of academic psychology, so much so, indeed, that apart from providing cautionary methodological tales with which to warn the unwary undergraduate, his work is not even covered in the Oxford syllabus. Or take it another way: has psychology affected issues of public concern on which it

could reasonably be expected to have a bearing, say economics? Here, surely, is a powerful mode of thought and of policy-making that treats psychological matters like risk, preference, delayed gratification in saving and investment. It even proposes notions like utility through which the values and probabilities of outcomes are assumed to combine to determine choice. Yet though economics had, in the lifetime of official psychology, been through the revolutions of Marshall, of Keynes, of Schumpeter, and of Morgenstern and van Neumann, there is not a trace of any influence exerted by psychologists. A minor exception, perhaps, is in the application of psychology to industrial relations—a not altogether successful venture at that, and one also sufficiently peripheral to psychology to be ignored (perhaps deservedly) in the syllabus of most major university departments.

And finally, since I do not wish to make too much of my initial gloomy thoughts, let me remark on the strange fact that, in recent years, the most conspicuous public voice of psychology has been radically Utopian and reductionist, motivated by the assertion that scientific psychology shows that the human enterprise is altogether wrongly conceived, that it would be better managed by human engineers than by law and that when ordinary people acted human they were muddled by notions like choice, freedom, dignity, intention, expectations, goals, and the like. B. F. Skinner, in his Herbert Spencer Lecture two years ago, implied indeed that human affairs so conceived could be shown to be "wrong" in much the same way as Copernicus had shown that the heliocentric universe was "wrong."

My winter of discontent did indeed lead me to explore the impact of psychology on common sense—and vice versa—but it lead me also to look more deeply into what might be called the interface between "expert psychology" on the one side and the common-sense views of man on the other. I was drawn to a disturbing conclusion on the matter of why experimental or

academic psychology had not had more of an impact on the broad cultural conception of the nature of man or why, perhaps, its contribution had been negatively reductionist. It was not that psychology had not yet found out enough, was not empirically advanced enough to enter the debate with authority. Rather it was the stronger conclusion that psychology had initially defined its task in such a way that it could never have had much of a direct impact, given the nature of its concepts of explanation. Its initial concerns, its theoretical orientation, its style of research were not fitted to the kinds of processes or patterns that shape human affairs as they occur in human societies: symbolic systems like language, conceptual structures in terms of which human beings carve up and interpret the world around them, and the cultural constraints imposed by human institutions were not within its terms of reference. These systems include everyday concepts like purpose, mind, responsibility, loyalty, even Cabinet responsibility—transmitted concepts that serve as the basis for human institutions like the law and economic exchange, institutions which, so to speak, provide a buffer against individual variation.

The founding contract of academic psychology was such that, in the main, these matters were ruled out as belonging elsewhere, or, more accurately, as nothing but second-order phenomena to be derived from first principles. The larger edifice of human affairs, it was felt, would be elucidated by the stones that comprised it. We had, I believe, painted ourselves into a very tight little corner where we had much control and certainty—like lower computer specialists who insist that their task is to describe the hardware and the machine language and not the properties of the programs they comprise—and the price we may have had to pay had we followed on this way would have been perpetual and justifiable modesty.

There are historical reasons why this was so, stemming from our early childhood of envy among the natural sciences and our attempts to emulate (or, better, simulate) their successes,

and I shall consider these in a moment. It seems to me that I have not exaggerated. Indeed, I am sure that there are still psychologists of the highest intelligence and good will who would insist today that the course upon which we originally embarked is a sound one for psychology, but after forty years of participating in the enterprise with mounting contrary conviction, I would be less than candid if I did not call it as I saw it. Indeed, I am encouraged to air my conclusions because I think that winds of change are blowing and that one can already sense the new course on which we are embarking.

All of this is *not* to say, please note, that psychology has not got on with it. For it certainly has. But our modest successes have all been, in a special way, *in vitro,* treating chunks of behavior out of the controlling contexts in which they ordinarily occur, even though the contexts have a massive influence over the chunks. The more rigorously isolated from context and the more tightly controlled the conditions of experiment, the more precise and the more modest the results have been. The justification of course has been that this is the traditional way to proceed in a line of inquiry called "the natural sciences," refining one's investigative procedure to a paradigm or model that is presumed to elucidate phenomena in real life. This brave and bold approach doubtless worked in physics, where the connection between controlled experiment and nature had become clear. For reasons that will concern us in a moment, it is not plain that such a program is yet suitable to psychology or will ever be. The disturbing symptom in our discipline has been its steady loss of conceptual unity. It increasingly consists of a collection of topics-cum-procedures, between which it is ever more difficult to discern workable conceptual connections. Each topic develops its paradigm and its literature, even its own heroes. Recently, Alan Allport (1975) has expressed the concern that each topic has a way of digging itself into an isolated trench, with less and less connection even with the neighboring trenches, the end of the digging being

reached not through success but boredom. Again, let me insist that this is not to say that some of the topics have not been of the greatest interest—the study of human perception being a conspicuous case of one topical success after another. But perception, on the other hand, is studied *in vitro,* and efforts to relate perception to motivation or to learning or to social behavior each begin as a new topic-cum-procedure.

Let me move on to a more detailed diagnosis of our historical difficulties, better to come to terms with what I think is needed to rescue psychology from its past and perhaps to assure it a place in the general debate on the nature of man.

Psychology paid its price of admission to the natural sciences in the nineteenth century by a tacit agreement to ban both mind and purpose from its past armamentarium of explanatory concepts. A decent nineteenth-century natural science had no truck with either mentalism or teleology. And, indeed, given the ghost-in-the-machine use of such concepts in that period, neither of them deserved a place. To anybody conversant with the history of psychology over the past century, it is surely plain that such an initial taboo could not be sustained, save in the form of an ideological preface. Mentalistic concepts were there all along—in Titchener's method of structural introspection, in concepts like 'imagery," and even in the hallowed doctrine of threshold and just-noticeable-difference. And intentionality was surely an implicit premise in theories of attention, with notions like "set" being used heuristically to deal with self-directed intentions to behave in a certain way. Indeed, we preferred to conceive of these as mental-like phenomena or purposive-like behaviors, as in Tolman's purposive behaviorism. Even the period of radical behaviorism, ushered in by J. B. Watson and now perhaps flickering to a close in the polemics of Professor Skinner, was, we should remember, accompanied by a rise of the phenomenological theories of Gestalt psychologists who, you will recall, insisted upon a distinction between man's physical or geographical environ-

ment and the effective phenomenal or behavioral environment that mediated between a world of physics and the world of experience as it affected man's conduct.

Three concerns of post-war psychology further hastened the trend away from radical behaviorism: the emergence of so-called "cognitive psychology," with massive reliance on concepts like hypothesis, strategies, expectations. Cognitive psychology soon found common cause with artificial intelligence, whose heuristic spirit was not in the least constrained by a fixation on the nineteenth century. The third hastening trend has been the arousal of interest among psychologists in the nature and use of language and other man-made rule systems.

In spite of all this, much of psychology has remained true (perhaps because there is something compelling about infantile fixation) to its early vow. We are still embarrassed by the possibility that purpose and intention will suck us back into the swamp of teleology. Mentalism and teleology are still four-letter words in psychology. And here is where the difficulty arises, I think, but in a rather surprising way.

For while we have become increasingly free of our ancient phobias about mind and purpose—most of us now being willing to treat them at least in the "as if" spirit of a heuristic—we have not altogether freed ourselves of the positivistic bias that goes with the older style of "hard-nosed" research. Let me explain more fully what I mean by this. The contrast that is relevant, I think, is between what can be called a structural approach and a point-by-point sequential approach.

Let me use as a typical example the notion of a stimulus and a response, the two of them being defined independently of each other. A light comes on or a buzzer sounds and an organism responds to it, the response again being an it. Stimuli and responses are then, in some sense, said to be connected or related, or the occurrence of a response after the appearance of a stimulus is said to change in probability by virtue of some

condition either in the stimulus presentation beforehand or in the consequences that follow the pairing, what is often called a reinforcement. Stimuli and responses have a kind of thing or event status, and each can be operationally defined—the former as a nonsense syllable or a light flash or what not; the latter, the response, of course, being an observable event like a button press or a verbal response.

Perhaps the first sign that all was not well in this positivistic heaven came as an offshoot of the theory of information, when it was shown that the nature of a stimulus could not be defined merely in centimetres, grams, and seconds, but also depended upon the ensemble of alternative stimuli that might have occurred, how many bits of information were transmitted, or more succinctly, what was the uncertainty in the event. Well, that could also be dealt with by a sleight of hand in which the set of permissible stimuli to be presented was controlled by the experimenter, and probability of occurrence could then be stated as another property of the stimulus—so that to c, g, and s could be added p. But suppose, now, the set of alternatives were not independent of each other but, rather, were part of a structure, a structure whose existence was in the head or mind of the subject, like his language and its rules. How are we to interpret the comprehension of a sentence?

Take an example from the linguist C. V. Fillmore (1971): May we come in? Is it a stimulus? Well, not really. The sentence itself appears, rather, to be a complex function which seems to be mapping a context into a proposition that "carries" a certain meaning. The elements are more like triggers than stimuli. "May" signals a speech act requesting permission and recognizes that the addressee(s) is on his own turf as defined by some code. "We" signals that one should consider contexts involving at least three participants in which at least one is the addressee, etc. "Come" indicates that the speaker and his companions want to move towards the addressee or to

where he will be when they all get there, and contrasts with "go"; it involves spatial deixis. "In" signals that the destination is enclosed, container-like—a room, a house, a pub, a sauna.

In order to translate such a sentence into a proposition one would need to know not only how the addresser and addressee organize their worlds, but also to have some hypotheses about where they might be or even what they are doing. The sentence might have been uttered by a dentist on behalf of himself and his nurse, the two poised with drill, addressing a patient open-mouthed on the chair! One could make no sense of such a sentence without taking into account the cognitive structures in terms of which the world is organized by the participants and, indeed, how language maps into those structures. The notion of a self-contained stimulus (or response) fades as, indeed, does a simple sequential account of the order of processing between input and final output. And what is the output?

Most of what humans respond to in the so-called real world has this property: without a structural description of the cognitive organization in the minds of the participants in an action, one cannot even locate, still less define the stimulus. Indeed, we have long been warned about this difficulty, even before our linguistic colleagues forced us to confront it. Was it not Sir Frederic Bartlett who argued so persuasively the impossibility of a theory of memory based on the storage and retrieval of such isolated elements as nonsense syllables? I think I have made clear enough what I intend by structure for us to go on to the next point.

It is another heritage of psychology's early alliance with nineteenth-century natural sciences that it cut itself off from considering the possibility that mental structures derive from what anthropologists call "culture": a society's set of theories, values, ways of acting, and thinking and respecting. Hoping to keep its biological base, to remain with the *Naturwissenschaften* rather than suffer the denigration of being a *Geisteswissenschaft,* psychology chose to avoid questions of how

human beings were able to operate with such complex rule systems as kinship, economic exchange, and the law, and did so in a most extraordinary way. It could keep its attention focused inside the individual skin (rather than upon the culture) by invoking a response system: call it a tendency to conform to social norms. Men had a tendency to conform, and in conformity-demanding situations normal distributions of response were transformed into J-curves. At least, two differentiable types of situations were thereby recognized, although the statistical criterion thus provided was not really used very searchingly. But then, it is not a very searching analysis of the rules of chess, or courtship, or investment, to say simply that people conform to them. As Roger Barker (1963) has been fond of pointing out, the best predicator of human behavior is a specification of where the person is: in post-offices, we *do* behave post-office.

The effects of these three historical habits that have so dogged psychology—its anti-mentalism, its tendency towards positivism of the old school, and its refusal to consider in detail how a culture patterns human action—put psychology in a curious light. It has come, in some inevitable way, to stand as a champion of reductionism, often against its will and its spirit. Partly this is because the three historical deformations are reductionist in their very nature: if you think responses are all and mind is a nonsense, if you do not take into account the structural complexity of what it is that men respond to, and if you take man to be a creature of biology tempered by a certain amount of learning, then it is a very dim picture indeed that one offers in the debate about man's nature.

But there is also something in the nature of the research we do as a result of our positivist tradition which tempts the reader of our results into reductionism. It stems from our built-in fascination with the methodology of one or at most three independent variables at a time and our delight in finding experimental situations where such small numbers of vari-

ables do account for a large part of the variance. I would offer as an example in my own field of developmental studies the extremely catastrophic experimental situations used by Harlow and his associates to demonstrate the enormous importance of terry-cloth clinging in the young rhesus monkey's attachment to a mother surrogate. Doubtless, when all else fails, terry cloth will do. But compare Harlow's results with the subtleties that have emerged from studying infant mother interactions *in situ* reported this year by the ethologist Robert Hinde in his Wolfson Lecture.

You might think that having said all that, I would now don sackcloth and ashes, resign my Watts Professorship in the University of Oxford and slink away to do penance, or perhaps battle. Not in the slightest! As I have already hinted, all is not lost. Consider my Oxford microcosm. Professor Weiskrantz is busily at work studying how certain brain lesions produce a state of "blind-sight" as he calls it, in which his patients manage to be able to supply correct answers to questions about visual events they have been presented with of which they claim to have no direct awareness. He would not blench if you congratulated him on his interesting work on the neurology of consciousness. My own work is shot through with reference to the role of intention in early language acquisition—intention as exhibited by the child and as perceived by the mother. And my distinguished colleague Dr. Broadbent is studying business games the better to understand how businessmen, civil servants, and politicians come to policy decisions. He would not stoop, I assure you, to the low-level nonsense of the leader-writer on *The Times* who found nothing more enlightening to say about the government's efforts to get hold of the sterling exchange crisis than that it was acting like Pavlov's dog now hitting the lending rate button, now the import control level, and so on.

The three of us, I suspect, are straws in the wind, and I would like to say why I think so by examining briefly how psy-

chology is coping with mind and intention, how we are faring in efforts to get hold of the structural contexts that determine the underlying significance of "stimuli," so-called, and how finally I see hope for psychology joining forces with the sciences of culture, even perhaps including economics. Having done that, I would like to pay a tribute to Freud, an appreciation of why he caught and transformed our thinking about man. Perhaps we can then assess what it takes to affect common sense.

Mind, intention, and culture. Let me look first at "mind" and "purpose" to see how these might be faring—whether psychology is addressing anything to common sense aside from spirited tracts about the non-existence of both of these in the style of the village atheist. To locate ourselves we shall need some analysis first.

I shall begin with the common sense distinction between "intended" or purposeful behavior in contrast to "caused" behavior. We say of intended action that it is carried out "for the sake of" achieving an end in mind, in contrast to caused behavior which is understood to be contingently related to a set of antecedent conditions. Typically, the cause of a behavior is determined by a method in which we control a set of antecedent conditions defined independently of the consequent behavior that the antecedents may be found to produce. When a relation is found between the antecedent and consequent, we invoke a contingent link between the two, usually in the form of a "mechanism" or "hypothetical construct." That, in any case, is the surface structure of what we do. In fact, there is much that is implicit in our selection of both the antecedent conditions, the consequent behavior, and the intervening contingent construct. For example, if it should be the case, as it most certainly would be, that the incidence of diarrhea in infants is highly correlated with the antecedent softness of asphalt highways, we would immediately recognize that this is an "empty correlation" and we would look for a

more sensible link between antecedent and consequent, like the temperature limits for the culturing of a relevant baccilus. "Theories" are what provide the causal glue between antecedents and consequents, but only certain kinds of theories.

Where the analysis of intended action is concerned, the principal objection is, of course, that to invoke intention as explanation is circular, that it explains nothing. Such explanations cannot help in the search for antecedents. But is the use of intention limited in this way? Antecedents and consequents must obviously be defined independently lest one become involved in the dizzy enterprise against which Hume warned us of defining the antecedent by the consequent, and vice versa. "Why did he attend Congregation?" "Because he wanted to." "Because he did." Plainly, explanation of the antecedent why of behavior gets nowhere by this route.

But now, let me pose two questions about explanation by cause and description by intention. The first is a question of distinguishability, the second of consequentialness. I shall be crude, I am not a philosopher. But psychologists trying to get their house in order must use philosophical analysis, and therefore, you will hear overtones (probably out of tune) of G. E. M. Anscombe, Quine, John Searle, Charles Taylor, and Rom Harre. If Wittgenstein was right, that the philosopher's task is to help the fly out of the bottle, I can only hope there will be a Wittgenstein in the wings.

I begin with the well-known example of two utterances that are both distinguishable and differ widely in their consequences: one is "I am going to take a walk," and the other, "I am going to be sick." The first implies that something is under my control as an agent. The latter implies a prediction made on the basis of antecedent sensations, and agency is not implied. In the first utterance, a noncontingent link is implied between intention and action. If a contingent link were intended, I would have said something like "The chances are I am going to take a walk," which would be an appropriate reply to the

question, "What do you think you will be doing next Sunday morning?" Now, the category distinction between actions implying intention and behaviors that do not is made all the time in all languages, all cultures, and is irresistible. I am ignoring for the moment whether, in Professor Skinner's curious sense, it is pre-copernican or "wrong" as a description, for that at present is irrelevant. The distinction is made and it is a compelling feature of man's experience.

As Mrs. Anscombe is at pains to point out, the consequences of the distinction are serious. Failure to do what one said one would do is, in the case of intentional actions, interpretable as lying (though extenuating circumstances are recognized). Failure in the second case is interpretable only as a mistake, unless one reinterprets the statement to be an intentional effort to deceive, but then it is relocated in the first category. At this point, very different consequences in terms of the behavior of others toward the speaker can be expected. Different Gricean cooperative principles apply. Mistakes are expected: lies are not. The first produce disappointment, the second indignation.

Now we may note that both lying and mistake-making are also amenable to analysis by antecedents: the liar may be more likely to be the child of a broken home: the mistake-maker may have undergone permissive schooling, but that is not the issue. The issue, rather, is whether the act in question was experienced as a lie or a mistake, whether something is or is not intentional. If the latter, if an intention is carried out, no further questioning need be asked.

For it is taken as axiomatic by human beings that what we do is congruent with what we intend to do. Only the exceptions require analysis. When intention is not carried out, contingency is not permitted as extenuating. Intention and execution are assumed to be structurally linked. Extenuating circumstances for an unfulfilled intention are either changed intention—"I decided not to go for a walk when I heard that lions were loose in the park," or alien forces—"I was locked into my room." There

is no objective test available for determining whether a "real" intention exists in the person who proclaims it. Intentions are inferred or attributed on the basis of conventional contexts and their recognition conditions depend upon what, in contemporary philosophical jargon, is known as "uptake." To describe an intention and the action on behalf of it is to give a structural description of an event as it is interpreted by the participants.

It is much as with a speech act. The intention implied in a speech act does not cause the procedures that are used in its execution, whether syntactic or semantic. But as Searle properly notes, the role of these in the meaning of the sentence cannot be analyzed without attributing an intent to the act: to inform, to warn, to praise, etc. If one says, "Would you be so kind as to pass the salt?" the constituents are to be understood in terms of a request that is made contrastive to a command, and not to be understood in terms of what it appears to be on the surface: a question about the limits of the addressee's compassion. The effort is to define the structure of a set of constituents in an act. And that is what we do when we assign an act to an intention structure.

The argument, thus far, is simply that human beings can and irresistibly do distinguish certain acts of their fellow men as intentional, that we see others as having something in mind and behaving on behalf of what they have in mind. Our response towards them and their acts is sharply affected by whether we categorize it as intentional. The argument extends beyond that. It would be a vain enterprise to explain or even to discuss the causes of any human behavior without taking into account whether or not intention had been attributed. At least where social or transactional behavior is concerned, even the causal chain between antecedent and consequent must contain an account of how the participants categorized each other's acts.

What all this suggests, at the very least, is that we adopt "the

perception of intention" and "the perception of mindfulness" as topics for research. We could at least find out what "cues" lead us to "see" certain behaviors as intentional acts or as leading to the inference that somebody or some thing is in possession of a "mind." Let it be said immediately that there is a flourishing "topic" in psychology, inspired by Fritz Heider (1958), that deals with just this issue, called "attribution theory." A recent incisive review by E. E. Jones (1976) suggests that there is indeed pay dirt here. Not surprisingly, people do distinguish between action caused by circumstances and action caused by intent, and with devastating consequences for their evaluation of what they have observed. To illustrate, when they themselves are involved in a situation, they are much more likely to see their own behavior as a result of circumstances. When they observe others, they see the action as produced by intention (when it is conventional or expected) or by quirky dispositional traits steering intention (when the behavior is unconventional or unexpected).

"Actors attribute to situations what observers attribute to actors" appear to be one conclusion. But the general conclusion from this work is that "Behavior belongs to the person: the 'field' acts on everyone." Yet the research has not really found the so-called cues by which the inference of intent is made. For, in fact, there are no simple cues in the conventional sense. What is involved is a structural inference, based on a constellation of events. In this sense, it is precisely as in linguistics. What is the cue by which we recognize a dependent clause or an imbedding? It is not marked by parentheses or tree diagrams, but inferred from the understanding of the rules of a sentence.

Stimulus and the anticipated input. I commented on the fact that the inference of intent was at once ubiquitous, universal, and irresistible. And indeed, one could go on to explore the biological roots of such perceptions. Heider and Simmel long ago produced an animated film involving the movement of

squares, triangles, and circles which is compelling seen as animate figures involved in a scenario of intent, much as Michotte has a like film for inanimate causality. There is little question that intention movements in lower organisms trip off appropriate, goal-linked behavior in their conspecifics, and Menzel (1974) has recently shown the manner in which young chimpanzees use the direction of locomotion of a better informed animal to guide their own search for a hidden reward object. Indeed the past two decades of research in neuro-physiology suggest that there is a feed-forward mechanism in neural functioning by which to put it metaphorically, an about-to-occur action is transmitted by an efference copy of that action around the nervous system. As von Holst and Mittelstaedt (1950) put it nearly thirty years ago, input stimuli do not impinge upon a neutral organism, but are processed by a comparator against anticipated input—the monkey knows when his hand is being shaken by a stick and when he is shaking the stick.

The perceptual processing of the organism that yields inferences of intent seems not to be all that illusory as an account of what is going on in the nervous system. Not only is there good reason to believe that human behavior is in fact organized into acts carried out "for the sake" of achieving certain ends, but also the receptive human nervous system is ready to perceive behavior as so structured, perhaps too ready. It should follow, then, that any description on human behavior must take into account this powerful if loose program of perceptual processing if it is to predict how human beings are going to behave in an environment containing other human beings. It must do so in the same spirit as the linguist who takes into account the fact that human beings process strings of words as sentences or the student of perception who takes into account the fact that human perceivers organize input into figure-ground configurations.

But I must reiterate that societies prescribe rules and codes

based on the kinds of perceptions and inferences we have been discussing. People starve to death biologically for these codes, turn away from sexual attractions, go to war, etc. All of these domains are more or less tightly regulated by systems of roles, of rules, of exchange, etc. Increasingly, anthropologists are developing formal procedures for describing such rule systems. Increasingly, psychologists are becoming interested in how such rule systems are acquired, and it is certainly not by the conventional linking of stimuli and responses.

The implication of all that I have said is certainly not just that we consider psychological phenomena at different "levels," this one molecular, a next one molar, still another yet more molar, *ad infinitum*. It is more revolutionary than that, I think. The conclusion is that a reaction to any feature of an environment is, to use Chomsky's (1976) phrase, most likely to be "structure dependent." By structure dependency he means, and I mean, that the significance of any feature is determined by its position in a structure. The position of a piece on a chessboard, the function of a word in a sentence, a particular facial expression, the color or placement of a light, these cannot be interpreted without reference to the person's internalized rules of chess or language, the conventions he holds concerning human interaction, the traffic rules in force in his mind. To set out with even so innocently positivistic an objective as studying, say, the threshold for recognizing different colors is a surprisingly empty exercise without a notion of how colors are contextualized in the task. Some years ago, for example, Postman and I showed (1949) that the recognition threshold for the color red varied in exposure time by a full order of magnitude depending upon whether red was conventionally expected in that setting or not.

What then is the status of experiments that strip expectancy down to a level, say, of chromatic equiprobability? It is said that by so doing one obtains a "neutral" situation which permits one to explore the basic "color discrimination" mecha-

nism. What is basic in this context? Well, it turns out to be the case under fairly simple conditions that the recognizability of colors to which one has been previously exposed is a function of their linguistic codability—roughly the number of elements in the linguistic description required to differentiate them from other colors in the array presented. Are not linguistic codability and expectancy as basic to a theory of color perception and color recognition as the spectral composition of the input?

It would seem to me—and this is very much in the spirit of the late Egon Brunswik—that the task of psychology as an experimental discipline is to investigate representative settings in which phenomena are contextualized in order to come anywhere near approximating what might be called a systematic description of ordinary behavior. If it cannot do this, it cannot achieve generality. But far worse than that. It risks ending up peddling paradigms designed more for narrow nicety than for descriptive or explanatory power, as in theories of learning where attentional factors are minimized to a point approaching zero, and where, it would seem, context and materials are designed for achieving maximum experimental control rather than representativeness.

My emphasis on structure sensitivity in "natural" situations leads me to look for leads in linguistics. For I admire linguistics not only for its willingness to look at natural, ordinary behavior—speaking of comprehending ordinary speech—but for its aim of describing the banal and the ordinary systematically. If I ask a linguist about sentences, he will not insist that we confine our discussion to the movements of lips, tongue, and glottis. If I ask him about reading, he will not go on about cross-modal matching. Chomsky, in his recent *Reflections on Language*, has an interesting point to make. He begins with what he chooses to call "science making," the manner in which people ordinarily put knowledge together. In some domains, this human capacity appears to be extraordinarily powerful, as in the creating of

physical sciences and mathematics, in other domains rather feeble, as in matters involving people exercising their will.

Science making, whether lay-modest or grand, depends upon a human capacity to make structure-sensitive distinctions and to do so easily, immediately, and with a minimum of prior tuition on the point at issue. There is, as always with Chomsky, an insistence that the capacity involved is innate, by which he means that certain capacities are species specific, including the human capacity to organize knowledge in a human way—with which I find no quarrel. One of these natural capacities is, of course, the faculty to proceed with astonishing speed and facility into the uses of language. He then goes on to say:

> Alongside the language faculty and interacting with it in the most intimate way is the faculty of mind that we might call "common sense understanding," a system of beliefs, expectations, and knowledge, concerning the nature and behavior of objects, their place in a system of "natural kinds," the organization of these categories, and the properties that determine the categorization of objects and the analysis of events. A general "innateness hypothesis" will also include principles that bear on the place and role of people in a social world, the nature and conditions of work, the structure of human action, will and choice, and so on. These systems may be unconscious for the most part and even beyond the reach of conscious introspection.

The starting point for Chomsky, then, would be to examine the natural ways, or better, the ecological representative ways, to use Brunswik's term, in which people look at and account for objects involved in events and how they look at and account for people and their actions.

As I read Chomsky, he is proposing that we begin our inquiry into the nature of human functioning with a structural description of ordinary knowing, to set as our goal the elucidation of those structures as we find them. It is the ordinariness of the enterprise that appeals to me. For it is just such ordinariness that has so often been lost from psychology in its efforts to deal positivistically with isolated variables. It is

what has led us in the past to get stuck in little trenches labelled "serial position curve" when the intent was to study memory. This is changing. It is not that we had to build upon the dreary, pioneering studies of Ebbinghaus on the rote learning of nonsense syllables, but to escape, to run away from our adoptive home. The study of memory like much else in psychology is beginning again to concern itself with what people ordinarily do when they remember, even with what they do to save themselves from having to remember. The study of cognition in general, with its new emphasis on natural categories, is making striking progress. Developmental psychology, as it moves away from a total reliance on narrow, single variable experiments is moving nicely, thanks in large part to the impetus given by Piaget and Vygotsky. The psychology of language and communication, the microanalysis of social psychology, all of these as they become more paradigmatic of the ordinary begin to have a broader impact within and beyond psychology. But what I also see, and I am deeply impressed by it, is the extent to which comparable structural descriptions in anthropology, sociology, linguistics and artificial intelligence begin to make possible for us a more fruitful exchange.

The "exemplary" case of Sigmund Freud. Now, finally, why Freud had such an impact on common sense. I think there are three crucial points to make. Before I do so, however, let me put in perspective one possible impediment to a proper appreciation. It has to do with his emphasis on sexuality, particularly his insistence that it was not only ubiquitous but had its origins in infancy. Undoubtedly this insistence (and particularly its oversimplification in the hands of both admirers and detractors) did seize the imagination of educated and uneducated alike. But had that been all, his views would have created a *frisson de scandale* much as Havelock Ellis's had done, and would soon have been converted to smut. His power in public discussion had rather to do, I think, with these things: his attention to and reinterpretation of the ordinary (the psycho-

pathology of everyday life, as he chose to call it), his deeply puzzling examination of the relation between the intended and the unintended, and finally his interpretation of the nature or meaning of "significance." A word about these.

For Freud, the ordinary conduct of everyday life was the starting point. Neurosis was not a blemish nor a disease, but a continuation of ordinary living. The ordinary, for Freud, was as much in need of interpretation as the extraordinary. One did what one intended to do, yes, but there was a hidden reason, a latent content as well as a manifest one. Intention, in Mrs. Anscombe's sense cited earlier, was reopened for examination. The Freudian slip became a tool for reinterpreting the ordinary.

But then, if the ordinary is not what it seems, what is it? Here is where Freud's literary genius took charge. Beneath the ordinary is a drama. Each of us is a cast of characters, acting out a script. Looked at carefully, our reactions to the world could be seen as an enactment of the script. It is in terms of these scripts that the surface of experience has systematic meaning or significance. Freud's scripts may have been culture-bound projections of *fin-de-siècle* Vienna. But for him they served as the cognitive systems in terms of which the symbolic significance of events could be understood. One of the scripts or codes was, of course, the epic struggle of the ego, the superego, and the id—the ego, as free agent trying to strike compromises between the priggish, societal demands of the superego on the one hand and the hedonistic, lusting, pleasure-principled id on the other. Indeed, he even tried his hand at a theory of perception in his essay on the "magic writing-pad" to account for the motivated way in which perceptual selectivity operated, balancing between a near-hallucinatory program in the service of drive and prohibition, and a reality-oriented one serving the sturdy little ego, almost like a judas eye through the middle of a distorting mirror. And as if these coding principles were not enough, Freud reinvented cultural forms like the Oedipal drama with its principles of categorization such that to the

experiencer, every older man was a father, every older woman a mother, every ingratiation a denied parricide or a maternal seduction.

The ordinary, in a word, was to be understood as explicable in terms of its symbolic, coded value; coded values were to be understood in terms of the way in which the world was organized in secret thought below the surface; the response of society and of the self—whether indignation or anxiety or guilt—was to be understood in terms of the sharing of these codes. Memory, perception, action, motivation were all to be seen as structure-sensitive constituents of this overall operation. The system may have been plainly wrong in content and detail, may indeed (as we know from a decade or two of principally American experimental research to tame it) have been totally unamenable to test by controlled experiment of the kind representing the older positivism. But surely it represented a modern ideal and, in an abstract way, constituted the kind of explanation that we speak of as structurally systematic. Various writers have pointed out its similarities in this abstract sense to the theoretical programs of Chomsky, de Saussure, and Piaget—all of them based on the analysis of surface phenomena derived from underlying structures through the interposition of transformation rules—in Freud's case, dream work and the distortion of ego defense mechanisms were the principal transformations. Perhaps, as intellectual historians, we should take seriously the fact that this type of formulation has had so powerful an impact on common sense, on interpretations of the ordinary. The details of the Freudian drama have by now receded, but the approach in its formal character has become part of educated common sense.

Please do not misinterpret. I am not proposing that only those theories which have a general cultural impact be taken seriously. God save all counter-intuitive ideas! My claim, rather, is that educated human beings, given their intrinsic "science-making" or theory-making capacities, know how to do things

and know that they do them. A theory of human behavior that fails to make contact with man's conceptions of his world and his way of knowing, that sets these aside as epiphenomena, will neither be an adequate theory of human behavior nor will it prevail in common sense. Physics had to make the world of nature, as experienced, comprehensible to man. The task of the psychologist is more difficult. For in making man comprehensible to himself, we start with man's knowledge of himself, his intricate sense of what he is like. Unless we begin from a better systematic description of that, we will fail. I doubt that we will, although our first century has not, I fear, been very impressive.

Contents

Rule Tables

Acknowledgements

Many of my colleagues have at one time or another helped towards the preparation of this book. Most of those who have been associated with the Cambridge Language Research Unit have contributed in some measure, and especially our director, Margaret Masterman, whose early advocacy of the role of lattice theory in the basic theory initiated, for me among others, new lines of thought; I am also indebted to her for many useful and stimulating discussions. I also wish to thank R. O. Anderson for his helpful comments on the manuscript.

Inferential Semantics

As you read this sentence, you are framing in your mind an understanding of what I mean it to say; and despite its being about your own response to it, you will probably succeed. I take no credit for this; my task is simply to express what is already formed in my mind. But your achievement is still beyond the frontiers of science, beyond anyone's understanding; in one sense of the word: a miracle. Equally miraculous is your ability to understand the words of someone who speaks and to follow conversations. While the speaker's task is to generate an utterance to convey a presumably preexisting thought, following rules of which we now have a certain understanding, thanks to the work of Chomsky and the generative grammarians, the listener has the harder job of deciding what one would have to have been thinking, in order to motivate the utterance he hears in the context he finds himself in. How is this possible?

Ours is a speakers' civilization, and our linguistics has accordingly concerned itself almost solely with the speaker's problems. This accounts for the rise of generative grammar and the prestige attached to this particular facet of the speech process. The skilful speaker wins praise; the skilful listener, despite the mystery of his achievement, is ignored. Though the listener's problem has always been an object of interest for a few, perhaps the first occasion for its being taken seriously as a subject for scientific research was the project, consequent on the development of the digital computer, of devising a method for the mechanical translation of languages. If a machine is to 'translate', it must first 'understand'. Naturally, the machine translation workers hoped that they could simply invert the process of expression, already beginning to be understood, in order to get a comprehension process which would serve their purposes. In the issue, the machine translation problem has so far proved insoluble, in all but the least demanding of its applications. It seems that the generation of a sentence to express a given idea is one of those processes, like the differentiation of an algebraic function in elementary calculus, which has in general no inverse.

This book is a by-blow from the same quest. Not that I have anything to say towards a 'solution' of the listener's problem; but thinking towards this goal soon leads one to ask about its end-product—the thought arising in the listener's mind as a result of his activity, which is (he hopes) the same thought from which the speaker's utterance arose. The way forward seems to me to require that we first get clear about the *structure of expressible thoughts*, as they 'exist' before and after the speech exchange has done what it can to transmit them.

This concern inevitably runs afoul of some contemporary trends in the philosophy of language. It is one which, once broached, is likely to become a main theme of controversy among linguists. It calls for the use of mathematical techniques—for mathematics is the only tool we have for avoiding fallacies in the treatment of mental constructs which lie beyond the limits of language. Some philosophers hold, of course, that all thinking is based on language, and this may perhaps be true; but the thesis implicitly regards mathematics as itself an elaboration of language. This is historically correct, but a distinction can still be made between articulate speech, which is my subject here, and the very differently structured devices of the mathematician. For these are neither Greek, nor English, nor Esperanto, nor Neo-melanesian, but are, as nearly as anything can be, common to all cultures.

It is obvious that thoughts, while still unformulated in language, are not amenable to empirical study. The speaker is normally quite unconscious of the original anatomy of his ideas, for they enter consciousness only in the course of their transformation into speech; it is the listener who has the opportunity, if only fleetingly, to observe the products of his comprehension. The natural methodology to adopt, then, is introspection: but this is denied to the scientific method, and that may be one reason why the listener's accomplishment is still beyond our grasp. But there is no objection to asking what mathematical properties pertain to these silent thoughts, if any kind of comprehension of them is to occur. I set myself, therefore, to investigate what this thing can be that the speaker says, that the listener understands, that the writer pins to the page. I look for a notation for things expressible, but unspoken.

CHAPTER I

Preliminaries

The first step is to get ourselves clear of the partial solutions of this problem which play so large a part in our traditional learning in this field. I mean the legacy of verbal logic, which seeks to separate a ruly and reliable core of language, conveying well-formed ideas subject to clear-cut laws, from the shapeless bed-rock of uneducated speech. The idea that language can and should be 'logical', so that for example someone who says "*I didnt never do that*" should be understood as confessing to having done it, is very deeply rooted, not indeed in our linguistic habits, but in our education. And it is on their education that linguists naturally expect to draw when they are doing their thing. For the present purpose, this habit of mind sets trip-wires all over the field of study; for it suggests a *kind* of structure for our thoughts which is, in fact, foreign to them. Logical thought, useful though it is in many situations, is a kind of circus-trick, making language walk on its hind legs. We need to see it going on all fours.

So I have to start by taking a tough line on looking only at 'natural language'. This means, in the first place, *spoken* language. To make it clear that the examples I shall use to illustrate the argument belong to a different register from the text in which they lie, I enclose them in double-quotes " ", and use *[an italic typeface]*. Of course, such devices are quite inadequate for the notation of real talk. They miss out on all the facial expressions, the gestures, the mannerisms of natural speech, the whole gamut of 'paralanguage'. Most of this must, regrettably, be lost sight of. But there is one feature of the same general kind which, in English at least (and I make no apology for all my examples being from this language), is not wholly paralinguistic, and can be notated, namely Intonation.

I have, therefore, in my examples, indicated the intonation as well as the usual material conveyed in writing. I have not used for this purpose an iconic notation; such notations either give a too narrow transcription, or else are too inaccurate to be helpful. Instead, from among the several systems available, I have chosen to use that of Halliday.[46] For those readers unfamiliar with this system, I have given a brief synopsis of it in Appendix I. Halliday's work has not escaped criticism, but as a notation its usefulness does not depend on the correctness of the theoretical analysis underlying it, which is the target of the critics. As it was based on a study of actual tape-recorded conversations, a few gaps exist, noted in Appendix I; but these are not represented in my examples.

1.1. The Semantic Background

My subject lies, in a broad sense, within the domain of semantics, so it is fitting that I should begin by looking at the origin and history of this study. This lies in India and Greece; the Chinese, pioneers in so many sciences, were not drawn towards an analytical study of the meaning of sentences. Perhaps, as many have suggested, the structure of their language was not such as to stimulate them to ask the appropriate questions.

The study of the meanings of human utterances is, however, at one level, as old as civilization itself. Among the Greeks, the first among Western nations to articulate so many of our still living preoccupations, this study was included in Rhetoric. The 'rhetoric' of the ancients was a combination of two disciplines, one concerned with *what* one should say, and the other with *how* one should say it. In the course of time, the field came to be divided into three main parts, the courses of the mediaeval *trivium*. 'Grammar' was the study of the correct surface form of utterances. Despite the favourable circumstance that the learned West was bilingual, there was too great a similarity between Latin and Greek (or it was held that there ought to be) to adequately exercise the minds of grammarians in comparative studies. 'Logic' examined the rules of inference obtaining among a special class of utterances, called in Latin *oratio pronuntiabilis*. 'Rhetoric', in its residual sense, was the most esteemed of the three, and taught how this knowledge might be used with the skill and address necessary to convince a jury in a courtroom, or a crowd in the market-place, of the rightness of what one wished to say.

None of this, however, was directly addressed to the meaning of ordinary remarks, with all their clumsiness and their lack of logical precision or even, no doubt then as now, grammaticality. Only educated speech was taken seriously, and the carefree foundation of natural conversation on which it rested was disregarded. The ancients therefore never developed a semantic theory of any generality. Almost everything that is directly relevant to our quest is of quite recent origin; I shall consider this in more detail in Chapter II. It is convenient to divide 'semantics' into 'determinative' and 'predicative' semantics. Those will be taken up again, here I consider only their ancient history.

Determinative semantics deals with single words, or with noun-phrases at most. Interest in the meanings of words is attested from the start of writing. Word lists, ancestral to present-day thesauri rather than to dictionaries, were compiled by the Sumerians;[68] such lists gathered together words of related meaning, just as we find in a modern thesaurus such as Roget,[84] but with a much less elaborate classification, and no index. Such lists contained, for instance, parts of the body, food-plants, gods, cities, and the like. Many other ancient civilizations showed parallel developments: this is, in fact, the most 'natural' way to approach the meanings of words. 'Wheat' suggests 'barley' suggests 'beans' suggests . . . But we soon encounter difficulties, especially that of metaphors. Interest in this propensity to shift their meanings which words pre-eminently show is also probably as old as poetry. But while exploited in art and used or misused in the practice of rhetoric, there was (and is) no analytical theory of metaphor. The ancient world went no farther than to foreshadow the thesaurus.

1.2. Predicative Semantics

More progress was made in studying the meanings of sentences; at least of well-behaved sentences. In certain limited directions, a kind of predicative semantics developed quite early. Aristotle, in his work on logic[6] for example, clearly was concerned with this topic, even though he confined his attention to a rather special class of sentences amenable to this kind of approach. In Aristotle's view, logic was primarily a technique for right thinking; right speaking was expected to follow from this as a natural consequence. This, however, was not the only view expressed in antiquity, though the pre-eminence accorded to Aristotle in the Middle Ages has tended to leave this impression on us.

Prior to the revival of Aristotelian studies in the thirteenth century, Apuleius[5] had a wider influence on mediaeval logic. He thought of logic as essentially a refinement of grammar; for him, illogical or contradictory utterances were ill-formed, in the same sort of way that ungrammatical sentences were. Despite Aristotle, this attitude was again exemplified by the 'universal grammarian' school, whose work, typified by the celebrated Port-Royal grammar,[67] proved the direct forerunner of contemporary trends.

This Apuleian approach is, however, apt to run into absurdities. This is shown in many a present-day paper on semantics, where one may find various sentences containing some kind of semantic oddity marked as 'deviant', very often on quite inadequate grounds. As an example of the dismissal of a non-Apuleian sentence, we find (in Fraser[36]) "*Even both Joe and Jane yelled*" asterisked as deviant; the point being made is that 'even' can't be followed by 'both', or so Fraser claims. But why not "*Unpractised though he was, Joe, urged by Jane, began to yell; after some time, even both Joe and Jane yelled. At last, help arrived.*" ? Apuleius was concerned with the same rather restricted range of contexts as Aristotle; the concept of semantic deviance, implied by this approach, has trapped many enquirers who have not been trained to ask on every occasion 'What is the context?' A non-Apuleian sentence (if not really ungrammatical) is simply one for which appropriate contexts are rarely encountered. A sentence is not deviant in itself: the deviance is in the context which calls it forth. But a sentence which no context ever calls for is never uttered (at least, never in good faith: people can always make up examples); and what is never uttered is not an utterance and is not within the purview of a realistic semantics. If no one has ever said, or ever might have said, "*Hurry and get paralysed, the train goes at six past tomato soup*" then this sentence is *unavailable* as an example for or against anything.

(Except, of course, as an example of a bad example!) Nevertheless, the category of 'deviance' retains a strong hold on many linguists. Lakoff[63] even goes so far as to propose a definition of 'grammaticality' of sentences, by reference to the truth of their presuppositions (this topic is discussed further in §4.1). This view comes near to labelling as 'ungrammatical' what many people would call a lie.

1.3. Introducing 'Rhematic'

There was, then, a large gap in the scope of classical semantics; they had no adequate theory of what kind of ideas can be communicated by speech, but only a clear grasp of some particular subclasses of such ideas. We still have no such theory. One motivation of the present work has been experience of the difficulties arising in the handling of texts by computers. While I cannot claim that my work will help to resolve these difficulties—it rather goes to show that they are irresolvable—attempts to contribute to this field certainly alerted me to the absence of any real model of what it is that is being exchanged when people talk. I hope that my work may go some way towards filling this gap.

My subject, as I have said, is the structure, relationships, and notation of thoughts (a purposely vague word, which I shall sharpen up in due course) in their pre-linguistic, pre-utterance condition. I want to discuss the meanings of sentences without consideration of the sentences through which they are expressed;* I am concerned with deep structures as independent as they can be (which is of course not wholly independent) from surface structures. For this discipline I adopt the term *rhematic*, proposed for a 'logic of sentences' originally by Coleridge.[24]† Its status as a 'logic' I shall revert to in §4.10. As soon as a 'thought' is expressed in words, questions arise as to how these words have been chosen; I assume that the choice is governed by four factors: (a) in what context the words are uttered, (b) what they

* I am of course aware that some philosophers would claim that this is an impractical or even unattainable goal. I ask the indulgence of any reader who thinks thus. Progress often comes through the disregard of warnings.

† I assign to "rhematic" the morphological paradigm of "logic"—adjective "rhematical", noun with null suffix. Various systems covering the same ground would be "rhematics".

are to express, (c) the grammar of the language spoken, which will furnish at least one sequence of rules generating the utterance from an appropriate notation for the thought; this will normally allow free choices at various points, where (d) considerations of style and register will determine the final choice of words.

In this schema, I shall be concerned here primarily with the factors (a) and (b). The factors (c) and (d) belong to grammar and rhetoric respectively; so, with the trivium in mind, we naturally expect that consideration of (a) and (b) may lead to some kind of logic. And, indeed, rhematic will turn out to resemble logic up to a point; notably in requiring a mathematical treatment, which linguists may find rather heavy going. It differs from Aristotelian logic in being mathematically weaker, and correspondingly wider in scope; its scope is, in fact, ideally that of all natural language utterances. I will not claim to have literally attained this ideal; but I do take the idea of natural language very seriously as the subject of study, and I believe that in a great deal of modern linguistic work 'naturalness' of language is not valued as highly as it ought to be.

1.4. 'Natural Language'

What then is this 'natural' language, and how does it differ from other varieties of language? My first criterion, which I shall apply to all the examples I give (other than those required to illustrate other kinds of approach), is that it must be easy to imagine a context in which they would actually be uttered by a character of some type known to us all. Occasionally I may suggest a context, if for any reason it may not be obvious. Next, I shall make no use at any point of the alleged deviance (or non-deviance) of a given utterance. This seems to me to be an inadmissible mode of argument; even for its original purpose of determining limits on the ways different words can be combined, it is dealing at best with *word-uses*, among which change-over is too continuous and often too rapid to make the enterprise worthwhile. Humpty-Dumpty's aphorism, that 'words mean what I choose them to mean, neither more nor less'[16] may not apply in some of the more uptight uses of language, but it is more valid than most of us care to admit in the case of what I here call 'natural language'.

Another class of enemies of natural language is found among

the philosophers. Their discipline requires certain conventions, which are not observed in ordinary conversation; if it did not, it would hardly be worth pursuing. Among such conventions are that some utterances have no meaning at all, and so needn't be taken seriously; that some statements though meaningful can be disbelieved without any quarrel over their context; and that misunderstandings are as likely to be the fault of the listener not having attended properly or not knowing one's own uses of words, as to be blamed on the speaker not making himself clear. Discourse conducted according to these rules is more likely than common talk to get to the heart of difficult problems; but it is not what I am considering here. It's not what I call *natural* language.

As a first example of a procedure which I shall adopt repeatedly throughout this book, I shall codify what seem to me to be defining characteristics of natural language in a set of formal 'rules'. In this form, they can be easily referred back to at need, and the relevance of particular rules to a particular point in the subsequent argument can be pointed our economically. Here, then, are my *Rules of Natural Language*:

L: Every utterance in natural language is
- *L1:* *meaningful* (that is, capable of furnishing inferences agreed among the participants in a conversation); and
- *L2:* *believed* within the limits of the context in which it is uttered; and
- *L3:* either
  - *L3.1:* *understood* as intended by the speaker, or
  - *L3.2:* according as the discrepancy does or does not become apparent to the participants, respectively
    - *L3.2.1:* the speaker proffers an alternative expression of his thought, or
    - *L3.2.2:* the participants come to entertain divergent models of the context.

All such rules, though more or less disguised as analytic statements, are essentially ethical in content. That is, they prescribe what ought to be done, and only in ideal circumstances describe what is done. In the above set, for example, the whole of L3 can be more briefly put in the form 'If I don't understand, it's your fault'. This may not be very philosophically expressed, but it is fundamental for the very existence of language as a social institution. Responsibility for getting an idea across can *only* rest with the speaker, if only because the listener can never reliably know when a misunderstanding has occurred. This rule has an important practical consequence, in that when an utterance produces not even the illusion of understanding, the listener can and does ask for an explanation, and usually gets it. This cancels, in effect, the obscure remark, and substitutes another; therefore, remarks which elicit this response do not count as having been uttered at all, and need not be covered by any theory which concerns itself explicitly with natural language. This disposes of quite a lot more so-called deviant sentences.

An illustration occurs in a recent monograph by Wanner,[100] who offers as an example, in another connection, the supposed sentence "*Beautiful though Elizabeth claimed everyone knew that Marcia was, she never appealed to John*". The author claims that, despite the number of intervening words, it 'remains clear' that Marcia was beautiful. It is admittedly clear to the *reader*: but, in the unlikely event of the utterance being heard in conversation, it would be quite unclear to the *listener*. If anyone was listening, the speaker would be pulled up and asked to explain. He would then say, presumably, something like "*Marcia never appealed to John. Not that she wasn't beautiful; everyone knew that, or so Elizabeth said.*" Indeed, in its previous form, the remark is not only difficult to understand, it is also perhaps even more difficult to generate as an utterance; some of the re-structuring rules which are called upon, operate only in literary registers and are blocked in the grammar of conversational English, so that some grammarians might wish to question even its well-formedness. It is obviously desirable that such examples should not be used.

1.5. Belief as a Truth-Value

Having dealt above with the rule L3, I shall now turn to look at L2. This rule requires us to believe 'within the limits of the context' everything that we hear. The qualifying phrase is not primarily intended to provide a loophole for the sceptic, but to emphasize that no utterance can, in general, be correctly understood in the absence of its context. Thus, if you admire a friend's walking-stick, and he tells you that it's made of beech, it matters not at all if your more expert eye detects that it is in fact hornbeam; you have the choice of either accepting a contextual model in which this distinction is not made, or of inviting its amendment by such a remark as "*I'd say it's hornbeam*". What is ordinarily called disbelief occurs when two participants in a conversation *persist* in adopting divergent contexts.

The normal purpose of conversation is to arrive at an agreed contextual understanding, or to celebrate its prior existence; it is frustrating when this purpose is not achieved, and we clearly need a word for saying so. It is natural, since a context is an obscure entity arrived at by complex mental process whereas words are immediately present to the senses, for contextual discrepancy to be attributed, formally, to the words rather than to the context; so we say 'I don't believe that', or even more pointedly 'I don't believe you'. But in fact these phrases do not impugn the sincerity of the speaker, so much as the accuracy of his information. What, then, can we say about deliberate lying?

A 'liar' is a person who chooses between two thoughts competing for expression on grounds of expediency rather than of truth. Fortunately it's not too hard for a discerning person to recognise this type of personality disorder, and to make the appropriate allowances. Whenever someone known to have this habit speaks, this information forms, for a listener forewarned, a part of his contextual map. This means that the liar's remarks are still believed, but they will be believed to be expedient for himself rather than to be true of *his* contextual map. Under these circumstances it will be difficult, perhaps impossible, to achieve the normal congruence between the two contexts. A community in which lying is very prevalent labours under a great handicap in all its social interactions on this account.

What I mean by 'believe', as the word is used in L2, is thus not quite what one might suppose; the rule means that a listener's understanding of an utterance is never blocked by a supposed state of unbelief. The latter applies only to the listener's reconstruction of the speaker's grasp of (or presentation of) the context. Natural language thus does not operate a system of truth-values like that of formal logic. There are no *false* statements, outside of special registers which exist in all civilized language communities for special purposes; at most there are statements which are rejected, in the sense that the listener refuses to modify his contextual map in the direction invited. This is very different from logical falsity, both psychologically and in its formal properties (which are in fact not unlike those of the 'negation' operator used in Intuitionist mathematics[51]). In fact, as this would lead one to expect, natural languages only develop a binary yes-no logic under special cultural circumstances; ordinary negation operates to block inferences rather than to contradict them (this topic is discussed in more detail in §14.2), and in natural language repeated negatives are understood to reinforce each other rather than to cancel out.

1.6. The Inevitability of Meaning

I come now to comment on rule L1. This denies the existence of meaningless utterances, or rather calls on all concerned to ascribe a meaning to whatever nonsense anyone chooses to utter. Rejection of this injunction, like that of L2, is permissible in special types of discourse; there are conversational modes where the participants are expected to adhere to special constraints, and where disregard of these constraints is formally equated with meaninglessness. But this is not 'natural' language, but rather a special kind of '*oratio pronuntiabilis*' devised for particular purposes, such as law or science. To show how L1 works out, there is no better way than to assemble some examples of the kinds of utterances which have been held to be 'meaningless'.

Here, then, is a selection:

1.6.1 "*He must be either alive or dead*"[44]
1.6.2 "*Good day, Father!*"[44]
1.6.3 "*Jesus was the Son of God*"[77]
1.6.4 "*Colourless green ideas sleep furiously*"[17]
1.6.5 "*The present king of France is bald*"[7]
1.6.6 "*All mimsy were the borogroves*"[16]
1.6.7 "*If book mother and And help the*"[75]
1.6.8 "*Aaaagh!*"[110]
You're too stupid to understand any of this.
1.6.10 "*This sentence is not true*"[100]

The first of these, (1.6.1), is in classical logic tautologously true; such a statement has been held to assert nothing since it excludes nothing. All and only true propositions are implied by it. That it is not linguistically meaningless is perhaps obvious. One can for instance infer from it "*He may be dead*", which is certainly not among the 'agreed inferences' from the equally tautologous remark "*If it's not a fish, it must be something else*".

A much better case can be made for the meaninglessness of (1.6.2). This, as a 'phatic' utterance, is not intended to convey information. Nevertheless, it does so; one will infer from it, for instance, that the speaker is friendly, that he knows the use of 'father' as a term of respect, that he is willing to participate in a further exchange. All this adds up to establish certain contextual points which might be otherwise; the remarks therefore convey meaning, even if it is not much.

The argument about (1.6.3) concerns whether it, or anything inferable from it, is empirically testable. If not, according to one school of philosophy, it is meaningless; this is, of course, a rather special sense of 'meaningless'. However, not only are there some inferences, or at least presuppositions, here, such as "*Jesus existed*", which are testable, but even if the positivist case is fully accepted it serves only to reduce (1.6.3) to the same form as (1.6.5) or (1.6.1). Both of these, I argue, fail to achieve meaninglessness.

The trouble with (1.6.4) is supposed to be 'semantic incongruity'; it is the kind of sentence that grammarians mark with a star, a practice which I have already mentioned adversely. If, however, we imagine it to be actually uttered, it is not too hard to make sense of. Obviously, it is a kind of poetry; it could be saying, with more elegance, that original but dull notions, while still awaiting public recognition, disturb one's peace of mind. But, of course, remembering rule L3, one would be wise to check this with the speaker.

(1.6.5) belongs to a context which well-informed listeners will be indisposed to adopt. One detects a discrepancy from widely accepted facts. How could one do that with a meaningless utterance?

In (1.6.6) we encounter, for the first time, undefined additions to the lexicon. Here we have no recourse but to apply L3, which we can do by following up the reference given; my source does in fact offer the required explanation. It turns out to be saying that the borogroves were neither happy nor strong. One may still have doubts about the actual existence of borogroves, of course; but in that case we have a situation the same as that of (1.6.5).

To find meaning in (1.6.7) might seem a bold claim; but again we must consider how we would react to someone actually uttering it. We might perhaps take it for an utterance in a foreign language, whose phonology allowed one by chance to pick out apparent English 'words'. If that were ruled out, we would suspect the speaker of suffering from some form of aphasia; and this, as a medical diagnosis, however amateurish, is a non-trivial inference, and one might even add a guess that the words 'book', 'mother', and 'help' were especially loaded for the patient. If, however, it were made clear that the speaker was not aphasic, we might well conclude that he was a linguist attempting to produce a meaningless utterance; if the attempt is judged to have failed, my point is made, while if it is admitted to have succeeded, the speaker has got his meaning across, as in all the other examples.

An inarticulate utterance such as (1.6.8) could be dismissed as not language. But any human cry is potentially an intended communication, and there are contexts in which an inarticulate noise is more meaningful, more expressive as we say, than many a more dispassionate remark. Articulateness admits of degrees—"//$_{1+}$***Ouch***" is about half-way to "*Aaaagh*".

The next example, lacking quotation marks and reference, must read as part of my running text. However, I hope it won't be taken literally; that is not my intention. This lack of serious intention opts out of the current context, and comes as close as any previous example to being truly meaningless. But if on this account you fail to take offence, you will at least concede that it is an insult which is not intended, rather than say a warning or a threat—so some meaning still comes over even here.

Finally, (1.6.10) need cause no difficulty at all. It is a correct assessment of the preceding sentence. However, it *is* possible to understand the pronoun "this" as referring to (1.6.10) itself; the sentence would then involve *self-reference*; to this I now turn.

1.7. The Problem of Self-Reference

Later in the book, when I have been able to be more specific about what I mean by the meaning of a sentence (in §6.2.4), I shall show that a self-referent sentence, if it is accepted by the listener as being truly such, yields a 'deep structure' which *precludes* it from belonging to any normal context. Such sentences therefore exist in a closed world of their own. My discussion of examples of supposedly meaningless sentences will have shown that, when actually using language, the search for meaning takes precedence over everything else; this shut-off world of self-reference is therefore only entered, in the listener's mind, as a last resort. To get the point across, a simple expression like (1.6.10) is not really sufficient: we would need to say something like "*The sentence of which these words form a part . . .*". It must, however, be conceded that language does have the capability of self-reference, and there is nothing in the definition of 'natural language' which prevents it; as I shall show, real examples exist.

Lakoff[65] has drawn attention to a class of sentences which he calls 'perfomrative antinomies'. These are, judging by his examples, no part of natural language; one example is "*I warn you to disregard this warning*". Nevertheless, real-life performative antinomies do occur, if only by oversight. An actual case is presented by a notice which said "*You are hereby required to show your permits*". If 'hereby' is understood to refer to the text in which it stands, this makes it equivalent to "this is an order to show your permits"; but in fact this is not an order at all, but a declarative sentence about an order. It thus reduces to a self-contradiction like the Epimenidean paradox (1.6.10).

The word 'hereby' is perhaps the commonest expression leading to self-reference. It is a favourite in legal jargon. A sentence beginning "*It is hereby provided that . . .*" is clearly intended and understood to refer to circumstances in the real world. It could be held that in such a context 'hereby' simply means 'formally' or 'authoritatively' or the like; but it is more natural to take such 'serious' instances as involving what I may call 'benign self-reference'. This occurs where there is no self-contradiction, but where, by the principles I shall describe in detail in Chapter XIV, one can obtain a legitimate inference which is compatible with a real context and therefore can be accepted as intended at one remove by the utterer of the self-referent remark. The conceptual oddity of this way of expressing oneself may perhaps have the effect of making the utterance seem self-authenticating, and therefore suitable for solemn occasions or legislative acts.

There remain two possibly legitimate uses of self-reference. One is in commands, and is more fully explained in §7.6. The other is illustrated by Ryle's thesis[88] that the sentence "The term 'heterological' is heterological" involves an infinite regress. If this is accepted, the representation of this sentence in my notation (which, however, will not be fully explained till Chapter XII) is as shown below as (1.1).

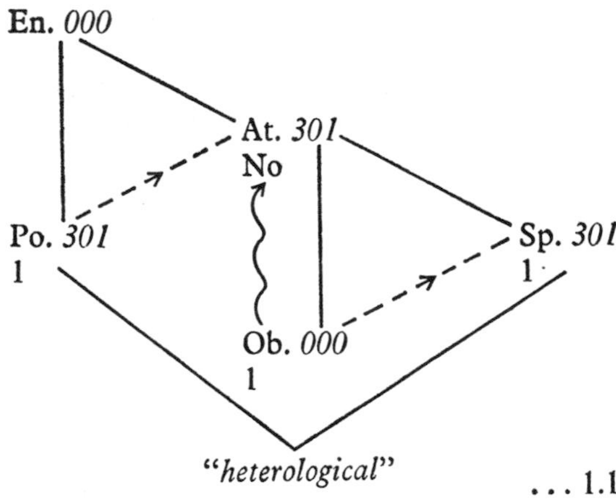

... 1.1

This asserts that the word "heterological" possesses no attribute of having the property denoted by (the word "heterological" which possesses . . .) and so on for ever. However, Geach[43] has argued that there is no necessary self-reference, and his analysis would be represented in my notation by (1.2); but in any case a self-referent rhema is required to explain the point at issue.

This book, like others of its kind, contains frequent references to other parts of itself. These references are not, however, self-references. The whole book is too long to constitute for anyone a single context; the topics discussed change and progress as the text proceeds and while it would be difficult to specify just where context boundaries could be drawn it is clear that there is no sense in which I am guilty of self-reference when I refer to another section or subsection than the one the reference occurs in. Bibliographic self-reference is in principle possible,[75] but is naturally not customary. The reference given for (1.6.7) will be found to involve a (benign) self-reference.

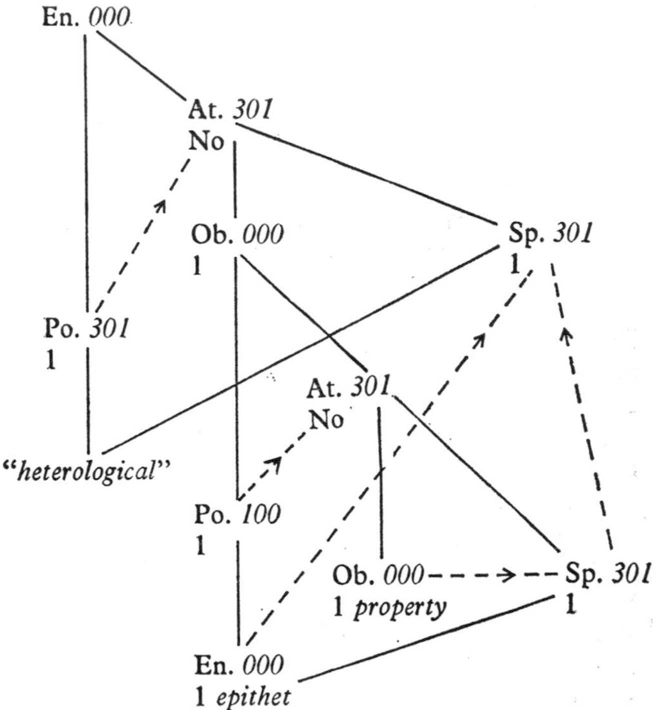

... 1.2

A frequent instance of benign self-reference, which is accepted in some circles, is the practice of writers to refer to themselves in the third person. It may be objected that to refer to oneself as "the writer" involves no more than a special form of the first personal pronoun, perhaps comparable with the forms in some Far Eastern languages used for addressing social inferiors. But literally it means "the writer of these words", which is a manifestly self-referent expression, just as if one should refer to oneself in spoken language as "the speaker". It might well be regarded as a point of good style to avoid all instances of possible self-reference, however benign; these expressions are only clear if overlooked. It is a possibility even in the most 'natural' language, but it has something pathological about it, and it certainly calls for no further consideration here.

CHAPTER II

The Speech Process

Having made clear my concern with the operation of language in as much isolation from written and formal distractions as possible, I shall in this chapter try to place Rhematic more precisely among the linguistic disciplines. My concern with actual speaking and actual listening leads naturally to the consideration of the speech process as a continuous or repeated cycle of exchanges between (ideally) two participants. Increasing the number does not materially increase the complexity of the cycle (so long as only one speaks at a time!); but there are simplified cycles to be taken account of with only one participant.

2.1. The Coversational Cycle

The basic cycle, assuming two participants, may be diagrammed as follows:

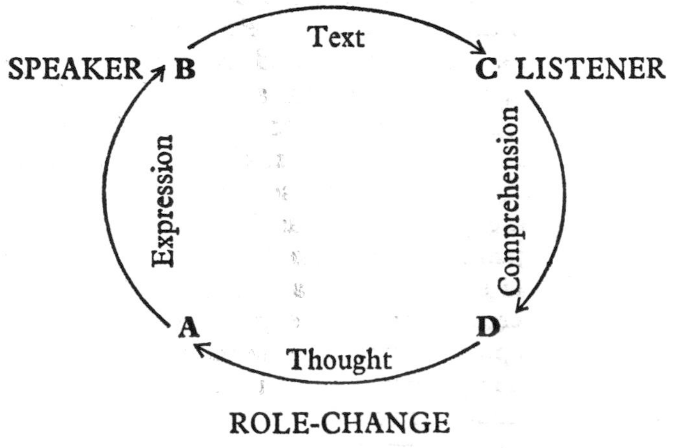

This cycle is divided into four phases: in clockwise order, they are Expression, Text, Comprehension, and Thought. Each phase has its own characteristic features and processes. Expression involves a procedure which takes as input a 'thought' (which we must think of as formalized in some manner), and yields as output a string of phonic material, that is, an utterance. Once uttered, this string constitutes a text, the next phase of the cycle. This phase is essentially static; under ideal conditions, the text is received by the listener as auditory input containing all the information imparted to it by the speaker. Of course, some attenuation takes place, and under non-ideal conditions hearing may be seriously impeded; but all this is outside the field of linguistics: it belongs to communication engineers, otologists, and other specialists. The third phase, that of comprehension of the text, is again of concern to linguists; but it has been comparatively neglected, in contrast with the rapid progress which we have lately seen in the analysis of the process of expression. The output of the comprehension process, as indicated by my diagram, is again a thought. This must be in some sense the 'same' thought that the speaker had intended to convey, if the cycle is to be judged successful; but once received, it will be processed in the listener's mind, and possibly result in the elaboration of a new thought. We then see a change of roles between speaker and listener, the new speaker expressing his new thought, thereby initiating a new cycle.

An important contrast exists between the two phases of overt action, that is expression and comprehension. There is no reason to doubt that the former is typically a determinate process of an algorithmic character. If we had a suitable means of encoding 'thoughts' in a non-linguistic manner, it is a process which could be realistically simulated by a computer programme. Unfortunately, linguists have hitherto lacked such a non-linguistic notation—a lack which I here try to fill. Some consideration has also been given to the inverse process of comprehension, to the extent that this is equivalent to the extraction of a deep structure from a surface text. The difficulties of this phase have lately been discussed at some depth by Wanner[100] and will be considered further in §2.3; it seems, from the lack of real progress, doubtful whether comprehension is an algorithmic process at all. It may rather be a questing search ('what would I have had to be thinking in order to say that?'), an open-ended enterprise bearing to expression something like the relation which, in the calculus, integration bears to differentiation. Failure to face up to this contrast may well have retarded our understanding of grammar in many ways.

Besides the full four-phase cycle represented above, there exists a mode of language use in which only the section A — B — D is operative, an alternation between expression and thinking. This gives rise to a lecture or monologue. This process is however strictly derivative from the conversational one: the lack of feedback from the listener(s) makes is possible for the speaker to become seriously incomprehensible, and public speaking or lecturing is well recognized to be a skill requiring patience and experience to acquire. A yet more 'degenerate' form of the cycle involves nothing but thought, albeit at least partly verbalized (*truly* wordless thought, if possible at all, is liable to become quickly disorganized). Both sustained analytical thought, and disciplined meditation, are also difficult but teachable skills. I would consider both to be within the field of linguistics.

2.2. Previous Linguistic Studies

The different phases of the conversational cycle present very unequal obstacles to their understanding. The simplest to examine is the text phase; and as one would expect this was the earliest to be the subject of systematic analysis. All ancient linguistics, both Sanskrit and Greek, was essentially a descriptive study of text, which easily passed over to prescription, if this indeed was not its original intent; text, for the most part, meant written text, though varying degrees of attention were paid to the spoken word as well.

With the revival of scientific interest in grammar in modern times the text phase was again the first to attract attention. There grew up in due course three main types of grammatical model, which have been characterized by Hockett[53] as the Word-and-Paradigm (WP) model, and the Item-and-Process (IP) model, to which must be added the Item-and-Arrangement (IA) model introduced by descriptive linguists familiar with non-Indoeuropean languages. The first descended directly from classical tradition; it surfaced, perhaps for the last time, in an interesting discussion by Robbins.[82] The IP model was essentially a generalization of this involving a freer, and partly generative, attitude towards 'paradigms', originated by Sapir.[91] The IA model stemmed originally from the obvious but long unexploited hierarchical structure of the sentence (Husserl[55]) and proved the most successful of the three lines. It led, by way of immediate-constituent grammars, to the development of phrase-structure grammar, the first strictly mathematical technique to be applied to language structure. All these techniques were applied to explain the surface features of texts, either written or spoken.

Linguistics finally broke through its confinement to this one phase of the cycle with the introduction of transformational grammar by Chomsky.[17] This made possible the development of a truly generative approach to grammatical structure, and with it a formalism for describing processes within the expression phase of the conversational cycle. True exploration of this phase began with the introduction of the 'deep structure' concept by Katz and Postal,[59] further developed by Chomsky.[18] Unfortunately, those who pioneered this work felt it necessary to pursue a strictly empirical approach to the elucidation of deep structures, that is, to work backwards from the surface structure of a text, by considering *from what* it could be generated, using the apparatus most economical of distinct transformations. This approach made it impossible for them to break out of language altogether, although it is possible that in the thought phase, from which expression starts, the material communicated is potentially free from the particularities of any one language. Evidence for this comes from the facts of bilingual competence, from the possibility (and also from the limitations) of translation, and from some psycholinguistic observations, in particular the well-known ability of people to remember facts long after they have forgotten the words through which the facts were first communicated to them. While one must concede that thinking with any pretence to rigorousness must be fully verbalized in some language (or visualized in a notation) what we more loosely call 'thinking' proceeds with only fragmentary verbalizations, some of which serve more as mantras to recall attention than as steps in the argument; despite which, conclusions may emerge intelligent enough to edge conversation forward.

To pursue this insight evidently calls for an explicitly mentalistic commitment. That transformational grammar is itself essentially mentalistic was perceived by Katz,[57] and has been generally admitted by members of this school; despite this, insistence on the empirical approach to deep structure has not abated. Watt,[107] for instance, goes so far as to criticize Katz's position on the ground that if Transformation Grammar were truly 'mentalistic' it should be open to psycholinguistics to furnish evidence for its theses, the existence of which evidence Watt queries. But the virtue of a mentalistic approach is that it allows *a priori* considerations to be relevant, not that it calls for confirmation from a science of the mind. I shall argue in Chapters III–V that such considerations are both available and productive.

2.3. Deep Structure and Comprehension

Present-day linguistics thus operates not only in the text phase, but also to a useful extent in the expression phase. Since, traditionally, expression and comprehension have been regarded as more or less mirror-images of each other, the techniques of Transformational Grammar have also been applied in an attempt to unravel the comprehension phase. The problem here is, How do we derive 'deep the structure', which we supposedly understand, from the surface structure of any utterance, which we hear? This naturally brings up the question of the logical status of what are called 'deep structures'.

It seems to be universally assumed at the present time that every well-formed sentence has a deep structure, and that in most cases it is known what this is. Deep structures are in fact presented as tree-diagrams with labelled nodes including such terms as 'noun phrase', 'verb phrase', and the like, and are to this extent not unlike the surface structures which they correspond to; despite a few exceptions (such as Sampson[90]) generativists seem uncritical of this model. The very term "deep" structure implies an adjectival rather than a substantive distinction from "surface" structures. Nevertheless, there is no adequate evidence that such structures exist (outside the theory that postulates them), or that they are supported by more than highly-trained intuition; this is the essence of Watt's[107] criticisms.

There is indeed the possibility of deriving such evidence from recall experiments of the type used in psycholinguistics. Work on these lines has been reviewed by Wanner,[100] who adds his own results to the corpus. The difficulty here, which Wanner does not remark on, is that it is scarcely possible to carry out such experiments on the recall of sentences *in a natural context* (or at least no appropriate technique seems to have been devised). In the absence of a context, it is quite unclear what factors are likely to affect the recall of different words or portions of a sentence. In an experiment of the usual type, where subjects are asked to recall, after varying intervals and in response to varying stimuli, different members of a set of usually very similar sentences, there seems to be little motivation for the subjects to think at any stage what the sentences mean (which, in the absence of a real context, may well be nothing since they are not felt to be really "uttered"). The relevance of such work to the structures arrived at by the normal process of comprehension is remote. It is noteworthy, however, that all these workers take it as established that the output of "comprehension" will be the deep structure of the given sentence as provided by the grammarians, and that their results should be explainable by a hypothesis framed in relation to this structure. Neither assumption seems to be warranted.

It is not surprising, in view of the dubious logical status of these deep structures, that they have given rise to a number of serious discussions of pseudo-problems. One such question, discussed at length by Partee,[76] asks whether transformations 'preserve meaning'; in the absence of an agreed notation for meanings independent of the language being discussed, the status of the question itself is unclear. However, it is always possible to furnish an answer to such questions if they can be cast in the form of a computer programme, and the answer so obtained can easily be dubbed 'empirical'. Thus, for instance, Katz and Postal[59] claimed to have established empirically that transformations involve no changes in meaning, using 'empirical' in this sense. Many similar pseudo-problems concerning deep structure arise in connection with speech act theory, discussed in the next section; all alike stem from the belief, which I hold to be mistaken, that such questions can, and therefore should, be settled by empirical evidence.

The claim has been repeatedly advanced that the whole theory of deep structures is in some sense empirically based. This claim is documented and discussed by Botha,[11] and he succeeds in my opinion in demolishing much of it. A definition, widely accepted as definitive, was given by Chomsky[18] for 'deep structure' in the form of four conditions which any such structure must satisfy; but these have been strongly criticized by Lakoff,[62] who argues that they are both logically and procedurally unworkable. From such claims and counterclaims, it seems likely that it is impossible to study deep structure effectively by an empirical methodology; it should therefore be a promising undertaking to approach the subject from a strictly mathematical, that is *a priori*, angle. I shall argue for the possibility of this approach in §2.6; and its results will be examined in the rest of the book.

2.4. Speech Acts

Before entering on to this, there is another topic which may be helpful in our study, at least partly independent of recent developments in linguistics, namely the study of 'speech acts'. This topic was originated by Austin,[7] and has been followed up by linguistic philosophers and less enthusiastically by linguists. The term 'speech act', as used by Austin, covers everything that can be achieved by articulate utterance; this is commonly interpreted as covering the three phases of the conversational cycle labelled in the diagram of §2.1 'expression', 'text', and 'comprehension'; but not 'thought' (in practice little attention is paid to comprehension either). A general account of speech act theory is given by Searle.[94]

The main 'achievements' of utterance are described as the 'illocutionary act' which is accomplished merely by pronoucing the words, and consists mainly in the transfer of meaning from speaker to listener; and the 'perlocutionary act' which consists in any intended effect the words may have on the listener. Thus, for example, the sentence "*He urged me to shoot her*" describes an illocutionary act, but says nothing about any perlocutionary force it may have had; this might be described by the sentence "*He persuaded me to shoot her*". A distinction is made between perlocutionary force, which is normally extra-linguistic, illocutionary force (such as that of a question, command, opinion, &c., any of which are open to finer classification), and locutionary or semantic force, which is what is ordinarily called the meaning of a sentence; the usefulness of separating the last two is, however, not obvious.

Nor is it clear what we can make of Cohen's claim[23] that certain subordinating devices 'extinguish' the locutionary force of an utterance; we may illustrate this by the example of "*He is going to town; I shall too*" as against "*If he is going to town, I shall, too*", where the locutionary force of "He is going to town" is said to be missing from the second sentence, though the words remain. It would be more apt to say here that the subordinate clause is *modified*, by a hypothetical ('perhaps') modifier, rather than to isolate a named meaning-component which is 'extinguished'.

More profitable is the help we can get from this study in classifying the varieties of inference, which I shall take up in §4.1. The term 'implicature' is associated with speech acts, and is one which, like the term 'presupposition', has been used in more than one sense. Two *levels* of inference have to be distinguished: there is what we may call 'delocutionary' inference from the locution itself, and 'sublocutionary' inference from what we suppose to underlie the locutionary act in the speaker's mind. Thus, Grice gives the example[45] of the utterance "*Joan has beautiful handwriting and her English is grammatical*" in the context (for once explicit) of an examination report; from this, as he says, one can infer that Joan showed little aptitude in the subject examined. This is a delocutionary inference, though a rather subtle one. On the other hand, Cohen gives[23] as an example of implicature, that one may draw from "*It's raining*" the inference "*I believe that it's raining*"; for this, one requires the additional premiss that every declarative sentence carries an 'implicature' of sincerity, deriving from the language rule L2 (see §1.4), which goes outside both the words and their context and is thus a sublocutionary inference. The term 'implicature' would be usefully confined to this type of inference, which has no direct relevance to comprehension and is not part of what one normally calls the 'meaning' of the remark.

A further topic arising in the study of speech acts is that of performatives. A 'performative' verb is one which, uttered in the first person singular and present tense, constitutes an example of what it refers to. Thus, any sentence beginning with the words "*I command*" is itself a command; similarly, *warn, advise, assert,* and many others are performative verbs. On the other hand, *go, discover, perform* are not performative, because they do not refer to speech acts, but neither are *joke, lie* which do do so. There are perhaps too many doubtful cases: is it, for instance, insulting to say "*I insult you*"? Performatives have a kind of self-referential quality, but sentences containing them avoid self-reference in the strict sense; they are discussed further in §7.10.

The existence of performatives has tempted linguists to find them in deep structures even where there is no surface indication of them; they can then be used to indicate the illocutionary force of a sentence in a neatly systematic way. The idea has been promoted by Robin Lakoff[66] and even for simple declaratives by Ross,[85] and rebutted by, among others, Fraser,[37] and by Anderson.[4] Ross's idea, that a simple declarative sentence is in reality framed in an imaginary performative clause, of the form "*I assert that . . .*" is, in part, motivated by a desire to enlarge the scope of the inferences *formally* derivable from the given sentence; even sublocutionary inferences could be accommodated in this way. In my view, however, this is only legitimate to the extent that the premisses so drawn upon can be regarded as forming part of the context (as defined in Chapter III); they should therefore, if they are warranted at all, be placed *in* the context in some suitable form, rather than incorporated into each utterance. Ideas present neither in the context, nor in the information directly presented by a given utterance, may not be regarded as making any contribution to the meaning of the utterance.

Disregard of the context as a real and independent element in any speech act has been a persistent tendency among linguists of all schools; it has had many unfortunate consequences, of which the desire to insert such imaginary elements into 'deep structures' is only one. Not all such attempts, however, originate from ignoring the context. Baker,[8] for example, has suggested that all questions contain, in their deep structures, a specific 'question morpheme'. But this too is a needless complication. Questions differ from statements, according to my treatment, given in §§6.6 and 7.7, in a simple and characteristic way, which enables them to be identified as such without any special morpheme. On the other hand, imperatives do contain a stimulus to action, albeit usually unexpressed in any specific word, which needs acknowledgment; these are treated in §§7.6 and 13.7.3. All such items, whose real presence may be in doubt, must be checked against the rule §2 given below in §2.6.2.

2.5. Semiotics

Another discipline which may be relevant to our enquiry is that called 'semiotics'. The term itself was first coined by Locke;[69] as regards content, it is equivalent to the mediaeval 'trivium'. In its modern sense, semiotics goes back mainly to C. S. Peirce,[78] who first formulated the definition generally accepted today. In his view, semiotics studies the three-way relationship between (a) a speaker or listener, (b) signs used between them, and (c) the things or ideas so designated. Having to do with meaning, in what many would claim to be its widest sense, its potential relevance to our subject is obvious. Nevertheless, though some semiotic topics are undoubtedly pertinent, and will be noticed in their proper place, semiotics has built-in limitations which prevent it from being what is needed.

First, it covers the same incomplete segment of the conversational cycle as is covered by the study of speech acts—indeed, the latter has often been presented as a branch of semiotics; it is thus not concerned with the thought phase, but only with the transfer or conveyance of thoughts. Second, it gives no account of the different, indeed contrasting, competences required of speaker and listener, which as we have seen cannot rightly be ignored. Third, it does not include the context among the three entities whose relationship is to be studied. The amount of effective transfer of ideas which is possible in the absence of a context is very restricted. This is, essentially, what computer-based systems of information-handling aim to do; while these are admittedly useful as clerical aids, and for other limited purposes, their power falls very far short of that of natural languages. For these reasons, the assistance we can expect from semiotics, despite its quite copious literature, is rather restricted.

I will exemplify this judgment by a consideration of three topics from the semiotic field. One of these is the distinction which, though known already to some of the classical writers, has been revived by semioticians, between 'signification' and 'designation'; this is discussed for example in a recent paper by Coseriu.[25] The *signification* of a sign is the class of entities which it points to, defined by intention. Thus "*subtidal plants*" signifies plants which grow below the level of the lowest tides; "*monocotyledons*" signifies a particular taxonomic class of plants; "*subtidal monocoty-*

ledons" signifies objects belonging to both classes. The *designation* of a sign is the collection of individials which satisfy its signification; thus, the designation of "*subtidal monocotyledons*" is the genus *Zostera*, the only one included by the description. The value of making the distinction in a general semiotic environment is shown by the sample of "*the victor of Jena*" and "*the vanquished of Waterloo*": though their significations are different, both designate Napoleon. One who was uninformed about the career of Napoleon would perceive the difference between these, but miss their identical designation. When speaking in a context where this particular piece of information can be taken for granted, they 'mean the same', but in a more general context they do not. Once again, we see how the context, properly taken account of, makes unnecessary a distinction which without it must be adhered to. Any well-formed noun phrase, it has been held, *signifies* something; but some, such as "*the present king of France*" *designate nothing*. But again this is true only in some contexts: a French royalist, for example, might not hold the designation of this phrase to be null. In rhematic, therefore, we are not concerned with this distinction.

My second topic from semiotics, which may be rated a near miss for relevance to our study, is the classification of lexical relationships. There is a full discussion of this in Lyons' 'Introduction to Theoretical Linguistics';[70] he gives here a potentially useful terminology for the various relations. For example, two words are defined as "incompatible" if there exists nothing to which both apply; the example given is "*red*" as against "*green*". Notice, however, that the incompatibility holds between a certain pair of *ideas*, for which the names 'red' and 'green' spring to mind, whereas the words, as *lexemes*, have a range of meanings which conflicts with their being incompatible: both might for instance be applied to a new recruit to the Communist Party. The respect in which they are incompatible is important for the speaker, for he has to choose words to express his ideas; but for the listener, who has to understand the words spoken, it is misleading to present as 'incompatible' words whose meanings may in fact not be so. Here, then, we are up against a different shortcoming of the semiotic approach.

A third semiotic distinction will, however, prove to be one which we shall have to have a means of making; this is between 'predicative' and 'determinative' syntagms. The former convey facts, or modalities of facts, while the latter denote participants in facts. Thus, "*this tree is old*" is predicative, while "*this old tree*" is determinative. My treatment of this topic is given in Chapter X.

2.6. The Methodology of Rhematic

Rhematic is concerned primarily with the 'thought' phase of the cycle. The purpose of this work is to devise a notation for utterable thoughts, independent of particular languages, and to show how such a notation can be used. My main contribution to this task is by the use of mathematical arguments; but, of course, the notation emerging from such arguments must still be related intelligibly to natural language utterances, if it is to justify the claim to denote the 'thoughts' which a speaker expresses in utterances and a listener comprehends. Such a notation has to satisfy three kinds of conditions, which together, as it turns out, determine it almost completely.

2.6.1. The Sequoyah Test: The proposed notation has first to play the part of a deep structure, in that it must contain the same information which appears in the utterances used to express it. Its relation to the phonic strings of natural language is one of translation, analogous to translation between two languages, or to the relation between the spoken and written forms of one language, though more abstract in that one relatum is non-linguistic in nature. It must therefore at least satisfy the tests appropriate to prove the adequacy of a system of writing as a transduction of spoken language.

The classic case of such a test was that which faced Sequoyah[34] when he wished to convince the Cherokee Indians of the usefulness of the syllabic script he had devised for their language. His procedure was to demonstrate that arbitrarily selected spoken input could be transduced into the medium under test by one scribe, and regenerated by another having no other means of communication with the first. Since my notation is not itself a language, but aims to express only such things as are capable of expression in any language (except where inadequacies in the lexicon prevent it), this test ought to be extendable so that the two communicating subjects need have no common language. Provided they are both adequately versed in the notation, it should be possible for them to communicate by its means.

So far as I know this test has never been explicitly applied to the deep structures proposed by the Transformational Grammarians, though in so far as these structures are adequate for their intended purpose they should be able to satisfy it. Note, too, that since it is ideas and not words that are being conveyed, there is no need for the output from the test to be the same string which served as input. I have no doubt that 'deep structures' could be prepared which would pass this test (though I suspect that not all such structures appearing in the literature would). Whether they could be constructed by *universally sufficient rules* so as to do so is another question; I would guess that such rules would probably produce output very like my notation. But it would be absurd to suggest that the Sequoyah test is sufficient to specify the notation to within isomorphism; it is, after all, only a minimum requirement.

2.6.2. Sincerity: Since I consider that 'thought' precedes its utterance, the primary operation the feasibility of which I must assume is the generation, from a formula of my notation, of a surface text in a given language, for which English serves as my example. It follows that we must ask under what conditions such an utterance is faithful to its original formula; in colloquial terms, we ask "Is it 'sincere'?". For this purpose I give below a set of 'Rules of Sincerity'. But because, for obvious reasons, most of my examples will *start* from a written sentence and then *proceed to* its rhematic notation, these rules are expressed in symmetrical terms of 'correspondence' rather than 'expression'. Here, then, are the Rules of Sincerity:

S: An utterance in a given context, and a given rhematic formula, correctly *correspond*, provided that
- *S1:* No element of the formula conflicts in any way with either
  - *S1.1:* any marker present in the (phonic) material of the utterance, or
  - *S1.2:* any contextual circumstance accepted by the speaker (or hearer, as the case may be); and
- *S2:* Every element of the formula corresponds to some

linguistically recognizable feature (which may be null) of the utterance; and

S3: Every feature of the utterance is determined (not necessarily fully) by either

S3.1: the accepted contextual circumstances, or
S3.2: the grammar of the language in use, or
S3.3: some element of the formula.

These rules will be used (for the most part without overt reference) to check for superfluities and omissions on either side whenever I present a rendering of any utterance in the notation. It is not possible, at this stage of the exposition, to comment usefully on the procedure for performing these checks; not till Chapter XII shall we have the full range of notational devices with which to exemplify the rules. It is important, however, to state the rules thus early, since they form an essential part of the method I shall use; and in attempting what some may judge to be a dubious enterprise, the freeing of 'meaning' from its customary clothing of language, I am obliged to give evidence that my equipment is not too obviously defective.

2.6.3. The Rhematical Calculus: Semioticians, in discussing how the users of a language relate its signs to the matters signified, have always begun by considering particular sign-signified pairs. No less important, however, are the relationships existing among the signs themselves. For it is on these that constructive thinking depends, the utility of which is the dominant factor in the biological usefulness of the language faculty itself. By 'constructive thinking' I here mean the comparing of one supposed fact with another, and the deducing of previously unnoticed facets of experience from what is already known. It is known to have, as one of its many modes though an untypical one, the capacity for rigorous logic, as well as for analogical and associative thinking. From this we may infer that the system of signs, that is in our case the system of formulae of my notation, must have among other things the structure of at least a rudimentary *calculus*.

This, the third condition to be satisfied by the notation, is a far from vacuous point: the mathematical theory of general algebra provides techniques for determining what systems can and can not be used as 'calculi' or inferential systems. We are here concerned not with properties of this or that sign, or with the different ways in which signs can signify significata, but with properties of the whole system of all signs, or at least of all except those which may for one reason or another be exempted from the requirement of inferential competence. Exclamations, phatic remarks, perhaps questions, suggest themselves for such exemption; but the rest must constitute a system bound by fairly exacting mathematical requirements, if they are to serve for the uses which we know that they are daily put to.

The relevance of such holistic properties of the system of signs is largely confined to the pre-linguistic 'thought' phase of the conversational cycle. In the other phases, where we have to consider the surface forms of the texts we exchange, a considerable degree of unsystematicness is tolerable—provided the 'deep structures' retain their system. Indeed, there is probably a psycholinguistic bias in favour of irregularities and special cases at least up to a certain limit: no natural language is free from them, and analogical levelling seems always to lose its impetus well before the last molehills are flattened—unless perhaps some new field with a more attractive topography has meanwhile been taken in. Chinese civilization seems to have lost nothing by its use of an almost totally unsystematic writing system, which is claimed to be little if at all harder for native speakers to learn than the highly systematized scripts of the Western nations. There is therefore no payoff, either in the study of the text phase, or for the generative grammar concerned in expression and perhaps comprehension, in seeking for some general system underlying the material; no such system exists or need exist. It is otherwise with the material which rhematic studies; the next three chapters will be devoted to elucidating the system involved.

I hope to show that the exigencies of this system, together with the requirements of the Rules of Sincerity, are sufficient to determine within very narrow limits the character of the underlying 'signs' of my rhematic notation. There is almost nothing arbitrary about it except for its graphical presentation (I shall give three forms of it: one diagrammatic, one matrix-type, and one using symbol-strings); and, of course, the lexicon, the contents of which are strongly culture-specific, even peculiar to each individual. This then is no wild goose chase: quite the contrary, the thought phase of the cycle is likely to prove the most circumscribed and the easiest of the four phases to give a full account of—not that I claim any finality for what I present here. Comprehension is likely to prove the hardest. But in every wider field of linguistics, the availability of a rhematic notation will be a useful tool.

CHAPTER III

Context and Comprehension

In the course of the next three chapters, I shall argue that certain non-trivial characteristics of meaning-structures can be deduced from the fact that these structures must be subject to the mental operation of 'comprehension'. It is, presumably, not essential for comprehension to work perfectly all the time, for successful communication to take place; but to ensure that it occurs with a low enough frequency of failure to be tolerable (in emergencies this may be zero), it must be *possible* for it to operate perfectly. The purpose of the present chapter is to make clear the implications of this kind of 'comprehension'. To define what I mean by 'perfect' comprehension, I shall, in Chapter IV, go on to construct a mathematical model of it.

3.1. Utterance and Context

If I were to say to you one Thursday "*I'll meet you on Thursday week*", you might, as a result of hearing this, expect to see me in a week's time. But in my usage, or idiolect, "*Thursday week*" means a week from next Thursday, and so, if spoken on a Thursday, it means in a fortnight's time. Your comprehension would be defective, and I would, therefore, pursuant to rule L3.2, be at fault. In the language of Chapter I, we would be 'entertaining divergent models of the context'. The immediate occasion for the divergence is that you draw an inference from my utterance which I did not intend you to draw.

I think anyone would agree that if a hearer agrees exactly with a speaker as to what inferences do and do not follow from an utterance by the speaker, then understanding of that utterance is satisfactory. Comprehension has occurred. But if, as in the above imaginary example, any one inference is not shared between the participants, comprehension is, at best, not 'perfect'. The various misunderstandings that can occur differ widely, of course, in how consequential they are; but to make such distinctions calls for value judgments which fall outside the linguistic sphere, and they must for the present purpose be rejected. I shall, therefore, consider only the case of 'perfect' comprehension: this is in accordance with the accepted strategy for mathematical models, which always represents more or less idealized situations. The usefulness of what is imperfect is not denied, but theoretical insight is held to start from what is perfect, actuality being seen in the first instance as an attempt at it. Only after further development of the theory can we hope to delineate the real world in more detail.

The example just given is intended to illustrate, yet again, the indispensability of the *context* to the understanding of an *utterance*. Both these terms have been used in a wide variety of ways in the literature; my use of 'context' will be explained in the next two sections, but before going on I shall make clear what I mean by 'utterance'. This term has been variously defined; Garner[41] has summarized its various senses fairly exhaustively. In this work, I shall consistently use it in the sense which Garner labels 'sentence object token'; that is, a particular instance of a piece of (graphic or) phonic material which constitutes a sentence in a given language. However, to avoid having to define prematurely what I mean by a 'sentence', I shall accept as an utterance any possibly incomplete sentence which a speaker offers as if completed; and I shall further treat any intended concatenation of utterances as (optionally) a single utterance.

3.2. The Logical Nature of Context

We have seen an example of an utterance whose meaning depends on whether it is spoken on a Thursday. Contextual relevance is perhaps usually less drastic than this, but is never wholly absent. At the least, if we are correctly to decode personal pronouns, demonstratives, and in many languages verbal tense forms, we have to refer to the immediate space-time situation, which must, therefore, be part of what we mean by 'context'. For most lexical items, there are some contextual data which can affect how they will be understood, if understanding is held to require agreement on all inferences. Here, 'context' has the rather vague sense of 'things not uttered which affect the meaning of what is uttered'. This formulation distinguishes between what is and what is not uttered; but since utterances exist only in the text phase of the conversational cycle (that is, at 'surface' level) this distinction is not acceptable in rhematic. Anything which forms part of the context *can* be uttered; but whether or not it *is* so is not relevant to its status as part of the context.

Further light on what we mean by 'context' can be got by considering what sort of questions can be asked about it. In almost every publication on semantics one can find examples of sentences being discussed without any reference to their context, as I have already had occasion to remark. Thus, in Fraser,[36] we find the example "*The statue was even photographed by the King*", no context being given. Since, according to the view which I take, there is no such thing as a 'null' context, this implies either that the sentence exists in a 'universal' context containing all knowledge (a notion which I demolish on set-theoretic grounds in §4.7), or that it *defines* a context rather than arises out of one. In that case, it is proper to ask questions about it which treat it as a context; such would be 'which statue?', or 'what other notice did it get?'. But it is improper to ask the sort of questions, which Fraser does in fact ask, such as 'Does it mean the same as "*Even the King photographed it*"?'; for to answer this we should have to have a context independently defined.

This kind of confusion implies a too easy disregard of the distinction between language and 'meta-language'. Utterances answer questions *about contexts*. Questions *about utterances* belong to a different 'aboutness' level. If we are to regard comprehension as involving some kind of delocutionary inference, this must be an inference *from* utterances, understood as being *about* the context in which they occur. This calls for illustration. Imagine, then, an establishment of sedentary workers; a newcomer, not yet assigned an office of his own, asks a superior "*//$_2$Can I /work in /**Tom's** /office?*". He gets the reply "*//$_{13}$Tom's /**in** his /office this /**morning**.*" The situation described, and the first sentence, together specify a rather simple 'context'. The second sentence can now be examined as an utterance *in* this context. As an example of a question about the utterance, one might suggest

"What is the theme?"; the answer to this would be "Tom" or "Tom this morning". One might also ask "What is essentially being said?", the answer being that Tom's office is *occupied.* Questions about the context are quite different: one would be "Where is Tom's office?" (this is something which both participants would know the answer to already): the answer might be "Here". Similarly, to "Who is in Tom's office?" (which supposedly is known only to the second speaker) one would give the answer "Tom". One of the more obvious *inferences* from the second sentence, which we would expect both to agree on after it has been comprehended, would be "*//$_1$Tom's /**here** /now.*". Another would be "*//$_1$Tom's /office is in /**use**.*". It is evident that both these are 'about' the context; neither is 'about' any of the *utterances* discussed, because they are on the same level as these.

Linguistics, in general, is about utterances in their various aspects; if there is a meta-language for discussing language, this should form part of linguistics. In fact, linguistic research has concentrated on utterances as texts, and has made relatively little progress in considering their antecedent 'deep structure'. An appropriate meta-language for this does not yet exist; in the rhematic notation I shall here describe, which is specifically about the meanings of utterances, we may hope to find a possible meta-language of this kind. Its lack hitherto has led to difficulties in distinguishing the two levels of abstraction, and so to confusion between discussing *what* a sentence means, and *how* it does it.

3.3. The Linguistic Nature of Context

It appears then that the 'context' of an utterance ideally includes everything both verbal and situational which may have a bearing on the interpretation of the utterances emanating from it. A context is then an entity of the same kind as the *meaning* of an utterance. Each utterance, as it is comprehended by the listener—and each potential utterance which occurs to him as a result of the work of the 'thought' phase of the cycle—is thus a contribution to the context, which it in general alters (for one or the other participant) in some point. The contextual map for each is thus built up in sequence, as the utterances are exchanged in sequence, and this sequence is not wholly arbitrary but represents evidence of the relative prominence that the various contextual data have for the participants. It is therefore necessary in general (though not necessarily on all occasions) to consider the utterances in the order in which they are given.

However, we must also admit as part of the context many things which are not uttered at all. For example, whenever I speak, the word "*I*" means "Frederick Parker-Rhodes"; but this piece of information is only rarely uttered. All the same, it can be (as for instance when one introduces oneself to a stranger). There are also pieces of general knowledge which everyone possesses and so never need to be said, such as that only human beings talk, which are also constantly latent items of every context, even though semanticists have often suggested that they should be included in dictionaries. Obviously, this kind of material could also be included among the utterances defining a context. If, on the other hand, there were anything strictly ineffable forming part of a context, then as such it would at some point affect the meaning ascribed to some utterance in that context; this altered meaning could be discussed, and the discussion would involve expression, in some form, of the supposedly ineffable matter. We are therefore entitled to propose that any context at all can be *represented by* a sequence of utterances.

Let me try to illustrate this with an example. There are two participants, Alfred and Beatrice (A and B); the sequence of the utterances is given to illustrate the build-up of the context, from Alfred's point of view. Unspoken context items are unmarked for speaker; those marked A or B are uttered by the persons indicated:

$//_1$ ∧ *There are /people /playing /**ten**nis.*
$//_1$ ∧ *They're /not /**here**.*
$//_1$ ***Alf**red would /like to /play.*
$//_1$ *Alfred /sees /**Bea**trice.*
A: $//_2$ *Want a /game of /**ten**nis /Beatrice?*
B: $//_5$ ∧ *I'm /dead /**tired*** $//_4$ ∧ *I'd /rather /**not**.*
$//_4$ *People who're /**tired*** $//_1$ *don't /**like** /playing /tennis.*
A: $//_1$ *Come and /watch the /**oth**ers /then.*
B: $//_4$ *Oh* ∧ *I'd /**like** to /sit in the /sun a bit.*
$//_1$ ∧ *It's /quite /**cold** today.*

Note that we start off with a sequence of context statements; these are not uttered, but I give them as if they were utterances because I am making the point that nothing would be changed if they *were* uttered by an imaginary commentator. They express a state of affairs which exists before Alfred starts the conversation. I don't mean them to be in any way *complete* as a statement of the context; they are selected only as being the points necessary to understand Alfred's first remark. Two other contributions come from the context-commentator later on; one of these tells us (we aren't supposed to know anything at all) what effect tiredness has on tennis playing. The other introduces a new point, not essential to any of the foregoing, but obviously relevant to how the conversation will proceed. The most likely thing is that Alfred will actually utter the last contribution, followed by a suggestion that Beatrice had better stay indoors.

By this time the context will have become quite complicated; in fact, I shall not get to the point of being able to work fully through any context as elaborate as this in my notation though I do so discursively in §13.3 (this is only for want of space: it should not prove too hard as an exercise for the reader, given plenty of paper!). Moreover, I have omitted from the above example all potential context items which are not particular to the given incident. The speakers are identified by the initials at the left-hand margin, but properly each role-change should be made explicit in the same form as the rest of the context information.

Besides depending on the identity of speaker and listeners, all speech acts occur in a spatio-temporal environment, within which are made at least the distinctions of here versus not-here, now versus not-now, and usually others; these distinctions are made in all languages, mainly by demonstratives and personal pronouns, and many go beyond this minimum and in so doing call for a more delicate structuring of their contexts. We are thus led to recognise two classes of context items: one 'general', applicable to all contexts, the scope of which is in some measure specific to the language used; and the other 'particular', describing the peculiarities of each individual context as required. To be truly free of all surface constraints, both should be made explicit; but I shall hedge a bit here, omitting the general items from consideration, on the grounds that they can be (and of course normally are) treated as part of the grammar of each language.

3.4. The Rhema

We have seen, from the example given above, how a context can be made explicit as a sequence of utterances. But this of course is only a *representation* of the context. A context is not identical with a sequence of utterances, but with the corresponding sequence of what the utterances mean. We are therefore brought back once more to considering how 'thoughts' can be notated otherwise than by expressing them linguistically. What, in fact, does an utterance 'represent'?

Now we know, from the feasibility of translation, that one can produce two utterances U_1 U_2 each a well-formed sentence in languages L_1 L_2 respectively, such that there will be something in common between the effect of U_1 on the behaviour of a hearer acquainted with L_1 and that of U_2 on a hearer knowing L_2, assuming that each is appropriately motivated. This way of putting it in terms of behaviour is the weakest possible formulation, but it will serve to make my point. The common element (of induced behaviour) is clearly not peculiar to either L_1 or L_2, and is therefore not something expressed *in* either language, and therefore is not an utterance. But since it can be expressed, in either language, *by* an utterance, it is at least part of what such an utterance *represents*. In general, of course, the common element includes many things not affecting overt behaviour, and these too must be included (except by strict behaviourists) in what the utterances represent.

It is this that I have hitherto loosely designated as a 'thought'. I shall from now on use the term *rhema** for that which an utterance represents, for a given participant in a given context, which is to be expressed as a formula in an appropriate notation. The word 'thought' can indeed be used of mental images insufficiently clear or conscious to be formulated as rhemata; but such 'arrhematic' thoughts will of course not concern us further. Two rhemata R_1 R_2 such that any utterance which is a sincere

* The term as here defined is close to its original meaning in Greek, though the later grammarians used it in the sense of 'verb'. 'Rhema' must not be confused with 'rheme', which is contrasted with 'theme' in the category of *focus*.

expression of either is a sincere expression also of the other (according to the rules S) will be said to be *equivalent*. I shall further postulate a relation between rhemata denoted by "$\supset$" representing 'delocutionary inference', such that for all rhemata R_1 R_2 the proposition $R_1 \supset R_2$ is either true or false. The nature of this 'inference' will be discussed in more detail in §4.1, where various interpretations of the term are surveyed.

3.5. The Lexigen

In general, the sentences of particular languages have a more or less complex 'surface' structure, and though this differs from one language to the next, at least parts of it are usually recognisable in a translation of a given sentence into a second language. Thus, if we may accept "*Il me fait chaud*" as a possible rendering in French of the English sentence "*I am hot*", we are entitled to make certain identifications between the words. Thus, in particular, there is a strong overlap in semantic application and grammatical status between the English "*hot*" and the French "*chaud*". There is also a correspondence between "*I*" and "*me*", which would be stronger were it not that the two forms are marked in their respective languages for different cases. But broadly speaking, in so far as the two sentences 'mean the same', these two word pairs also 'mean the same'. But there is nothing in the English which 'means the same' as the French "*il*", and it is stretching things a bit to say that "*fait*" means the same as "*am*". There are, therefore, structural elements identifiable across translations and others which are not identifiable; but the two classes are not sharply separated. The most predictably identifiable are those referring to particular perceptual isolates, such as "*dog*", "*chien*", "*Hund*", "*gouzi*", or "*come*", "*viens*", "*komm*", "*lai*".

It thus appears that not only is there a rhema which represents both "*I am hot*" and "*Il me fait chaud*" in suitable contexts, but this rhema must be expected to contain structural elements corresponding to "*hot* = *chaud*" and to the first person singular as the common element between "*me*" and "*I*". On the other hand, it is likely that no other structural elements will appear, unless perhaps there is one for the present tense. A rhema, therefore, has a structure some of whose elements are likely to receive expression in linguistic units *below* the rank of a sentence.

I shall call such structural elements, of whatever 'size' they may be in relation to the whole rhema, *lexigens*. This name indicates that in a procedure for generating an utterance from a given rhema, the identity of each *lexigen* is likely to be a major factor in selecting an appropriate *lexeme* from the *lexicon* of the language. It is not the case that every lexigen *must* be expressed as a lexeme, or (as the above example shows) that every lexeme registers the presence of a lexigen in the rhema expressed. A further example of this may be given: the Russian sentence "*U men'a kniga*" translates into English as "*I've got a book*". The juxtaposition of the two case forms in Russian, possessive and nominative, requires for its rendering in English the insertion of a full (one might almost say over-full) verb form, which evidently does not represent any lexigen in the rhema common to the two sentences. As we shall see in Chapter XI, where the case system is examined in detail, this is a common situation in languages which like English have a wholly periphrastic system for indicating case relations. There are other situations also where we shall find seemingly load-bearing words which serve to express material carried at the rhema level by lexigens which find their main expression elsewhere, as well as words which serve no purpose but to satisfy a grammatical rule like the "*It*" in "*It's nice to get away*". What we do *not* find are lexigens which find *no* expression in a corresponding sincere utterance.

3.6. The Rhema Structure of Lexigens

As defined above, a lexigen is any structural component of a rhema which might, in one language or another, call for expression in a particular lexeme; to which I added the qualifying phrase 'of whatever size'. This hints at the fact that we may discern a structure within a single lexigen. An obvious illustration of this is the existence of phrases, such as "*take to pieces*", which have one-word synonyms, in this case "*dismantle*". The latter word corresponds to a lexigen which can (perhaps must) be represented as having its own rhema-like structure with at least two lexigens of its own, meaning say "transform into components", with an appropriate relationship ("into") between them. Such examples perhaps naturally prompt a search for 'atomic' lexigens which can be analysed no further, and out of which all others can be constructed; hopefully, these may constitute a manageably small 'universal vocabulary' for the rhematic system.

Unfortunately, this quest proves to be open-ended and circular. Any lexigen can be explained, in dictionary fashion, as equivalent to some more or less expanded rhema; and a large class of simple rhemata can be expressed, in any given language, by a single word, which would justify their condensation, in an appropriate context, to a single lexigen. Consider, for instance, the group of words "*knife*", "*cut*", and "*sharp*". A '*knife*" is a "*sharp*" thing used for "*cutting*"; "*cutting*" is done with a "*knife*", best if it is "*sharp*"; and "*sharp*" in the attribute of a "*knife*" which makes it good for "*cutting*". In any cultural context where knives exist, we are likely to find lexigens corresponding to all three terms. Any two of them could be represented as complex structures derived from the third. Thus, a knife could be a "cutter", and sharp could be "cutsome"; or sharp could be rendered as "knifish" and cut as "beknife". But there is no reason to choose any one as the basic element; there is no clear-cut primacy among them. Clearly, this will usually be the case; if there is an 'obvious' choice in the matter, it depends on the conceptual structuring of our world, which is certainly not the same for all languages. It may be in this sense obvious that "*intrude*" means "*enter without permission*", but it is a feature of our culture, that one is not supposed to go into someone's house without announcing oneself or having prior permission; there are cultures (as in parts of Nepal) where this convention is not observed, and there, perhaps, the notion of entering *with* permission would be the 'marked' term. There is then no clear basis for the idea of 'atomic' lexigens, in that any such class is at some point or other bound to a particular language, and no vocabulary of atomic lexigens can claim to be a universal of language.

Any lexigen, then, can, if desired, be regarded as semantically equivalent to various structures of lexigens; that is, since a lexigen is by definition a component of a rhema, one may always replace a single lexigen in a given rhema by a structure of lexigens so as to produce a rhema equivalent to the first, in the sense of §3.4. The converse, that a structured portion of a rhema can be replaced by a single lexigen, may equally hold, of course. This means that the structure we impute to rhemata must be such as to permit of this operation; this point I shall deal with in its proper place. It also, however, raises the question as to what sort of structures can represent lexigens in this way. This can easily be answered: if one were to ask what is meant by the word "knife", one might answer "*It's what people use to cut things*". This is an utterance which expresses, like any other utterance, a rhema; the rhema which it expresses can obviously be used, therefore, as a definition of the meaning of "*knife*". It may turn out to be the case that the class of rhemata serving as definitions in this way is in some manner restricted, but at least we may conclude that what I have been calling 'structures of lexigens' are in every case themselves rhemata. It follows that the internal structure of rhemata is hierarchical, in that big ones contain, in general, smaller ones as part of themselves. In the actual writing-out of rhemata, when we have the notation to do it, it is a question of the delicacy of description where one chooses to stop.

3.7. Inferential Relations between Lexigens

I have already introduced the notation $R_1 \supset R_2$ for an inferential relation between two rhemata. Now suppose that in such a case R_1 differs from R_2 only in that one of its lexigens l_1 is replaced in R_2 by a different lexigen l_2. We then expect that there will be an evident inference-like relation between the words used to express l_1 and l_2, which we may write $l_1 \supset l_2$. I shall consider in detail in §4.1 the various ways in which this 'inference' can be thought of; here I shall consider the consequences of following up one simple type. If I were to say "*I've got a poodle in this basket*", you would be entitled, without doubt, to infer from this that "*You've got a dog in that basket*", and from this that "*You've got an animal in that basket*", and further "*You've got an object in that basket*". The feature of the world which this relation reflects, and from which it derives its usefulness, is that there is an inclusion relation between the classes of things designated by the respective lexemes, in their appropriate word-uses. Representing these designation-classes by the words enclosed in parentheses ( ), and the inclusion relation by $\geqq$, we have (*objects*) $\geqq$ (*animals*) $\geqq$ (*dogs*) $\geqq$ (*poodles*). This is not, from the linguistic point of view, a 'fact', but rather a contribution to the lexicographic definition of these four words; if anyone were to dispute the assertion (*animals*) $\geqq$ (*dogs*), for instance, he would not be criticizing a widespread opinion, but showing his ignorance of the accepted usage of one or both words.

It is evident that, whenever such inclusions hold, the corresponding inferences are legitimate between rhemata differing only by the substitution of one of the lexigens for another (provided the rhemata contain no general or negative terms: see §9.6). The converse is also true. Thus, if one hears a word unfamiliar to one, say for example "*sgiandubh*", and discovers in the course of conversation that "*Sandy's lost a knife*" is accepted as an inference from "*Sandy's lost his sgiandubh*", then one has discovered that a sgiandubh is a kind of knife. It follows that not only is inclusion between designation-classes a lexigen-relation pertinent to inferences between rhemata, but also that whenever delocutionary inference is traceable to a relation between particular lexigens, this relation is an inclusion of one designation-class in another.

We are therefore directed to consider the system of lexigens as being structured by designation-inclusion, this being the most relevant property of this system for understanding inference relations between rhemata. What I here call the 'system of lexigens' is not, of course, the same as the system of lexemes of any given language. The latter involves many other types of relationship besides inclusion; but while most of these are, in detail at least, pecular to a particular language the system of inclusions is in one sense a language universal. For while it gives us no more than definitions for *words* (as I mentioned above), the inclusion-relation is *factual* as between what the words *mean*; that is, designation-inclusions between *lexigens* derive from extra-linguistic facts, and are thus common to all languages. The system of lexigens, then, is an inclusion system.

3.8. Introducing Lattices

The lexicon of a given language is much more complex than

this, and much more fluid in that words are for ever changing their meanings, for most words are more or less subject to the whims of Humpty Dumpty. But it would be strange if there were no similarity between lexemes and lexigens at all. There are two ways of presenting a 'lexicon': one presentation enables one to find the meaning of a given word, usually by arranging the words in a conventional order (easy in an alphabetic script, not impossible even in an ideographic one); this is called a 'dictionary'. The other enables one to find, or helps one to choose, a word to express a given meaning; this is much harder, since there is not, perhaps cannot be, a conventional order for the meanings of words. Nevertheless, there have been numerous attempts to do just this, and the result is called a 'thesaurus'; one classic example of a thesaurus, for English, is that of Roget.[84] Credit for first recognising the importance of thesauri in semantics belongs to Masterman;[72] the 'thesaurus principle' is now widely accepted, at least as a tool of research or an aid in computational linguistics, and I here propose to carry it still further, though applying it to lexigens rather than to words.

The mathematical structure of a thesaurus is, ideally, that of a *lattice.*[72] As this notion will be heavily exploited in the sequel, it is necessary to explain what is meant by it. Suppose you have a set of entities, which we may think of as 'classes' since we are going to consider them as 'including' one another; that is, we suppose that if a, b are any two classes, we can assert that either $a \geqq b$, or $b \geqq a$, or both are true (which we write $a = b$), or neither is true (which we write a//b). Now let us denote the set of all these 'classes' by L. If, for *any* pair of members of L such as a, b, there is a *unique* smallest member of L, x, such that both $x \geqq a$ and $x \geqq b$, and a *unique* biggest member y such that both $a \geqq y$ and $b \geqq y$, then we call L a *lattice.* The element x we denote by $a \smile b$, and we call it the *least upper bound* or *LUB* of a and b; and the element y is similary called the *greatest lower bound* or *GLB* of a and b, denoted by $a \frown b$. The operations $\smile$ and $\frown$ are called the *join* and *meet* respectively.

As an example of a lattice, we may take the factors of a given whole number. One factor is said to include another, for this purpose, if the first *is divisible* by the second; thus, $12 \geqq 3$, $15 \geqq 3$, $3 \geqq 3$, but 15//12. That the factors of a given number do form a lattice we can see from the following diagram; in this diagram, each factor is connected by one or more descending lines with all its divisors. I take the number 60 as my example:

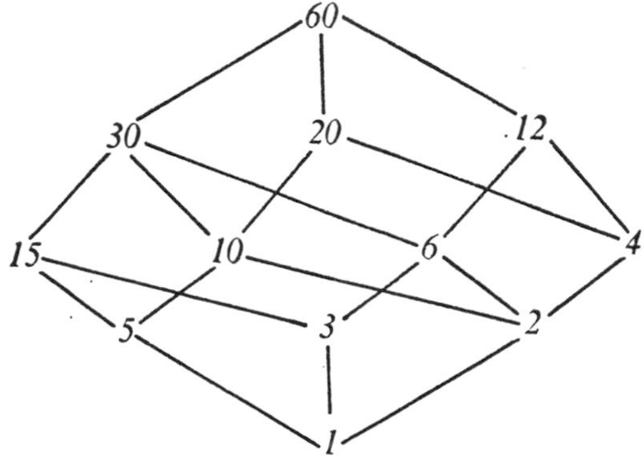

. . . 3.1

Since, as is well known, the expression of any number as the product of its factors is unique, we know that this system must satisfy the lattice property; for $a \smile b$ stands for the least common multiple of a and b, and $a \frown b$ for the greatest common divisor. One can check, by tracing the lines up and down by eye, that (3.1) does indeed represent a lattice; in more typical instances the set is too big for this to be practicable. As an example of a set which is *not* a lattice we may take the living descendants of a given individual. Suppose that G is the mother of a son F and a daughter M; that F has a daughter W, and that M has two sons H and L; that H married W and they had a son S and a daughter D, and that W also had an illegitimate son B by L. S, D, and B have no descendants, and so nobody O is descended from all three. The diagram for this is on p. 46.

This is *not* a lattice because there is *no* unique 'least upper bound' for S and D, since both H and W 'include' both S and D, but H//W, that is, neither of H, W 'includes' the other. Fig. (3.2) exhibits another point which needs to be watched. If we were to eliminate say D from the diagram, the remaining part would satisfy the lattice condition; but this fact is obviously fortuitous, since it is clear that family trees are very unlikely to be lattices unless they are very small. The moral is, that diagrams

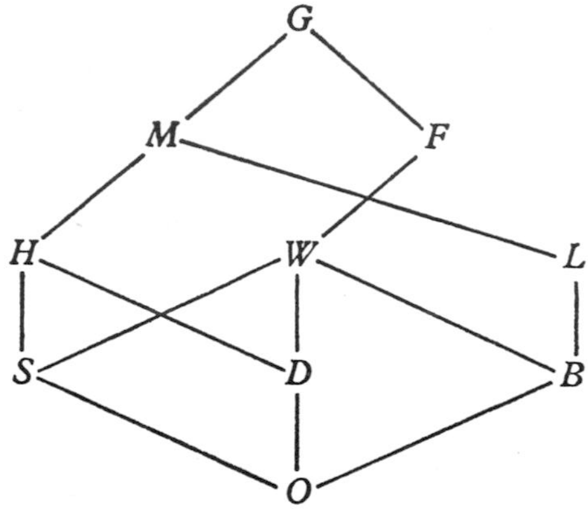

. . . 3.2

such as (3.1) and (3.2) should not be thought of as anything but diagrams. A system which happens to 'be' a lattice, for any other reason than that it is constructed according to rules which show that it ought to be one, is unlikely to yield any useful insights through its adventitious lattice property.

3.9. The Lexical Lattice

In stating above that the mathematical structure of a thesaurus is 'ideally' a lattice, it was this last point which I had in mind. The introduction by Masterman[72] of the lattice model of a thesaurus did not depend on finding that any arbitrary vocabulary embodied in an actual thesaurus satisfied the lattice definition, but on the advantages to be obtained from *representing* a thesaurus by a lattice, in which the ordering relation was that of designation-inclusion. In such a representation, the elements stand for designation-classes, not for actual words; most of them will have one-word *names* (otherwise the representation is unlikely to be close enough to be useful), but some will always have to be designated by (usually brief) noun-phrases. A selection of moderately complex examples of such constructions are given in Chapters VIII to XI, which will illustrate this point. Here is a simpler case: A "*saw*" and a "*chisel*" are each both an "*edge-tool*" and a carpenter's tool; for the latter class we have no one-word name in English (though 'tool' itself originally had this meaning), but *"carpenter's tool"* is a perfectly good two-word name, and is how we ordinarily designate the class. We now notice that these four designation-classes violate the lattice condition, for they do not include a unique LUB for chisels and saws, nor a unique GLB for edge-tools and carpenter's tools. In constructing a thesaurus, according to the lattice principle, we would have to *insert* such a class, for which the name *"carpenter's edge-tool"* is the best we can do without resorting to neologism.

However, for considering the structure of the system of lexigens, we are not limited by the actual existence of words. I shall prove, in Chapter IV, that *proper* lexigens (that is, those which do not correspond to empty designations) do constitute a lattice. If it were the case that every pair of designations had a join (union) which was not nameless in a given language, and a meet (intersection) which was not empty in real contexts, then the set of all designations (of proper lexigens) would be a lattice of a special type called 'Boolean'. That this is not in fact realized is shown by such examples as *"children"* and *"windows"*: probably no language has a name for their join (*children*)$\smile$(*windows*), unless by an accident of homophony, and their meet (*children*)$\smile$(*windows*) is certainly an empty designation (that is, there is nothing which belongs to both classes).

We can, however, as mentioned above, show that the system of all proper lexigens is a lattice; this I shall call the *lexical lattice*. It is understood to be common to all languages, but it cannot be called a language universal, since 'lexigen' is not a linguistic concept. One may legitimately wonder whether it is admissible to speak of 'all lexigens'—for I shall show later that we can attach no mathematical meaning to the phrase 'all rhemata', which seems similar. In fact, the class of all lexigens, though indefinitely large and in the limit potentially infinite, is certainly not more than denumerably infinite. For let L be an incomplete version of the lexical lattice. The upper bound of L is the designation which includes all others, and which I shall call the designation of the *null* lexigen; the lower bound is the empty designation-class, which is the designation of the *empty* lexigen. Now let C be a concept needing to be introduced into the incomplete system of lexigen L; however unrelated C may be to the material already included it necessarily is included in the null lexigen and includes the empty lexigen. The worst possible case is then the accession to L of an infinite succession of such unrelated concepts; but this generates at most a denumerable infinity added to the original L. If L was finite, it will become denumerably infinite; and if L was infinite already, its cardinality will not be affected by the accessions; but L cannot exceed in cardinality the quantity 2^w where w is the sum of the numbers of words in all known languages, which is finite. The completed lexical lattice is therefore at most denumerably infinite; as an individual entity it is not a member of itself, for its members are classes (one of them has indeed the lexical lattice as its only member); and it is a non-unique member of at least one other class (that of lattices). It is therefore not only a class but a *set*, free from the antinomies which affect the class of all rhemata.

3.10. The Rehearsal and Repertory of a Context

We must now return, after this lengthy excursion, to the original object of this Chapter, which was to give a logical description of what I mean by a 'context'. Now we saw in §3.3 that a context is something which can be represented by a sequence of utterances. Now an utterance represents what it conveys to a hearer of it, namely a rhema. So what is represented by a sequence of utterance is a sequence of rhemata; in one sense, then, that is what a context is. Though as we have seen not all these rhemata need receive verbal expression, we obviously need for notational purposes to formulate in the same way everything which goes to specifying a given context. We may thus regard a context as being represented, and therefore fully specified, by a sequence of actual or potential utterances; this sequence, which we now regard as a single complex utterance, I shall call the *rehearsal* of the context. The complex rhema which could find expression in this rehearsal is then identified with the *context* itself.

A point has here to be made in regard to highly complex rhemata such as actual contexts often are. This is that, while they can be comprehended easily enough by listening to the context-rehearsal, they usually defy re-expression by such rules as are adequate in the case of rhemata expressed by a single sentence. If the listener is asked to do this, he may either attempt to reproduce the rehearsal verbatim, or he will produce a quite different sequence of sentences which (on processing by the rules described in Chapter XIII) will yield (more or less) the same result as the original one. In such a case the listener is presumably using a different, though no doubt equally ruly, procedure from what he uses to express a simpler rhema. There is a problem here for the transformational grammarians to look into.

Whatever may happen in the rather artificial situation where a listener is asked to re-rehearse a context, it is a fundamental assumption of my theoretical position that if a context has been comprehended fully, the listener has grasped not only the separate sentences in the rehearsal, but all and only the permissible inferences from them as well. Now the understanding of a contextual situation, though commonly assisted by linguistic means, is a goal definable independently of any particular language, and can be attained, by appropriately informed and sufficiently intelligent observers, irrespective of the languages they use. This is one reason for considering inference as a relation between rhemata, not between sentences. To grasp a context is to grasp every rhema inferrable from the context, that is, from those conveyed by the rehearsal of the context.

Thus, side by side with the rehearsal of a context, which is a sequence of utterances, and the context itself, which is a single complex rhema, we need a term for the complete set of rhemata generated by an appropriate inference procedure from the context. This set of rhemata I shall call the *repertory* of the context. Note here that 'rehearsal' is a term referring to the object language, whereas 'context' and 'repertory' both belong to a different level of abstraction, that of rhematical notation, which can be used as a metalanguage for discussing what an object language expresses. An utterance which expresses any rhema which belongs to the repertory of a given context will be said to be *compatible* with that context.

It will have been apparent, from my discussion of the concept of 'natural language' in Chapter I, that we may not be able to maintain the same attitude to contradiction as is adopted in traditional logic. This point is of relevance here, in that we shall find it possible for the repertory of a context to contain rhemata which would be held to contradict each other in Aristotelian logic; indeed, there is no reason why 'contradictory' utterances should not cooccur in the rehearsal itself. In Aristotelian logic, the rule is that *any* proposition is inferrable from a contradiction. This has always been felt irksome by non-logicians, and the effect of the rule is of course simply to forbid the use of contradictions, so that it is never applied. In real life there is no one to forbid contradictions, and the constraints of formal logic do not apply to the study of natural language. As we shall see, there are a variety of 'impediments' to inference which we shall have to formulate; one of these is that *nothing* (not anything!) may be inferred from any rhema containing a contradiction (see further in Chapter XIV). There are, however, still some constraints on what may be accepted as the rehearsal of a context (see §13.2); these are designed chiefly to eliminate incoherences, such as those exhibited in "*They came in the evening. Nineteen is a prime number*" which might co-occur in a rehearsal but could hardly be juxtaposed. But the avoidance of contradictions is not one of the rules which can properly be required.

CHAPTER IV

The Context Lattice Theorem

We have now reached the point of having a basic set of terms with which to discuss the subject-matter of rhematic: utterance, context, rehearsal, repertory, rhema, lexigen. The task of this chapter will be to show that the concepts thus designated import into the thought phase of the conversational cycle sufficient mathematical structure to impose useful constraints on the permissible relationships between a rhema and its component lexigens. In Chapter VI these relationships will be formalized as a description of rhema structure. Both this, and still more the next Chapter, will involve fairly detailed mathematical argumentation; those readers who wish to avoid this may turn now to the summary of conclusions given at the beginning of Chapter VI.

4.1. A Characterization of Inference

The notion of 'inference' has been repeatedly mentioned in the foregoing pages. I have suggested that 'comprehension' of an utterance may be defined as requiring that the listener should agree with the speaker regarding all the 'inferences' which legitimately follow from an utterance in a given context. But I have also pointed out (in §2.4) that different interpretations have been put on this term by different investigators, and before we make use of the concept we shall have to show that it is capable of proper definition.

A frequent term in the literature on this topic is 'presupposition', deriving from Frege;[38] many writers contrast this with 'inference' by saying, as does van Fraassen,[35] that a sentence A presupposes another sentence B if B can be inferred either from A or from its negation. Thus, it is said to be a presupposition of "*John realized that Mary was pregnant*" that "*Mary was pregnant*", since this is equally presupposed by *"John didn't realize that Mary was pregnant"*. The discussions about presupposition have generally accepted this poisition, and no writer has really exposed all the muddles involved. One result of this has been to promote the view, expressed for instance by Kuroda,[61] that there is no such thing as *the* formal representation of the meaning of a sentence; this would in any case follow from the neglect of context which is conventionally accepted, but the confusion about presuppositions is Kuroda's immediate pretext. I will not repeat what I have said about context, nor will I labour the point about language and metalanguage, but the idea of 'the' negation of a sentence must be looked at (a fuller treatment will be found in §14.2).

Consider the utterance "*Edwin has given me the documents*". According to most contributors to the topic, this carries the presupposition "*Edwin has had the documents*". However, even confining attention to cases where the sentence is pronounced with the simple falling tone, there are five possible tonicities (only "the" cannot be tonic), and up to three possible negations (of "*has given me*" in all cases, on "*the documents*" except when "*has*" has tonic stress, and on "*Edwin*" when this term is tonic). There are therefore at least ten distinct ways of negating this sentence; of these, three support the presupposition proposed—those with "*hasn't*" replacing "*has*" and with tonic stress on "*hasn't*", "*given*", and "*documents*". Neither "*//₁ **Edwin** /hasn't /given me the /documents.*" nor "*//₁ Edwin /hasn't /given /**me** the /documents.*" presupposes that Edwin has had them; nor do any of the forms in which "*Edwin*" or "*the documents*" are negated. The form with "*me*" tonic depends critically on the context: if Edwin had a duty to pass the documents to someone, it would be 'presupposed' that he has had them, but only in the sense that this was *known* to be so (the utterance in question would not be compatible with this context if this was not known); if he had no such duty, there is only a pertinential inference (§14.5) that he hasn't got them *now*. In the other cases, the 'presupposition' is valid in all and only those cases where it is a rhematical inference in the sense I shall define in the sequel. The attaching of this special term to an ill-defined subset of inferences does not seem to me to be a useful contribution.

To illustrate the range of different kinds of 'inference' that have been proposed as useful or interesting, let me take one utterance from which a paradigm of 'inferences' can be derived. From "$//_5$ *Larry's /passed his /**finals**.*" we can infer variously

4.1.1. "$//_1$ *Larry has /passed an /**exam**.*" by direct inclusion;
4.1.2. "$//_1$ *Larry / has the /**results** of his /finals.*" ditto;
4.1.3. "$//_1$ *Larry has /answered some /**questions**.*" ditto from (4.1.1);
4.1.4. "$//_1$ *Larry has /passed /**previous** /exams.*" by inclusion using lexical information relating to the word "*finals*";
4.1.5. "$//_1$ *Larry was /taking his /**finals**.*" ditto using "*passed*";
4.1.6. "$//_5$ *Larry might /well have /**failed**.*" by pertinential inference;
4.1.7. "$//_4$ *Either /**Larry** or $//_1$ **Chris** have /passed their /finals.*" by logical inference, using $A \supset A \smile B$ on the word "*Larry*";
4.1.8. "$//_4$ *Larry /passed his /**finals** while $//_1$still /**alive**.*" by logical inference from lexical expansion of "*pass ones finals*";
4.1.9. "$//_1$ *∧ I /**believe** that $//_1$ Larry's /passed his /**finals**.*" by sublocutionary inference (implicature of sincerity);
4.1.10. "$//_{13}$ *∧ I'm /**happy** that /Larry's /passed his /**finals**.*" by sublocutionary inference from the use of tone 5;
4.1.11. "$//_5$ *∧ He's /probably /**failed**.*" by pertinential inference from (4.1.2);
4.1.12. "$//_1$ *Per/haps /**Chris** has /passed his /finals.*" by inclusion from (4.1.7);
4.1.13. "$//_5$ *Larry's /**dead**.*" by pertinential inference from (4.1.8);
4.1.14. "$//_1$ *∧ I'm a /happy /**believer**.*" by inclusion from (4.1.9 and 10).

It will be noted, of the several different kinds of inference exhibited here, that not all are 'correct' in any colloquial sense of the term, some by themselves and most of them in combination. It will also be observed that all of (4.1.2) to (4.1.5) are 'presuppositions' according to van Fraassen's definition,[35] since these also follow from "$//_1$ *Larry's /failed his /**finals**.*". Let us now consider, in the light of these examples, what kind of 'inference' we require to use in rhematic.

4.2. Rhematical Inference

One obvious point of difference between the varieties of inference illustrated is that some are, and others are not, transitive. That is, it may be the case that whenever $A \supset B$ and $B \supset C$ we can state also that $A \supset C$, or not. What I have called 'direct inclusion' is so; this fact, which will probably be obvious, is illustrated by the acceptability of (4.1.3), obtained by two stages of inclusion via (4.1.1). So, as is well known, is logical inference. But these varieties cannot be successfully mixed: (4.1.12) is not acceptable as any kind of 'inference' from the original utterance.

Others are non-transitive on account of their definitions. What I have labelled above as 'pertinential' inference consists in the elucidation of unuttered context items, from the observation that in the absence of these items we would have a context with which the given utterance would not be compatible. If Larry were certain to pass, no one knowing this would utter (4.1.0) at all; at best, they would put it in tone 1 (simple falling). Therefore, we can give (4.1.6) as a 'pertinential' inference. But this restricts the operation to actual utterances, and it cannot be applied a second time to inferences such as (4.1.6) so derived. Similarly, sublocutionary inference, which involves making explicit the speaker's presumed state of mind evoking his locutionary act, precludes its being used as a premiss; if we disregard this, we get such nonsense as (4.1.14). Pertinential inference misapplied to unuttered inferences also predicatably yields nonsense, as in (4.1.11) and (4.1.13).

On the other hand, there is no objection to the use of information such as might be obtained from dictionary-entries relating to the words used. This bears out what we would expect from the remarks in §3.6, which indicate that we can construct a rhema equivalent to a given one by incorporating in it, in the place of one of its lexigens, a rhema expanding this lexigen so as to indicate in greater detail what it means in its given context. Thus, we might expect to find, as lexical information relating to "*finals*", something to the effect that before one can take one's finals, one has to have passed previous examinations, which is stated in (4.1.4). The same model of how such information can be used indicates that every step of this kind is equivalent to a step of inference by inclusion; it is not really any different. Accordingly, combination of the two methods should give acceptable inferences, as in (4.1.4), as against (4.1.5) which (given a plausible kind of dictionary) could be reached in one step.

The reason for our being interested in transitivity of inference is not only that it is a property which 'inference' in the ordinary sense ought to have. I shall show, in §4.3, that for the purposes we are using it for, it *must* be transitive (proposition 4.2). More discursively, we need it to impose some relevant and appropriate structure on the repertory of a context, and the structures derivable from non-transitive relations are too limited a class to be useful to us. This requirement leaves us, in the light of these examples, with a choice between inference by inclusion, and logical inference. One might wonder here whether this exhausts the possibilities; all one can say here is that the topic has been under careful study at least since the time of Frege, and no one has come up with anything not exemplified in the above paradigm. But this must remain an open question.

In regard to logical inference, this has been the type universally regarded as proper to exact thought, from the time of Aristotle[6] to Russell and Whitehead[87] and beyond; it has been, in the form of the predicate calculus, the tool used by all workers in Artificial Intelligence (see Wilks[106] for a review of this work). But it nevertheless cannot be relied on to produce good sense in the structuring of contexts. Neither (4.1.7) nor (4.1.8) gives a good view of the context of Larry's success in his finals. These examples are not chosen to guy them, but only as being not also explainable in terms of inclusion (most inferences by inclusion are also logical inferences). It requires only a little thought to convince one that inclusion is the relation which gives us 'good' inferences, and that in its absence, logical inference is unlikely to do so. The fact that in combination they produce nonsense, as in (4.1.12), is enough to show that logical inference, for all its prestige, is not what we're looking for.

One further point may not be out of place before I pass on. In a recent paper, Zwicky[109] has introduced a new confusion into the terminology, by using 'inference' to refer explicitly to statements derived from two or more 'premisses'; this of course harks back to Aristotle,[6] but is hardly in accord with modern usage. Those consequences which can be derived from a single premiss Zwicky would subsume under the term 'presupposition'. I here regard this last term as having too many uses to be useful any longer. 'Inference' is too strongly established to be discarded; but its many varieties illustrated in §4.1 need to be distinguished by adjectives: logical, sublocutionary, and pertinential have already appeared. In the sequel, I shall adopt, pursuant to the following argument, the term 'rhematical' inference for that relationship which depends on inclusion. This, however, is not yet a formal definition; I shall now attempt to provide one.

4.3. Definition and Properties of Rhematical Inference

I first postulate an undefinable predicate U, defined over utterances, such that Ua may be read as 'the utterance a is understood'. Note that I here use the term 'understood' rather than 'comprehended'; I wish the latter to be confined to the process, properly within the subject-matter of psycholinguistics, whereby a listener *achieves* the understanding of an utterance in a given context. It is his having done so that I denote by U, and it is for my purposes an undefinable because it models a situation analyzed in another discipline, psychology. For simplicity, I do not explicitly mention the context here; but, of course, if Ua is true of a given a in a context C, it may not be true of the same a in another context C′.

I have already introduced the sign $\supset$ for 'inference'; I shall from now on restrict it to be used as in the proposition below, and I shall use for the inference relation of the predicate calculus the sign $\Rightarrow$. I then begin as follows: by *rhematical inference* I shall mean a relation $\supset$ defined over rhemata by

$$(\forall a)\,(\forall b)\colon (a) \supset (b)\,.\,\&\,.\,Ua\;.\Rightarrow .\;Ub \qquad \ldots 4.1$$

where (a), (b) denote the rhemata expressed by utterances a, b respectively, and where a given context is assumed to apply throughout.

This proposition can be paraphrased as follows. For any two utterances a, b both compatible with a context C, we assert that the rhema conveyed by b is rhematically inferrable from that conveyed by a if and only if the understanding of a in context C implies, in the logical sense, the understanding also of b. The particular form in which (4.1) is written is intended to show its formal analogy with the *modus ponens* of classical logic. This analogy is of course not fortuitous (I would wish to say that (4.1) furnishes the intuitive basis on which *modus ponens* is founded), but is no more than an analogy. For U, though it syntactically replaces an assertion operator, does not represent assertion, nor truth, but an (often unconsious) assent to something heard or read, whose further analysis belongs to psychology rather than linguistics.

To continue: the 'premiss' a is represented as a single utterance; however, in view of the discussion in §3.1, the distinction between a single utterance and a sequence of them is not of first importance. A sequence of utterances is in the domain of U, being 'understood' if and only if every component utterance is understood. In particular, we shall often consider the a in (4.1) as being the rehearsal of a context. Several properties of rhematical inference can be derived directly from (4.1). Thus, it follows from the properties ascribed to $\Rightarrow$ in the predicate calculus that, for any u, $Uu \Rightarrow Uu$; substituting u for both a and b in (4.1), we have:

$$(\forall u) \;.\; (u) \supset (u) \qquad \ldots 4.2$$

Next, from two successive applications of (4.1),

$$(\forall u)(\forall v)(\forall w): (v) \supset (w) \,.\, \& \,.\, (u) \supset (v) \,.\, \& \,.\, Uu \Rightarrow (v) \supset (w) \,.\, \& \,.\, Uv \Rightarrow Uw$$

thus proving that

$$(\forall u)(\forall v)(\forall w):.\ (u) \supset (v) \,.\, \& \,.\, (v) \supset (w): \Rightarrow :(u) \supset (w) \quad 4.3$$

Since we take U as indefinable, we have no means of distinguishing rhematically between two utterances u, v such that $Uu \Rightarrow Uv \,.\, \& \,.\, Uv \Rightarrow Uu$. We may write this condition simply as $(u) = (v)$. It now follows, again from two applications of (4.1), that

$$(\forall u)(\forall v):.\ (u) \supset (v) \,.\, \& \,.\, (v) \supset (u): \Rightarrow :(u) = (v) \quad \ldots 4.4$$

We have now shown, in the results (4.2)–(4.4), that rhematical inference is *reflexive* (4.2), *transitive* (4.3), and *antisymmetric* (4.4). Any relation having these three properties is called a 'partial ordering', and its domain constitutes a 'partially-ordered set' under it. The kind of system called a 'lattice' described in §3.8 is a special type of partially-ordered set (generally abbreviated to 'poset'). It is now clear, from the definition of the repertory of a context as given in §3.10, that this will always be a poset under rhematical inference. I shall now ask whether there is anything further we can say about it.

4.4. The Context Lattice Theorem

In this section I shall give a proof that the repertory of any context is a lattice under rhematical inference. This will proceed in the following steps. I will first define the lattice-theory terms 'ideal' and 'sublattice'. Next, using these definitions, I will prove a lemma or intermediate theorem, which I shall repeatedly refer to in later chapters. Thirdly, I will prove the proposition stated above, using this lemma.

4.4.1. Some Lattice Definitions: If L is a lattice, and if a is an element of L (which in our present context we think of as a designation-class), then all the elements of L which are included in a constitute together the *lower ideal* of a in L. Conversely, the set of all elements of L which include a constitute the *upper ideal* of a in L. The union of the lower and the upper ideals of a given element a is called the *double* ideal of a. If S is any subset of a lattice L, an element x of S, such that S is identical with the double ideal of x, or is contained in the double ideal of x, is called a *separator* of S.

If s is an arbitrary set of elements of a lattice L, and if S is the smallest set containing s, together with the join and the meet in L of every pair of elements of S (not only of s), then S is a lattice and a subset of L; this S is called a *sublattice* of L. We further say that S is *generated in* L *by* s.

These terms may be illustrated by reference to the lattice diagram (3.1) in Chapter III. The upper ideal of the element '3' in the lattice represented by (3.1) consists of the elements '3, 6, 12, 15, 30, 60', i.e. all the multiples of 3. The lower ideal of '3' contains only '1, 3', i.e. the divisors of 3. The double ideal of '6' contains '1, 2, 3, 6, 12, 30, 60'. In this subset of the lattice, '6' is called a separator, because there are no elements of the set, say x, such that x // 6. It is the case for example that 10 // 6, but

10 is not in the double ideal. Now consider the elements 6, 20; since neither includes the other, they generate a sublattice of four elements, namely that containing 2, 6, 20, 60. The sublattice generated by 4, 6, 20 contains the elements 2, 4, 6, 12, 20, 60; there are six elements here, not the maximum of eight, because $20 \geqq 4$ in the generating set.

4.4.2 The Partial Replacement Lemma: Using this terminology, we may now state this lemma in the following way.

> If L is a lattice with bounds I,O; if A is the union of an arbitrary set of ideals in L; and if B is the sublattice generated in L by an arbitrary set of elements of A; then the set L″, formed from L by deleting A except for I,O and replacing those elements which are in B, is a lattice. . . . 4.5

To prove this, we prove the existence of a unique meet and join for every pair of elements x, y in L″, going through a hierarchy of different cases. First, we distinguish cases 1, 2, 3 where A is a single lower ideal, a single upper ideal, and a union, respectively. In case 1 we distinguish case 11 for the join and case 12 for the meet of x,y. In case 11, since necessarily neither x nor y are in A–B, and A is a lower ideal, $x \smile y$ is not in A–B and is therefore in L″; this clears 11. In case 12 we distinguish 121 where x,y are both in B; 122 where they are both in B* (i.e. in L″ not in B); and 123 where one is in B and the other in B*. In 121, since B is a lattice, $x \frown y$ is also in B and therefore in L″. In 122 we distinguish 1221 where $x \frown y$ in L was in A, and so in L″ $x \frown y = O$; and 1222 where $x \frown y$ in L was not in A and is therefore still in L″; these clear 122. In case 123, suppose that x,y have in L″ two distinct GLB's p,q, of which also one is in B and the other in B*; if this were so, then x,y would both be LUB's of p,q, but we know from case 11 that $p \smile q$ is unique in L″, and so $p \smile q$ either is, or is included in, the unique GLB of x,y, and we have cleared 123 and all of 12 and all of case 1. In case 2, where A is an upper ideal, the preceding argument is repeated with $\smile$ and $\frown$ systematically interchanged. In case 3 suppose for case 31 that A is the union of two ideals A_1,A_2. Then let L′ be formed from L by deletion of A_1, B being null; then this L′ is a lattice, and L″ will be formed from it by deleting A_2 and supplying B which yields again a lattice by the preceding cases. By iteration, the lemma follows, for every union of ideals as A. QED.

4.4.3. The Completion of the Proof: Let (c) be a rhema rehearsing a context c. Let **S** be the repertory of c, that is the set of all rhemata (u) inferrable from (c). And let **R** be the set of lower ideals in **S** of each of these (u), which I denote by Rep(u). Thus (u) $\supset$ (v) if and only if (v) is in Rep(u). Now consider u,v,w such that (v) is in Rep(u), and (w) in Rep(v). Now, from (4.3), (u) $\supset$ (v) and (v) $\supset$ (w) imply (u) $\supset$ (w), so that (w) is in Rep(u), and therefore Rep(u) $\geqq$ Rep(v). Therefore, if every (u) could be taken as the rehearsal of a context, **R** would be isomorphic with **S**, differing only in using the inclusion relation $\geqq$ instead of $\supset$. But in fact some of the u might be non-rehearsals, as we have seen in §3.10, and for such utterances x, Rep(x) = (x). But since every element of **R** is by definition the lower ideal of an element of **S**, this means that we must delete from **S** every rhema which is inferrable from (c) *only* through (x), whenever x is a non-rehearsal; that is, we must delete from **S** the whole lower ideal of (x), except those elements of whose upper ideals (x) is not a separator. If we now denote by **Q** the set of elements whose upper ideals contain (x) but not as a separator, it is clear from the lemma (4.5) that if **Q** is a lattice, then **S**, modified as described, is a lattice provided it is so in the case where *all* the utterances involved can be accepted as rehearsing a context. We have therefore to prove that both this unmodified **S** and **Q** are lattices.

If every utterance (in the given repertory of c) rehearses a context, and, as we know by definition, every context can be rehearsed by an utterance, it follows, from the fact that the elements of **R** are repertories of contexts rehearsed by inferences from c associated by the set-inclusion relation $\geqq$, that **R** is a lattice (for any two *sets* are included in a unique join and both include a unique meet); therefore **S**, which we have proved isomorphic with **R** is also a lattice in this case.

As for **Q**, we note first that (x) is in **Q**, since it does not separate its own upper ideal. If (y),(z) are both in **Q**, then so is (y)$\frown$(z) whose upper ideal contains that of (y) and so *a fortiori* is not separated by (x). If (y)$\smile$(z) is not itself (x) it must be included in (x), else (y),(z) would not be in **Q**, and the upper ideal of (y)$\smile$(z) cannot be separated by (x), else that of (y) would be also, *contra hypothesi.* Therefore the meet and join of any (y),(z) in **Q** are in **Q**, and so **Q** is a lattice. It now follows from (4.5) that whether or not there are 'non-rehearsals' among the utterances inferrable from a given context c, the repertory of c under rhematical inference $\supset$, that is our **S**, is a lattice. We have therefore proved that

> The repertory of any context constitutes a lattice under rhematical inference . . . 4.6

I shalf refer to this result as the *context lattice theorum.* We must remember that 'rhematical inference' has been defined in terms of inclusion between designation-classes, in contradistinction to logical, pertinential, and sublocutionary inferences; the first two of these excluded types will later be shown to be in many cases definable in terms of rhematical inference, but the requirement for inclusion is primary.

4.5. Objections to the Theorem

To the mathematician it may seem strange to discuss 'objections' to a theorem that one has just proved. But a proof involves many definitions and postulates, any of which may be found on closer inspection to be less than realistic, so there are many loopholes for a keen objector to shoot his arrows through. In fact, as we shall see, this theorem is likely to meet with many objections from conventional linguists. Some of its consequences are unexpected and in some quarters will be unwelcome.

Among the objections I have in mind are the following. The result leads us to discredit the existing theory of 'deep structures' in (what will seem for some time) a radical manner; it will be replaced by a theory which is perhaps not so new as it must at first appear, but will be indigestible to many accustomed to the prevailing one. Secondly, we shall be led, albeit by linguistic rather than mathematical arguments, to promote the category of 'focus', hitherto generally treated as unimportant and obscure, to a high place in grammatical theory. Thirdly, we shall have to question the validity of many of the transformations currently used without hesitation by transformational grammarians; one such is the 'passive transformation'. Fourthly, we shall find ourselves going against a long-standing current of opinion in believing that any well-formed utterance in a sufficiently explicit context has a precisely formulable meaning (this is, for example, denied by Kuroda[61]), which we shall express in a notation which is irksomely, if not unexpectedly, rather complex and necessarily unfamiliar.

There will therefore be a predictable rush to the loopholes, and before proceeding I must try to show that they are already plugged. The theorem can be demolished *a priori* by either finding a flaw in the argument, or discrediting one of the assumptions on which it rests, and *a posteriori* by finding an empirical counter-example (which of course would imply contradiction of at least one of the premisses). The mathematical argument is in fact simple, consisting of an enumeration of cases each of which is by itself trivial. The prior assumptions have empirical reference at one point only, in the assertion that every context can be rehearsed; the rest are all essentially definitions, which might be inappropriate but could not be technically 'false'. I shall therefore consider (a) whether every context *can* be rehearsed, and (b) what a counter-example to the theorem might look like.

One way of rehearsing a context, the extreme of redundancy, would be to express, in a suitable sequence, all the rhemata forming its repertory. This would be possible for any context, provided that none of the inferences composing it were inexpressible. I have already alluded to the notion that there might exist contexts including some item of an 'ineffable' character in §3.3, and argued that such items could not in practice affect our understanding of the context. That is to say, if there were any such items, i.e. inexpressible rhemata, included in the repertory of a context, their omission would make no empirical difference. It seems, therefore, that the possibility of rehearsing a context by expression of its whole repertory, though not a very practical idea, is sufficient to establish that *any* context *can* be rehearsed.

A counter-example to the context lattice theorem requires us to find a context in whose repertory there are two rhemata whose coassertion is irresolubly ambiguous (or undefined). Since these will already have been covertly coasserted in the rehearsal, either the rehearsal is ambiguous itself, or it is possible for coassertibility to depend on the accompanying material, which merely replaces an ambiguity at the upper bound of the context 'lattice' by one lower down in it. Now there is a minor literary genre, the 'shaggy dog story', which consists in a more or less elaborate narrative designed to rehearse a context in which an otherwise deviant (i.e. non-Apuleian, §1.2) utterance becomes acceptable, such as "$//_{13}$ ∧ *I* /*wouldn't* /*keep a* /***knight*** /*out on a* /*dog like* /***this***.". It is evident that, given time and a lively imagination, this can always be done; given, that is to say, a pair of utterances alleged to be incompatible in the required sense, one can construct a context to which they both belong. Thus, any proposed counter-example to the theorem will involve an evident incompleteness in the context rehearsal, a stimulus in fact to extend it by the 'shaggy dog' method. This implies, of course, that not every sequence of utterances can be accepted as a context rehearsal; this I have already stated in §3.10. If what one is given is *really* a rehearsal of a context, therefore, the context lattice theorem will apply to it.

The mere notion of 'understanding', as represented by U, does *not* require the truth of (4.6). It only requires that, if Uu, then for all (v) the proposition (u) ⊃ (v) should be decidable. The context lattice theorem adds to this that the set of all rhemata inferrable from (u) will be a *lattice*; this lattice can be used, in the manner I shall explain, as an *inferential calculus* for the context rehearsed by (u), and this certainly looks like an enhancement of the bare notion of 'understanding'. For this enhancement to fail, through the existence of 'forbidden' coassertions inferrable from (u), would preclude a fully analytic treatment of something which in a weaker sense, is yet 'understandable'. Put this way, it seems not unreasonable to think that counter-examples to (4.6) might be forthcoming. But it appears that when one is actually confronted with such a situation, one finds that the alleged context rehearsal u is *not* understandable as it stands, and accordingly one supplies, with more or less abatement of the confidence of one's comprehension, such additional conjectures as may serve to restore the situation. That is, besides the rule of natural language L1 (§1.4) which bids us attach meaning to *any* utterance, we have also an urge to understand *any* context. When this is frustrated we feel mystification or puzzlement; and if these feelings are relieved by purely verbal means, we laugh. What we never do, it seems, is to behave as if the context lattice theorem might be false.

4.6. Mathematical Properties of Rhemata

If, then, we must accept (4.6) as an unavoidable consequence of the link I have assumed between understanding and inference, it becomes by such acceptance the foundation theorem of rhematic. This is why I have used the phrase 'inferential semantics' as the title of this book, rather than the neologism 'rhematic'. It is easy to show that it imposes non-trivial (and indeed far-reaching) constraints on the way in which we can represent rhemata in our notation. For rhemata have to be such that those representing the inferences which are the members of the repertory of any context constitute a lattice under rhematical inference. This property must be reflected in any consistent notation, to the extent that it must be possible to determine from the formulae representing any pair of rhemata whether or not either is inferrable from the other, the relation in question being a partial ordering relation definable in terms of the formulae *alone*, without re-converting them into any linguistic form.

As far as I know, no one has previously tried to impose this kind of constraint on any system of representation of sentence 'meanings', however these may be conceived or defined. Certainly, the usual type of representation of 'deep structures' used in transformational grammar does not have the appropriate form. The generative approach, powerful tool though it undoubtedly is, does not encourage its users to see the totality of things generated as a mathematical entity of which questions might usefully be asked. The first twist that (4.6) gives to linguistics, is to force such questions on our attention.

As we have seen in §3.5, a rhema can be regarded as a structure whose elements include lexigens. The structure must be such as to allow of the existence of two contrasting types of correspondence between rhemata. Intuitively, for instance, there is a 'replacement' type of correspondence, illustrated by the conceptual isomorphism between "*My aunt's in the hall*" and "*Your brother's in the loo*"; and the 'rearrangement' type of relationship, like that between "*I think George knows you*" and "*George thinks you know me*". The first pair of sentences 'ought' to differ only in the replacement of lexigens in an otherwise unchanged structure; while the second pair 'ought' to differ in the rearrangement of a fixed set of lexigens in, again, an *unchanged* structure. On the other hand, in the pair "*Celia believes that Daphne's superiority is unassailable*" and "*Daphne is unassailable in her belief in Celia's superiority*", a fixed set of lexigens partakes in *different* structures in each case. Evidently, then, a rhema is a *structured* set of lexigens, of the kind that can be represented by a graph, with the lexigens associated with the nodes of the graph. For example, the last pair of sentences could be represented, using the conventional tree-type graphs, with eight nodes each, as follows:

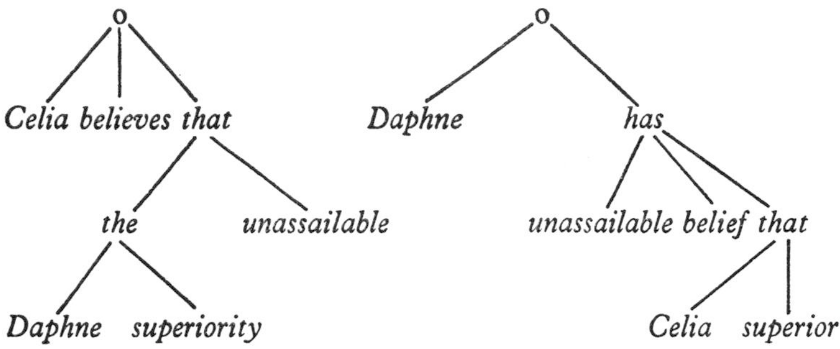

The type of structure represented above is mathematically a graph structure; but this is not all that can be said. It is firstly a special kind of graph (in fact a tree, which we shall find out *not* to be the right kind); and secondly, it is a labelled graph, in that the various nodes are associated with the lexigens. However, if these graphs are to be capable of representing, through their own structure, the possibility or otherwise of one being inferred from another, and if one instance of the kind of inference we are looking for is inclusion between the designation-classes represented by the lexigens, as I argued in §3.9 and exemplified in §§4.1 and 4.2, the lexigen-labels used in the graphs are not *merely* labels, but stand for elements of the lexical lattice. Our rhema structures are therefore labelled graphs in a stronger sense than that in which the term 'labelled graphs' is usually interpreted in graph theory. I cannot therefore refer here to a standard textbook, but shall have to give an exposition of the few scraps of theory which we shall have need of in the sequel; this forms the topic of Chapter V. I need hardly add that no one has ever tried to represent sentence structures *except* by 'labelled graphs' in this sense: the concept is a very wide one; but in linguistics these representations have never been expected to bear any mathematical weight.

4.7. The Importance of Finiteness

An important point concerning the theorem (4.6) is that it includes mention of a given context; being 'given' implies that it is finite. It has therefore a finite repertory (though the apparent size of the repertory depends on the delicacy with which the context has to be described to account for the inferences which the participants in the conversation choose to make about it). The context lattice theorem refers only to this finite set of rhemata; it says nothing at all about the class of *all* rhemata.

It is not immediately obvious that there is anything objectionable in making assertions about 'all' rhemata. One might imagine a theoretical 'universal context', and suppose, in view of the finiteness of the accessible world, that its rehearsal could be completed in at most a denumerable infinity of sentences. However, it will be clear from what has been said already, that an utterance expressing the coassertion of two rhemata expresses a third rhema distinct from, though in general containing, both its constituents; and we shall find in the sequel that for any two rhemata there are in general many different ways of combining them into a larger whole, the choice between which again lies in the context as known to the participants. Moreover, the results will depend on the order of succession between the rhemata being combined. Thus, the class of all rhemata will contain in general many members corresponding to each of its own subclasses. Such a class runs into many antinomies, which spring from the fact that, if we suppose it to have a cardinality c, it can be shown that its cardinality is greater than c, whether c be finite or infinite. The class of 'all rhemata' is therefore *not a set*, and no predicate defined only for sets can be meaningfully applied to it; this precludes almost all mathematically interesting statements.

This conclusion is not without some significant consequences. It firstly reinforces the point, which I apologize for bringing up yet again, that there can be no rational semantics without a stated context. Any supposedly context-free sentence is either itself a context-rehearsal, or the beginning of one; or it lies suspended in that 'universal' context which, as I have just argued, is a logical surd. Secondly, the claim, conventionally made by generative grammarians (as by Chomsky[18]) that they aim to generate "all and only the well-formed sentences of a language", needs examination in the light of this result. In practice, of course, actual generative procedures impose an upper limit on sentence length, which permits a finite subclass to be selected, and this may be hoped to furnish examples of all the rules there are. But it is very far from 'all' the sentences which there could be, and should not be claimed as such. In the present work, I do not formulate any such claim, attractive though it is, nor shall I use generative procedures in devising an acceptable mathematical representation for my rhemata. On the contrary, I shall aim at a notation which shall provide a formula to represent any *finite* rhema; 'any' rhema, *without* qualification, I may not mention.

It is unwise to set out on an open-ended procedure, without first investigating what kind of a system one will end up with. And once one has surveyed the field, as this advice requires, what would have been generative rules are more naturally seen as *selection* rules, operating on a preexistent totality. This is how I shall develop the theory. (Later, in §7.9.3, I shall introduce a generative definition G to supplement the primary constructive one; but once this latter is to hand, and the finiteness of the domain assured in any actual context, the objections indicated above no longer apply.)

There is another objection, which may be made against the generative method, and in particular to the description of syntax in terms of 'rewrite rules': namely, that such rules seem to imply actual mental processes which they summarize, processes which some generativists have been tempted to see as 'innate faculties' of the brain. Indeed, they may be so. But, from what we know of brain function, selection rules seem to offer a more likely model, being supported by the analogy of the known functions of memory and attention, for example, whereas there is no convincing independent analogue of the supposed rewrite-rules. If so, the latter can only be an indirect way of denoting what happens. But this is a point which empirical evidence may at any time be obtained to settle more certainly one way or the other.

4.8. The Lattice Property of Lexigens

Although I have already asserted that lexigens can be regarded as elements of a 'lexical' lattice, I have given no convincing proof of this at the mathematical level. Before leaving the topic of the context lattice, this omission will now be repaired; though it would certainly be odd if rhemata were subject to the lattice condition and lexigens, out of which they are constructed, were not.

There is a sense in which a lexigen 'exists' corresponding to any arbitrary designation-class, provided this can be described in a finite rhema; for such a rhema, as we have already seen, could be used itself as a lexigen. But this principle is incompatible with practical aims, for it would leave us with a lexicon equal to the power-set of the universe. We need, therefore, some procedure for limiting the proliferation of lexigens threatened by their 'free creation'. There is no harm in admitting the existence, for any two lexigens a,b of their meet $a \frown b$; that is, a lexigen whose designation-class is the intersection of those of a and b. Thus, given the lexigens selecting in English words such as "*flail*" and "*machine*", we can allow also the existence of one which will select "*threshing-machine*"; or again, to recall a former example, from the lexigens corresponding to "*children*" and "*windows*", we can construct one whose designation-class contains everything which is both a child and a window. The great majority of these 'meet' lexigens will, like the last, be empty. What we cannot admit, however, is the free formation of lexigens by the *union* of designation-classes. Whenever there is a need for one of these, a word or phrase can be coined for it; but when no such word has been found necessary, we do not need, and therefore should not postulate, any element in the lexical lattice to accommodate it. 'Meet' lexigens on the other hand can always be specified by standard linguistic devices (the simplest being adjective plus noun), and since they so quickly become empty as the number of terms increases, they pose no threat of impracticable numerosity.

The system we thus envisage could be constructed by the following imaginary procedure. We start from the set of all referents which we may ever need to designate, which I assume to be finite, and the lattice whose elements represent each and all of the subsets of this: this will be what is called a 'Boolean' lattice, which has the maximum number 2^n of elements, n being the number of the 'referents', and I shall call it B. Now the actual lexical lattice which we want is obtained from B by taking an arbitrary set of elements, representing the conceptual repertory of a given language C, and deleting from B the upper and lower ideals of all its elements not in C, and the upper ideals only of the elements in C. To the small rump left of B we may add new lexigens, as they are coined to meet communicational needs, and with each such addition will come their lower ideals (containing the new meets, whose existence we allow), but not their upper ideals. Every step of this process will be an example of that described in the replacement lemma (4.5), and will consequently leave the system still a lattice. The proposed limitation on the creation of new lexigens is therefore compatible, as required, with the system of all the lexigens being a lattice. The 'lexical lattice' is unimpaired.

It may be questioned, however, whether the 'designation-class' of a lexigen need be a discrete collection of unit entities; while this might be true of such a lexigen as that behind "*dog*", it would seem not to hold for abstract ideas such as "*difference*" or "*white*", still less for processes such as "*eat*". Once again, however, we are saved a lot of trouble by having to consider the relationships existing within one context at a time. In one context there is usually no difficulty in enumerating, as a small discrete class, the instances of any such abstraction; there are never very many white things or instances of whiteness, and if "*white*" say is being used in a strictly general sense, then its referent in this context is a singular class. Similarly, the process of "*eating*" may be itself the subject of interest, but most often we shall have in mind one or more particular instances of its being done, which will form a discrete set. Such sets are each included in one or more other more general lexigens, and in turn may or may not have non-empty intersections. Though each context calls out a different selection from the total lexical lattice as being immediately relevant, the same argument as used in the general case will show that what we obtain, for each context, is still a lattice.

4.9. Ambiguous Rhemata.

This confinement to one context at a time also means that the meaning we attach to any rhema is defined by its position in the context lattice, relative to other rhemata in the repertory of the context; any meaning it may have in a wider field of comparison is not immediately relevant, though of course the phonic string expressing a given rhema in one context is likely in any other context to express essentially the same, or at least a closely similar, rhema. For this reason, the question of synonymy between rhemata is not an urgent one. There are, however, at least two senses in which rhemata can be 'ambiguous', and these we must look at briefly.

The simplest sense in which a rhema can have two distinct 'meanings' is when, in a given context, we can reasonably hesitate between two or more possible ways of expressing it. Such hesitation can arise because for some reason the language used does not allow the expression of exactly the relationships within the rhema. I purposely avoid saying that all rhemata are expressible, not merely because the expression 'all rhemata' is guarded by a logical taboo, but also because I wish to keep the term rhema for *all* elements of the context lattice, including its upper bound, and this at least *is* typically too complex to be expressed directly in one sentence. I have, however, mentioned that a context can contain mutually contradictory inferences, and in general all the rhemata in the upper ideals of both of such contradictories will be difficult to express unambiguously, and indeed must be inherently ambiguous in the logical sense too. It is unfortunately not practicable to give examples of this, before I have explained the rhematical notation which I shall build up in the following chapters; there are, however, examples of this type of ambiguity in the diagrams (7.4.4) and (15.5.3).

Another way in which a rhema might be called 'ambiguous' is if its *expression* is fairly described as itself 'ambiguous'. The case of (7.4.3) is of this kind, to the extent that, besides allowing different inferences which are typically incompatible, it has itself an expression in English which permits the *same* ambiguity. This is probably rare. Quite common, however, are rhemata expressed by sentences which are potentially ambiguous, but in a given context can convey only the one meaning intended. In such a case, however, the rhema in question is not truly ambiguous, since its meaning is as mentioned above only defined within a given context.

It should also be said, now that, as I hope, the indispensability of the context has been sufficiently emphasized, that it is a topic which *can* be made too much of. An arbitrary sequence of rhemata, culled from different contexts and strung together, does not necessarily constitute the rehearsal of a new context. But just as we have a strong inbuilt drive to attach meaning to any string of words we hear actually uttered, such as say (1.6.4), so we have a tendency to weave any set of data together to make a context of some kind. The rules of rehearsal R given in §13.2 are accordingly rather weak; on the whole, many arbitrary strings of rhemata will get through, or can be made to pass the test by 'obvious' supplementation. This means that, even though we are primarily concerned with rhemata within a given context, cross-contextual comparisons of rhemata are possible, and the concept of 'the' meaning of a rhema, though at times logically treacherous and always a bit fuzzy, is by no means nonsensical; its status is in fact very like that of the 'meaning of a word', an expression which semioticians have wisely frowned on, but which is none the less still useful in less exacting circles.

4.10. Rhematic and Logic

The context lattice theorem (4.6) has a further consequence, that it raises once again the question of whether, or in what sense, we can claim rhematic as a 'logic'. For rhemata in their contexts are subject to lattice relations; and a lattice is, mathematically, an algebra, albeit a weak one, and is capable of being used as a 'calculus'. And if rhemata represent meanings, we have then a calculus of meanings; which is more or less what one means by 'a logic'. One could even go further, and say that, since rhematic denotes meanings of utterances non-linguistically, while the same meanings are or can be expressed in language, which I have been at some pains to insist must be 'natural' language, one might describe rhematic as a 'natural logic'.

Unfortunately, this term has a history. It was perhaps first used in philosophical discussion by Moore.[73] A recent wide-ranging discussion of 'natural logic' is that by Lakoff;[62] he regards 'natural' logic as a special variety of logic which underlies and is conveyed by ordinary discourse, as symbolic logic is conveyed by its special notation, and (to go beyond Lakoff) one might add Aristotelian logic by '*oratio pronuntiabilis*'. But this is precisely what rhematic does not do. It provides a notation (which I have yet to develop) which is quite as abstract and non-linguistic as that of the predicate calculus, for example, and this notation can be operated in a calculus the existence of which is guaranteed by the context lattice theorem, and is in this sense anything but 'natural'. The relationship of natural language sentences to the rhematical formulae of the notation is also by no means one-to-one, except within the confines of a given context, and the theory gives no warrant for the idea that sentences of natural language *themselves* constitute a logical or quasilogical notation. They are logic only at one remove; and even if I have succeeded in making this 'remove' as it were computable, it remains a remove. This is not what most authors have meant by 'natural logic'.

There are also direct contrasts between rhematic and logic. One is that they work with different kinds of inference (see §4.1). The 'inference' assumed in rhematic could almost be defined in behaviourist-terms, by experiments analogous to those of von Frisch[39] on bees. These animals in fact operate a simple kind of inference, in that, when 'told' to go from A to B as if in a straight line, they can 'infer' the sufficiency of a circuitous route. Analogously, one might show that a person told "*This room is too hot*" can infer from this a request to open the window, or some similarly appropriate response. The question I ask is 'What properties must this kind of inference have, in order to do what it is observed to do?', with results beginning to become apparent. Logic, on the other hand, starts with a notation, and then defines, in terms of the syntax of the notation, what *shall* count as 'valid inference' by a set of axiomatic propositions.

Thus, while *logic* studies the validity of inferences within a given 'language' (either an artificial notation or, in case of 'natural logic' the language, familiar though obscure, of natural discourse) *rhematic* studies the competence of languages to mediate a given inferential system, in particular the system, familiar even if obscure, underlying our everyday experience of 'understanding' speech. Logic depends on clearly-defined truth-value relations; but for rhematic truth-values are of secondary importance; inference is a kind of inclusion relation between designation-classes. Truth-values in the logical sense can be extracted from a rhematical background by using an artificially restricted language; this is, historically, the clear origin of Aristotelian logic, and indirectly of modern mathematical logic. But it has come a long way from natural language, and with good reason; natural language is not primarily logical and logical thought is not natural to man, but an acquired skill, very differently valued in different civilizations. What we have now to do is to construct a model of the relationship between rhematical inference and the characteristics exhibited by natural languages. Meanwhile, however, we need to establish our rhematical notation: this I do in Chapter V.

CHAPTER V

Labelled Graphs

In this chapter I shall give an elementary account of the theory of labelled graphs, confining attention strictly to those aspects of the subject which will prove useful in constructing a rhematical notation. I do not, for this purpose, use the definition of 'labelled graphs' given by Harary,[49] which is that most commonly accepted, but a slightly wider one, which is necessary to adapt the theory to our present purposes.

5.1. Definitions

A *graph* may be defined, on any set V, as an arbitrary subset A of the self-product of the set, V^2. The elements v_i of V are called the *vertices* of the graph, and the elements a^i_j of A are called its *arcs*.

As an illustration, let V be the set of numbers less than eight, that is, 1, 2, 3, 4, 5, 6, 7. Then the self-product of V is the set of all ordered pairs of these numbers, such as 11, 12, 13, 35, 53, 71 etc., of which obviously there are $49 = 7^2$. Let A be the subset of V^2 containing those pairs v_iv_j in which v_i is a divisor of v_j, and no others. Then the members of A are 11, 12, 13, 14, 15, 16, 17, 24, 26, 36, 22, 33, 44, 55, 66, 77; it is *this set* which is defined as the graph [V, A]. It can be *represented* in a variety of ways, of which the easiest to take in at a glance is the diagram on p. 75, where each arrow goes from one number to a multiple of it.

The fact that V was stated to consist of numbers is relevant to the construction of the graph, and gives an example of what sort of reasons can lie behind graphs; but the graph represented in (5.1) would be regarded in unlabelled graph theory as identical with any other having the same pattern of arcs, represented by the arrows, whatever labels were attached to the vertices; in

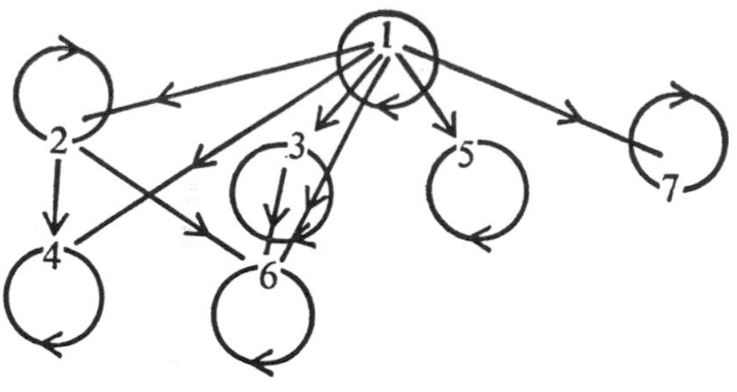

. . . 5.1

general, no labels are used, just dots and arrows. The following, for example, is in this respect a more typical example of a graph:

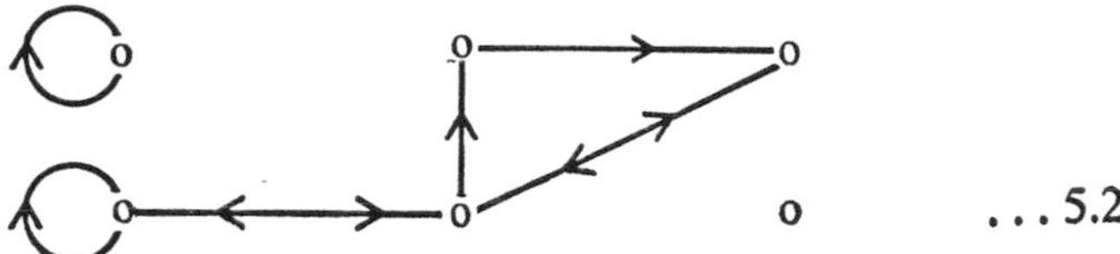

. . . 5.2

5.1.1. Terms used for Unlabelled Graphs: In the above diagrams I have represented arcs by arrows. Some arcs in (5.2) have the arrows going both ways; that is, the two vertices connected by them occur in *both* possible orderings, among the vertex-pairs which are the elements of the graph set. This represents an undirected connection, and it is usual to omit the arrow-head in such cases; this kind of arc is sometimes called an 'edge'. In (5.2) there are six vertices, and of the thirty-six members of their set-self-product, eight are included in the graph; two are connected to themselves, two pairs are connected both ways, and two pairs one way only. One triplet of vertices are joined in a circuit. One of the vertices is not connected to any vertex, and another is connected only to itself. This graph is not *connected*; its largest connected part contains four vertices. In what follows I shall be concerned only with connected graphs.

A vertex which is connected by an arc to itself, that is one v_i such that $(v_i v_i)$ is in the set A, is called here a *node* (this distinction between 'node' and 'vertex' is not made by all graph theorists). We shall be concerned here only with graphs in which *all* the vertices are nodes (like 5.1); that is, being or not being a node is not a point in which vertices differ for us. When this is the case we can slightly simplify the representation: we can omit the self-loops from the diagrams, and can incorporate labels more conveniently.

A closed loop, such as the triangular one in (5.2), is called a *circuit*. A graph with no circuit* is said to be *oriented*. A graph with no symmetrical arcs or 'edges' is a *directed* graph or 'digraph'. We shall only be concerned with digraphs (but this will need demonstration in linguistic terms); moreover, with only marginal exceptions (§7.11) they will be oriented digraphs.

5.1.2. Definition of Labelled Graphs: A graph [V, A] is said to be *labelled* in a domain **B** if there is a many-one mapping L from A to **B**, such that for all i, j the mapping image $L(v_iv_j)$ of the pair (v_iv_j) is an element of **B**. It is convenient to define L as a mapping not from A but from V^2 into **B**, and for this purpose we select (or supply) a special element 0 of **B** such that $L(v_iv_j) = 0$ whenever the pair (v_iv_j) is *not* in the graph set A. The effect of this definition is that *every* arc and every node has a label, possibly 0, and any vertex which is not a node has 0 as its label. We can now describe (5.1) as an oriented digraph *labelled* in the domain of the integers. The domain containing the labels of a labelled graph is called its *base* domain.

In standard graph theory, the base domain of a labelled graph is taken to be an unstructured set; that is, identity or difference of labels is relevant, but any relations between one label and another are disregarded. Here, however, I shall assume that the base domain *has* some structure. (In general, this structure is that of an algebra; but in our applications it is, more specifically, a *lattice.*) This introduces certain complications into the theory which make it impracticable for me simply to refer the reader to a standard text, but to include as much exposition as is necessary here. Those who are deterred by mathematical expositions should pass on to Chapter VI, where I return to linguistics.

5.1.3. Nodes and Arcs: It will now be evident, if we recall the discussion in §2.5, that representation of a rhema structure as a graph will require some means of distinguishing 'lexigens' from

* Two nodes connected by an 'edge' constitute a minimal 'circuit'; a node is not counted as a circuit.

whatever relations between or among them we may need. One way of doing this, and probably the only one deserving serious consideration, is to use the distinction between nodes and arcs for the purpose. This entails that there will be no overlap between node labels and arc labels since it is hardly appropriate that either type of structural element should share a common designatum with one of the other type. This, however, is by no means an inevitable feature of labelled graphs in general, and to keep the matter in perspective I shall not make the corresponding simplifications till §5.1.4.

The simplest possible kind of labelled graph is one where the base domain consists of the set 0, 1 (represented as a lattice diagram in (5.3) below). Labelled graphs of this type are identical, in the distinctions which they can make, with unlabelled graphs; the simplest non-trivial base domain contains three elements, say 0, 1, 3 (5.4). This domain allows for distinguishing two kinds of nodes and arcs, without requiring that nodes and arcs are differently labelled; alternatively, one of the non-zero labels could be reserved for nodes and the other for arcs, but since this distinction is also apparent in the structure (self-links versus other–links) it is otiose if neither nodes nor arcs are to be further distinguished among themselves.

In general, labelled graphs are used in applications where there is a call for multiple distinctions among the nodes, but none, or a relatively simple system, among the arcs; this is indeed the case for the application I have in mind here. Accordingly, there exist terms based on the *variety of arcs* to describe different kinds of labelled graphs. In *uniform* graphs, all the arcs have the same label (other than 0 formally applied to non-existent arcs); in *multiform* graphs there are more than one kind of arcs. In conventional graph theory a multiform graph is often considered to be a set of uniform graphs defined over a single set of vertices; but this way of describing the situation is needlessly complicated when we have in any case to reckon with a non-trivial base domain. I shall here use the term *biform* for graphs with just two kinds of arc.

In the case where the base domain **B** is an algebra of any kind, we can usefully call the subalgebra generated in **B** by the arc labels the *arc subalgrebra*, and conversely that generated by the node labels the *node subalgebra*. In general, neither need be disjoint from the other, and either may be identical with the whole base algebra. I shall hereafter use the symbols **A** and **N** for these two subalgebras.

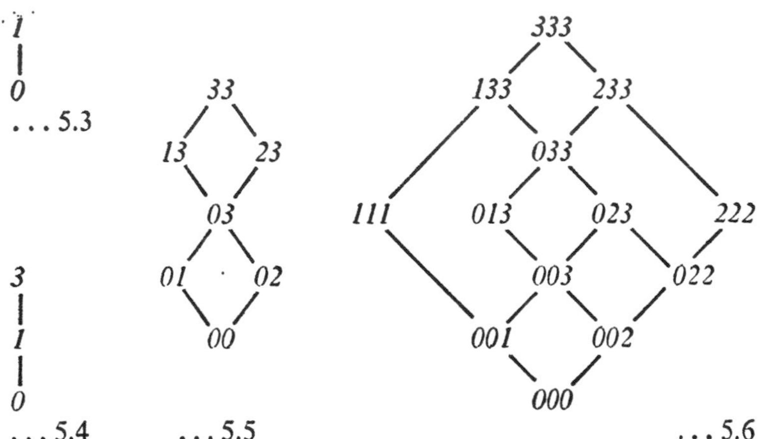

5.1.4. Distinctly Labelled Graphs: I shall now define the class of *distinctly* labelled graphs as those whose arc and node subalgebras have at most one element in common. All the graphs I shall use in the sequel will be distinctly labelled, and I shall commonly refer to them as DLGs.

It is helpful to consider a little more closely the relationships between the two subalgebras; the terminology here introduced will be taken up again in §5.4. In our present application, we have seen that in general nodes will represent lexigens, and arcs the relations between them. We have already seen that the system of lexigens can be consistently represented as a lattice, the lexical lattice; and consequently we can identify the node subalgebra of our base algebra with this lattice. It is not yet apparent how many arc labels we shall need, but it will be small enough for any algebraic relations among them to be subsumed in a lattice also. So, if both **A** and **N** are lattices, we can assume without loss of generality that **B** is also a lattice.

Let us illustrate the matter by reference to Fig. 5.6. above. Let us suppose that the node subalgebra is represented by the elements 003, 013, 023, 033 in the middle; it is easily verified that these constitute a sublattice of the whole. Those elements of **B** which are lower bounds of **N**, that is, which are included in every element of **N**, will be called *infranodal*; in (5.6) they are 000, 001, 002, and the GLB of **N** 003 itself. Conversely, we call those elements which are upper bounds of the whole of **N** *supranodal*; these are 033, 133, 233, 333 in (5.6). Besides these two classes, we may also have *extranodal* elements of **B**, characterized by their joins and meets with elements of **N** being respectively supranodal and infranodal. This class includes in (5.6) 111 and 222; for example it will be seen from the diagram that the join $111 \smile 033$ is the supranodal 133, while the meet $111 \frown 033$ is the infranodal 001. These terms do not exhaust the possibilities, and it may be useful to have in reserve the description *abnodal* for such elements as 022 which do not satisfy any of the criteria given. If (5.6) with the node subalgebra given above, is the base domain **B** of a DLG, there are various possible locations for its arc subalgebra. If **A** contained 000, 001, 003, for example, it would be infranodal and would have only the one point in common with **N** that a DLG is allowed to have. We would still have a DLG if **A** consisted of 000, 001, and 111, but then we could not say that **A** as a whole was infranodal. Again **A** could contain 033, 133, 233, 333, all supranodal, and again qualifying for a DLG. Or we could go for 000, 111, 222, 333. As we shall see, many of these choices for the arc subalgebra have bizarre consequences which we wish to avoid. But so far as the definition given for a DLG goes they are all still available.

5.1.5. Paths in a DLG: Before leaving our definitions, there is a further term in graph theory which we shall need, together with some satellite terms. A sequence of vertices $(v_1 v_2 \ldots v_n)$ all of whose juxtaposed pairs $(v_1 v_2)$, $(v_2 v_3)$, etc. have non-zero labels in a DLG is called a *path*. The sequence of these n-1 labels constitutes the *track* of the path, and the sequence of n node labels is its *route*. Here is an illustration:

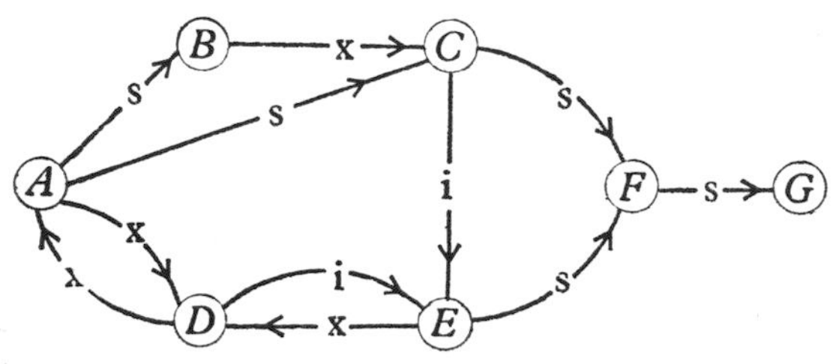

. . . 5.7

The graph shown on p. 79 is understood to be labelled in the following base domain:

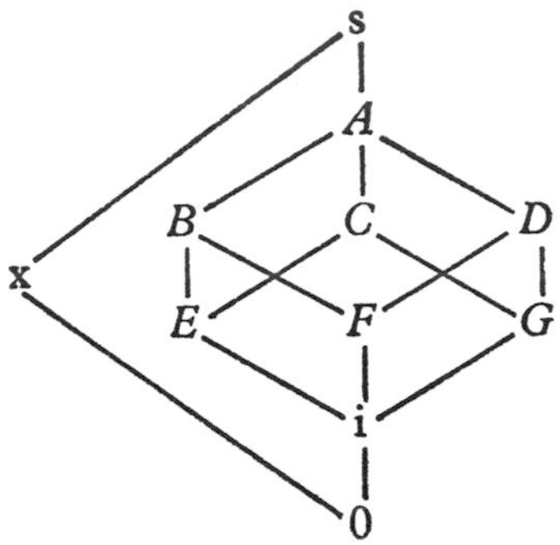

. . . 5.8

It will now be observed that in the graph represented in (5.7) there is a path of length 5 whose route is *ABCEFG* and whose track is *sxiss*; this is the longest path which does not contain a circuit. The longest circuit in (5.7) has route *ACEDA* and track *siix*; shorter ones are of two steps, routes *ADA* and *DED*, tracks *xx* and *ix* respectively. Of the three arc labels used here, *s*, *x*, *i* are supranodal, extranodal, and infranodal respectively, as can be checked in (5.8).

5.2. Representations

There are a variety of ways of representing graphs. I shall use here essentially only two, the diagrammatic (of which several examples have already been given) and the tabular. The general trend in graph theory is to study properties of individual graphs, but for the present application we are more interested in the relations between different graphs each representing one of a mass of objects, in particular of course the rhemata in a given context repertory. For this reason, I shall lay rather more stress on one particular tabular representation than is customary; but the diagrammatic representation is much more easily grasped by the reader, and will be preferred everywhere except in this chapter.

5.2.1. Diagrammatic Methods: It is only necessary under this heading to point out two things. One is that a diagram is not a graph but a representation of a graph; this is perhaps a pedantic distinction, but as in the case of lattice diagrams it occasionally causes confusion if the distinction is forgotten. Nevertheless, I shall not scruple to refer to diagrams as graphs from time to time. The second point to make arises from this, namely that a given graph can be represented by a variety of diagrams. Thus, the two diagrams below are both diagrams of the graph sometimes called the 'Fibonacci generator':

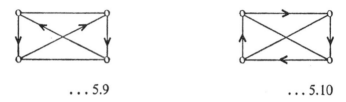

. . . 5.9 . . . 5.10

It need hardly be said that typographical conventions can also differ without their affecting the graph concerned. I shall adopt a special set of conventions when I come to construct diagrams to represent rhemata as graphs; these are adopted for convenience only and have nothing to do with what is represented.

In general, when a diagrammatic representation is given for a labelled graph, the nodes are identified by some symbol referring, in a conventional notation, to the element of the base domain used as their label. The arcs on the other hand are either drawn simply as arrows, or in an oriented graph as (conventionally *descending*) lines, and if there are differently-labelled arcs the difference is indicated by such devices as whole versus dotted lines or the like. Only if the arc subalgebra is of comparable scope to the node subalgebra is it expedient to mark arcs with special symbols, as is done in (5.7) for the sake of clarity. In most instances where labelled graphs are used, the base domain, if its structure is relevant, will be defined separately; but if for any reason a special domain is used its definition should always accompany the diagram. For example, in the following graph, the base domain is the set sum of the real numbers and the lattice of two elements (I, Ø):

$$1 \longrightarrow -3.57 \longrightarrow \pi \longrightarrow 3.34_{10}{-11} \qquad \ldots 5.11$$

This could represent a space-time vector; its status as a graph is only marginal.

5.2.2. Tabular Representations: There are many different ways in which a graph can be represented by a table or array. I shall here use only one method, which is immediately suggested by the definition which I use for a graph. This consists in assigning one row of the table to each vertex set, and one column to each vertex (conveniently in the same order), and in writing, in each of the cells of the table, the label on to which the corresponding row-column pair is mapped by the label-mapping of the graph.

This is exemplified in the two tabular representations for the graphs represented by diagrams (5.10) and (5.11):

	A	*B*	*C*	*D*
A	0	1	1	0
B	0	0	1	1
C	1	0	0	1
D	1	1	0	0

. . . 5.12

	A	*B*	*C*	*D*
A	1	I	∅	∅
B	∅	–3.57	I	∅
C	∅	∅	π	I
D	∅	∅	∅	3.34_{11} –11

. . . 5.13

(5.10), as an unlabelled graph, is represented adequately by a table containing only 0's and 1's; that is, it is equivalent to a labelled graph with a two-element base domain. (5.11) *is* labelled, and its tabular representation has a diagonal row of components representing the node labels, which are real numbers, while the other components corresponding to arc labels are either ∅ or I (which I use here because 0, 1 are preempted). In both cases, what we have is an array of $n \times n$ components, each being an element of the base domain in which the graph in question is labelled and n being the number of nodes; an 'array' is simply a table with the row and column headings removed, and is no more than a special kind of structured set. It is important to distinguish between the terms 'array 'and 'matrix'.

5.2.3. Matrix Representations: The term *matrix* refers to an array whose components are defined to be elements of a specified *scalar algebra,* and which is a member of a domain of matrices over which operations of 'addition' and 'multiplication' are defined in terms of this scalar algebra, to which the matrix *components* belong. The scalar algebra is usually required to belong to the class known in general algebra as a 'ring'; most of the classical properties of matrices survive, however, if the concept is widened to allow of the scalar algebra being only a semi-ring (Braithwaite[12]), and for us this is more convenient, since all lattices belong to the latter class. It follows that (5.10) has a matrix representation, since there is a ring of two elements (identical with elementary arithmetic *modulo* 2), which allows the array in (5.12) to be treated as a matrix, provided it is one of a family of others of the same kind. But (5.11) has no matrix representation, since its base domain is not even a semi-ring.

As an example of a matrix representing a graph, of the type we shall be concerned with here, is the graph matrix of (5.7); note that we use square brackets [ ] to distinguish a matrix from a mere array:

$$\begin{bmatrix} A & s & s & x & . & . & . \\ . & B & x & . & . & . & . \\ . & . & C & . & i & s & . \\ x & . & . & D & i & . & . \\ . & . & . & x & E & s & . \\ . & . & . & . & . & F & s \\ . & . & . & . & . & . & G \end{bmatrix} \qquad \ldots 5.14$$

Zero components are often represented, for greater clarity, by dots rather than by 0's.

There are two points to be made about matrix representations. The first is that there is little purpose in using such representations for isolated graphs (such as (5.7)); the characteristic usefulness of the matrix form arises from the possibility of attaching significance to the sums, products, and other functions, of different matrices representing different graphs. In the application to rhematic, the members of the repertory of a context, which together form a lattice, form a 'natural' set of graphs whose matrix representations could be used in this way; just how, I will explain in the next section. The second point is that, just as there are many diagrams which represent a single graph, differing in how the vertices are set out, as in (5.9, 10), so there are many different matrices, differing again in the order in which the vertices are set out along the principal diagonal; all these 'permutations' represent the *same* graph.

The two points made above are related in the following way. If we have a family of graphs, all represented as having the same vertex set, and a given abitrary ordering of the vertices is adopted for one of them, then their matrix representations form a *coherent domain* if and only if *this* ordering is applied to the matrix representation of *every* graph in the family. It is obviously necessary to have a coherent domain if matrix operations are to be meaningful in graph terms and if the identity of each vertex is to be respected. If there are n vertices, there are $n!$ ways of arranging them, and therefore $n!$ coherent domains for the matrix representation; no one domain has any logical edge over the rest, though some may lead to neater layouts of the matrices than others do. But for us it is important that every rhema we have to represent should have within itself sufficient *clues* to enable a 'correct' order of its vertices (lexigens) to be ascertained; if not, it has no unique matrix representation and therefore no defined place in the context lattice.

5.3. Covertical Graph Algebras

To give a concrete idea of what it is like to have a family of graphs represented collectively by a coherent domain of matrices, I shall now set out *in extenso* a diagrammatic representation of a 'context repertory'. First, I shall take the *base domain* to be the lattice shown below as (5.15); and the '*repertory*' of the context will be represented by the graph (5.16).

5.3.1. Introductory Example: This example is highly artificial, first because it is impossible within one page to set out the whole repertory of a real context in this complete way; and second because for the same reason I must use a very simplified base domain. The latter will be understood to have the form

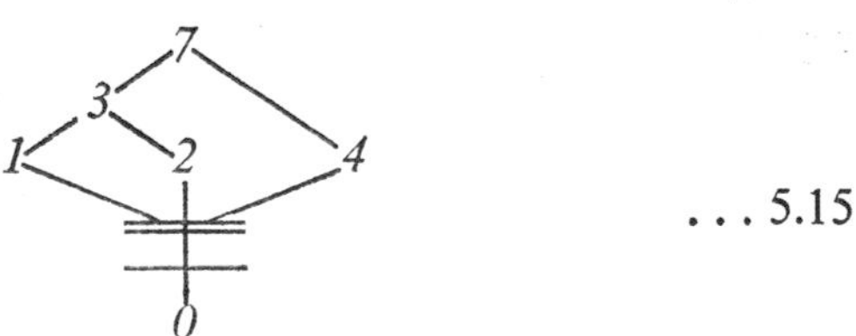

The bottom three elements constitute the arc subalgebra, and the top six the node subalgebra; I shall not use 7 as a label, and I shall simply omit any node having the label (∅) identical with the arc ==. I shall observe the conventions that every graph representing a rhema of the repertory must have the initial node of the 'rehearsal' as its unique starting-point, and that only oriented graphs are used. (These will also appear, for reasons I have yet to explain, as rules of the rhematical notation.)

The context repertory is then represented by the following diagram

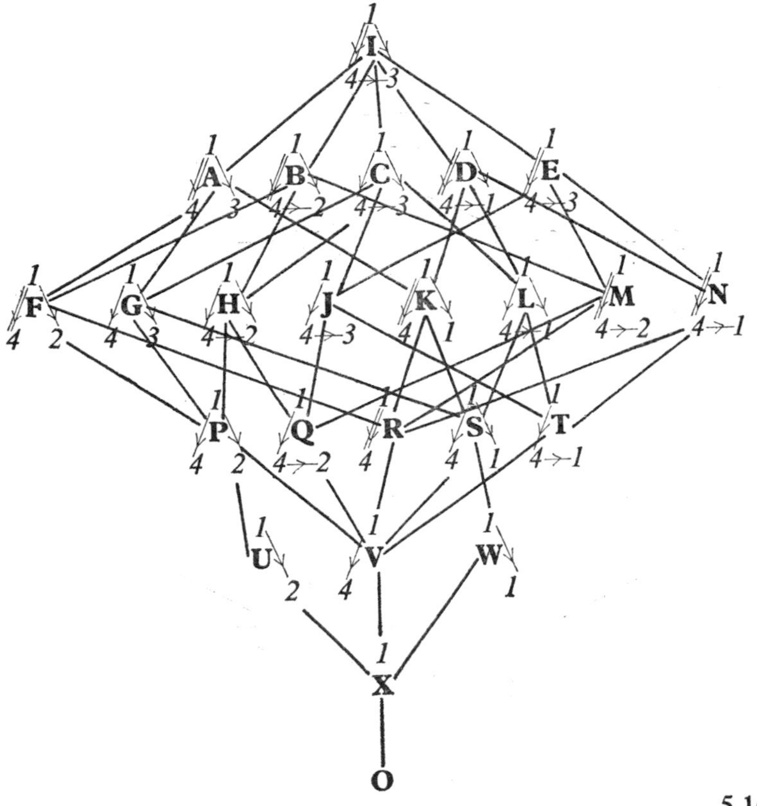

...5.16

The structure of each rhema graph is indicated by *light* lines with arrows, and that of the *repertory* by **heavy** lines. 'I' represents the context 'rehearsal'.

The figure (5.16), like (5.17) to follow, may well be confusing at first, since it contains two different kinds of sub-diagram: one representing rhemata, the other representing the context repertory. The latter, but not of course the former, is a lattice, as required by (4.6); the reader may check this by visual inspection against the lattice definition in §3.8. The point may be made perhaps more clearly by using the matrix representation for the rhemata, which I have described in the previous section; for the representation of *oriented* graphs, such as these rhema graphs are, we may use *triangular* matrices, that is, those in which all the components below the principal diagonal are omitted, since they are all zero. The resulting figure is:

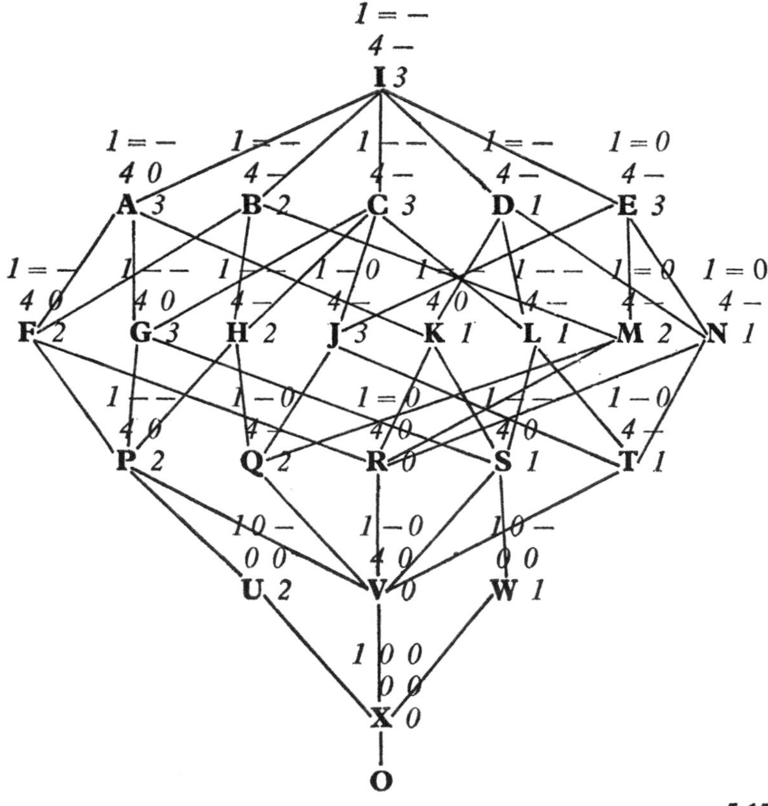

. . . 5.17

It can be seen that, in the above diagram, one matrix is represented as 'included in' another, as R is in D for instance, if and only if the corresponding pairs of matrix components are all so included in the base domain (5.15). Thus, the components, *other* than in the last column, of R are equal to those of D, while the last column is all zeros in R as against -1 in D (equality counts as inclusion).

Note, in passing, that a matrix is said to be made up of *components*, not of 'elements'; the latter term is confined to members of a given set, domain, algebra, lattice, or the like. Neither term is used for the parts of graphs.

5.3.2. Conformal Operations on Matrices: In (5.17) the convention is adopted, that every triangular matrix is represented as having three diagonal components, even in the case of those which represent graphs with less than three nodes, such as U, X, or O; moreover, those vertices which are nodes are always written in the same order for every matrix. The result of this convention is that the matrices form a coherent system; one example of the value of this is the rule that has just been given, regarding the inclusion-relations of 'corresponding' matrix components between different matrices. This particular relation is called *conformal* inclusion.

However, since as mentioned in §5.2.3, any permutation of a matrix represents the same graph, the use of this conformal inclusion rule presupposes a restriction of an unusual sort on the graphs themselves; for, in general, there is no unambiguous ordering of the vertices of a graph which could form a basis for attaching significance to 'corresponding' components of the matrices. Indeed, the only class of graphs whose vertices are simply-ordered is that of *chains*, of which (5.11) is an (untypical) example. Since, however, rhemata have a more complicated structure than this, their arcs must be of at least two kinds, i.e. have at least *two labels*, if they are each to be a chain as well as have some characteristic structure of their own.

A family (set) of graphs over a given vertex set, each of which is an identical chain of vertices under arcs of one label, irrespective of how they may differ under arcs with a different label, is said to be *covertical*. For a given n, one can identify the n-th vertex in every graph belonging to a covertical family. In particular, the matrix representations of such graphs have a preferred permutation, that in which the vertices appear in the order given by the common chain. It is convenient to define a matrix in any *other* permutation as an *abnormal* representation of a graph belonging to a given covertical family; unless otherwise stated, matrix representations of such graphs will be understood to be *normal.* The arc label defining the common chain of a covertical graph family is called the *accessory* label, and is denoted by a. In a normal matrix representation of such a graph, no component below the principal diagonal is in the upper ideal of the accessory arc label (assuming that the graphs are labelled in a lattice as base domain with infranodal arc labels); if all the components above the diagonal belong in this ideal, this makes normal matrices very easily recognizable. With the type of base lattices we shall be using, such matrices are *triangular* (like those shown in (5.16)).

If M, M′ are two such normal matrices, and a, a′ are corresponding components of M, M′ respectively, and if + is any two-argument function defined in the base algebra, then a + a′ is an element of this base algebra, and the matrix, which we shall denote as M + M′, each of whose components is the '+'-product of corresponding components of M and M′, will be a normal representation of a labelled graph belonging to the same covertical family. We can in this way *define* a '+-product' of two matrices, and therefore also of two graphs; it is called the *conformal analogue* of + for matrices. Since there are in any algebra at least two such two argument functions, we can always define a conformal analogue of the *base algebra* for any covertical family of labelled graphs. An example of such a 'conformal algebra' is the lattice shown in (5.16) and (5.17), the one in **heavy** lines, which represents the 'context repertory', the element 'I' representing the 'rehearsal' of the context. It can be shown that this must be a lattice,* because the base algebra (5.15) is one.

It also follows that, in order to satisfy the context lattice theorem (4.6) the rhema graphs in any one context repertory must be a covertical family; for if not, their representative matrices will not have a unique preferred permutation, and the relation of conformal inclusion will not be definable (at least,

* It is in fact a sublattice of the product $\mathbf{N}^n\mathbf{A}^{n(n-1)/2}$ where **N** and **A** are the node and arc sublattices of the base domain **B**, and where n is the number of nodes in the graph family (in the example: $n = 3$).

not so that $a \geqq b$ is always either true or false). As a corollary, rhema graphs must be (at least) *biform* graphs (i.e. with two arc labels).

5.3.3. Sums and Products of Graphs: In conventional graph theory the only 'sum' and 'product' of two graphs are what I shall here call the *direct* sum and product. The *direct sum* of two graphs is the pair of them considered as one graph; if their vertex sets are disjoint, their direct sum is a disconnected graph. For example,

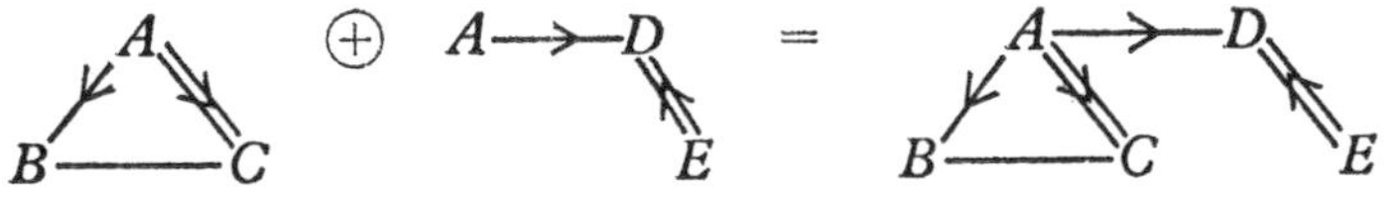

A ⊕ A—D = A—D
B—C E B—C E

... 5.18

The corresponding relation between their matrices is

$$\begin{bmatrix} A & 1 & 2 \\ . & B & 1 \\ . & 1 & C \end{bmatrix} \oplus \begin{bmatrix} A & 1 & . \\ . & D & . \\ . & 2 & E \end{bmatrix} = \begin{bmatrix} A & 1 & 2 & 1 & . \\ . & B & 1 & . & . \\ . & 1 & C & . & . \\ . & . & . & D & . \\ . & . & . & 2 & E \end{bmatrix}$$

... 5.19

That is, the matrix of the direct sum of the graphs is formed by juxtaposing the two matrices diagonally, identifying as one any pair of vertices shared in common between the two graphs. This is *also* what is known as the 'direct sum' of the two *matrices*.

The *direct product* of two graphs is rather easier to understand in the case of labelled graphs than for unlabelled ones. It is ordinarily defined only for graphs whose vertex sets are disjoint (though this proviso is not needed for graphs labelled in a common base algebra). If one graph has n nodes and the other m nodes (I ignore vertices which are not nodes), then they have matrix representations as $n \times n$ and $m \times m$ matrices respectively. Their direct product has a matrix representation as a $mn \times mn$ matrix, each of whose components is the product, in the base algebra, of the components corresponding to it in the separate matrices. Thus:

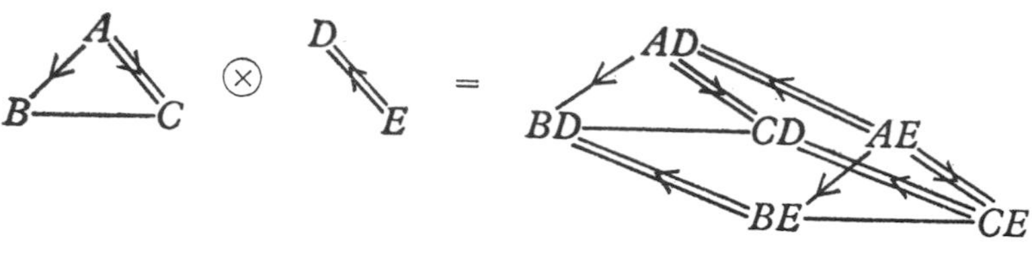

... 5.20

or, in matrix terms:

$$\begin{bmatrix} A & 1 & 2 \\ . & B & 1 \\ . & 1 & C \end{bmatrix} \otimes \begin{bmatrix} D & . \\ 2 & E \end{bmatrix} =$$

$$\left[\begin{array}{ccc|ccc} AD & 1D & 2D & . & . & . \\ . & BD & 1D & . & . & . \\ . & 1.D & CD & . & . & . \\ \hline 2A & . & . & AE & 1E & 2E \\ . & 2B & . & . & BE & 1E \\ . & . & 2C & . & 1E & CE \end{array}\right]$$

... 5.21

In drawing the graphs in diagrammatic representation (5.20), I have assumed that the base algebra is such that the 'product' 1D = 1, likewise 2D = 2, 1E = 1 and 2E = 2. This need not necessarily be so, of course; it is true if the base algebra is a lattice in which the 'product' is represented by the 'meet' operation $\frown$, and if all the arc labels are infranodal. If there are supranodal arc labels, the direct product matrix will have components off the diagonal which belong in the nodal part of the base algebra, the interpretation of which may well be obscure. This is a reminder that we may encounter additional conditions on the structure of the base algebra besides those we have already met.

We must note, however, that the direct product of two members of a given covertical family of graphs, though it is defined unambiguously, is not a member of the same family, since its vertex set is not the same, but in fact the self-product of the original set. Since two members of one covertical family have identical vertex sets, the direct sum in this case is identical with the algebraic conformal sum. It follows that a covertical graph family is closed (albeit trivially) under the direct sum operation, but *not* under the direct product.

5.4. Matrix Products

The most distinctive operation defined for matrices is that of the matrix product. All the matrices we shall be concerned with are square (or triangular, i.e. half-square), and for any two *square* matrices with the same number of components there is defined a *product* which I shall now explain.

5.4.1. Definition of the Matrix Product: We shall denote the component in the i-th row and the j-th column of a matrix A by the symbol a_i^j. The *whole* i-th row is then $a_i = a_i^1, a_i^2, \ldots, a_i^n$, where n is the number of diagonal components. Similarly, the whole j-th column of a matrix B will be $b^j = b_1^j, b_2^j, \ldots, b_n^j$. The *inner* product of a row a_i and a column b^j is then defined as the sum of the terms of the conformal product $a_i b^j$ of the row and column as thus set out.

The *matrix product* of two square matrices A, B both with n diagonal components is then the matrix C whose component c_i^j is equal for all i, j to the inner product $a_i b^j$. That is to say

$$\begin{array}{c} \mathbf{a}_1 : \\ \\ \\ \end{array} \begin{bmatrix} a_1^1 & a_1^2 & a_1^3 \\ a_2^1 & a_2^2 & a_2^3 \\ a_3^1 & a_3^2 & a_3^3 \end{bmatrix} \times \underset{\mathbf{b}^2}{\begin{bmatrix} b_1^1 & b_1^2 & b_1^3 \\ b_2^1 & b_2^2 & b_2^3 \\ b_3^1 & b_3^2 & b_3^3 \end{bmatrix}} = \begin{bmatrix} a_1b^1 & a_1b^2 & a_1b^3 \\ a_2b^1 & a_2b^2 & a_2b^3 \\ a_3b^1 & a_3b^2 & a_3b^3 \end{bmatrix} \qquad \ldots 5.22$$

where $$\mathbf{a}_1\mathbf{b}^2 = \mathbf{a}_1^1\,\mathbf{b}_1^2 + \mathbf{a}_1^2\,\mathbf{b}_2^2 + \mathbf{a}_1^3\mathbf{b}_3^2 \text{ (etc.)} \qquad \ldots 5.23$$

Clearly, the matrix product of two square matrices is another square matrix of the same number of diagonal components as its factors. Since all the components in the product are elements of the same algebra which was used as scalar algebra in the factors, if the latter represent labelled graphs in a given covertical family, so does their product. I shall refer to matrix products formed in this way as 'M-products', as distinct from the direct products which I shall call 'G-products', these being the only ones defined for unlabelled graphs. Thus, while the G-product does not produce closure of a covertical family, the M-product does do so.

5.4.2. M-products with a Lattice as Base Algebra: There are two bivalent operations definable in any lattice; they are usually denoted, as in §3.8, by $\smile$ and $\frown$, and called 'cup' and 'cap', or more formally the 'join' and the 'meet' of the two elements affected. Although some purists object (since a lattice is only a semi-ring), they are also known sometimes as the lattice sum and product respectively. These identifications can be carried over to define M-products of graphs labelled in a lattice as base domain. For this purpose, we define the product in the same way as in (5.22), but to evaluate the inner products $a_i b^j$ we make use of the formula

$$a_i b^j = a_i^1 \frown b_1^j \smile a_i^2 \frown b_2^j \smile \ldots\ldots \smile a_i^n \frown b_n^j \qquad \ldots 5.24$$

which can be abbreviated as

$$\bigcup_k^n a_i^k \frown b_k^j \qquad \ldots 5.24a$$

The inappropriateness of the terms 'sum' and 'product' for the meet and join operations remains, however. A main reason for it is that whereas a real sum and a real product are quite different operations having different properties and an unsymmetrical relationship, the meet and join of a lattice algebra are largely interchangeable. Thus, in ordinary algebra $x(y + z) = xy + xz$ but $x + yz \neq (x + y)(x + z)$; but in a lattice algebra both relations hold:

$$x \frown (y \smile z) = (x \frown y) \smile (x \frown z); \text{ and}$$
$$x \smile (y \frown z) = (x \smile y) \frown (x \smile z) \qquad \ldots 5.25$$

There exist, then, besides the M-product defined using the inner product formula of (5.24), a *coproduct* of any two square matrices with the same number of diagonal components over a lattice algebra, whose definition resembles that of the M-product except that $\frown$ and $\smile$ are interchanged throughout.

We have, then, up to now, characterized *five* bivalent operations on lattice-labelled graphs in terms of their matrix representations; these are (a) the *sum* (conformal join, G-sum in a covertical family), (b) the *meet* (conformal product), (c) G-product, (d) M-product, and (e) coproduct. All these have at least a marginal role in the theory we shall need, but it is the conformal operations (a), (b) which we shall make the most use of. I shall only briefly consider what significance attaches to M-products.

5.4.3. M-products of DLGs: Conventional graph theory makes some use of M-products; we must, however, explore their meaning for *labelled* graphs by the examination of examples. Consider first the case of M-self-products, using as our example the distinctly-labelled (§5.1) graph **G**:

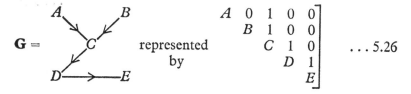

$$\mathbf{G} = \quad \text{represented by} \quad \left.\begin{array}{ccccc} A & 0 & 1 & 0 & 0 \\ & B & 1 & 0 & 0 \\ & & C & 1 & 0 \\ & & & D & 1 \\ & & & & E \end{array}\right] \qquad \ldots 5.26$$

This is a uniform graph (with only one arc label other than zero); as always with labelled graphs, we need to know the form of the base domain, and I shall consider two possibilities, as follows:

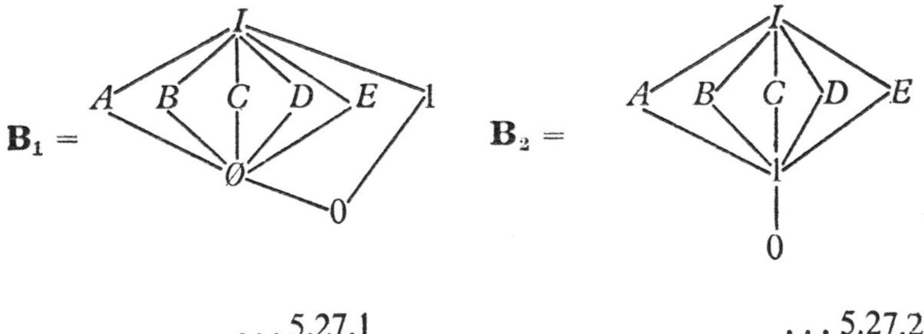

. . . 5.27.1 . . . 5.27.2

It will be seen that $\mathbf{B}_1$ makes the arc label (1) extranodal, while with $\mathbf{B}_2$ the arc label is infranodal. In both cases, the M-product of two DLGs labelled in each of these domains is itself a DLG, with node labels along the diagonal, and arc labels off it. If the base domain has *supranodal* arc labels, M-products of DLGs are themselves not distinctly labelled, and require a different interpretation; such cases will not concern us.

The M-self-product of the graph **G** shown in (5.26) can be worked out, using the formula (5.24) in conjunction with (5.22), and getting the joins and meets of the components from one or other of the base domains shown in (5.27). The results may be written $\mathbf{G}^2(\mathbf{B}_1)$, $\mathbf{G}^2(\mathbf{B}_2)$; in the same way we can evaluate also the two $\mathbf{G}^3$ products. They are

$$
\begin{array}{rrrrr|}
A & 0 & 0 & 1 & 0 \\
 & B & 0 & 1 & 0 \\
 & & C & 0 & 1 \\
 & & & D & 0 \\
\mathbf{G}^2(\mathbf{B}_1) & & & & E
\end{array}
\quad
\begin{array}{rrrrr|}
A & 0 & 1 & 1 & 0 \\
 & B & 1 & 1 & 0 \\
 & & C & 1 & 1 \\
 & & & D & 1 \\
\mathbf{G}^2(\mathbf{B}_2) & & & & E
\end{array}
\quad
\begin{array}{rrrrr|}
A & 0 & 0 & 0 & 1 \\
 & B & 0 & 0 & 1 \\
 & & C & 0 & 0 \\
 & & & D & 0 \\
\mathbf{G}^3(\mathbf{B}_1) & & & & E
\end{array}
\quad
\begin{array}{rrrrr|}
A & 0 & 1 & 1 & 1 \\
 & B & 1 & 1 & 1 \\
 & & C & 1 & 1 \\
 & & & D & 1 \\
\mathbf{G}^3(\mathbf{B}_2) & & & & E
\end{array}
\qquad \ldots 5.28
$$

which correspond to the following diagrammatic representations:

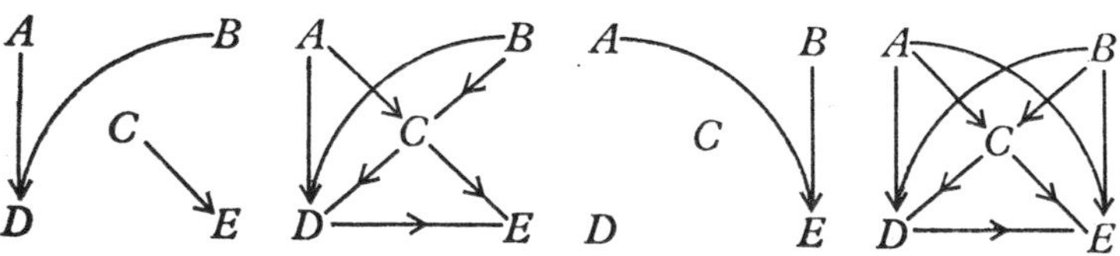

. . . 5.28a

It will be observed that $\mathbf{G}^2(\mathbf{B}_1)$ has all and only the arcs corresponding to *two-step* paths in **G**, and the only arcs which survive in $\mathbf{G}^3(\mathbf{B}_1)$ are those corresponding to *three-step paths* in **G**. There are no four-step paths in **G**, and the reader may check by forming the self-product of $\mathbf{G}^2(\mathbf{B}_1)$ that $\mathbf{G}^4(\mathbf{B}_1)$ has only zeros off the diagonal. When arc labels are extranodal, therefore, the n-th M-power of a DLG is the graph of its n-step paths. If instead we use $\mathbf{B}_2$ as the base domain, the graphs we get contain arcs corresponding to all paths of *up to* n steps.

5.4.4. Transitive and Intransitive Arcs: Comparison of the two base domains of (5.27) shows us that if an arc label is required to identify an arc representing a *transitive* relation, it may be convenient to use an infranodal element of the base domain for it, while for an intransitive relation, an extranodal arc label is indicated. It will be recalled that a 'transitive' relation is one T such that (for any a, b, c), a T b and b T c together imply a T c; both partial-ordering and simple-ordering are transitive, and in particular any simply-ordered set (soset) is constructable from such a relation. Since, as we have already seen, in §5.3.2, every rhema graph must have an arc label under which its nodes form a chain, that is a soset, it is convenient to regard the relation represented by the accessory arc label a as a simple-ordering and therefore transitive. It is not obligatory to do so, since a chain is still a chain, even if each link is defined by a non-transitive relation; but in that case we can obviously define a derived relation which *is* transitive.

For the purpose of drawing graph diagrams, non-transitive relations have a lot to be said for them; compare the following

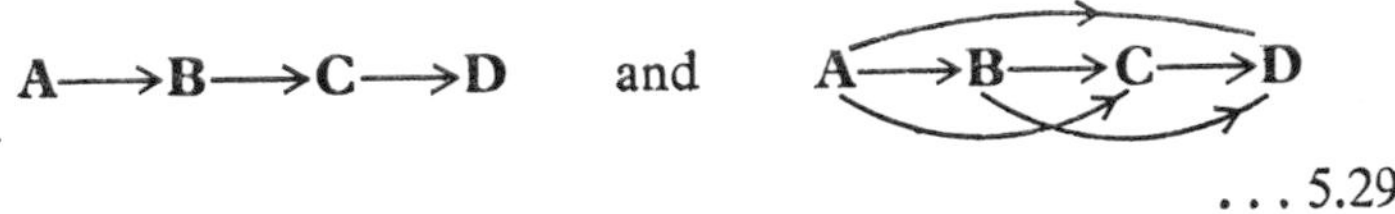

. . . 5.29

in which the first is shown with intransitive ordering relations and the second with transitive ones. If the arc label involved is infranodal in the base domain from which the labels are drawn, however, we can quite easily have it both ways; for the matrices of the two graphs of (5.29) are respectively

$$\left.\begin{array}{cccc} A & \mathrm{a} & \mathrm{o} & \mathrm{o} \\ & B & \mathrm{a} & \mathrm{o} \\ & & C & \mathrm{a} \\ & & & D \end{array}\right] \qquad \left.\begin{array}{cccc} A & \mathrm{a} & \mathrm{a} & \mathrm{a} \\ & B & \mathrm{a} & \mathrm{a} \\ & & C & \mathrm{a} \\ & & & D \end{array}\right] \qquad \ldots 5.30$$

of which the second is the third self-M-power of the first; or indeed *any* power n where n ≧ 3, for it can easily be verified that the M-product of the two matrices shown is equal to the second one. On the other hand, if a is extranodal, the n-th M-power has all its non-diagonal components zero whenever n ≧ 4. It is therefore convenient to have the accessory arc infranodal, though other arc labels may well be extranodal if they represent non-transitive relationships.

Let us further consider the case where there are different arc-labels in a single graph; again, I take a simple chain, but with a slightly more complex base domain:

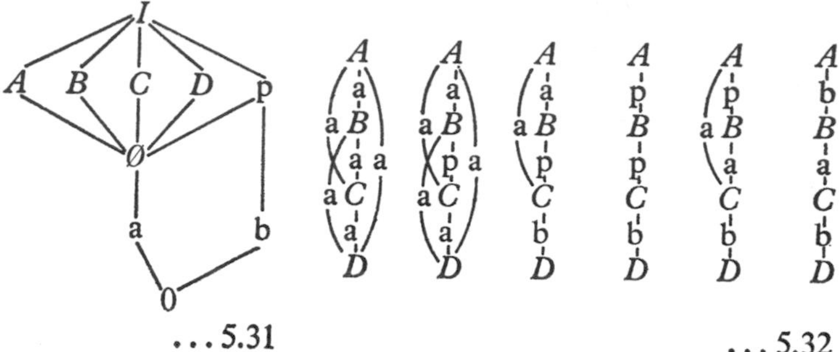

. . . 5.31 . . . 5.32

Each of the diagrams on the right (5.32) consists of a simple chain with one-step arcs, labelled as indicated, to which I have added its 4th M-power in each case, to show which connections are transitive and which are not. It will be seen (and can be checked by writing out the matrix representation and forming its self-M-product and then the self-M-product of that, for each chain) that the one with three a links is fully transitive; that the occurrence of a p link does not interrupt the transitivity of the a's; but that any b link takes no part in transitivity relations. This is because $a \frown b = 0$. If the chain condition is to be maintained, as required in *covertical* graphs, the accessory arc label a must be included in *all other* arc labels.

This example also shows that it is a useful device to use, as the ordinary matrix representation of a graph, *not* its immediate matrix equivalent G but the derivative $G + G^n$, where n is the number of nodes in the graph; in this way we economize on the numbers of arcs in the graph *diagram* (as in (5.29)) while representing *all* the transitive relations in the graph *matrix*. I shall call $G + G^n$ the *transit* matrix of the graph.

5.5. The Algebra of Rhemata

We introduced the idea of a Covertical Graph Algebra (CG**A**) in §5.3 and in §5.4 we defined and explored in several examples the operation of M-product formation from two covertical graphs (represented by their matrices); though only self-products were looked at in detail. I shall now formally define a CGA as any subset of a covertical family of DLG's which is closed under the operations of sum and M-product.

5.5.1. The Context Repertory as a CGA: In thus citing the M-product, which we have already defined in §5.4.1, in the definition of a CGA, we are committed to using only infranodal and extranodal elements of the base domain as arc labels; for no set of graphs using supranodal arc labels can be closed under the M-product operation without abandoning the requirement that the graphs be distinctly labelled (DLG's). However, it can easily be shown that any CGA is also closed under the meet and coproduct operations. It would therefore have been equally possible to take as our basic operations the meet and the coproduct. There seems to be little advantage in either choice: the way I have taken leads to our having to use the lexical lattice 'upside down', as I shall shortly show, and some may find this disquieting; but the opposite way of presenting the theory would have led to the context repertory being 'upside down', which is no less disquieting. Either feeling is equally unsupported by any real arguments: these are matters of representation, not of substance. So I carry on.

We are also committed, by the fact that the nodes of the rhema graphs represent, ultimately, lexigens, to using a *lattice* as the base domain, of which the lexical lattice is a sublattice. This means that the CGA whose elements represent the rhemata of a given context repertory can also be no more than a semi-ring, which is the class of algebra to which lattices belong. Like other semi-rings, such an algebra has a 'zero' and a 'unit', but it does not have for every element an additive inverse (that is, most elements x do not have a y such that $x+y=0$, like positive and negative integers), nor does it have a multiplicative inverse (like a number and its reciprocal); a 'ring' has the first but not the second, and a 'field' has both.

The 'zero' of a rhematical CGA is the null matrix representing the null rhema (expressed linguistically by silence). The 'unit' of the CGA is the matrix, with I for every diagonal component, and the upper bound of the arc subalgebra everywhere above the diagonal and zeros everywhere below, which represents a wholly self-contradictory rhema, and has *no* linguistic expression. However, within any given context, the context rehearsal, which has a usually very complicated but not self-contradictionary structure, and can be in principle expressed by a string of sentences, serves as the 'unit' of the relevant subalgebra. This subalgebra is all we shall ever require. The diagram (5.17) represents a very simplified case of such an algebra *in extenso.*

5·5.2. Arc Labels as Designation-Classes: Like the node labels, which we have already identified as designation-classes with an appropriate delimitation of the designata, the arc labels are elements of the base domain. We have already had one case of a base domain which made no sense: this was the one got up to present a vector as a labelled graph (5.11). It could therefore be that for our present purpose the base domain may be equally unhelpful. However, we have found out a number of consequences of assuming different lattice relationships between the arc and the node labels, which seem to be material to our argument; and the elements of our context CGAs are 'really' labelled graphs in a sense that a vector is not. Our arc labels must therefore be interpretable as sets related in some intelligible way with the node labels.

We must therefore ask, what sort of members do these sets contain? If it is not to be one of the node labels, an arc label must obviously represent some set having at least one element which is *not* the designatum of any lexigen; such an entity I shall call an 'indesignable'. One possible candidate is the act of designation itself. It will be objected, of course, that since in the preceding sentence I have designated this entity, it is obviously not indesignable. Here, however, we come across one of the very confusing properties of natural language; it can discuss itself without showing any signs of doing so in its syntax and with at most a few unusual vocabulary items. This book is written in a quite natural variety of English. But whenever it refers to the internal workings of language in general, or of English in particular (which is after all what it's about) it is using a 'meta-language', though one which is confusingly indistinguishable from the object language it is discussing. As such, it 'demotes' the language phenomena under discussion to the logical status of referents. The designation-acts which it *contains* are still beyond its power to refer to; those which it *refers to* are not those which it *uses*. Thus, in finding a designant which designates an act of designation, I create a new level of designation to which the acts referred to do *not* belong. It is therefore legitimate to assert that the acts of designation belonging to the level of the languages used are indesignables, even though there are *other* such acts, at a lower level, which do indeed have designants.

I therefore conclude that an arc label may be said to denote a set which includes, as one of its members, the 'act of designation', and is by this circumstance distinguished from any node label, all of whose members are ordinary designata.

5.5.3. The Bounds of the Base Domain: Obviously, one could analyze this matter further, either by making distinctions within the vague concept of an 'act of designation', or by thinking up other items of the same conceptual level. I shall not do so, because it seems sufficient to have only one such indesignable; but the way is open for anyone who wants to elaborate. Not to be too subtle, one might say that the sentence "//$_{13}$***Here*** *is some* /***paper***" involves two 'acts of designation', one referring to a place, and the other to an object. On the other hand, in an appropriate context, "//$_{13}$***Here*** *is* /***some***" could mean the same thing, but the concept of 'paper' would be reached in two designative steps, one reaching as far as "*some*", and the other interpreting this pronoun by the appropriate antecedent. I have been able to find no case where failure to distinguish between these two potentially distinct acts could cause confusion; but obviously this is a possibility, and if it could be exemplified, it would suggest the need for an extra node label.

Apart from this source of node labels, there is one other consideration which can generate them. We assume the potential existence of a designant whose designatum is the totality of all designables. It would 'mean' nothing, because it would include everything; but it is necessary to serve as one of the bounds of the lexical lattice and so of the node subalgebra. No language has a word for it; I shall call it '∅'. But if there were an element in the total base domain which *included* ∅ but was distinct from it, such element would contain inevitably some set-member which was not ∅ and not included in ∅ and therefore not a designatum at all. This additional element would then belong to the arc subalgebra.

Thus, ∅, though the bound of the node subalgebra, is not a bound of the base domain. We have in fact two possible arc labels, one containing only the 'act of designation', and the other containing this together with ∅. Neither of these can be identified as the bound of the base domain lattice however; for we need to *distinguish* at least two arc labels from 0. This last is the bound, and includes both the arc labels just mentioned, together of course with something else; for this extra something I suggest the *speech act* itself.

The other bound of the base domain (which, as a lattice, must have both an upper and a lower bound) is the node label I whose designation class is *empty*. Since there is nothing less than nothing, this must obviously be a bound also of the whole domain. We therefore come up with the following representation of the base domain as a lattice; in (5.33) it is in the form in which a descending line from x to y denotes that $x \geqq y$ or x includes y. On the right in (5.34), the convention is reversed. We note that it is the second which corresponds with the form we have previously entertained.

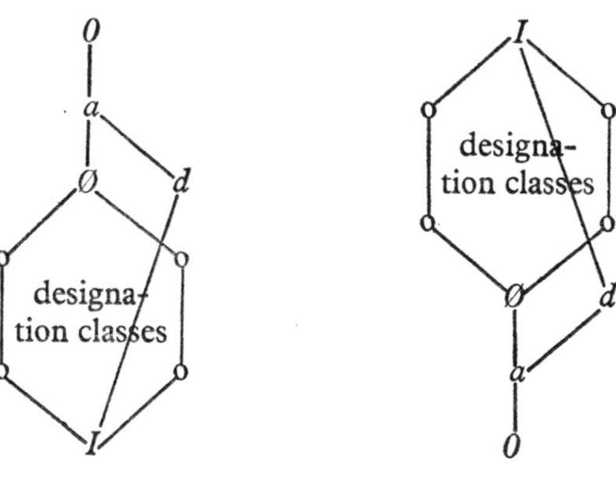

. . . 5.33 . . . 5.34

5.5.4. The Inversion of the Lexical Lattice: It is now clear that if we are to use the second form of the base domain shown above, which is required by the conventions I have adopted for characterizing the CGA we are using, the lexical lattice, which constitutes the greater part of the domain, must be contained in it in the 'inverted' position; that is, with the element representing the empty designation at the top, and the universal designation ∅ at the bottom. Inclusion-relations between lexigens thus run the opposite way to inclusion-relations between rhemata interpreted as inference. This is evidently correct and inevitable: from "*I am* *typing*" one may infer "*I am writing*", but not conversely, since "*writing*" includes and is not included in "*typing*".

Although we shall find in due course that the actual structure of the lexical lattice is by no means as simple as the designation-inclusion model would at first suggest, the above conclusion will hold. With it, once we are given the lexicon of a given language or variety, or that part of it concerned in a given context (which is often quite a small part) together with the two arc labels which I believe will be found sufficient, the base domain of our rhema graphs is fixed. The form shown in (5.34) illustrates the relationship between the two subalgebras **A** for arcs and **N** for nodes; this ensures that rhemata shall be represented as DLG's.

Fully to describe the rhema algebra we shall have to work out the principles governing the graph structure of different rhemata. But if we observe the principle that throughout any one context they will be a covertical family of graphs, the existence and nature of the 'algebra' for a given context is assured. It will be, as we have seen, a lattice; and all inferences within it will be represented by inclusion-relations as represented in this lattice.

5.5.5. Circuits in Covertical Graphs: Another point regarding rhema algebras in general will prove a helpful determinant in the fitting of the rhema structure to linguistic categories which will be our concern in Chapter VI. This is the question whether rhema graphs can contain circuits.

Any biform graph with two arc labels, which is a chain under the arcs labelled a, and which contains any circuit of more than two steps, will contain as a subgraph one of the three-membered rings shown in (5.35). This can be interpreted in two ways; in one, we take the extranodal arc label d as forming the circuit, using the base domain of (5.34), while in the other we introduce a third arc label s whose position in the base domain, expanded to accommodate it (and two others to be discussed later) is shown in (5.36). Let us now form the transit matrices for each of the two circuit graphs under each of the two base domains (dotted arrows show accessory arcs *a*, unbroken ones show the arcs labelled *d* or *s*):

...5.35

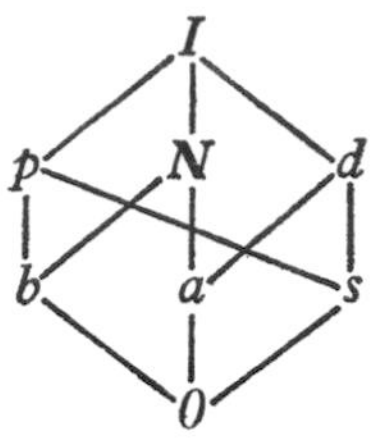

... 5.36

The transit matrices are as follows:

	Graph (5.35.1)	Graph (5.35.2)
Assuming base domain (5.34)	$\begin{bmatrix} A & \mathrm{a} & \mathrm{d} \\ \mathrm{d} & B & \mathrm{a} \\ \mathrm{a} & \mathrm{d} & C \end{bmatrix}$ ... 5.37.1	$\begin{bmatrix} A & \mathrm{d} & \mathrm{a} \\ \mathrm{a} & B & \mathrm{d} \\ \mathrm{d} & \mathrm{a} & C \end{bmatrix}$ ... 5.37.2
Assuming base domain (5.36)	$\begin{bmatrix} A & \mathrm{a} & \mathrm{d} \\ \mathrm{s} & B & \mathrm{a} \\ . & \mathrm{s} & C \end{bmatrix}$ ... 5.37.3	$\begin{bmatrix} A & \mathrm{d} & \mathrm{a} \\ . & B & \mathrm{d} \\ \mathrm{s} & . & C \end{bmatrix}$ ... 5.37.4

It will be observed that both (5.37.1) and (5.37.2) are nonsense, in that not only the supposedly circuit-forming arcs d but also the accessory arc a which is supposed to form only chains are now in circuits. It follows that if the base domain is *strictly* (5.34), there is *no* possibility of circuits appearing in our graphs. This is not the case for the other two; if the base domain contains the arc label s as in (5.36), genuine circuits can be formed.

This is an interesting conclusion; for, it will be recalled, I interpreted the element 0 in (5.34) as containing among its set-member the 'speech act', alongside of the universal designation ∅; accordingly the element s, here used as an arc label, may represent the set containing the speech act alone. (Obviously, a speech act *subsumes* acts of designation, as the diagram indicates (designation alone is represented by d); but besides this it includes 'acts of predication' (indicated as p) not contained in d.) Thus rhema graphs can contain circuits if they have arcs representing speech-acts. There is only one occasion where such an arc might be necessary, namely the representation of utterances involving self-reference; these do, as I shall show further in §7.11, involve circuit formation. This is an interesting confirmation of the general principles of interpreting arc labels suggested here. Since "acts of predication" do not exist outside "speech acts", the labels p and b of (5.36) have no use at all.

5.6. The Rhematical Notation

We are now in a position to use the principles of distinctly labelled graph theory to propose a systematic representation of rhemata. This representation can then be reduced to the form of a notation, which will be used in the remaining chapters of the work.

5.6.1. The Requirements: We have seen that graphs representing rhemata must be biform oriented digraphs distinctly labelled in a lattice domain, with one transitive arc label under which they are chains, and (at least) one intransitive arc label. Besides these specifications of internal structure, we must also arrange for the graphs representing the rhemata of a given context repertory to form a lattice under conformal inclusion.

This latter requirement is not wholly nugatory. Some possible types of graph, acceptable in themselves, do not collectively satisfy the lattice condition, which stems from the context lattice theorem (4.6). For example, if the rhema graphs are required to be lattices, then the totality of such graphs conformally included in a given one representing the context rehearsal can be shown not to be a lattice in the general case. Nevertheless, the additional constraints which are motivated by linguistic considerations do not impair the lattice property of the context repertory. The only 'additional constraint' we need examine here is that every rhema graph should have a unique node of origin; that is, that one and only one node is the terminus of no incident arcs. That every graph is *connected* follows from this, remembering that they have to be oriented digraphs. The unique origin must in fact be the node which stands first in the chain order imposed by the accessory arc labels a; this follows from accepting the structure (5.34) for the arc subalgebra of the base domain, which requires that the designatory arc label d includes the accessory arc label a.

That the system of graphs we are left with by these requirements forms a lattice with a given one as upper bound can be proved thus. First, if we might delete from the upper bound U any designatory arc to get another member of the set included in U, the set would be a lattice; for given any two graphs produced by such deletions, the deletions of both together would produce a unique 'meet', and those deletions common to both would leave us with a unique 'join'. But for a given U there are some arcs we must not delete; we must therefore eliminate from the lattice just described certain elements together with their lower ideals. But some members of these lower ideals will still occur, since all the arcs of U can be deleted if it is done in an appropriate order; and obviously the elements restored to the set in this way bring with them their own lower ideals, subject only to a further application of analogous deletions and reinsertions. The formation of the set of permitted graphs from the original set which is known to be a lattice thus involves the procedure described in the lattice replacement lemma (4.5), and therefore yields a lattice as the resulting set.

5.6.2. Specification of the Notation: We have now arrived at a fairly restricted model of rhema structure, according to which every rhema is to be represented by a graph of a special kind, selected, from the very wide field available initially, on the basis of two different kinds of constraints, one arising from the linguistic nature of the structure to be represented, and the other from the lattice property required of the collectivity of rhemata representing a given context repertory.

This model has the following properties. First, the *rehearsal* of a given context is represented by a DLG with two arc labels a, d such that in the base domain $d \geqq a$, which DLG is a chain under the arcs labelled a (including those also labelled d), and a poset originating from the head of this chain under the arcs labelled d alone. Second, any graph of the same type whose matrix representation is conformally included in that of the rehearsal graph represents a rhema which is *inferrable* from the rehearsal. Third, that the complete system of such inference relations defines a lattice of rhemata, whose lower bound is the null rhema in which all arc labels are 0. (Since the graphs must each be connected, the label of any node disconnected from the rest must be 0; a node still having any connection by a d arc may have ∅ (the lower bound of the node subalgebra) but not 0 as its label, since 0 belongs to the arc subalgebra.)

Each rhema must therefore be represented notationally by its graph in this system; that is, either as a diagram, or as a matrix (for this purpose, triangular matrices are sufficient), or as some symbol-string equivalent to such matrix and diagram. For many purposes, symbol-strings are the most convenient representations of anything; it is usually such strings that we think of as meant by the term 'notation'. Clarity in representing graph structures is not, however, one of their virtues. I shall therefore use, in the sequel, *diagrams* as the preferred notation for any rhema structure. I shall only exceptionally present matrices beside them, and symbol-strings never. I shall, however, mention as I go along how these strings are to be constructed, since firm conventions for this purpose are useful whenever the structures are to be handled by computers.

The following example will illustrate the three notational methods described: it is based on the utterance "*It is commonly found that symbol-strings are notationally obscure*", which I interpret rhematically as:

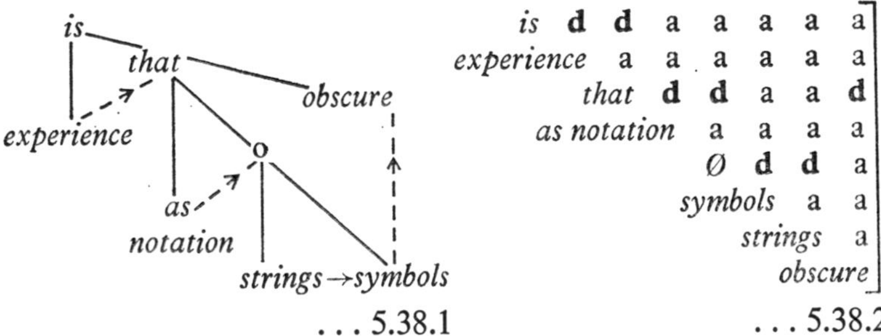

... 5.38.1 ... 5.38.2

(is): 01 / (experience): / (that): 014 / (as notation): / (): 01/ (symbols): / (strings): / (obscure):. ... 5.38.3

In the diagrammatic notation, the designatory arcs are indicated in solid lines, the accessory arcs, where they do not coincide these, as dotted lines (with arrows, since they sometimes have to run upwards, whereas the designatory arcs can always be drawn running downwards). So far as possible, the nodes are arranged so that they can be read in chain order from left to right (but this is not always possible). In the transit-matrix form (5.38.2), the arcs are denoted by a and d respectively, the latter being made more prominent by *black-letter* type; the node labels are written to *end* on the diagonal of the triangular matrix. The symbol-string notation (5.38.3) has each node separated from the next by a slash and divided into two parts by a colon; the first part is the node label (in which the lexical contribution is enclosed in (); later, in §12.3, I shall introduce other material before the lexical), and after the colon are written the *relative* positions of the nodes *to* which d-arcs lead *from* the whose label has just been given. Terminal nodes end in : /, and the end of the whole formula is marked by :. .

CHAPTER VI

Linguistic Interpretation of The Structure

The argument has now reached the point where we have arrived at a specific proposal for the representation and notation of rhemata by a particular, though still rather broad, class of labelled graphs. The class chosen cannot be claimed as necessarily the only one available, for the arguments which have led to it have not been of strictly mathematical rigour; this has been due to the need to bring in linguistic considerations at various points, rather than to any laxity in the mathematics. In this chapter I shall try to strengthen the case for the notation I have proposed, by providing a more detailed interpretation of the various elements of the graph structures. I hope that in this way I can show that the notation is adequate, even if it is logically impossible to prove its uniqueness.

6.1. The Structural Elements

It will be recalled that my proposal is that each rhema in the repertory of a given context should be represented by a biform graph which is a poset with unique origin, under one arc label, and a chain with the same origin under the other, the second (accessory) arc label being included in the first (designatory) arc label in the base domain, which is a lattice containing the lexical lattice (in inverted form) as its node subalgebra. The rhemata of a given repertory will form a covertical family, which will be a lattice under conformal inclusion. The upper bound of this lattice will be the rhematical representation of the context rehearsal; the lower bound is null. The common ordering of the vertices required for coverticality will be that defined by the accessory arcs.

In general, each rhema will be expressible in linguistic form in any chosen language possessing adequate lexical resources. There must therefore be a procedure for the generation of its expression, requiring as data only (a) the lexicon of the language, (b) the data present in the graphical representation of the rhema, and (c) all previous contributions to the rehearsal of the context to which it belongs. This entails that there must be a definite correlation between every feature of the graph structure representing a rhema and the linguistic structure(s) which may be used to express it, found by such a generative procedure; this is the counterpart to the 'sincerity' of §2.7.2. These features may be summarized as consisting of the node labels and the two non-zero arc labels; these together with their sequential ordering determine the matrix representation of the rhema graph, and since the sequential ordering is itself determined by the accessory arc label, the labels alone determine the structure.

In looking for a linguistic interpretation of the two arc labels, it is helpful first to consider the alternatives. The condition for a rhema graph to belong to the repertory of a given context may be put in the form, that it must have the vertex set required by the context, and that its matrix must be triangular, with every component below the diagonal 0 and every one above it either a or d. If a is to be meaningfully distinct from 0, we must be able to state what it would mean to have a matrix with a 0 above the diagonal, or with a non-zero component below it; for only then is it clear that both 0 and a are conveying real information. Of course, the structures represented by such matrices will not be rhemata inferrable from the context rehearsal; but they may, nevertheless, be linguistically identifiable. Both types of aberrant rhema will be in fact identified in the sequel, in §§6.2.3 and 6.6.

I shall now look in turn at the designatory arc label and the accessory arc label; the node labels, which I have already explained must represent the lexical content of the several lexigens in the given rhema, will not detain us long. We must, however, remember that any lexigen is in principle capable of explication as a rhema of greater or less complexity; this, as stated in §3.6, means that a lexigen may either itself designate some extra-linguistic designandum, or it may designate two or more subordinate lexigens belonging to an explicating rhema. Even if, in a given context, we accept a given lexigen as directly corresponding to a given node label, we may still find it necessary or convenient to provide for it a rhematical explication in the dictionary, and this explication (if it carries information which the context allows us to assume the participants in the conversation possess) is automatically available for substitution for the node label wherever it occurs within the given context, as a permissible step in any inferential procedure. Thus, the sentence "*Cedric hit the man with a gold watch*" could occur in a context where no gold watch had been mentioned up to this point, and would then be potentially ambiguous; but one would expect all concerned to know that watches make poor weapons, and this expectation is formalized by assuming this information to be contained in their common mental dictionary. That is, we suppose that they all have available, under the tag "*watch*" something like "*Watches are rarely over two inches in diameter*", and under "*hit*" perhaps "*instruments for hitting are not much use under a foot long*". Though psycholinguistically the realism of the procedure is dubious, one could in principle infer from all this that the man Cedric hit had a gold watch on him. *Every* node label is then potentially a cross-reference to a 'dictionary' of this kind.

6.2. The Designatory Arc Label

I have applied the term 'designatory arc label' to the element d of the base domain, as set out in (5.36), on the supposition that it can be interpreted as designating the 'act of designation', in a sense analogous to that in which a node label 'designates' the semantic content of its underlying lexigen. We would therefore expect an arc labelled with d in a particular rhema graph to denote an *occasion* of designation. Ultimate designants designate extralinguistic entities, and can therefore find no place* in a structure intended to represent the specific contribution of language to a context; but between the unanalysed utterance and the ultimate designatum we may interpose any number of partial designation-acts, each in turn penultimate and therefore appearing in the rhema graphs.

* Except where the designation is itself a word or utterance, for an example see (12.3).

6.2.1. Acts of Designation: Consider, for example, the game of Snap: the two players turn up cards simultaneously until it happens that the two shown form a pair, whereupon the first to shout 'Snap' takes all. In this context, the only utterance allowed for is a simple one, "$//_{1+}$ ***Snap.***"; rhematically this could be represented (as indeed any utterance can) by a single node label (*snap*). However, using the lexical information I have just given, this node label can be explicated by a rhema. Instead of referring by an act of 'ultimate designation' to the contextual situation described, we can represent it as involving penultimate designations. The simplest such explication uses two designants, one designating 'our two cards', and the other alluding to the fact of their 'correspondence'. Thus, we arrive at the rhema:

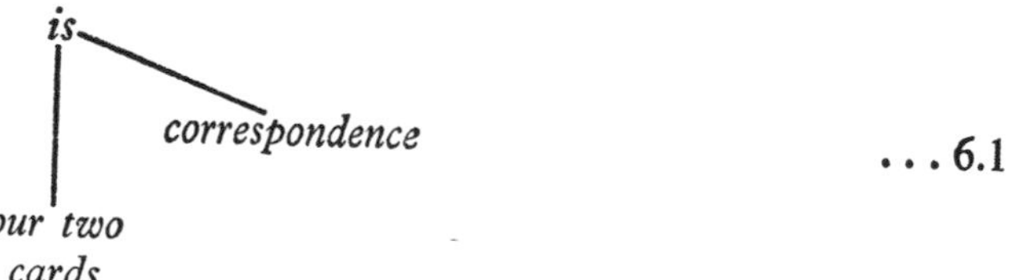

...6.1

Here the node labelled "*is*" represents what we may think of as an act of *predication*; such an act requires to be accompanied by acts of *designation*, and these are (in this explication) two in number, represented by the two 'designatory arcs', *from* "*is*", *to* "*our two cards*" and "*correspondence*" respectively, which are the *designants* involved in the respective acts. The relationship does not of course depend on the presence of an act of predication: this is a peculiarity of the word "*snap*" which we are explicating. If we take the explication a stage further, we may analyse "*our two cards*" as "*your card and mine*", or rhematically

...6.2

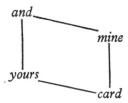

In this case, the original node of the subgraph, labelled "*and*", represents the designant which is being explicated by the rhema

shown; the label indicates that what is designated is a conjunction of two or more designata, calling for two acts of designation represented by the two arcs leaving "*and*". Each of these arcs arrives at a secondary designant; these could have been labelled "*your card*" and "*my card*", but I have taken the opportunity to exemplify a further instance of designation presented by the fact the two designants have a common element in the class of 'cards' within which they form a contrasting pair. The word "*mine*" refers anaphorically to "*card*", and while in English the first of the pair has to be given a different grammatical form from the second, they both have the same conceptual structure, which I represent as a two-act designation involving the ultimate designant "*card*".

6.2.2. Trees: The conventional method of setting out the structure of a sentence is as a tree diagram; this is of course a labelled graph, though usually represented as uniform only, and without any consideration of the base domain from which the labels come. This pattern reflects the obvious fact that in all languages there is (at surface level) a hierarchical structure. A sentence consists of clauses, a clause consists of groups, and so on. This hierarchy is certainly not a *purely* surface feature. In passing from an utterance "//$_{13}$ ∧ *There's a* /**man** *at the* /**door**." To the more explicit "//$_{1}$ ∧ *There's a* /*big* /**man** *who* //$_{1}$*seems to be*/ **drunk** //$_{-3}$ ∧ *at the* /**door**.", we are replacing the simple lexeme "*man*" by a complex structure incapable of expression in English by a single lexeme. Where the first sentence conveys a rhema with a node labelled by the lexeme "*man*", the other has in place of this node a structure which, as an independent rhema, might be expressed by "//$_{1}$ ∧ *The* /*big* /*man* /*seems to be* /**drunk**.". The last contains in turn the group "*The big man*" which invites further analysis.

This shows that the hierarchical structure apparent in surface grammar corresponds to a hierarchical structure of subgraphs at the rhematical level; and, obviously, this is a nearly universal feature in all but the simplest utterances. Since acts of designation tend to be composite, a predilection for tree diagrams is natural and broadly correct. Nevertheless, not every constituence relation in surface structure corresponds to an act of designation in any interlingually valid sense, such as calls for representation in the rhema graph. Many examples to the contrary are given in Chapter VII. To give one case here, consider the utterance *//₅ ∧ I /haven't /found the /***page**."; this could be set out, in conventional form and in my notation, thus:

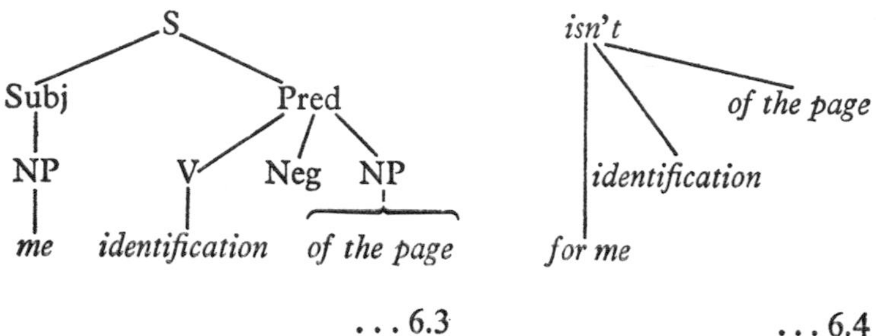

. . . 6.3 . . . 6.4

The difference between these, apart from the labelling conventions, is that the conventional tree diagram has an extra branch-point at the node labelled "Pred". Now there is no means in English, or perhaps in any language, whereby "finding a page" can be designated by a single word (unless anaphora is involved: but this already calls for special treatment); only the simplest intransitive predicates can be so designated. Thus, the arc in (6.3) from "S" to "Pred" does not represent an act of designation, but a stage in the parsing of the sentence, or conversely one of a possible sequence of generative steps used to construct the sentence from its 'deep structure'. For this reason I omit this detail; the 'predicate' of a sentence is not an identifiable constituent at the interlingual rhematical level, and indeed there are many languages which would use one word for "*I havent found*" and another for "*the page*". I don't claim that it is 'wrong' to have a sentence component labelled 'predicate', of course; but it appears, in those languages which have it, at a relatively superficial level, and it is unnecessary and therefore inexpedient at rhematical depth.

One can also adduce cases where rhema structure seems to involve *greater* complexity than is apparent on the surface. Thus, the sentence "*//₄ ∧ He /***ques***tionably suc/ceeded.*" could be a polite way of saying that he failed, and in that case the 'predicate' could legitimately appear in the structure as a node, designating one of the varieties of unsuccess further particularized by additional designants. We thus find that the relation represented by the arcs labelled with d bears a general though not a detailed correspondence with that of constituence in surface structure. It does generate tree structures, but not necessarily those conventionally used. Furthermore, as the example (6.2) already shows, our structures are not necessarily trees at all.

6.2.3. Coincident Designations: The departure from the strict tree pattern in formulating 'deep structures' is of course no novelty. The awkwardness of treating all allusions to a given referent as formally distinct at a deep as well as a surface level has struck several writers; a recent attempt to popularize non-tree representations among linguists has been made by Sampson,[90] whose formulations are in this respect essentially the same as mine. A simple case of this is in such an utterance as "//$_5$ *Brian's /brought his /new /***bat.**", in which 'Brian' is designated twice, first by name and second as the referent of "*his*". Both acts of designation have one and the same designatum, and are thus fittingly represented by two designatory arcs coinciding on one node. The structure is therefore (showing d-arcs only):

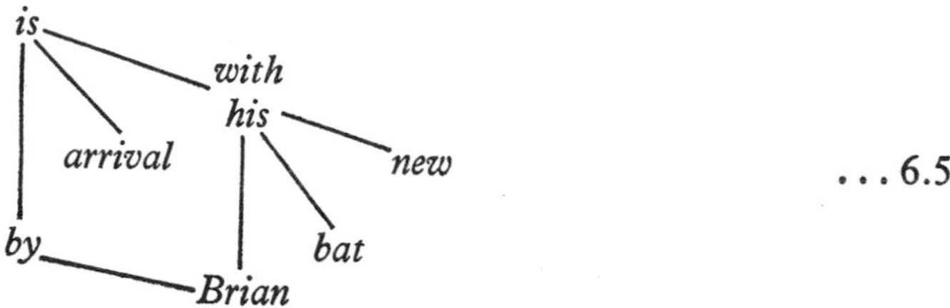

...6.5

This example is essentially the same as (6.2), involving one pair of coincident designatory arcs. More complicated is the structure proposed for "//$_4$ ∧ *You /know /***Gavin** //$_3$ ∧ *the /young /man with the /***limp** //$_4$ **Well** //$_{13}$ ∧ *his /friend /***Ted** *has a /***limp** //$_1$ **too.**", namely: (see p. 114).

From these examples, it will be evident that our structures are by no means confined to trees, even if we look only at the designatory arcs.

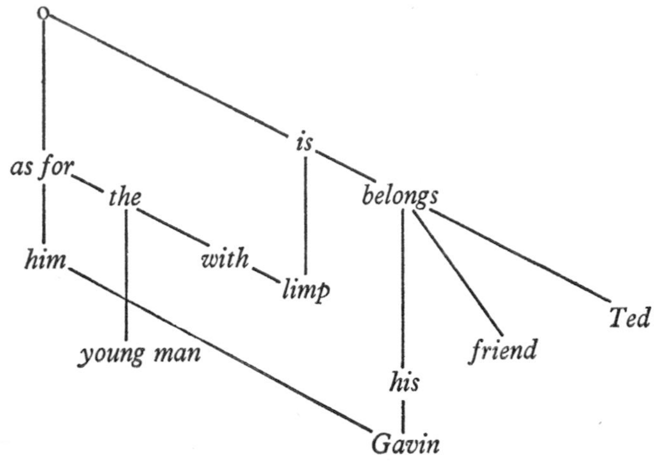

. . . 6.6

6.2.4. Designation of Speech Acts: The discussion in §5.5.5 gives colour to the suggestion that we may occasionally have a need to designate speech acts; I there proposed a special arc label for such designations. I shall now look at this idea more closely.

In colloquial English one may say “$//_1$ ∧ *The sug/*__*ges*__*tion* that *she's* $//_4$ *alco/*__*hol*__*ic is un*$//_1$**kind**.”; it would generally be taken as more or less synonymous to say “The statement ‘she's alcoholic’ is unkind”. However, the second form is not colloquial as to register; it is in fact not really at home except in a rather academic style of writing. It is deliberately contrived to enable a speech act, namely the utterance “*She's alcoholic*”, to be desig-

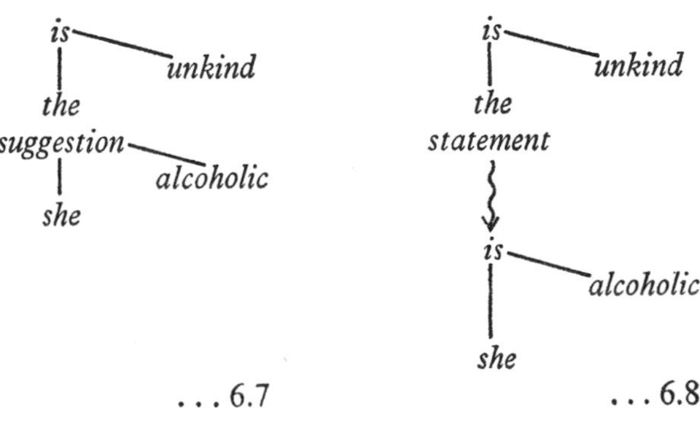

. . . 6.7

. . . 6.8

nated at the same time and in the same sentence that the utterance appears in; its penultimate designant is the word "statement". In contrast the former utterance does not designate any such statement, though it presupposes (in the everyday sense) that someone has made such a statement. I would present the structures of these two sentences as shown at foot of facing page.

The wavy line in (6.8) denotes an arc labelled with s (see (5.37)).

Another example of speech-act designation, in an idiom acceptable in certain registers, is in the phrase "The present writer does not agree": though here too we obviously have to do with writing not with speech. This would have the structure

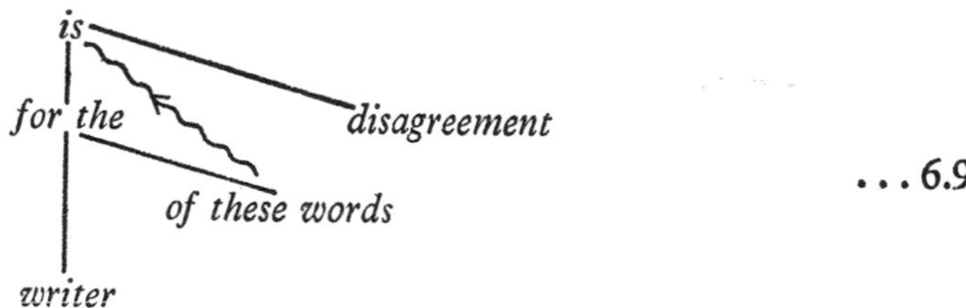

...6.9

In this case the s-arc introduces a circuit into the graph, as self-reference necessarily does. In general, however, it seems that s-arcs are not required in either the declarations or the interrogations of normal spoken language; but see §7.6.2.

6.3. The Accessory Arc Label

We have thus arrived at a fairly convincing identification, in linguistic terms, of what the designatory arc label means in rhema structures; it can be formally described as representing an 'act of designation', and more informally as being the analogue, at the rhematical level, of the relation of 'constituence' at the surface level, with due caution against expecting a one-one correspondence between these two relations. It is this type of arc that causes tree diagrams to be the most popular form of representation of both surface and deep structures. I now turn to the accessory arcs, those labelled with a.

6.3.1. Formal Properties of the element a: In proposing the structure (5.37) for the lattice to be used as the base domain of the labelled graphs representing rhemata, I pointed out that a was shown as included in d. Moreover, if there were any arc label x such that $x \frown a = 0$ (the suggested arc label s for speech act designation has this property $s \frown a = 0$), the transitivity of a would be interrupted by any x-arc, while this transitivity would not be interrupted by an arch such as d which includes a (i.e. $d \frown a = a$). Thus, for any three nodes P, Q, R, two arc links P-d-Q and Q-a-R together imply P-a-R, as can be checked by forming the transit matrix for the graph on P, Q, R as vertex set (see §5.4.4).

This means that, to find a linguistic interpretation of a, we must look at cases where it is the *only* link between two nodes. It has this role among the designants under a common node; thus, this arc should be inserted between "our two cards" and "correspondence" in (6.1) between "your" and "mine" in (6.2), and so on. The examples we have already had also show that more than two designants can be linked in this way; thus (6.5) has two groups of three needing a-arcs to show their linear ordering. In theses cases its transitivity means that its significance must be in some sense 'the same' as between *any* pair of designants taken in the appropriate order.

This property largely excludes any dependence of the accessory arcs on the nature of the node labels; for such dependence would entail that the node labels, that is the lexical lattice, should have some kind of simple ordering among themselves, or at least be subject to some kind of selection rule such that the labels cooccurring in one sentence could be simply ordered. It is difficult to conceive of a rule of this kind operating on an open set such as is the lexical lattice as a whole.

6.3.2. Closed Categories of Node Labels: There are, however, as we shall see in Chapters VIII–XI, certain closed categories within the node subalgebra, to which some selection rule could be applied which might, in principle, dictate a particular ordering of the nodes within a given clause. The kind of categories I have in mind are those reflected at surface level in cases, demonstrative pronouns, numbers, and the like. If any of these were subject to a selection rule which would exclude any two nodes in one rhema (or dependent on one preceding node by designatory arcs) having labels agreeing in one of these categories, this could be interpreted as an ordering of the nodes in question in the way required.

The only one of the categories in question for which such a rule is in any way plausible is that of case. Simple examples quickly dispose of quantification as being subject to such a rule: "*Both dogs chased both cats*"; and equally 'identification' as defined in Chapter X: "*Her brother insulted her aunt*'. But just such an exclusion rule as I have described has been claimed to operate with cases; this was first suggested by Fillmore,[32] and is still entertained in some quarters.

There are, however, serious difficulties in explaining the role of the accessory arcs in this way. First, the exclusion rule for cases can only be maintained at the cost of some artificiality. For example, the members of conjunct pairs or lists normally have the same case, and if the case is to occur only once, the whole of such a list must be counted as subject to one act of designation; but in reality such lists can be enlarged while one is speaking. Consider, for example "*//$_1$ ∧ You'll /want to /use a /**spade** for/ that //$_2$ or a /**pick** //$_2$ maybe a /**mat**tock, //$_1$ whatever you /**like**.*". Quite apart from the sufficiency of whatever selection rules exist, the variety and interrelationships of the cases available will be found to preclude any effective exploitation of them in this way.

6.3.3. The Subject-Predicate Relation: Conventionally, as I have already remarked, the principal division within a clause is seen as that between the subject and the predicate. The predicate can, in turn, be divided (in many cases) into a verb and a complement, which is in many ways an analogous relation. In "*She made the boys return the ball to him*" we can in this way arrange the terms in order, from 'outermost' to 'innermost', thus: *she—boys—him—ball—return.* This procedure, perhaps, might enable us to order the nodes in any one clause in the manner required.

Several difficulties arise, however. If the matter is interpreted in strictly conventional terms, it does not obviously cover all types of clause; equative sentences, for instance, or correlatives such as "*The longer you leave it the worse it gets.*". The requirement that the relationship be 'the same' between any pair of nodes is also not well maintained. Worst of all, for a relationship required to operate at the rhematical level, the ordering of the nodes obtained in this way is far from being translation-invariant; it is not even invariant within one language. Consider the sentences "*//₁Ralf re/ceived the /lordship of /**Westbury** from the /king*", "*//₁The /king /gave the /lordship of /**Westbury** to /Ralf*", "*//₁The /king en/dowed /Ralf with the /lordship of /**Westbury***"; these are all synonymous, in that they say the same thing, but they all give different orderings of the terms under 'predicate-stripping', respectively Ralf–king–Westbury; king–Ralf–Westbury; king–Westbury–Ralf.

It is clear then that this relation would, at least, have to be radically reconceived if it were to provide what we need in the way of a linguistic interpretation of the accessory arc label. The proposal which I shall now make can, perhaps, be seen as such a re-consideration of the essence of the subject-predicate relation. As will have been already gathered, the terms 'subject' and 'predicate' play no part in my conception of rhema structure; the time has come to examine what takes their place.

6.4. Focus

Briefly, my conclusion is that the only linguistic category which has the requisite structure is that which has been described, among many other names, as 'focus'. I here use Halliday's term,[47] which seems to have become marginally more popular than some others; but I admittedly depart from Halliday's conception of the matter, in the use that I make of the focus category here.

6.4.1. Historical: Focus is one of the more recent additions to the list of contrasts which have interested linguists. That every sentence can be seen to have some term which is understood to be a point of reference, known to both participants, and another which constitutes some addition to the information about it, could not become obvious so long as the written text was the main object of study; and even if attention is given mainly to spoken language, the elusiveness and subjective quality of the distinction makes it peculiarly difficult to study without recourse to introspection, which prevailing philosophies discourage.

Doubtless a careful study would reveal earlier references, but the first really systematic treatment of the subject seems to be that of Halliday's already cited; it is, however, preceded by an interesting paper by Hultzén,[54] primarily concerned with intonation, in which the idea of what was later called focus appears, under the description 'information points'—a term from information theory used by Hultzén for what I call 'rhemes'.

A common view on focus is that it is basically a class of *syntactic* forms or transformations which serve to "focus attention" on one word or clause. Such a form is the cleft sentence ("//$_1$ ∧ *It's* /***Dad*** *that* /*pays*.") (thus Schachter[92]). Some attempts have been made to treat focus by transformational methods, as by Hirst;[52] the difficulty revealed by these efforts is that the notion of 'context'—which is for me what focus is all about—is not susceptible of transformation unless it is already verbalized, and so already 'focussed'. Saltarelli[89] takes focus as a relation between 'propositions', and takes the active-passive contrast as marking it; but his distinction between focus and 'contrastive stress' (which I regard as the main surface expression of it) suggests that Saltarelli's use of the term "focus" is for a more 'surface' level than I would wish. Nevertheless, Saltarelli expresses views close to my own on the importance of focus, and on the primacy of meaning over its syntactic organization.

In general, the impression conveyed is always of a two-term opposition between a *theme* (given term, topic) and a *rheme* (new term, comment). The picture is to this extent analogous to the subject-predicate distinction (but, as in that case, one can extend the two-term opposition into a multi-term ordering by further analysing the primary moieties of the clause). For example, in the sentence "//$_1$ *Jane's got* /***married***." the theme is "Jane" and the rheme is "got married"; in another context, however, one might be discussing marriages more generally, and someone, citing Jane as an instance, would say "//$_1$***Jane****'s got* /*married*.", using "Jane" as rheme and "married" as the theme. English has a preference for placing the stress late in a sentence, and when a transitive verb is present a change of focus *can* be marked by exchanging active for passive constructions; but in a sentence such as the above this resource is not available, and focus can only be indicated by the tonicity. In spoken English, in fact, the main focus terms are usually unambiguously indicated; but this is not the case in all languages because the matter is so often self-evident to the participants that marking of theme and rheme is unnecessary. This reluctance to mark focus explicitly (or to recognise the markers if they are present) is doubtless a major cause of the obscurity which many linguists find in the category.

Thus, as recently as 1971, Partee[76] could say, of 'topicalization', that it is 'poorly understood', and suggest that it is not part of 'deep structure' (whereas it is more nearly surface structure that it is not part of). Writers on focus, even such as Boadin,[10] who has examined in detail its expression in certain African languages, seem content to treat it as a rather peripheral matter. But there is increasing recognition that it may play a primary role in language: thus Venneman[98] has recently made a good case for regarding it as the prime mover in changes of word-order pattern, such as from SOV to SVO types. It is therefore no longer out of the question to find it important; though the role I suggest for it here is a particularly fundamental one.

6.4.2. Focus as an Odering: Let me now illustrate how in a multi-term sentence we can identify terms as *ordered* by focus, or at least by a focus-like relation to which the term seems acceptably extended. I take as my example the utterance "//$_{13}$ *Anne /gave me a /cake for my /birthday /**last** year /**too**.*". In this sentence the rheme is marked, by the tonicity, as "last year"; there is no marking of focus contrasts in the preceding theme section of the clause, though there is a presumption in favour of the word order corresponding to it, and if for instance the next most rheme-like term were say "cake" one would expect the sentence to be pronounced "//$_{1}$ *Anne /gave me a /**cake** for my /birthday //*$_{13}$ ***last** year /**too**.*" We therefore identify 'inside' the theme a potential utterance "//$_{1}$ *Anne /gave me a /cake for my /**birth**day.*". Removing the new rheme "birthday", we again hesitate. But, since cakes are associated with birthdays in our culture this term is a weak candidate for being the next rheme; if it were so, we would expect to hear "//$_{4}$ *Anne /gave me a /**cake** for my //*$_{1}$ ***birth**day.*". I therefore prefer to see the theme in isolation as "//$_{1}$ ***Anne** /gave me a /cake.*"; if from this sentence we remove the latest rheme, we get "//$_{5}$ *I've got a /**cake**.*" which, as a two-term sentence, leaves no room for further analysis.

The parallel of this procedure with predicate-stripping is clear. But the difficulties attending the acceptance of the latter as underlying the accessory arc label no longer apply. It is the same relation being indicated all through, and not, as in the predicate-stripping case conceptually distinguishable relations more or less assimilated by the syntax; focus, whether between adjacent items or at a distance, can always be described as a contrast between a point of reference and a point of interest. Moreover, the relation is presumably invariant under translation into another language; though it would be difficult to put this to the test, since the intrusion of an interpreter would inevitably affect the context materially and perhaps in itself alter the focus relations.

6.4.3. Focus within Groups and Phrases: In the above description, I have concentrated on focus relations between the main constituents of a clause. If focus is to be available to explain *all* instances of the accessory arc it must be shown to hold equally between any two ultimate designants. This is not difficult in subordinate clauses which involve a predicative, since these can be transformed into independent sentences by relatively superficial modifications; but there is a little more difficulty to applying focus to determinative constructions.

Thus, we may ask what are the focus relations in "$//_1$ ∧ *The* /**big** /*old* /*house at the* $//_1$ *edge of the* /**town**". This phrase can be progressively turned into predicative form; the first step, in English, requires the insertion of "is" before "at", but also, interestingly, the transfer of the tonic stress from "big" to "house". This gives us two items to examine further: "$//_1$ ∧ *The* /*big* /*old*/ **house**" and "$//_1$ ∧ *is at the* /*edge of the* /**town**.". The former corresponds to the predicative "$//_1$ ∧ *The* /*old* /*house is* /**big**." ("The big house is old" could give a determinative "The old big house"), whose determinative in turn gives "$//_1$ ∧ *The* /*house is* /**old**.". We thus see that the focus order comes out as *house* (theme)—*old*—*big* (rheme): in noun groups the tonic stress falls on the noun itself in most situations, and does not mark the rheme as it does in most constructions in English.

This is sensible enough, in that the existence of the house is presumably the first thing understood, and its properties of being old and big are successively added to it as points of further distinction. But what of "$//_1$ ∧ *at the* /*edge of the* /**town**"? Do we not have first that there is a town, and only as a later addition that we are interested in its edge? This is possible; but if the matter *were* being looked at in this way, on account of the way the context was being built up, one would have to say rather

"*//$_1$ ∧ at the /***edge** *of the /town*". In such extended locative constructions, using an auxiliary noun such as "edge", the auxiliary noun, though the head of the phrase, does not attract the tonic stress as a semantically full noun such as "house" does. In the form originally given, therefore, the theme is "edge" and the rheme is "town". The whole phrase, therefore, has the structure shown below (accessory arcs are indicated by broken arrows):

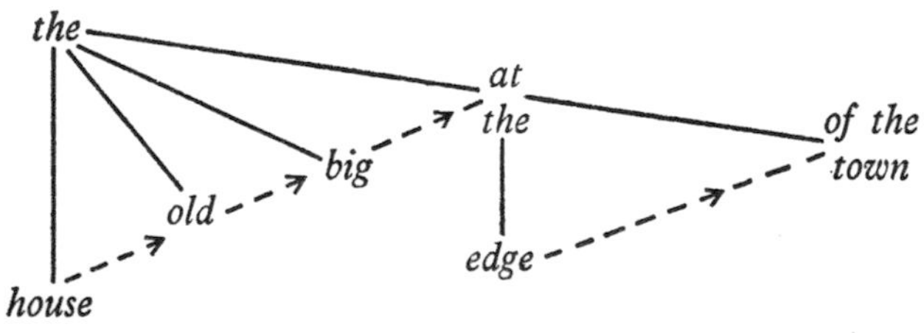

...6.10

In later chapters we shall encounter a wide variety of construction illustrating the application of focus relations within low-ranking syntagms. Though in some instances the relations indicated may not be obvious, perhaps even ambiguous, there is no reason to suppose that in principle focus relations are ever absent, except in the circumstances discussed in §6.6.

6.4.4. Focus and Synonymy: There remains a major obstacle which may lead many readers to question the correctness of my identification of focus as the relation signified by the accessory arc label. This is that it forces us to make a distinction between the two sentences "*//$_1$* **Jan***ice is /coming to /lunch.*" and "*//$_1$ Janice is /coming to /***lunch**." of a kind which not only disguises their synonymy, but as we shall see precludes either being inferrable from the other. Surely, this must be nonsense?

On the contrary, I deny that they are in any sense synonymous as natural language utterances. Can you imagine a context in which both forms would be equally admissible? The idea that these two utterances 'mean the same' is one of the fallacies arising from disregard of context; perhaps, indeed, the most striking and important of such fallacies. Paraphrased in prose format (where intonation is conventionally not marked), they might appear respectively as "We shall need an extra place for lunch because Janice is coming" and "Janice is arriving soon after twelve so she'll be having lunch with us". There is indeed an element of common meaning between them, but this is curiously difficult to express in any but a deliberately stilted idiom; perhaps it comes across in "Janice will be present at our midday meal". If it had been thought that she wouldn't come at all, but hardly in any other context, the neutral predication could perhaps be expressed in spoken form as "$//_5$ *Janice is* /**com***ing to* /*lunch.*". The fact is that what one says is always strongly circumscribed by the context of the moment, so much so that except for special purposes, such as I shall allude to in the next section, this kind of 'pure' meaning, free from the complications of focus, *does not exist at all.* This is a strong and perhaps a startling statement; but I hope that by the accumulation of examples its truth may become apparent.

The conclusion that there is (in most contexts) no rhematical inference between utterances differing in their focus relations, even such simple ones as "$//_1$ *Here's* /**Wal***ter.*" and "$//_1$ *Walter's* /**here.**", may seem at first sight paradoxical. I suggest, however, that our view of the matter is heavily influenced by the intellectual history of our culture. Relatively early there arose a concept of 'logic' based on treating such pairs of utterances as synonymous—a brilliant piece of creative intelligence. But the respect in which this technique was held has over the centuries so taken hold of our educational routine that we now find it 'obvious' rather than 'brilliant'. What we have come to call rational thought makes use of the far-reaching simplifications, made possible by identifying such utterances, in every department of life (including no doubt some where it is hardly the appropriate tool). What I bring forward here is an alternative rationality, technically much more complex (but at the same time more 'natural', in that we do it all the time after a fashion), of which the other is a very special case; its advantage, if any, is in its being closer to real life.

6.5. Inference without Focus

I have already drawn attention to the fact that 'inference' is a term capable of diverse interpretations; some of these are described in §4.1. I am proposing to explore a model of inference based on inclusion, defined within a lattice representing the repertory of a given context. The possibility of doing this we have seen to depend on the existence of a relation between the lexigens of every rhema which imposes on them a simple ordering, and which I have claimed to represent the linguistic category of focus. However, inference is usually regarded as independent of this or any other *linguistic* category. If, then, my model is sound, and in particular if it includes classical logic as a special case, I have to explain why and how such other kinds of inference work—or show that they don't work.

6.5.1. Aristotle: One way of imposing enough order on discourse to make it the basis of a rigorous system of logic, without bringing in focus, is to start by imposing transformations on our utterances designed to bring them all within a common framework, simple enough to make possible unambiguous matchings between their terms. It is the matching of term to term that is the real contribution which I look for to my ordering of them by focus; if this can, in some reasonably extensive class of cases, be done in some other way, then we have at once an alternative logic. Though Aristotle[6] naturally did not consider transformations as such, he was explicitly aware of the possibility of restating a variety of utterances within the limited set of canonical forms which his syllogistic theory allowed. Some such undisciplined remark as "*Socrates was like the rest of us: we all have to die, and so did he*" could be, as we would say, transformed into the ruly equivalent "*All men are mortal. Socrates was a man. Therefore, Socrates was mortal.*"

In my notation the unruly version looks like this*

It is by no means obvious how one might derive the conclusion from the premisses, if these had to be expressed in this format; I shall explain the procedure in detail, when we come to Chapter XV. But the ruly form of the syllogism, if we assign the unexpressed focus-relations appropriately, reduces to the same form too. In this case, however, there is a much simpler algorithm for obtaining the conclusion; this is in fact the obvious method to use, whenever we are given input premisses which can be transformed into one of Aristotle's approved 'figures'. The only trouble

* I suggest the following way of reading it:
"both are all to (and) was one of Socrates, so died he
of us *die* us Socrates"

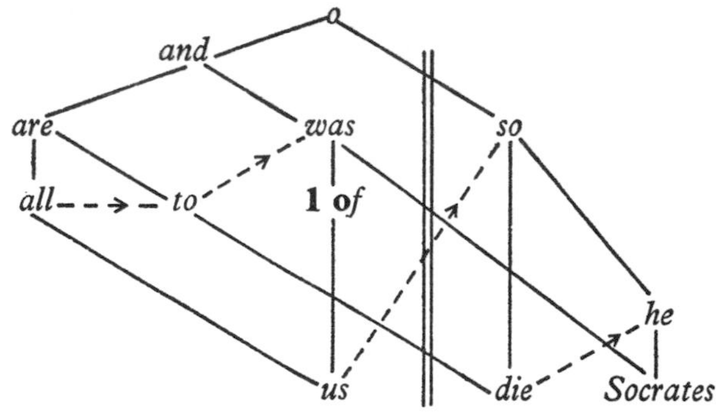

. . . 6.11

is that in most cases there is no transformation which will serve for this, so that a sharp division appears between '*oratio pronuntiabilis*' and '*oratio vulgaris*'. This division, which is strictly an artifact of a particular methodology, has come to be reified as a special kind of 'rational' thought as opposed to the loose thinking of the masses, with many baneful consequences to our culture.

6.5.2. Kungsun Lung: Another baneful effect of Aristotle's elegant logical method has been to discourage proper concern with the context of utterances (which in his method is strictly irrelevant). In the Chinese philosophical tradition, context was never lost sight of. One result of this was that they never succeeded in producing an algorithmic system of logic at all (Chinese logic is still a very obscure field in the West; a good survey is given by Needham[74]). As an example of what can be done in this direction—selected more for being comprehensible to me than for its own merit—I take the contribution of Kungsun Lung,[30] who desired particularly to be remembered for his aphorism

—"a white horse is not a horse".

The explanation of this appears to be that in the comparison of sentences any inherent ordering of the terms, such as for us is furnished by focus relations, is to be disregarded (except, possibly, the order provided by the surface structure of the text—discussion is illustrated exclusively from the one example). Thus, any sentence containing the term "horse" (or alternatively "white horse") is an instance of the said term, and two terms are synonymous if and only if their instances are appropriate to the same set of contexts. But the set of contexts where one might say “Bring me a white horse” is not the same as the set where one might say “Bring me a horse”: either you care about the colour or you do not. Thus, what Kungsun Lung is really claiming is that the null qualifier actually means “any-coloured”, and contrasts with “white” without including it.

We have here a type of inference, though it is both weak and of restricted application. It is easy to understand why it did not survive its inventor. But it is of interest as showing how little in the way of useful inference can be done without some strong structural relationships between sentences, whether this be natural or artificial.

6.5.3. Rhetorical Forms: For the Greeks, as mentioned in §1.1, logic and rhetoric were closely connected; both were seen as ways in which discourse could be improved by discipline, the one constraining content, the other form. As we now see, more clearly than did the ancients, form and content are complementary and can in principle exchange roles; though the extent to which this can happen in language is limited by the rules of syntax. Nevertheless, the form of an utterance can carry meaning of a kind; and most of the ‘figures’ catalogued by ancient and modern rhetoricians owe their effect to just this.

The main effect produced in this way is to suggest analogies. Two sentences which exhibit a detailed parallelism of structure, if uttered consecutively, carry the suggestion that corresponding rhemata ‘match’, in the sense that meaning can be attached to their joins and meets (in the lexical lattice) as well as to the two sentences themselves. To take a case of the simplest of the rhetorical figures, isocolon, we may say (as St Columba did, starting a war with it): “*//$_4$ ∧ To /every /cow her /**calf**, //$_1$ to /every /book its /**copy**.*”. This saying gives in my notation, omitting the accessory arcs, the form:

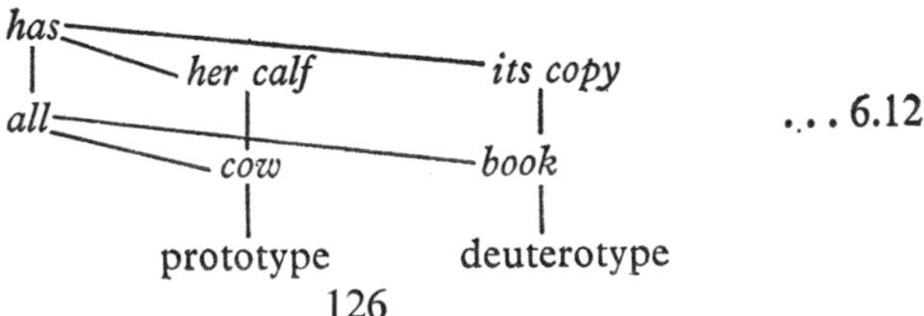

The obvious parallel is reflected in a sufficiently rigid structure to impel its suppletion by the two terms at the bottom. If this is combined with the legal precept that the borrower of a cow possesses the calf born while he has her, it can be 'inferred' that the borrower of a book may keep a copy of it, without having to appeal to either Aristotelian logic or to focus relations. Such inference *could* be accepted as valid (its rules can easily be made definite enough for that) but, according to the legend, it was not. A logic of analogy is not at all impossible; an interesting beginning has been made for instance by Hesse.[50] But its results are too erratic to be socially acceptable, even if the strict formality of the utterances which it depends on were a commoner mode of natural speech than it in fact is. I need not add that there are many other rhetorical figures, all importing into utterances enough geometrical regularity to enhance the apparent meaning conveyed, but as likely to deceive as to enlighten the listener.

6.5.4. Categorization: In §6.3.2 I mentioned the possibility that in a sufficiently restricted mode of discourse, the node labels of the rhemata could be 'categorized' in such a way that in different sentences they could be matched if and only if the node labels belonged in the same categories. It is not hard to see that such a principle could not be extended to unrestricted natural language, but nevertheless, there are quite a lot of occasions when this kind of matching-rule can seem obvious enough to substitute for, and even to override, the rules (given in §13.5) using focus relations.

This method is the one generally used in artificial information-retrieval systems, operated on computers; such systems normally aim to deal with a fairly limited range of data, for which categorization is by no means impossible, and, for this very reason, tend to become unmanageable when applied to wider fields. The possibility of categorization also arises in more natural language situations, characterized by a relatively limited vocabulary or 'restricted code'. Pidgin languages, for example, normally have no means of marking focus relations, and while very often focus may be clear from the context of situation it is likely that understanding such languages may depend very largely on some kind of categorization.

The acquisition of language by young children inevitably passes through a phase where vocabulary is very restricted, and here too it may be that categorization is for a time a serious rival to focus, though I know of no direct evidence about this. The essential limitation of the method is its lack of generalizability; it can never be more than a temporary prop, or an artificial expedient. But it can at times be in *conflict* with matching by focus, and this can lead to misunderstanding. Reasonably disciplined speech avoids such conflict, but one thing that natural language never consistently achieves is reasonable discipline. There is a wide field of research here into what actually happens when such conflicts arise; but this is for the psycholinguists, and I shall not pursue the matter at this point.

6.5.5. Non-Human Communication: Language is usually restricted by definition to the human species. While this remains broadly true, the borderline now seems less rigid than it once did. It is now well known, for example, that bees (at least of the genus *Apis*) use a system based on analogue coding to convey detailed quantitative information on where to find food sources and nesting sites (von Frisch[39]). The structure of this code, with simultaneous transmission of two or more signals but no segmentalization, is as different as it could well be from human language, and detailed comparisons are thus hardly relevant. But it does serve to show that factual communication can occur by means radically different from our own—or, for that matter, from the sharing of emotional 'settings' accomplished by the phonation of mammals and birds.

Of more immediate interest is the work of Gardner and Gardner,[40] who taught the young chimpanzee Washoe to use a sign-language designed for deaf-mutes. Washoe's progress in this art has exceeded the accomplishment of any other non-human animal, to the extent of using multi-term sentences which can reasonably be understood as conveying simple (one-level) rhemata. But whereas the system has, when used by human deaf-mutes, a regular syntax of the isolating type, Washoe's grasp of syntax is unsure at best. In particular, her utterances seem to lack focus; though, in a restricted code, its place may be taken by categorization. It would be of great interest to study the mechanism of this communication, which is good enough to be useful in daily life, from a rhematical point of view, especially as its use is now being established in a small colony of young chimpanzees.

6.6. The Zero Arc Label

As already mentioned, it is important for the interpretation of the non-zero arc labels, d and a, that both should be distinct from zero, the label formally attached to arcs which are, in diagrammatic representation, absent from the rhema graphs. That is to say, it makes sense to ask what the zero arc label *represents*. Given that rhemata are to be represented by oriented digraphs, that is by triangular matrices, all of whose components below the diagonal are formally zero, we have only to ask what a zero means when it appears *above* the diagonal.

6.6.1. Things not in the Repertory: The first point is that a rhema matrix with any component other than a or d above, or other than zero below, the diagonal, does not represent an unambiguous element of the lattice which (4.6) requires any context repertory to be. We therefore have to seek an illustration something which is *not* in the repertory of any context. We have already encountered one entity of this kind, namely utterances involving any form of self-reference, such as (6.9); these have an anomalous s arc label *below* the diagonal. Such a remark can never be inferred from the rehearsal of a context, and is therefore not a member of the repertory. It is true that it could be inferred from a rehearsal which itself contained a self-reference; but such a context occurs only in the discussion of self-referent utterances, an enclave of thought which we need not waste much time on.

There are, however, two, more ordinary, kinds of remark which have the same property of not being inferrable from a rehearsal which is not of the same kind. The first is commands: but there is nothing odd about a context rehearsal incorporating a command, for the whole point of a command (or request, which is only a polite command) is to change the existing state of affairs, which requires that it should be itself insinuated into the prevailing context in some form or other; this entails, in fact, a type of self-reference—see §7.5. The second kind of remark which cannot be inferred is a question. Here the possibility of finding a question in the rehearsal itself does not arise; a context is necessarily given, actual, not requiring an answer, even if it may often fail to carry much information. Thus, while commands must conform to the general type of rhemata, and in particular must have a gap-free simple-ordering among their nodes, questions must *not* have such a structure. They must have something above the diagonal in their matrix representation other than a or d; or an anomalous component *in* the diagonal.

This then is, perhaps, a unique identifying feature of questions. But is it really? As we have seen, there is a strong tendency in most languages to leave focus unexpressed, and what is unexpressed may sometimes not be there. One might think that in many statements of moderate complexity, not all the focus relations need be bothered with. Do we need to know them, for instance, to understand "*They emptied the water out of the tank with a siphon in a few minutes.*"? (Note that I load the dice by omitting intonation!) Now, in any actual context in which these words might be uttered, it will be the case (as with Janice coming to lunch) that either they are intent on emptying the tank, or they are demonstrating the use of a siphon, or possibly just trying to see what can be done in a few minutes. Moreover, within each of these cases, which each fix a theme for the sentence, there will be sub-cases fixing the focus relations between the other terms. We end up with one of many particular versions (most of which are in English, perhaps exceptionally, distinguished); thus, with "$//_1$ ʌ *They /emptied the /**water** out of the /tank* $//_4$ *with a /**siphon*** $//_1$ *in a /few /**minutes**.*", the focus order (theme-rheme) is fixed as *tank—siphon—minutes—water.* I maintain that, in statements, focus relations are in real contexts fully determinate. There are also a kind of questions (see §6.6.3) which contain no zero arc labels, but **I** as a node label instead.

6.6.2. Closed Questions: A question expecting a yes or no answer, or, or posing a fixed list of alternatives, is called a 'closed' question. From the above argument, we would expect its rhematical structure to be that of a conflation of its possible answers with no mutual focus ordering between them. Here is an example:

$//_1$ *Pat's* /***here.***

is d	d	
Pat	a	...6.13
	here	

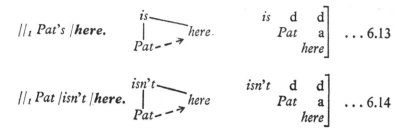

$//_1$ *Pat* /*isn't* /***here.***

isn't d	d	
Pat	a	...6.14
	here	

These two forms can be combined in more than one way; the details of the representation of closed questions will be left till §7.7, and I shall give here only the simplest type, in which the predication is queried without any biassed expectation. This is:

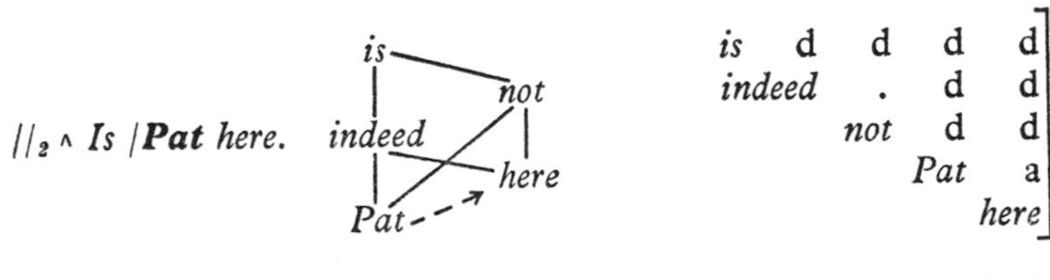

...6.15

This last, it will be observed, contains each of the two possible answers as subgraphs. That is to say, we can 'infer' from the rhema representing a question any admissible answer to the question. Once an answer is given, a contribution to the total context is made, just as it would be if the statement were made spontaneously. The question is not a contribution to the context, but an *invitation* to contribute.

6.6.3. Open Questions: A closed question can also be expressed by stating the possible answers. Thus, the one discussed above could have been expressed by "$//_2$ ∧ *Is* /*Pat* /***here*** $//_1$ *or* /***not***.". This method is not limited to two alternatives; for example, one might say "$//_2$ ∧ *Is my* /*coat in the* /***car*** $//_2$ ∧ *in the* /***cupboard*** ∧ *or* $//_1$ *be*/*hind the* /***door***.". But if one were not sure whether any such list of alternatives were really exhaustive, or in any case to save time, one can say simply "$/_1$*Where's my* /***coat***.". The interrogative pronoun "where" can be analysed rhematically as equivalent to "what place", where "what" is a completely indefinite qualifier, representable by the node-label **I**, complementary to the node-label 0. Using this representation, the above question takes the form:

...6.16

As in the case of a zero arc-label, the presence of a node-label **I** can be seen as an invitation to fill in the totally vacuous node, and so contribute to the context. In this case, as in the other, the possible answers to the question are all included in the rhema graph for the question.

6.6.4. Questions involving Focus: It would seem to follow from the argument in §6.6.2 that to delete one of the arc labels from a normal rhema structure would give us a form representing some kind of question. But, if the node labels connected by the arc being deleted are not a yes-no pair, or a list of alternatives, what sort of a question would it give us? In most cases, it appears, the result of such a deletion is nonsense, in the sense of a question whose proposed answers are not both acceptable in any normal context. But there is one type of question, of rare occurrence but perhaps useful occasionally, in which focus and that alone is asked about. It would seem possible to say "$//_{12}$ *Do you /mean Van/**ness**a's /**gone** ∧ or Va//$_1$nessa's /**gone**.*" though the contexts in which it would be appropriate must be rare indeed; either focusing of "Vanessa's gone" would be acceptable as an answer, and the rhema structure involved would be:

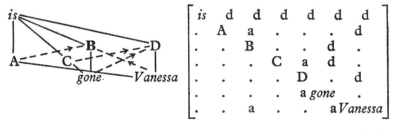

is	d	d	d	d	d	d
.	A	a	.	.	.	d
.	.	B	.	.	d	.
.	.	.	C	a	d	.
.	.	.	.	D	.	d
.	.	.	.	a	*gone*	.
.	.	a	.	.	a	*Vanessa*

...6.17

Such cases are, however, only of marginal interest.

6.7. The Inference Relation

It now remains only to show that the interpretations we have proposed for the node and arc labels are consistent with the inference relation being correctly modelled by conformal inclusion between the matrix representations of the rhemata. For the context lattice theorem (4.6) requires that whenever $P \supset Q$ (rhema Q is rhematically inferrable from rhema P) the matrices $[P]$ and $[Q]$ representing these rhemata shall satisfy $[P] \geqq [Q]$.

However, it should be noted that the converse has *not* been proved. It may well be that in some cases, where $[P] \geqq [Q]$, we do not have to accept an inference $P \supset Q$. For such exceptions would still be compatible with the context repertory being a lattice under the inference relation $\supset$, provided that they were such as to allow us to apply the lemma (4.5) to them. It is indeed evident that in some cases inclusions do not correspond to inferences. Thus, whereas "*//$_1$ ∧ I'll |**do** it.*" is certainly an expression of a sub-rhema included in that conveyed by "*/$_1$ ∧ I |didnt |say I'd |**do** it.*", the former is not inferrable from the latter.

It follows then that we shall have to supplement the simple inclusion model by a list of exceptions, and then prove for each item in the list that it does not disrupt the required lattice property. These rules are discussed in full in Chapter XIV. But I may anticipate by citing an approximate formulation, in relatively few words:

> A rhema Q is rhematically inferrable from P if and only if:
> (a) $[Q]$ is conformally included in $[P]$; *and*
> (b) no successor of a *negative* node N in P is also in Q, unless
> (b1) it succeeds a *definite* successor of N, *or*
> (b2) N and *all* its successors are also in Q; *and*
> (c) no successor of a *hypothetical* node H in P is also in Q, unless
> H itself is in Q
>
> . . . 6.18

The proof that the rules I, of §14.6.2, on which (6.18) is based, preserve the lattice property of the context repertory (which is defined as including all and only the legitimate inferences from the rehearsal) is given in §14.6.

The inclusion in a question of its possible answers is not part of the theory. It is, rather, a useful rule by which to construct rhema graphs to represent questions, subject to the requirement that such graphs shall *not* be conformally included in the relevant context rehearsal. There is an analogous relationship in the case of commands, namely that one may infer from a command, if it is not accompanied by a refusal (which, in real life, may well be tacit), its own fulfilment. This must not be confused with the *pertinential* inference of its previous *non* fulfilment.

6.8. Summary of the Linguistic Interpretation

We have thus arrived at the following position. The repertory of any context is represented by a covertical lattice algebra of biform oriented digraphs, each of which is a one-origined poset under arcs labelled d and a chain under arcs labelled a. The upper bound of the lattice, for any given context, represents the rehearsal of the context; this will usually not be expressible in a single sentence but only by a string of sentences (typically a very long string if all the points which may be relevant are to be included). The inclusion relation in this context lattice is interpreted as rhematical inference. It corresponds to conformal inclusion of the triangular matrices which furnish one possible representation of each of the graphs, subject to certain conditions, summarized in (6.18), the conformity of which with theorem (4.6) has yet to be proved; this conformal inclusion is defined in terms of the base domain of the labelled graphs.

This base domain is itself a lattice; this lattice I have denoted by **B**. The elements of **B** are the node and arc labels available for labelling the graphs which represent rhemata; they are subject in **B** to an inclusion relation which can be interpreted as inclusion of designation-classes, with the proviso that the node subalgebra in **B** is inverted, that is to say it is the 'dual' of the lattice of designation-classes, its upper bound being the *emptyd* e-signation-class **I** and its lower bound the *universal* designation-class 0. **B** contains as sublattices a node subalgebra and an arc subalgebra; the former is a complex open set whose structure we have yet to examine, but the latter contains, beside 0, only two arc labels which we shall normally call upon, though there is at least one other denoting the designation of a speech act which can enter into language structures though in those commonly thought of as constituting 'natural' languages it appears only in commands.

The lattice **B** must not be confused with the lattice representing a context repertory. The elements of the latter can be represented by graphs labelled in **B**, the characteristics of which are described above, or by triangular matrices with components in **B**. And, of course, neither of these lattices must be confused with the graphs representing rhemata, even if these may accidentally resemble lattices diagrammatically.

Within the graph structures representing rhemata, the node labels represent lexigens. These labels evidently have a complex structure of their own, reflecting the complexity of a thesaurus required to express the lexicon of even an artificially simplified language; the details of this structure will engage us in Chapters VIII to XI. The arc labels we have identified as representing two basic linguistic 'acts'. The non-transitive arc label d, every instance of which is understood to subsume an instance of the transitive arc label a, is interpreted as an 'act of designation', the node to which it leads being the correponding designant. The designatum, that which is designated, is either another designant, reached by another act of designation, or, if it is an 'ultimate' designatum, it is an object or conceptual isolate in the extra-linguistic environment and consequently does not appear in the rhema graph at all. The accessory arc label a is interpreted as an 'act of adduction', whereby is adduced, upon whatever items are already specified, another item intended to throw light on these or to advance the conversation in some direction or other. These 'acts of adduction' reveal the speaker's attitude to the context, and correspond to the linguistic category of 'focus', the importance of which is accordingly greatly enhanced if the point of view of this work is accepted.

Finally, allowance has to be made for rhemata of a kind which are linguistically possible, but which from their nature are either not members of any context repertory, as are questions, or are members only of such contexts as are specially marked in the rehearsal, as in the case of commands. The former are distinguished by the occurrence of zero arc labels above the matrix diagonal, or by the otherwise unused node label I. The latter have no such peculiarity, though a command we shall find in due course contains an arc with the label s not otherwise used. There are also certain types of rhema which belong to no context but such as they generate themselves; here fall, among possibly others, most self-referent utterances, whose place in 'natural' language is at best marginal.

This, then, is the material now at our disposal. The next chapter will be devoted to illustrating it by numerous examples.

CHAPTER VII

Some Examples of Rhema Structures

The purpose of the following examples is to illustrate the use of the graphical representation of rhema structures, described in the preceding chapters, as a notation, applying it to as wide a range of rhemata as possible. At the same time, I hope that the reading of this chapter may help to habituate the reader to the new medium. In principle, of course, the notation could be transduced into phonic material and serve as a language itself, given only an adequate lexicon; one might even learn to think in it. But such thinking could never be very fluent. The wide and pervading discrepancy of all known syntaxes from one-one correspondence with the structures which my system calls for indicates, either that my theory is wide of the mark, or that the neurological facilities of our brains are imperfectly adapted to its implementation. If so, it is no more evidence against the theory than the deficiencies of the eye are evidence against the theory of optics; indeed, if we can suggest what actual syntaxes may be seen as modifications of, we may thereby help the psycholinguists to formulate productive questions about the language faculty.

7.1. The Nature of the Examples

As an introduction, it may help to recall what it is I propose to use the notation for, and where it fits into the overall methodology of linguistics.

7.9.1. Their Content: A rhema structure, formulated in this (or any other adequate) notation, refers to that phase of the speech cycle before the speaker begins to utter, or after the listener has understood an utterance. It represents thought ready to be expressed, not its expression. The examples below must therefore not be looked at as proposed new analyses of English sentences. Each one is accompanied by a suggested expression of it in English (any other language would serve as well) as an aid to comprehension; these expressions are in this chapter all given with the intonation marked (using Halliday's notation, explained in Appendix I). The question is not whether the graph correctly gives the content of the English, but whether the English translation or paraphrase correctly conveys the given rhema: and I can't promise to have avoided all errors here.

In principle, if no conditions are placed on the length of the utterance required, every rhema structure can be expressed in English; but in some cases considerable circumlocution may be called for, and I admit to having selected the examples among other things to avoid this. It would therefore be rash to claim that the selection has not been influenced, in Whorfian fashion, by the peculiarities of my native tongue. But even if this is so, it should not detract from the value of the examples; for just as one may learn a language B (up to a point) from a textbook written in another language A by someone only superficially acquainted with the culture of B, so one's learning of rhematical notation need not be thwarted by the biasses of the medium of instruction.

In the examples, the question of context should not cause particular trouble. Though we must have a sufficient context to comprehend a given utterance, that is, to 'translate' it into a rhema, the process I am asking you to carry out here is the reverse of this. Each rhema contributes something towards a context, and can do so just because its content (in contrast with natural language utterances) is not context-dependent; though of course the context will determine what rhemata are relevant to the occasion, and also affect what surface forms may be used for their expression. When I give an English rendering of a given rhema, I aim to suggest the semantic nuances conveyed by the rhema as given, not those derived from its possible context: though from what I have repeatedly said about context in general, this is necessarily an error-prone operation. One has sometimes to fall back on the idea that the rhema given is the beginning of a context rehearsal itself—which is always of course admissible—if one is to avoid the clumsy device of manufacturing a context for it.

7.1.2. Their Validity: An important question which any such collection of illustrations presents is, How do we know they are right? How can we test whether or not the given rhema is 'correctly' rendered by the English sentence which I offer? The answer to this question lies in the 'rules of sincerity' set out in §2.7.2. They are called so, it will be recalled, because 'sincerity' is the quality expected of the speaker when expressing his thoughts: and this is what I am trying to do in my English paraphrases of the examples given.

One might further add that, according to the theory, any such translation is correct if and only if it carries, for a fully competent user of the language in question (English), precisely the same set of inferences which could be drawn from the rhema as given by the rules of inference of the system. These rules, though summarized in (6.18), are given in more detail and after full explanation in Chapter XIV.

We are thus still in the language-learning stage, during which the only effective criterion is what the teacher says.

7.1.3. The Graphical Conventions: In the diagrammatic representation of rhema graphs, which I use in this and all later chapters, the following conventions are adopted.

Node Labels are represented by English words or word-groups. This is more or less inevitable, but it can be confusing if not understood correctly. For node labels are not *words* of any language: they are lexigens, that is elements of the lexical lattice, which is supposed to be isomorphic with an idealized thesaurus of the language in question, but can never be strictly isomorphic with any actual set of words, if only because the 'meaning' of a word depends, even more sensitively than that of a sentence, on the context in which it occurs. Thus, the 'words' appearing in the diagrams must be understood to suggest a designation-class only; they do not stand for the words used in the way that the letter-strings appearing in a connected text do.

Usually a node label will include some indication, equally informal, of its 'case' (typically by a preposition), and sometimes also of 'quantification' (including negation) and 'Identification'; these terms are more fully discussed in Chapters VIII–XI. Lexically-specific items are found for the most part only in ultimate nodes, which have no successors under designatory arcs. Fully formalized node labels are introduced in Chapter XII.

Designatory arcs are represented by unbroken lines, which are understood to be directed downards (arrow-heads are not used here). These arcs represent the 'deep structure' equivalent of immediate constituence. As such, they are understood to be non-transitive. Under these arcs every rhema is nevertheless potentially a poset, with a unique upper bound and of course no circuits. Many of them, but far from all, are trees.

Accessory arcs are shown as dotted lines with arrow-heads, which are arranged to go from left to right whenever possible. These are transitive, and only the minimum set of them required to establish the covertical ordering of the nodes is shown as a rule. But in some cases the structure is sufficiently non-obvious for others, inferrable from the rest by transitivity, to be usefully inserted. Remember that every designatory arc subsumes an accessory arc which is not shown.

Wherever possible, the designatory arc leading from a superior node to its *first* successor is drawn vertically. This makes the structure a little easier to take in at a glance. It also has the useful effect that complicated structures are more likely to come out elongated horizontally rather than vertically, which assists their layout on the page.

7.2. Determinative Expansion

There are two main types of process by which a rhema structure may be built up from smaller and simpler components. In one, a particular node in one of the parent rhemata is replaced by the whole of the other parent, the second being a determinative, that is, a rhema which does not involve an act of predication. In the other, both parents involve acts of predication, and the replacement of a node of the first by the whole of the second involves the creation of a subordinate predication; this is the process underlying what Halliday has called 'rankshift'. In this section I shall deal with the first process only, which I call 'determinative expansion'.

7.2.1. The Method: The basic procedure involved here is to replace a node N by a pair of nodes joined by a designatory arc. Thus, while the expression "*for my brother*" can if desired be represented by a single node label, it can equally and equivalently be expanded into two, the first representing *"for him"* and the second representing the ultimate designant, designated by *"him"*, namely *"my brother"*. In setting out rhemata such an expansion is a useless complication, except in the case where the ultimate designant is itself designated twice over, for then the two penultimate designants may very well differ, for example in their cases.

To use such an expansion one must already be within a context where the two nodes in the expanded form are separately warranted. That is, before one expands *"for my brother"* in this way, one must amplify the context rehearsal in such a way as to justify it, for example by a rhema which refers to *"my brother"* a second time. For if not, the expansion involves an alteration in the vertex set of the rehearsal, which we have seen is not permissible *unless* the context is modified. If one reference to *"my brother"* introduces one node, a *second* reference expands this node into *three*, two penultimates and an ultimate designant; but every subsequent reference only adds one more node, an extra penultimate. The result is that the ultimate designant is reached by several designatory arcs.

Essentially similar is the operation by which we replace a single node label, say *"to a bachelor"*, by an expansion of it into three (or more) nodes. In this case, the contextual justification is usually the adduction of a rhema expressing lexical information; this could be the statement that a "bachelor" is an "unmarried man". With the help of this (which must first be incorporated into the context rehearsal) we can expand *"//$_4$ ∧ she /**won'**t /marry a //**bach**elor."* as follows:

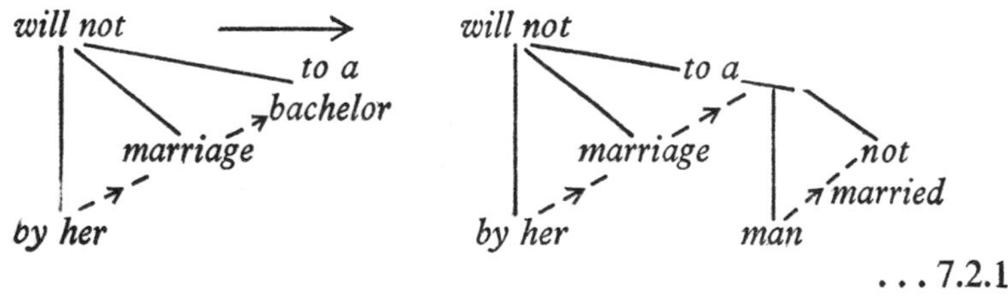

...7.2.1

7.2.2. A More Realistic Example: Let us illustrate this procedure in a more realistic context. Let us begin with the rhema:

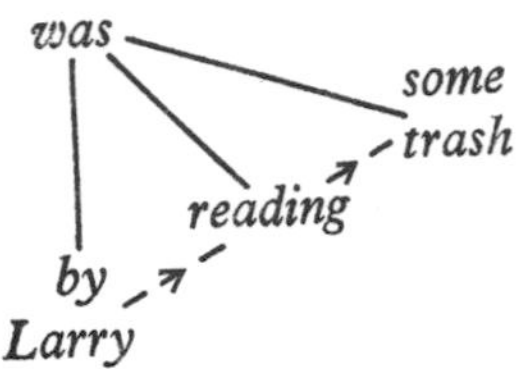

. . . 7.2.2

which one may express by "$//_1$ *Larry was* |*reading some* |***trash***.". Hearing this, you may be prompted to ask what precisely I mean by "trash". So I will then expand the context by additional material, the role of which will be the same as that ascribed above to dictionary information, though in this case it is unlikely to be found in a dictionary, being (as most such information really is) specific to the occasion. The effect of my expansion may be to produce the following rhema:

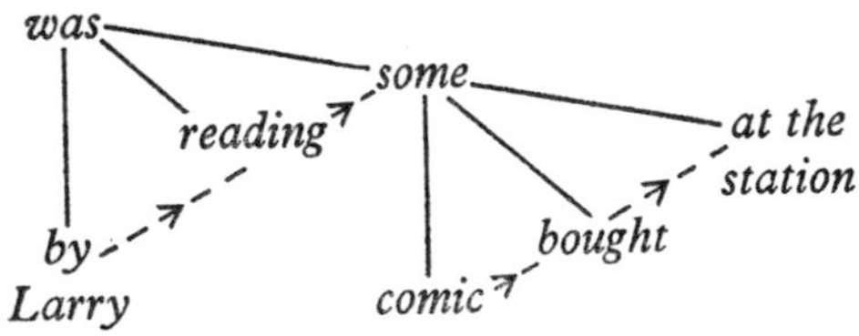

. . . 7.2.3

Here the queried lexigen, forming the node label "*some trash*" in (7.2.2) has been expanded into a four-node rhema, which, as an independent sentence, could represent "$//_1$ ∧ *A* |*comic was* |*bought at the* |***station***." but which the indefinite identifier "some" marks here as being the determinative form "$//_1$ ∨ *A* |*comic* [which was] |*bought at the* |***station***".

7.2.3. Cross-Linking: However, it would be more natural to give the extra information in the form "$//_{1+}$ *Oh* $//_{1-}$ *it was some* |*comic he'd* |*bought at the* |***station***."; this includes the pronoun "he" and so involves a second reference to "Larry", bringing in another type of expansion. The two together produce a fairly complicated structure:

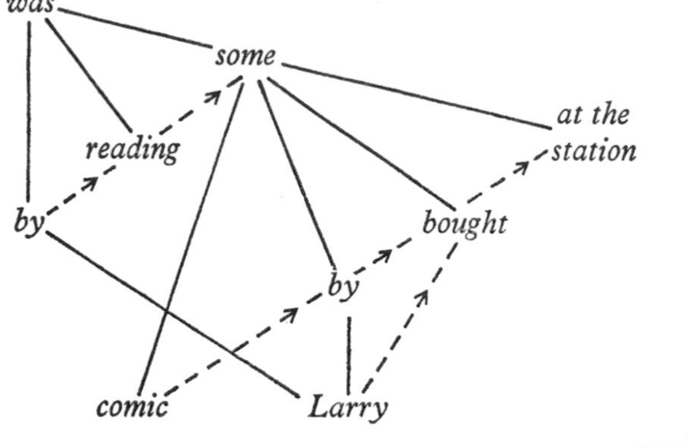

. . . 7.2.4

which means "$//_1$ *Larry was |reading a |***comic** *he'd* $//_1$ *bought at the |***station**." .

It is now clear that expansion of determinatives either produces or requires a compound rhema structure; that is, one in which there are intermediate nodes between the initial node and the ultimate ones. Thus, (7.2.2) is a simple rhema; but (7.2.3) and (7.2.4) are compound rhemata. It is also evident that there is a close correspondence between this type of hierarchical structure in the rhemata, and the syntactic structure of the expressions which convey them in surface texts. Up to now we have looked at determinative expansions only; these do not involve rankshift, but they do generate, as in this example, sentences involving different ranks, a main clause and a relative clause within one of the noun groups. Let us now pass on to the other main type of expansion.

7.3. Framing of Predications

Here it is convenient to start from the rhema which will become subordinate, and expand it 'upwards'; that is, to expand its initial node into a member of a 'framing clause'. Such a framing clause is usually hardly worth uttering if there is no predication for it to frame.

7.3.1. Initial Example: Consider then the rhema

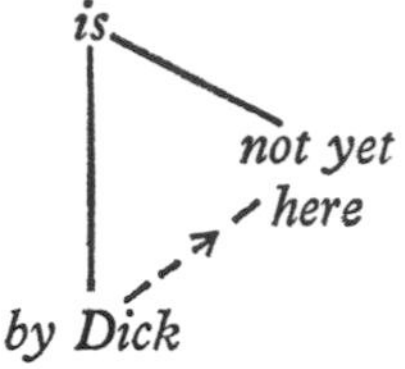

. . . 7.3.1

which can be expressed in English* by "//$_5$ *Dick* /*hasn't ar*/***rived.***" Note that here "*Dick*" is the theme, and the statement is intended to draw attention to his non-arrival, which is therefore the rheme. This may well be a cause of annoyance, and this might be the occasion for an utterance conveying

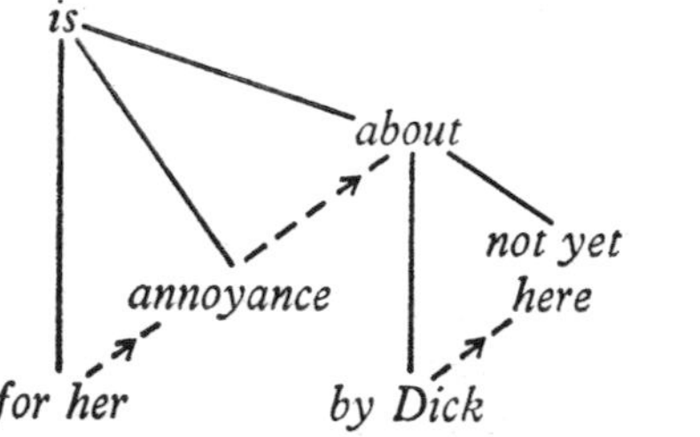

. . . 7.3.2

such as "//$_4$ ∧ *She's an*/***noyed*** *that* //$_1$ *Dick* /*hasn't ar*/***rived.***"; the focus relations within the subordinate clause are unchanged. The only modification required to (7.3.1) to adapt it to its framing clause is a change of 'case', informally notified by the label "*about*" in (7.3.2). The focussing in (7.3.2) is of course, not the only one possible. Still keeping (7.3.1) intact, one could say "//$_{13}$ ∧ *She's an*/***noyed*** *that* /*Dick* /*hasn't ar*/***rived.***", which would express

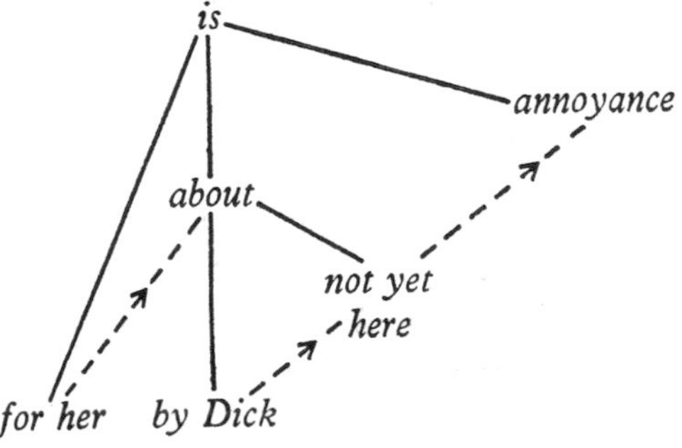

. . . 7.3.3

* An actual utterance depends not only on the rhema but also on the context. Thus, the use of tone 5, rather than tone 1, is likely in the kind of context in which the following elaborations might be motivated.

(Note that in the tone 13 the second tonic normally marks the first item after the theme, which is here the whole subordinate clause, represented by its rheme "arrived".)

We can also start from a rhema differing from (7.3.1) in focus, such as would be conveyed by "$//_{1+}$ ***Dick*** */hasn't ar/rived.*"; in this context anxiety would be more appropriate than annoyance, and with the framing clause we would have

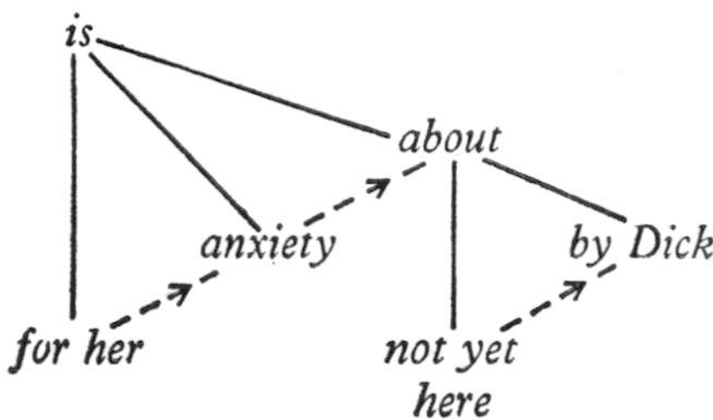

. . . 7.3.4

to be Englished as "$//_4$ ∧ *She's /**worried** that* $//_1$ ***Dick*** */hasn't ar/rived.*" And, of course, there is a corresponding form with the subordinate clause as the theme relative to "anxiety".

7.3.2. Omission of Intermediate Predications: We may properly ask at this point, in view of the strictures which I made earlier on the inclusion, in conventional sentence structures, of nodes labelled with such marks as 'predicate', whether any of the nodes in (7.3.2) etc. might be eliminated without loss. The initial node must necessarily remain, since otherwise the graphs would not be connected under the designatory arcs. Each of the ultimate nodes could be eliminated, provided the information carried by their labels could be accommodated in the node above, but in this example there are no cases where this can be done. The interesting case is the intermediate node, labelled 'about' in each of (7.3.2)to(7.3.4). This node serves as a separate initial for the subordinate clause; while this clause is unmistakable in the surface forms I have presented, it might not always be a true part of the rhema structure. However, since its deletion would call for some change in the expression of the rhema, at least in English, it is not strictly redundant.

If, for example, we delete the "about" node in (7.3.3), we get

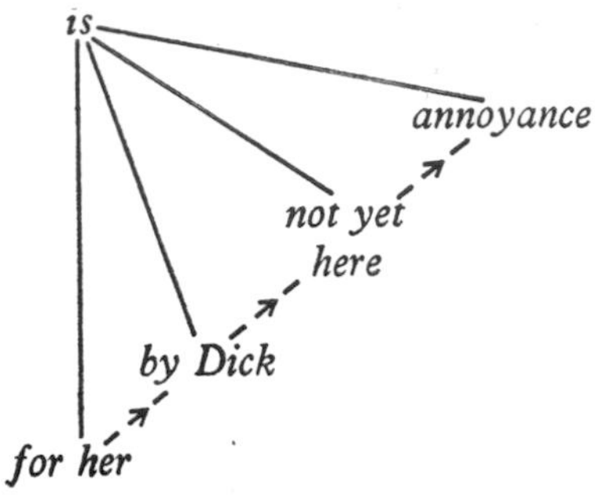

. . . 7.3.5

This rhema could be conveyed by "//$_{-1}$ *Dick's /not ar/riving an/* **noys** *her*." The difference in attitude is not great, but tends to make Dick the source of the annoyance more personally than before; the absence of an intermediate node also makes possible the interchange of "by Dick" and "for her" which would perhaps be more likely to fit the context, though this shift of focus is not one which English can easily express.

7.3.3. The Potential of a Simple Rhema: In this connection, it should be shown how little is lost in terms of real expressive power by the absence of a 'predicate' node. For this purpose, I take a relatively complicated case, which can still be given sufficiently as a simple rhema:

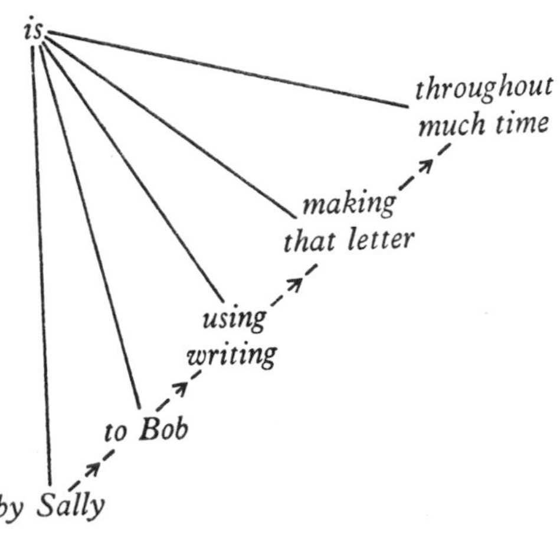

. . . 7.3.6

This we can render in English as "//$_{13}$ *Sally's /taking a /long /**time** /writing that /letter to /**Bob**.*". In the customary type of representation, this sentence would appear in a diagram such as

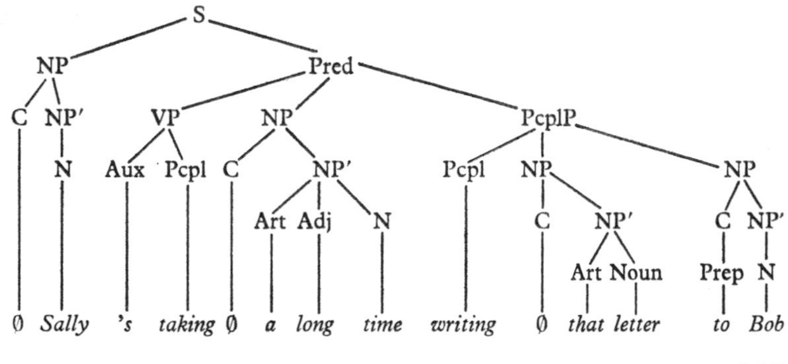

. . . 7.3.7

The purpose of the structure (7.3.7) is of course not the same as that of (7.3.6). Whereas that was a specification of the semantic content of an utterance, (7.3.7) aims also to represent its surface structure, or at least to furnish the specifications for such structure. It is therefore to be expected that it is considerably more complicated. The additional material is precisely that which is liable to alteration on translation into another language. As an obvious example, the group labelled 'PcplP' would in French go most naturally into a prepositional construction: '*en ecrivant à Robert cette lettre*'. It is also the case, of course, that there are alternative ways of expressing (7.3.6) in English. Here are some near-paraphrases:

(a) //$_{13}$ *Sally's /given /Bob a /lot of her /**time** /writing him that /**letter**.*
(b) //$_{13}$ *Writing /Bob's /letter's being a /slow /**job** for /**Sally**.*
(c) //$_{4}$ *Sally's /writing that /letter to /Bob /**very** /slowly.*

None of these reproduces (7.3.6) identically: all involve a few changes of case, and since focus relations cannot be fully marked in one tone-group over five constituents, all expressions of (7.3.6) are necessarily context-dependent in this respect, especially (c) with only one tonic. Though all three would be possible utterances in the same context, they would not be equally natural. But the point to be made is that each of them has a structure grossly different from (7.3.7) while these differences reflect at most minor differences in the semantic content.

A particular point to be made here is that, in generating expressions for (7.3.6) in English, a variety of alternatives present themselves between which the choice is determined largely by considerations of style, or even personal whim. These include, among others, the selection of which of the nodes to realize as the verb, if any. In (c) the node with the "writing" lexigen is chosen; but in the other renderings the surface 'main verb' does not appear in the rhema as a node at all. In (b) we have an equative form, and in (a) the verb is based on the case marker attached to "Bob". All this serves to show that we are working here at a much 'deeper' level than is usual; but it also raises the question of what the 'usual' level really is. Perhaps it is the level at which all the arbitrary choices (and no others?) have been made: but this is already half-way from thought to speech. Moreover, during the utterance of (7.3.7) one still has the chance to reconsider what is to come, up to the time that the first section has been completed; thus, one could still substitute say "doing" for "writing" while already beginning to utter the NP "a long time". This implies that it is quite artificial to relegate all the 'arbitrary choices' to an initial stage of the generative process.

7.2.4. Predication without a Predicate: We thus see that the category of 'predicate' has no place at the rhematical level. It is worth pointing out that it is not present even in surface structure in all types of sentence. Here for example is a predicative rhema which suggests itself for this form of expression:

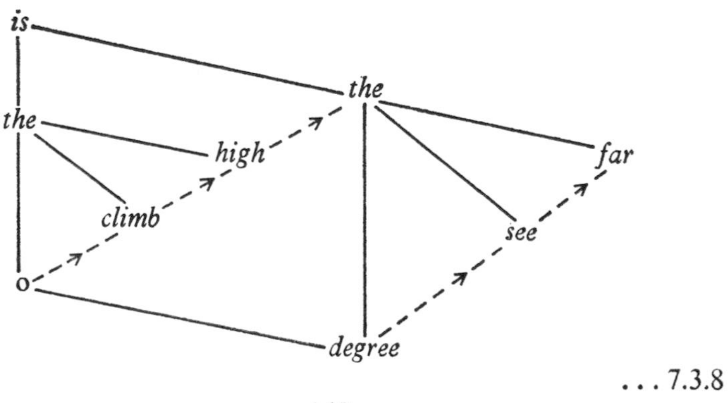

. . . 7.3.8

whose most natural translation is “$//_4$ ∧ *The /higher you /**climb*** $//_1$ ∧ *the /further you /**see**.*”. Note that the idea of ‘degree’, which gets no explicit mention in English, appears in the rhema structure as the common designation of the two themes, whose identity is expressed by the parallel structure. The lexigen specifies what is being compared; it surfaces only in the comparative form of the adjectives. The logical structure can be paraphrased as “The climb-high degree is [a monotonic function of] the see-far degree.”. Comparable constructions exist, of course, in many languages.

7.4. Epistemic Modifiers

In the previous section I introduced the topic of framing-clauses for predications. This has long been a favourite of grammarians of the generative school, who like to incorporate into their deep structures as many implicatures as possible. However, we have in the present system a definite criterion for judging whether a proposed framing clause is or is not legitimately a part of the rhema expressed by a given utterance. For the rules of sincerity (see §2.7.2) require that every feature of the rhema structure shall correspond to some feature (which may be null provided it is contrastively so) of its expression (rule S2). The question is then whether these may be a ‘null’ feature of an utterance which might justify a suggested framing clause.

Now a ‘null’ feature can only be claimed to exist if it is in contrast with an alternative which is not null. Thus, if it is claimed that there is such a feature in, say, “*I have it*”, which might justify a rhema structure based on “*I assert that I have it*”, there must be non-null alternatives available, presumably with “*I deny*” or “*I suspect*” or the like as prefixes. These are, perhaps, possible utterances: but what they contrast with is obviously “$//_4$ ∧ *I as/**sert** that* $//_1$ ∧ *I /**have** it.*”, and not just “$//_1$ ∧ *I /**have** it.*”, whose alternatives are in natural style “$//_1$ ∧ *I /havent /**got** it.*” or “$//_4$ ∧ *I /**may** /have it.*”

7.4.1. Expressions of Belief:

A more subtle application of the same criterion concerns what is acceptable in conversation. If a null framing clause is really present, it must be available for comment by a listener. Consider, for example, the rhema:

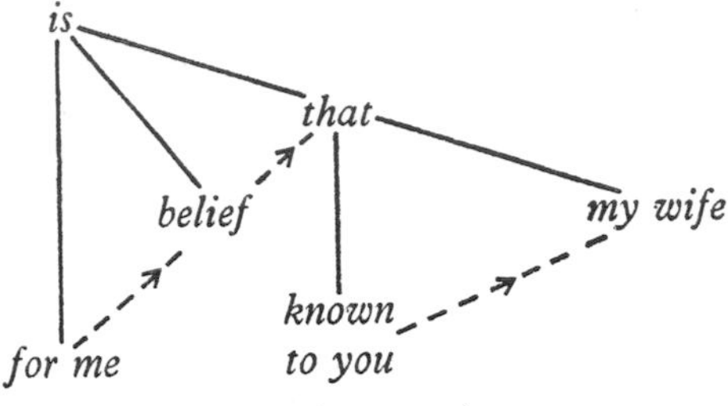

. . . 7.4.1

To express this unambiguously in English calls for a two-group tonality thus "*//₄ ∧ I be/**lieve** you //₁ know my /**wife**.*". To this utterance, it might well be acceptable to reply "*//₅ ∧ I'm a/fraid you're /**wrong**.*"; which, however, would be definitely impertinent if the utterance were "*//₁ ∧ I be/lieve you /know my /**wife**.*". The latter in fact is not understood as containing a statement of belief at all, despite its overt framing-clause, but as a factual statement weakened by an epistemic qualifier. That is, it expresses the rhema

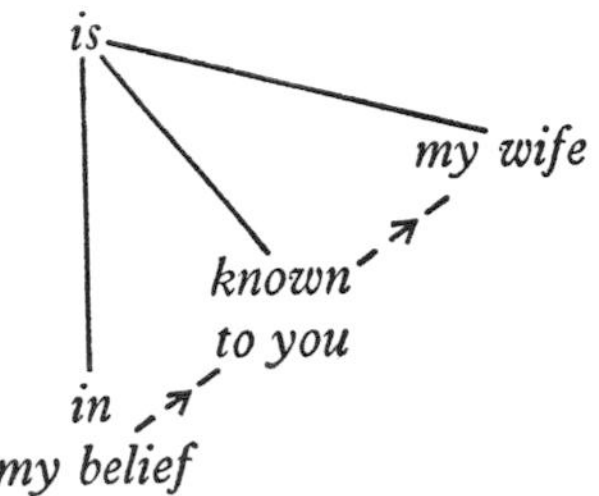

. . . 7.4.2

in which the framing clause is replaced by a single constituent which, in typical contexts, is likely to stand as the theme of the utterance.

On the other hand, a framing-clause *may* be legitimately present which is not manifested in the surface utterance. For instance, to the utterance "*//₁ Jim'll ar/rive /half /**drunk**.*" it would be quite in order to answer "*//₄ Oh /**come** //₄ ∧ he /doesnt /**always**.*"; such a reply understands the first speaker to have meant "*I expect Jim'll arrive half drunk*" and addresses itself accordingly to the framing-clause. In this instance, the odd case is the one where the framing expectation is ignored, allowing only such brusquer answers as "$//_1$ ***No*** $//_1$ ∧ *he* /***wont***." or perhaps "$//_1$ *How do you* /***know***.". The important point is to be on the lookout for possible framing-clauses which are not overtly indicated, and for their absence from utterances which purport on the surface to have them. In the absence of a context we are of course reduced to guessing—which is presumably why there has been so much argument in the literature on this topic among those who do not always ask what the context is supposed to be; but when the context is given the matter usually admits of a quick decision.

7.4.2. Reported Speech: A frequent occasion for epistemic modification, which is usually tacit, is in contexts where someone reports what another has said. What sort of reply would be expected to such an opening as "$//_1$ ∧ *I* /*hear you're a* /***trumpeter***." depends very obviously on the context. If the listener had not recently been practising his instrument, he would no doubt reply "$//_1$ ***Yes*** $//_4$ ∧ *as a* /*matter of* /***fact*** $//_{1+}$ ∧ *I* /***am***.", whereas if he *had*, it would be more polite to say "$//_4$ ∨ *I* /*hope I've* /*not been dis*/***turbing*** *you*.". In the first case the surface framing-clause is interpreted analogously to the one in (7.4.2); but in the second case, there is no alternative to (7.4.3):

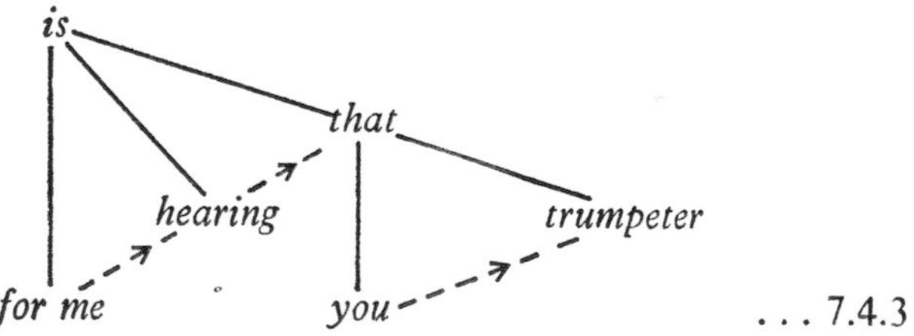

. . . 7.4.3

As this example suggests, however, reported speech is a frequent occasion for ambiguities. Such ambiguity is not necessarily confined to surface expression in a given language. A typical case is illustrated by the utterance "$//_{13}$ ∨ *He* /***said*** *it was* /*done a* ***week*** *a*/*go*.". In some contexts this would be quite clear, and would express a rhema with two levels of predication, as exlained below; but the tone indicated usually goes with a single predication, and would in other contexts be taken as expressing rather

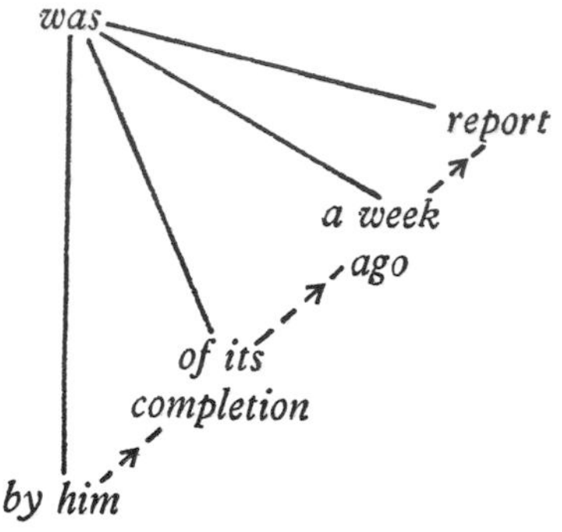

. . . 7.4.4

This is an example of the first type of ambiguous rhema mentioned in §4.9, in which one may hesitate between two possible expressions of it. In the present case, English has a form, given above, which reproduces just this ambiguity, so there is no need to 'hesitate'. The point is, that the speaker himself may not know exactly what to say. If he does know, he will be expected to use one or other of the unambiguous expressions below. If the *report* was made a week ago, we shall have the rhema (7.4.5), while if 'it was done' a week ago, and he now reports so, we shall have (7.4.6):

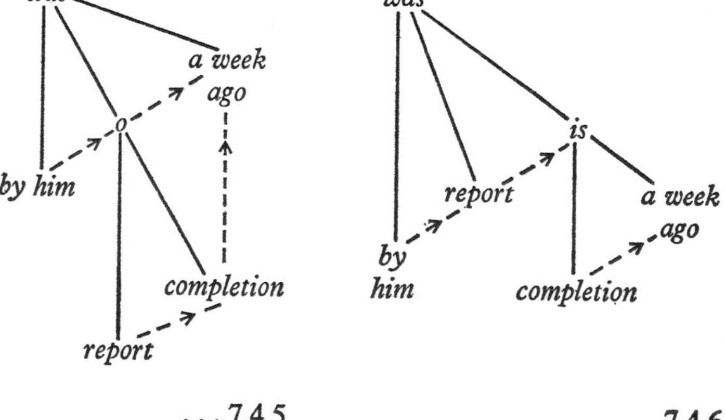

. . . 7.4.5 . . . 7.4.6

The best rendering of (7.4.5) is "//$_4$ ∧ *He* /***said*** *it was* /*done* //$_1$ ∨ *a* /***week*** *a*/*go*.", while (7.4.6) can be expressed by varying the tonality to "//$_4$ C *He* /***said*** //$_1$ C *it was* /*done a* /***week*** *a*/*go*.".

There is no question that the use of the 'ambiguous' tone 13 with this sentence is quite natural and acceptable (in my variety of English). It is not to the point to call this a 'careless' utterance, as if the speaker were unsuccessfully trying to convey either (7.4.5) or (7.4.6). The ambiguous (7.4.4) is a perfectly possible rhema, and as it happens there is a way of expressing it in English. It shows that people can not only express ideas ambiguously, which we all know, but also that they can entertain ambiguous *ideas*, which can be faithfully represented in my notation, and this is more interesting. Confusion occurs in the commoner case, where there is available only an unambiguous but possibly incorrect expression for an ambiguous thought.

7.5. Modal Constructions

The epistemic modifiers and framing-clauses discussed in the last section are only one example of a wider type of modifiers, which are usually classified as 'modalities'. These are most often expressed by special verbs, forming a class known as 'modal verbs'. In English, this class is not too well-defined; but there is a class of verbs with special syntactic constraints, which I shall discuss now.

7.5.1. Modalities with Free Subordination: Modal verbs come, in English, in two main subclasses; in one, the subject of the framing clause need not be that of the subordinate clause, and such modal verbs may be characterized as involving 'free' subordination. Take, for example, the utterance "$//_1 \wedge$ *She /wants me to /***go.**"; this again is an ambiguous expression, in that it may express either (7.5.1) or (7.5.2):

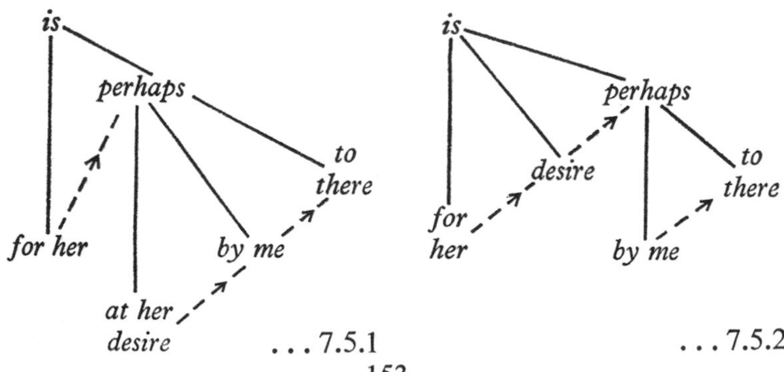

... 7.5.1 ... 7.5.2

These differ in part, as do (7.4.5) and (7.4.6), in which of the two clauses the notion of 'desire' is expressed; but here there is a framing-clause in both, which clearly cannot be ignored because it is the only place where "*for her*" can be located. (7.5.1) with 'desire' in the subordinate clause indicates that she is aware that I may go at her wish, a thought more clearly expressed as "*//₄ ∧ She'd /**like** me to /go.*". On the other hand (7.5.2) says that she has a wish for me to go, my possible going being unqualified by the fact that she desires it, which one might make more explicit by "*//₁ ∧ She /wants to /have me /**go***". In the first, "desire" is represented as a modality of action, while in the second it is a modality of experience related to a possible action.

In real life, of course, the contrast is typically very slight; normally both rhemata are meant, and this calls for one from which both can be inferred, such as (7.5.4) below. With this may be contrasted the much weaker rhema (7.5.3) which is inferrable from both, and might

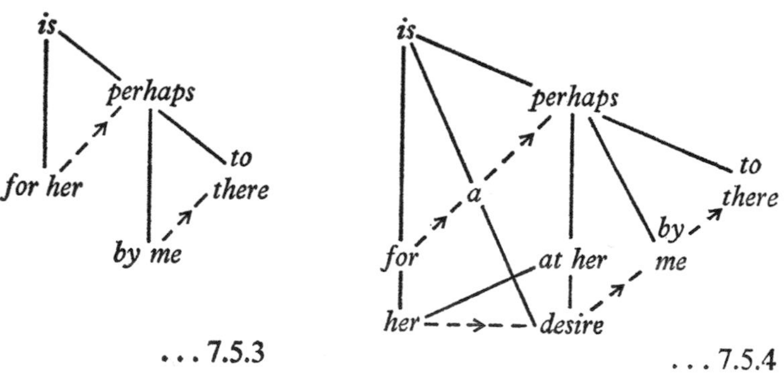

...7.5.3 ...7.5.4

be expressed by the utterance "*//₁₋ ∧ She /thinks I/ might /**go**.*".

7.5.2. Modality as Rheme: In the above examples, I have assumed that the modality, here that of wanting something, will be thematic in relation to all other terms except the subject "*she*"; this is the commonest situation in daily life. However, it is possible for the modality to be the rheme; for example, in a context when one is considering whether to fall in with a request. Such a situation might call for an expression like "*//₄ ∧ She /**wants** me to /go.*".

Once again, starting from the two models (7.5.1) and (7.5.2), we arrive at two possible rhema structures:

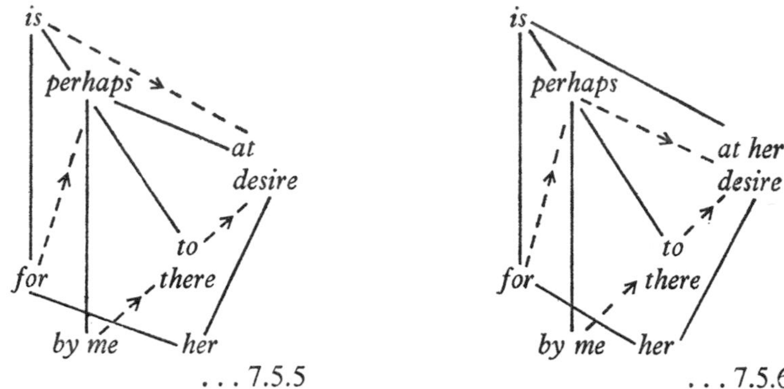

These two, however, are very much more alike than (7.5.1) and (7.5.2); they differ only in the interchange of designatory and accessory arcs from (*is*) and (*perhaps*) to (*desire*). Their inferential 'join', from which both can be inferred, would have both arcs designatory, which indicates that the notion of "*desire*" is designated in both clauses, as in (7.5.4). Note here in passing that if the designatory arc were assumed to be transitive, this 'join' would be identical with (7.5.5); this is clearly wrong, for (7.5.5) might well be rendered more explicitly as "*//$_4$ ∧ She |thinks I might |**go** for //$_{1+}$**her**.*", which would not be taken as implying that she wants me to go, which is certainly implied by (7.5.6).

7.5.3. Modalities with Identical Subjects: There is no *logical* reason for classifying modalities into those which do or do not require the subject to be the same in the subordinate and the framing clauses; but there are nevertheless modal verbs which have this property in English grammar and it is of interest to see what kind of rhemata they generate.

If we take the restriction seriously, as an initial hypothesis, it is natural to construct a rhema in which the modality is unmarked for which of the two clauses it falls under; this can be done in the following form:

is *desire* *to* *for* *by* *there* *him*

. . . 7.5.7

is *right* *to* *for* *by* *there* *him*

. . . 7.5.8

is *possible* *to* *for* *by* *there* *him*

. . . 7.5.9

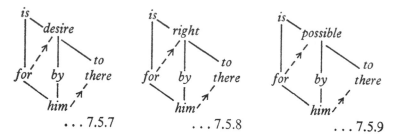

which can be translated respectively as "$//_1$ ∧ *He /wants to /***go**.", "$//_1$ ∧ *He /ought to /***go**.", and "$//_1$ ∧ *He /can /***go**.".

We have already seen that the first of these can operate naturally enough with different subjects, and here English grammar presents no obstances. But the other two can also be constructed with separate subjects; following the same rhema form as we have above, which makes the subordinate clause a predicative expansion of the modality, we have the rhemata:

is *right* *to* *for him* *there* *by me*

. . . 7.5.10

is *possible* *to* *for him* *there* *by me*

. . . 7.5.11

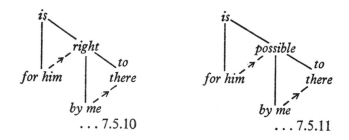

These can be expressed by such utterances as "$//_1$ ∧ *He /feels I /ought to /***go**." and "$//_4$ ∧ *As /far as /***he***'s con/cerned* $//_1$ ∧ *I can /***go**.".

It is perhaps because in these cases the primary subject is less materially concerned with the matter, than in cases of wishing or hoping or the like, that English (and of course many other languages) requires a more elaborate construction to express (7.5.10, 11) than for the previous rhemata. Nevertheless, such moral judgments as (7.5.10) are common enough; but the lack of a modal verb allowing free choice of subject is a frequent feature at least of European languages. Is this a mere accident of history, or is there a psycholinguistic explanation?

7.6. Commands

I mentioned in §6.6.1 that two kinds of remark, commands and questions, are not inferrable from statements, and so can occur only in contexts whose rehearsals already have the corresponding quality (for questions there are no such contexts), but yet play an essential part in normal conversation. In this section I shall look at commahds.

7.6.1. The Marking of Commands: They need a distinctive feature; the first question is, must we assume a special marker, perhaps located in a framing clause, for some or all commands? As before, the way to find out is to ask whether it is acceptable, in reply to a command or a request, to answer the supposed framing-clause rather than the substance of a command. Consider the imaginary exchange A: "//$_2$ *Would you /mind /shutting the /* ***door***." B: "//$_{1-}$ ***No*** //$_{-3}$ ∧ *I /wouldn't /****mind.***". Obviously, B is refusing to treat A's request seriously in answering the overt framing-clause; this is unacceptable except as a joke. One may conclude, then, that in contexts where the request is appropriate, the reply as given is not; the framing-clause is not really present in the rhema conveyed. This is not an invariable rule: it is possible to convey framing-clauses of the same import which invite a reply at their own level; but to do this needs a certain amount of circumlocution, as in "//$_2$ *Could you /****do*** *something /for me* //$_1$ *Please / shut the /****door.***". The need for this kind of construction makes it very clear that ordinary commands do not have framing-clauses.

But, since commands, unlike questions, have otherwise a normal type of rhema structure, the fact that they are different from statements calls for *some* marker. The only alternative is to place this marker as a constituent in the rhema itself, normally as the theme of the whole. However, we have to take account of the fact that there are two ways of refusing a command, typified as "won't" and "can't". One can either merely refuse obedience to the command, or one can claim incompetence (or material impossibility of compliance). This implies that a command carries two distinct inferences, one being that the action called for will take place, the other that it is requested (or commanded, which I take to include requested as an inference). In either type of refusal, the objector is saying in effect "you're assuming a wrong context": in one case, the error is in supposing that anything will happen because in reality (as seen by the objector) it can't, and in the other case, it lies in assuming that a command to him is in order.

We therefore need, not one, but two special node labels. One has only to convey future time, and can properly be placed at the initial node of the command rhema (for analogies, see Chapter XII). The other has to carry the "command" lexigen in a suitably generalized form. An appropriate phrase, reasonably accommodated within one label, would be "*at my request*" or "*by this request*" or the like. These phrases, however, raise the question of self-reference; if the idea of "request" is to appear within the command rhema, that rhema itself must be the request referred to. It seems, therefore, that we have here a characteristic structural peculiarity of commands, analogous to the zero arcs which we have already noted as distinctive of questions. But, of course, there are other occasions beside commands where self-reference occurs, though these are only marginally within 'natural language'.

7.6.2. A Simple Command Rhema: We are now in a position to propose a rhema structure for a command or request. I take as my example a context in which Jill and Herbert are in their sitting-room, and the phone rings. They both recognize this as in itself a call to action; but the situation is as yet extralinguistic. Herbert is the first to speak. He says "//$_{13}$ *Your /turn to /answer the /**phone** /**Jill**.*". Jill, as listener, comprehends this utterance as embodying a call to action on her part; she thinks "bother", and goes to the telephone. What she has comprehended is shewn at top of opposite page.

Had Herbert thought it worth while to add some polite phrase such as "*please*" or "*if you dont mind*", the whole rhema could have been labelled as a request (as opposed to a command), and the label could be placed on the initial node or equivalently on the next node which designates the whole speech act. Conversely, an even brusquer order could have been labelled as a command in the same place.

But when Jill comes back, she doesn't mean to be caught

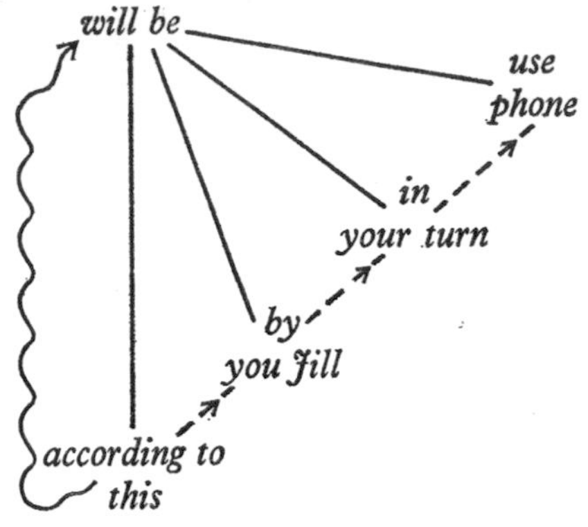

...7.6.1

again; so she says "//₅ *Next* /*time* /***you*** /*go*.". Here the context is different, because there is no immediate call to action providing the theme of the message; on the contrary, the fact that this is a request is now the rheme. The rhema structure is therefore

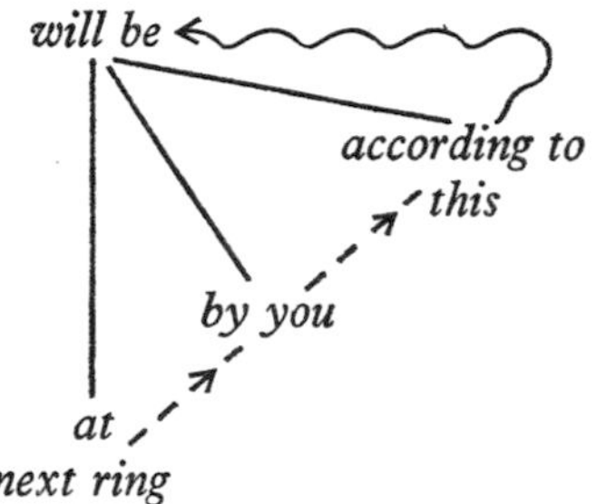

...7.6.2

We note that each of these forms, on deletion of the node carrying the speech-act designation arc, we recover as inference that the action called for will be done; if this is not the intention of the person addressed, it's up to him to correct the context assumptions. Conversely, we can also infer from them, by deleting all the nodes except the first and that with the case-marker "according to", a two-node graph embodying the self-reference circuit "*it will be according to this*", which is perhaps a more basic self-description of a command than even the actual lexigen for "*command*" itself.

7.6.3. Commands in Indirect Speech: A command can not

only be issued, but also reported on. This involves, in surface grammar, some kind of rankshift; many languages have special syntagms for this purpose. At the rhematical level, the main effect corresponding to this rankshift is the elimination of the self-reference. Its place is taken by a lexigen designating the action reported on, such as "*request*"; but the request itself does not appear, but rather the intention behind the request, which calls for no self-referential designation. Thus, continuing the previous example, Herbert might say "$//_4$ ∧ *I /asked* /***Jill*** *to* $//_1$ *go to the* /***phone***."; this would express the rhema

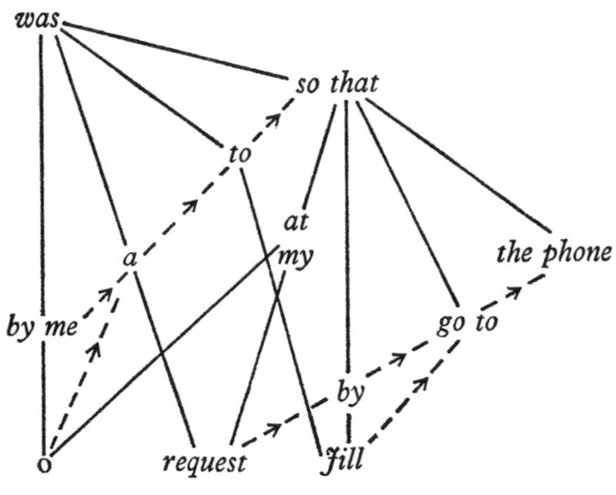

. . . 7.6.3

The structure is rather complex; but then the notion of a reported command is itself a complex one.

We may perhaps profit by looking at some versions of this embodying altered focus relations. Two such are shewn at top of opposite page.

These may be expressed respectively by "$//_1$ ∧ *I /asked* /***Jill*** *to /go to the /phone.*" and "$//_4$ ∧ *I* /***asked*** */Jill to /go /to the /phone.*". The reader is invited to trace out the order of the vertices in each of these rhema graphs.

7.7. Questions

I have already given some relatively simple examples of rhema graphs for questions in §6.6, in order to illustrate the interpreta-

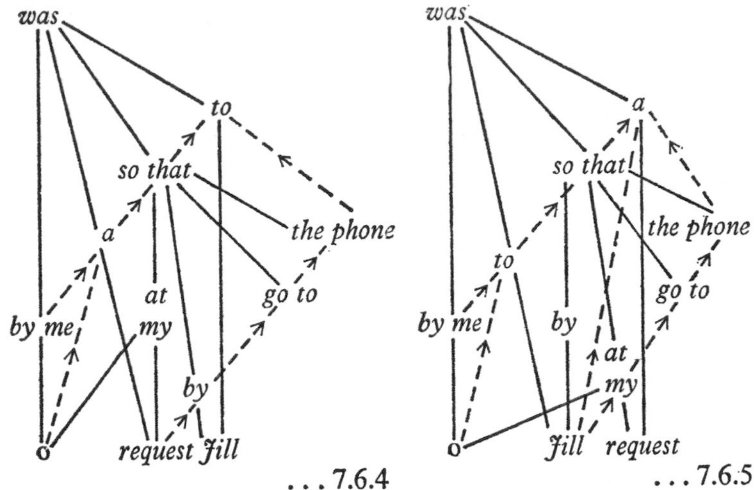

. . . 7.6.4 . . . 7.6.5

tion required for zero arcs. Here I shall add to these a wider selection, designed to illustrate some of the complications which attend the rhematical form of questions.

7.7.1. Framing Commands: The first complication is that for any question there are, in principle, two forms of refusal to answer. One may say simply "I don't know", or one may say "I won't tell you". These obviously correspond to the "can't" and "won't" answers to a command; in fact, they answer in their respective modes an assumed command to answer the question. But whereas "don't know" is always an acceptable response, the availability of "won't tell" is contextually restricted. Very often, indeed usually, this response is unlikely enough for it to be treated as deliberate restructuring of the context. In such cases, the natural form of the question rhema is one with no framing-clause; if such a refusal is anticipated by the speaker, he will be likely to use an explicit request to frame his question, such as "*||$_4$ Can you |**tell** me |whether . . .*" or the like.

In this respect, there is a difference between closed and open questions. Only rather trivial open questions, such as "*||$_1$ What's the |**time**.*" can safely be presumed to lack such a frame; in general, such questions are always more likely to be refused than closed questions. We can, of course, say that the context will decide whether or not there is a framing command; but it is the purpose of a question to elucidate the context in some particular, and therefore the asker of the question necessarily lacks context information which may well include whether the question itself is in order. This is, of course, a well-known conversational problem, and is usually met by making the framing-clause explicit. Nevertheless, there are grounds for supposing that the listener will understand the framing clause to be present, except in trivial cases, in any open question.

The main evidence is that one can indicate focus relations within the framing-clause even when it is unspoken. Thus, the utterances "//$_1$ *What have you* /***got.***" and "//$_5$ *What* /***have*** *you* /*got.*" differ in that the 'command' is the theme in the first and the rheme in the second. They are represented by the structures:

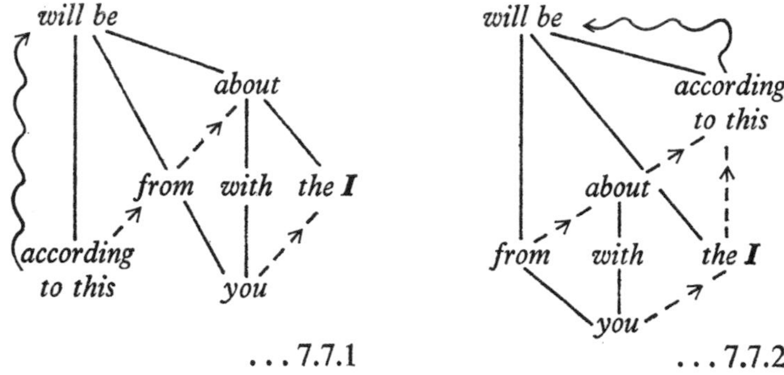

. . . 7.7.1

. . . 7.7.2

An alternative way of expressing (7.7.2) would be to add some such expression as "//$_1$ ***Please.***" to the simple interrogative.

There are several points about these rhemata which call for explanations; they will be alluded to again in Chapter XII. Here it is only necessary to point out the factors affecting focus. The extra-contextual position of questions means that focus relations within them do not, as in other rhemata, stem directly from the context and the attitude of the speaker to it; instead, they are determined by what answers would be acceptable. It would not be acceptable to reply to "//$_1$ *What have you* /***got.***" by saying "//$_1$ ***I've*** /*got an* /*onyx.*"; the required form is "//$_1$ ∧ *I've* /*got an* /***onyx.***". This shows that the node representing "what" must be the rheme in the question as its value is in the answer. For this reason, the node label (**I**) which stands for the interrogative pronoun marker is placed last within the question-clause.

7.7.2. Rankshifted Questions: Where there is a genuine framing-clause, a question can be rankshifted (as it appears in surface structure) merely by substituting the new governing clause for the framing-clause which calls for an answer to the free question. Thus, "*//₁ ∧ They /asked him /what he'd /**got**.*" has a form directly parallel to (7.7.1):

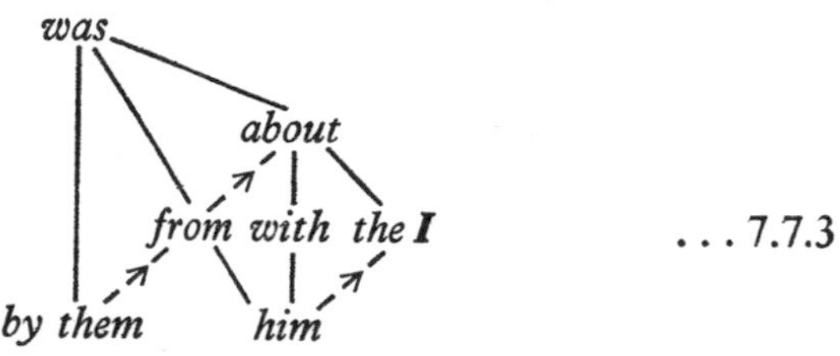

. . . 7.7.3

The new governing clause can still be a command, even if not the original command to answer the question. This is illustrated in the case of the warning "*//₄ ∧ Re/member /whose /**house** this /is //₋₃ **dear**.*" which expresses the rhema

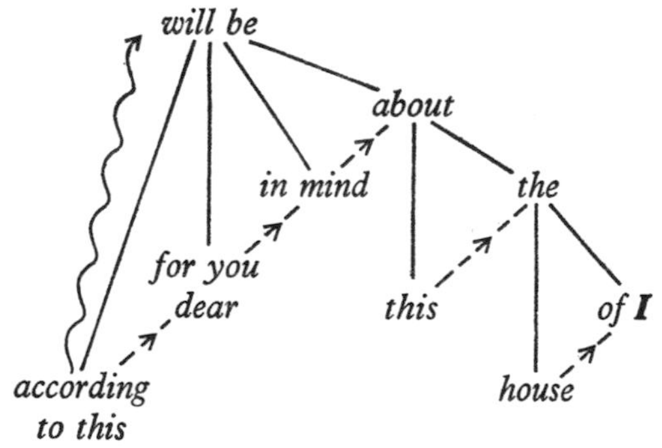

. . . 7.7.4

One can also of course subordinate a question to another question as in "*//₁ **Who** did he /ask //₋₁ what we'd /**come** for.*". A question such as this asked about a third party is unlikely to have its own tacit framing-clause; one does not anticipate a refusal to answer, and altering the tonicity does not seem to change the assumed content of the framing-clause, so much as to change it into an "I wonder" one. Thus, "*//₅ Who /**did** he /ask //₋₁ what we'd /**come** for.*" seems rather to mean "I wonder who he asked"; that is to say, it has the structure

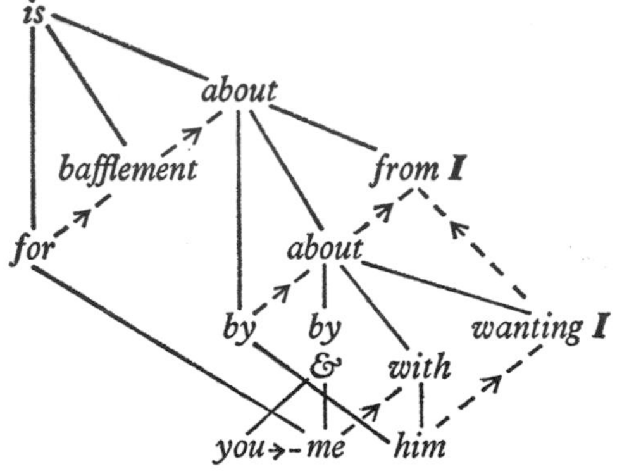

. . . 7.7.5

7.7.3. Closed Questions: In regard to closed questions, such as those which call for a yes-or-no answer, an important problem is again that of focus. A question such as “Is Pat here?” can be asked in different ways, expressing different forms of bias about the expected answer. Most languages have different syntagms for this purpose. In English, the most nearly ‘neutral’ form would be “$//_2$ ∧ *Is* /***Pat*** /*here*.”. One who expected the answer to be “*No*” would say “$//_2$ ***Is*** /*Pat* /*here*.”, while an expectation of “Yes” calls for the unexpected form “$//_2$ *Isn’t* /***Pat*** /*here*.” (perhaps because “$//_2$ ***Isn’t*** /*Pat* /*here*.” is the unmarked form for a negative question and therefore ambiguous). One can also express hope rather than bias; hoping for “*Yes*” one says “$//_2$ ∧ *Is* /*Pat* /***here***.”, while fearing “no” leads to “$//_2$ ∧ *Isn’t* /*Pat* /***here***.”. Here then are the three main forms of this question; the first is the same as (6.15). In (7.7.7) it is the phrase “not here” which is subjected to the interrogative construction, while in (7.7.8) the zero arc separates the two alternative predicates.

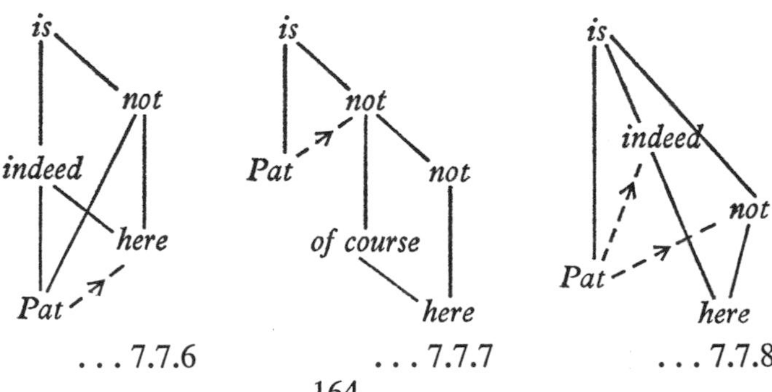

. . . 7.7.6 . . . 7.7.7 . . . 7.7.8

"$//_2$ ∧ *Is* /***Pat*** /*here*." "$//_2$ ***Is*** /*Pat* /*here*." "$//_2$ ∧ *Is* /*Pat* /***here***."

The form "$//_2$ *Isn't* /***Pat*** /*here*." is represented by (7.7.7) with the first "not" replaced by "so" (the lexigen (*so*) is used simply as a positive alternant to "not").

Closed questions are not limited to only two answers, nor need the answers expected be either yes or no. Here is an example with a three-way choice. It has an overt framing-clause, but this is partly an artifact of English syntax; it appears not to be subject to change of focus within the framing-clause, but on the other hand there are a number of quite polite ways of answering "I won't tell you". It would be more or less in order to reply "$//_5$ ∧ *Which*/*ever you* /***like***." or "$//_4$ ∧ ***I'm*** /***sorry*** $//_5$ ∧ ***I*** /*dont* /***drink***." to the three-way question "//. *Which do you pre*/***fer*** $//_2$ ***gin*** $//_2$ ***whiskey***, *or* $//_1$ ***sherry***." which would express:

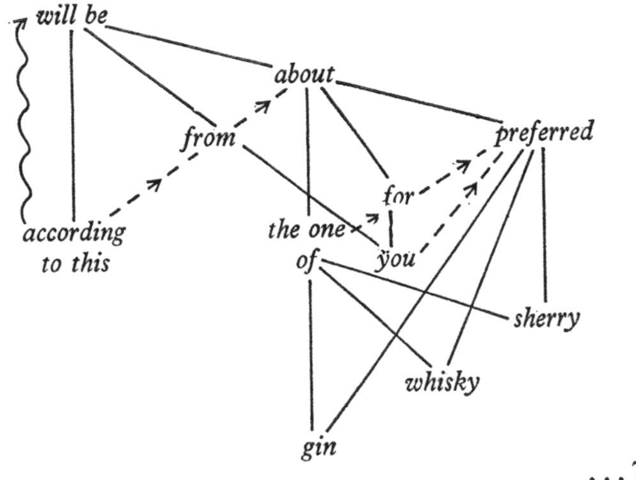

. . . 7.7.9

Note that each of the mutually unordered alternatives is designated penultimately in two ways, once as a member of the set of choices (one of), and once as a member of a field of preference. Though one cannot make the request-to-choose the rheme while using the words given above, the use of a quite different framing-clause, such as "$//_1$ *Choose your* /***tipple*** . . ." would serve to direct attention to this node.

One can also frame a question with an *open* list of given alternatives. Such questions though logically open questions need not contain an interrogative pronoun and express rhemata with zero arcs; they have none of the symptoms of having tacit framing-clauses (though such a clause can be added overtly, as by "//₁ ***Tell*** *me* . . ."). Here is an example:

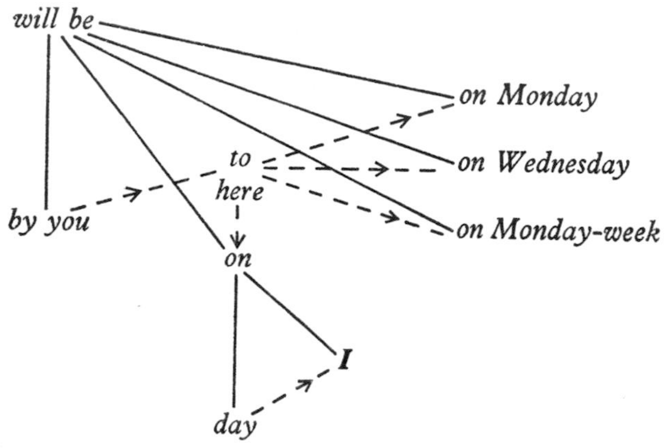

. . . 7.7.10

which can be translated as "//₂ *Will you /come on /**Mon**day //₂ **Wed**nesday //₂ Monday /**week**.*". The tone on the last clause is sufficient to indicate an open list, though one could optionally add a final "//₁ *or /**when**.*" which is in any case understood, and appears as the subrhema "on day **I**". Notwithstanding that it need not be expressed, this last alternative seems to have the role of a rheme; but it is so only in relation to the question, and in fact an answer naming any of the alternatives would be just as much a rheme in the answering rhema as would say "//₁ ∧ ***I'll*** */make it /**Tues**day.*" answering the pronomical clause. Therefore I have indicated all four terms as connected by zero arcs.

Finally, here is a closed question in rankshifted position as shewn at top of opposite page.

7.8. Vocatives and Exclamatives

A 'vocative' noun is essentially one in the second person. In the past many grammarians have held that vocatives are outside the sentence structure altogether, largely because they are usually not integrated into the syntax and can be omitted with no adjustments. But this is not the case in all languages, and anyway it is

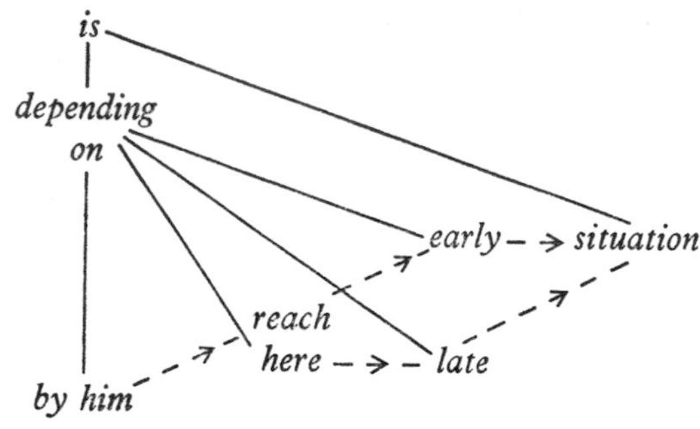

...7.7.11

"$//_4$ ***All*** *de/pends on /whether he /gets here* $//_2$ ***early*** *or* $//_1$ ***late***."

usually easy to determine the rhematical role of a given vocative. Their only constant peculiarity is their identification with the second person. Overlapping with vocatives as a class are exclamative utterances; these are often more or less inarticulate, but may have a well-defined syntactic structure and presumably a corresponding rhematical structure. But they raise other questions, their association with a context being of an unusual kind.

7.8.1. Some Examples of Vocatives: Consider the utterance "$//_{13}$ *Raymond's /still /**here** /**Ken**.*". This would be acceptable in a context where Ken was wanting to see Raymond, but didn't know whether perhaps he'd gone home, and if so presumably Ken would be off himself. The addition of the final "*/**Ken**"* to the sentence thus conveys in summary fashion the additional point, which some would call an 'implicature' and others a 'presupposition', "perhaps you'd like to know". Thus Ken, while not a participant in the action described, is involved in an information-exchange. The structure is therefore

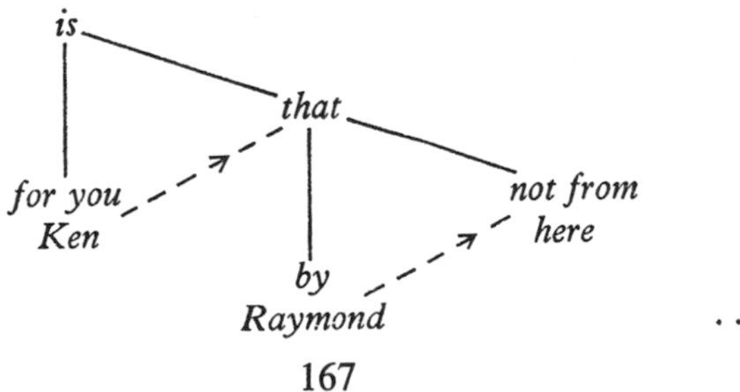

...7.8.1

The reality of the framing-clause represented by such a vocative as this is shown by the possibility of expressing changes in its focus. Thus, for instance, the calling of Ken is marked as the rheme of the framing-clause in "//₂ ***Ken*** //₋₁ *Raymond's /still /**here**.*". In many cases these vocative-clauses may be of interrogative or imperative form ("are you there?", "listen!").

However, many instances of vocatives involve no framing-clause, and the vocative appears as a participant in the primary rhema. Examples of this are (7.6.1) and (7.7.4).

7.8.2. Exclamatives: Heather has been telling Connie one of the exploits of her uncle George; Connie comments "//₅ *What an ex/**traordinary** a/chievement.*". What are we to make of this? First and perhaps most relevantly, one spots at once that Connie disposes of what is currently called an 'extended code'; that is, she's educated. Some people in that context would have said "//₁₊ ***Gosh.***" or "//₅ *Well I/**never**.*", and we would have felt less inclination to investigate the rhematical content conveyed by these phatics. Perhaps Connie deserves no better, either.

It can't be claimed, however, that nothing is conveyed by this exclamation. It stands in meaningful contrast to say "//₅ ∧ *Just /**like** him.*" or to "//₁ *What /happened to the /**bear**.*", conveying respectively the ideas "another of your stories about George" or "tell me some more". It seems to me that such exclamatives are rhetorically motivated abbreviations of assertive rhemata involving a kind of framing-clause, expressing in effect "I agree with you that that was an extraordinary achievement", the structure being then

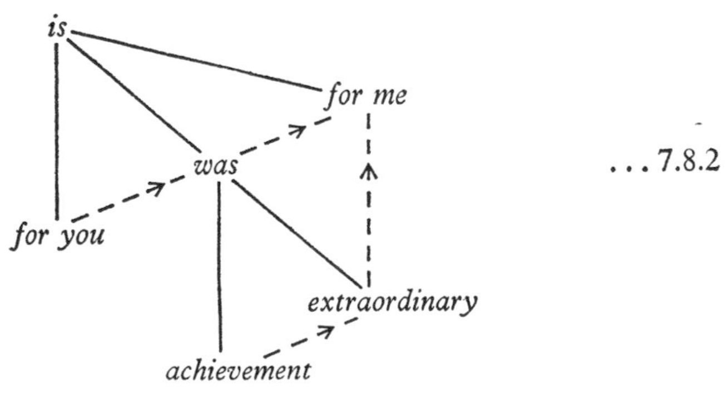

7.9. Forbidden Rhema Structures

It will by now be apparent that, despite the complications introduced by multiple designations and the appearance of self referential arcs and zero arcs in commands and questions, the graphs representing rhema structures are essentially trees or modified trees. This raises two questions: first, what might be represented by a structure which, while still being a graph involving designatory and accessory arcs and forming a chain under the latter (which we have found to be a necessary condition for all members of a context repertory), did not have a tree-based structure? and second, if the answer is 'nothing', can we find a simple definition of the permitted forms?

There does seem to be one type of structure which fails to represent the semantic content of any possible utterance. In its simplest form it is that shown as (7.9.1), which is itself contained in a perhaps more plausible structure, namely (7.9.2):

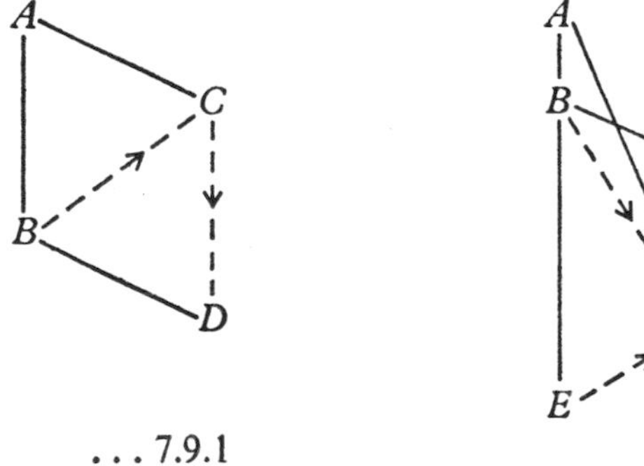

. . . 7.9.1 . . . 7.9.2

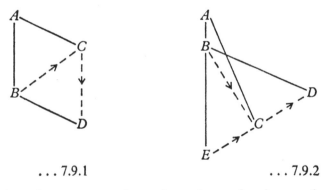

(7.9.2) involves the sequence of two dependents of a given node B being interrupted by a node *not* dependent on B. Can we exemplify this?

7.9.1. The House that Jack Built: What is involved is a focus anomaly, and a *locus classicus* for focus anomalies is the rigmarole "The House that Jack built". Here we have a string of clauses of the form "$||_1$ *This is the |**cow** that* $||_1$ *tossed the |**dog** that* $||_1$ *chased the |**cat** that . . .*"; syntactically we have a sequence of enchained relative clauses, which English (unlike Chinese, for example) can manage quite happily, but at the cost of confusing focus relations. The tonic stress falls obligately on the head noun in each case, and so gives no clue to the focus. The simplest representation would be

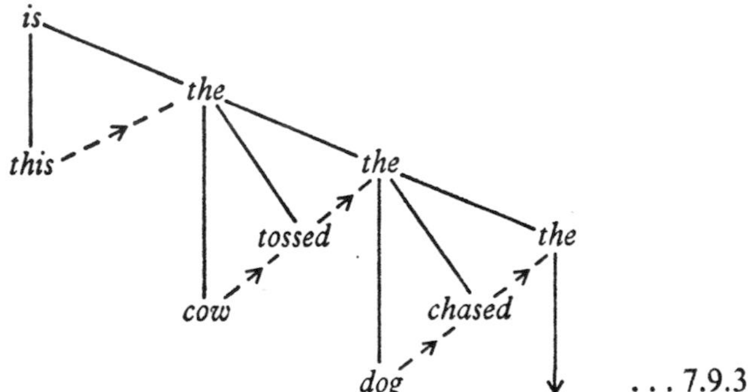

. . . 7.9.3

But within the context of the total build-up it is obvious that it is the successive verbs which are the rhemes of each verse. So what about the following?

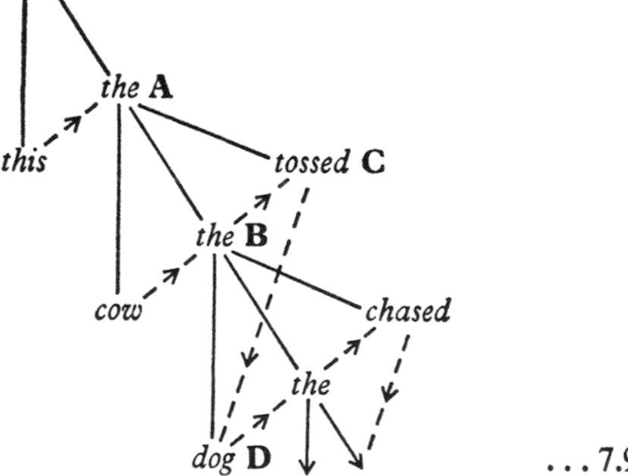

. . . 7.9.4

This structure contains instances of (7.9.1); thus we have the four nodes marked ABCD which correspond to those so marked in (7.9.1). If, however, we build up the whole utterance step by step from the beginning we find no actual anomaly at all, but only a pathological conflict between focus and word-order. This is represented, without any conflict with the patterns evidenced so far, by the admittedly bizarre rhema structure (7.9.5) below.

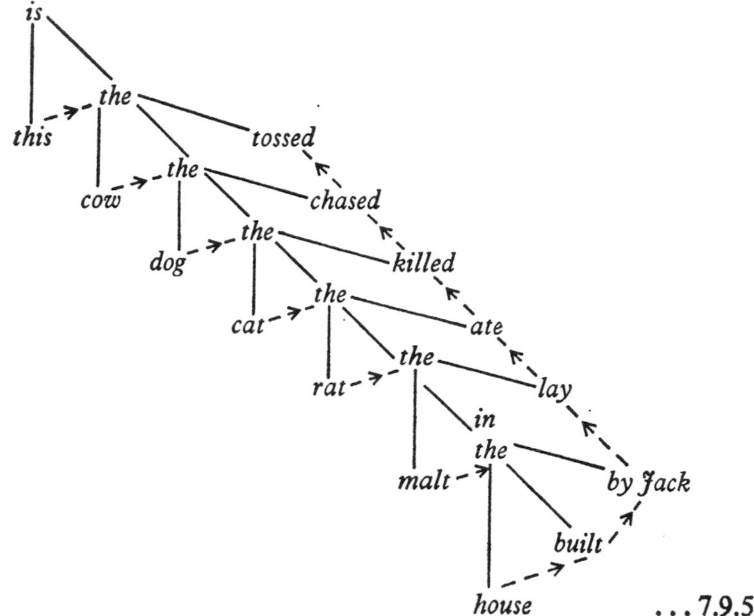

...7.9.5

7.9.2. Attempt to Construct a Counterexample: Let us instead see what happens when we try to fit words to the structure (7.9.2). Take the sentence "*Here is the lost ring*" and try to find a way of expressing it which will give the focus order represented by

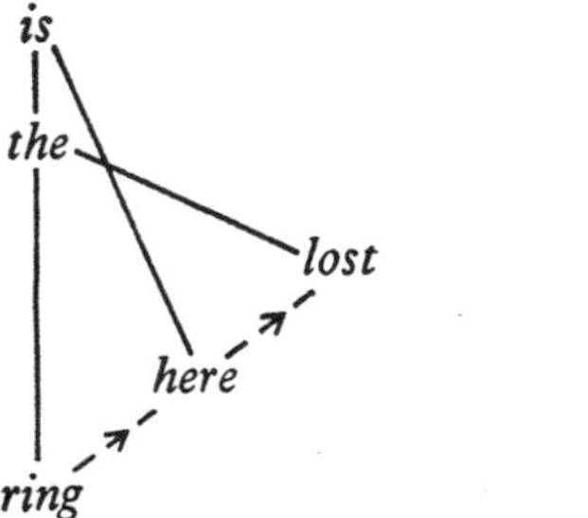

...7.9.6

There does exist a tonal pattern in which the theme as well as the rheme can be marked; it is the tone 13 of which we have had several examples. It would give in this case "$//_{13}$ *Here's the* /***lost*** /***ring***.". But this is obviously not a well-formed sentence; the two tonics cannot fall on an adjective-noun pair in this way, indeed they cannot be juxtaposed without at least a pause between them. We can do the same in a two-clause utterance: "$//_{1}$ ***Here****'s the* /*ring* $//_{5}$ ∧ *the* /***lost*** *one*."; but the effect of this is to propound a more detailed designation of 'ring', the rhematical content of which is better represented by the form (7.9.7) which, though somewhat unusual, is still of the familiar pattern:

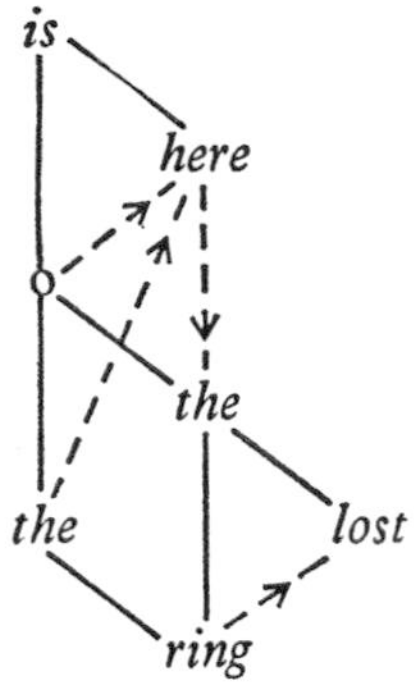

. . . 7.9.7

It would therefore seem that the type of structure represented by (7.9.1) *may* perhaps represent nothing capable of communication in speech. Failure to think of an example proves nothing, of course, and the conjecture may be wrong. But if not, we would be justified in saying that (7.9.1) is not a rhema graph for any utterance at all. However, it turns up in the context-rehearsal (15.5.3), though this is a rather unusual context.

7.9.3. Suggested Definition of Rhema Graphs: One definition which would exclude any structure containing (7.9.1) could be formulated in 'generative' terms, at least in form. The definition will not refer to the node labels, since for the time being at least we can envisage any labels at all being used in any position of the structure. This is analogous to the acceptance in surface grammar of any words at all to fill the slots of a syntactic structure; there will also be selection rules, which prevent many of the resulting structures being accepted as well-formed, but these are conveniently listed separately from the strictly structural rules. In the same way there are certainly rules of selecting lexigens in rhema structures; we shall encounter some of these later on, though I shall not venture on a comprehensive listing of them. The worst we need expect from disregarding such rules is the rhematical equivalent of 'colourless green ideas'.

My suggested definition of a rhema structure is by the following *Rhema Generating Rules*:

G: An expressible rhema structure *either*
- *G1:* consists of one node only; *or*
- *G2:* is derived from an acceptable rhema structure by
  - *G2.1:* replacing a node N with no designatory successors by
    - *G2.1.1:* two nodes N_1N_2 connected by a designatory arc, together having the same precessor and successor under accessory arcs as N had; or
    - *G2.1.2:* two nodes N_1N_2 connected by an accessory arc, each having the same precessor under designatory arcs as N had;
  - *G2.2:* to any set of nodes N_1–N_n adding a node N_o with a designatory arc incident from each and the same accessory successors as N_n.

These rules do not cover questions or commands. Both these have special characteristics pertaining to the fact that their rhemata are not required to belong to the repertory of a normal context; but obviously the rules G could be extended to include them. It is less obvious that the rules G as they stand can account for elaborately parallel structures produced particularly by the term 'respectively'. Perhaps hardly at home in natural language, but becoming so, this word has some remarkable rhematical offspring. For example, the utterance "$||_4$ ***Peggy** and* $||_4$*Bill are |coming to* $||_1$ ***lecture** and* $||_1$*play |**chess*** $||_5$ *re|**spec**tively.*" expresses the structure shewn at top of p. 174.

This, almost the simplest "respectively"-structure, can be generated from the initial rhema containing 'to-by-for' by successive applications of G2.1.1 and G2.2 (only a minimum set of the transitive accessory arcs are shown). The more natural "$||_4$ *Peggy's |coming to |**lecture** and* $||_{-1}$ *Bill to |play |**chess**.*" could be represented more simply, with the initial "o–to–&–&" rhema condensed to a single &; but even so the effect of the

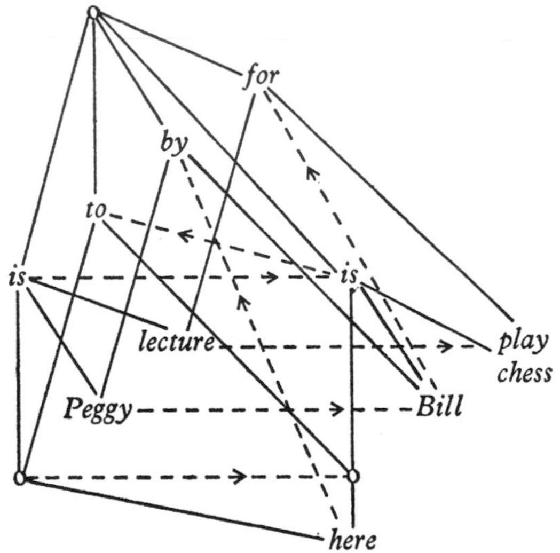

. . . 7.9.8

evident isocolon, only mildly disguised by the intonation, would be to reproduce (7.9.8).

7.10. Performatives

Sentences containing performative verbs are not uncommon in perfectly natural speech. The fact that such a sentence is itself an example of the action of the verb raises the suspicion that it involves an irreducible self-reference. However, such utterances belong in ordinary contexts, and can be inferences in context repertories, and it would therefore be a point against my theory if they had to be represented as self-referent in rhematical notation.

That performative utterances may not be irreducibly self-referent is suggested by comparing them with commands. A command is intended to cause action, and not merely to carry information; it has thus a special role not shared by other types of utterance. Moreover, we have seen that formal registers, of European languages at least, tend to express commands by explicitly self-referent constructions, such as "It is hereby ordained that . . .". Let us look more closely at a typical performative: "*//$_4$ ∧ I must /**warn** you that //$_1$ your appli/cation /may be re/* ***jected***." The second clause *contains* the warning, though the whole utterance is also what we would colloquially call a warning. It could be paraphrased in the form "This is a warning that your application may be rejected", which is explicitly self-referent; but equally one might put it thus "I give you warning that your application may be rejected". I suggest the following rhema structure:

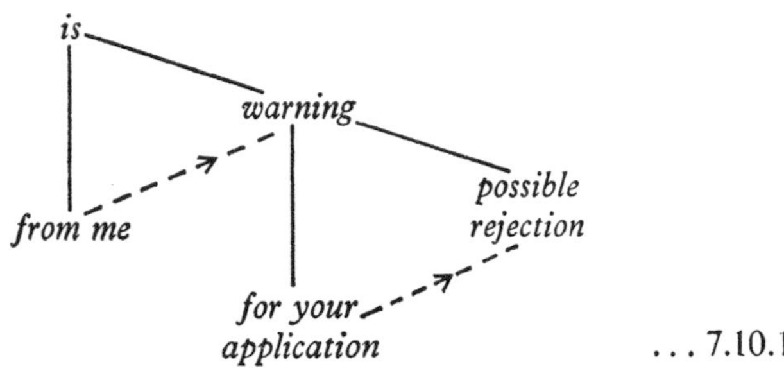

... 7.10.1

The solution of the problem being to attach the lexigen (*warning*) as a label to the governing node of the clause expressing the substance of the admonition, to show that "*//₁ ∧ Your appli/cation /***may** *be re/jected.*" is a 'warning' by itself.

The same device may be used in other cases of performatives, even those which are sufficiently formal in character to attract self-referent formulae in written form. Such a one would be "*//₁ ∧ I de/clare /***David** */***Lane** *e/lected //₁ member of /parliament for /this /***city**." which expresses the rhema

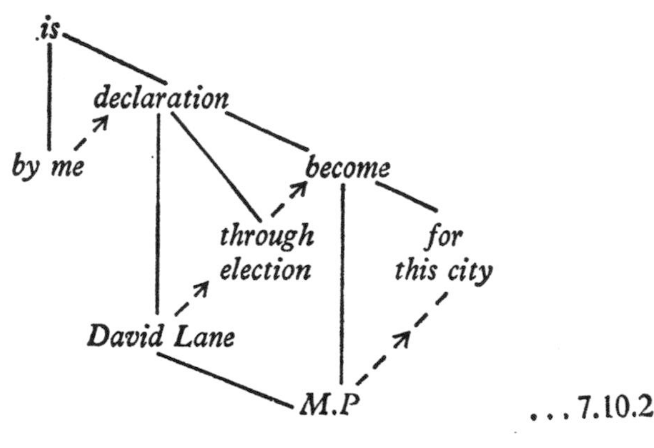

... 7.10.2

As before, the logical justification is that the declaration as such does not include its syntactically (or conventionally) required framing-clause, which is where the imputation of self-reference resides.

CHAPTER VIII

The Node Labels

We have now seen that there are only a limited range of types of structure which can be used to represent the 'meanings' conveyed by utterances in any given context; these are the rhema graphs, which I have defined as oriented digraphs labelled in a lattice algebra as base domain, including two arc labels a, d such that $d \geqq a$, and such that every graph is a chain under the arc labels a, further subject to the rules G for rhema generation. The arc labels were fully discussed in Chapter VI, but hitherto I have given no proper treatment of the node labels, except to indicate that they are to represent 'lexigens', a discussion of which is found in §3.5 and following sections. The purpose of this chapter is to introduce a more detailed study of lexigens, which I propose to carry to that point where only that part of the 'lexical lattice' (the one whose elements are the lexigens) which is not concerned with closed categories remains to be examined. To describe this last is an open-ended task, even for a reasonable corpus of text in a given language, and I shall not pursue it very far.

8.1. Word Uses

As I remarked in §3.6, the quest for objectively definable units, in terms of which all word-meanings could be defined with the help of rhema structures, has no prospect of success. Whereas we can set non-trivial limits on the possible *structures* of meaning, from considering constraints inherent in the process of communication by speech—the result of which I have already described—no such limits exist for the *content* of the messages so structured, which is what we are now concerned with. This is because there exist an infinite variety of contexts which form the subject of such messages, as well as an infinity of ways of analysing and apprehending them. It does not follow, as we shall thankfully discover, that no progress can be made in bringing some order into the system of lexigens; it does mean that there will always remain a residue unaccounted for in any systematic way. What's more, this will include the largest part of any realistic dictionary.

This irreducible part concerns the meanings of what are often called 'full' or 'semantically loaded' words. To call it 'irreducible' is not to imply that there may not be within it some meanings (sememes) which are required in all languages; but if there are any such, this is an empirical fact, not a logical or mathematical requirement. Some of these empirical universals of language will refer to items which are of significance to all men because of their common humanity, rooted in biology. Everyone, for instance, has a mother, and almost everyone knows who it is; so we would expect (and, with minor reservations, find) that every language is able to express this idea. Even here, however, some languages require a compound expression, as when the social system imposes on the child a mother-like relationship with several women, one of whom only is the womb-mother. The principal parts of the body are also strong candidates for a place in every lexicon; but here too there are differences, such as our insistence that a foot is not a leg, a distinction habitually disregarded by the Russians (actually their word, *noga*, is cognate with *onukh-* or ὄνυχ (Greek), *ungul-, nail*). Perhaps in the end the only really universal lexemes are those for the natural numbers, at least up to ten.

Categories derived from the 'objective' world are thus not likely to introduce any really firm structure into the lexical lattice. More promising are those involving closed systems of contrasts concerned with the internal workings of language itself: these are the raw material for the 'syntactic' words which, while relatively few in the number of their types, head the list in frequency of their tokens in running text. The relationships existing between the nodes of one rhema furnish one system of such contrasts; another arises from the structure of the speech act and the speech situation, which are perhaps truly universals of language. There is also a category of quantification, of which the numerals are a specialized subclass.

If we set these aside for the moment, the unit which carries the residual semantic information in its specific form is the 'full word'. But of course 'words' can have more than one meaning apiece, and some meanings fall within the area of application of more than one word. We therefore cannot use this term itself: I prefer the term *word-use* coined by Sparck-Jones.[95] Every word-of-a-language (lexeme) has a set of word-uses, each of which is associated with a more or less narrowly defined area of meaning. And to every such meaning there are often a set of words, in each language, which have a word-use referring to it. There is no necessary connection between the uses of what native speakers regard as a single word; their diversity arises from various historical processes of which most speakers are wholly unaware. These include fixation of metaphors, speech taboos, loss of phonetic distinctions, folk-etymology, and many others. We have thus to avoid conjectures about origins, and take them as they come. Only when (and if) a word-use can be defined in the semantic sense can we have a firm basis on which to explore its history; and even then, there are words arising by convergence from two equally valid etymologies (such as "bottle", both a diminutive of "butt" and the reflex of Latin "*botulus*").

Individual word-uses have very different degrees of importance in a language. Some are much more context-dependent than others; and some are much more frequent than others. Strong context-dependence generally leads to large families of uses of the words affected and conversely to large sets of words which have uses which, in a given context, more or less coincide. Such a word in English is "*drink*"; in different contexts it can be replaced by (a) "*imbibe*", "*swig*", "*swallow*"; (b) "*the sea*"; (c) "*alcohol*", "*booze*", "*tipple*"; (d) "*wellwishing*", "*toast*", etc. On the other hand, a word like "*barley*" almost always refers to *Hordum sativum* and nothing else; characteristically, there is no synonym in current use.

As to frequency, there are common word-uses known to all competent speakers, less common ones known only to more or less specialized groups of people, and at the other extreme there are nonce-words, whose purport is (the speaker hopes) apparent from the immediate context but are not, strictly speaking, 'known' to anyone at the time. One word-use can rise or fall in this scale as time goes by, often quite rapidly. Highly context-dependent ones are buffered against such change, but they may go out of use in time; some, nevertheless, have lasted for thousands of years with little change in meaning. Some disappear with their referents, like "*pony-trap*", others decline leaving their referents flourishing, like "*cur*". Word-uses can become common without any obvious change in the situations to which they refer; people must always have "*liaised*" with each other, and "*chortled*" on occasion, but only recently under these names. Among the more frequent words, some have wider emotional connections than others. Such a series is "*girl*", "*cloud*", "*ruminant*", "*catasterism*"; people are more interested in girls than in clouds, many don't know even what a ruminant is, and very few could correctly define "catasterism". Thus, while there is a lot to be said for dictionary-makers beginning with the commonest word-uses, such work is not very durable.

Finally, word-uses are subject in general to restrictions arising from register. They may be classed as 'learned', 'obscene', 'poetic', 'slang', and the like; some meanings have representatives in all these categories. Their effect is, that the uses of a given word in a given language usually do not constitute a well-defined set; this is one of the difficulties in compiling a realistic dictionary. Registers intergrade, and only manifest as a rule through changing the frequency with which different items occur. These, however, are complications which, for my present purpose, can be deferred; I am concerned not with the nature of word-uses, but with their meanings, and how to begin to systematize them.

8.2. The Inferential System

I have already alluded, in §3.7 and §4.8, to the fact that lexigens can be regarded as forming among themselves a lattice, which I have called the 'lexical lattice', under the relation of inclusion of their designation-classes. But this was argued before I had properly defined and exemplified the structure of the rhemata within which, in actual speech acts, lexigens always appear. In this section I shall consider the extent to which this inclusion-relation can be properly assimilated with rhematical inference, as defined in §4.3, when the lexigens are accommodated in rhemata.

As I have already said, each lexigen is located at a node, and forms the label attached to this node. Some node labels, especially those which appear in a non-ultimate position in a rhema, will not correspond to semantically loaded sentence components; they will be represented in surface structure, if at all, by 'empty' or syntactic words. For the time being we can think of these nodes as carrying only information in the closed categories mentioned above, and being unmarked in the open lexical system which I am here mainly concerned with. There are, needless to say, inferential relations among the closed category items also: these are discussed in the following three chapters. Here I consider only the 'full' words which carry lexical meaning.

Each such word contributes something to the position, of the rhema which it helps to express, in the inferential system of the given context repertory. Take any utterance, such as "*//₁ ∧ I /left my /hat and /**coat** be//₁hind the /**door**.*", and replace one of its words by one of a vaguer meaning; say "*things*" instead of "*hat and coat*". We thus get the utterance "*//₁ ∧ I /left my /**things** be//₁hind the /**door**.*" This conveys a rhema which, because of its total meaning includes that of the previous one, is inferrable from it by the rules of rhematical inference. Conversely, if one tightens up any of the terms, or adds additional words, one gets an utterance, such as "*//₁ ∧ I /left my /hat and /coat on the /**peg** be//₁hind the /**door**.*", from which the original form can be inferred.

Considering these relations, which are strictly inferential since they hold between rhemata conveyed by complete utterances, we can infer inclusions between designation-classes, namely (*things*) ≧ (*hat and coat*) and ∅ ≧ (*on the peg*). This exemplifies the basic test which must be applied, empirically, to any inclusion-relation we may be led to postulate within the lexical lattice. In any pair of rhemata differing by substituting one lexigen for another, an inclusion may be postulated between the lexigens if and only if the corresponding inference holds between the rhemata. To adopt this test at once raises the question, whether it necessarily has an unambiguous result. From all I have said about the necessity of the context, it might be that the inference might run one way or the other according to the context; let alone the possibility that it might also depend on what rhemata we use to illustrate the given lexigens.

Here is an example of what I mean. Suppose that I say "*//₁ Lets /have a /little /**food** /now.*" in a situation where, as it happens, we have nothing to eat except biscuits. In this context, my utterance allows the inference to (the rhema expressed by) "$//_1$ *Lets /have some /**bis**cuits.*". According to the test I have just proposed, we ought to conclude that (*biscuits*) ≧ (*food*); but of course in any actual dictionary we shall find that the reverse is implied to hold. There is, however, a fallacy in the argument. Because the inference which I suggested as holding between the two rhemata does not actually go from the first (with "food") *by itself* to the second (with "biscuits"), but from the first together with an unspoken but equally relevant rhema to the effect that we only have biscuits to eat. The premiss is thus a combination of the two rhemata (8.1), (8.2):

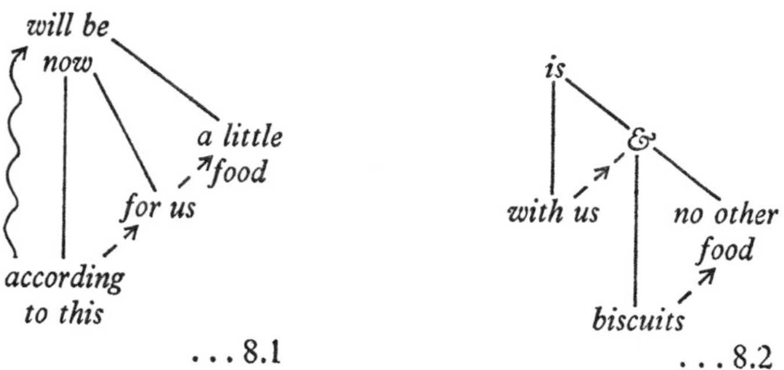

These can be combined (by methods described in Chapter XIII) to form the rhema:

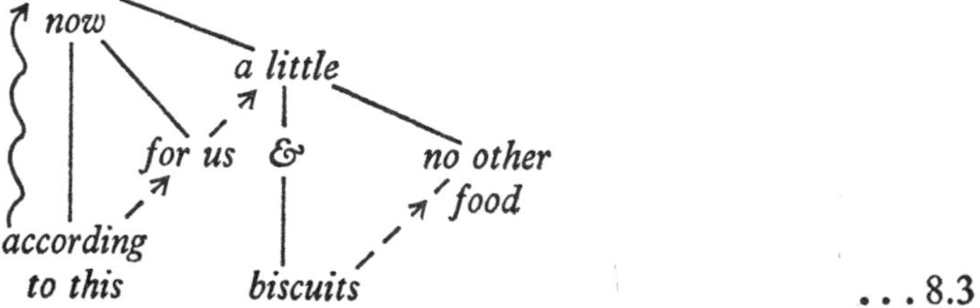

...8.3

Obviously, now, the inference to "$//_1$ *Lets /have some /**bis**cuits.*" is valid (by merely deleting the node labelled "food") even though in the lexical lattice we are given the natural information that (*food*) ≧ (*biscuits*).

Let us now look at a case where one word implies another in

one utterance and not in another, thereby suggesting that the relationship between the lexigens involved may depend on the rhemata they occur in. There can be two views as to whether one can infer from "*//₁Jim's /bitch has got /**puppies**.*" that "*//₁Jim's /dog has got /**puppies**.*". This is because there is a conflict among the word-uses attached to "dog": it may refer, as the unmarked term to any member of the species, or specifically to the male. One can argue that the second utterance clearly precludes that the "male" word-use is intended, and so justify the inference by inclusion of designation-classes. On the other hand, it can be argued that in a real context where the word "*bitch*" is used, the word "*dog*" is only acceptable in the 'male' sense, and so disallow the inference. The first argument, however, cannot be used to establish inclusion-relations between the lexigens, since it relies on the additional information that male animals don't have young. The second argument also falls down, since it makes the two utterances belong to different contexts and therefore not directly comparable. We must conclude that the instance cited does not allow any decision to be arrived at about the inclusion-relations involved. We have, in fact, to deal with different word-uses, and therefore with different lexigens; and it is, I think, obvious that this is so whenever this kind of indecision arises.

It should perhaps be added here that one favourite method used by semanticists (I have already given several instances of it) is barred to us. This is the use of supposedly 'deviant' utterances as an aid in defining meanings. Such an utterance would be relevant only if it occurred in an actual or imaginable context, and in that context it would not be deviant; a *context* cannot be deviant if it actually occurs for the linguist does not criticise the world. The sentence "*Jim's male dog has had puppies.*" is syntactically well formed; it is no doubt a lie, but if not it is no business of the semanticists to go putting asterisks on it. Take it to the vet!

8.3. Constitution of the Node Subalgebra

I have already had occasion to explain what is meant by the 'direct product' of two graphs. This is a very general term, and can be applied equally to lattices. If the node subalgebra of our base domain is a lattice, as we have seen it ought to be, then it might be the direct product of two or more lattices. Here is a simple example of the nature of such a product, illustrated diagrammatically. Each of (8.4) and (8.5) represents a lattice, and (8.6) represents their direct product, formed by combining three (8.4)s in the pattern of (8.5) or equivalently four (8.5)s in the pattern of (8.4):

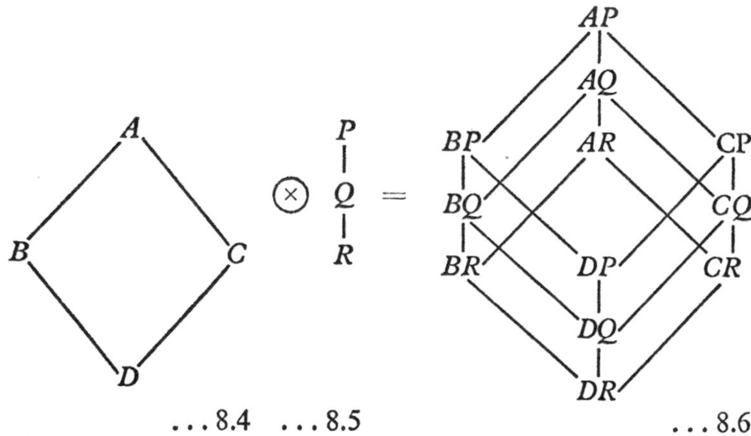

. . . 8.4 . . . 8.5 . . . 8.6

Suppose now that we can find some general category, to one term of which every lexigen must belong. Then if this category can be represented as a labelled graph, its various terms being the labels attached to the nodes, and if the lexigens when we ignore the category constitute a lattice, the system of lexigens taking account of both their parts will be represented by the direct product of these two, which is a lattice if and only if each of its direct factors in one. Such a category might be that of 'case'; every lexigen, we could say, had to have a definite case marker giving one aspect of its relation to others designated by the same preceding node. We could then look to see whether the system of cases could be represented as a lattice, using the same inclusion-relation under which the lexigens *without* their cases form a lattice. In our case, this would be designation-inclusion. If this were so, then the total system of lexigens would also be a lattice, namely, the direct product of the lexical lattice and the case lattice. But if not, and the involvement of the 'case' category were indeed demonstrable, then the total system would not be a lattice, nor would the base domain of our rhema graphs, and the context lattice theorem (4.6) would not hold.

To maintain the theory we have therefore to accept, as valid components of the lexigens, besides the lexical lattice itself, only such additional closed categories as can be represented as lattices under the same inclusion-relation. There appear to be three such categories, which form the subject matter of Chapters IX–XI; these are 'quantification', 'identification', and 'case'. In order that they should combine with the lexical lattice in the required manner, that is as factors of a lattice product, they must not only be representable as a lattice under designation-inclusion on their own, but they must be such that each is universally expressed by one and only one term at every node, so forming a constant component of the node-label which represents the lexigen. 'Absence' of a given category at a given node gives us no trouble, since it can be represented by the upper bound of the category lattice; but representation of one category by two terms simultaneously must not be allowed. The first question is, how to recognize which such categories exist.

It is no part of the theory that there are exactly three of them. Any others could remain hidden within what I choose to regard as the unanalyzed component of the lexical lattice. The value of making as many as possible explicit is twofold; first, the less information remains in the residual lexical lattice, the better for all concerned, especially those who compile dictionaries; and second, if the categories are well chosen, they may express essential and distinctive contributions to the inferential process. Possible additions to my three categories will be briefly looked at in Chapter XII. As an example of the kind of category which one might give special recognition to, but which in fact seems not worth the trouble, I may mention here that of 'classifiers'.

Fairly complex systems of classifiers, classifying nouns into partly arbitrary and partly conceptual classes, exist in several languages; for example, Chinese and Bantu. A simpler system of the same sort in Indoeuropean is that of gender. The main difficulty about accepting such systems as a possible basis for a universal category (and if it is not universal in *some* sense it is of no use to us) is that there seem to be very few terms with any claim to this status. Contrasts between animate and inanimate, and between human and non-human, are very widespread but hardly universal; moreover they are not very useful inferentially. And any attempt to construct an artificial system of this kind leads to the same kind of indecision that one encounters in trying to find an uncontroversial set of elementary semantic concepts underlying empirically attested lexigens. If there is anything here (which I doubt) it is hardly worth the trouble of recording.

8.4. Quantification and Inference

In contrast with this, I shall in this section consider in a general way the category of 'quantification' which will be dealt with in detail in Chapter IX. The importance of this category is precisely that it is very strongly involved with the inferential relation; so much so, that if it cannot be defined and shown to have the required lattice property the whole theory collapses. This is the category whose terms are concerned in answering the questions "how much" or "how many" of the members of the class designated by the lexigen are involved, or more generally how large a part of the designation-class is designated at the particular node concerned. Its importance in inference arises from the relevance of this information to deciding what follows from what.

Examples of the effects of some quantification terms on inference are soon come by. From "*Tom is going to Ireland this summer.*" we can rightly infer that "*Tom will not be at home.*" and that "*Tom will be travelling overseas.*" But from "*Tom isn't going to Ireland this summer.*" which carries a quantification 'at no time' as against the 'sometime' of the preceding sentence, we can infer neither "*Tom will be at home.*" nor "*Tom won't be travelling.*". But there are clearly some inferences we can make, such as that "*Tom won't be in Dublin this summer.*" whose negation conversely does not follow from the positive sentence.

The effect of negations on inference is of course well-known, but equally drastic are those arising from general quantifications. If I say "*Your pony is in my yard.*" it can be inferred that "*One of your animals is in my yard.*"; this is a simple instance of (*animal*) $\geqq$ (*pony*). But from "*All your ponies are in my yard.*" it does not follow that "*all your animals are in my yard.*", but of course the converse. For just as any reference to a pony is a reference to an animal, so is any reference to 'all' animals aslo a reference to 'all' ponies. The quantifier 'all' signals an inversion of the inclusion relations between the designation-classes of the lexigens containing it.

It is no accident that it is precisely negative and general terms that are singled out for attention in classical logic. It is as if simple inclusion between designation-classes were felt as the intuitive norm of inference, departures from which are therefore striking and exceptional and so worthy of particular attention, in contrast with the main body of inferential processing in ordinary speech which can be left to function without special attention or learned notice. The rather paradoxical result has been that the predicate calculus, as the modern successor of Aristotelian logic, based on the same exceptional quantifications, is now commonly seen as the standard type of inferential system, against which the claims of rhematical inference have to be laboriously argued.

It is general quantifications I wish to look at here; complementations and suppositions have the simpler effect of ruling out certain otherwise permissible inferences, an effect which can be codified simply enough by appropriate additions to the rules of inference, but the effect of general quantification is to invert inference relations, and this can only be understood as a modification of parts of the lexical lattice itself. Let me illustrate what happens by the following example.

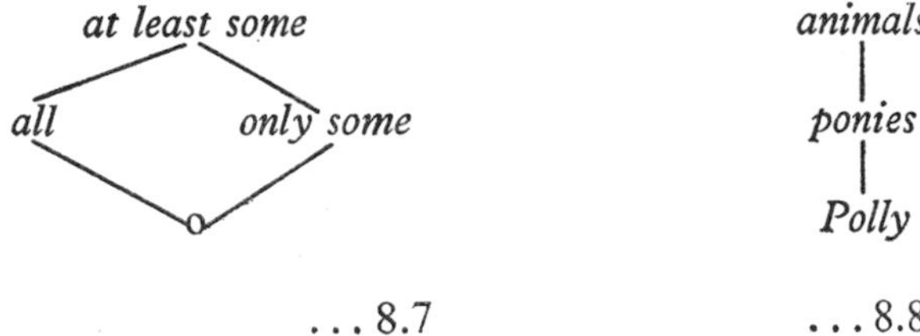

. . . 8.7 . . . 8.8

(8.7) is a portion of the quantification lattice, and (8.8) is a portion of the lexical lattice, including reference to an individual pony called Polly. We would expect, from these sublattices, to be able to construct part of the overall node subalgebra as the direct product of these two. The model for this is already to hand as (8.6); the only modification required is to delete the self-contradictory entry for "*only some Polly*", apart from disregarding all distinctions subject to the empty quantification. This would give us

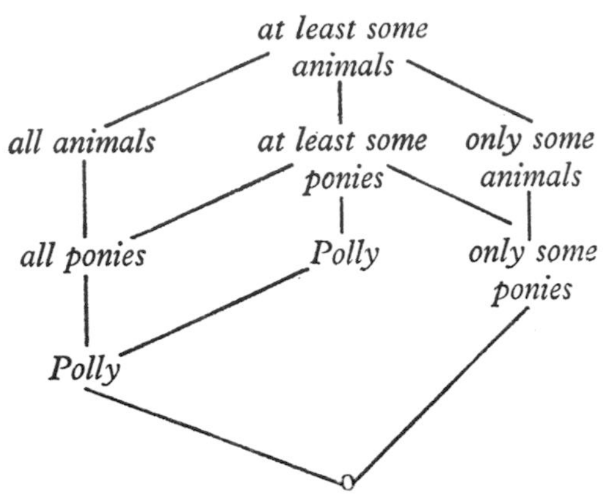

. . . 8.9

We at once see, however, that if this correctly indicates the inclusion-relations between the designation-classes, we should be able to infer, not only from "*At least some ponies are piebald*" that "*At least some animals are piebald*", but parallel with this that if "*All ponies eat grass*" then "*All animals eat grass.*" To avoid this, we have to invert the part of the product lattice concerned with "all"-terms. If we do this, and identify the two occurrences of "Polly", we get the following, which is only partly a direct product, that is to say, not a direct product at all in any mathematical sense:

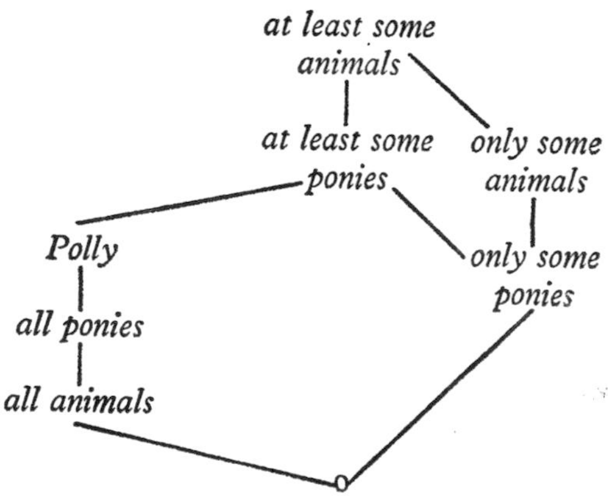

. . . 8.10

It can be proved, in fact, that this process (essentially, forming a direct product and then inverting parts of it corresponding to certain elements of one of the factors) will always yield a lattice from lattice factors. I shall call the result a partially-inverted or PI-product.

8.5. The Node Subalgebra Reconsidered

We can now see that the model of the node subalgebra, as simply the direct product of a set of lattices representing the various closed categories we elect to distinguish and the unanalyzed lexical lattice, is an over-simplification. This is so, because the designation-class of a phrase such as "*all ponies*" is the class of all occurrences of the concept of "all ponies", and this class is included within the class of occurrences of the concept "at least some ponies", just as the designation-class of "*all animals*", that is of the occurrences of the concept of "*all animals*", is included within that of "*all ponies*", and that of "*at least some ponies*" in that of "*at least some animals*".

Fortunately, it turns out that this effect applies only to certain quantification terms, and not to any terms of either identification or of case; moreover the quantifications producing this inversion are themselves a sublattice of the quantification lattice. The inverting effect extends, as can be seen by working out a few further examples, to all factors of the node subalgebra other than quantification. Thus the node subalgebra can be presented as a PI-product of the quantification lattice with the direct product of the identification, case, and lexical lattices. This is not as convenient an arrangement as one might have hoped, but is still a considerable simplification over the practice adopted in the examples in the last chapter (and earlier) where the node labels were left implicitly unstructured.

It still allows us, moreover, to present each node label as a sequence of four terms in a conventional order; in doing so, no explicit reference to the inversion wrought by some of the quantification terms is required. The simplest way to deal with this, at the computational level, is not to use an inverted form of the lexical lattice but to invert the inclusion relation if, and only if, this is called for by one of the inverting terms of quantification.* But when computation is not in question it is probably

* This is equivalent to a re-structuring of each context-repertory, which is the form in which the operation is specified in the Inference Rules (§14.6.2).

easier to think of the node subalgebra as a PI-product with parts of itself inverted, after the model of (8.10).

In an ordinary dictionary of an inflected language, it is customary to give as entries only the uninflected stem of each word, rather than to give each inflected form in the paradigm a separate entry. In the same way, we can separate the terms of the closed categories from the residual lexical terms, in envisaging a rhematical dictionary. These categories will be the same for all languages; they must not be mistaken for a set of inflectional forms, or a list of case-markers or demonstrative pronouns or whatever it is that most frequently represents them in the surface form of a given language. They are conceptual only, and the terms which we distinguish in each category are as many, and no more, as can be exemplified in at least one of the world's languages. This sets a limit (perhaps a not very practical one—but it may not be very practical to think of all languages at once in this way) to the *delicacy* to which the conceptual analysis is carried out; otherwise there would be no rational limit at all.

The conceptual analysis is the subject of the next three chapters. But given that it can be done, if only to a first approximation in this work, it is essentially a construction based in part on *a priori* considerations. There is nothing comparable to this kind of analysis which can be done on the lexical lattice, except to the extent that additional similar categories can be extracted from it (which is probably very limited). The temptation to construct this factor of the node subalgebra in a similarly *a priori* manner must be resisted. In the past, it has not been easy to resist; the notion has captivated many minds, from such pioneers as Timothee Bright[13] and Bishop Wilkins,[104] down to Peter Roget, who adopted an aprioristic approach to his classification of ideas, to which he attached great importance.[83] The difficulty with such approaches is that the contents of the world (the whole world, including man's subjective attitudes as well as objective entities) are essentially contingent, and cannot be predicted by any finite intelligence; and it is these contents which make up the designation-classes whose inclusion-relations are represented in this factor of the total system. *A priori* methods are bound to fail, and their products to be seriously misleading.*

* A partial exception to this generalization may be found in Leo Jolley's posthumous book *The Fabric of Knowledge*.

In the present climate of opinion this hardly needs saying, perhaps; it is more remarkable, and perhaps to some objectionable, that I should recommend an *a priori* approach, even if pruned and tamed by consideration of actual language competences, for the closed categories. It is, however, made possible by constant appeal to the test of rhematical inference, which enables us (if the theory as a whole is accepted) to trace out the structure of each of the lattices in relation to whatever terms may occur to us to start with, and from these to predict new ones. The latter may always turn out not to be taken account of in any known language, and can then be discarded (so long as the lattice structure allows it). In this way what was originally set to be a symmetrical and comprehensive pattern capable of indefinite refinement in delicacy will end up as a lopsided and finite structure. But so long as it is a lattice this does not matter; each of the categories can be constructed in this way, and I have attempted to make a start on them. If I have not altogether succeeded in getting them right, that is to be expected; the means exist for others to do better.

Finally, a word must be said about a point which is purely one of convention, but a convention which there may well be two views about. I have explained how, in the base domain of the rhema graphs, the whole of the node subalgebra is inverted, if the order of the inclusions among designation-classes is to be our criterion. It may be asked, why I should not have inverted instead the base domain itself and left the designation-classes in their 'natural' order, with the empty class at the bottom of the diagram and the universal class at the top. This, however, would have had undesirable consequences, as it seems to me. For, with this presentation, the inference relation operates *upwards* in the base domain (i.e., $a \supset b \equiv b \geqq a$), but, according to all precedents, *downwards* in the context lattice. We have thus two conventions in mutual conflict, and in this situation it seems right to make the younger give way to the older of them.

CHAPTER IX

The Quantification Lattice

I now turn to giving a detailed account of the terms relating to quantification. The function of such terms is to specify what parts or members of the designation-class indicated by the accompanying lexical term, or of its complement, are being designated in the given context. We must remember that the 'terms' I am classifying are not words of any language, nor particular word-uses or meanings conveyed in any given language, but logically possible distinctions. There is no *logical* limit to the number of such distinctions, nor to the delicacy with which they can be sought out; but terms which can be exemplified by *no* word-use in *any* language do not concern us, and of course I shall have to give up long before that point. The 'quantification lattice' I present here is therefore, of necessity, incomplete; though probably not grossly so. It has at least the merit that it can conveniently be printed on one page.

9.1. Survey of Terms

The nucleus of the quantification system is the subsystem of what we may call *formal quantifiers*. These are the terms expressed in English by "all", "some", and "none", and their special status is indicated by their role in Aristotelian logic. Together, they generate a 'Boolean' lattice of eight terms (one being a null designation), as follows:

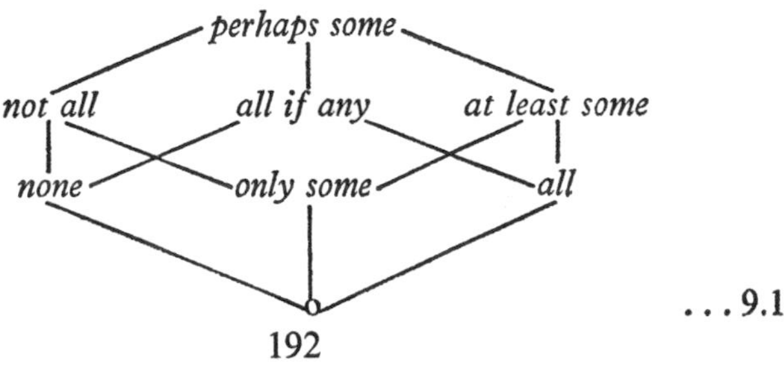

. . . 9.1

The application of these terms is not to be thought of as limited to concrete designation classes, though this applies largely to the English words I have used for them in (9.1). With predications, such as "*I eat apples*", they refer to the class of possible occasions designated by the predication. We thus have "*I dont always eat apples*", "*I never eat apples*", "*I only sometimes eat apples*", etc.; though expressed in terms primarily referring to time in English, these sentences are really modifications of the unmarked form concerned with the class of occasions to which the predication refers. "*At least some*" is the most unmarked term, and its complement "*none*" indicates its simple negation.

It might be thought that the upper bound of the lattice, which I have labelled "*perhaps some*", would be the unmarked term. But it is a general rule that upper bounds, in these categories, are uncommon in daily life, if not indeed so vacuous as to be absurd, and this infrequency leads to their being *marked* terms in linguistic expression, if they occur at all. In the present case, the upper bound occurs almost only with predications, and conveys the sense of uncertainty or unreality, that of the 'hypothetical' modality of some grammars. The lower bound of (9.1) represents the designation-class which is contained in all three of "all", "some", and "none": there is no such except the empty class. It is a very general rule that lower bounds of all our lattices represent the empty designation-class; needless to say, no language has a word for it, but it is nevertheless a lattice element. Don't make the mistake of thinking that "*nothing*" conveys its meaning: it refers to what is both nothing and something and everything, and a lot of nonsense could have been avoided if (9.1) had been borne in mind by philosophers in early times.

9.2. Partitions and Collections

In building up the quantification lattice, we need to take account of the fact that there are two ways of specifying parts of a designation-class. We may either consider the class as being partitioned (which is the primary meaning of the English words used in (9.1), but not specifically of the terms which they there represent); or we can think of subclasses being built up from the elements. The quantification lattice has corresponding parts, with the respective upper bounds "possibly intact part" and "possibly empty set", as well as a part where both processes interact.

These two terms (neither of which is specific enough to attract any particular attention in most languages) stand at the head of the lattice, immediately followed by the upper row of terms from (9.1); most of the rest of the quantification terms are interposed between the lower row of (9.1) and the empty designation. This part at first sight seems rather complicated, as it is set out in (9.2). It lacks the relative symmetry seen in the identification lattice and still more in the lattice of the case system. This is largely due to its including the numerals. Notwithstanding that the quantification lattice is 'closed' (in one sense of the term), it is, unlike any of the other closed categories, actually infinite, since the numeral system has no limit. I have indicated this feature by the use of a special representation for the arcs concerned.

It is not, however, the infinity of the numerals which causes the complication, so much as the existence of four different series of numerals by which one may select from a possibly larger designation-class. There are, to start with the widest designations, a series exemplified by the phrase "two of" in "*//$_{13}$ **Two** of the /books I /**not**iced were //$_{1}$ written by him/**self**.*"; though admittedly in perhaps most contexts "two of" means precisely two, I can find no better way of indicating the use of numerals as *exemplifying* a possibly larger class, but in the diagram (9.2) I have written them "2 etc." to avoid confusion. More precisely one can say "two or more"; this form is rather pedantic, as is the complementary "at most two", but both are useful at times. The third level of precision is attained by citing a specified range, such as "two or three"—though this particular expression is current in English for any small number, which is not what is intended here. The limit is reached in what is perhaps the commonest type of numeral, which simply states the number, as "two" for example. There is a widespread tendency for terms with narrow designations to be commoner than those with wide ones, and a corresponding tendency for them to be used where a wider designation is really what is meant. This is a systematic confusion, by no means confined to quantification; it helps language to function, but hinders those who seek to systematize it.

One quantification term which I have not included is "few". As the complement of "many" it simply serves to deny a rhema containing that term; but in the vaguer sense, "a few", it represents a designation inferrable with progressively less plausibility from 2, 3, 4, . . . This term can be located from general inferential principles in the sublattice headed by "RANGE" in (9.2), but within this sublattice it has no precise position. Its inferential capacities are wholly determined by the context in which it occurs, and it comes nearer than any other phrase or expression I have come across to defeating the assumptions of the theory. Its function is evidently to confine attention to the

Explanation of conventions used in Fig. (9.2):

Abbreviations for Lattice Elements

Bold italic type = the formal quantifications (see (9.1))
CAPITALS = upper bounds of sublattices associated with modifications of the inference relations
(words in brackets) describe quantifications having no simple expression in English

AIA — all if any (i.e. either all of or none of)
All — all (as formal quantification); always
all — all the
ALS — at least some; the unmarked positive quantification
am1, etc. — at most 1, etc.; numerals with upper bound
hol — whole of; one whole item
ltl — little of
mch — much of
mny — many (not 'many of', which is negation of 'few')
NAl — not all
non — complement of the lexical element
OSo — only some
pll — plural, exclusive of dual
plu — plural, inclusive of dual
Prh — perhaps; perhaps some
sev — several but not necessarily very many
som — some of
1, etc. — singular number
2, etc. — dual number
3, etc., etc. — particular numbers, not implying a complete set
1 om, etc. — at least 1, etc.; numerals with lower bound
$\frac{1}{2}, \frac{1}{3}, \ldots$ — particular fractions
1–2, etc. — specified ranges of numerals, describing complete sets
1, etc. — exact numerals, describing complete sets.

——————— unbroken arcs denote immediate inclusions
— — — — broken arcs denote inclusions inferable by transitivity
(triple line) stands for an infinite set of arcs of ordinal ω
(thick line) stands for single arcs of the formal quantification lattice
(thin line) stands for other single arcs

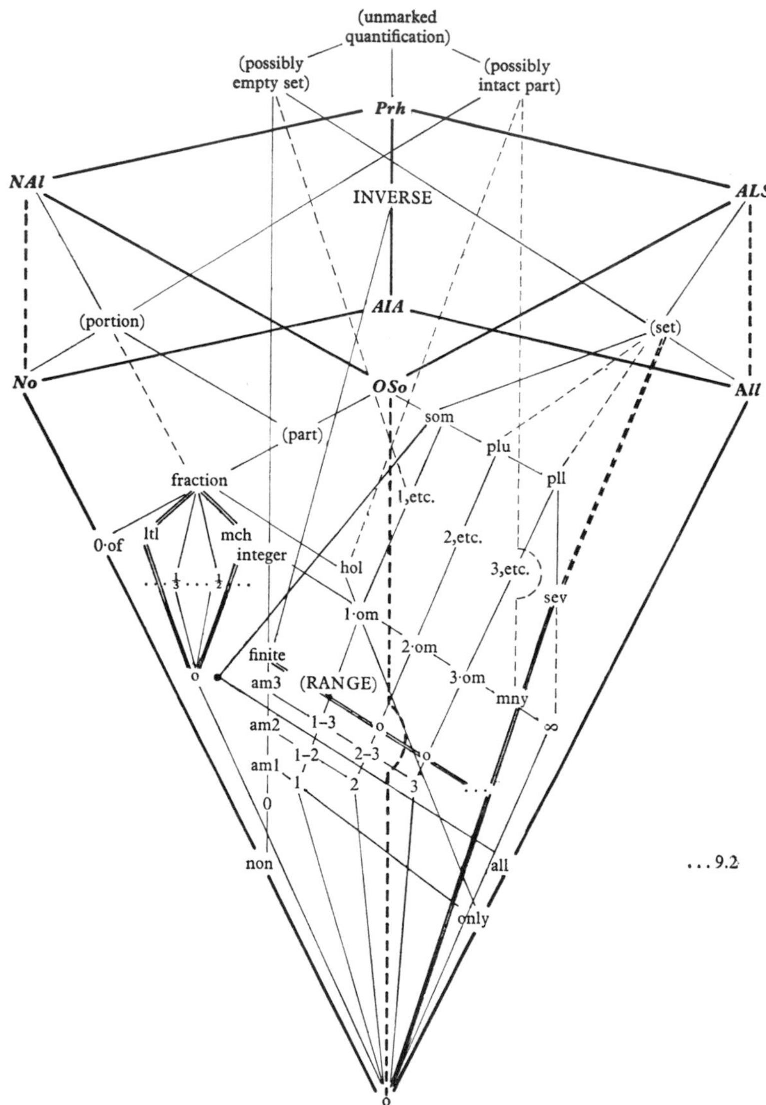

. . . 9.2

The Quantification Lattice

more manageable moiety of an infinite system, and its exceptional irreducibility is a by-product of the potential infiniteness of the quantification system. That this should cause trouble is not very surprising, though nevertheless a blemish in the theory.

Parallel to the numerals, though without any inferential connections with them, there is a subsystem concerning fractions. These terms are of low frequency in use compared with the numerals, but are represented in all languages and need to be included.

9.3. Examples of Inferences among Quantifications

The following examples, selected to show the inferences implied in (9.2) actually working in rhemata, do not include any of the formal quantifications; there will be plenty of those in the rest of this chapter. Some of the 'inferences' will be found more true than useful; they are inserted to justify the structure of the lattice rather than to exemplify how people think. It is in general the case that the kind of inference which involves replacing a stated quantification by a vaguer one is not one that springs to mind in conversation. This is equally true of the other closed categories also; these are not terms which we naturally question or think about at all, and we normally don't think of them as subject to this kind of manipulation. But it does not follow that such inferences are impossible, still less that once pointed out they would be rejected, but they do have a comical quality about them which seems connected with the relative semantic 'emptiness' of the words used to express them.

My first example is "$//_{1}$ ∧ *He's /got at /**least** /three /horses.*" From this we can infer correctly that he has three or so horses, that he has two horses, that he has some horses, that he has a whole horse. We may not infer that he has half a horse, nor (without additional information, widely known though it is) that he has a finite set of horses. We may also infer that he has perhaps got horses; but the further particularity involved in saying that he's got perhaps four horses is not a valid inference, though it *is* a likely comment on the utterance as given.

Next, consider "$//_{1}$ ∧ *At /most /**two** of us'll be /coming.*". This can be inferred from "*At most two people will be coming*", but not conversely; on the other hand it allows the inference that at most two of the girls will be coming. The element "am2", being included in (INVERSE), reverses the inclusion-relations between (*people*), (*us*), and (*girls*). On the other hand it does allow the inference that at most three of us will come, but *not* that all of us (nor that not all of us) will; the inversion only applies to parts of the node subalgebra *outside* the quantification lattice.

Thirdly, "*//₄ ∧ She at/tended /**two** or //₁ at most /**three** //₁ bi/**ology** /lectures.*" permits the inference that she attended at least two lectures, and also some lectures, both of which are within the quantification lattice. But we can't infer that she attended two or three lectures of all kinds, because the element "2–3" is included in (RANGE), and this *also* prevents the inference that she attended two or three genetics lectures, because she might have gone to none of those.

As a last example, let us consider "*//₄Joe /**didnt** /fly here //₁ after /**all**.*". The negation here represents a complementation, that is, that Joe came by *non*-aerial transport. As seen from the position assigned to the element "non" in (9.2), this allows, though it hardly invites, such reflections as that Joe came by at most three flights. But "non" is also one of the inverting quantifications, and this is borne out by the correctness of the inference that Joe didn't come in a Jumbo Jet (though (*aerial transport*) ≧ (*jumbo jet*)), and the futility of the reverse inferential relation with "*//₁ ∧ He /must have /come by /**bike**.*" (though (*powered transport*) ≧ (*aerial transport*)). The element "non" is a confusing one, as these examples show, and its place in the quantification system might be questioned. But the fact that it corresponds to a type of negation which all languages can express (though usually without clear distinction from other types)—and particularly the fact that unless it is represented by a whole set of complementary designation-classes in the lexical lattice it induces inversion as otherwise only quantifications do—makes this the most convenient treatment of it.

9.4. Four Modes of Quantification

The examples given above introduce us to the effects of certain quantifications on the inferential relations of their accompanying lexical terms, already mentioned in §8.4. These, however, are only part of the classification of quantifications on this count; I shall here set out the rest of this scheme.

The largest and most frequent class is that of *direct* quantifications. These include "*NAI*", "*ALS*", and the whole lower ideal of "*OSo*". If the quantification term of a node label belongs to this class, inference proceeds in the normal manner. The class can be specified as those quantifications which are in *either* ideal of "*OSo*" but in *neither* ideal of "INVERSE". This class is then the first and simplest *mode* of quantification.

The second 'mode' comprises inverse quantifications—those in the lower ideal of "INVERSE". As we have just seen, these have the property that they invert the inference relations otherwise obtaining in respect of the lexical terms which they accompany, and also of the other closed categories of identification and case. This does not involve any inconsistency with the principle that inferences depend on inclusion of designation-classes. The designation of a word such as "*chair*" does not consist of all and only those objects called 'chairs', but only those which form part of the context of a speech act (or a potential speech act, such as a thought to which utterance is refused). That is, the designation-class is the intersection of the class of 'chairs' and the class of 'speech context items'. In the same way, the designation of the phrase "*at most two chairs*" is in a one-one relation with the class of contexts in which such a set of chairs is involved. This class is included among those in which one or no chairs are mentioned, and in particular all contexts involving at most two pieces of furniture; and in its turn includes the class of contexts involving at most two arm-chairs. As the reference to 'chairs' is common to all, the designation of "*at most two chairs*" shares the same inclusions, and justifies the inferences involved.

These two modes of quantification, direct and inverse, generate two more; those which belong to the lower ideal of both "INVERSE" and "*OSo*", that is, which are in the lower ideal of "RANGE", may be called *exact* quantifications. Their characteristic is that they forbid any inference which involves altering the lexical term associated with them, unless the quantification is also loosened up. Thus, from "*Three craftsmen were working*" we can infer neither that "*three people were working*" (for there may have been more), nor that "*three potters were working*" (for there may have been less). On the other hand, we can infer that at least three people were working, and that at most three potters were working, for in both these cases the quantification is removed from the exact mode.

Finally, there is one element of the lattice (9.2) which is in the upper ideal of both "INVERSE" and "*OSo*", namely "*Prh*";

this may be called the *free* quantification, and allows inferences obtained by substituting for the accompanying lexical term any other in either its upper or its lower ideal in the lexical lattice. Examples are, however, apt to be trivial. From "//$_1$ *Perhaps* /*Trish is up*/***stairs***." we may infer either that she may be in the bath or that she may be in the house. But because "perhaps" inevitably invites mere speculation we are apt to entertain notions which are not really inferences at all, such as that she may be in the garage.

9.5. Illustrating Lattice Inversion

It is necessary, before I go on, to present an illustration of the kind of diagrams actually generated by the incorporation of inverse quantifications into the completed node algebra. For this purpose, I shall construct the PI-product of the formal quantification sublattice (the elements underlined in (9.2)) with the following small sublattice concerning sheep:

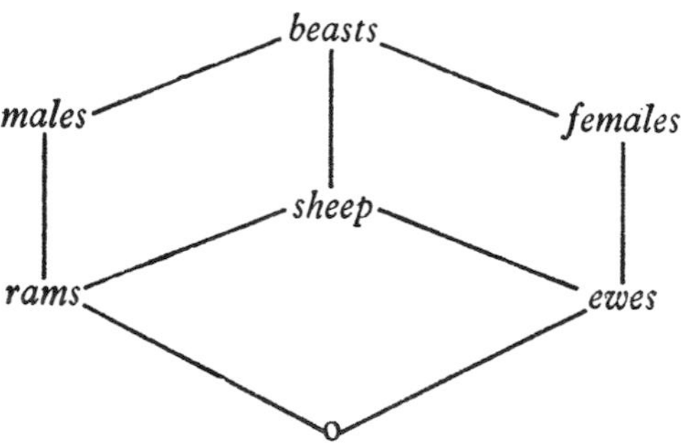

. . . 9.3

The PI-product takes up a lot of room, and is shown on page 201.

It will be seen from (9.4) that the sublattices corresponding to the quantification terms "not all", "at least some", and "only some" are isomorphic with the diagram shown above as (9.3), omitting the empty lower bound in each case. But corresponding to the inverse quantifications "all", "no", and "all if any" are, on the contrary, inverted relative to (9.3). The validity of particular inferences obtained from (9.4) can readily be checked, if it is borne in mind that the diagram is oriented so that inferences which do not involve inverse quantification go *up* the lattice. So

The Quantification Lattice

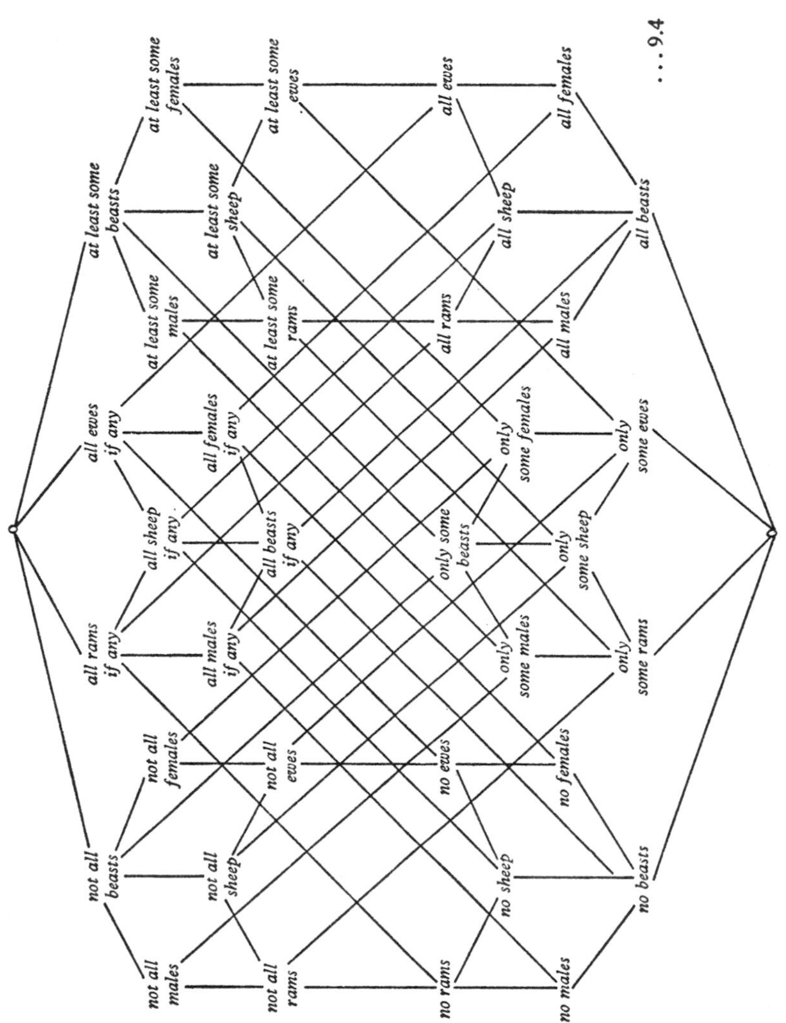

of course do the others but only because the inversion has been explicitly performed in constructing (9.4). I am *not* recommending the use of such constructions as a computational device; it is a great deal simpler to perform the inversion at a late stage in the programme.

For example, we can see that "*Only some rams have horns*" ⊃ "*not all sheep have horns*"; that "*no females have horns*" ⊃ "*if any ewes have horns all have*"; and that "*all rams have horns*" ⊃ "*at least some beasts have horns*". These three inferences illustrate, respectively, proceeding from a direct sublattice to another direct sublattice; from an inverted to an inverted one; and from an inverted to a direct one. The lattice allows no inferences from a direct sublattice to an inverted one; this is because, in Aristotelian terms, one can't deduce a general from a particular.

It should be noted that the lattice (9.4) is based on one-to-one inferences. This means that it can't be used, as one might perhaps expect, for syllogistic algorithms. For example, a predicate which applies both to "no ewes" and to "only some sheep" must apply to "at least some rams"; but there is no lattice algorithm which will derive this result from (9.4). To do this, one needs to know also that all sheep are either ewes or rams; this knowledge is a separate contribution to the context, and needs a separate rhema to be incorporated into the context rehearsal. We have here a general characteristic of rhematic as opposed to logic; only the presence or absence of an inclusion between two elements can be directly utilized to derive inferences. Any other property of the lattice has to be mobilized indirectly, by being stated in rhemata and in that form incorporated into a context rehearsal.

This distinction parallels the psychological distinction which people tend unconsciously to make between 'intuitive' knowledge, which seems to be immediately available, and 'verbal' knowledge which we have no access to in the absence of some measure of verbalization. I do not claim that there is any exact correspondence here; but the agreement is sufficient to suggest that the one may underlie the other. Certainly it is hard to see how there can fail to be a difference in ease of access between the two kinds of knowledge, if my theory is reflected at all in the organization of our memory.

9.6. Secondary Quantification

It will be conceded by most native speakers of English, that the two utterances "$||_1$ ***All*** */dogs /bark at* $||_4$ *least /**sometimes**.*" and "$||_1$ ***No*** */dogs* $||_4$ ***never*** */bark.*" are in normal contexts equivalent; that is, they carry the same set of inferences. Since, however, they seem to carry quite different quantifications of identical lexical items, it must follow that the variety of distinctions which can be made among sentences with two terms carrying marked quantification is less than the square of the number of distinct one-term quantifications. That is to say, the set of possible combinations of quantifications within one simple rhema is not represented by the self-product of the single quantification lattice—which one might have expected—but by a lattice smaller than this.

In pursuing this line of thought I shall consider only the formal quantifications shown in (9.1); not only is the self-product of (9.2) itself impossibly complicated, but the effects of dual quantification on inference are confined to the formal quantifications. The lattice which actually represents the inclusion-relations among (otherwise similar) sentences carrying two formal quantifications I shall call the *secondary* quantification lattice; in this section I shall consider what form it has.

The full self-product of (9.1) has 64 elements. The reason why some of these turn out to be identical with others lies in two well-known principles of elementary logic. First, we know that if $A \supset B$, then *not-B* $\supset$ *not-A*; and second, if a predicate ***P*** is true of a given set of objects, then *not-P* can be asserted of *at most* the complementary set. The first principle can be illustrated by the pair of sentences:

At least some dogs always bark $\supset$ *Not all dogs never bark.*
A B not-B not-A

. . . 9.5

The second principle is similarly illustrated by:

No dogs never bark ≡
All dogs at least sometimes bark $\supset$ *Not all dogs never bark*
A P A* not-P

. . . 9.6

To apply these principles, we need to know which of the formal quantifications are related to each other as negatives, and which as complements. The negatives are fairly obvious with the help of suitable verbalizations; the complements refer to the sets *excluded* by each quantifier. The lattice complement of each term in (9.1) represents its negative, however, *not* its complement as that term is used here. Here is a table of the correspondences:

	Quantification	*its Negative*	*its Complement*
0	perhaps some	[empty]	perhaps some
1	at least some	none (≡ not even some)	not all
2	all if any	only some (≡ not all, even if any)	all if any
3	all	not all	none
4	not all	all	at least some
5	only some	all if any (≡ not merely some)	only some
6	none	at least some	all
7	[empty]	perhaps some	[empty]

. . . 9.7

In setting out the reduced secondary quantification lattice which results from these relationships, I have represented each combination of possible quantifications by a pair of numbers, using the coding given in the left-hand column of (9.7). The heavy lines connect the elements which have "1" (at least some, the unmarked quantification) as their second term; it will be seen that these form a lattice isomorphic with (9.1). Each of the self-complementary terms, 0, 2, 5, generates a set of six identical secondary quantifications because each of them is too imprecise to rule out any term as the second term. For the rest they combine in pairs; thus, "43 ≡ 14" means that "*not all dogs always bark*" is identical with "*at least some dogs dont always bark*". As usual, the bottom element of the lattice represents the empty quantification, which in this case includes any sentence with either term empty in respect of quantification.

It must be emphasized that (9.8) contains no information not already implicit in (9.1), from which it is generated. Its use is simply as a convenient summary of the quantification inferences subsisting between rhemata or sub-rhemata containing two formal quantifiers at different nodes.

The Quantification Lattice

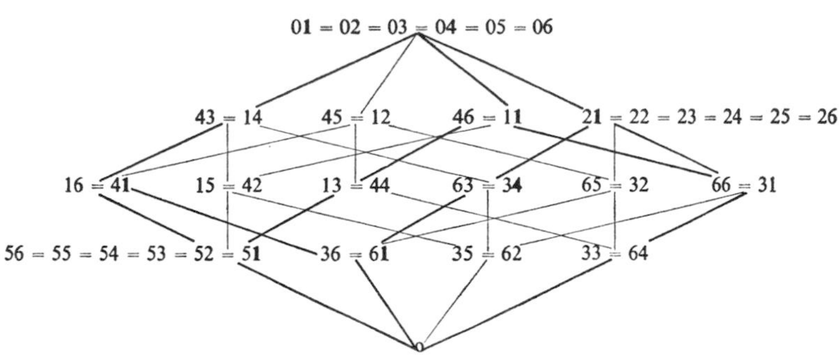

. . . 9.8

9.7. Tertiary Quantification

There is no reason in principle why, since a rhema may have any number of components, it might not involve more than two formal quantifications on different terms. One would suppose that to describe the varieties of quantification of such rhemata, a lattice analogous to (9.8), but more complicated, would be required. And indeed if it were logic we were studying this would be so. But there is a good reason why this complication need not be pursued.

The purpose which guides our development of the node subalgebra is to provide a conceptual basis for describing and predicting what people actually understand of what is said, and how they can make themselves understood by others. Although we seem able to handle certain kinds of complexity with amazing fluency, in other directions we falter before the difficulties really start; for we are apt to judge what is 'complicated' by what we are used to seeing discussed. It is hard to make a rhema structure such as say (7.6.3) seem other than complex, but it represents a simple enough utterance; it is equally hard to analyse the bafflement which many people feel for simple arithmetic, such as is embodied in "If a hen and a half lays an egg and a half in a day and a half, how many hens lay two eggs a day?". The fact is that ordinary natural language understanding breaks down for most people in certain relatively simple contexts; and these are, for this reason, outside the scope of rhematic. It is here that specially learned modes of thinking are required to take over, such as logic and more generally mathematics. This fact furnishes a useful limitation on the delicacy with which we have to pursue our enquiries.

One such case, where we may refrain from further investigation for this reason, arises where more than two formal quantifications occur together in one rhema. Utterances of this kind have, in society at large, too small a chance of being correctly understood to be acceptable. Even the simplest case, a triple negative, which careless writers sometimes fall into, will not be misunderstood only if not read at normal speed, if you see what I mean. Tertiary quantification is therefore a barren subject for us, even if it may have interest for the psycholinguists.

9.8. Quantification at Intermediate Nodes

So far I have considered only the effect of quantifications on terminal nodes of rhemata, those which designate actual referents. We must expect all our closed categories to have some role on other nodes as well, even if the terms usable there are only a subset of those available at terminal nodes. Non-terminal nodes, as I have already remarked, can be classified into two types; one type denote predications, and the other determinations. The first govern subordinate clauses in surface structure, the second normally noun-groups. Determinative intermediate nodes present no special problems, except that their presence makes possible the attaching of more than one quantification to a given lexigen.

Consider the utterance “$//_1 \wedge$ *She /wore /two /**flowers** she'd* $//_{-1}$ *picked by the /**road**side.*”. This belongs in a context where she had been picking flowers by the roadside, and then selected two to put in her hair. First of all the flowers are quantified merely as ‘some’ or ‘plural’, and then these find their place in a higher-ranking structure where they are re-quantified as “two”. The result is the rhema:

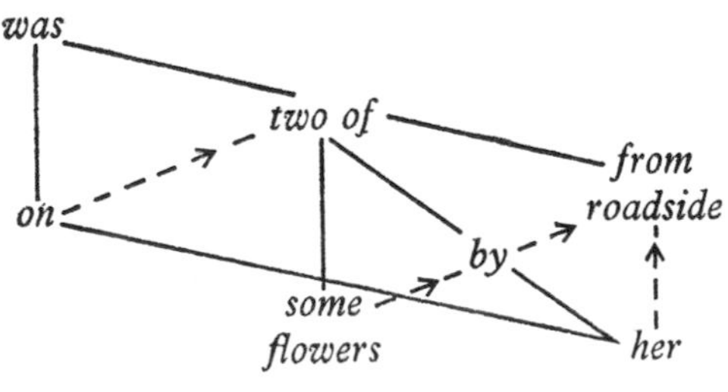

. . . 9.9

It is clear that this kind of thing can very easily happen, and is unlikely to cause much trouble, except when formal quantifications are involved; but notice that if two such quantifications are linked by a designatory arc, rather than an accessory one, they do not normally involve the secondary quantification lattice, since each operates in a different sub-rhema. It is of more interest to consider what quantifications can be applied at predicative nodes, and what significance can be attached to them.

As I have already made free use of expressions, normally referring to time, as more or less equivalent to timeless quantifications, identifying, for instance, "all" with "always", in order to generate plausible English sentences, it will be clear that in this language at least the quantification of a predicative node can refer to *how often* the predication it heads is true. If we weaken this to saying only on what subset of occasions it applies, we have a formulation which is likely to be valid for all languages. For the experience that a sentence can be true in some contexts and not in others is elemental and presumably universal. In this way one can indicate, by quantification terms, how frequently something happens, or what is the probability of its being the case. Thus "$//_4$ ∧ *She can* |***gen****erally be con*|*tacted in* $//_1$ *Kathman****du****.*" could be represented as:

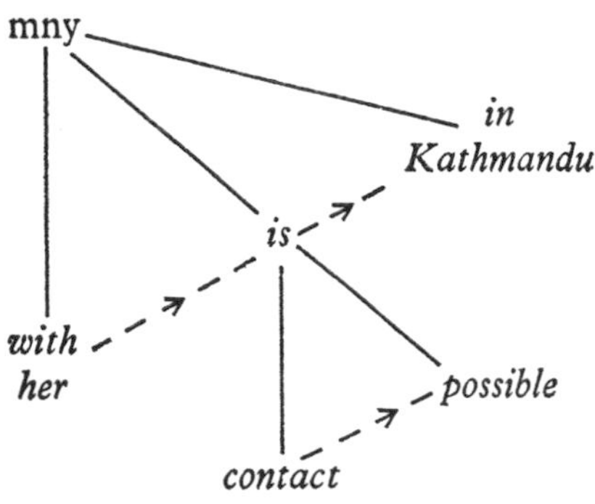

. . . 9.10

But equally, it should be noticed, we could have interchanged the nodes "*mny*" with "*is*" to produce the same effect.

This raises an important question, which will be taken up again in Chapter XV, concerning the manipulation of quantifications at non-terminal nodes; in general, there are various places they can be put with no change in the meaning of the rhema. This arises especially with negations, and I shall give a further example to show how many different things can be meant by 'negation' of a sentence, since this is a point which seems to have been too often overlooked. In each of the following rhema structures, the abbreviation *N* marks an alternative position of the negation "not" (coded *No* in (9.2)), while *not* stands for an occurrence of the same element with no alternatives.

The utterance whose negation is in question is "$//_1$ v *Our /baby's /got /**measles**.*". The negations are all expressed in the words "*Our baby hasn't got measles.*" and the example is chosen so that only the intonation needs to be varied. Under each graph is given tone and tonic:

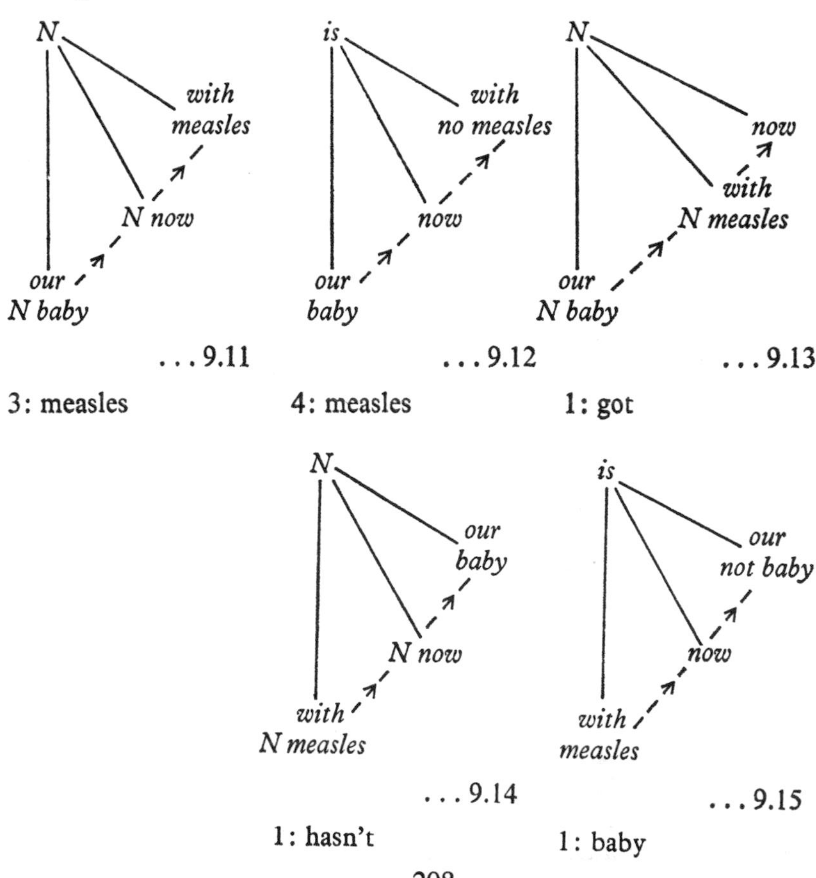

. . . 9.11 — 3: measles

. . . 9.12 — 4: measles

. . . 9.13 — 1: got

. . . 9.14 — 1: hasn't

. . . 9.15 — 1: baby

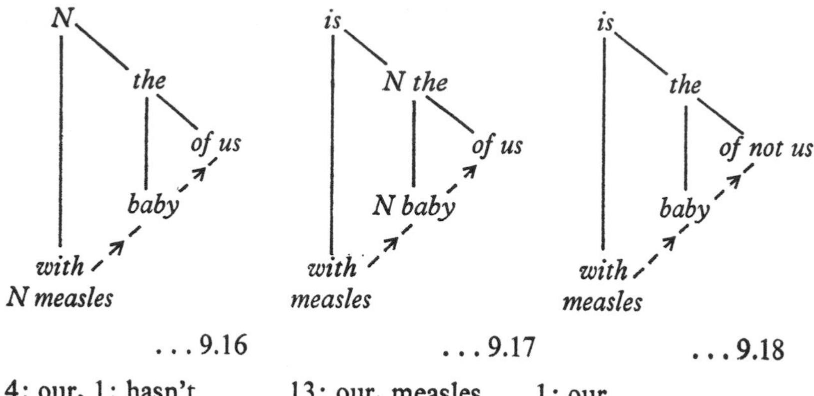

. . . 9.16 . . . 9.17 . . . 9.18

4: our, 1: hasn't 13: our, measles 1: our

In most cases the sincerity of the expression is tolerably unambiguous, though the clarity of the distinction between the last two is perhaps questionable. The distinctions between the various negations can be made plain by indications of the implied context, as follows:

11. *//$_3$ ∧ Our /baby /hasn't got /**measles**.* [as you supposed]
12. *//$_4$ ∧ Our /baby /hasn't got /**measles**.* [it's chicken-pox]
13. *//$_1$ ∧ Our /baby /hasn't /**got** /measles.* [but it mayn't be long now]
14. *//$_1$ ∧ Our /baby /**hasn't** got /measles.* [as we had feared]
15. *//$_1$ ∧ Our /**baby** /hasn't got /measles.* [it's Jemima]
16. *//$_4$ **Our** /baby //$_1$ **hasn't** got /measles.* [but there's a lot around]
17. *//$_{13}$ **Our** /baby /hasn't got /**measles**.* [whatever made you think so?]
18. *//$_1$ **Our** /baby /hasn't got /measles.* [it's the one next door]

It may be worth noting that the behaviour of the 'free quantification' is closely parallel to this: "*//$_5$ Perhaps /**our** /baby's got /measles*".

9.9. A Comment on Previous Studies of Quantification

No reference has been made, in the course of the foregoing discussion, to the work of the many linguists, especially of the generative grammar school, who have paid attention to the topic of quantification. This has seemed unavoidable, since the questions asked within the context of generative grammar have so little in common with what appears pertinent here, where we are concerned with what inferences can be derived, rather than with how surface sentences are generated. To be able to answer questions of the latter type, one needs to know (a) what is the rhema to be expressed, (b) what devices (transformations, rewrite rules, etc.) are available in the target language for expressing quantifications, (c) where each node of the rhema appears in the finished sentence structure, and (d) what quantifying transformations are available in each place. One should add also that the force of any quantification is strongly dependent as a rule on the context, without attention to which these questions may get wrong answers. Of these questions, I am here concerned only with (a).

In the light of this difference in viewpoint it is difficult to comment at all usefully on what has been said in the literature about quantification. Take, for instance, the proposal that this is one of the categories open to expression in an imaginary framing-clause; this opinion is argued for instance by Carden,[14] who represents quantifiers by special 'verbs' in such clauses.* Of course, this proposal could be implemented in a generative programme, provided its input is not required to be in rhematical form, and might well give satisfactory results. But it sheds little light on the inferential relations involved, nor does it come anywhere near dealing with the wide variety of forms typified by (9.11–18) which differ in their effects on the listener in just this point.

Conversely, my notation affords no opportunity to ask at what stage in a generative procedure any given quantifier has to be taken into account. They come attached to their nodes, and it makes no sense to remove them, except within the narrow scope of the rules of equivalent quantification (I3 in §14.6) which owe more to Aristotle than to Chomsky. So far as I have been able to learn, no previous author† has undertaken systematically to study the terms of quantification as an inferential system, and build this system into a wider one competent to deal with a

* It is worth mentioning here that there is no formal objection to representing the four terms of each node label as *separate nodes* of the rhema graph (in a fixed conventional order); this would turn each node into a sort of 'clause', and go some way towards the type of analysis favoured by many linguists besides Carden.

† That is, among linguists. The topic is of course basic to logic.

usefully wide range of natural language inferences. On this narrow front, at least, there seems little in the way of previous work to discuss.

The same remarks go for the other closed categories as well. The contributions of generative grammarians to identifications, for example, though numerous and for their own purposes insightful, have little in them that can be put to use in constructing an inferential system. The essential difficulty is that the 'deep structures' used for such work are not 'deep' enough to figure in this kind of system; they fall a long way short of being elements in an algebra. Work on case, though more relevant for my purposes, is nevertheless inappropriately oriented. In all this field, I am asking questions which have virtually not been asked before, at any rate not of the utterances of natural language. These questions need to be asked, and even if the answers I suggest may not be correct, it will be found useful to have made the attempt.

CHAPTER X

The Identification Lattice

The second of the closed categories to which I devote special attention on account of their effects on inference is that of identification. The terms of identification serve to relate the accompanying lexical items to the context. While quantification terms help to answer questions of 'how much' or 'how many', those of identification answer 'which'. In surface grammars, these terms are most frequently conveyed by demonstrative or indefinite pronouns. In English these are separate lexemes, and relatively easy to find and catalogue; but as in every language there are gaps in the system, and the total number of possible terms exceeds those actually exemplified in any given language.

10.1. Survey of Subcategories

There are at least three different questions which might be asked about the relation of a given lexigen to a given context in which it occurs; each of these generates a separate sub-category, the identification lattice being a suitably pruned derivative of their direct product. The first question is whether the identity of the item is known to the speaker or the listener or both, and the corresponding subcategory is that of *definition.* Next, items can be distinguished according to the order in which they occur to the speaker, or are introduced into the conversation, giving the subcategory of *seniority.* Lastly, we may ask whether an item belongs in a context by nature or by animadversion, and in the former case whether it is related or not to the locus of the conversation, these questions giving us the subcategory of *provenance.*

10.1.1. 'Definition': Something which has been identified by neither the speaker nor the listener is not within the speech situation at all. There are therefore three terms in the subcategory. For the listener, the class of things already identified is included in the larger class of things which might be identified, so that 'unknown' ≧ 'known'. The speaker cannot refer at all to what is unknown to him, except to ask what it is; and this is appropriate only if the listener knows. There is therefore a term of interrogation, which, as we saw in dealing with questions in Chapter VII, must be represented as included in all its possible answers.

The lattice representing the subcategory of definition is thus

Known to Sp., not to Li.	0	*indefinite*	
	|		
Known to Sp. and to Li.	1	*definite*	. . . 10.1
	|		
Not known to Sp.	3	*interrogative*	

Of these terms the 'definite', as might be expected, is by far the most productive; there are a smaller number of 'indefinite' terms, rather poorly reflected in actual lexemes; and still fewer interrogatives.

10.1.2. 'Seniority' Under this subcategory we distinguish between earlier- and later-mentioned representatives of otherwise similar designation-classes. The essential distinction is that between 'one' and 'another', also conveyed by 'the former' and 'the latter'. In natural language the terms are limited to two, but writing allows a wider range, represented usually by the ordinal numbers (the first two of which are in many languages drawn from the demonstrative pronouns). The use of nonce-markers, such as A,B,C, and the like is also an attempt to widen the subcategory of seniority. The structure contributed to the general identification lattice is, however, simply

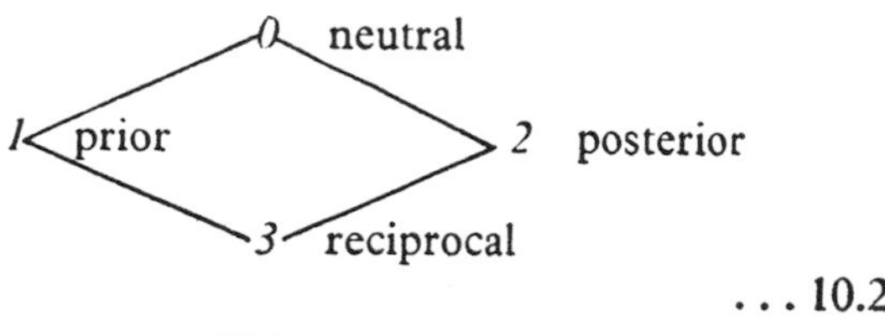

. . . 10.2

The last term 'reciprocal' arises when, in plurals, items previously distinguished are brought together, either in parallel (respectively) or in complementation (each other). The prior–posterior distinction is not confined, as might be supposed, to things introduced into a context only by specific mention of them; it is also inherent in at least one pair of contextual isolates, namely 'me' and 'you' respectively. The speaker, in fact, is 'prior' in his own eyes to all others, and the listener is relative to the speaker 'posterior', meaning introduced later, by the act of addressing him.

10.1.3. 'Provenance': This is a more complex category which involves two distinct questions, each of which generates a four-element lattice. The first distinguishes between items which belong by nature to the context, which are *constitutive* of it, independedently of the course of the particular conversation, and those which form part of their context only through being mentioned or adverted to, which I call *adductive* items. There are also *common* items which are both constitutive and also specially mentioned; in fact, specifically adductive terms are few in number and low in frequency. There are no terms in actual use which are neutral in this subcategory, but the corresponding lattice elements are needed to complete the identification lattice as a formal system, and occur in the node labels of most predications.

The second question arises only in connection with constitutive items, and relates to placing them in relation to a division of the context which seems to be a strict universal of language, namely into *proximate* and *remote* moieties. The former include the speaker and the listener and things felt as intimately related to them and thus 'here', while the remote moiety of the context includes all that is not so related and thus 'there'. Here there are both neutral and common terms also, the former for things not subject to the context dichotomy or at least not marked as such (this is a small class of terms) while the latter are confined to plurals, particularly the 'exclusive' plurals of the first and second personal pronouns denoting 'I and they' or 'you and they'. The resulting system of four terms is repeated for constitutive and for common terms, giving the following lattice for the subcategory of provenance:

The Identification Lattice

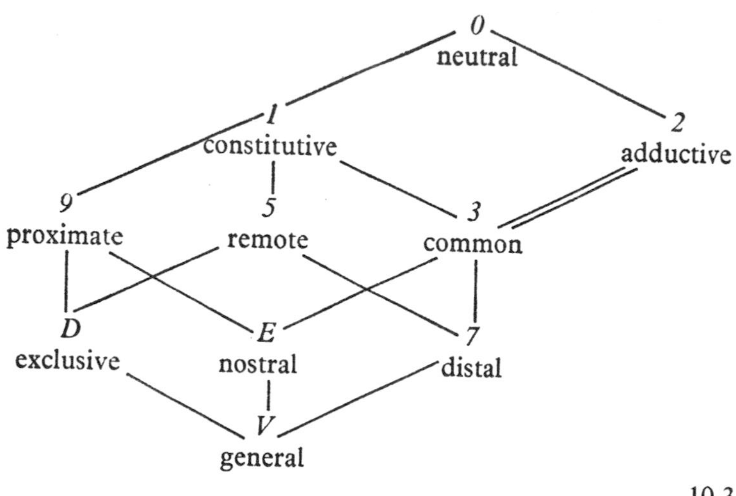

. . . 10.3

The numerical codes attached to the elements of the lattices (10.1–3) are used again in the diagram (10.4) setting out the completed identification lattice; they are there given in reverse order, first the code from (10.3) for provenance, second that from (10.2) for seniority, and last that from (10.1) for definition. For want of enough numerals, the letters D,E,V are used to complete the codes in (10.3).

10.2. The Identification Lattice

This is represented in (10.4), where I have included all elements which are either required to complete the lattice or correspond to actual identifications for which some language has a corresponding term or morpheme. A considerable number have no simple English equivalents, and this is likely to be a common situation. Despite its relative complexity the information contained in the identification lattice is not very important, except for defining the personal pronouns which are found in all languages; there is a strong tendency for identification terms to acquire secondary meanings, for example as pejoratives, or to be used illogically (why should "*each other*" mean what it does?). And, as is well known, many languages, especially those with SOV word order, have no definite article; though it is noteworthy that while there are many instances of languages which have evolved such an identifier in the course of their history there is no proven instance of its having been lost (a British dialect of the Hull area has a phonologically null pronunciation for 'the', but the indefinite article survives, and the dialect itself may not have a long life).

The lattice (10.4) is based on the direct product of (10.1–3),

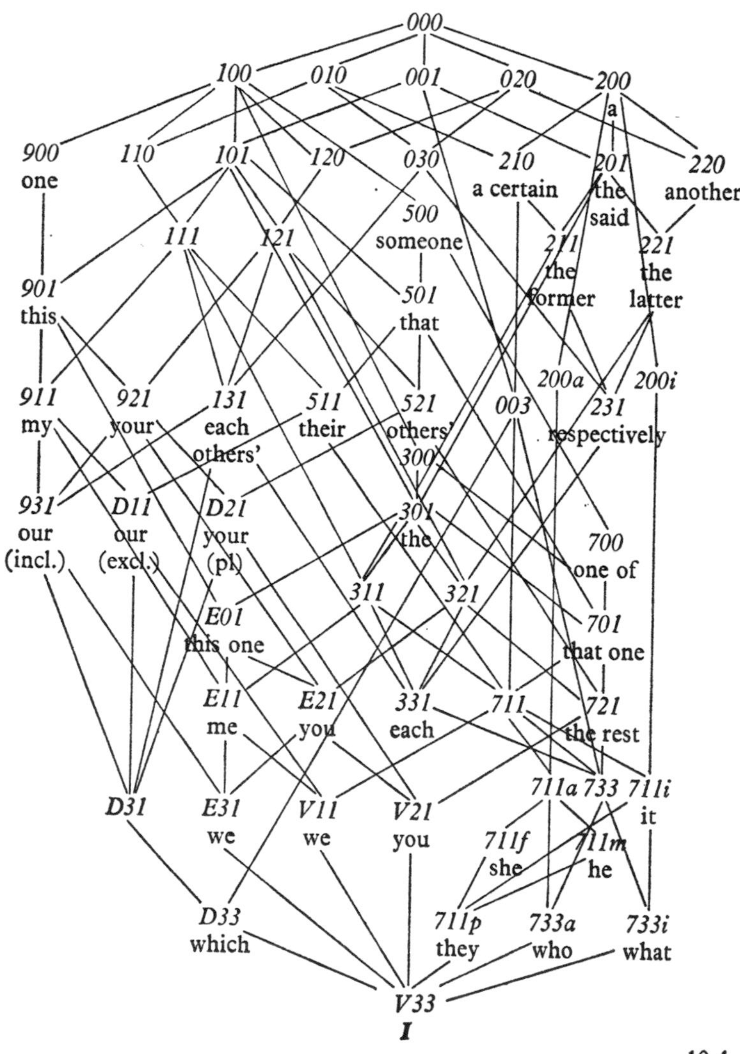

. . . 10.4

Description of Unmarked Elements

000	unmarked identification
001	unmarked definite
003	unmarked interrogative
010	prior indefinite
020	posterior indefinite
030	reciprocal indefinite
100	constitutive indefinite article
101	constitutive definite article (contextual "the")
110	constitutive prior indefinite
111	constitutive posterior definite ("*own*"); with null lexis, "*self*"
120	constitutive posterior indefinite
121	constitutive posterior definite; with null lexis, "*partner*"
200a	animate adductive
200i	inanimate adductive
300	common indefinite article
301	common or existential definite article
311	common prior definite
321	common posterior definite (vocative marker)
711	third person pronoun
711a	the same (for animates only)
733	interrogative third person
D31	bilocal inclusive
V33	general interrogative marker

with a large number of deletions. The following points call for some explanation:

1. The pronouns "*one*" and "*someone*" (the latter including "*something*") are attached to the proximate and remote indefinite constitutives; this may seem rather arbitrary, but is based on the idea that most uses of "*one*" as a pronoun tend to include the speaker, while those of "*someone*" do not. Certainly one could equally justify attaching "*one*" to the element 100.
2. The *ideas* of '*self*' and '*partner*' as an elementary contrast are suggested in the notes on (10.4) as appropriate for 111 and 121 respectively; but these *words* do not properly correspond.
3. There are in English three main uses of '*the*' (besides a vast number of finer distinctions), corresponding to the elements 101, 201, and 301. The second I have labelled for greater distinctiveness "*the said*" but it applies to all cases where there is reference to a previous mention of the same lexical item; it is the 'anaphoric' definite article. The element 101 is the 'contextual' definite article, denoting something forming part of the context such as "*the window*" or "*the heat*", irrespective of previous mention. The element 301 is the 'existential' "*the*", as applied for example to "*the sun*" or "*the government*", which belong potentially to *all* contexts and have thus always "been mentioned before". An example of 201 would be "*the lattice*", applied here, after previous discussion, to the diagram (10.4).

4. Personal pronouns have been entered on three levels: First, they appear as possessives (“*my*” etc.); next, the meets of these with the existential “*the*” are identified as the substantive pronouns (cf. Portal[80]) on the grounds that “*me*” = “*my self*”, etc., and that “*you*”, “*me*” and the like are both constitutive of, and adductive in, their context. The third level of pronouns contains special combination which allow inference of terms on the second level. Thus, “*we*” allows inference of “*I*”, and may allow either for “*you*” or “*they*” also, according as the “*we*” is taken as inclusive or exclusive; this distinction is not made in English, and the English “*we*” is identified as *E11* with plural quantifier.

10.3. The Effect of Identification on Inference

This category is less involved in inference than is either quantification or case; but it has nevertheless one important effect aside from the inferential relations represented within (10.4) itself. This is in the information ostensibly conveyed by every definite identification that the referent actually exists. That is, the phrase “*the shirt Kit gave me*” (whatever its focus relations) carries the implication “*Kit gave me a shirt*”. In this section I shall explore some of the ramifications of this effect.

10.3.1. The Definite Presupposition: This type of inference is one of those which has often been included under the term ‘presupposition’. As required by Van Fraassen’s definition[35] both the sentence and its negations (or at least some of them) carry it. It has been discussed in some depth by Katz.[56] In my notation, the utterance “$//_4$ ∧ *I /haven’t /got the /****shirt*** $//_1$ ***Kit*** */gave me.*” expresses the rhema

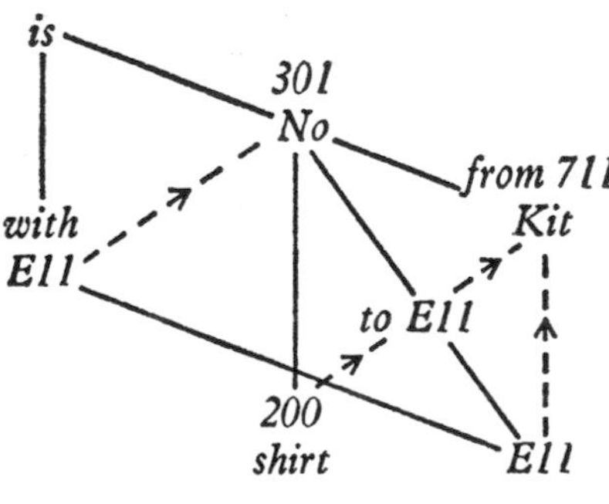

. . . 10.5

But, of course, this allows perfectly well the inference expressed by

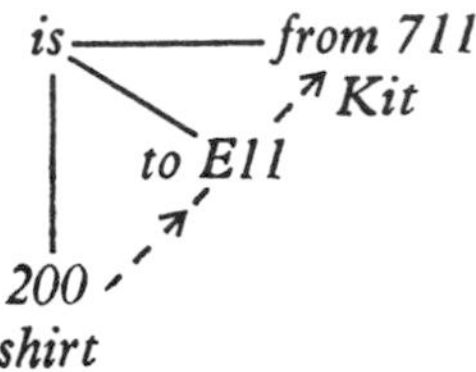

. . . 10.6

obtained by deleting the node label which appears as "301No()" together with the first two nodes of (10.5). The interesting point is that, in general, the occurrence of the negative quantifier "No" in a node label is sufficient to forbid its deletion, unless all its successors are deleted as well. What overrules this is the presence of the identifier "301", the 'existential definite article', which is evidently one of the identifiers possessing the property of shielding a negative from deletion. It raises the question of which identifiers have this property.

10.3.2. Identification of the Shielding Terms: Here again we can usefully resort to the device of a series of closely related utterances which convey slightly different sets of inferences. I have been calling at a friend's house, while they were out, and telling of it later I may say one of the following:

(a) *$||_4$ ∧ I |**didnt** |find an $||_1$ excellent |**cake** $||_{1-}$ made by |**Pam**.*
(b) *$||_1$ ∧ I |didnt |find an |excellent |**cake** $||_1$ made by |**Pam**.*
(c) *$||_1$ ∧ I |didnt |find the |excellent |**cake** $||_1$ made by |**Pam**.*
(d) *$||_1$ ∧ I |didnt |find an |excellent |**cake** that $||_1$ **Pam** had |left.*

Of these, (a) and (d) suggest the continuation "because I didn't know to look", (b) suggests, say, "but a soggy one left by Pete", and (c) might go on "though they'd left it there for me". As for their rhematical forms, these are:

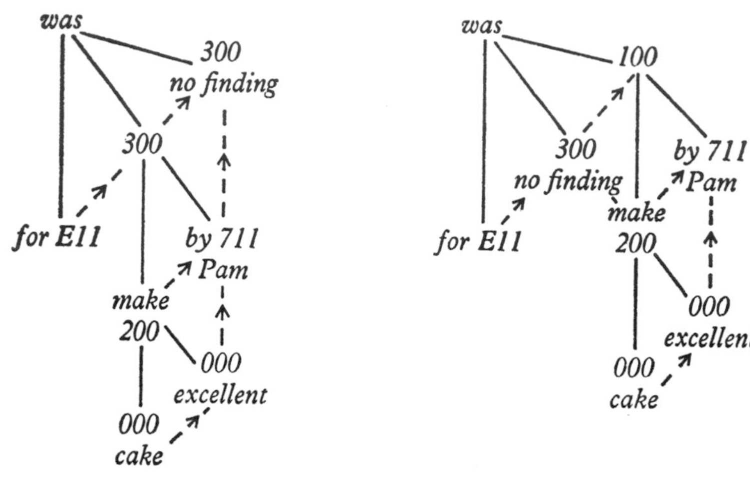

. . . 10.7 . . . 10.8

(10.7) goes for (a), the negated node being in the rheme position and thus subsequent to the subrhema containing 'cake', while (10.8) is the rhema for (b) as it stands, but the identifier 100 at its fourth node must be replaced by the *definite* 101 to give (c) and by the common (i.e. both constitutive *and adductive* 300) to give (d). The implication is that in (b) the "cake" was part of my context albeit not what I'd expected, and therefore constitutive, but it is not marked as adductive, because another cake from the one expected is up for mention instead. In (c) again the "cake" is again not adductive, but it *is* definite, because I know and acknowledge that it existed. In (d) it is again indefinite, but it is now marked as adductive as well as constitutive by the relative pronoun "that" (at least, this is one of the circumstances favouring the non-omission of relative pronouns in colloquial English).

Of the four sentences given, it is clear that all except (b) imply that Pam *had* made an excellent cake, despite the negative main clause. In (a), the effect of the negation is avoided since it follows in the order of the accessory arcs the subordinate clause about the cake. In (b) the negation affects the subordinate clause as well as the main clause, because it precedes it in the accessory arc order. In (c) and (d) the structure is the same as in (b), but in these cases the identifier attached to the initial node of the subordinate clause (and so by indirect designation to the cake) is either definite or adductive, and *both* these classes of identifier effect negative-shielding. That is, the nodes they fall on and their designatory successors are exempted from the blocking of inference which the negative would otherwise entail.

Another question one might ask about these examples is, Does Pam make excellent cakes? She clearly does, except in (b) where the matter is strictly undecidable, since the whole subordinate clause is blocked to inference. But suppose I had said "$//_1 \wedge$ *I've /never /seen an /excellent* ***/cake*** $//_1$ *made by* ***/Pam.***", then I am clearly denying Pam's competence in cake-making. The difference is caused by the strengthened negation, in effect denying the existence of the entity described in the subordinate clause; in (b) the reference is to one occasion only, but here to all possible occasions. This brings us to the next question.

10.3.3. The Interaction of Identification and Quantification: It is well known that puzzles, at least, arise through the combination of identifications such as the definite article with terms of formal quantification. In particular, there is a difference between "*all the*" in the sense of "all of the . . ." and in the sense of "the whole class of . . .". If in each node label each category is represented by one term, this difference clearly cannot be represented by their order, as it is in some surface grammars, for the terms within one label are unordered.

The solution to this problem is inherent in the sublattice shown as (10.1) dealing with definiteness. Here the indefinite term is shown as including the definite, not as alternating with it; that is to say, definite identification is an additional restriction placed on what would otherwise be indefinite. This is the difference between "*all*" and "*all the*". Where the reference is to a whole class, definite identification may serve to specify what class is intended, but does not affect the wholeness. "*All the big cups*" specifies a particular class of "big cups" known to the listener, and is included in the wider designation of "*all big cups*", precisely as "*the*" (001) is included in (000). In such expressions, of course, "*the*" can be replaced by a more specific identification, such as "*our*", with corresponding effect.

There is thus no problem, provided the principles of the theory are followed in combining the lattice elements. Neither is there any trouble with other formal quantifiers such as "*No*" (none of);

the differentiations possible in surface forms in each case involve in no case a contrast, but only alternative designations one including the other.

10.4. Predication and Determination

I have already had occasion to mention the distinction between subrhemata which denote predications and those corresponding to determinative expressions, that is (in surface terms) noun-groups. While it is perhaps obvious that neither quantification nor case terms can help here, it is less clear that it belongs in the category of identification in any genuine sense.

One might almost expect, in view of the sharp difference which from some viewpoints exists between a statement and a term in a statement, which is part of what this distinction is about, that I might advocate a special arc label to indicate it; but, of course, from the more strictly linguistic point of view the difference is not so sharp, since one statement can be a term within another, and any "horse which is white" *is* white, even if it may not be a horse. Moreover, the difference is concerned precisely with the relation of things to their contexts, which is what identification is about, even if in a limiting sense. For a predicative rhema *is*, or at least contributes to, the context, while a determinative rhema designates some constituent *part* of it. We are therefore within the competence of this category.

Let us suppose that Joe says to me "$//_1$ *Stephen's |got a |new |**job**.*". Later I meet someone whom I want to make conversation with, not knowing him too well, and I relay "$//_4$ ***Joe*** *|tells me* $//_1$ ***Stephen's*** *|got a |new |job.*". This expresses the rhema

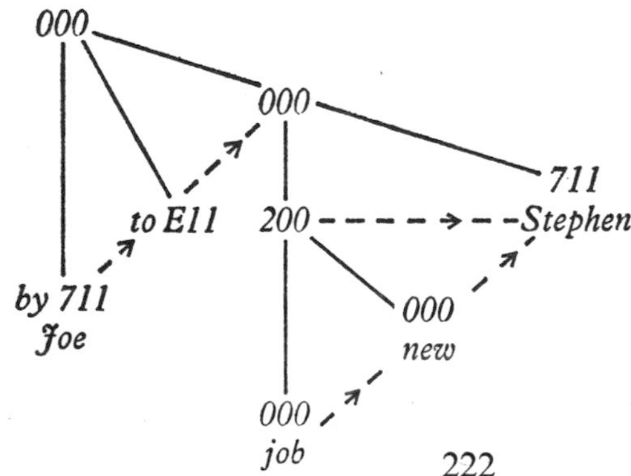

. . . 10.9

There are two predications here, one subordinate to the other. Neither has any mark to warrant its having a marked identification, so both are labelled "000". So also are the nodes for "*new*" and "*job*", whose proper identification is assigned to the determinative node for "*new job*". If, on the other hand, I were to say the like to someone whom I knew knew Stephen, say his wife, then I would make the subordinate predication definite (that is, known to both of us); speaking English, I could not express this point directly, but it would become apparent through my use of a different intonation pattern: "*//$_4$**Joe** /tells me //$_1$ Stephen's /got a /new /**job**.*" since "Stephen" would not function as the rheme in a remark addressed to his wife. The rhema in question would differ from (10.9) (a) in the order of the two terms under the dependent predication, and (b) in having the identification "001" instead of "000" on the initial node of this predication, to show that it is 'definite' in this context.

Alternatively, I could have expressed my thoughts a little differently; I could have left unsaid that Stephen had obtained the job, lest any emphasis here might be taken as a slur on his competence, and come up with "*//$_4$ **Joe** /told me about //$_1$ Stephen's /new /**job**.*", which would sincerely express the rhema

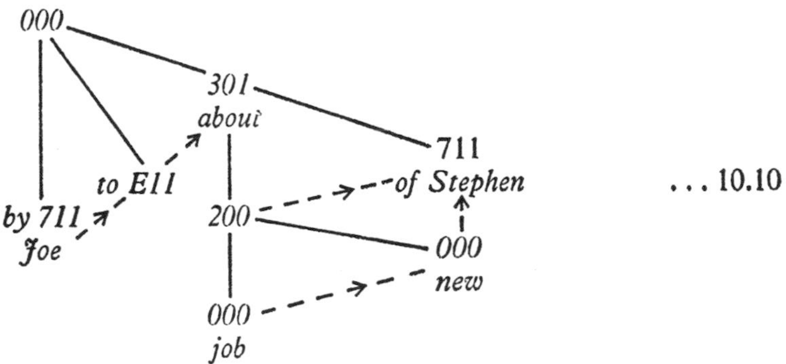

... 10.10

Here we see the second predication reduced to a determinative subrhema; it is given the identification "*301*" equivalent to the existential 'the' since it is both constitutive of the context (the part introduced by Joe) and adductive (because I am making it the subject of talk with a new listener). The rest of the structure is the same as in (10.9). But of course the use of the determinative form is also possible talking to someone of whom I know less. To such a one I might well say "$||_4$***Joe** |told me about* $||_1$ *this |**Stephen** who's* $||_1$*got a |new |**job**.*". This has the effect of making "Stephen" the theme of the subordinate clause (as the qualifier of a determinative, "Stephen" is both rheme and non-tonic in (10.10). Moreover, the name is indicated as unknown to me, equivalent to "a certain person called Stephen", not the Stephen we all know and thus rating only the relatively indefinite identification "200". The whole determinative group is identified with "301" as before (though the note of enquiry in my remark might prompt rather "303"). The rhema structure expressed here is then as follows:

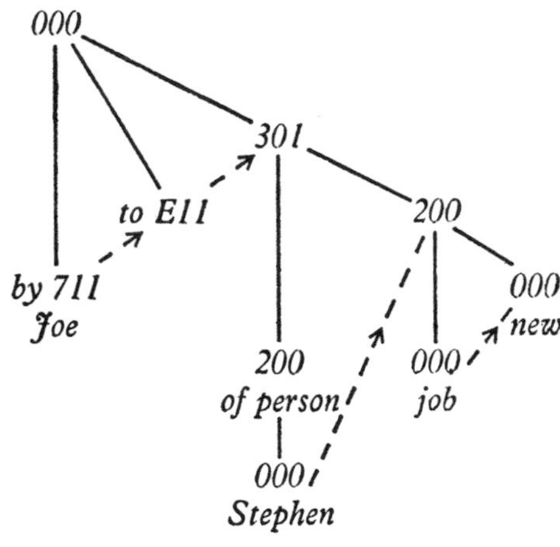

...10.11

Let us now look at these various forms of the utterance in question, and see what clues they offer us for the representation of predication. It is first evident that we need to look at the identification of the nodes to be differentiated; but it is also clear, too, that this alone will not suffice; at least the identification "200" can be found on nodes of both types. We must therefore look at the following nodes also; in fact, however, we need look no further than the first node after the predicative or determinative one, that is its theme. For it is plain that any identification at all may be required for the rheme nodes added to this.

We find that for predication we get the following pairs of identifications: 000–711, 000–200 (10.9), 001–711 (rhema not set out); and for determinatives: 200–000 (all rhemata shown),

301–200, and perhaps 303–200. A little consideration will show, indeed, that the theme of a predication must needs have all the identification elements which its predicative node has, and perhaps more; but there is no such rule for determinatives, and indeed we could make a case for the opposite, that the determinative node must have at least the identifications assigned to its theme.

Thus, while it would in one sense be simpler to invent a special identification term or digit to mark the distinction, such a special marker would inevitably be redundant, and the system is already too complicated to make such redundancy welcome. The rule for identifying nodes across this contrast is then

> A node whose identification includes (in the sense of (10.4)) that of its immediate successor (i.e. theme) is thereby marked as *predicative*; while
> Any other intermediate node is determinative. . . . 10.12

This rule is sufficient to mark the two types of intermediate nodes, which distinction is one we shall often need to make. I shall not use any additional distinguishing mark for them.

10.5. Vocatives

The lattice (10.4) presents a number of inferential relations between different identification terms; most of these are fairly self-evident and can easily be verified by examples. Those who try to do so will, however, encounter a snag with the possessive pronouns. The lattice indicates that the designation of "*your doctor*" includes that of "*you doctor*", which is apparently false.

The resolution of this difficulty is that the pronoun terms corresponding to "*I*", "*you*", "*he*" and the like are already so fully identified that they cannot be accompanied by any lexeme which adds to their circumscription. That is to say, "*you doctor*", as "*E21 (doctor)*", must be interpreted as having an *empty* designation-class (unless by chance you happen to be one), and as such *included in* every other class. Nevertheless, in ordinary English the expression "*you doctor*" is quite acceptable; it is a kind of vocative form, and is only slightly different in effect from "*you*" alone. If then it does not express "*E21 (doctor)*", what does it stand for?

Let me take a fuller example. Suppose I say "*//₁ **You**'re no /good at /sewing //₄**Jane**.*"; my adding the final tone-group with "Jane" indicates that I am either speaking in the presence of more than one person, or expecting that Jane won't be listening. That is, in this context, "you" by itself will not bite; it will not be understood as "E21", but in some weaker sense, for which a proper name is a required supplement. This sense must be, from (10.4), the second-person modification of the existential "the"; this is the term coded as "321". It is this otherwise unexpressed identification which is the essential ingredient in vocatives, and not, as one might suppose, "E21". See (10.14)

Although seldom given overt expression, there seems to be a niche for a first-person analogue of a vocative. It is possible to say, for example "*It seems to me as a parent that . . .*" or "*I the only witness swear that it's true*". And we have the term "311" in readiness for such use. But in reality these are not comparable to ordinary vocatives, but rather to such expressions as "*you, my son*" where the presence of a second identifier shows that two separate nodes are involved. The fact that "E11" and "E21" are not compatible with non-empty lexical items need not prevent their referents being designated twice over for rhetorical effect, but this expresses a different rhema structure. This is illustrated in (10.13), as against the true vocative in (10.14) below; (10.13) could be expressed by "*//₅ ∧ It's for /**you** my /son //₁ ∧ to con/tinue what /I've be/**gun**.*".

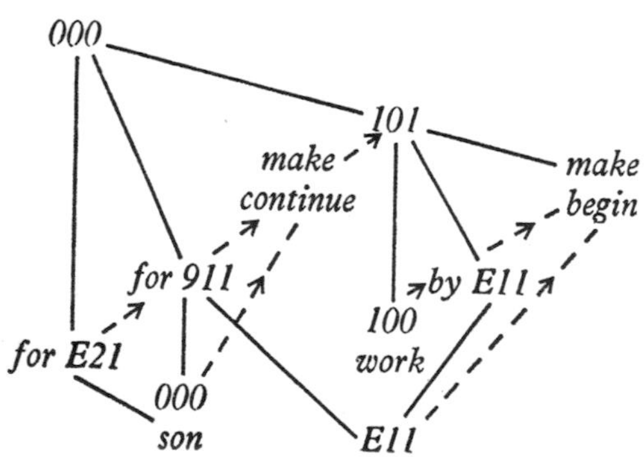

. . . 10.13

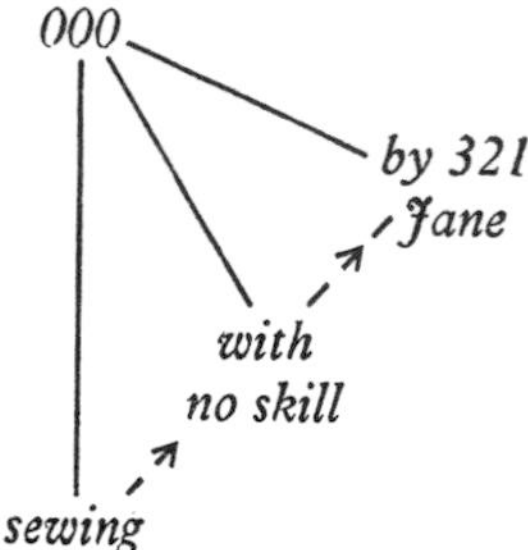

. . . 10.14

10.6. Identifications at Predicative Nodes

There remains, despite the convention stated in §10.4, a considerable range of choice for the identification terms to be attached to the initial node of a predicative rhema. I shall mention here some of the uses to which such identifications can be put. It is the function of identifications to relate what they refer to to their context. In the case of a rhema which makes a direct contribution to the context itself, not determined by previous context except through the particular lexigens or subrhemata that it contains, this fact is clearly indicated by the identification "000". This will be the commonest case.

If, however, what is said has already been established as part of the context, perhaps with the hypothetical quantifier, or in some other way less than plainly stated, then it merits marking as definite with "001". This will be the case for example with the second clause in "*//₋₁ ∧ I /didnt be/lieve he'd /**seen** it //₅ ∧ But he /**had**.*". Closed questions might be identified with "003", even though their status is already apparent from the presence of zero arcs; but some questions so heavily expect a positive answer that the latter may well be a less appropriate way of indicating their status than this identification. To this class belong question-tags to commands, as in "*//₁ Tip him the /**wink** //₂ ∧ you /**know**.*".

A slightly wider range of possibilities exists for subordinate predicatives. These can certainly be *constitutive*, as in "*//₁ ∧ He /**knew** that /this had /happened.*". The particle "*now*" usually serves to mark a sentence as *adductive* in some sense, and if there are no adductive terms within it it can be identified with "200"; thus "*//₄ Now her //₁ brother was a /**Free**mason.*".

CHAPTER XI

The Case Lattice

Whereas the closed categories of quantification and identification are involved in the process of inference through having to be cited in the rules of inference *I* (§14.6) which I shall eventually draw up, the category of case plays a rather different role. The function of the case system is to specify the mutual relationships of the nodes of one rhema, which represent the roles of the things designated in respect of one another. Being more intimately concerned with the content of a rhema than the previous categories, the case system provides the most effective classification of the terms affected which can be obtained from the closed categories; it thus plays a most important role in the matching of nodes between one rhema and another belonging to the same context, which as we shall see is a necessary step in the inferential process. In fact, a substantial part of the information conveyed by a rhema may be located in the case terms of its node labels.

11.1. Fillmore's Case System

As compared with the preceding categories, that of case is considerably more fundamental for the general linguist. Though errors and omissions in the quantification or identification lattices will certainly matter when we come to test our inferential algorithms, they are unlikely to obstruct the application of the theory to the description of a given language. This is because the mapping of the lexical or other resources of a language onto these lattices is not subject to very strict logical controls—as is shown by the wide tolerance of most languages for lacunae and illogical constructions in these areas—and is therefore not a very effective method of detecting defects in the lattice structures proposed for them. In contrast, the case system represents a set of relationships which have to be expressed with reasonable precision in every language, and at least a minimal apparatus for doing so is no doubt to be found in every language.

Case occupies a central position in the logical construction of sentences, intimately concerned with the verbal system, with subordination of clauses, with noun-group structures, and much else; and it interacts at surface level in one way or another with most other systems. Its importance has been in recent years ably argued by Fillmore [31, 33], and I need not repeat his arguments here. While I shall make use of his findings in what follows, it will be necessary to adopt a rather different approach to the problem from his. For my purposes, it is necessary to establish a system of inferential relations between the various case terms, which is a consideration that does not enter into the purview of the orthodox linguist, at least not in the rigorous manner used here. For me it is important to have a complete set of case terms, such as constitutes a lattice providing for the expression of every kind of case-based inference which we shall encounter in actual applications.

It must at once be said that, in fact, inferences from one case or set of cases to another, while possible, are for the most part quite trivial: to *produce* something implies *aiming* for it, to *pass through* a place implies *arriving* there and *leaving*, and so on. Correspondingly the 'complete' case system, as compared with the kind of case systems exemplified in a more strictly linguistic analysis, is something of a disappointment. It is arrived at by closing the logical gaps which we find in such a system as Fillmore's, as we must do to adapt the system to our inferential requirements; but for practical purposes the 'gaps' can always be filled by the use of appropriate lexical items, and while unfilled serve to economize on overt case markers.

The effect of this is that no real language has anything like as many distinct 'cases' as I distinguish here; the tendency is to reduce the complexity of the system, often (as in English) by relying on separate lexemes, mainly of course prepositions, to mark case distinctions, or by making verbs do the job (as in Chinese). For the linguist, the aim is to work out a minimal case system in which the fewest possible distinctions and contrasts are represented; and this, in particular, is the nature of Fillmore's system, and of all those which derive, as does Anderson's,[2] from his approach. According to a fairly recent proposal[33, 2] eight cases can be distinguished. These are named Experiencer, Agent, Object, Instrument, Source, Goal, Place, and Time. Of these, Fillmore uses the Object case as the unmarked member of the system (which is thus an 'ergative' type of case system, as opposed to an 'active' type like that of IE where there is an unmarked 'subject' case). Except that this could mean that the Object includes designation-wise the other cases, there are no inferential relations based on designation-inclusion among these eight; this is of course a measure of their economy as a system.

11.2. Inferences between Cases

A simple example of this type of inference is as follows. Suppose I say "$//_5$ ∧ *I've /had a /letter from /**Toby**.*"; it is legitimate to infer from this that "$//_1$ ***Toby**'s /written a /letter.*". In the first sentence, "Toby" will have a case which in Fillmore's system would be that of the Source; while in the second, "Toby" would be Agent. In both sentences "letter" has the Object case. But of course Fillmore's system does not allow an inference from Source to Agent; one may not infer a "letter *by* Toby" from a "letter *from* Toby". In order to correct this, and make what is evidently a proper inference apparent from the lattice relations of the case terms, we have to concoct a variant of the Source case which will be included in the Agent (or contrariwise); this new case is the one I call Donor. At the same time, we have to have also a Source case which does *not* carry this implication, since if someone comes from Liverpool there is no sense in which Liverpool is cited as an agent of anything. The effect of this kind of modification is to increase the delicacy of the case system, by dividing each of the Fillmore cases into more finely delineated components.

This consideration raises the problem, which we have met before, of where to stop. Clearly, there must be a limit to what can be incorporated in a closed category; but we can gain no help from the usage of actual languages, since however restricted their formal 'case' systems may be, all languages can express any relation of this kind which we may be able to think up an illustration for. The answer probably lies, as in the previous categories of quantification or identification, in listing the basic contrasts which the category requires, forming the corresponding product lattice, and striking out those elements which appear to represent no logically possible relationship. The first step of listing the 'possible' contrasts is, however, difficult to do in this instance, and involves an inevitable element of arbitrariness; I take the view, for example, that we shall not need a case denoting "on the left of", nor one corresponding to "out of love for". But I have no theoretical justification for these rejections; to say they are allowed for in the lexicon is true enough, but could be equally true of instruments or goals. What I have in fact done, is to take Fillmore's eight cases, and to ask what sub-categories can be derived *from these.* That I shall thus avoid objections to calling the result a 'case' system is perhaps the best that can be said for it, unless the following list of subcategories should strike anyone as self-evidently exhaustive.

11.3. The Sub-categories of Case

Having said this, I at once renege on it to the extent of throwing one item back into the lexicon; I see no need to distinguish Place and Time within the case system. Whether a thing is a city or a day is inevitably part of its lexical meaning, and those few instances which might be either temporal or spatial could very well be distinguished by additional rhema nodes; thus for "marriage" we can when necessary put "time of marriage" or "place of marriage" as required. I shall therefore merge Time and Place into a single case of Circumstance.

With this amendment, I shall illustrate within the system examples of three sub-categories, which I call *Phase*, *Mode*, and *Grade.*

11.3.1. Phase: is my name for the contrast exemplified in the pair Source and Goal. These are not incompatible, for a thing can be both a goal and a point of departure. If I say "*//$_1$∧ I / usually/ /go to /London via /**Dunton**.*", I allude to both my arrival at and my immediate departure from Dunton, which is thus *both* Goal and Source. And if I further add that I thereby avoid Royston, then that town is neither Goal nor Source. The lattice for the Phase sub-category is therefore

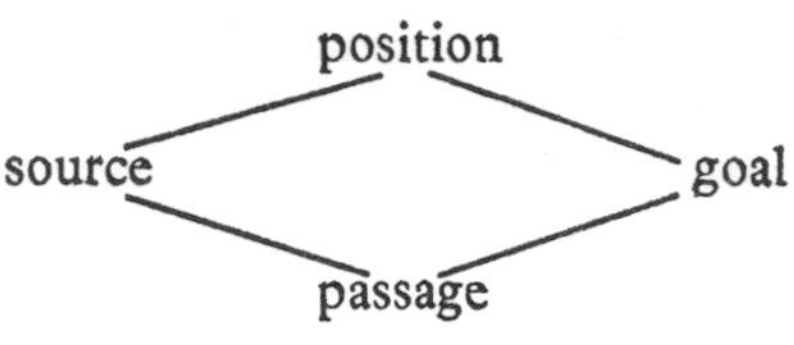

. . . 11.1

Apart from Source and Goal themselves, only one of the Fillmore cases seems to belong specifically to either of these types. The 'Experiencer' receives experiences, and in this sense he is in regard to them in the position of a goal. The Instrument, at least when applied to a concrete tool, is something taken up and then put down again and thus both comes and goes, and may be assigned to the 'passage' term of this sub-category. The remaining cases are all unmarked for Phase.

11.3.2. Mode is the sub-category under which things are described as either a state or an action. Either something happens, or not. Everything can be regarded as static (in the sense that whatever changes it may be subject to are not under consideration); but not everything can be seen as in action, since there may be no action to see. A philosopher may object that there may equally be no static object underlying supposed changes (as for instance in "*It is getting late*"), but the use of language at all seems to require the supposition that there always is a word for it (in the given instance, it is "*time*"), even if philosophically it might be argued that there is nothing for such a word to mean. So, in effect, there are two 'mode' terms, the one including the other:

Some kind of activity is always in question in regard to the cases of Agent, Instrument, Source, and Goal. Those of Experiencer, Object, and Circumstance do not depend on anything happening, and thus correspond to the state term of this sub-category.

11.3.3. Grade is a three-way distinction, the terms of which I call Primary, Secondary, and Tertiary. The terms 'subjective', 'objective' and 'circumstantial' might be more explicit, but carry too many overtones to be acceptable.

The 'primary' cases are those which identify the lexigens which they mark as independently or spontaneously involved in an action or in a state. These things are the reference-points for the description of what is going on, in relation to which the roles of other participating entities are determined. Bearers of primary cases are often people or animate objects, but their use is not confined to such; we can say that a falling branch breaks a window in the same sense that a boy can break a window. Weather can close roads as effectively as the police can. No element of 'personification' is involved here, but of course there *is* a latent invitation to picturesque elaboration.

The 'secondary' cases mark those lexigens which are involved in the situation in consequence of the primary case-bearers. Whenever a window is broken, it is a consequence of some person or thing breaking it (or if not, the window will take a primary case such as Experient). It is not compulsory to mention the primary source of the trouble, so we cannot make a rule that every complete rhema contains at least one primary case; nor can we insist that there is at least one secondary case; but the presence of both is the most usual situation. The secondary cases in the Fillmore system are the Object and the Instrument; Experiencer and Agent are the primary ones.

The 'tertiary' cases, typified by that of Circumstance, denote things which form part of the background or setting in which events occur, irrespective of whether they are deliberately involved by an agent or not. Change or removal of tertiary case bearers does not alter the essential nature of what is being described, in the way that primary or most secondary cases affect it. The commonest items here are the places and times concerned, but also more abstract circumstances may be tertiary in some statements, such as "*//$_1$ ∧ He /got /up in a /bad /**temper**.*". There is an important complementarity between the secondary and tertiary cases, in that the secondary ones refer to what moves or changes or arises, while the tertiary apply to what is stationary. Thus correponding to the tertiary Source, which applies to the place where something comes from, there is the secondary Product, which applies to what comes from some other thing or process.

There seem to be no valid inferences from one grade to another; that is, the designation-classes produced by the assignment of a primary case are disjoint from those produced with the same lexigen by substituting a secondary or a tertiary case. If A is given to someone by B, then B is primarily involved, and it is a confusion to use the same case for this relation as for the tertiary relation that A comes from B; for in the first case B does something and A undergoes it, whereas in the second case A takes the initiative and B takes the consequences. It therefore seems that the lattice for the grade subcategory is

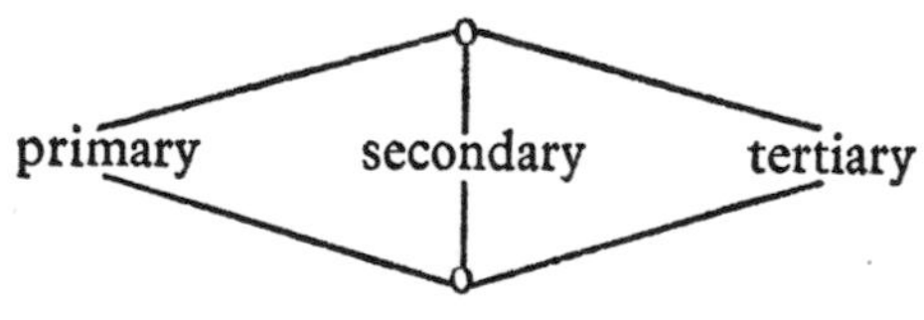

. . . 11.3

which is simple but uninformative; the two bounding nodes of this lattice are empty: that is, they represent no case-relations except the unmarked case which I call Entity.

11.4. The Case Lattice

The direct product of the three lattices (11.1–3), omitting elements corresponding to the bounding elements of (11.3), is a lattice of 26 elements; these are an upper bound, a lower bound, and three copies of the Boolean lattice of eight elements obtained as product of (11.1) and (11.2). The upper bound is a usable though vacuous case, but the lower bound is linguistically empty. There are thus 25 cases, arranged as shewn on opposite page.

The case terms, or 'cases' as I shall call them, will generally be denoted not by the numerical codes but, for moemonic purposes, by the first two letters of the names given them in (11.4); not all these names are wholly satisfactory, because some of the cases correspond to rather obscure notions, as is only to be expected when they are generated by a logical process rather than by appeal to frequency of usage. There is likely to be found a very wide variation in the frequency of occurrence of the different cases in ordinary conversational usage, a variation reflected in part in the following examples of the cases in use.

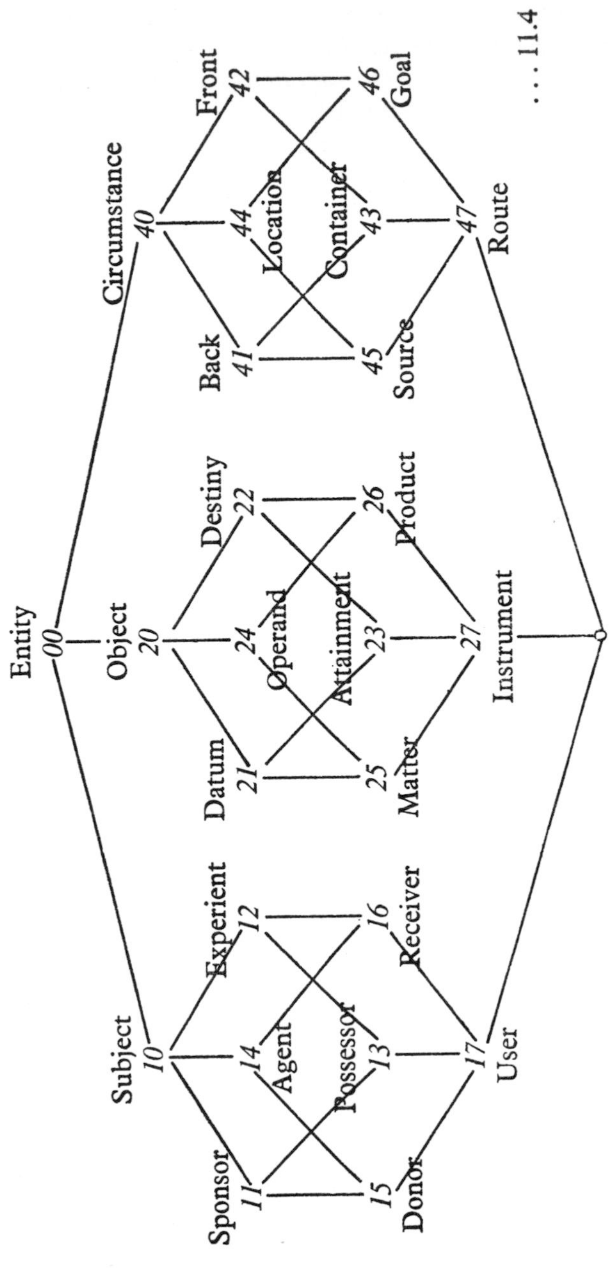
Entity 00
Subject 10
Sponsor 11
Experient 12
Possessor 13
Agent 14
Donor 15
Receiver 16
User 17
Object 20
Datum 21
Destiny 22
Attainment 23
Operand 24
Matter 25
Product 26
Instrument 27
Circumstance 40
Back 41
Front 42
Container 43
Location 44
Source 45
Goal 46
Route 47
. . . 11.4

The arrangement of the examples is as follows: each case is illustrated by one occurrence, followed by contrasting occurrences of each of the cases *immediately including* the one illustrated in (11.4). Most of them have additional illustrations incidentally in other examples which are referred to by the cases under which they occur. The use of the cases in the labels of predicative nodes is treated separately in §11.5.

00: ***Entity***: As the unmarked case, this is used (a) as the case assigned to a complete free sentence or clause, and (b) at nodes designating the common referent of two or more other nodes, where the proper cases will be given. But besides these special uses, the Entity case is appropriate for indicating mere existence. Thus:

Spanning the gorge[Ro] *there is a suspension bridge*[En] 11.4.1
(further examples under 10, 20, 40)

10: ***Subject***: This is the unmarked one among the primary cases, which is therefore the case to use for equative clauses and for the 'subject' of a clause which has neither the position of Experient or of Sponsor. Thus:

Peter[Su] *is always available in Cambridge*[Lo] . . . 11.4.2
There's always Peter[En], *in Cambridge*[Lo] 3
(further examples under 11, 12, 14, 23, 45)

11: ***Sponsor***: denotes possession without enjoyment, offering without relinquishing, or in general a responsibility for something; as a stative case it lacks the implication of something happening which the Donor gives. Thus:

Jasper's car[Sp] *has four doors*[Ob] . . . 11.4.4
Jasper's car[Su] *is four-doored*[At] 5
(further examples under 13, 21)

A car may be called 'four-doored' even if three of the doors have been nailed up; the use of the Sponsor case implies that they really work.

12: ***Experient***: This is a frequently required case, since it is from some experience that so many utterances spring. It covers the subject of a verb which does not denote deliberate action (such as "see" as opposed to "look"), many instances of passive subjects, and some of the objects of an active verb, which may have a primary role even though logically 'object' implies a secondary case. Thus:

Frank[Ex] *felt disillusioned*[Ob] *with them*[Da] . . . 11.4.6
Frank[Su] *was disillusioned*[Ob] *by them*[Ag] 7
(further examples under 13, 16, 22, 44)

Note that though "disillusioned" is a verb in English, this will be rendered in rhematic notation by its own node, to which some case must be assigned; I assume this will be the Object case, the lexigen designating 'disillusionment'.

13: ***Possessor***: from being a Possessor we must be able to infer both being a Sponsor and being an Experient; it therefore denotes that kind of possession involving both responsibility and enjoyment, even if often in weak senses. A door, for example, can as Sponsor have a lock, and can as Experient have dents in it, while in relation to carvings on it (if these are valued by the speaker) it will be Possessor. But more typically the Possessor case operates as in:

I[Po] *have at least Nathan's skill*[At] . . . 11.4.8
I[Sp] *can vouch for Nathan's skill*[At] 9
I[Ex]*'ve found Nathan skilful*[At] 10
(further under 17)

14: ***Agent***: This is a very common case, being the unmarked active primary one. It is to be used whenever neither giving nor receiving is involved, and implies action rather than merely being in a certain state (an element of 'deliberate' is valid, but only for persons, of course; 'action' as here understood need not be 'deliberate' action). Thus:

Peter[Ag] *lives in Cambridge*[Lo] . . . 11.4.11
Peter[Su] *is now in Cambridge*[Lo] 12
(further under 12, 16, 24, 25, 26, 27, 41, 42, 43, 46, 47)

15: ***Donor***: Differs from the Agent in being involved in a transaction with something that passes from the Donor to somewhere else. It is distinguished from the Source (where its instances are included in Fillmore's system) by being in a primary role, the initiator or at least the centre of interest in the action involved. Thus:

Jim[Do] *has given £30*[Ob] *towards the work*[De] . . . 11.4.13
Jim[Sp] *has promised £30*[Ob] *towards the work*[De] 14
Jim[Ag] *has secured £30*[Ob] *towards the work*[De] 15
(further under 17)

16: ***Receiver***: complementary to the Donor, this is the primary correspondent of the Goal, implying an active taking or acquiring of an object or idea. Thus:

Guy[Re] *has learnt a new tune*[Ob] . . . 11.4.16
Guy[Ex] *has heard a new tune*[Ob] 17
Guy[Ag] *has played a new tune*[Ob] 18
(further under 17)

17: ***User***: This seems the most apt name for a rarely-needed case, applicable to lexigens used to designate what is both a Donor and a Receiver, though there are many uses of "use" to which it has no application. It can be used (as in the illustrations for case 27) as a complement to the Instrument, but only if the listener is really expected to think of the Instrument being first received and then laid down again. More often it denotes buying and selling, thus:

Caroline[Us] *handles Esperanto journals*[Ob] . . . 11.4.19
Caroline[Do] *distributes Esperanto journals*[Ob] 20
Caroline[Re] *subscribes to Esperanto journals*[Ob] 21
Caroline[Po] *has some Esperanto journals*[Ob] 22

20: ***Object***: Fillmore uses this name for what he regards as the unmarked case; but for me it is unmarked only among the secondary cases. It is still of very frequent occurrence, being required for all secondaries when no ideas of readiness, intention, or treatment are attached to the designatum of a node. Thus:

The Elians[Ag] *held games*[Ob] *in honour of Heracles*[Da] . . . 11.4.23

There used to be games[En] *held in honour of Heracles*[Da] 24
(further under 11, 12, 15, 16, 17, 21, 22, 24, 44, 45)

21: ***Datum***: This is the case denoting that something is ready for use, available, presupposed, relied on, and the like; it is also the case for the content of a message, for a precondition for a current state of affairs, or a standard of comparison. Only a few of these uses are illustrated here; thus:

Hares[Sp] *rely on their great speed*[Da] *in danger*[Lo] ... 11.4.25
Hares[Sp] *are capable of great speed*[Ob] *in danger*[Lo] 26
(further under 12, 20, 23, 25)

22: ***Destiny***: This denotes what is intended or foreseen, also for things hoped for or feared. Thus:

I[Ex]*'d like to have a better example*[De] ... 11.4.27
I[Ex]*'ve seen better examples*[Ob] 28
(further under 23, 26, 27)

23: ***Attainment***: This case, as the meet of the last two, implies both Datum and Destiny, that is, it applies to what is both required and foreseen. It is thus the case for any permanent attribute consciously possessed or in the case of an inanimate object deliberately imposed or ascribed; it is perhaps less infrequent than one might expect. An example is:

Leila[Su] *has always suffered from poor health*[At] ... 11.4.29
Leila[Su] *has to reckon with her poor health*[Da] 30
Leila[Su] *must be prepared for poor health*[De] 31
(further under 11, 13, 21, 27)

If attention were directed particularly to Leila, for example if this term were the rheme of the utterance, one might alter the case of Subject to Possessor, Experient, and Sponsor respectively to allow of the range of inferences resulting from neutralizing what in English is the varying verb in these sentences. (Compare 27.)

24: ***Operand***: This differs from the object case only in being active as against stative; it is thus to be used whenever there is an implication of something *happening* to whatever it is, but without any indication about *what* happens. It is relatively infrequent; thus:

Geoffrey[Ag] *was observing*[In] *the pelicans*[Op] . . . 11.4.32
Geoffrey[Ag] *was watching*[In] *the pelicans*[Ob] 33
(further under 25, 26, 46)

Note that the latent lexigens given the Instrument case are the same in each of these sentences, designating "vision"; it is the verbs used for this action in English which express the case distinction on the object of the sentence.

25: ***Material***: Here we are more specific as to what is going on; the designatum is being used up or consumed. Thus:

Atterwoods[Ag] *use refractory bricks*[Ma] . . . 11.4.34
Atterwoods[Ag] *need refractory bricks*[Da] 35
Atterwoods[Ag] *keep refractory bricks*[Op] 36
(further under 27)

26: ***Product***: This indicates what is produced, brought into action or existence, or made. Outcomes being always more interesting than the complementary requirements, this case is more frequent than Material. Like the other active secondaries, it tends to be expressed in the verb:

They[Ag]*'re going to start a furniture business*[Pr] . . . 11.4.37
They[Ag]*'re hoping to start a furniture business*[De] 38
They[Ag]*'re running a furniture business*[Op] 39
(further under 27)

27: ***Instrument***: This denotes what is input at the beginning of an action and recovered in tact at the end of it. It can be used for tools used, for materials partly or incidentally consumed, or more abstractly for methods employed. It makes many adverbs of manner, and verbs describing how something is done (such as seeing, as in (11.4.32) or saying, etc.). On account of its position in the lattice it carries many implications, some of which can be reinforced by the case assigned to the primary term if this is also the rheme of the utterance. Thus:

Tom[Us] *used some matches*[In] *to light the fire*[De] ... 11.4.40
Tom[Re] *used the matches*[Ma] *to light the fire*[De] 41
Tom[Do] *produced some matches*[Pr] *to light the fire*[De] 42
Tom [Ag] *procured some matches*[At] *to light the fire*[De] 43
(further under 24, 47)

If "Tom" were theme rather than rheme, the case assigned would be the Agent throughout. If the fire ever got lit, we would have the Product case for it in place of that of Destiny.

40: ***Circumstance***: This is the unmarked member of the tertiary case subsystem, and thus indicates any attendant circumstance of an action which is not marked for its location or active involvement; it is the commonest tertiary case except with lexigens designating space or time concepts. Thus:

It[Ob]*'s held in the church*[Lo] *when cold*[Ci] ... 11.4.44
In the church[Lo] *it's cold*[En] 45
(further under 41, 42, 44)

41: ***Back***: indicates what is at one's back, in the past, or overcome. There is a certain confusion regarding this case, and the next, used with predicative nodes, referred to in §11.5. Thus:

Jack[Su] *is over his exams*[Ba] ... 11.4.46
Jack[Su] *is busy with his exams*[Ci] 47
(further under 43, 45)

42: ***Front***: indicates what is in front of one, or in the immediate future. Thus:

He[Ag]*'ll be going*[So] *before the new year*[Fr] ... 11.4.48
He[Ag]*'ll be going*[So] *next year*[Ci] 49
(further under 43, 46)

The verb "going" stands for the node label "So901.1(place)", that is, "from here"; it might also have been given as "Go501.1 (place)".

43: ***Container***: This case indicates what is both in front of one and behind one, and so usually all round as well; it is the case involved in the more narrowly locative uses of "in". Applied to a term designating time, it means "in the course of". Thus:

They[Ag] *live in the wood*[Co] . . . 11.4.50
They[Ag] *live beyond the wood*[Ba] 51
They[Ag] *live this side of the wood*[Fr] 52
(further under 41, 45)

44: ***Location***: This is the unmarked tertiary active case, and marks the place where something happens or the time when something occurs; it is much commoner than the Container with temporal designata since almost always these involve things happening (but "my birthday is in November" could have the month as Container). Thus:

He[Ex] *injured*[Ob] *himself while climbing*[Lo] . . . 11.4.53
He[Ex] *injured*[Ob] *himself on a climb*[Ci] 54

The difference is that he could injure himself "on a climb" by cutting his finger on a sardine tin during lunch; but this would not count as an injury while climbing.

45: ***Source***: I here restrict Fillmore's case term to tertiary use. With places, it denotes the origin where something comes from, and with times the 'terminus post quem'. Thus:

She[Ex]'*s been ill*[Ob] *since that party*[So] . . . 11.4.55
She[Ex] *fell ill*[Ob] *after that party*[Ba] 56
She[Ex] *was ill*[Ob] *at that party*[Lo] 57
(further under 42, 47)

46: ***Goal***: This denotes the place where one is going to, or the time till when something occurs. Thus:

We[Ag]'*ll keep talking*[Op] *till lunch*[Go] . . . 11.4.58
We[Ag]'*ll have the talk*[Op] *before lunch*[Fr] 59
We[Ag]'*ll have the talk*[Op] *between lunch and tea*[Co] 60
(further under 47)

47: ***Route***: This denotes what is both 'Goal' and 'Source', and therefore applies to any place one passes through, or to a period of time which falls within the course of an action. It can be used for the completion of an action, that is both its beginning and its ending. Thus:

The boys[Ag] *ran*[In] *through the yard*[Ro] ... 11.4.61
The boys[Ag] *ran*[In] *out of the yard*[So] 62
The boys[Ag] *ran*[In] *into the yard*[Go] 63
The boys[Ag] *ran*[In] *about in the yard*[Co] 64

Note that the idea of "running" is expressed by the Instrument case with a lexigen designating this action; that is, the boys passed through the yard by means of running. Their action includes the idea that they started to run [Pr], eventually used up running [Ma], and also had the running as an attainment [At].

11.5. Cases at Predicative Nodes

In the preceding examples, I have confined attention to situations where the case terms are placed on terminal nodes, or on what can plausibly be represented as such, that is nodes having no designatory successors. The same principles apply of course to those intermediate nodes that head determinative subrhemata, for these are equivalent to surface noun-groups. But, more than either of the other closed categories, case has an important role at predicative nodes. In this section I shall survey this field.

11.5.1. Case Terms realized as Verbs: As we have already seen in some of the examples, many verbs in English and many other languages have no real semantic content apart from what derives from the cases assigned to their formal subject and complements. In such instances, it is usually immaterial whether the cases concerned fall on predicative, determinative or terminal nodes. Apart from such one-term examples as "fly" (= "air" in the Route case), "spit" (= "saliva" in the Product case), and the like, there are many instances where a certain pattern of cases specifies a verb. Thus a Donor, a Receiver, and an Object together generate a verb of giving. For example, "*Millie's cousin gave Derek a plastic gnome*" is a three-node rhema, with no node assigned to 'giving' at all; but hardly so in "*Millie's going on* *like that gave Derek a headache*", for it can be claimed that a predicative could not be a Donor, but rather a Datum (secondary grade).

Verbs of this kind may be called *casual* verbs; besides the obvious example of 'giving', 'having' is one which in many languages lacks a proper verb (thus Russian), another is 'making', and most of the less specific verbs of motion can be sufficiently rendered by the use of tertiary cases. An interesting though speculative extension of the idea of casual verbs is to the expression of modalities; in §7.5.3 I proposed rhema structures for modal expressions in which the modal labels "desire", "right", "possible" appear at the predicative node introducing a modal clause, and it is these which I suggest we might represent as cases. I shall not argue this case in detail, as it is not of any far-reaching importance, but merely draw attention to the isomorphism between the two sublattices (11.5.1) and (11.5.2), the former giving one plausible system of inference-relations among modalities and the other pairs of cases, stative primary and stative secondary, applied to the subject and object of the modal 'verb'. The figures only show six* combinations, out of a total of sixteen, with the uncomfortable implication that the other ten should have some kind of 'modal' interpretation as well; but it may be worth thinking about.

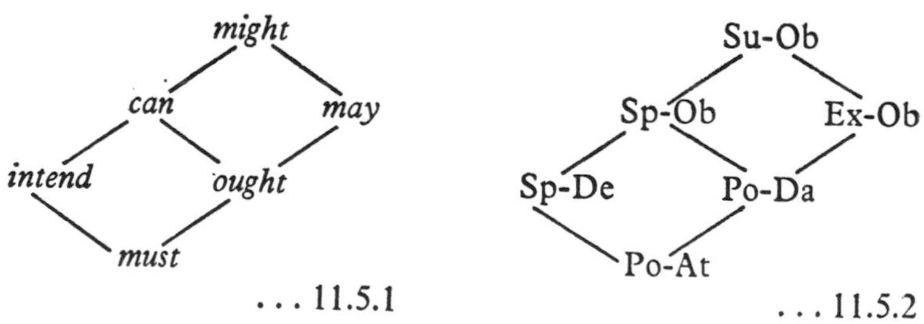

. . . 11.5.1 . . . 11.5.2

11.5.2. Subordinate Clauses: The preceding speculation about modal verbs employs only stative cases; in contrast, we would expect the active case terms to describe, when applied to predicative nodes, relations of a more concrete sort. In fact, the four active secondary cases seem to fit closely to four main types of subordinate clause. These are illustrated by the following:

* Perhaps "ought" does not imply "can" in most of its uses; if so, Ex-Da would be better than Po-Da.

The problem was solved by (John going himself)[In] ...11.5.3
Solving this problem needed (John to go himself)[Ma] 4
Not solving the problem made (John go himself)[Pr] 5
This problem led to (John going himself)[Op] 6

In each example the first part of the sentence may be represented by a clause (expressing 'solve the problem' or the like) with the Object case at its predicative node, though a more specific case (Destiny or Datum) might be more appropriate for the last two. In each also "John" could be extracted from the second clause to function as a surface subject, in the Agent case, but sharing a second (tacit) designant in the position shown. It is evident that many other inter-clause relations could be expressed by varying the cases of two clauses together; still within the active secondary group of cases there are sixteen combinations, and again we are tempted to look for some kind of 'interpretation' for them all. This is almost certainly a waste of time; they will arise in real life situations with very unequal frequency, and actual languages will evolve means for expressing a few of them systematically, and leave the rest to be expressed by whatevery periphrasis the speaker's skill or want of it suggests. Such periphrases arise without effort in languages of the isolating type, but present a much harder problem in the highly inflected Indo-european type of language. (Can this be why users of the latter have been stimulated to the sustained examination of grammar and logic, studies which the Chinese have managed largely without?)

11.5.3. Tense and Aspect: If the secondary cases are thus able to express what we may roughly term 'causal' relations between clauses, we must expect to find that the tertiary cases will do the same for their time relations. How far, we may ask, can 'tense' relations be handled by the use of different cases at the predicative nodes?

We must remember in this connection that it is the function of the tertiary cases to describe the 'background' of actions, whose 'foreground' is occupied by the main (primary) actors and their (secondary) appurtenances. Thus, if say the Front case is applied to a clause, that clause will be marked as something 'in front of' the main action, that is, as in the future. This manner of expressing time is imposed on us by the system I have already built up; but is not the only one possible. On the whole, most authors have felt rather that the future turns its back on us, marching on ahead as it were, as for instance does Clark;[21] this is the natural consequence of seeing the tense of a clause from the viewpoint of its own actors, rather than from that of those outside. If tenses are to be represented by cases, they must be seen relatively, *not* from within, because cases mark relations between the terms of one rhema. There is an interesting discussion of this problem by Traugott,[97] from which it is clear that the equation of 'back' with 'future' appears more natural to more people than the converse identification which the present approach imposes; Fillmore[32] for example also accepts it.

The kind of relations which my system leads to are illustrated by the following:

(*They had finished*)[Ba] *when* (*I saw them*)[Lo] . . . 11.5.7
(*They will have finished*)[Ba] *by next Friday*[Fr] 8

Note that in (11.5.8) the element of futurity depends on the Front case assigned to "*next Friday*". It is evident that in general no actual date of this kind needs to be expressed or even thought of, in order for futurity to be felt as needing expression; this is clearest in negations, such as "*They won't have finished*", where the point of reference is only present in the context. In order for such a rhema to be extracted from an overall context without losing its tense reference we shall have to allow it to be the only dependent in a truncated framing-clause. That is, the rhema structure corresponding to "*They will have finished it*" will be

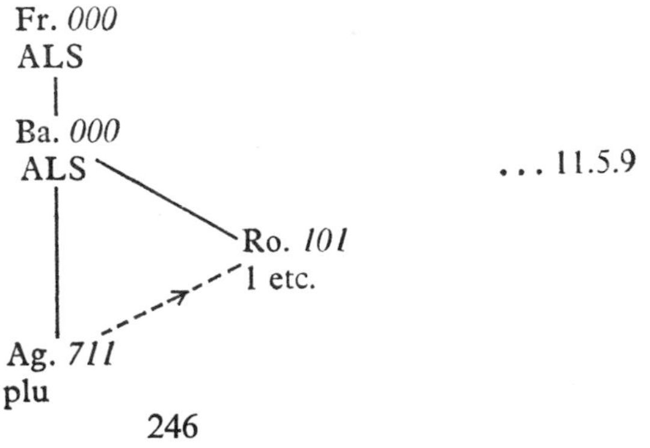

In a crude paraphrase we may put this as follows: "In *front* (of us now) is that *behind* (us we shall have) that *by* them is *through* one thing." The items enclosed in ( ) represent potential nodes, such as would be present in the complete context rehearsal, but are omitted from the diagram (11.5.9) as semantically vacuous.

A further example, of rather greater complexity, of the use of tertiary cases to denote tense or aspectual relations, is as follows:

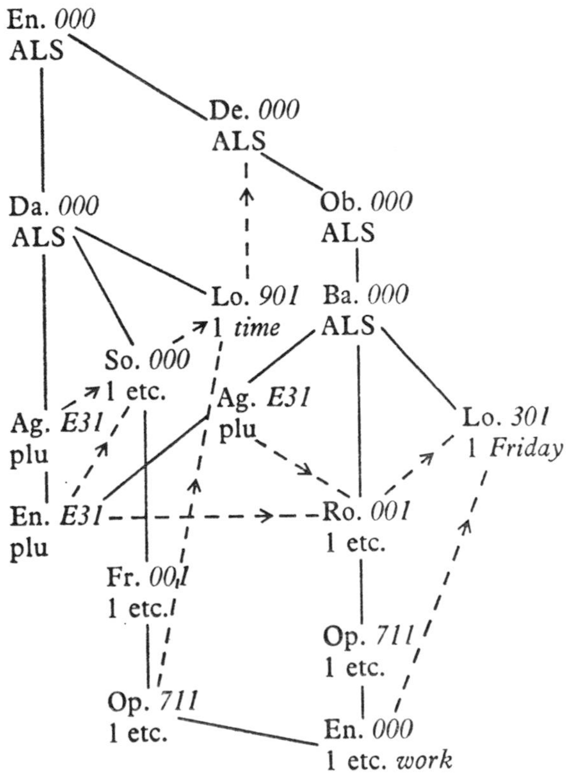

. . . 11.5.10

This can be expressed by "$//_{-1}$ ∧ *We must /start /doing it /**now** $//_4$ so as to be /able to've /**finished** it $//_1$ by /**Friday**.*". The idea of 'start' is represented as "leaving [So] being in front of [Fr] the processing of [Op] it [711]", that is, leaving the stretch of time before the work begins; finishing is analogously analyzed as "getting through" [Ro] the work (with shared ultimate designant with the previous Op.711). The clause connective "*so as to be able to have*" comes out as the chain of nodes De–Ob–Ba. One could insert a third reference to the original subject under the "Ob" node, with the case [Sp]; but this is not unambiguously called for in the English version (the work might have been finished by someone else) and would of course complicate the graph yet further.

CHAPTER XII

Summary of Rhematical Notation

In this Chapter I propose to summarize the position we have arrived at up to now, and, in particular, to give a brief resumé of the principles of our notation. This I have called 'rhematical' notation; and its formulae, variously presented as graphs, matrices, or symbol-strings, denote the content or meaning of what is to be expressed in speech, or the contribution which the hearing of it should make to the listener's context. I would not wish to claim that the notation is, as presented hitherto, complete and sufficient for this purpose, though I consider it justified to think it more suitable and effective than current 'deep structures' in the form of tree diagrams. Moreover, I would hope that defects, which surely exist in it, may be rectified by adding elements to the general schema, without radically restructuring the system.

Some of these possible gaps I shall try to fill in this chapter, and look at briefly at some others; but the main function of what follows is to summarize what has gone before.

12.1. The Possibility of Further Closed Categories

I have identified just three closed categories which are concerned with inferential relations, and whose terms consequently call for explicit recognition in the notation: these are Quantification, Identification, and Case. That there are only these three is certainly not self-evident, and requires supporting argument before proceeding.

There are at least three directions in which we might look for possible systems of contrasts, hopefully closed, relevant to the notation of utterable thoughts. There are, for example, a variety of moods and attitudes which are usually conveyed by para-linguistic means—facial expression, voice quality, gestures, and the like—but which can presumably also be articulated; such might constitute a useful addition to my three categories. One may, for instance, speak facetiously, or in anger, or conspiratorially; how, if at all, should we register these nuances in our notation? On examination, the kind of things conveyed paralinguistically seem to be rather a mixed lot. It is, certainly, relevant to what inferences may be drawn from an utterance to know that it is 'facetious', for example; it might in such cases help to have a warning lexical item, say "*joke*", attached to the initial node of such a rhema. But paralanguage has many uses; thus, the effect of a 'stage whisper', which may sometimes convey a 'conspiratorial' intent, is something entirely different; it is a way of defining the boundaries of the conversation, a thing which is also done, in the opposite sense, by climbing on a chair and calling for attention. If we are concerned with the content of what is said, or implied, these matters are outside our field; they pertain to the switchboard rather than to the microphone.

Another set of distinctions finds expression, at least in English, through intonation, which is in this language mainly governed by grammatical rules, though none would deny that there remains within it a large paralinguistic residuum. There is no doubt, however, that selection of what tone to use for one's next tone-group depends among other things on a desire to express such moods as detachment, surprise, reservation, admonition, etc. Do these constitute a 'closed category', and if so is it one that can affect inferences? They certainly help the listener to relate the speaker to the context, and give obvious clues to the speaker's emotional stance towards the matters conveyed; in these ways they may be said to affect inference, in the 'sublocutionary' sense of §2.5, but for the most part through altering the weight that may be laid on it, rather than by altering its content. In my terms, I would say that these moods do not bear on the context *repertory*, whose items are the inferences from the context, but only the *importance* of the context or rather of the particular aspect of it expressed in a given utterance. It would indeed be useful to have some means of labelling some parts of a context as weightier than others; but doing so would greatly complicate the notation, and the nuances involved would inevitably be subjective and possibly misleading, I would therefore not be in favour of incorporating these matters in the notation.

Some of these moods, which may be expressed through intonation, may be more inferentially useful than others. The contrast between assertive and reserved expression, for instance, enters in part into the category of quantification, though the only expression I have allowed for it in (9.4) is in the element "*Prh*" (perhaps). There are other similar qualifying attitudes, some of them expressed by particles (even in English, which is poor in them): the functions of the initial particles "*well*" and "*now*" fall here. Thus, "*well*" serves to recall attention to the speaker's own contribution to the context, especially after a digression or threatened digression; and "*now*" introduces a further material contribution to the context. There probably is material here for a category of "attitude", having the function of delimiting the boundaries of the context (not, as in whispering, of the conversation), which is on the face of it relevant to inferential relations. Nevertheless, its utility is questionable. The listener who hears the introductory "*well*" will not automatically erase the contribution he has just made, which the particle may invite him to do, but may well resign himself to another spate of talk before being allowed to continue his own train of thought. And from the rhematical point of view, the listener is always right.

Finally, there are a few points which I have made no provision for expressing, though in some languages at least they are well within the field of regular grammatical contrasts. Such a one is narration. It is not uncommon for a language to have special tense forms of verbs for this purpose, or other markers, which suggests that it is felt to be something worth being clear about. its relevance for our purposes is, however, rather marginal. The main reason for wanting to mark off 'narrative' is presumably to invite a suspension of interruptions till the tale is told; this is a social rather than a linguistic concern. The matter of 'facetiousness' with which I began this section is perhaps comparable, as in that case, if it is desired to mark a narrative as such, it can be done by the lexical term of the initial node.

There are, therefore, possibly additional materials which might be incorporated in special terms in the node labels of a rhema graph; but none are so important as to require such treatment, at least at the stage of development of the enquiry which I shall reach in this work.

12.2. Complete Node Labels

If, then, it is agreed, at least provisionally, to give up the search for additional categories, we have four kinds of contribution to each node label; these cover respectively Case, Identification, Quantification, and Lexis. The first three are 'closed' categories, which we can represent, given any finite degree of delicacy to be attained, by a finite lattice of elements representing the terms of the category; the last is 'open', in the sense that its terms cannot be definitively listed in this way. Within this lexical residue there may perhaps be further closed categories concealed, but even if so the major part of it remains unsystematic.

It follows that each node label should consist of four terms; they are not to be considered ordered relative to each other, in the sense that the nodes are ordered, but as simultaneous. They must, however, for notational convenience be written in a fixed order, and for this I choose the order opposite to that in which I have expounded them, that is, Case first, then Identification, then Quantification, and lastly Lexis. The motivation is English word-order: "*using these four terms*" we completely specify the node label.

The case term is represented by a two-letter code, being the first two letters of the case name as given in (11.4); the identification is given as a three-digit code,* as given in (10.4); then comes the quantification using at most three characters as given in (9.2); and finally the lexical term in the form of an English word enclosed in (. . .). If the lexis is null, it is given as ( ), and the quantification ALS may be omitted.

These conventions are illustrated by the following diagrammatic and matrix representations of the rhema expressed by "//$_4$ ∧ *They /may /finish it to/**day**.*" (See top of opposite page).

In this example, we have only one node in which the lexis is not null; this is a lower frequency than usual, but there are on the average about half of the nodes which have null lexis. Node labels written in this form are necessarily less perspicuous than when all the terms are either null or indicated by English words; but of course it is not possible to make this kind of representation

* The suffixed letters a, m, f, i appearing in (11.4) can be regarded as part of the lexical term.

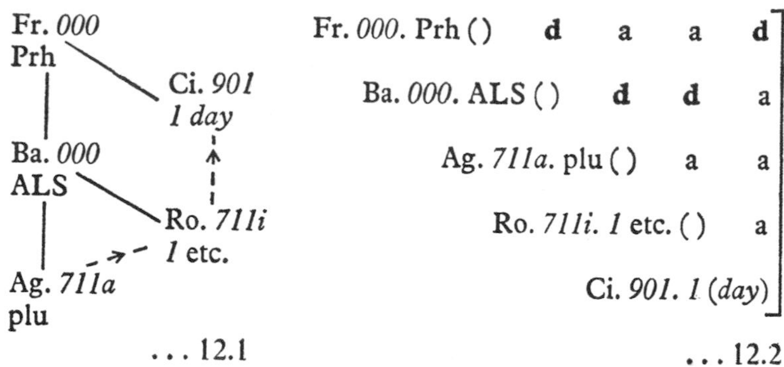

both perspicuous and rigorous, and a certain amount of arbitrary or numerical coding is unavoidable. Accordingly I shall use the conventions just illustrated in all further formal examples, though to help read the graphs I give an English 'translation' (for that is really what it is) for each example.

12.3. String Formulae

While the graph diagrams are the easiest form to take in by eye, and the matrix equivalents are the most suitable for mathematical manipulation, neither is at all suitable for input to or output from a computer, not to mention the convenience of writing or printing. We therefore need to have a third mode of representation for any rhema structure, in the form of a symbol-string. This type of formula has already been illustrated in §5.6.2. In this section I shall give the full rules for such formulae, and provide additional illustrations of their use.

We have first to make a distinction between the written form of the string formulae, and their representation by binary digits in a computer; I give first the written form. In this, the nodes are given in the order determined by the accessory arcs; accordingly these arcs do not need special mention, but the absence of such an arc, that is a zero arc as found in questions, needs to be marked. Each node label is written according to the conventions outlined in the preceding section, except that all the omissions there allowed for are here positively recommended. The lexical term, in ( ), is followed by a colon (:). In the case of a terminal node, this is at once followed by the 'end-of-node' sign (/); but if the node has designatory successors, these are indicated by a string of numbers, each of which gives the number of following *nodes skipped* to reach the terminus of each designatory arc. These arc 'addresses' need not be separated by punctuations, unless a two-figure number is required whose first is greater than the immediately preceding figure (in which case they may be separated by commas ,).

Zero arcs are indicated by substituting a (.) for the (/) at the end of the node. The last node in a formula is also marked in this way. If an s-arc is present, leading to a speech-act, it will usually have a negative 'arc address' which sufficiently identifies it, but if it goes to a later node in the formula, then it may be marked by (+).

Here is an illustration of the string formula conventions. The following rhema, may be expressed by "$//_1$ ∧ *The |present |writer |calls him|self |"I"."*

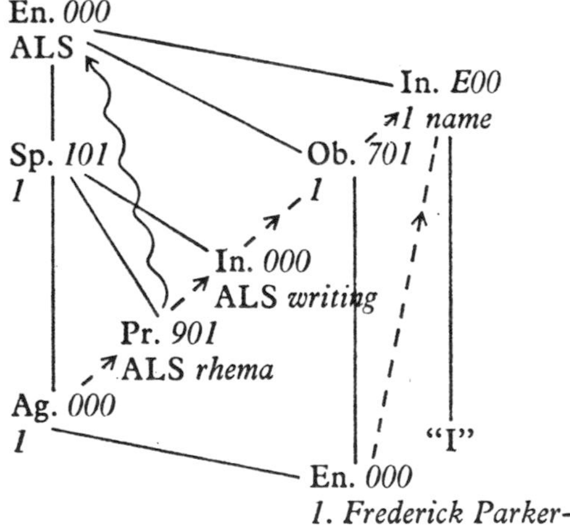

. . . 12.3

This has the following string formula: 000():046/Sp101.1():012/Ag000.1():3/Pr901(rhema):–4/In000(writin):/Ob701.1():0/000.1(FP–R):/InE00.1(name):O/"I".

The following points may be noted in this example: (1) lexical terms are confined to six characters, as in "(writin)"; this is of course arbitrary, and derives from the aim to reduce the codes to a form suitable for computers; (2) the s-arc following the fourth node is indicated by '–4', it being assumed that an arc returning to the same node (which is in fact not permissible) would be coded '–1', which is also a convention derived from computer practice; (3) the reflexive pronoun is not given a special identification, since it is sufficiently indicated by "701" together with a shared designation with the node to which it refers back; (4) the final node "I" is anomalous, in that it is not a designant at all, but a designatum; the actual occurrence of designata in speech is possible only in contexts, such as telling one's name, where utterances as such are in question. The distinction can (and must) be made in rhematical notation (quote-marks are sufficient for this), but is inevitably unmarked in the surface structure except through recognizing 'verbs of utterance', such as "call".

The encoding of a symbol-string formula could well be done character by character according to one of the standard systems for converting the common printed signs into seven- or eight-bit codes. But a considerable saving of space is possible if the coding incorporates the lattice structures assigned to the closed categories in (9.2), (10.4), and (11.4). This requires for Case, Identification and Quantification respectively, 6, 8, and 10 bits (with supplementary bits if specific numerals are involved); the lexical terms can be sufficiently coded alphabetically at 5 bits per character. Internal occurrences of . and (can be omitted, and the 'unmarked' terms "En" and "ALS", together with): can be all coded "111", while / is "11110" and terminal (or zero-arc) . can be "11111". The arc 'addresses' can probably for practical purposes be assigned 4 bits each, allowing notation of entries up to 12, +, & –; in very complex rhemata such as context rehearsals this may be insufficient, but these will not normally be required to be presented in this form at all.

Rhematical notation is appreciably more redundant than the surface expression of a given rhema. Using the coding outline above, the example (12.3) can be conveyed in 394 bits, whereas the character-by-character transcription of the English, including the Halliday notation, in ASCII code (8 bits per character) goes into only 376 bits, which in other codes could be considerably reduced. This is in accord with the fact that whereas the generation of the English from the rhema is in principle an algorithmic procedure (the speaker's task), the converse listener's task is *not* so.

12.4. Types of Intermediate Nodes

Another topic which needs to be summarized before we proceed is the classification of the nodes of a rhema, and particularly the intermediate nodes which have both preceding nodes and succeeding ones under the designatory arcs. Some distinctions between such nodes have already been made, but a few more are required for a complete understanding of the system.

After having classified nodes into Initial, Intermediate, and Terminal, we need to make further distinctions within the last two classes. Terminal nodes are either 'ultimate designants' (further classified as singly or multiply designated according as they have one or more designatory precessors), or designata, such as the "I" of (12.3) above. Intermediate nodes are more diverse.

Besides the two classes we have already named, that is 'predicative' and 'determinative' nodes, which are distinguished by their identification terms in relation to those of their successors, there are also 'conjunctive' and 'designative' nodes. The last class includes those nodes which designate something other than merely an ultimate extralinguistic designatum; usually a multiply designated terminal node. There have been many examples of this type of node in the preceding chapters; only the term 'designative' is new. Thus, the 6th node in case Ob of (12.3) is designative of the 7th in case En, but *not* the 8th. The fourth class, of 'conjunctive' nodes, is however up to now unexplored, and must be illustrated and explained by examples.

The key word here is "and". In English, and many other languages, the same word is used both to connect noun groups and to conjoin otherwise independent sentences; and also all ranks between. The rhematical status of these different uses of "and" are different; I shall begin with the kind of "and" that joins nouns or noun-groups. From the utterance "//$_5$ *John and /**Penny** have ar/rived.*" we may infer both that John has arrived and that Penny has arrived. On the other hand, from "//$_{13}$ *John or /**Penny** can /do /**that**.*", we can infer that John or someone can do it, but the rhema conveyed by "//$_{13}$***John*** *can /do /**that**.*" is not among the admissible inferences, since it rules out the alternatives which the former rhema explicitly put in. To get this inference legitimately one would also have to know that Penny has already declined to help; and this of course is available if at all only in the context. But we *also* may not infer "//$_{13}$***John*** *can /do /**that**.*" from "//$_{13}$ *John and /**Penny** can /do /**that**.*" where we have "*and*" again, as in the first example, this time because (without further contextual information) it may need at least two people to "*do that*".

The rhema structures involved here are as follows: for the two uses of "and":

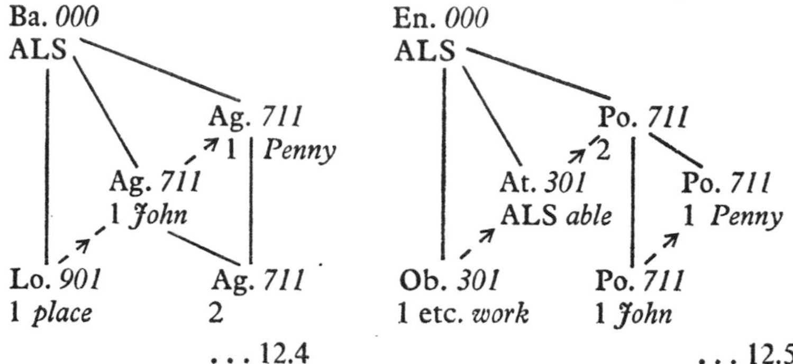

. . . 12.4 . . . 12.5

"//$_{5}$ *John and /**Penny** have ar/rived.*" "//$_{13}$ *John and /**Penny** can /do /**that**.*" and for the case of "or":

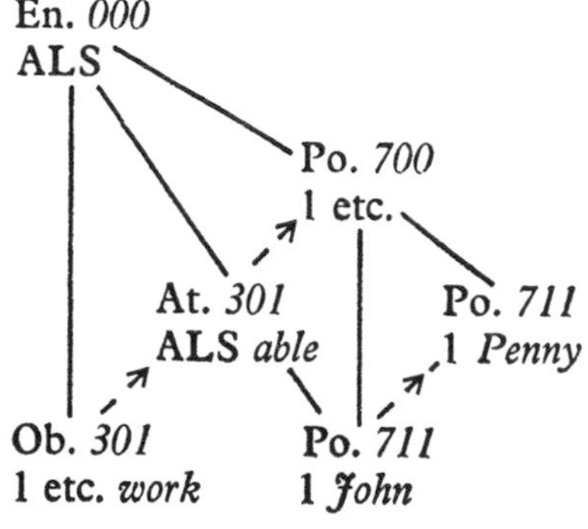

. . . 12.6

"//$_{13}$ *John or /**Penny** can /do /**that**.*".

The final node in (12.4) indicates that both "John" and "Penny" help to designate a pair whose arrivals are understood to be correlated; if this were not so the last node would be omitted, and its absence would probably be marked by the use of the tone ...1 instead of 5, with final tonic. In (12.6) we can distinguish the 'inclusive' from the 'exclusive' "or" (a point rarely felt useful in natural speech) by making the quantifier under "Po.700" "1om" or "am1" respectively. Conjunct subrhemata are recognized by having the same case on *all* their nodes, and in the case of "and" the same identification, while with "or" the alternants will have the same identification and the conjunctive node a weaker one (as with predicative nodes).

Note that in (12.5) and (12.6) the two nouns depend on an intermediate node (Po.711.2() or Po.700.1()); since designatory arcs are nontransitive these nodes cannot be omitted, unless all their peculiar successors are so too, because this would disconnect the graphs (see rule I2.1.3 in §14.6.2). It is this which prevents the derivations of the 'forbidden' inferences in these cases. We can, of course, drop say "*Penny*" and keep "*John*"—the result carrying the meaning "*John and another*" (12.5) or "*John or someone*" in (12.6).

The use of "and" to join clauses (that is, subrhemata headed by predicative nodes) can denote many things. It may mark mere collocation, for which posterior identification "020" is a sufficient indication; but very frequently it introduces a rhematical isocolon, a pair of rhemata, that is, whose parallelism is part of what they are intended to convey. This can be illustrated by "*//₁ Ned's a /**fool** and his //₁ brother's /**worse**.*" which expresses the relatively complex structure as shewn at top of opposite page.

Here the first three nodes (I have indicated only the minimum accessory arcs to facilitate discerning their order) are saying "Ned and his brother are foolish and worse", with two terms cased Su and At. This whole rhema designates separately and in parallel the two rhemata more precisely indicated by the spoken forms, one after the other. Thanks to the parallelism each of the dependent rhemata *can* be inferred from (12.7) since they are represented by connected subgraphs, even though there are conjunctive nodes of the type used in (12.5).

12.5. Summary of Terms at Predicative Nodes

In the course of the last three chapters I have indicated the

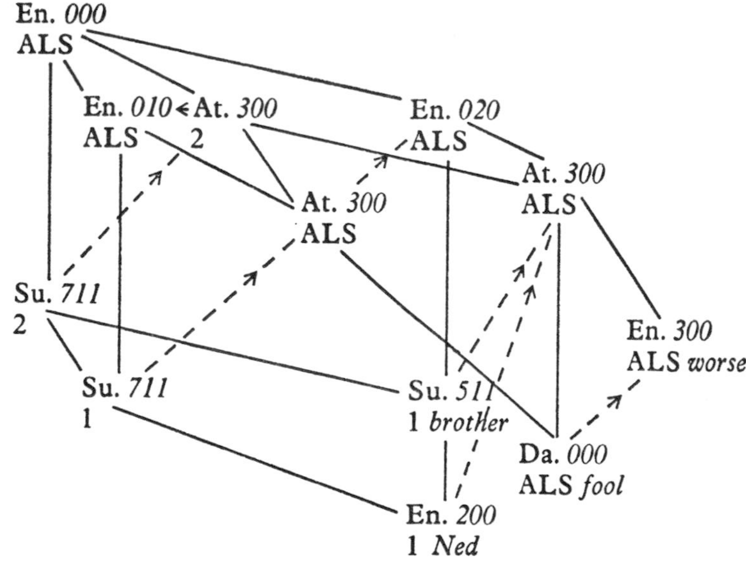

. . . 12.7

possible uses of each of the closed categories at predicative nodes. In this section I shall add little fresh but summarize the conventions there proposed, with some general comments.

In most instances the *quantifier* at a predicative node will be the (linguistically) unmarked "ALS". Uncertainty can be expressed by "Prh", but for specific degrees of *probability* separate nodes with appropriate lexical terms are required. A limited range of other quantifiers can be used to indicate frequency: a predication which is true only on one occasion (usually expressed in English by "*once*" or the like) may be marked by the quantifier "1"; repeated or recurrent events will take "*mny*"; and if it is a marked feature of the rhema that it holds permanently or invariably, "*All*" may be used. However, care must be taken with formal quantifications, especially negatives, in relation to the rules "*I*" in §14.6.

Identification plays a minor role at predicative nodes, but is nevertheless required to mark a clause as adductive, that is as containing a significant enlargement of the context (other than the mention of a new term, which would carry the adductive marker itself); to indicate a marked comparison between two clauses (as in (12.7) above) as 'prior' and 'posterior'; and to mark a statement as 'definite', in the sense of something already known to both participants. The expression "*The fact that . . .*" though in surface grammar treated as a noun group will be rhematically headed by a predicative, not a determinative, node, with the existential identification "301".

The following logical relations can be indicated by the use of *case* markers at predicative nodes: tense (aspect), modality, temporal relations, causal relations. These are mediated by the appropriate assignment of cases from the following sublattices of the case lattice (11.4), in the same order: tertiary stative, secondary stative, tertiary active, secondary active. The interpretation of the secondary cases at a predicative node depends on what other cases occur on nodes coordinate with it; and, with the secondary stative cases at least on whether the 'subject' of the predication is identical with that of the framing-clause or not (see here §11.5.1). When associated with another clause in a complementary case, the cases In,Pr,Ma mark clauses as a means, a result, or a cause of another; while the corresponding statives At,De,Da may express a condition, a purpose, or a pretext respectively. One might possibly extend these associations to express the ideas of 'believing' and the like as 'casual' verbs. Thus, with a clause governed by a predicative node with Datum case, subject cases Su,Sp,Ex,Po would express belief, expectation, assumption, and knowledge; while with a clause in case De subject cases Sp,Ex would correspond to advising and hoping respectively.

The temporal relations indicated by cases are those which are often called 'aspects', rather than merely indications of the time when things happen. (Absolute time, present as against non-present, corresponds closely with the constitutive versus adductive contrast in the Identification system; and past as against future might be associated with prior versus posterior.) The relations indicated by cases are of relative time, that is, whether something has been completed, is in progress, or has not yet begun, at the contextual moment (which normally requires no node to represent it) or at a time defined by another clause or designated by a coordinate node. Thus, the cases Co,Ba,Fr,Ci mark the predication of a habitual, completed, future or continuing action respectively; "I have done it" is interpreted as "my doing it is behind us", and "I had done it before they came" as "my doing it was behind their coming". That this interpretation is not the intuitively-obvious one for many people I have remarked in §11.5.3; but it is forced on us by the logic of the system. The tertiary active cases Ro,So,Go,Lo mark a clause as subject to the subordinating conjunctions "throughout the time that", "since", "till", and "when" respectively.

These uses of the closed category terms at predicative nodes are all, more or less, in accord with the inferential relationships which most frequently occur to a listener on hearing the forms indicated; unfortunately we have to qualify this as 'more or less' since the uses of the various surface forms, indicated as equivalents (more or less) of the given cases, identifications, or quantifications, of predicative nodes, are somewhat erratic and strongly context-dependent. The problem of deducing a rhema from a heard utterance, that is the listener's problem, is an open-ended one, and the result may always differ from what the speaker intended. But the converse procedure, the speaker's problem of expressing in an utterance a rhema already formulated in his mind, though open to various arbitrary (or at least rhematically irrelevant) choices along the way is in principle 'testable', in the sense that he may *fail* to express his intended thought.

12.6. The Application of the Rules of Sincerity

This test I have already formulated, in discursive style, in the rules of sincerity *S* of §2.7.2. I will conclude this chapter with a few remarks on their use. The first point which must be made, to avoid misunderstanding, is that although the problem confronts us here in the form of a comparison between an utterance and a rhema, represented as a graph (in one of three notational forms which I have provided), it is obviously unrealistic to imagine that there exists in the speaker's brain anything like either a graph, or a matrix, or a symbol-string. Not enough is known about brain function to be able to guess what form the 'rhema' does take. It is hard to doubt that there is something 'present' before speech begins (I am aware here that some authorities would not agree); and I claim to have shown that this 'something' must be transducible into the general form I have used to represent rhemata hitherto, though not necessarily containing *all* the information which I have indicated rhemata as containing. But I would not wish to perpetrate the kind of simplistic assumption which linguists have recently been tempted into by the great power of transformational notations, which has led them to imagine corresponding 'programs' coded somewhere in people's heads.

However, I do assume that it is possible to mean one thing and say another, through accidental failure of the generative procedure by which one's utterance is produced, and that if this happens then there is a discrepancy between rhema and utterance of the kind which infringes one or other of the rules *S*. And what can happen by accident can of course be effected 'on purpose', though how one discriminates between the two kinds of failure is a moral rather than a scientific question. I shall now give a series of examples of these discrepancies.

I have turned up very late for an appointment with my friend Di, and feeling apologetic I entertain in my mind the thought:

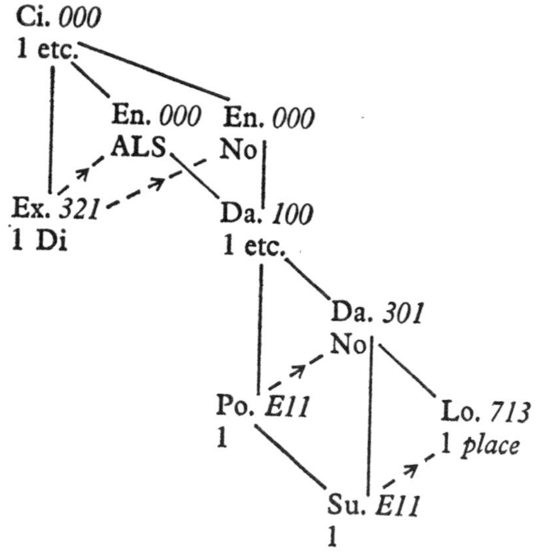

. . . 12.8

which, in my confusion, I seek to express by the utterance "//$_2$ *Did you |think I'd |got |**lost**.*". Though it is perhaps strained to describe all of them as a want of 'sincerity', there are several errors here. Rule *S1.1* requires that no element of the rhema structure should conflict with any marker present in its expression;

but the case Ci on the initial node conflicts with the simple past tense of the question; it would require rather "Are you thinking . . .". Rule *S1.2* requires accord between rhema and context; but although I started from the idea that "she must be thinking I was lost", the resulting case Ci *is* in conflict with the context of an opening remark, which should have either "Did you think" or "Have you been thinking" (En or Ba–Ci).

Rule *S2* requires that every element of rhema structure should reflect something in the utterance, but the lexis (*Di*) of the second node has no expression in the utterance given. Finally, against rule *S3*, the utterance has two features unjustified either by the rhema, or by the context, or by grammatical rules. First, the use of the tone *M*$\underline{2}$ implies that Di wasn't *really* thinking any such thing; but the rhema structure is that of a 'neutral' question, requiring tone 2 not $\underline{2}$.

The other point is the use of "I'd got lost". The tense is unsupported by the relevant part of the rhema; the last five nodes by themselves, following the interpretation of the cases suggested in §12.4, might be translated as "*I didn't know what place I was at.*" which is conveyed by "$//_1$ ∧ *I was* /***lost***." and says nothing about 'having got' lost. However, though not 'justified' by the rhema, nor of course by any rule of grammar, it is possible to justify the tense chosen on contextual grounds; Di might have been thinking "He's got lost", but hardly just "He is lost".

This example is of course artificial, in that I have compressed into it offences against every one of the 'rules of sincerity'; but it is not absurd or unnatural. The situation chosen is one in which such errors are very likely to arise on account of one's embarrassment, and at the same time the rhema which is intended to be expressed is one which is appropriate under the circumstances, provided I'd waited for Di to open the exchange. The errors too are all quite slight in the sense of affecting only minor points in the structure, except the one about the bias in the question which would call for more radical restructuring; but this is after all a matter which is not very seriously regarded; the difference between the tones 2 and $\underline{2}$ is acoustically small.

Some readers may wonder whether this comparison, ostensibly between a 'thought' and its utterance, is essentially different from, say, the predicament of a man who thinks in French and frames what he has to say in English with less than complete success. I claim the difference is that, whereas French and English are both fully articulate languages, my rhematical notation denotes what is not yet articulated in any language. 'Thinking' no doubt always involves verbalization of a kind but much of it is fragmentary, in some sense ascribing to the fragments much more rhematical content than their utterance, unprocessed, could convey; it uses also visual, auditory, or haptic imagery. And whatever thought one comes up with can always be expressed in a variety of ways, corresponding to minor transformations of the rhema structure, or determined by alternatives arising in the course of linguification. To translate from one language into another involves at least a partial return to the rhematical level, even when the main building-blocks of the surface structure can be processed in a more or less one-to-one manner. Even if the *delicacy* of a structure such as (12.8) exaggerates the degree of detail lodged preformed in the mind—though in my example I give myself ample time to perfect it—its *texture* (mathematical description) mirrors its prelocutionary form more faithfully than that of any 'surface' language can. Thought is not speech, and their congruence is praiseworthy.

CHAPTER XIII

Construction of the Context Rehearsal

The first problem arising for us, now that we have a fully developed system of rhematical notation for the representation of thoughts to be expressed in speech, is the problem of how to construct a realistic representation of a *complete context*, given that this cannot be expected to correspond, in most cases, to any single utterance. This chapter will be devoted to this problem; the procedure for deriving inferences from a representation of a context will be examined in the following chapter.

13.1. Characterisation of the Problem

It has been established, in Chapter IV, that the system of inferences acceptable from a given context C can be represented as a lattice under the inference-relation; and that the inference relation can be represented as conformal inclusion between the matrix representations of the rhemata between which it holds, as shown in Chapter V. The upper bound of this lattice represents the *rehearsal* of the context C, which we may imagine as a sequence of utterances conveying all the information available about the context to its participants, even though in practice much of this information will not need to be stated. The lower bound of the context lattice is the null rhema, represented by a graph with all its vertices and arcs labelled with the zero of the base domain. The set of elements of the context lattice is identified with the total set of legitimate inferences, that is, with the context *repertory*.

13.1.1. The Data: All else, it therefore appears, depends on the rhema structure by which we represent the upper bound of this lattice; that is, the rhematical notation of the context rehearsal. The data we are given, from which this construction must start, can be regarded as a string of natural language utterances defining the context. I shall not here consider that part of the process, which results in reducing each of these utterances to rhematical form; this is the mathematical representation of the listener's task, comprehension, and as I have already said this is likely to be an open-ended problem, any proposed algorithmic solution of which must be incomplete or at least not *demonstrably* complete, I shall therefore assume that our data take the form of a string of rhemata; and the problem I shall tackle will be the combining of these into a single rhema representing the context rehearsal.

This is also, of course, a part of the listener's problem; for what the listener has to do is to attain a comprehension of the total context, and not merely of the separate utterances which go towards it. It may, therefore, be asked whether my division of the problem, involving rejection of the 'difficult part' and concentration on the mathematical construction, is either realistic or justifiable. My answer here would be that it is the rhemata which are the essential thing throughout the speech cycle; the surface utterances, with all their complexity and often arbitrary rules and limitations, serve merely to build up and convey the rhemata, which are the stuff of thought. Natural language is in this respect a typical biological device, which has to meet certain minimal requirements, but has no need to do so in the most efficient manner, still less to exhibit the kind of elegance which delights the mathematician or the artist. It is like the eye, which produces a seriously distorted image, but one normally free from those errors, such as astigmatism, which could not be computed out by the brain, while admitting, for example, chromatic aberration which (surprisingly) can be corrected algorithmically; the collection of makeshifts which is surface grammar has the same character of getting the essential items across, but without regard to elegance of coding. Nevertheless, we know that its reduction to rhematical form is somehow possible; for this is essentially the same as a translation procedure, as if from one language into another. Anyone who knows the source language, and the principles of the rhematical notation which I have described, can effect the translation; and (as in the case of inter-language translation) there is a range of permissible outputs, each proper to a different contextual background, but each attaining a greater precision than natural languages are usually able to achieve.

13.1.2. Node Matching: The main problem at the mathematical level, which is the appropriate level of discussion once the data are given in rhematical form, is one whose existence is not at first sight apparent to the listener. This is, to represent all the rhemata, input as data, as matrices of the *same order*, that is with the same number of components, where most of these components are, in any given instance, likely to be zero. This problem does have a simple linguistic interpretation, of course; but it will require a little explanation to show what this is.

The easiest way to start is to consider the relation of an inference rhema to a rhema from which it can be inferred. Let us look at the utterance "$//_{-1}$ *Sentences of /up to /seven /**words** will be con/sidered.*"; I shall take this in the role of a context rehearsal, and consider alongside it an inference to the effect that "*Sentences will have up to seven words.*". The 'rehearsal' (absurdly rudimentary though it is) can be given in rhematical notation as:

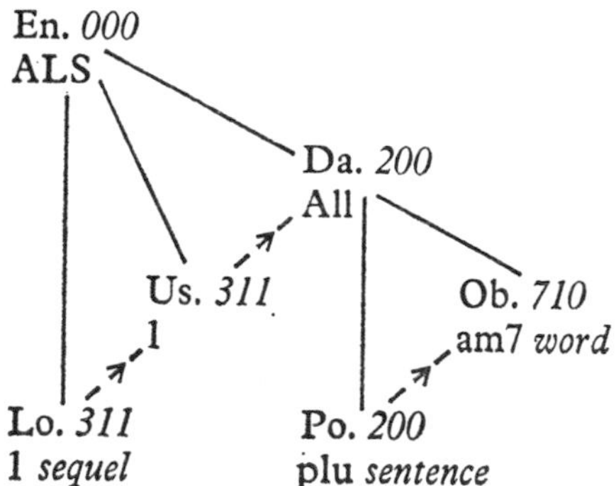

...13.1.1

corresponding to the matrix representation:

En. *000*. ALS ( )	**d**	**d**	**d**	a	a
	Lo. *311*. 1. (*sq*)	a	a	a	a
		Us. *311*.1. ( )	a	a	a
			Da. *200*. All ( )	**d**	**d**
				Po. *200*. plu (*sn*)	a
					Ob. *710*. am7 (*wd*)

...13.1.2

It is convenient at this point to introduce a new term: a triangular matrix such as (13.1.2) can be regarded as made up of L-shaped pieces called *gnomons*, each consisting of a vertical arm and a horizontal arm, which have one of the node labels on the diagonal in common between them. Thus, the second gnomon in (13.1.2) is the sequence d, Lo311.1 (sq), a, a, a, a. Each node of the graph (13.1.1) has its corresponding gnomon in (13.1.2), and it is this gnomon, rather than just the node label, which properly represents the node in the matrix.

The inference, that sentences will have up to seven words, is obtained from (13.1.2) by 'deleting' the first three gnomons (that is, replacing their components by zeros) and replacing the case Da of the fourth gnomon by En which includes it in (11.4); this gives us:

0	0	0	0	0	0
	0	0	0	0	0
		0	0	0	0
			En. *200*. All ( )	**d**	**d**
				Po. *200*. plu (*sn*)	a
					Ob. *710*. am7 (*wd*)

. . . 13.1.3

which corresponds to the graph diagram:

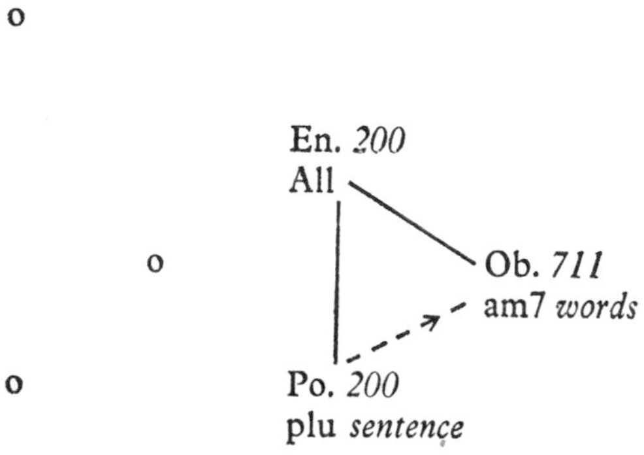

o

En. *200*
All

o

Ob. *711*
am7 *words*

o

Po. *200*
plu *sentence*

. . . 13.1.4

where for completeness sake I show the three unlabelled vertices as points unconnected with the fully labelled residue. So much is plain; but supposing we were given (13.1.4) as input, together with another utterance such as "//₁ ***Sen****tences will be con/sidered.*", how would we know which of the nodes conveyed by the latter would correspond to nodes already present in (13.1.4)? Out of the two we can evidently make up the six-node graph (13.1.1), but given each alone, there is no way to tell *which* of the six nodes each has; this only becomes apparent through comparing them. We must therefore find rules for *matching* the nodes of separate rhemata, so that they can be combined unambiguously into a larger whole.

13.1.3. The Matching Problem Defined: If the theory which I am expounding is to hold, there must be an unambiguous result; for if not, two rhemata which represent possible inferences from a given context will not have a unique least upper bound in the context repertory, which would then not be a lattice. In the example just given, we must know, and be able to ascertain by fixed rules, that the first node of (13.1.4) corresponds to the fourth gnomon of the completed rhema (13.1.1), and not, as it might, to the first. If such rules could not be found, or even if they could not be given a linguistic justification, the theory would be discredited.

In the illustration, it is, of course, 'obvious' that the only node which matches between the two proposed constituent rhemata is the one whose lexis is (*sentence*). But a little thought will show that we may not rely on identity of lexical terms for matching; for people can use synonyms, or pronouns, or replace a single word by a more or less complex periphrasis, and expect to be understood without difficulty. We can no doubt exclude as possible matches nodes whose lexical terms intersect only in an empty designation-class; but much tighter rules will be required to make matching unambiguous in all cases. We have no justification for expecting such rules to be simple when expounded in the analytical manner, nor do I claim that the rules I shall give are complete, or even without errors. The task of formulating matching rules is, perhaps, one of the major challenges which this approach to the understanding of how language conveys meanings presents. Its successful accomplishment will require the repeated study of individual instances and the search for ever more infrequent anomalies. In the course of this there will be a danger that the fascination of the search will take over from common-sense, and so lead to the whole approach being discredited. But a reasonable approximation to a complete statement of the rules must be possible, for if not it would be hard to understand how people do in fact arrive at any consensus in the course of a conversation.

We shall be able, when we have some matching rules to work with, to decide which nodes of two given rhemata contributing to a given context rehearsal 'match' each other. We shall then know also which do not match. Any node in a given rhema which has no match in another corresponds, therefore, to a null gnomon in the matrix representation of the latter; and there will be a null gnomon in the first corresponding to each node of the second which finds no match. We can, therefore, restate the matching problem as the problem of locating the null gnomons with which the matrix representation of each rhema must be filled out to give it its proper order as a member of the context repertory, considered as a lattice of matrices related by conformal inclusion. After this, however, there remains the problem of how to combine the nodes which do match; this is mainly a question of calculating the label of the combined node, but we also of course have to find *every* component of the gnomon, including the arc labels.

13.2. Rules Governing Context Rehearsals

Not every sequence of sentences is equally satisfactory as a rehearsal of a context. Some are obviously nonsense, in the sense that, if they are taken as context rehearsals, the context rehearsed is either bizarre, incomplete, or grossly improbable. It will help to formulate some rules which 'proper' context rehearsals must obey; such rules, if they can be trusted, will be helpful in finding the rhema structure of the completed rehearsal. It is, of course, useless to hope for *truly* rigorous rules of this kind: in natural language anything may happen, and the participants in a conversation will resort to wild guesses rather than conclude that either of them is incapable of connected speech. My so-called 'rules' of rehearsal are therefore only guidelines for such conjectures; but (a) in most instances they will be effectively directives rather than guidelines, and (b) other instances lie beyond the scope of the present work—that is, I shall avoid 'pathological' situations.

13.2.1. Connectedness: The first principle is that a completed rehearsal must be non-trivially connected; that is, it must be a connected graph, if all zero arc or node labels are ignored. If it is not connected, it represents two contexts rather than one. It is another question whether the rhema graph for a complete rehearsal must necessarily have a single initial node, such as we have hitherto required an ordinary (single) rhema to have. Intuitively, the rhema structure for an extended narrative, perhaps the simplest model for a rehearsal, would consist of a sequence of single rhemata, with whatever shared designations may be called for, all dependent on a single initial node labelled with the lower bound of the node subalgebra. One would therefore suppose that if an initial node were made a requirement for any complete rehearsal, nothing would be lost. But I suppose to go one step further, and require that this initial node shall itself be the initial node of one of the constituent rhemata. In this form, the rule of connectedness introduces a useful limitation on the choices to be made subsequently. But, as we shall see in §13.4.1, this initial node need not be that of the first-uttered constituent.

13.2.2. Anaphora: Another rule which comes to mind is that in a complete context rehearsal any anaphoric pronoun or identifier must have something to which it refers. In speech, forward anaphora is within limits allowable ("*He's a decent chap, is Bert.*"); but a context rehearsal is not speech, but a formalization of speech, involving explicitly many items of information which are too obvious or too trivial to require utterance, and not necessarily respecting the order in which the utterances are in fact made. For such a construction, it is reasonable to make it a rule that every anaphora must be prepared for by an explicit designant.

This is, of course, a pedantic rule; every 'must' in language generates a literary device based on flouting it. A short story can well open with such a sentence as "*Bjorn entered the bunker, swinging the cow's tail.*", where both occurrences of "*the*" involve anaphora, as does the name "Bjorn" seeing that we don't yet know anything about him. It could be a 'good' way of beginning the story, not because it could begin a context-rehearsal, but precisely because it couldn't, thereby engaging the reader's imagination from the start. If we had instead *"Once there was a man called Bjorn, who . . ."* we would find it relatively uninteresting and unstimulating.

This shows us that what I call 'rehearsing a context' is a highly unliterary activity, still less a colloquial exercise. It is a thing one has to do to operate an algorithmic inference system, rather than a need encountered in daily life. The relation of such a formal context rehearsal to the succession of random hints which ordinarily serves its turn may be seen as analogous to that between a formal syllogism, as understood in Aristotelian logic, and the loose way in which arguments reducible to this form are framed in conversation. Rhematic is, after all, a kind of alternative rationality beside that of logic, its spontaneity contrasting with the formality of the latter. Good writers, while generally eschewing a too meticulous following of the kind of rules I set out here, commonly begin with some kind of defining paragraph which sets out their subject; such opening paragraphs may perhaps be compared with the 'enthymemes' in which rhetoricians used to disguise their syllogisms. The fact that formal syllogisms are rarely if ever encountered in ordinary discourse does not invalidate the type of logic they are intended to formalize; neither does the absence of formal context rehearsals from real language invalidate the present system.

13.2.3. Adduction: A context rehearsal departs from reality in another way. It is required to make explicit everything that the participants in a conversation know about their context, or of which they become aware through their talk. Set out in full, it must thus give the impression of addressing a moronic comprehension. An obvious parallel is a computer programme, likewise addressed to a grossly unintelligent executant; and this analogy will be helpful. In a typical programming language (as, for instance, FORTRAN,[79] still widely used) there is a rule that no variable can be used until it has been 'declared'—that is, incorporated in an instruction to the computer to recognise the chosen symbol as a variable of a stated kind. In rhematic terminology, we can analogously stipulate that the first node in a rehearsal which designates a given designatum must have an *adductive* identification if indefinite (or be definite if it is constitutive).

This turns out to be a rather weak restriction, since in fact most identifications are marked as adductive. Constitutive identifications, marking an item as already located within the context, are in English mainly exemplified by demonstratives and possessives ("*my hat*" , "*that spider*", etc.). Thus, the sentence "*A certain man found a hoard of coins in his house.*" would be acceptable as a rehearsal; each of "*man*", "*hoard*" and "*coins*" has an adductive identification (the last two constituting a determinative sub-rhema to the effect that "*a certain hoard consisted of certain coins*"), while "*house*" has the anaphoric identification "*his*" which, however, refers back to "*a certain*" man within the same rhema.

13.2.4. Rules of Rehearsal: The foregoing considerations may be summarized in the following rules, bearing in mind that a context rehearsal is by definition something given as such, so that 'rules' can be said to govern it only in so far as the listener, who has to grasp the context rehearsed, mentally adjusts his comprehension so that the 'rules' hold. That is to say, the rules may not in all cases be exemplified in unedited context rehearsals; this, however, is not open to empirical verification, since the greater part of most contextual material is in normal circumstances unuttered, and to correct this is already an unnatural proceeding, whose ruliness tells us nothing objective. Thus, as I stated above, the rules given are best thought of as guidelines for the completion of a rehearsal, rather than a description of any existing object.

R: If a rhema Y contributes to the rehearsal of a context already in part rehearsed by a rhema structure X, then
- *R1:* The initial node of either X or Y is matched by a node of the other; and
- *R2:* Every node of Y has *either*
  - *R2.1:* an identifier which is either
    - *R2.1.1:* adductive indefinite, or
    - *R2.1.2:* constitutive definite; *or*
  - *R2.2:* at least one designatory successor which either
    - *R2.2.1:* has an identifier satisfying R2.1, or
    - *R2.2.2:* is also a designatory successor of a node in X.

This statement of the rules of rehearsal will be assumed in the sequel; but, with the foregoing provisoes regarding their interpretation, there may well be additional rules which could be added to them.

13.3. Construction of the Rehearsal

What we now have to do is to construct, from a given sequence of rhemata as data, a single rhema structure which shall represent the rehearsal of the context defined by the input rhemata. We shall start by taking two of the input rhemata and forming a product, which I shall call their *concatenation*, from which both the operands can be derived by the inference procedures to be defined in the next chapter. We shall then take a third of the inputs, and form its concatenation with that from the first two; and so on, until the data are exhausted. The procedure is thus a succession of concatenation operations, each performed on two operands only, though the first operand will be progressively more complex as the work proceeds.

This raises the question of what order the input rhemata should be taken in; for in general we cannot expect that the concatenation operation will be commutative. If the data are given in the form of a conversational exchange, we may presume that the order in which they are uttered will be acceptable for the purpose; this, however, may well prove optimistic, since real-life conversations are full of repetitions and back-trackings, which may or may not be signalled by interpellate ("what do you mean?") questions. In general, too, there will be material relevant to the contextual situation which is never uttered because it can be seen, or is taken for granted, by the participants. Even when we have got the spoken contributions into their proper order, we shall have to examine each of them to see what unspoken assumptions it embodies, not already warranted by what has gone before, and insert these before this latest utterance. There is thus a certain amount of preediting to be done before the concatenations can begin.

In the illustrations I shall give of the procedure, I shall work with material already 'preedited' in this way. This will look perfectly 'natural', in the same way that most of my single-sentence illustrations have appeared 'natural'. But the appearance is, of course, misleading in both cases, and for similar reasons. I would not burden you with an example such as "$||_2$ *Is* ʌ $||_4$ ***what**sername* ʌ ʌ $||_1$ *I* |***say*** $||_2$ *Is* ʌ ʌ *er* |***Pat*** |*here.*", when I wish to illustrate the rhema structure (7.7.6), more elegantly if less 'naturally' rendered as "$||_2$ *Is* |***Pat*** |*here.*"; likewise, the conversations I shall use to illustrate the concatenation procedure will be either artificially simplified, as in Chapter XV, or at least tidied up considerably, as in §13.4.4 below. We must not forget that if anyone wishes to apply my theory to material from tape-recordings, the tidying up will be a necessary preliminary, and one whose outcome may not always be unambiguous, since in any kind of recorded conversation so many clues obvious to the participants will be missing.

13.3.1. Illustrative Example: Before giving a formalized presentation of the procedure involved in forming the concatenation of a sequence of rhemata which rehearse a given context, I shall now set out in some detail a particular example. First, I give the verbalized form of the rehearsal, what I shall afterwards call the 'raw input'; this will consist, like the context illustrated in §3.3, of utterances from a conversation, interspersed with actually unuttered, but relevant, items of background information. I shall call the participants A, B as before, and the unuttered contributions will be assigned to an imaginary X. Here, then, is my example:

A^1 $||_4$ ***Well*** ʌ $||_{13}$ ***This*** *is* |*where I* |*live* |***now.***
B^2 $||_{1+}$ ***Oh*** ʌ $||_2$ *Do you* |***like*** |*living in a* |*caravan.*
A^3_4 $||_4$ ʌ *It* |*doesn't* |***cost*** *much* $||_4$ ʌ *Be*|*sides* $||_1$ ʌ *It's a* |*very* |***big*** |*one.*
X^5 $||_1$ *All* |*caravans have* |***win**dows.*
B^6 $||_{-2}$ *Don't the* |***win**dows* |*leak.*
A^7_8 $||_{53}$ ʌ *They* |*often* |***do,*** *of* |***course*** $||_5$ ʌ *But* |*I've been* |***lucky.***
X^9 $||_1$ *Luck is when* |*windows* |***don't*** |*leak.*

The rhema structures corresponding to these nine sentences are set out on the following page. For the sake of simplification, one or two conversational elements of no consequence to the illustration have been left out: such is the phrase "of course" in A7. Long double-lines have been inserted to connect the nodes which we shall decide 'match' each other; these matches will be

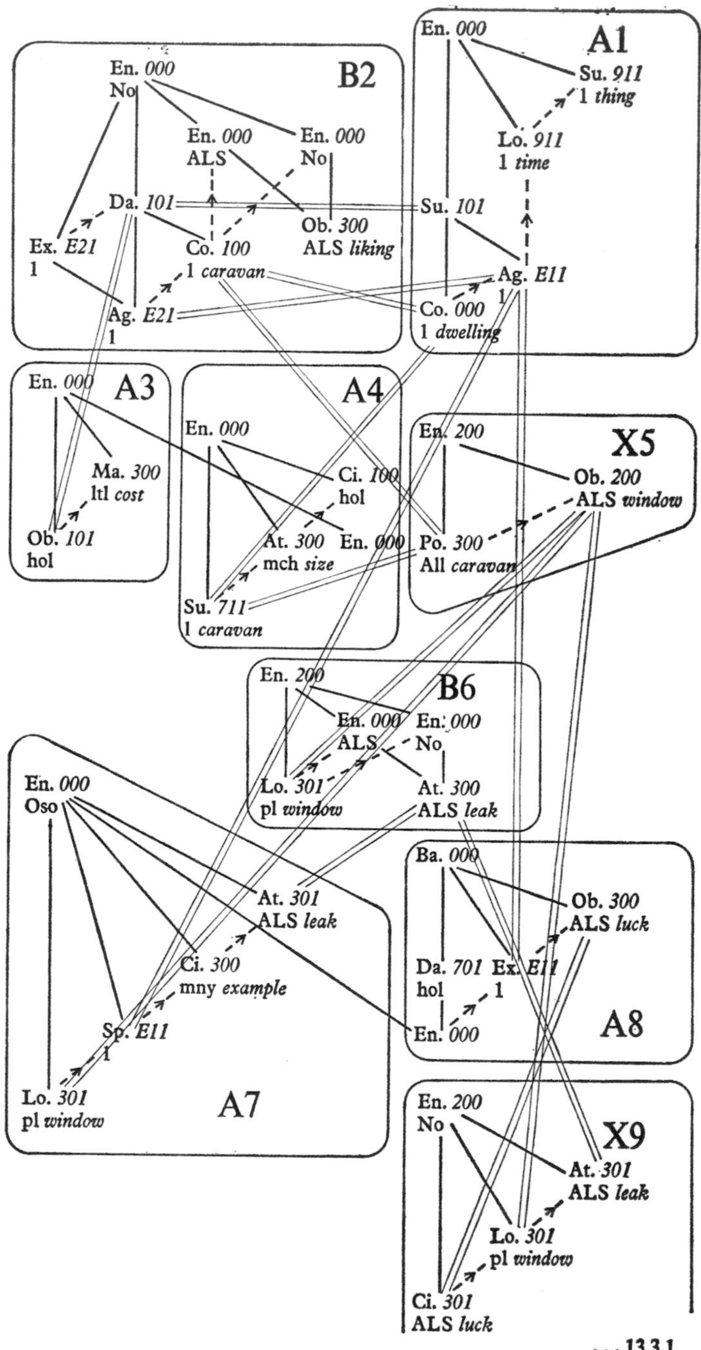
B2
En. 000
No
En. 000
ALS
En. 000
No
Da. 101
Ex. E21
1
Co. 100
1 caravan
Ob. 300
ALS liking
Ag. E21
1
A1
En. 000
Su. 911
1 thing
Lo. 911
1 time
Su. 101
Ag. E11
1
Co. 000
1 dwelling
A3
En. 000
Ma. 300
ltl cost
Ob. 101
hol
A4
En. 000
Ci. 100
hol
At. 300
mch size
En. 000
Su. 711
1 caravan
X5
En. 200
Ob. 200
ALS window
Po. 300
All caravan
B6
En. 200
En. 000
ALS
En. 000
No
Lo. 301
pl window
At. 300
ALS leak
A7
En. 000
Oso
At. 301
ALS leak
Ci. 300
mny example
Sp. E11
1
Lo. 301
pl window
A8
Ba. 000
Ob. 300
ALS luck
Da. 701
hol
Ex. E11
1
En. 000
X9
En. 200
No
At. 301
ALS leak
Lo. 301
pl window
Ci. 301
ALS luck

. . . 13.3.1

explained later. The rhema expressed by each sentence is *enclosed in a box* for greater clarity. In the following subsections I shall examine each of the concatenation operations starting with that between A1 and B2, and then between the product of these two with A3, and so on; there is no example here of a case where the next rhema will not match at all with the previous concatenation, though this is in theory possible and must be allowed for in the formal procedure.

13.3.2. Concatenating A1 and B There are three nodes in each of these rhemata which could match with each other. "Su101()" in A1 refers to 'living in a caravan' (though the caravan is ostended rather than mentioned, hence the lexical term "dwelling"), and, of course, so does "Da101()" in B2. Nodes which, in the context, designate the same thing are taken as "matching"; this is the basic idea of the matching relation. Unfortunately, of course, it may be quite unobvious from the words used when two nodes have such a common designatum. In the example here, this is perhaps obvious to the reader, but it could hardly be so to a computer programmed to carry out the concatenation. What would be obvious, even to a computer, is that "AgE11.1()" in A1 matches "AgE21.1()" in B2; the alternation of identification, 'me' versus 'you', is a simple function of who is speaking. It is convenient when, as here, there are two nodes within one rhema having the same designatum, such as "ExE21.1()" and "AgE21.1()" in B2, to prohibit one of them taking part in a match, since they are only vacuously alternatives. For the sake of getting a unique concatenation, we therefore refuse to accept a match between the *first* of such a pair and any node in the other rhema.

However, the most important match here is between "Co000.1 (dwelling)" in A1 and "Co100.1(caravan)" in B2. This is the one which tells us most about the context. But it is not the primary match in the order in which we shall search. This is because it runs counter to the focus ordering, in that it matches the theme of the first rhema with the rheme of the second, leaving most of both rhemata in the 'wrong' order: 'wrong' that is if we are right in taking the two rhemata in the order A1, B2. As I have said, it is possible that the order in which utterances are pronounced may not always reflect their contextual position; but this is likely to be a rare anomaly, and unsuitable for an example such as this. I therefore propose to build the concatenation of A1, B2 round the match between "AgE11.1()" and "AgE21.1()", which are respectively the rheme of A1 and the theme of B2, and so involves no barrier to the subsequent recognition, as 'secondary' matches, of the other two pairs. This preference for rheme-theme matches will be incorporated into the formal procedure.

13.3.3. Introducing A3: The result of concatenating A1, B2 is now the first operand, with which A3 must next be concatenated. It is:

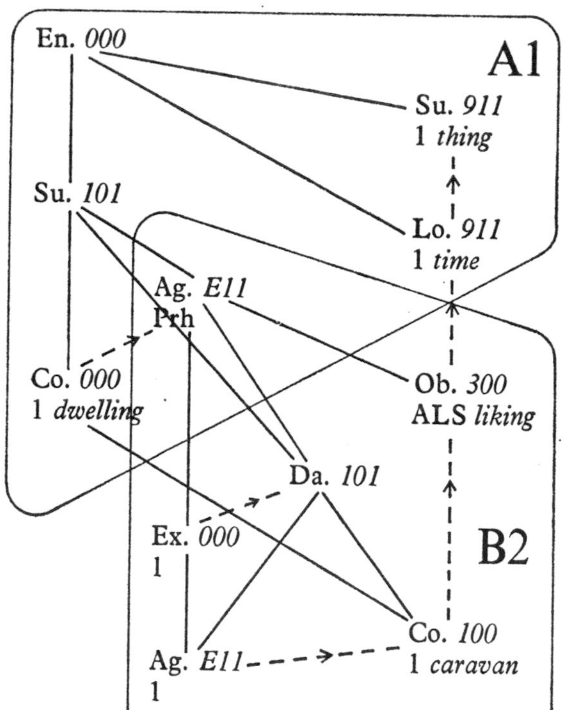

... 13.3.2

There are several points here which call for explanation. First, the linch-pin of the construction is the node "AgE11Prh()", which comes from conjoining the initial "En000()" of B2 with the "AgE11.1()" of A1. In this operation, we retain the case of the node in the first rhema for this is the one which furnishes the syntactic context, and for the other terms of the node label we take the intersections, using the appropriate sublattices (9.4), (10.2), and (11.4). However, in this case the second rhema is a question. This question is never actually answered; this is a common situation, but in a context rehearsal we cannot accept any zero arcs (the characteristic of closed questions), and so we have to have a way of regularizing unanswered questions. This is, in the last resort (which in the actual procedure we should not be reduced to till we reach the end of the input, but for brevity I here anticipate), is to introduce the quantification "Prh", which accordingly turns up at this node as representative, in the concatenation, of the initial node of the question B2. Next, the two *secondary* matches are represented by linking the nodes affected by new designative arcs; this is the 'obvious' way of showing that they have the same designata. These are the arcs joining Su–Da and Co–Co, which have no warrant in either of the two operands. Finally, since in the concatenation the subrhema governed by "AgE11Prh()" is determinative, that is, it means "I who . . .", the "Ex" node from B2 appears with null identification, which marks this relation (. . .) by *including* the former.

If we were to try to express (13.3.2) in English, we should have to say something like "$//_4$ *This is /where /**I** $//_4$ who /may or /may not /**like** /living in a /caravan* $//_{1+}$ ***live***.". It will get worse as we go on: contexts are not normally 'rehearsed' as a single sentence; the function of the rehearsal we are here constructing is not to be uttered, but to serve as the upper bound of a lattice, all of whose elements will represent, we hope, all the of the inferences legitimately derived from the given context.

When we bring in A3 to concatenate with (13.3.2) we find that only one of its three nodes gives a match: "Ob101hol()" matches with "Da101()", because the 'object' referred to is the same, namely 'living in a caravan'. Of course, we can't use this method of spotting matches in a formal procedure, for there we have to rely solely on clues given in the input rhemata. I shall in due course suggest some simple (over-simple) rules for this; but in working an informal example it is legitimate to use commonsense to illustrate what's going on. When we find a match, as here, between an intermediate node and a theme, we have to carry over the whole of the second rheme into the place occupied by the matching node in the first. As before, we conflate the initial of A3 with the intermediate node which matches it in (13.3.2); A3 is then turned into determinative form (it now means 'living in a caravan, *which* is cheap'), and the dependents of "Da101()" in (13.3.2) are transferred to become dependents of the now equivalent node "Ob101hol()". The result is:

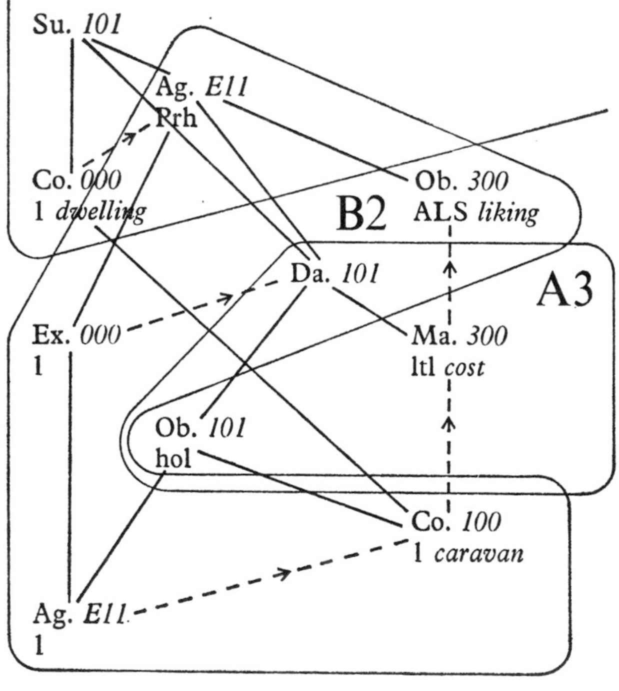

. . . 13.3.3*

I omit the top parts of the total rhema to save space. The part remaining is determinative, not predicative, and says "*I, who perhaps like living in a caravan, which doesn't cost much* . . .".

13.3.4. Introducing A4: The next rhema, A4, removed from its position in the narrative, says that "*Besides* [*being cheap to*

* Note that here there are designative arcs linking Da. with Ag. and Co., as in B2, which I have omitted to avoid overloading the diagram. Immaterial at this stage, this convention avoids the final (13.3.9) becoming unreadable.

live in] *the caravan is a very big one*". We have two matches here with (13.3.3). "Su711.1(caravan)" obviously matches with "Co100.1(caravan)"; and the node "Ci100hol()" has a shared dependent with the initial of A4 which marks these two as having the same designatum. The latter node is represented in (13.3.3) by "Da101()". The first of these matches is precisely of the preferred rheme-to-theme type, and is thus the primary match; the latter, notwithstanding that it is even more clearly marked, must then be secondary, and marked by an added designatory arc replacing the shared successor. The result of these operations is shown in (13.3.4). Here again I have cut out the initial nodes to get a manageable diagram; the parts shown are combined by the same procedure illustrated for A1, B2 in (13.3.2), could be expressed by "*My living in a caravan, which nevertheless is large, doesn't cost much*".

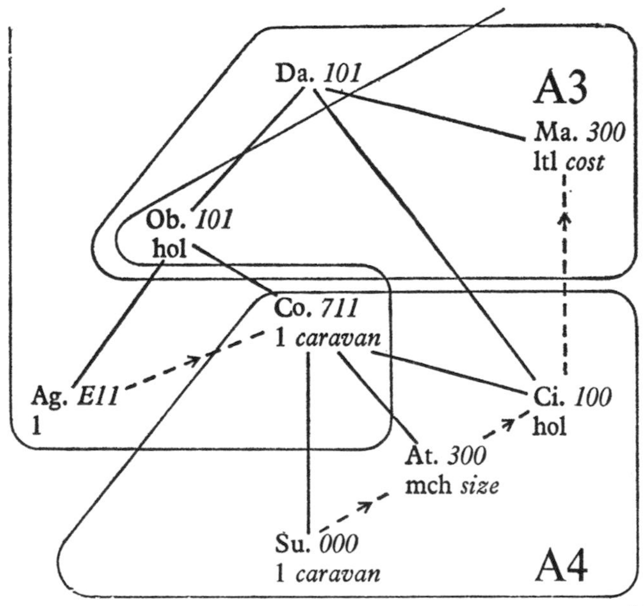

. . . 13.3.4

Two points call for comment. First, since the subrhema governed by 'Co100.1(caravan)' is now subsumed as a component within a larger rhema, it is determinative, no longer predicative; on this account the identification of its theme is reduced to 000 and the identification appearing in A4 is transferred to the governing node which becomes "Co711.1(caravan)". The second point is that since the two nodes which formally were represented as having a common designatum are now explicitly associated by a designatory arc, that from "Da101()" to "Ci100hol()", the shared successor "000()" is now deleted.

13.3.5. Introducing X5: We now come to the first unuttered contribution to the rehearsal. It is needed so that the reference to "windows" in subsequent contributions shall be understood as designating a part of the caravan already introduced. This is, of course, 'obvious' to the human participants; but since the statement that caravans have windows is needed to complete the designatory chain from "dwelling" to the last occurrence of "windows", to which it supplies the third of five such arcs, it has to be included in the rehearsal *as if* uttered. Its effect is very simple: it is simply to amplify the node "Su000.1 (caravan)" of (13.3.4) by a determinative subrhema describing it as having windows. The result is:

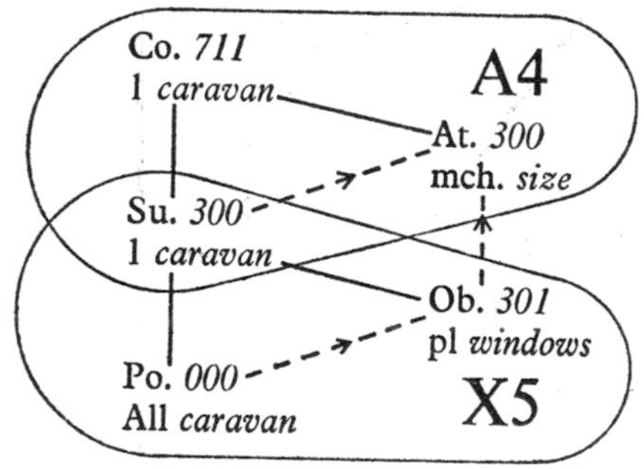

. . . 13.3.5

Note that in deriving (13.3.5) from (13.3.4) we have transformed X5 from predicative to determinative form, changing the identification of its theme to 000 and assigning the 300 identification instead to the matching node "Su300.1(caravan)" of (13.3.5)

13.3.6. Introducing B6: We now come to another question, asking whether the windows don't leak. This, too, gets no *firm* answer, but A7 constitutes formally an affirmation. Before reaching this result, however, we can introduce the following simple step into the concatenation. It follows exactly the same lines as the last, with only one match, from "Ob301pl(window)" to "Lo301pl(window)". As in previous instances, this requires that we conflate the former node with the initial of B6, and that we reduce the identification on "Lo301pl(window)" to 000 to make the newly introduced rhema determinative of "windows". We thus get:

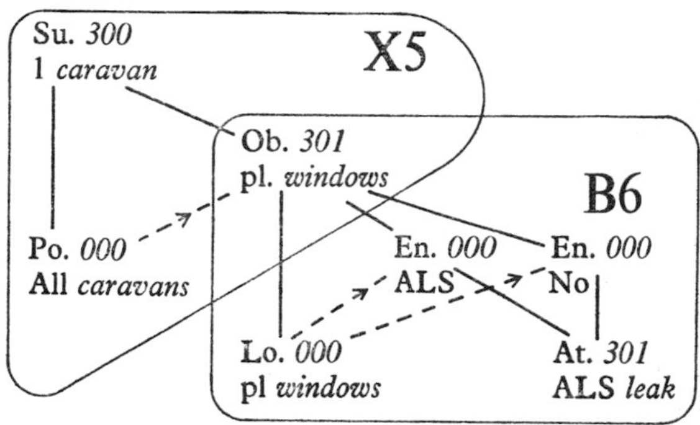

. . . 13.3.6

This stands for "*A caravan, which like all such has windows which leak, dont they?*"; English lacks the means to use an interrogative as a relative clause, but it is logically possible for something to be characterized by a question asked about it.

13.3.7. Introducing A7: This sentence admits, albeit grudgingly, that caravan windows usually do leak. The rhema A7 gives three matches with (13.3.6). The intermediate nodes "En000()" of (13.3.6) and "En000Oso()" of A7 do match, even though a match between two nodes, both of which have dependents, is only allowable if some pair of dependents having the same case also match. In this case, they do so, for clearly both the "Lo" and the "At" nodes have the same designata. We have not encountered this situation before: it requires that we 'conjoin' the two non-terminal nodes, and 'fuse' the two pairs of matching nodes. The procedure leaves one of the two nodes which in (13.3.6) had a zero arc connection unmatched; "En000No()" has a quantification contradictory to that of its only possible match in A7, "En000()" which prevents matching. The appearance of such an unmatched *and* unordered node is clearly the sign that the question, still extant in (13.3.6), has been 'answered'; we have therefore to delete "En000No()" from the product. Another modification called for in this case arises from the fact that in fusing the two node labels "Lo" we would be combining the theme of a determinative rhema with that of a predicative rhema; this is not allowable, since every rhema or subrhema must be either the one or the other. Thus, this fusion has to be disallowed, though the match stands; as before, the thing to do in such a case is to keep the two nodes separate, and insert an additional designatory arc to join them. We thus get:

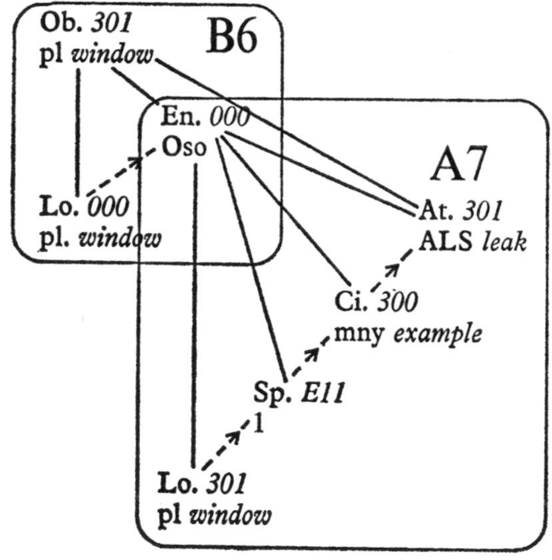

... 13.3.7

13.3.8. Introducing A8: But, having made this admission, quantified as shown by "only sometimes", A goes on to claim that with his caravan he has been 'lucky'. We don't yet know what he means by this; or, more exactly, *we* know very well, but what we know cannot be extracted from these utterances alone, and must await the unuttered contribution X9. Meanwhile, we have only A8, and this has one matching node, signalized by a shared successor, whose match in (13.3.7) is "En000Oso()". This is like the situation at A3, where also an intermediate node was matched with a theme. Nevertheless, as a match with a theme, it takes precedence over the other match, between

"SpE11.1()" and "ExE11.1()", which both designate A himself. These then are to be joined by a new designatory arc. Repeating the procedure used for A3 we get the result shown as (13.3.8) below.

Coming to X9, which tells us what 'luck' means in this context, we find, for the first time, that all the terminal nodes have matches. The theme "Ci301(Luck)" matches obviously with "Ob300 (luck)", and determines the pattern of the concatenation; the other two nodes have labels identically the same in (13.3.8) and simply fuse. The resulting structure will be found at the bottom of (13.3.9) where I set out in full the rhematic structure of the context rehearsal, which we have now completed.

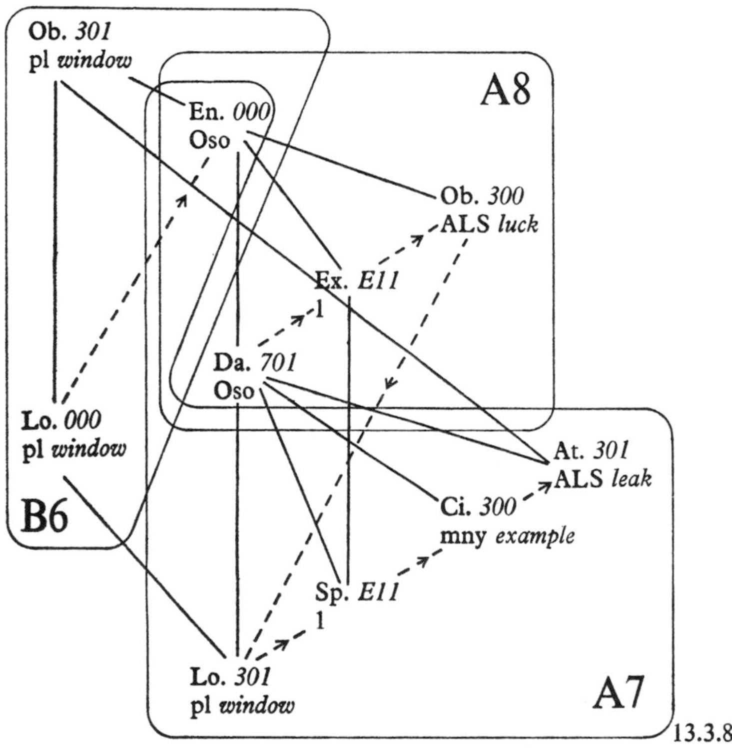

13.3.8

The completed context rehearsal is shown on the following page. There is one point to note in its construction, namely the rearrangement of the quantifications in A7 and X9. The last

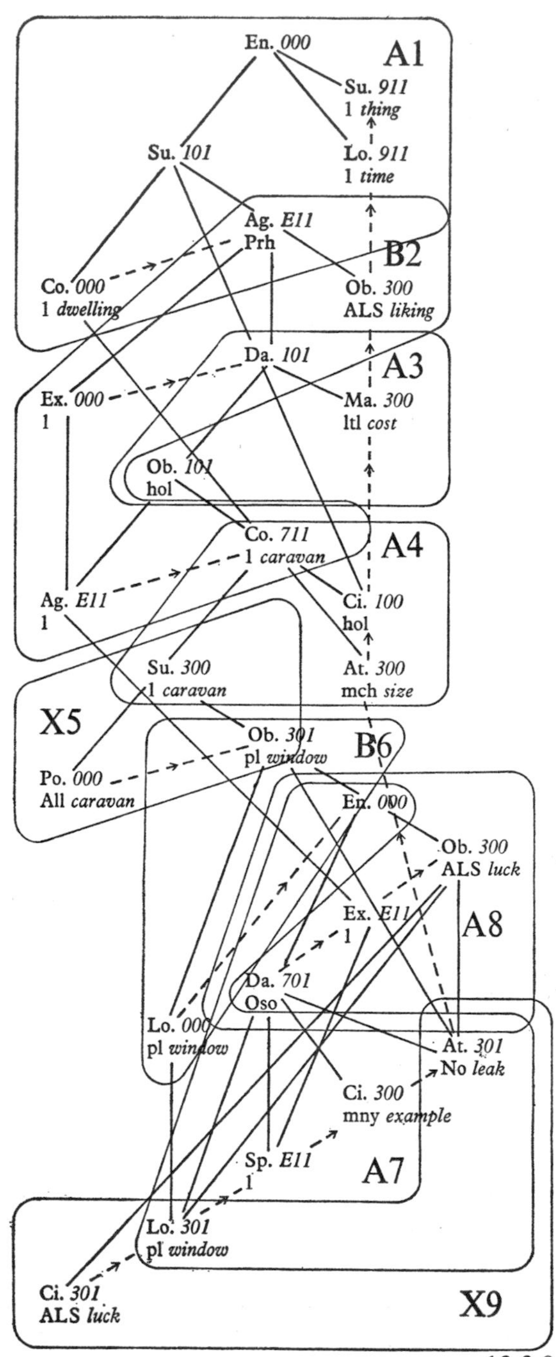

En. 000
A1
Su. 911
1 thing
Su. 101
Lo. 911
1 time
Ag. E11
Prh
B2
Co. 000
1 dwelling
Ob. 300
ALS liking
Da. 101
A3
Ex. 000
1
Ma. 300
ltl cost
Ob. 101
hol
Co. 711
1 caravan
A4
Ag. E11
1
Ci. 100
hol
Su. 300
1 caravan
At. 300
mch size
X5
Ob. 301
pl window
B6
Po. 000
All caravan
En. 000
Ob. 300
ALS luck
Ex. E11
1
A8
Da. 701
Oso
Lo. 000
pl window
At. 301
No leak
Ci. 300
mny example
Sp. E11
1
A7
Lo. 301
pl window
Ci. 301
ALS luck
X9

... 13.3.9

can be represented either as in (13.3.1) with "Not" at the initial node, or, among other variants, with the "Not" transferred to the "leak" node; the rules governing these equivalent quantifications are given in the next chapter. Though all equivalent (in relation to X9 by itself), they are not all equally compatible with A8 which says "I have had luck", not "I have had no luck". Thus, we have to place the "Not" at "At301*Not*(leak)". But this entails modification of A7, which says that windows leak but only sometimes. The modification required by the equivalent quantification rules is to replace the quantification of the initial node, here "Oso", by its complement (see table in §9.6), which is "Oso" again; this is, of course, correct, since if the windows "only sometimes" leak, they "only sometimes don't" leak. These quantifications have been shown in (13.3.9).

13.4. The Concatenation Algorithm

Having now described the concatenation procedure discursively, with the help of a particular example, I shall now reduce the procedure to a more formal shape. Essentially, what follows is a computer programme, though I avoid the excessively imperspicuous expressions commonly involved in the use of formal 'programming languages'; but it is unavoidable to present it as a sequence of numbered steps, nor can we do without the *ad hoc* naming of the entities involved. It is thus not an easy thing to follow, and those who will trust me that the procedure I have outlined can be formalized somehow or other should proceed at once to §13.5. (It is, of course, far from obvious that the formal procedure really does reach an unambiguous result, let alone the result aimed at. It is laborious, but not impracticable, to check it against the example just given.)

Besides the main concatenation procedure, I give also similar specifications of the operations used therein, and called "Match", "Conjoin", and "Fusion" respectively. These are, of course, required for the procedure to be fully explicit.

13.4.1. The Main Concatenation Procedure: We assume that the data is given in the form, represented by (13.3.1), of a sequence of rhemata, represented, for example, by their triangular matrices (this is the most convenient form for computer handling) or simply as graph diagrams as in the example just worked (which is easier for a reader to follow). I assume that the term "next" (i.e. the first unused member of the sequence of rhemata) will be clear, even when there is no next.

0. Let Z be null, and let A with n nodes be the next rhema, and let B with m nodes be the next rhema;
1. If B doesn't exist, return A as the result required;
2. Let j be 1; Bj denotes the j-th node of B;
3. Let i be n; Ai denotes the i-th node of A;
4. If Ai, Bj *match* (see §13.4.2), go to (10); else
5. Take 1 from i;
6. If i is still greater than O, go to (4); else
7. Add 1 to j;
8. If B(j–1) has d-successors, let k be j;
9. If j is still not greater than m, go to (3); else to (20)
10. Let C be the *Conjoin* of A and B (see §13.4.3) and let y be 2;
11. Let x be 2;
12. If Ax, By *don't match*, go to (15); else
13. If (x–i (y–j) is positive, replace Ax and Bx in C by their *fusion*/(see §13.4.4), and go to (15); else
14. If (x–i) (y–j) is negative, insert in C a designatory arc **d** from Ax to By in C; and in any case
15. Add 1 to x;
16. If x is still not greater than n, go to (12); else
17. Add 1 to y;
18. If y is still not greater than m, go to (11); else
19. Let A be the conjoin of Z and C, let Z be null, and go to (21)
20. Let Z be A, and let A be B;
21. Let B be the next rhema;
22. If Z is null or if B exists, go to (1); else
23. Report that the input data do not constitute a context rehearsal.

13.4.2. The Matching Rules: To determine whether two given nodes 'match', we must ideally decide whether they refer to the same designatum. This, however, is beyond our power to decide if all we have to go on are input rhemata whose context is still in process of construction; we have, therefore, to substitute a set of rules, based on this type of data, which will be likely enough to lead to such ideal matches being detected, and nodes with different designata being rejected as matches. We must remember that the whole process of constructing a context rehearsal is part of the comprehension phase of the speech cycle, the task of the listener. This, as explained in Chapter II, is inevitably an open-ended and indeterminate process, for which computer-type operations can at best give an approximate solution. The rules which I propose, and I must emphasize that they are offered only tentatively and as a basis for argument, are as follows:

M: Two nodes are accepted as matching
- *M1:* provided that
  - *M1.1:* neither has a single designative successor not shared with the other, and
  - *M1.2:* if both have more than one designative successor, then either
    - *M1.2.1:* no one case occurs among the successors of both, or
    - *M1.2.2:* at least one pair of successors with the same case match; and
- *M2:* they have either
  - *M2.1:* a designatory successor in common; or
  - *M2.2:* non-contradictory quantifications, and either
    - *M2.2.1:* identical lexical terms, or
    - *M2.2.2:* null, or if non-null then intersecting, lexical terms, and identifications of which one includes the other; or
  - *M2.3:* contradictory quantifications, and either
    - *M2.3.1:* contrasting identifications and intersecting lexical terms, or
    - *M2.3.2:* non-intersecting lexical terms.

Note that, in dialogue, the identifications must be corrected for the alternation of persons wherever necessary.

Some of these rules are exemplified in the example worked through in §13.3. Thus, M1.1 is used to exclude the node ExE21.1() of B2 from matching AgE11.1() in A1. M1.2 is not illustrated. M2.1 is used for example in A4, whose node

Ci100hol() is allowed by this rule to match with En000() in the previous concatenation. M2.2.1 is used several times, for example to allow Co000.1(dwelling) and Co100.1(caravan) to match, and at A3 the match of Ob101hol() with the previous Da101(). M2.2.2, likely to prove the commonest type of match, occurs for example at A7, where At300(leak) matches At301 (leak). Many other situations, including contradictory quantifications, will be illustrated in Chapter XV.

13.4.3. Conjoining Rules: These rules, many of which have been illustrated in our example, may be formulated thus:

C: Given two rhemata A,B whose primary match (found at step (4) of the concatenation procedure) is between the nodes Ai,Bj, the Conjoin of A,B has
- *C1:* if j = 0 (the initial node of rhema B),
  - *C1.1:* in place of Ai, a node whose label has
    - *C1.1.1:* for case, that of Ai, and
    - *C1.1.2:* for the other terms, those of B0; and
  - *C1.2:* as designatory successors of the above node,
    - *C1.2.1:* for each successor of Ai in A,
      - *C1.2.1.1:* if it matches with a successor of Bj with the same case, the Fusion of these nodes, or
      - *C1.2.1.2:* the label unchanged; and
    - *C1.2.2:* the remaining successors of Bj in B in order; *but*
- *C2:* if j = k (as formed at step (8) of the concatenation procedure), i.e. Bj is the theme of B or of a subrhema of B,
  - *C2.1:* in place of Ai, a node whose label has
    - *C2.1.1:* for case, that of Ai, and
    - *C2.1.2:* for identification,
      - *C2.1.2.1:* if Ai is predicative, that of Ai, or else
      - *C2.1.2.2:* the meet of those of Ai,Bj; and
    - *C2.1.3:* for the other terms.
      - *C2.1.3.1:* if Ai is predicative, that of Bh, or else
      - *C2.1.3.2:* the meet of those of Ai,Bh, where

Bh is the nearest interrogative precessor of Bj if any, or if not the nearest predicative precessor;

C2.2: and as additional designatory successors of the above node, those of Bh, except that Bj,

C2.2.1: if Ai is predicative, takes the quantification of Ai and retains its own identification, but otherwise

C2.2.2: Bj takes the identification 000 and retains its own quantification;

C2.3: and as designatory successors of Bj the former successors of Ai unchanged; *but again*

C3: if j exceeds k, then

C3.1: in place of the designatory precessor of Ai, its Fusion with that of Bj, and

C3.2: as designatory successors of the above node,

C3.2.1: for each node preceding Ai in A,

C3.2.1.1: if it matches with one of the same case after any previous match, but before Bj in B, the Fusion of these nodes, or else

C3.2.1.2: the node label unchanged; then

C3.2.2: any remaining precessors of Bj in B;

C3.2.3: then, for Ai and Bj,

C3.2.3.1: if the cases agree, the Fusion,

C3.2.3.2: else Ai followed by Bj; then

C3.2.4: the nodes after Ai in A treated as in C3.2.1; and finally

C3.2.5: any remaining successors of Bj in B.

13.4.4. Fusion: The 'fusion' of two secondarily matching nodes can be defined relatively briefly, but for the sake of conformity with the other operations, I set it out in the same manner:

F: Given two nodes A,B their Fusion is a node in whose label

F1: the case is that common to A,B

F2: the identification and quantification are each the join of the corresponding terms in A,B in (10.2), (9.4), resp.;

F3: the lexical term is the meet, in the lexical lattice, of those of A,B.

13.5. Adjustments

The concatenation of a series of rhemata presented as the rehearsal of a given context, as it is delivered by the preceding algorithm, is not always in the most convenient form for the computation of inferences from it. To enable the inference procedure to be simplified, and its conformity with the context lattice theorem (4.6) to be more readily proved, it is helpful if certain 'adjustments' are made to the raw concatenation before proceeding further.

13.5.1. Nature of the Adjustments: The governing condition on these adjustments is that they must in every case yield an equivalent thema to the one adjusted. To neglect this would be to risk an arbitrary alteration of meaning, after which any inference would be under suspicion. The reason why they are worth making at all, is that the raw product of concatenation, which as we have seen is rarely capable of intelligible expression except when fragmented into the same kind of sentences out of which it was composed, is for this reason liable to contain needlessly obscure distributions of the essential information. In principle, of course, the adjustments could be omitted, or made to the products rather than to the input of the inference procedure. But it is best to ensure that the inferences, when we get them, are as perspicuous, that is to say as easily expressed in natural language, as they can be. The adjustments are intended to secure this end.

The fundamental principle of the theory is that every legitimate inference from a context rehearsal C should be represented by a rhema structure, whose matrix representation is conformally included in that of C, using an inclusion relation such as is defined in Chapter V. But it is *not* required that every rhema so included should be an inference. As already mentioned, one could by this rule obtain an 'inference' by deleting "not"! This means that, in the next Chapter, we shall have to catalogue the various 'impediments' to inference. It is this catalogue which the present adjustments are mainly intended to simplify.

13.5.2. The Adjustment Rules: The rules, which effect the transformation of the raw output from the concatenation procedure into the proper form both for further concatenation, and for application of the inference rules, may be formulated thus:

A: If there is, anywhere in the raw concatenation,

A1: any pair of nodes unconnected by an accessory arc, and

A1.1: *if* only one of them has been involved in a match *then* the other must have its label deleted to the zero of the base domain, and the resulting vertex subsumed in its designatory precessor, or

A1.2: *if*, with no further input rhemata awaiting concatenation, both or neither have been matched, *then* both must be deleted and subsumed in their precessor, whose quantification becomes "Prh"; or

A2: any pair of nodes juxtaposed under both arc labels, where the identification of the first is included in that of the second (i.e. a determinative node and its theme), *then*

A2.1: the quantification of the first must be changed to the meet of the two quantifications, and

A2.2: the lexical terms of both must be changed to their meet in the lexical lattice; or

A3: any pair of nodes with a common designatory precessor and the same case, and *if*

A3.1: the same identification and lexis, contradictory quantifications, and if any designatory successors at least one in common *then* both are deleted and subsumed under their precessor whose quantification is negated; *but if with*

A3.2: non-intersecting identifications or lexes, *then*

A3.2.1: if they are neighbours under accessory arcs, *then* a common designatory precessor must be inserted, with

A3.2.1.1: the case common to both, and

A3.2.1.2: for quantification if both are numbers, their sum, otherwise their join, and

A3.2.1.3: other terms null; *but*

A3.2.2: if they are not neighbours, then both are deleted as under A3.1; *or*

A4: any node with the quantification "non" and at most one designatory successor,
then its lexical term (or that of its successor) must be replaced by its complement (see below), and its quantification changed to "ALS".

13.5.3. Comments on the Adjustment Rules: *A1* deals with the answering of closed questions; its effect is to eliminate from the final form of the rehearsal rhema all zero arcs, as required by the theory if conformal inclusion is to be unambiguous. In the example in §13.3, the effects of this adjustment were anticipated immediately after concatenating A3 rather than waiting to the end, to save retaining the doomed node in the intermediate concatenations; but at A7, which gives a definite answer to B6, rule *A1.1* is applied in the normal manner at once.

A2 serves to normalize newly-created determinative rhemata, giving them a standard form. This avoids unwanted alternative formulations, and facilitates the subsequent inferential procedures. The effects of this adjustment are seen in the appearance of the quantification "only" (the meet in (9.4) of "1" and "All") at two nodes in A4 in (13.3.9).

A3 deals with 'isoptotic' nodes, that is, those which have the same case. These may indicate conjunct pairs (see §12.3), or they may contradict each other either by quantification* (*A3.1*) or what is in effect by focus (*A3.2.2*); if all these situations are avoided, they will normally have been fused in the course of applying the rules C. Only one of the three types of conjunctions mentioned in §12.3 is provided for: the 'simultaneous "and" ' of (12.4) cannot be derived by concatenating two rhemata, and constructions with "or" (12.6) are likely to arrive ready-made by the process of concatenation. But this last is a questionable point, and *A3* may need tightening. These rules are not illustrated in §13.3.

A4 normalizes the treatment of the special complementing quantification "non". This is not a formal quantification in the sense used in the inference rules, and, while too useful an item

* It is probable that *A3* should not be applied to the *input rhemata* from which the concatonation is constructed; such utterances as "$//_4$ *That /tree **isn't** a /tree.*" can occur, and yield valid inferences—based on the first "*tree*" standing for "*which you call a tree*".

to be given up, it is best eliminated by this rule before proceeding to inferential processing. Of course, the lexical lattice is not strictly a complemented lattice (though it could very simply be converted into one, at the expense of an extra coding bit), and so the term 'complement' as applied to a lexical term is not wholly explicit. It is, however, perhaps sufficient to let the quantifier stand as "non" in cases where complementation is ambiguous or unavailable. This rule is not illustrated by any of my examples, but the use of "non" may be seen in the rhemata of (14.3.2) and (14.3.3).

CHAPTER XIV

The Derivation of Inferences

We have now arrived at a set of rules which, used in conjunction with a definite algorithmic procedure, should enable us to construct a rhema representing a context rehearsal from the string of rhemata which we shall normally be given as the initial form of the rehearsal. Though the rules may well need modification in the linght of experience, those given may be accepted as a starting-point. The purpose of this exercise is to construct a formal representation of the upper bound of the context repertory, which, according to (4.6), must be a lattice. This is a necessary first step towards the derivation of the complete set of inferences possible in the given context. This will be a subset (usually a proper subset) of the set of rhemata conformally included in the rehearsal thus constructed: in general, some of these included rhemata will not be acceptable as inferences. The purpose of this chapter is to identify and define certain classes of these 'forbidden' inferences, and to prove that their recognition does not run counter to the context lattice theorem (4.6).

14.1. Conspectus of Impediments to Inference

The various factors concerned may be called 'impediments' to inference; in each case, we would have a valid inference *but for* the presence of a particular blocking situation. It should be added on the other side that there may well be inferences which would normally be accepted as 'valid' which are not obtained as conformally-included rhemata in the context repertory: what I here call 'rhematical' inference is not the only type of valid inference; several others are referred to in §4.1, though reasons are there given for thinking that most of these can be subsumed under rhematical inference if this is rightly defined. One type of inference which can, in many instance at least, be so treated is the 'pertinential' inference, discussed below in §14.5. So, as I shall try to show in the next chapter, are all cases of Aristotelian syllogism. Nevertheless, we have no right to be dogmatic about this: rhematical inference is a plausible model of delocutionary inference (as defined in §2.5), but is not necessarily identical in extension with it. And sublocutionary inference which is certainly of great importance in everyday communication is not dealt with here at all.

Many of the impediments to inferences have already been alluded to. That negative quantification prevents many inferences that would otherwise be acceptable has been noted; there is an analogous effect from the 'hypothetical' quantification "Prh". The well-known 'presuppositions' arising from the use of definite identifications are certainly delocutionary inferences (for they do not depend on conjectures not warranted by the spoken words), and can in fact be included quite easily among the rhematical inferences.

Not previously mentioned are the effects of focus on inference; it is obvious that the theme-rheme distinction must affect the usefulness of different potential inferences from a remark: but one can say a little more than that. This is dealt with in §14.4. Somewhat analogous to this effect are certain restrictions which apply to the quantification associated with tertiary cases, discussed in §14.3.

Hardly an 'impediment' to inference, but requiring mention in this chapter, is the possibility of reducing some at least of 'pertinential' inferences to rhematical form; this is done in §14.5.

I do not, of course, claim that there is here anything like a complete list of the possible complications affecting what inferences may and may not be accepted, of all those covered by the basic rule of conformal inclusion, established in Chapter V. But, for every category of exclusions, due to some 'impediment' or other, I am obliged to show that its recognition does not conflict with the context lattice theorem (4.6). If there were such a conflict, it would indicate that recognition of the supposed 'impediment' conflicts with the comprehensibility of utterances, and must therefore be wrongly stated in some way: unless the whole theory is at fault. This proof is given in §14.6.3.

14.2. Negative and Hypothetical Nodes

In §9.8 a series of examples were given to illustrate the many ways in which a sentence can be 'negated'; the topic was also discussed earlier in §4.1 in connection with the allegedly misleading category of 'presuppositions'. I take the theme up again here from the point of view of what inferences are and are not acceptable from negated sentences.

The example I shall start with is:

(1) $//_{1}$ ∧ *We /bought some /melons in Mid/***elt.**

which I take to express the rhema given below as (14.2.1). The least specific form in which this sentence can be negated is perhaps that expressed by the utterance:

(2) $//_{-1}$ ∧ *We /***didnt** */buy any /melons in Mid/elt.*

produced by negating the verb alone, together with the replacement, by grammatical rule, of "some" by "any". The correspond-modification required to

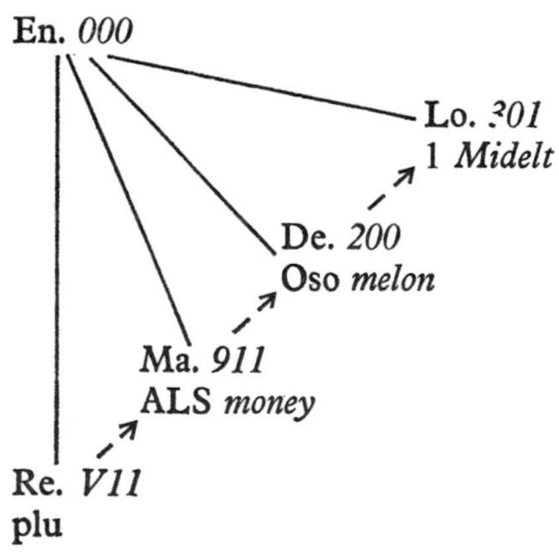

. . . 14.2.1

is then simply to replace the unmarked ("ALS") quantification of the initial node by "No."

Now it will be noted that every deletion or weakening of any of the nodes of (14.2.1) as given leads to a good inference. Thus, to delete the "Re" node leaves us paying for the melons but without asserting that we actually got them; loss of "Ma" says that we got the melons, but maybe as a gift (or by theft); loss of "De" says we went shopping but not what we bought; and omission of "Lo" merely keeps silence on the place. The same goes for weakening any of the nodes: thus, we can substitute "fruit" for "melon". Some of these inferences are logically valid but what one might call 'impertinent', in that they cannot rightly be used as the starting point for pertinential inference.* Thus, if we weaken the case "Ma" to "Ob", the meaning is that we had some money for melons, but does not indicate that we actually spent it; this omission could lead to misleading conclusions, such as that we got it from a bank in Midelt and then bought the melons elsewhere.

On the other hand, strengthening of any of the nodes in (14.2.1) gives a rhema *from which* (14.2.1) can be inferred. Thus, if we substitute "ten dirhems" for "money", or substitute the definite identification "201" for "200" after "De", (14.2.1) will be inferrable.

If, however, the initial node is quantified with "No", none of the weakenings give valid inferences. But we can infer from (2) that, for instance, we didn't buy any melons in Midelt for ten dirhems, and again that we didn't buy the particular melons which the context might specify. It will now be apparent that the whole system of inferences among the successors of a negative node is *inverted*, as compared with those with the corresponding positive node. This procedure, which could as well have been listed among the 'adjustments' in §13.5.2, is specified below in the preamble *I1* to the rules of inference in §14.6, specifically in *I1.1.2*

14.2.2. Other Negations: The various forms obtained from (2) by retaining the tone –1 and changing the tonicity gives us only variants of the same rhema agreeing with different contexts; this is in accord with surface grammar rules. Thus, in the context set by the question "*//$_{1}$ Where are the /melons from Mid/**elt**.*", one would say, to express (14.2.1) with negative quantification at the initial node, not (2) but "*//$_{-1}$ ∧ We /didnt /**buy** any /melons at Mid/elt.*". In order to express rhemata in which *particular* ter-

* Though this type of inference cannot be validly applied except to actual utterances, *some* rhematical inferences appear to be valid as pertinential premises.

minal nodes carry negative quantification we need a different tone. Thus, to convey

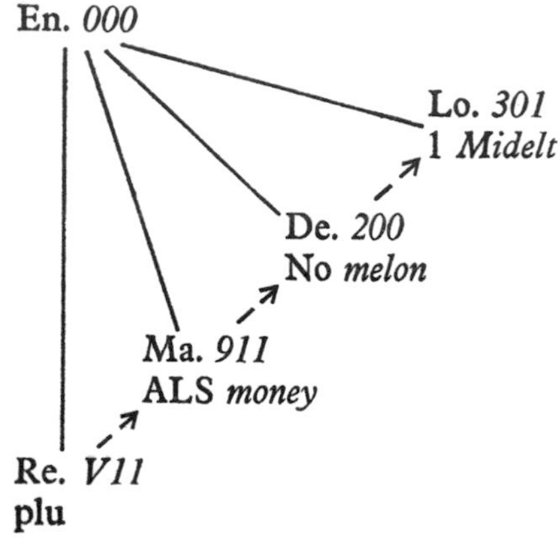

. . . **14.2.2**

one might use the form "$//_4$ ∧ *We /didnt /buy any /***mel***ons* $//_{-1}$ *in Mid/***elt***.*". From this, it is permissible to infer that we bought something in Midelt, that we paid for no melons in Midelt, that we got no melons on some occasion etc.; one thing we can't infer is that we got no fruit in Midelt. As before, but of course less restrictively, we cannot derive a valid inference by deleting or weakening the negative node. If we were to increase the delicacy of the rhematical representation by substituting a definition for "*melon*", say as "fruit of *Cucurbita melo*", which would expand the "De" node of (14.2.2) into

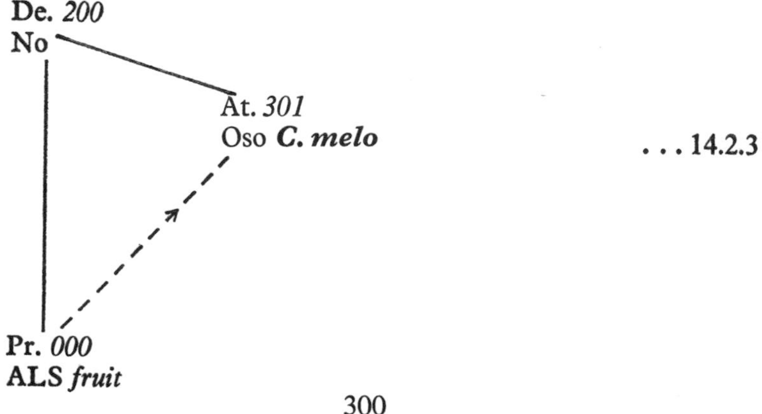

. . . 14.2.3

we would then have to apply the inversion procedure to (14.2.3) because its initial node is negative. Thus, if we were to strengthen the "At" node to specify, say, the cantaloupe variety, we should get a valid inference from (14.2.2): as indeed we do.

By shifting the tonic to other words of the sentence, any of the terminal nodes can be negated instead of this.

14.2.3. Hypothetical Nodes: The effect of hypothetical quantification by "Prh" is different from that of negation. Consider the sentence

(3) "$//_{-1}$ ∧ *They /may've got /stuck on some /bad bit of /***road***.*"
whose meaning we might represent by the rhema

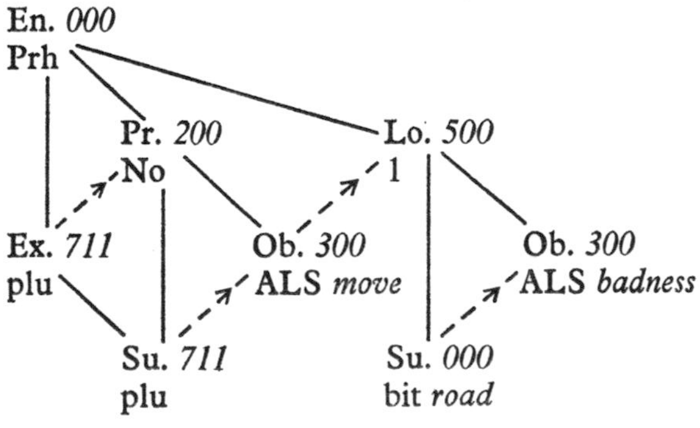

. . . 14.2.4

Acceptable inferences from this include both weakening and strengthening of subordinate nodes, excepting those under "Pr" with negative quantifier. Weakening might give us, for example, that they might have got stuck on the way; a strengthening of the *whole* "Pr" subrhema would give the inference that they might have had a broken suspension. Logically, of course, anything might follow from a 'perhaps': but not rhematically. There is nothing in (3) which would justify the inference that they'd stopped for a drink, however hypothetically; the words are not compatible with the speaker's having thought this possibility worth mentioning.

Like negations, hypotheticals can in principle be located also at terminal nodes; but this is not a frequent requirement, and the idea generally calls for some circumlocution to get it across. To localize the "Prh" on the "Pr" node instead of initially, we could for example say

(4) "*//$_5$ ʌ They /may've got /**stuck** or /something on //$_1$– some /bad bit of /**road**.*"

This allows the same inferences in respect of the hypothetical subrhema as does (14.2.4), but not as regards the last clause, which is now free of the hypothetical element. It can be weakened to, say, "somewhere"; but it cannot now plausibly be strengthened to, say, "at Jenkins Bridge" unless additions are made to the contextual background. It must however be remembered that in English, and probably in many languages, the means of expressing hypotheticals are relatively less developed than for negations. Though the relevant rules, given as *I1.1.1* and *I2.1.4*, are correct in principle, there may be difficulties in recognizing when to apply them in practice.

14.3. Tertiary Cases

In Chapter XI, in describing the case system we would require, one of the distinctions made was that of 'grade' between primary, secondary, and tertiary cases, denoting respectively an inherent or spontaneous involvement in the predication, one imputed by the observer or derivative, and finally a relationship helping to define the time place or circumstance concerned. The peculiarity of the tertiary cases is that, in accordance with their role as environmental indicators, they cannot meaningfully be accompanied by negative quantifications.

In view of the rule *I3.2* of 'equivalent quantification', we can, perhaps more plausibly, state this by saying that whenever we might otherwise have had a negative quantification at a node with a tertiary case, we must apply *I3.2* so as to negate the designatory precessor of the affected node, and leave the tertiary case with a non-negative quantification. An utterance such as

(5) "*//$_1$ ʌ He's /not /**once** been to my /class //$_1$ this /**year**.*"

would thus not naturally be represented as expressing

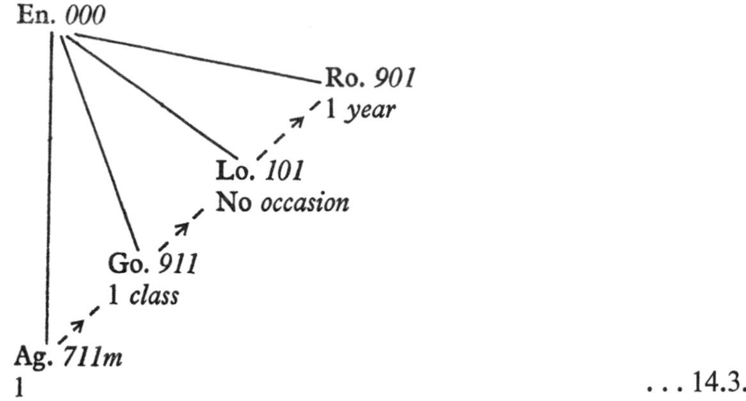

. . . 14.3.1

as if he *had* attended on an *empty* set of occasions (logically true, but not the form in which one naturally thinks). The natural form would rather be to apply the quantifier "No" to the initial node, and to replace the quantification of the "Lo" node by its

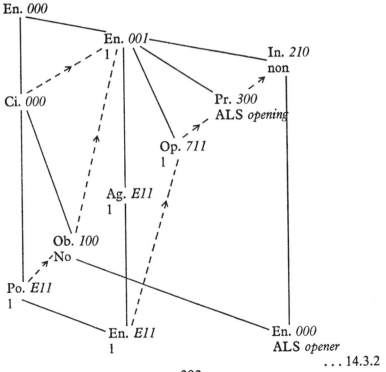

En. *000*
En. *001*
1
In. *210*
non
Ci. *000*
Pr. *300*
ALS *opening*
Op. *711*
1
Ag. *E11*
1
Ob. *100*
No
Po. *E11*
1
En. *E11*
1
En. *000*
ALS *opener*

. . . 14.3.2

negative, in this case the unmarked quantification "ALS". This would mean that he had not attended my class this year: the "Lo" node in its new form adds nothing to the meaning.

The impropriety (it is not more than this) of using "No" as a quantifier with a tertiary case depends on the meaninglessness of the affected node when *I3.2* has been applied, as above. By contrast, "non" can often be meaningfully used with a tertiary case, which could be expressed by "*//₄ ∧ I /hadnt /***got** *an /opener //₁ so I /opened it with /something/* ***else.***", but has no tertiary case, but a "non" at the "In" node. From this one can infer, simply by replacing "non" with the weaker "No", that "*//₁ ∧ I /opened it with/***out** *one.*", and so of course that I did open it. An analogue with a tertiary case, showing the same non-trivial inferential behaviour, is expressed by

(6) *//₄ ∧ We /***hate** */long /drives so we //₁ never /***come** *by /road.*":

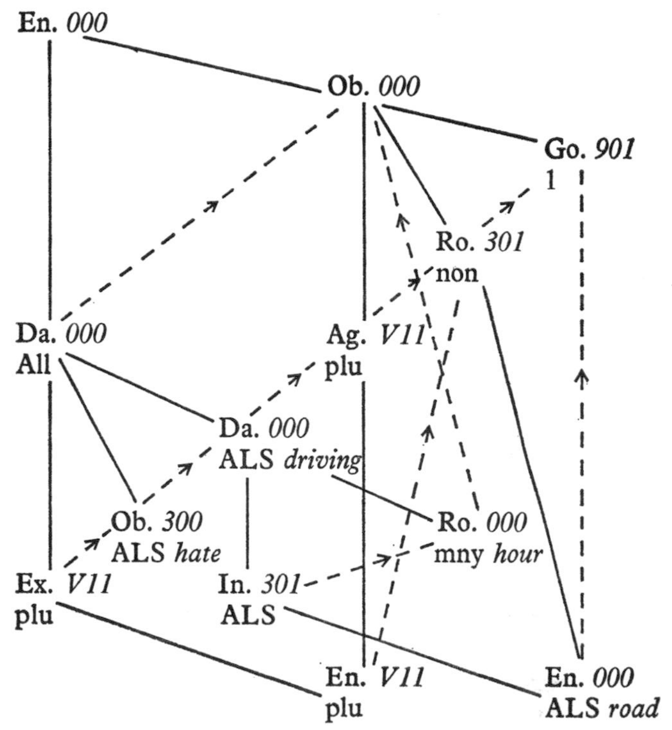

. . . 14.3.3

Just as the last example allows the inference that I did open it, so this one allows the inference that we do come, though not by road. If we insisted on removing the "non" quantification on the tertiary "Ro" node, and correspondingly negating at "Ob", this inference would be blocked by the inversion affecting negative subrhemata.

The rule which we deduce from these examples is not strictly an impediment to inference, but a rule against certain types of node label being used in the construction of rhemata from the start. In fact, it rules out *only* the use of "No" with a tertiary case; for example, not only is "non" acceptable (as we have just seen), but also "NA1". Thus, we can represent

(7) "*//₁ ∧ He /gave a /shilling to /each /**boy**.*"

by the rhema

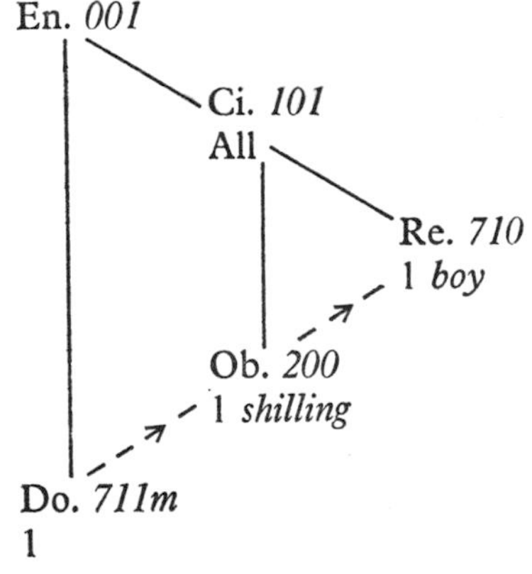

. . . 14.3.4

There are two ways of negating this: one is to attach "No" to the initial node, or equivalently, in view of *I3*, but prevented by the rule just formulated, changing "All" to "No" under "Ci". This would be expressed by "*//$_{-1}$ ∧ He /**didnt** /give a /shilling to /each /boy.*" (but maybe handed round some chocolates). The other distinct negation is produced by replacing "All" by its own negative "NA1", giving the meaning as "*//$_1$ ∧ He /gave a /shilling to /**some** of the /boys.*" (and perhaps 10p to others). This could not be expressed in the rhema without admitting "Ci101NA1()" as a well-formed node label.

14.4. Determinative Themes

Another, more genuine, 'impediment' to inference concerns the themes of determinative subrhemata. There is no sufficient reason to bar 'inferences' involving the deletion of either the rheme or the theme of a predicative subrhema: though the effect of the first is to produce a pointless remark, and of the second an unmotivated one. Practical utility cannot be a governing consideration for validity of inferences. But if we try to tamper with determinative subrhemata with the same freedom, we quickly get into trouble.

Thus, from "$//_1$ ∧ *The /trainer /gave the /blind man a /***dog**.", we can legitimately, though pointlessly, infer that the trainer gave the blind man something, and equally legitimately, but unaccountably, that someone gave the blind man a dog. But suppose we turn this into determinative form, as

(8) "$//_1$ *Jack's the /trainer who* $//_1$ *gave the /blind man a /***dog**."

expressing the rhema

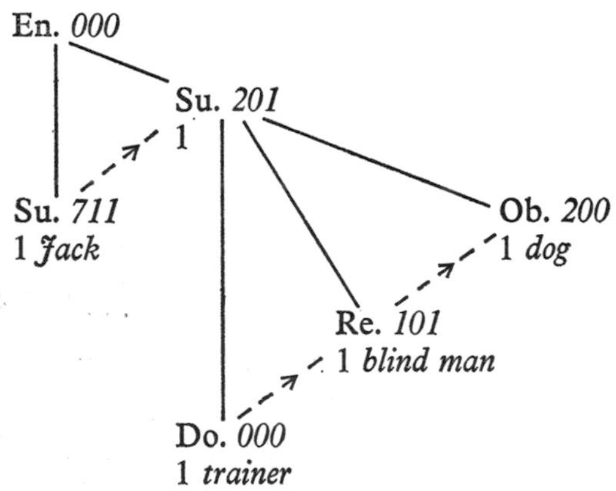

. . . 14.4.1

Merely to weaken the node label on any of the nodes of this rhema yields an acceptable inference. Thus, Jack is the person who gave the blind man a dog; Jack is a trainer; this person is a trainer who gave a dog; and so forth. What one can't do is to *omit* the theme of the determinative subrhema altogether. This gives a rhema which means that Jack is when the blind man got a dog: or with identification 000 on the "Re" node, Jack is the blind man who got a dog. Yet each of the four terms of the node label with case "Do" *can* be weakened, even to 'deletion', without producing this kind of nonsense.

The paradox is unaffected by applying the adjustment rule A2, which would require us to insert the lexical term "trainer" under the second "Su" node. If we after this delete the "Do" node altogether, we find that Jack is a blind trainer, which is equally unacceptable as an inference from (14.4.1). The solution to this problem lies in the mathematical structure of the base domain in which the rhema graphs are labelled. What I have been calling 'deletion' of a node, interpreted strictly, means replacing the node label by the zero element of the base domain; in the terminology of Chapter V, such a node becomes a mere vertex and no longer contributes anything to the rhema graph. But to 'delete' any *term* of the node label is to replace this by the 'zero' element of the categorial lattice, which is within the node subalgebra; to 'delete' in *this* sense all the terms of the node label is to label the node with the 'zero', i.e. the lower bound, of the node subalgebra. This is the element marked $\emptyset$ in (5.34); it is *not* the same as the lower bound of the whole base domain, the 0 of (5.34). If we substitute $\emptyset$ for the whole of the "Do" node label, we get the label which I denote by "En000()"; the meaning thus given for (14.4.1) is one of those too vague for straightforward expression, but it evidently indicates that Jack is the theme of the context in which the blind man got a dog—if it hadn't been for Jack the blind man wouldn't have the dog now.

The conclusion from this argument is that $\emptyset$ is the limit to which the theme of a determinative subrhema may be weakened; this is stated in the inference rule *I2.1.2*. Note, however, that this restriction does not apply to the other nodes in (14.4.1): rhemata obtained by total deletion, to 0 of the base domain, of, say, the "Re" node are valid inferences. But, of course, the second "Su" node may not be reduced to a mere vertex, since this would disrupt the connectedness of the graph (not strictly so in graph-theoretic terms, but the resulting graph has no interpretation as a rhema); hence the rule *I2.1.3*.

14.5. Pertinential Inference

Some cases at least of what I have called, in §4.2, 'pertinential' inference can be presented as rhematical inferences, as I shall show below. As explained in Chapter IV, however, this type of inference is not transitive, and cannot even be applied successfully to inferences from a given context other than items in its rehearsal; the incorporation of this type of inference is therefore something of a marginal gloss. Certain elements of the context repertory may be labelled 'pertinential inferences': but this fact is more a curiosity than a part of the theory. It will be recalled that this is one of several types of inference other than rhematical which may be recognized in speech act theory, depending on the recognition of something not actually said as necessarily belonging in the context in order to justify the utterance of what is said. Here is an example:

(9) "*//₄ People who /eat no /***meat** *are //₋₁ welcome to /***join**."

This utterance could figure in an address outlining the aims and objects of a vegetarian society. But we do *not* need any such wider context to make the following inference. We have only to apply some of the inference rules given in §14.6, and it comes out. For the sake of clarity, I begin with the rhema which I take (9) to express:

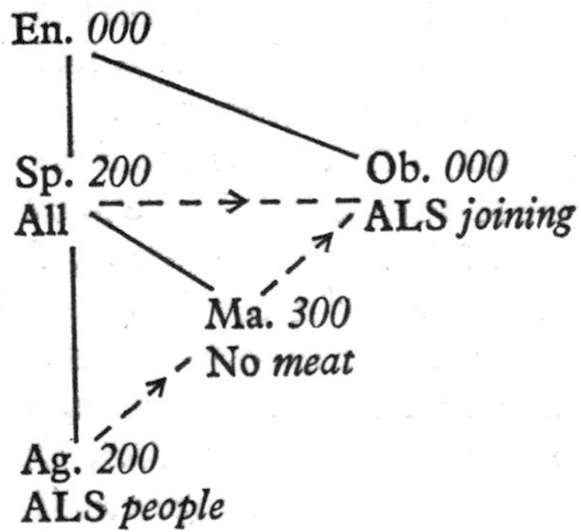

. . . 14.5.1

If we apply the rule *13.2.2* to the "Sp" subrhema, we can substitute for the quantification "All" its negative "NA1", and at the same time change "No meat" into "ALS meat": the resulting rhema says that not all people who eat meat can join, which *is*, of course, a legitimate inference. This in turn, by *13.2.1*, is equivalent to saying that at least some meat eaters can't join. Thus, while *logically* (9) says nothing about anybody being excluded, it wouldn't be worth saying if this were not the case. The inference we have just found is therefore an example of a 'pertinential' one.

Common sense would, of course, wish to go further, and conclude from (9) that *no* meat eaters will be welcome. This depends on the presupposition that statements of this kind are meant to be *complete* statements of the rules. It is a fact of life, which no one could deduce *a priori*, that most vegetarian societies do not, for example, admit meat-eaters under 21 years of age. Common sense is not inference.

The above example prompts us to proceed to various extensions of the principle. Thus, there is a pertinential inference from "*All dogs sometimes bark*" to "*Some animals never bark*". "*Dogs*" can be expanded into the non-obvious equivalent "*animals which are not non-dogs*", and this gives an exact analogue of (14.5.1) leading as before to the inference "*Some non-dogs never bark*" and so to the form given. Similarly, we can infer from "*//$_5$ Fine /**weather** to/day.*" first, that it is fine on days *like* this, and from there that there are days on which it isn't fine. It seems fair to conclude that the intuitive notion underlying pertinential inference can in some cases be comprehended under the present theory; but this very sentence could, using the same methods, be used to infer that some cases of pertinential inference are *not* covered!—which is no doubt the case.

Thus, there are cases where the asking of a question reveals the fact that the speaker doesn't know the answer. This is, perhaps, more a sublocutionary than a delocutionary inference. For example, a man who has just spent the night with a friend's wife might greet him with "*//$_2$ How's /**Molly** /these days.*". In the same way, one habitually infers from a request that the situation requested does not currently obtain; this too is sublocutionary. Whether such cases can be included in the scope of 'pertinential' inference is of course purely a matter of definition. It is of interest that the classes do overlap: but the wider field of 'inference' which these examples open up would take us too far from the topic of the present theory.

14.6. The Rules of Inference

I shall now give, in a formal layout, the 'rules of inference' which I propose to use. After a brief description of their content and origin, I shall give them in detail. In §14.6.3 I shall then prove that, considered as modifications to the simple lattice inclusion model, they do not involve any breach of the theorem (4.6). It is not of course to be inferred from this that this is the *only* criterion we need to apply. They must be tested by being applied to numerous examples before we can be sure that they are correct. The task I set myself in Chapter XV is to examine a few examples of this kind.

14.6.1. Description of the Rules: There are three main sections. The rules given under *I1* prescribe the actual operation which I interpret as the drawing of legitimate inferences. It is, as already adumbrated, an operation on lattices. But, since we have seen that the lattices involved are not simply the ones given by the conformal inclusion relation defined in Chapter V, we need a specific statement of what we are in fact doing. Most readers will find *I1* hard to follow in detail: what matters is that it should be possible to incorporate it into a computer programme, the *successful* running of which would help to justify the statements made in *I1*, or contrariwise. It is hardly possible to test a rule like this in any adequate way 'by hand': the operations are in practice too complicated and laborious.

The next section *I2* lists the 'impediments' to inference which we have found in this chapter, and a few others mentioned elsewhere. These should be easy to follow and easy, too, to check.

In *I3* are listed another class of exceptions to the rules as left by *I1*, due to the equivalence posited between certain pairs of rhemata derived from each other by manipulations of the quantifications of their nodes. These reflect the Aristotelian quantification laws. The need to refer to them explicitly arises from the nature of the notation; a subtler, but less perspicuous, notation using the secondary quantification lattice (9.8) would have enabled 'equivalent' rhemata to appear as notationally identical.

14.6.2. The Inference Rules may now be formally stated thus:

I: There is an acceptable inference from a rhema A to a rhema B *iff* both are elements of a lattice R in which A ≧ B, where

I1: R is the direct lattice product of

I1.1: for each arc label in Q (see below)

I1.1.1: if it is the last d incident at a given node, the label itself, or

I1.1.2: else its lower ideal in the arc subalgebra; and

I1.2: for each node label in Q among whose direct and indirect d-precessors (including itself) are

I1.2.1: any quantification "Prh", the *double ideal;*

I1.2.2: or either

I1.2.2.1: sequences of both odd and even numbers of inverting quantifications, or

I1.2.2.2: any exact quantification, the *label itself*; or

I1.2.3: no sequence with an even or zero number of inverting quantifications, the *upper ideal*; or

I1.2.4: in any other case, the *lower ideal* of the node label in the node subalgebra, where

I1.3: Q is either

I1.3.1: the rehearsal rhema C of §13.5, *or*

I1.3.2: any determinative subrhema of C with either a definite or an adductive identification at its initial node;

except that

I2: no acceptable inference is obtained

I2.1: by deleting (to 0 in the base domain)

I2.1.1: any arc label except s; or

I2.1.2: the first d-successor of any node whose identification is included in its own (designation-wise); or

I2.1.3: any node with an extant unshared d-successor; or by eliminating from any extant node label

I2.1.4: any negative quantification or "Prh"; *nor*

I2.2: by any alteration of

I2.2.1: the label of a node two of whose d-successors are related by a zero arc; or

I2.2.2: anything in a subrhema containing more than two formal quantifications; *nor*

I2.3: by assigning different cases to nodes which have the same case in the rhema A;

and accepting certain formally distinct rhemata as *equivalent*, namely that

I3: whenever

I3.1: two of the immediate designatory successors of one node, both with formal quantifications,

I3.1.1: have cases of the same grade, *then* an equivalent rhema is formed by replacing both quantifications by their complements; or if they have

I3.1.2: cases of different grades, *then* an equivalent rhema (subject to re-application of rule *A3*, §13.5) has

I3.1.2.1: the *complement* of the quantification associated with the primary case, and the *negative* of the other, or

I3.1.2.2: the *negative* of the quantification associated with the secondary case, and the *complement* of the other; *or*

I3.2: a node with formal quantification has one and only one immediate designatory successor also with formal quantification, *then* replacing the latter by its negative and the former by its

I3.2.1: complement, gives an equivalent rhema; and by its

I3.2.2: negative, gives an acceptable inference from the original rhema A.

14.6.3. Conformity of the Rules with the Context Lattice Theorem: We observe, first, that the whole of *I1* is concerned with defining the lattice in which the inference relation is represented; given that the system so defined is a lattice, as stated, this rule cannot infringe the theorem. Rule *I2* deletes certain elements from this lattice, as not being members of the inference lattice (i.e. of the context repertory); such deletions do not infringe the lattice property provided that for every element removed all those included in it are also removed. Now *I2.1* specifies the deletion of certain nodes or terms of rhemata, and it is obvious that any rhema included in one having such a deletion must also have this deletion, and so also be rejected by the same rule: therefore *I2.1* does not infringe the lattice condition. *I2.2* rejects all inferences involving certain parts of a rhema; what it eliminates is thus the whole inference sublattice headed by the rejected element, that is, its lower ideal in the complete inference lattice. These alterations also therefore are allowable. *I2.3* has the effect of restricting the independent variation of certain pairs of terms which otherwise might take other values; this is equivalent to making one of such a pair a constant, which is a special case of the operation specified in *I2.2*. Finally, *I3* (except *I3.2.2*) has the effect of identifying pairs of lattice elements (rhemata) which might otherwise be counted as distinct. Since the effect of this is necessarily to diminish the variety of elements of the lattice, it cannot result in an infringement of the lattice property provided the identifications extend to both the upper and lower ideals of the affected elements. Now the rule applies "whenever" the stated conditions appear, which means that it must be applied, along with any given pair of rhemata, to all elements of their respective upper ideals which are not in the upper ideal of both; and it specifies the affected rhemata as 'equivalent' which implies that the same inferences follow from both, that is that their lower ideals are to be identified throughout. Thus this rule also preserves the lattice property of the system of inferences; *I3.2.2* is a direct corollary of *I3.2.1* and causes no trouble. We have thus shown that the system if inferences from any given rhema defined by the rules *I* is a lattice, in accordance with the context lattice theorem.

It will be noted that *I3.2* leads to postulating equivalence between rhemata whose initial nodes differ as to whether or not they have a negative quantification. One of the equivalents will therefore, at *I2.1*, invoke *I2.1.2*, while the other requires *I2.1.3*: the equivalence therefore applies to two different ways of constructing the inference lattice (the formula which introduces *I3* is intended to mark it as an amendment to the preceding rules). This, however, does not invalidate the argument used above, since it is there shown that *both* the upper *and* the lower ideal of any such rhema are identified, between the affected lattices, even if they are mutually inverted.

CHAPTER XV

Examples of Inference

Having in the last two chapters set out the procedure for the construction, from a sequence of contributions represented by rhemata, of a single rhema representing the context rehearsal, and listed a variety of impediments and reservations attending the inference relation, I shall in this chapter give a series of simple examples of the overall process of deriving inferences from a given context. Ideally, as I have stated, the set of all inferences derivable from a given context constitutes a lattice, which I have called the repertory of the context, and whose upper bound represents the rehearsal as constructed by the procedure of Chapter XIII. The total number of elements of this lattice is likely to be large, and every one represents an acceptable inference from the context.

Space forbids (and tedium deters) a complete listing of these elements in even the simplest cases. It is, however, worth noting that whereas classical logic finds only one valid conclusion from given premisses, and present day mathematical logic draws a sharp line between a finite set of valid and an infinite set of invalid inferences, it is unrealistic to see rhematical inference in this way. Though the context repertory is of course a finite lattice, much that is within it is only formally acceptable as 'inference': for example, those which omit the theme of an input rhema. Thus, from "*//$_1$ Terence is /off to Nai/**robi** to/morrow.*" we can 'infer' that something will happen in Nairobi tomorrow; but who cares? Classical logic has an analogue in that a tautology can be inferred from all premisses true or false; but in our case we are confronted with a closed set of vacuous inferences, which between them make up the greater part of the context repertory. It is idle to hope for a rule to detect and ignore these, just as it is idle to expect an information retrieval system to reject low-quality information.

15.1. A Simple Syllogism

I shall start with an example which I shall examine in particular detail, partly to illustrate the computational side of the procedure, and partly to underline the complexity involved even in an artificially simple case. The 'context' I shall take to be rehearsed by the two sentences:

(1.1) "$//_1$ ∧ *You |often |tell the |***truth***.*"
(1.2) "$//_1$ ∧ *No |***liars*** |tell the |truth.*"

Hardly a realistic conversation, I admit; but I shall be unable to work through any examples which are not absurdly simple-minded, since I am here aiming at a more thorough analysis than I gave to the relatively natural conversation in Chapter XIII, and at the same time wishing to illustrate a wider variety of complications. The rhemata conveyed by (1.1) and (1.2) may be presented as

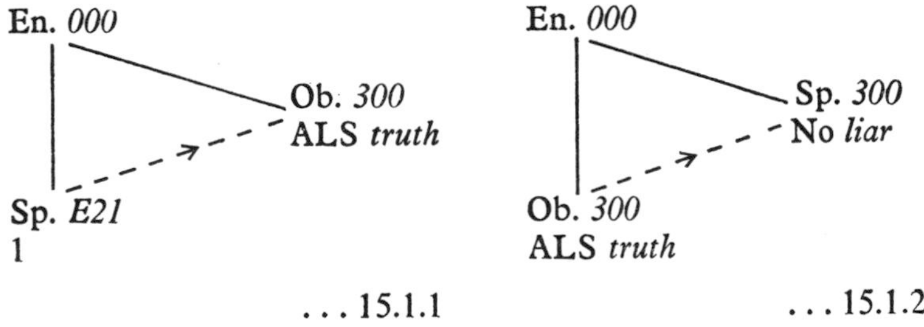

. . . 15.1.1 . . . 15.1.2

These are equivalent to the matrix representations

En. *000*.ABS ( ) **d** **d**
Sp. *E21*.1.( ) a
Ob. *300*.ALS (*truth*)

. . . 15.1.3

En. *000*.ALS ( ) **d** **d**
Ob. *300*.ALS (*truth*) a
Sp. *300*.No (*liar*)

. . . 15.1.4

The first step is to concatenate these two rhemata, following the procedure of §13.4.1; I shall not follow through the algorithm in complete detail, but in narrative form. We start by looking for primary matching pairs, beginning with the most favoured case, where the last node of (15.1.3) matches the first of (15.1.4), and then taking successively earlier nodes of (15.1.3), and only then proceeding to later nodes of (15.1.4). To accord more nearly with what happens in computation, I shall work with the matrices rather than the graphs. We find, first, that Ob300ALS(truth) / En000ALS() is not a match, because, referring to the rules M, M1 does not apply (one has two and the other no successors), nor does M2.1, but M2.2 does, and their lexical terms are neither identical, nor both null, nor intersecting. Next, SpE21.1() / En000ALS() are not a match, again failing at M2.2 because though the lexical terms are both null, their identifications are not identical. Next, however, we come to the identical initial nodes, which obviously do match. Here, then, at step (5) of the algorithm, we record the match and go to step (10) as directed; we form the conjoin of the two rhemata about the match found by the rules C. Since $j = 0$, we observe C1; since the nodes are identical, C1.1 defines again the identical node, and C1.2 assigns to this node four successive designatory successors derived from the two rhemata. The remaining part of the concatenation algorithm sets us to look for additional matches, and to substitute their Fusion if their order permits.

What we find in this search for secondary matches is that the two identical nodes Ob300ALS(truth), one from each rhema match (obviously), and no others. This match reduces the number of terminal nodes from four to three. Performing the (trivial) 'fusion', the rhema we arrive at as the rehearsal of this context is

En. *000*.ALS ( )	**d**	**d**	**d**
Sp. *E21*.1.( )		a	a
Ob. *300*.ALS (*truth*)			a
Sp. *300*.No (*liar*)			

. . . 15.1.5

From this, the matrix representing the rhema (15.1.1) as an element of the repertory (as opposed to its representation as a contribution to the rehearsal which is (15.1.1) itself) is obtained by substituting zeros for all the last column. This matrix differs from (15.1.3) in being of order 4 instead of order 3, and being thus conformable for matrix operations with (15.1.5). Similarly, the form of (15.1.2) as an element of the repertory is obtained by substituting zeros for the second gnomon (row and column) of (15.1.5). As elements of the repertory, both these rhemata are 'inferences' from the context; but of course, as being identical with the input, their status as inferences is nugatory. The rhema structure represented by (15.1.5) is of course

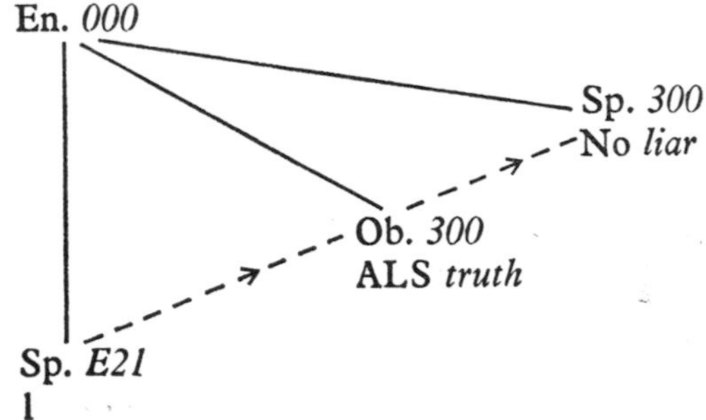

. . . 15.1.6

As in the case of the constructed rehearsal rhema (13.3.9), this though much simpler does not lend itself to expression in English.

Applying the inference rules *I* to (15.1.6) leads to identifying the repertory as the lattice product defined in *I1*, that is, the product of the lower ideals of each node label except the last, which with the quantification "No" is inverted to the upper ideal. Rule *I2.3* prevents us from assigning different cases to the second and fourth nodes in any valid inference, and *I2.1.4* forbids deleting the "No". Permitted is any weakening of the third "Ob" node, including its total deletion. This last gives us first the rhema

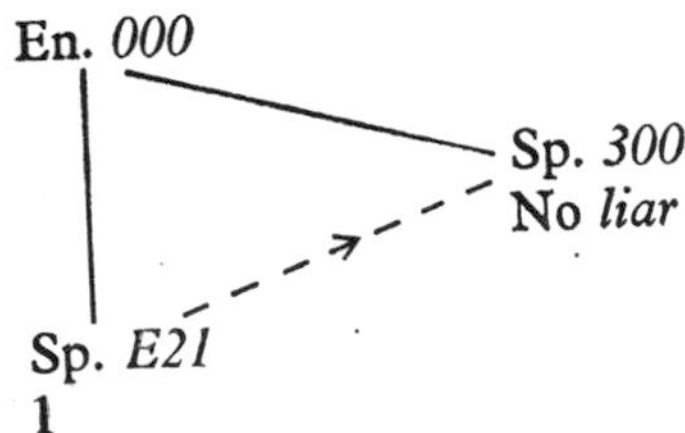

. . . 15.1.7

which means something like "*According to you is according to no liar*" but which clearly carries the implication, allowed by *I2.3*, formed by weakening the two case markers to "Su", which can be expressed by the utterance "$//_1$ *You're /no /**liar***.".

A long road to an obvious conclusion, one may legitimately comment. But it is a road which permits us to explore, much more exhaustively than more summary procedure, the surrounding terrain of allowed and forbidden inferences. For example, the rhema (15.1.2) comes within the scope of the inference rule *I3*, where *I3.1.2.2* specifies that it is equivalent to

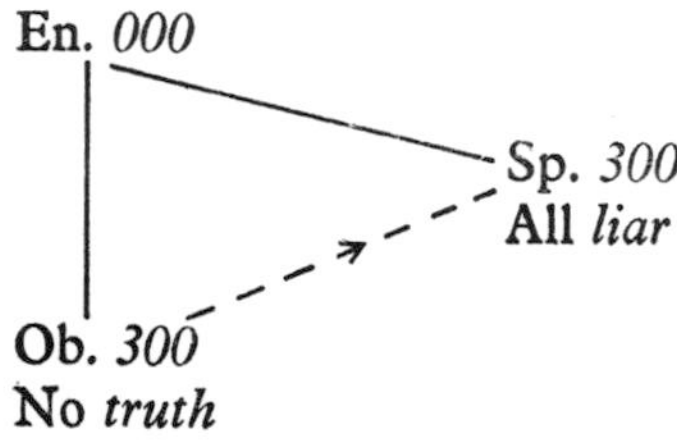

... 15.1.8

If we go through the concatenation procedure with this rhema following (15.1.1), we reach the five-node stage

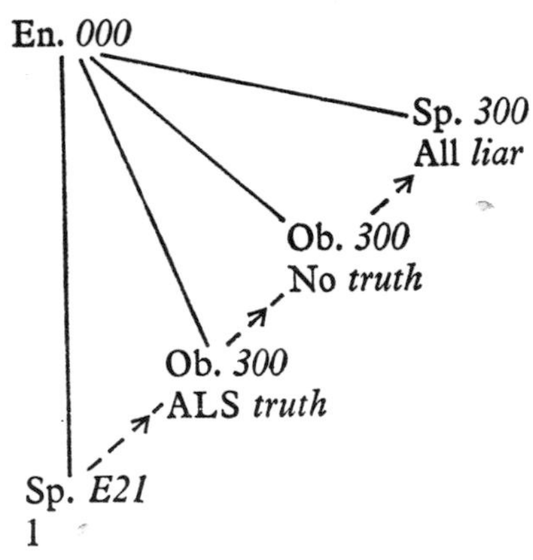

... 15.1.9

but for this the search for secondary matches fails, blocked by the contradictory quantifications on the third and fourth nodes. However, when we come to apply the adjustments *A*, the rule *A3.1* requires that we delete both these nodes and negate the quantification of their precessor, and from this we may draw the inference

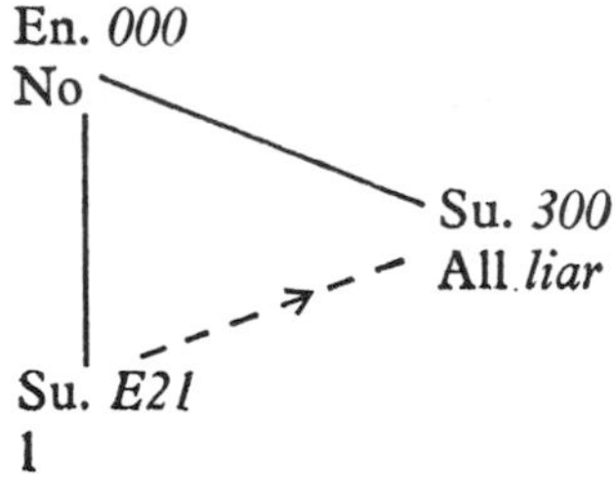

. . . 15.1.10

Here, with the theme quantified by "1", we are referring to a singular class, so that the "All" of the rheme is equivalent to "1" also, and once again we have a rhema expressible by "//$_1$ *You're /not a /**liar**.*"

We may note also that (15.1.10) is subject to rule *I3.2*, which makes it equivalent to one with "All" at the initial node and "NA1" at the rheme. Once again the quantification of the theme, together with the information (supposedly available from the dictionary) that liars are indivisible, leads to the conclusion that you are (always) not a liar. More realistically, of course, liars *are* 'divisible', in the sense that a liar is not invariably such, and we could perhaps more correctly express this equivalent of (15.1.10) by "//$_1$ *You're /necessarily not /**always** a /liar.*"

15.2. A Syllogism with a Compound Rhema

There are, of course, many more inferences available from (15.1.1) mostly trivial variants of the ones given, or remarks trivial in themselves; but it would be tedious to search for these. I now, therefore, move on to a case of slightly greater complexity, from the rhematical point of view, even though not for classical logic. I take as my context what is rehearsed by the utterances:

(2.1) "//$_1$ *Peter /eats /**garlic**.*"
(2.2) "//$_4$ *Everyone who /cooks /**garlic** //$_1$ **smells**.*"

which correspond to the rhema structures as shown at top of following page.

When we take this pair through the procedure of §13.4.1, we

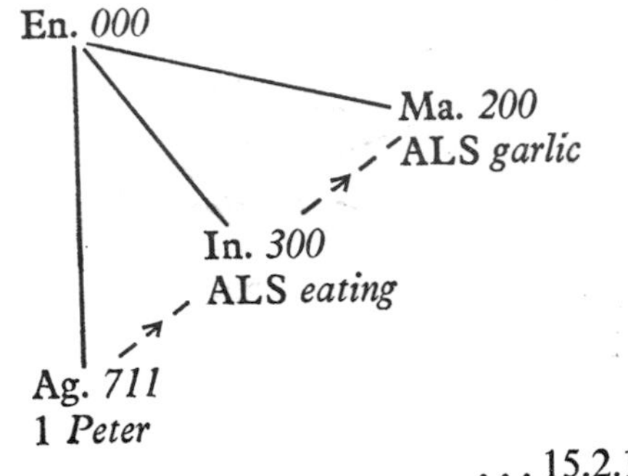

. . . 15.2.1

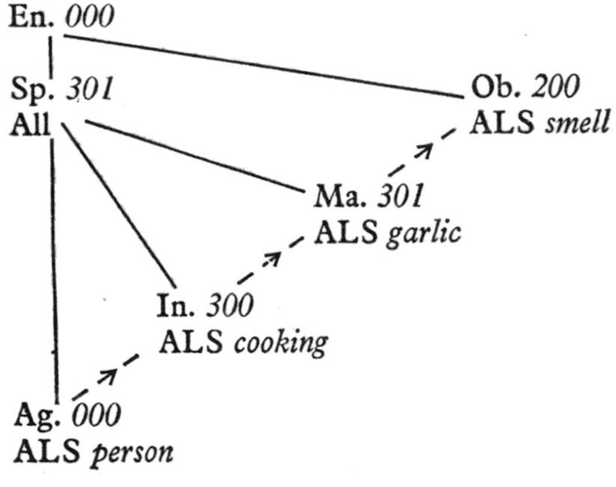

. . . 15.2.2

find that the last node of (15.2.1) will not match with any of the first four nodes of (15.4.2), but does match with the fifth one, Ma301ALS(garlic). This is a rheme-to-rheme match, and calls for the rule *C3* to 'conjoin' the two rhemata; this rule includes the rather complicated provisions of *C3.2* for matching and fusing the accompanying nodes, which will be found to allow both the two "Ag" nodes to match, giving us:

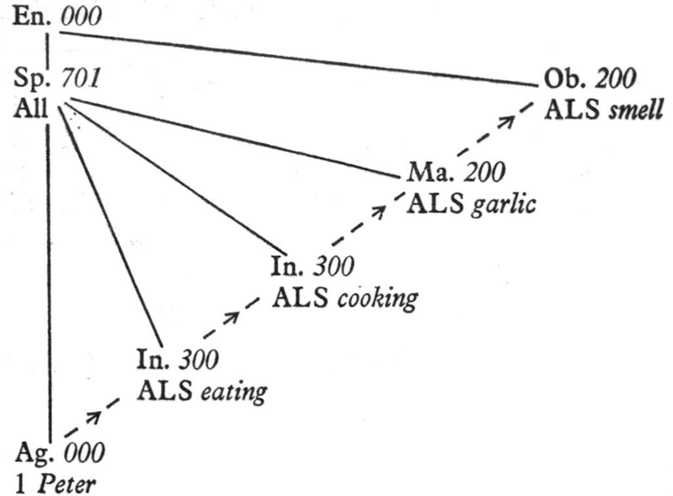

... 15.2.3

This calls for application of the adjustment rule *A2*, which inserts the lexis (Peter) under the "Sp" node; and *A3.2* inserts a conjunctive node of which the two "In" nodes are d-successors. The context rehearsal rhema is now complete. Among various permitted inferences from this, one of the few which are not already contained in one or other of the premisses is

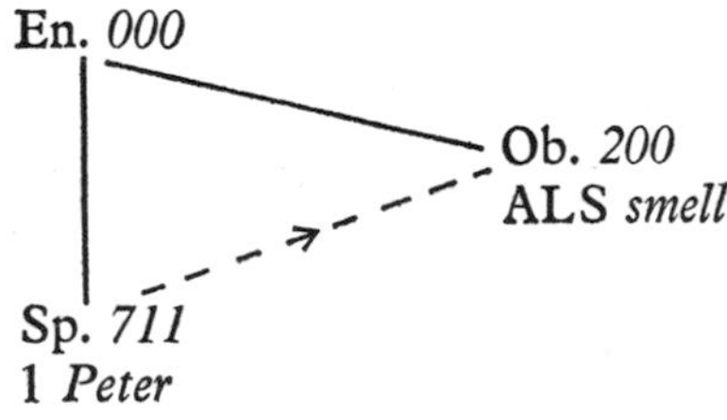

... 15.2.4

which may be expressed by "$//_1$ *Peter* /***smells***.".

It will be noticed, first, that this is quite a natural inference from the context as represented by (2.1) and (2.2), but that it is *not* a logically-valid one. If Peter eats the garlic but takes no part in cooking it, he could, if strict logic were to the point, avoid the unpleasant consequences. The ordinary casual listener is unlikely to notice the discrepancy unless it is pointed out; and, if it is pointed out, will tend to think of it as a 'catch' rather than as a serious point. This is not to say the 'ordinary' listener finds the involved procedure prescribed above more perspicuous than the comparatively simple rules formulated by Aristotle. But in this instance, as in many others, the procedure described here models more closely the results of whatever processes go on in a listener's brain. That this accuracy is not wholly fortuitous is suggested by a simple modification of the example. If for the second contribution to the rehearsal we substitute

(2.3) "$//_1$ *Everyone who* /***cooks*** /*garlic* $//_1$ ***smells.***"

the effect is to interchange the "In" and "Ma" nodes in (15.2.2). As before the two "Ma" nodes give our primary match, but now the "In" nodes lie on opposite sides of the matching pair, and *A3.1.2* now calls for their deletion from the concatenation, along with the negation of their precessor, the "Sp" node, to "Sp711 No()". The meaning now is, "*No Peter who uses garlic smells.*" from which we cannot infer that "*Peter smells*" because of rule *I2.1.4*, while *I1.2.3* eliminates from the context repertory all forms in which the "Sp" node (15.2.3) remains without its d-successors. Thus, (2.1) with (2.3) does *not* allow the inference (15.2.4), because it is blocked by the focus relations indicated in (2.3) by the altered tonicity. Once again the 'ordinary listener' would agree.

15.3. A Rehearsal with Three Contributions

As we saw from the large example in Chapter XIII, a typical context requires a large number of contributions to rehearse; it is out of the question to attend in the detailed fashion of this chapter to an example of that magnitude, but we can do better than the two contributions of the preceding cases. Here is a set of three:

(3.1) "$//_{13}$ ***Andrew*** /*made this* /***table.***"
(3.2) "$//_1$ *Tables* /*have from* /*three to* /*six* /***legs.***"
(3.3) "$//_4$ ***One*** *of the* /*legs is* $//_1$ ***short.***"

This can be considered as a dialogue, with two speakers uttering the first and last contribution, while (3.2) is an unuttered contribution from the participants' general knowledge (which helpfully ignores a large part of the class of 'tables'). The rhemata expressed are:

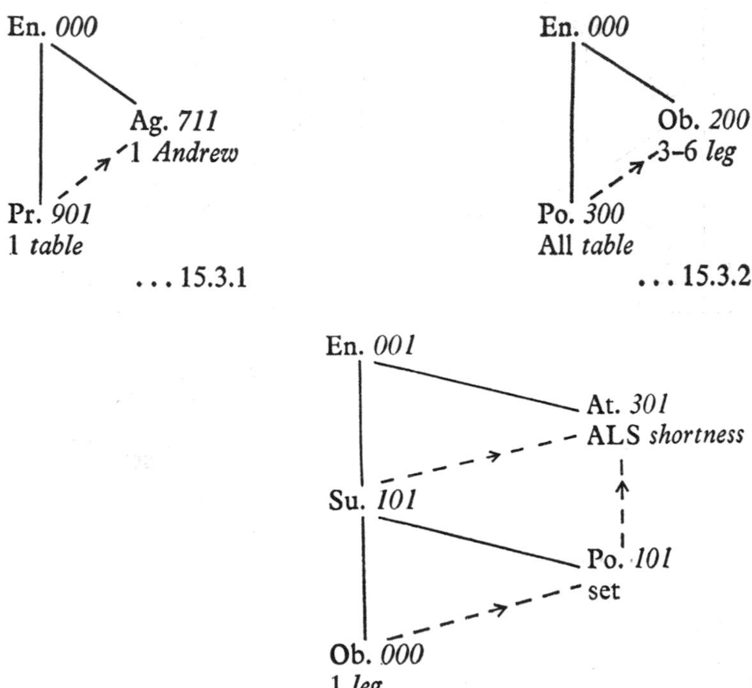

... 15.3.3

We begin the concatenation with the first two of these. The rheme node of (15.3.1) finds no match, but the node "Pr" node matches by rule *M2.2.1* with the theme "Po" of (15.3.2). On applying the appropriate rule of conjoining *C2,* we get the concatenation shown below as (15.3.4). Going on to bring in (15.3.3), we find once again that the "Ag" node has no match, but that "Ob" and "Ob" match by *M2.2.1* thanks to their common lexis (leg); this match again calls for *C2,* with the complication that here the 'nearest predicative precessor' of the second matching node is not its immediate precessor (which heads a determinative subrhema, marked by the identifications). Following through the prescriptions under *C2,* we eventually come up with the rhema (15.3.5) as the concatenation; the only adjustment required is the addition to the "Su" and "Ob" nodes, by *A2,* of "1.(leg)".

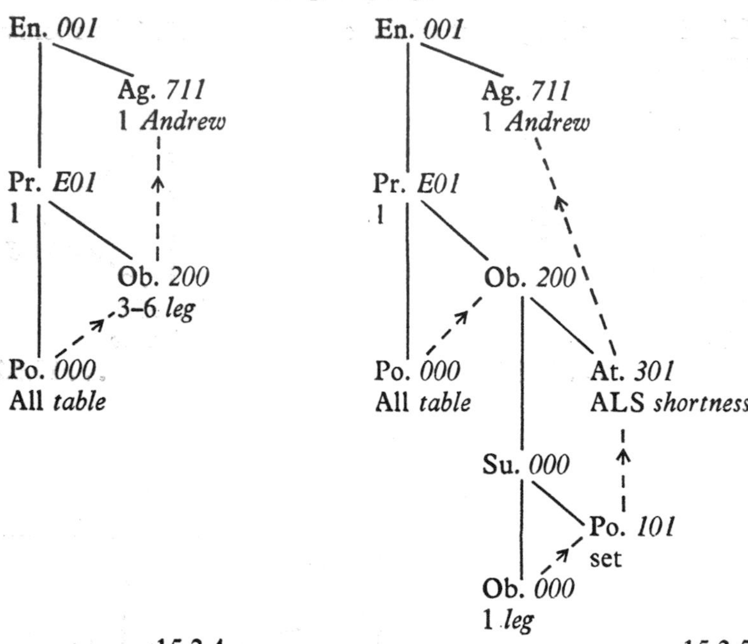

. . . 15.3.4 . . . 15.3.5

One inference, obtainable from (15.3.5), which depends on all three of the contributing utterances, is given by deleting both "Po" nodes (it is acceptable to delete *entirely* a node such as "Po000All(table)" with an inverting quantification), and the node "Ob000.1(leg)" leaving the following rhema

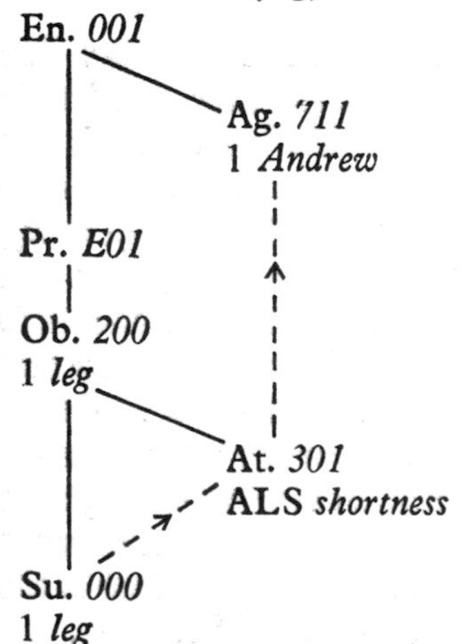

. . . 15.3.6

Which can be translated into English as "*//₁ **Andrew** /made //₄ one /**leg** that was //₅ too /**short**.*".

To reach this, admittedly elementary, conclusion, we need to have the middle contribution (3.2) since otherwise we cannot obtain by construction from the defective input that "the legs" means "the legs of the table": the fact that tables have legs, though known to all, and arguably subsumed in the definition of 'table', has to be made explicit in order for the conclusion to follow, if we stick to the procedure described. Since, without doubt, people do habitually draw on unspoken knowledge in deriving inferences from what they hear, this seems fair, even if very often the linking sentence contributes nothing to the final output. In (15.3.6) only the arc from "Pr" to "Ob", which is ignored in any plausible expression of the rhema, derives from (3.2).

15.4. Illustrating the Effects of Contradiction

The next example, though still very simple, and involving again only two utterances, is somewhat less elementary than the foregoing, in that it enables us to reach a conclusion beyond the capacities of classical logic, or for that matter the predicate calculus, without the addition of extra information. In the case I give below, the extra information is not something known to both participants, but only to one of them; nevertheless the other can successfully infer it. I need not emphasize that items not known to all concerned *cannot* be included as contributions to the context rehearsal, unless publicized by being uttered; a secret context is a contradiction in terms.

Here is such a case:

(4.1) A: "*//₁ Dick /doesnt /**know** //₄ whether /Jane's /**married**.*"
(4.2) B: "*//₁ **Everyone** /knows when //₄ someone with /children /**isnt**.*"

It is supposed that A knows nothing about Jane at the start of the conversation. The rhemata conveyed by these utterances are then, from A's point of view:

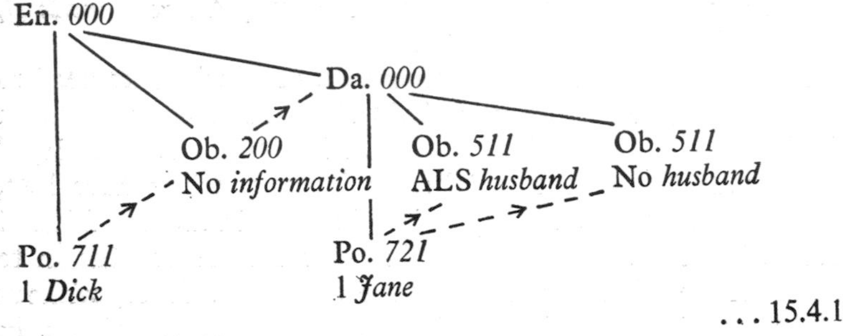

. . . 15.4.1

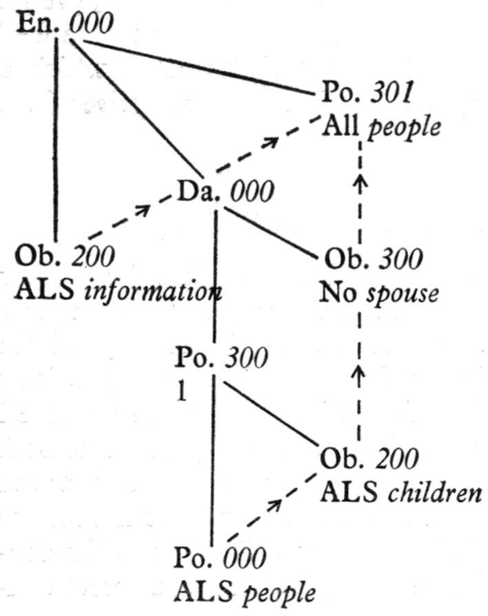

. . . 15.4.2

From B's point of view, of course, it would be legitimate to indicate by an extra cross-arc that the node "Po000ALS(people)" has the same designatum as "Po721.1(Jane)", but A could not at this stage use this item. Nevertheless, on going through the concatenation algorithm, we quickly find a match for the last node of (15.4.1), namely the 7th node "Ob301No(spouse)". This is a rheme-to-rheme match, and thus calls for *C3*. *C3.1* requires that we fuse the two "Da" nodes, but all matches other than the primary one are blocked either by position, as are "Po711.1(Dick)" and "Po301All(people)" or by the contra-

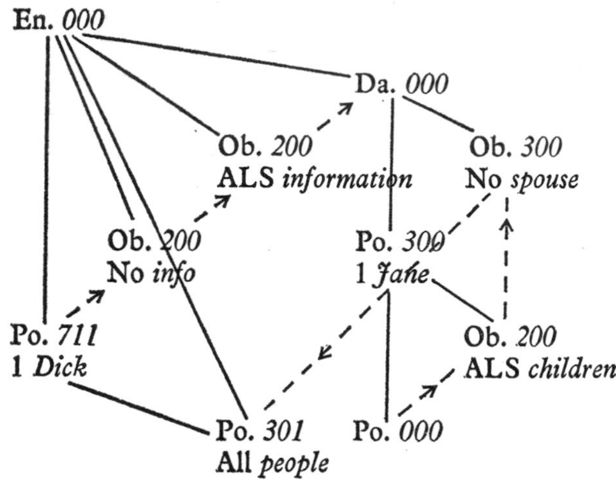

. . . 15.4.3

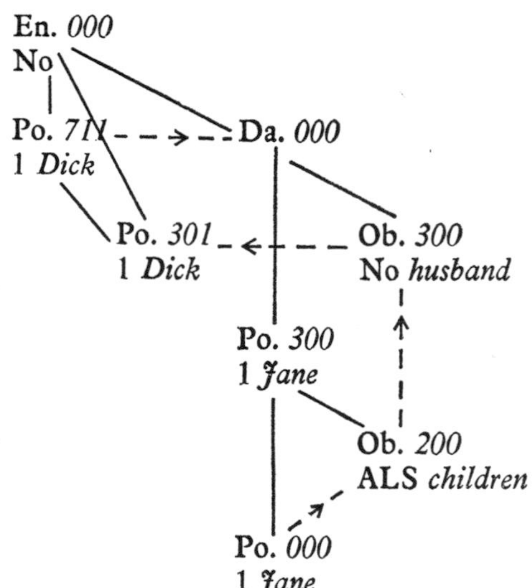

. . . 15.4.4

dictory quantifications on the "Ob" nodes. Subsequently, however, as we go on through the concatenation procedure, we find the Jane/people match mentioned above as a secondary match. The concatenation is therefore the rhema shown above as (15.4.3).

This is subject to the adjustment rule *A3.1* which eliminates the two "Ob" nodes and in compensation negates the initial node. The result of this adjustment is shown as (15.4.4). This last is of course the definitive concatenation, the C to be employed with the inference rules *I.* It will be found that the following are among the non-trivial inferences which can be obtained:

(4.3) *Dick doesn't know that Jane who has children is unmarried.*
(4.4) *It is not the case that Jane who has children is unmarried.*
(4.5) *Jane has children.*

The whole of (15.4.4) yields (4.3), though the occurrence of "Dick" at both ends of the focus-ordering cannot be rendered in spoken idiom. Deletion of both these nodes gives (4.4); and (4.5) arises as a result of applying the Inference rule I1.3.2, ignoring the initial negative.

It is (4.5) which was originally known to B, but is news to A. Together with (4.4) it carries the second-stage rhematical inferences that Jane is married, and that Dick doesn't know she has children.

15.5. Re-focussing

The last example contains an instance of double 'focus', but has too many conflicting complications to reveal its effects. I therefore present next an example relating to the point, alluded to in Chapter VI, that in rhematic, as opposed to other kinds of inferential procedures, one cannot derive from "$//_1$ *Anne /gave me the /**ring**.*" that "$//_1 \wedge$ *The /ring was /given me by /**Anne**.*", nor conversely. These sentences are not rhematically equivalent because, since they differ in focus, they are compatible with different contexts. One has therefore to ask why it is that almost everyone thinks their synonymy self-evident. The reason evidently is that in dialogue, which is after all the basic form in which speech is used, the two participants start by having divergent contexts, and may thus each entertain one or other of the above forms as his own view of what is the case. If this is correct, it should be possible to see how it works out under the procedures that I have described.

The simplest case is presented by a two-utterance dialogue:

(5.1) Doe: "//$_1$ *Who /gave /Ray that /**ring**.*"
(5.2) Me: "//$_1$ ***Anne** /did.*"

where the utterances express the following two rhemata:

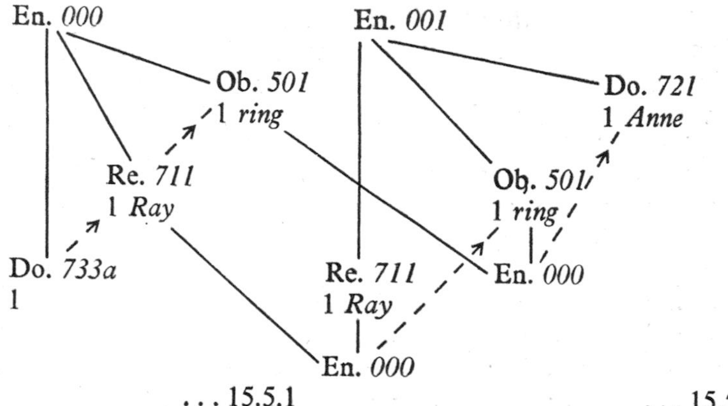

The anaphoric use of "did" in (5.2) is indicated by repeating the nodes of the first rhema, with common successors to indicate their common designata. The primary match, indicated by the second of these links, is that between the "Ob" nodes; as a rheme-to-rheme match it goes to *C3*, and on going through the prescriptions there we emerge with a rhema which, after registering the two secondary matches as prescribed by the concatenation procedure, gives the concatenation shown as (15.5.3) below. It is evident that, by deleting the appropriate nodes, which nothing in the inference rules forbids, we can extract two inferences from this, which are respectively expressed by:

(5.3) "//$_1$ *Anne /gave /Ray the /**ring**.*"
(5.4) "//$_1$ ***Anne** /gave /Ray the /ring.*"

The first requires the last node of (15.5.3) to be deleted, and (5.4) depends on deleting the "Do" node.

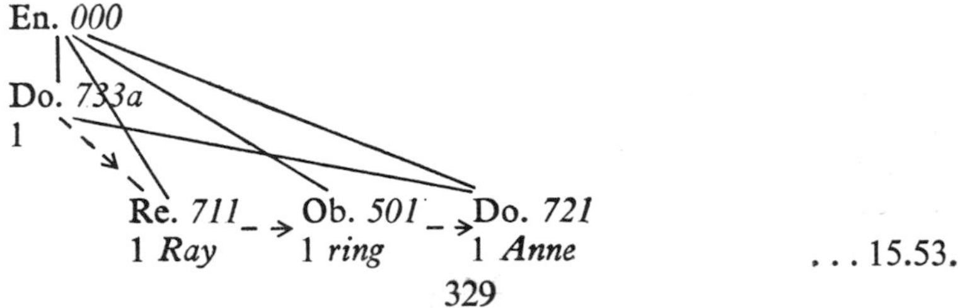

We thus see that, though we still can't get either of (5.3) or (5.4) from the other, both can be inferred from the same context. This, however, requires that the two participants adhere to their original contextual attitudes, as they may but certainly aren't likely to do. In fact, we would expect both to entertain (5.4) as their common thought about the matter. It is also impossible to produce a plausible example involving the first person pronoun except as one of the participants. We have, in fact, demonstrated the *logical* equivalence of the two sentences, in being consequences of a single statement involving the same terms in the same relationships (cases); but, in so doing, have only underlined their failure to correspond in the sense required by rhematic.

It is interesting to note that (15.5.3) contains the 'forbidden' structure (7.9.1), which I conjectured would never occur in any expressible rhema. (15.5.3) represents a context rehearsal, and need not therefore be 'expressible'—but it is still possible that there exists some language which *could* express it.

CHAPTER XVI

Retrospect

In this last chapter, I shall briefly survey the road we have come, comment on how far we have advanced along it, and speculate a little on what may come after. To what extent have the goals which I set myself been attained?

16.1. The Lost Dimension

One of these goals was to keep my attention on 'natural language'. This has not been easy, and attention has at times wandered. Some of the examples given in the previous chapter are too simple to be really 'natural': but then this is necessary if they are to be examined in any convincing detail (and in no case did I, for instance, list all the inferences obtainable). A more serious departure from naturalness was undertaken very early, when I dismissed 'sublocutionary' inference as outside my enquiry. A universe of discourse where one has to think only of what inferences can be drawn from the actual language spoken, without a glance at the paralanguage inevitably accompanying it, is a long way from any natural behaviour. As always with these methodological austerities, there is a payoff: in this case, the applicability of a known branch of mathematics; for the winks and groans, the angers and enthusiasms, which enlighten everyday conversation between people of the same speech community, outrun any existing theory even if they are capable of systematization at all.

I have, indeed, kept to 'natural language' only in the sense of avoiding some of the familiar absurdities of the textbooks. Some corners have been cut for brevity's sake, but a certain ration of over-simplifications is perhaps allowable. But the total disregard for all the interpersonal understanding that is possible without the use of words, or in spite of it, is not only regrettable, but it might be held to vitiate some of my main conclusions. In particular, the implied claim that my system models an important aspect of our actual handling of language communication could be refuted, if it could be shown that in the absence of paralinguistic aids we are incapable of fully understanding an important fraction of our habitual utterances.

This is, in my opinion, unlikely to be the case, but proof is as yet lacking. The best evidence comes from the usefulness of telephones. Communicating in this mode, at least half the paralinguistic information is blocked, winks but not groans for instance, yet understanding is not seriously impaired. But since the redundancy of this information is likely to be much greater even than that of spoken language, there is room for many doubts about this.

Moreover, at least some parts of what some people would wish to include as 'paralanguage' can be systematized. For example, I have throughout assumed that we shall have intonation to help us understand the utterances that I have looked at, though this has often been regarded as paralinguistic. I have also assumed the availability whenever needed of factual information about the context, much of which is in real life conveyed by gestures or the like, which also are 'paralinguistic'. But one feels that these things are only the top of an iceberg, which may yet hole my craft.

16.2. The Comprehension Problem

I have assumed, perhaps too unquestioningly, that 'in principle' it would be possible to generate, from any given rhema representing an utterance in a given language, given an adequate lexicon and a set of grammatical rules, a set of utterances in the same language (and except in marginal cases any other language possessing the needed vocabulary) any of which would also express the given rhema. Certainly not all rhemata can be 'expressed' in this sense, otherwise than by first breaking them down into simpler fragments, but I have assumed that for those which are not too complex, an algorithm could be devised to do this. But the converse process, of deriving from a given utterance a rhema of which it is the expression, is very much harder.

It is also, unfortunately, very much more useful. If this could be done, by purely mechanical means at an acceptable cost, we would have the makings of a breakthrough in Artificial Intelligence. Existing programmes in this field (see the recent survey by Wilks[106]) almost invariably rely on the Predicate Calculus for any inferences they may attempt, or on some system derived therefrom. In comparison with what rhematic seems able to achieve, this looks a very blunt instrument; but it can be worked, which is more than can be said, as yet, for rhematical methods.

Of course, we know in one sense that this problem can be solved, since we do it every day; but do we do so in any way which can be adequately modelled on a digital (or any other) computer? If the countless conventions of an integrated speech community are required as aids in understanding, if paralanguage is essential, then for all practical purposes such a computer model is probably unattainable. Even if, as I believe, such aids are not necessary, the actual processes of the brain need not reflect at all closely those which I have described.

16.3. The Neurological Angle

If there were such a parallelism between my model and the workings of the brain, then the comprehension problem would be 'in principle' (these words must work hard) solvable on existing hardware; though probably something quite different from a digital computer would be needed if the process were to be quick enough to be useful. But we come up here against one of the well-known weaknesses of the use of mathematical models, such as the one I present in this book. For the success of a model is not necessarily a guide to the processes which it models. In the beginning of steam-powered transport, people tried to build steam-driven models based on the mechanism of a horse's legs; but it was a quite different device, disregarding that model, that drove the horses off the roads.

It does not therefore follow, even if the 'success' of my theory is granted for the sake of argument, that it shows us 'how we think'. All it does is to reach the same conclusions from the same contexts; often enough, at least, to be perhaps misleading. But, all the same, it need not be so utterly different as is a locomotive from a horse. The interesting question is, is it like enough to offer helpful suggestions to neurologists and others whose concern it is to understand the higher functions of the human brain?

On the one hand, it is just as difficult to believe that we acquire in our earliest years a built-in equivalent of the material in Chapter XIII and elsewhere, as it is to imagine the existence 'in the brain' of the transformational grammar needed to specify a speaker's competence in his language. On the other hand, the fact that my rules and algorithms are based on a mathematical theory, founded on a few reasonable abstractions from the nature of the language game and linked at many points with the actualities of language (at least of English), suggests that the rules have some kind of neurological equivalent, even though there is no counterpart of "If Ai, Bj match, go to 10" and details at that level. There is then, I would say, an even chance that this type of approach to language might suggest some of the right questions to ask in this field. I need hardly add, that any real progress in this direction would probably help in the design of more appropriate hardware for implementing this kind of system than existing computers provide.

Inevitable, also, are questions regarding 'innate faculties'. The more closely we look at human performance with language, the more remarkable it seems. Obviously, we have an innate faculty for talking, but what precisely does this involve? Almost certainly, it is mainly a learning faculty: children in a certain age range can pick up the required mental skills with facility and certainty. Congenital aphasia is extraordinarily rare, considering the relatively recent acquisition of the language faculty, and its near-total lack in our nearest relatives. But if, as the underlying theory of rhematic seems to show, there is a body of elaborate mathematical processing both necessary and common to all languages, might it not be reasonable to expect the existence of some neurological organization preadapting the human brain for this kind of processing? It could, perhaps, be no more than the ability to carry out inference by inclusion (probably to be found in many of the more intelligent animals); but it is a permissible speculation that it includes also the ability to handle vast arrays of exceptions and inversions and special cases. Could we possess an 'instinctive' ability to handle large non-Boolean lattices?

16.4. Reflections on General Semantics

What I have described is, indeed, a calculus: a well-defined mathematical system, operating with proper mathematical rigour. Even if this is a better model of our actual competence than it may prove to be, it is notably lacking in mathematical elegance. It is, from the mathematician's point of view, complex, cumbrous, and (at least as I describe it) dreadfully slow to work. Nevertheless, it is still a calculus, a mathematical totality, defined by construction and by sets of rules; it is not simply a set of rules for generating something the totality of which is not considered significant.

This is, I believe, a novelty in semantics, if we set aside those approaches which deliberately circumscribe the field (ignoring the requirements of 'natural' language) such as classical logic. It is obtained at the cost of expecting semanticists to do more work than some have needed to do in the past. I mean, that to disregard the context of an utterance is no longer an available option, and that to discount the added power which mathematics gives, while always 'available', is shown to be a questionable strategy.

The mathematical 'ugliness' of the theory is, on the other side, the price I have to pay for a system which, in comparison with ordinary calculi, possesses far greater 'power'. That is, it can handle, in its clumsy fashion, a range of inferences and types of reasoning very much wider than any kind of mathematical logic. It is, if not (unfortunately) natural language itself, at least more like natural language in its competence than it is like mathematics.

Apart from making the context a compulsory item in any semantic analysis, the main linguistic innovation which the system brings is the attention paid to 'focus'. This, it seems, is the essential linguistic category which makes most inferences possible. Under certain conditions, we can make inferences of a kind by attending only to the lexical similarities of the words we use: we can use categorization as a partial substitute for focus. But in the ordinary use of ordinary language, in which we feel no limitations of this kind on our ability to understand what is said, focus plays the decisive role. This is, I anticipate, a point which linguists will find highly controversial; but that is the position I have been driven to adopt, and others confronting the same problems may or may not see it in the same light.

16.5. Philosophical Epilogue

The great question, which optimistic readers may be looking for an answer to, is 'What is language?' Of course, I don't pretend to answer that, except to say that it is certainly a great deal more than can be represented by the mathematical model of 'inference' described here. But I think that the present system does shift the context of the question appreciably. My theses, first that all speech is intended to be understood by someone, and second that understanding involves among other things a substantial agreement about what inferences can be drawn from what is said, perhaps do no more than direct attention to the most accessible level of speech function. But they imply a search for this kind of understanding even in improbable places (see §1.6), and thus raise the question of the relative importance of the rhematical and arrhematical functions of speech.

Obviously, this varies enormously between utterances, between social contexts, between people; much less, probably, between different speech-communities, though one would expect some correlation between educational level and rhematical awareness. It is an intriguing speculation that historically the weight attached to the rhematical component has risen smoothly from zero (the animal level) to its present value, which may well be above the limit of psychological health for many people in advanced communities. At any rate, the 'rhematicality' of discourse ought to be a major point of consideration when discussing the 'nature of language'.

In this connection, it is of interest that for the *speaker* there is probably little difference in the mental work required to utter with a strong rhematical intention and that needed to aim at a less rhematical but equally effective utterance, as judged by its perlocutionary effect; but there is a wide difference for the listener in the kinds of response called for. Almost certainly, the rhematical component of comprehension (I here widen this term 'comprehension' to include other components) involves a more difficult kind of processing for the listener. If so, we must expect a higher level of rhematicality of utterance in a speaker-dominated culture, such as ours, than in a listener-dominated one.

But our ideas of 'what language is' must depend in the main on the extent to which our understanding of the speech process extends round the various phases of the speech cycle. The advent of transformational grammar has made a big difference here, by breaking out of the once exclusive concern with what I have called the 'text' phase. My theory does little to increase our understanding, perhaps, but it does look seriously, if as yet only wistfully, into the comprehension phase as well. My main claim, however, is to open up the 'thought' phase, albeit only from one aspect, to rational enquiry. If this idea prospers, it may alter the balance in the philosophy of language from a preoccupation with the empirical component, towards a renewed interest in the content, and intent, of utterances. Linguistics is, today, perhaps too much beholden to sociology, and insufficiently so to mathematics. I urge, therefore, a greater stress on the inward look. Ask not so much "//$_1$ *What does /that /**mean**.*" but rather "//$_5$ *What /**do** you /mean.*" That, after all, is always the humanly important question.

Appendix

The Halliday Notation for Intonation

In the following pages I give a brief guide to the notation I have adopted for showing intonation. It is based on Halliday's work,[46] but it is employed only to specify the 'tunes', and does not carry any detailed implication regarding the theoretical analysis of the system. This system seems to me the most usable notation so far devised chiefly because it makes use of what seem the right set of contrasts, in a relatively perspicuous manner. The actual shape of the 'tunes', as given in the second column, applies strictly only to the variety of English studied by Halliday (which happens to be mine also, which may account for my approval of it); they are no doubt realized differently in other dialects, and the contrasts involved may not always correspond, but speakers of American English will probably not find it too hard to read in their own manner.

Each sentence is distributed over one or more 'tone-groups', the way in which this is done being called the 'tonality'. To each tone-group is assigned a 'tone', and one stressed word among those covered by the group is selected as the 'tonic'; but in some tones (such as 13) there can be two tonics, and more rarely there may be no tonic at all (though this may be regarded as an uncompleted sentence). The placement of the tonics is called 'tonicity'. The beginning of a tone-group is marked by a double slash //, and each stressed syllable within the tone-group is marked by one slash /; tonic syllables are in **bold** type. The tone assigned to each tone-group is indicated, by the numerical codes shown in the third column, directly after the //.

Besides the tones separately indicated in the following examples, there are a few others which occur, such as "1+3" and other bitonic versions of the "1" tones. There is a similar series of bitonic forms of the "2" tones, not mentioned by Halliday (and accordingly excluded from the examples used in the text). Likewise, the "climbing" tone has not been used, for the same reason. The names given in the first column are my own invention; as is also the order in which they are listed, where all the falling tones are given first, followed by the rising ones.

I need hardly say that this is not a complete account of Halliday's paper. In particular, the description of the uses of the tones is condensed (perhaps over much), and not all the uses have been included. The examples given are also my own, as are the mistakes. My hope is that the practice of always showing the intonation of grammatical examples may become general; its absence leads to a great variety of confusions and ambiguities, which can and should be avoided.

Tone	Tune: pre-tonic	Tune: tonic	Tune: post-tonic	Tune: 2nd tonic	Tune: coda	Halliday code	Principal Uses		Examples
Drop atonic						...	Runup to verbatim quote	//	*Then that /ass /Bob said* $//_{1+}$*Go to hell.*
							ctr. 1— ***apathetic*** final dependent clause	$//_1$	*∧ He /got the /**sack**//not that it /matters.*
Drop monotonic						1—	Final dependent clause	$//_1$	*∧ He /got the /**sack**//*$_{1-}$*∧ if you /**want to** /know*
							ctr. 1 ***weakened*** declarative	$//_{1-}$	*∧ An/**other** /poor /day to/day.*
Fall monotonic						1	Declarative	$//_1$	*John ex/pects a /**rise** /soon.*
							Open question	$//_1$	*Who's the /guy with the /**stick.***
							Injunction	$//_1$	*You must /get it /**finished** /this /week.*
							ctr. 1+ stative with ***tonic theme***	$//_1$	*∧ The /**window's** /open.*
							ctr. 2 ***emphatic*** closed qu.	$//_1$	*Are you /**sure** about /that.*
							ctr. 2 ***final*** of choice-string	$//_2$	*Either they're on /**time** $//_1$ or **they** /**lump** it*
							ctr. 3 ***emphatic*** prohibition	$//_1$	*Dont /come /**in** with /dirty /boots.*
Fall bitonic						13	Declarative with final vocative	$//_{13}$	***Minnie's*** */here /**Margaret.***
							Dec. with postponed antecedent	$//_{13}$	*∧ He's a /**queer** /bird is /**Harry.***
							Sentence with rankshifted clause in one-tone group	$//_{13}$	*∧ I /**think** /Jane /got it to/**day.***
							ctr. 1 decl. with ***marked theme***	$//_{13}$	*Susan's been /**ill** the /last /**two** /days.*
Fall deuterotonic						3	Prohibition	$//_3$	*Don't /come /**in** with /dirty /boots.*
							Non-final coordinate clause	$//_3$	*∧ He's /not /**here** /yet* $//_1$ *ring a/gain **later.***
							Second conjunct predicate	$//_1$	*∧ I've /**read** your /draft,* $//_3$ ***guess it's** o/**kay.***
							Question-tag	$//_1$	*Jill's /**married*** $//_3$ ***isn't she.***
							ctr. 1 ***mild*** injunction	$//_3$	*∧ You must /get it /**finished** /this /week.*
							ctr. 1 ***non-committal negative*** declarative	$//_3$	*James /can't /**swim.***
							ctr. 2 ***confirmatory*** rejoinder	$//_3$	*∧ You're /right a/bout /**that.***
							ctr. 3— vocative of ***warning***	$//_3$	*Silly /**fool*** $//_1$ ***Don't*** */go in /there.*
							ctr. 4 ***confirmatory*** dep. cl.	$//_1$	*∧ They've /**brought it,*** $//_3$ *as they /**pro**mised.*
Dive						1+	Stative sentence (tonic rheme)	$//_{1+}$	*∧ The /window's /**open.***
							Final item of list	$//_{-2}$	*He's got /**tongs*** $/_{-2}$ *a big /**hammer*** $//_{1+}$*∧ and /**nails.***
							ctr. 1 ***emphatic*** declarative	$//_{1+}$	*∧ This /**is** going to be /**fun.***
							ctr. 3 Question-tag *inviting assent*	$//_1$	*Bill's /done /**well*** $//_{1+}$ ***hasn't he.***
							ctr. 3— Vocative of ***summons***	$//_{1+}$	*Jere/**miah** your* $//_1$ ***dinner's*** */ready.*
Wave monotonic						5	Exclamation	$//_5$	*What a cat/astrophe.*
							ctr. 1 Decl. with ***commitment***	$//_5$	*That's /**very** sur/prising.*
							ctr. 2 ***emphatic*** question	$//_5$	*Is he /**certain** /of it.*
							ctr. 3— Vocative of ***insistence***	$//_5$	*Esmer/**alda*** $//_1$ *you must /take /**more** /**care.***

Tone		No.	Function		Example
Wave bitonic	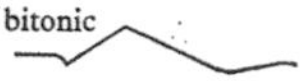	53	Emphatic declarative with ***marked theme***	$//_{53}$	*I* |*never* |*said* |***that.***
Wave deuterotonic		–3	Vocative (unmarked)	$//_{-3}$	*Jere*|***miah*** *your* $//_{1}$ ***dinner's*** |*ready.*
			ctr. 1 ***detachment in*** declar.	$//_{-3}$	∧ ***I'd*** |***think*** |*that'd* |*do.*
			ctr. 1 ***deliberate*** injunction	$//_{-3}$	*Please* |*look* |*through this* |***letter.***
			ctr. 2 ***detachment*** in question	$//_{-3}$	*Do they* |***really*** |*mind.*
Waver		$\underline{5}$	ctr. 3– Vocative of ***reproach***	$//_{5\bullet}$	*Oh*|***Jenny.***
			ctr. 5 ***emotive*** exclamation	$//_{5\bullet}$	*What a* |***wonderful*** |*picture.*
Bounce		–1	Answer to supplementary question or careful answer	$//_{-1}$	∧ *The* |*long* |*teeth are for* |*holding* |***prey.***
			ctr. 1 ***precise*** declarative	$//_{-1}$	∧ *The* |*train is* |*due at* |*four* |*thirty****one.***
Lift	monotonic	2	Closed Question	$//_{2}$	*Are they* |*all* |*equally* |*dangerous.*
			Non-final item of Choice-string	$//_{2}$	*Either they're on* |***time*** $//_{1}$ *or they* |***lump*** *it.*
			ctr. 1 declarative ***question***	$//_{2}$	∧ *You're* |*going to* |***France*** |*this* |*year.*
			ctr. 1 injunctive ***question***	$//_{2}$	*Tie it with* |***two*** |*knots.*
			ctr. 1 ***mild*** open question (tonic on the rheme)	$//_{2}$	*What's a se*|***lachian.***
			ctr. 1 ***echo*** open question	$//_{2}$	***Who's*** *the com*|*poser.*
			ctr. 3 Question-tag of ***doubt***	$//_{1}$	*That's* |***true*** $//_{2}$ ***isn't*** *it.*
			ctr. 3 Q.-tag of *acknowledgement*	$//_{1}$	*That's* |***true*** $//_{2}$ ***is*** *it.*
	bitonic	. . .	Closed Question with postponed antecedent	$//_{26}$	*Is she* |***still*** |*busy, the* | ***typist***
			ctr. 13, 2 Cl. Q. with ***marked theme***	$//_{26}$	*Has* |*Pam* |***said*** |*anything to* | ***Bob*** |*yet.*
	deuterotonic	. . .	Elicitation of background	$//_{-6}$	∧ *D'you* |*mean* |***both*** *came.*
			ctr. 3 vocative of ***identity***	$//_{-6}$	*Roger* |***Beale*** $//_{1}$ ***No*** $//_{1}$ ∧ *I'm* |*Ted* |*Sanders.*
Stoop		$\underline{2}$	ctr. (2) ***surprised*** elicitation	$//_{2\bullet}$	*Is* |*Fiona* |***dead*** *then.*
			ctr. 3 ***contradictory*** rejoinder	$//_{2\bullet}$	*Kit was* |*never in Bhu*|***tan.***
Rise		–2	ctr. 1, 2 ***supplementary*** question	$//_{-2}$	∧ *So* |*where* |***did*** *you* |*find it.*
			ctr. 3 vocative of ***search***	$//_{-2}$	*Alex*|***ander.***
Jump		$\underline{-2}$	ctr. –2 ***surprise*** in supplementary question	$//_{-2\bullet}$	*Is* |*Fiona* |***dead*** *then.—*
Dip		4	Dependent Clause	$//_{4}$	∧ *If* |*all the* |*members are* |***here*** *now* $//_{1}$ *lets* |***start.***
			ctr. 1 Compound declarative with ***displaced negation***	$//_{4}$	∧ *I* |*don't* |*do it for* |***moral*** |*reasons.*
			ctr. 3 vocative of ***address***	$//_{4}$	∧ *Su*|***sanna*** *its* $//_{1}$ ***your*** |*turn* |*now.*
Dipper		$\underline{4}$	ctr. 1 ***reserved*** declarative	$//_{4\bullet}$	∧ *There's* |*not* |*more than* |***thirty*** |*of them.*
			ctr. 2 interrogative of ***assertion***	$//_{4\bullet}$	*Aren't we* |*short of* |***money*** *then.*
			ctr. 1, 3 ***minimal*** request	$//_{4\bullet}$	*Anyway* |*lets* |*keep the* |***window*** |*shut.*
			ctr. 4 ***contrasting*** dep. cl.	$//_{1}$	∧ *It* |***wasn't*** *but* $//_{4\bullet}$ *Ted* |***thought*** *it* |*was*
			ctr. 3 ***contrasting*** non-final coordinate clause	$//_{4\bullet}$	∧ *He's* |*not* |***here*** |*yet but* $//_{1}$ *do* |***wait.***
Climb		. . .	ctr. 1 Declarative ***not expecting attention***	$//_{6}$	∧ *He* |*doesn't* |***mean*** *it.*
			ctr. 2 Question ***presumed unanswerable***	$//_{6}$	*What do they* |***know*** *about it.*

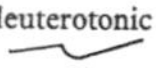

Bibliography

1 ALSTON, W. P. (1964). *Philosophy of Language*, Englewood Cliffs, NJ

2 ANDERSON, J. (1971). 'The Grammar of Case: towards a Localistic Theory', *Cambridge Studies in Lingustics, 4*

3 ANDERSON, S. (1970). 'On the Linguistic Status of the Performative-Constative distinction', *M.L.&A.T. Report*, Nat. Sci. Fn., *26*, p. 1

4 ANDERSON, J. M. and JONES, C. (1974). *Historical Linguistics*, The Hague

5 APULEIUS MADAURENSIS, L. *Peri Hermeneias* (ed. Thomas: Apulei Madaurensis Opera quae supersunt III.176), Leipzig, 1907

6 ARISTOTELES. *The Organon, or Logical Treatises* (tr. O. F. Owen), London, 1853

7 AUSTIN, J. L. (1962). *How to do things with Words* (ed. J. O. Urmston), Oxford

8 BAKER, C. L. (1970). 'Notes on the Description of English Questions: The Role of an abstract Question Morpheme', *Folia Linguistica, 6*, 197

9 HOCKETT, C. F. (1970). 'A Leonard Bloomfield Anthology', *Studies in History & Theory of Linguistics*, Indiana Univ.

10 BOADIN, L. A. (1974). 'Focus-marking in Ahu', *Linguistics, 140*, 5

11 BOTHA, R. P. (1970). 'The methodological Status of grammatical Argumentation', *Linguistics*, Jan.Ling. (Ser. Minor), *105*

12 BRAITHWAITE, R. B. (personal communication)

13 BRIGHT, T. (1588). *Characterie, an arte of swifte and secrete writing by character*, London

14 CARDEN, G. (1967). 'English Quantification', *Harvard Comp. Lab.*, NSF, *20*

15 CARNAP, R. (1961). *Introduction to Semantics* (2nd ed.), Cambridge, Mass.

16 CARROLL, L. (1872). *Through the Looking-glass, and what Alice found there*, London

17 CHOMSKY, N. (1957). *Syntactic Structures*, The Hague

18 CHOMSKY, N. (1965). *Aspects of the Theory of Syntax*, Cambridge, Mass.

19 CHOMSKY, N. (1971). 'Topics in the Theory of generative Grammar' in Searle, J. R. *The Philosophy of Language*, Oxford

21 CLARK, H. H. (1973). 'Speech Theory, Semantics, and the Child' in Moore, T. E. *Cognitive Development and the Acquisition of Language*, Academic Press, New York

22 COHEN, D. (1973). 'On the Misrepresentation of Presuppositions', *Glossa*, *7*, 21

23 COHEN, J. L. (1974). 'Speech Acts', *Current Trends in Linguistics*, *12*, 173

24 COLERIDGE, H. N. (1836). *The Table-talk of S. T. Coleridge* (2nd ed. p. 108), London

25 COSERIU, E. (1968). 'Semantik, innere Sprachform, und Tiefenstruktur', *Folia Linguistica*, *4*, 30

26 COSERIU, E. and GECKELER, H. (1974). 'Linguistics and Semantics', *Current Trends in Linguistics*, *12*, 103

28 DANEŠ, F. (1969). 'Order of Elements and Sentence Intonation' in *To Honor Ramon Jakobsen*, I, p. 499, The Hague

29 FARRADINE, J., DATTA, S. and POULSON, R. T. E. (1966). 'Report on Research on Information Retrieval by relational Indexing', The City University, London

30 KUNGSUN LUNG. *Gungsun Lungzi*, ch. 2, cited in Feng, Yu-Lan. *History of Chinese Philosophy*, vol. 1, p. 204, Beijing and London, 1937

31 FILLMORE, C. J. (1968). 'The Case for Case', *Universals of Linguistic Theory*, Bach & Harms, New York

32 FILLMORE, C. J. (1971). *Lectures on Deixis*, University of California at Santa Cruz, Summer Language Program

33 FILLMORE, C. J. (1972). *Some Problems in Case Grammar*, Rept. of XXII Round Table Meeting on Linguistics and Language Studies (ed. R. J. O'Brien SJ), Washington DC.

33A FILLMORE, C. J. and LANGENDOEN, J. (1971), *Studies in Linguistic Semantics*, New York

34 FOREMAN, G. (1959). *Sequoyah*, Norman, Oklahoma

35 VAN FRAASEN, B. C. (1968). 'Presupposition, Implication, and Self-Reference', *Jour. Philos.*, *65*, 136

36 FRASER, B. (1971). In (33A)

37 FRASER, B. (1970). 'A Reply to "On Declarative Sentences" ', *Math. Linguistics & Automatic Translation Rept.*, Nat. Sc. Fn., *24*, 305

38 FREGE, G. (1892). 'Über Sinn und Bedeutung', *Zeitschr. f. Philos., u. phil. Kritik, 100*, 25
39 VON FRISCH, K. (1967). *The Dance Language and Orientation of Bees'*, (tr. L. Chadwick), Cambridge, Mass.
40 GARDNER, B. T. and R. A. (1968). In *Behaviour of non-human Primates IV*, p. 117, Schreiter & Stellnitz, New York
41 GARNER, R. (1967). 'Austin on Entailment', *Philos. Quarterly, 17*, 216
42 GAUGER, H. M. (1969). 'Die Semantik in der Sprachtheorie der transformazionellen Grammatiken', *Ling. Bericht., 1*, 1
43 GEACH, P. T. (1972). *Logic Matters*, Oxford
44 GRAMSCHI, G. (1962). *Don Camillo & the Devil*, Penguin, London
45 GRICE, H. P. (1961). 'The Causal Theory of Perception', *Proc. Aris. Soc.* (suppl. series), *35*, 123
46 HALLIDAY, M. A. K. (1972). *Intonation and Grammar in British English*, Edinburgh
47 HALLIDAY, M. A. K. (1961). Categories in the Theory of Grammar *Word, 17*
48 HALLIDAY, M. A. K. (1967). 'Notes on Transitivity and Theme in English', *Jour. Linguistics, 3*
49 HARARY, F. (1969). *Graph Theory*, Menlo Park, California
50 HESSE, M. (1960). 'On Defining Analogy', *Proc. Aristot. Soc., 59/60*
51 HEYTING, F. (1956). *Intuitionism, an Introduction*, Amsterdam
52 HIRST, D. J. (1974). 'Intonation and Context', *Linguistics, 141*, 5
53 HOCKETT, C. F. (1954). 'Two Models of grammatical Description', *Word, 10*, 210
54 HULTZÉN, L. S. (1959). 'Information Points in Intonation', *Phonetica, 4*
55 HUSSERL, E. (1915). *Logische Untersuchungen* (2nd ed.), Halle
56 KATZ, J. J. (1972). *Semantic Theory*, Harper & Row, New York
57 KATZ, J. J. (1964). 'Mentalism in Linguistics', *Language, 40*, 124
58 KATZ, J. J. and FODOR, J. (1963). 'The Structure of a Semantic Theory', *Language, 39*, 170
59 KATZ, J. J. and POSTAL, P. M. (1964). *An integrated Theory of linguistic Description*, Cambridge, Mass.
60 KEENAN, E. L. (1971). In (33A)
61 KURODA, S. Y. (1974). 'Geach and Katz on Presupposition', *Foundation of Language, 12*, 177
62 LAKOFF, G. (1968). 'Instrumental Adverbs and the Concept of Deep Syntax', *Foundations of Language, 4*, 4

63 LAKOFF, G. (1970). *Irregularity in Syntax*, New York

64 LAKOFF, G. (1970). 'Linguistics and Natural Logic', *Studies in Generative Semantics*, No. 1. Univ. of Michigan, Ann Arbor

65 LAKOFF, G. (1972). 'Performative Antinomies', *Folia Linguistica*, *8*, 569

66 LAKOFF, R. (1968). *Abstract Syntax and Latin Complementation*, Cambridge, Mass.

67 LANCELOT, C. and ARNAUD, A. (1664). *Grammaire générale et raisonné*, Paris

68 LANDBERGER, B. (1937). *Materialen zum Sumerischen Lexikon*, Rome

69 LOCKE, J. (1690). *Essay concerning Humane Understanding; in IV Bookes*, London

70 LYONS, J. (1968). *Introduction to theoretical Linguistics*, Cambridge, England

71 MCCARTHY, J. and HAYES, P. (1971). 'Some philosophical Problems from the Standpoint of Artificial Intelligence', *Machine Intelligence*, *4*, Edinburgh

72 MASTERMAN, M. (1960). *What is a Thesaurus?*, Cambridge Language Research Unit ML 90

73 MOORE, G. E. (1922). *Philosophical Studies*, London

74 NEEDHAM, J. (1954). *Science and Civilization in China*, Vol. I, Cambridge, England

75 PARKER-RHODES, A. F. (1978). *Inferential Semantics*, Sussex

76 PARTEE, B. H. In (33A)

77 JOHN, SAINT. 'Gospel according to St. John', Ch. 20, v. 31, in *New English Bible*, Oxford and Cambridge

78 PEIRCE, C. S. (1906). 'Prolegomenon to an Apology for Pragmaticism', *Monist*, *16*, 492

79 PETERSEN, W. W., and ITO, J. L. (1971). *Fortran IV and the IBM 360*, McGraw Hill & Co., New York

80 POSTAL, P. M. (1966). 'On so-called Pronouns in English', in Dinen, R. *Report* of XVII Round Table Meeting on Linguistics and Language Study, Georgetown Univ. Press, D.C.

81 POSTGATE, J. P. (1900). 'The Science of Meaning', *Semantics*, Bréal & Michel, New York

82 ROBINS, R. H. (1959). 'In Defence of W.P.', *Trans. Philol. Soc.*, *59*, 112

83 ROGET, P. M. (1852). *Thesaurus of English Words and Phrases* (Preface), London

84 ROGET, P. M. (1936). *Roget's Thesaurus*, Longmans Green & Co., London

85 ROSS, J. R. (1968). 'On declarative Sentences', *Readings in*

English transformational Grammar, Jacobs & Rosenbaum, Waltham, Mass.

86 Ross, J. R. (1967). 'Auxiliaries and Main Verbs', *The Structure and Psychology of Language*, Bever & Wechsel, New York

87 Whitehead, A. N. and Russell, B. (1925). *Principia Mathematica* (2nd ed.), Cambridge, England

88 Ryle, G. (1954). *Philosophy and Analysis*, Blackwell, Oxford

89 Saltarelli, M. (1973). 'Focus on Focus: Prepositional Generative Grammar', *Studies presented to R. B. Lees*, Sadock & Vanek, The Hague

90 Sampson, G. (1975). 'The Single Mother Condition', *Jour. of Ling, 11*, 1

91 Sapir, E. (1921). *Language*, New York

92 Schachter, P. (1973). 'Focus and Relativization', *Language, 49*, 19

93 Schank, R. (1969). *A conceptual Dependency Representation for a Computer-oriented Semantics*, Stanford Univ. Comp. Sci. Dept., CS 130

94 Searle, R. (1969). *Speech Acts*, Cambridge U.P.

95 Sparck Jones, K. I. B. (1961). 'Mechanized Semantic Classification', *First Internat. Conf. on Machine Translation of Languages*, No. 25, Nat. Phys. Lab., Teddington, U.K.

96 Sparck Jones, K. I. B. (1965). *May's Thesaurus*, Cambridge Language Research Unit, ML 168

97 Traugott, E. C. (1974). 'Explorations in Linguistic Elaboration, Language Change, and Language Acquisition; Genesis of Spatio-temporal Terms'; in (4)

98 Venneman, T. (1974). 'Topics, Subjects, and Word Order: from SXV to SVX and TVX'; in (4)

100 Wanner, E. (1974). 'On Remembering, Forgetting, and Understanding Sentences', *Janua Linguarum* (Ser. minor), *170*

101 Watt, W. S. (1974). 'Mentalism in Linguistics, II', *Glossa, 8*, 3

102 Wells, R. P. (1947). 'Immediate Constituents', *Language, 23*, 81

103 Werth, P. (1974). 'Accounting for Semantic Change in Current Linguistic Theory'; in (4)

104 Wilkins, J. (1668). *An Essay towards a Real Character, and a Philosophical Language*, London

105 Wilks, Y. A. (1972). *Lakoff on Linguistics and Natural Logic*, Stanford Artificial Intelligence Project, AIM-70, Stanford California

106 Wilks, Y. A. (1974). *Natural Language Understanding Systems within the AI Paradigm*, Stanford AI Project AIM-237. Stanford, Cal.

107 WINOGRAD, T. (1971). *Procedures as a Representation for Data in a Computer Program for Understanding Natural Language*, MIT Project MAC, TR-84, Cambridge, Mass.

108 ZWICKY, A. M. (1971). In (33A)